CHRISTOLOGY
IN EARLY CHRISTIANITY

Photo by Matt Cashore / University of Notre Dame

Christology in Early Christianity

COLLECTED ESSAYS

Brian E. Daley, SJ

Edited by Andrew Hofer, OP

William B. Eerdmans Publishing Company
Grand Rapids, Michigan

Wm. B. Eerdmans Publishing Co.
2006 44th Street SE, Grand Rapids, MI 49508
www.eerdmans.com

Published 2025
Printed in the United States of America

31 30 29 28 27 26 25 1 2 3 4 5 6 7

ISBN 978-0-8028-8341-4

Library of Congress Cataloging-in-Publication Data

A catalog record for this book is available from the Library of Congress.

The author and publisher gratefully acknowledge permissions listed on pages 389–90.

Contents

Introduction *by Andrew Hofer, OP* 1

Part 1: Christological Surveys of the Early Church

1. Christ and Christologies 15
2. Seeing God in Flesh: The Range and Implications of Patristic Christology 38
3. "One Thing and Another": The Persons in God and the Person of Christ in Patristic Theology 59
4. The Word and His Flesh: Human Weakness and the Identity of Jesus in Patristic Christology 93
5. Antioch and Alexandria: Christology as Reflection on God's Presence in History 112

Part 2: Cappadocian Christology and the Apollinarian Challenge

6. Divine Transcendence and Human Transformation: Gregory of Nyssa's Anti-Apollinarian Christology 137
7. "Heavenly Man" and "Eternal Christ": Apollinarius and Gregory of Nyssa on the Personal Identity of the Savior 148

Part 3: Augustine's Christology

8. Word, Soul, and Flesh: Origen and Augustine on the Person of Christ 171

9. The Giant's Twin Substances: Ambrose and the Christology of Augustine's *Contra sermonem Arianorum* 201

10. A Humble Mediator: The Distinctive Elements in Saint Augustine's Christology 218

Part 4: Christology after Chalcedon

11. Unpacking the Chalcedonian Formula: From Studied Ambiguity to Saving Mystery 235

12. Apollo as a Chalcedonian: A New Fragment of a Controversial Work from Early Sixth-Century Constantinople 256

13. Leontius of Byzantium and the Reception of the Chalcedonian Definition 283

14. Nature and the "Mode of Union": Late Patristic Models for the Personal Unity of Christ 303

Part 5: Christ in Philosophical and Apocalyptic Traditions

15. *Logos* as Reason and *Logos* Incarnate: Philosophy, Theology, and the Voices of Tradition 339

16. "Faithful and True": Early Christian Apocalyptic and the Person of Christ 366

ACKNOWLEDGMENTS 389

INDEX OF AUTHORS 391

INDEX OF SUBJECTS 397

Introduction

Andrew Hofer, OP

In his review of Brian E. Daley's edited *opera omnia* of Leontius of Byzantium, Andrew Louth comments parenthetically, "Incidentally, a collection of Daley's articles, not just on sixth-century Christology, would be a boon to scholarship."[1] After reading that statement in 2020, I contacted Brian about whether a collection of his essays would be published. He told me that James Ernest (his friend, doctoral student, and editor-in-chief of Eerdmans) had already suggested that possibility. To my delight, Brian and James allowed me to assist them in the process of collecting the essays for Eerdmans.

After Brian and James agreed to limit the collection of essays to just two volumes, one dedicated to early Christian biblical interpretation and the other devoted to early Christology, Brian invited me to write the introduction to the second volume. Brian's Jesuit confrere Brian Dunkle—following his doctoral mentor and friend closely in patristic translations, scholarship, editorial board service, teaching, and mentoring as a leading scholar—has contributed a marvelous introduction to the first volume.[2] It is a great honor to present Brian Daley's work and, in a way, to introduce readers unfamiliar with the author of these writings to Brian himself. Peter W. Martens aptly writes in the introduction to Brian's Festschrift in 2008, "I cannot introduce

1. Andrew Louth, review of *Leontius of Byzantium: Complete Works*, edited by Brian E. Daley, SJ, *Journal of Ecclesiastical History* 71, no. 2 (2020): 395–97, at 396. Since that review, two volumes of Louth's own collected works have appeared: Andrew Louth, *Selected Essays*, vol. 1, *Studies in Patristics*, and vol. 2, *Studies in Theology*, ed. Lewis Ayres and John Behr (Oxford: Oxford University Press, 2023).

2. Brian Dunkle, SJ, introduction to Brian E. Daley, SJ, *Biblical Interpretation and Doctrine in Early Christianity: Collected Essays* (Grand Rapids: Eerdmans, 2025).

Brian Daley more succinctly or more faithfully than by describing him as a Jesuit priest. It is the Jesuit way of life that has ordered and shaped the rest of his life, including his vocation as a scholar."[3] While both Dunkle's and Martens's introductions stress the Jesuit character of Brian's life and work, I want to add a Dominican appreciation.

Dominican friars have taken, shall we say, a keen interest in Jesuit theology since the days of Ignatius of Loyola, who was himself, for a time, a student of Dominican friars and who mandated the teaching of Thomas Aquinas in the constitutions of the Society of Jesus.[4] The keen interest has produced much material for the history books over the past five centuries—fruitful collaboration between the two religious orders on one hand and acrimonious rivalry and accusations of heresy on the other. When I was teaching in Nairobi, Kenya, in 2003–2005, I contacted Brian about the possibility of studying under him for my PhD at the University of Notre Dame. At one point he wrote back that he thought this arrangement would work. But, mindful of the *de auxiliis* controversy in the late sixteenth and early seventeenth centuries, he had one condition: that we not discuss grace. Humorous—and true. Given certain limits, knowing Brian as my professor and dissertation director has been one of the great blessings of my Dominican life. What other Jesuit would wish me "happy feast" on the feasts of not only famous Dominican saints but also obscure blesseds?

From friends, colleagues, students, and readers in many Christian communities and scholarly academies from around the globe, Brian has received various accolades, including the Ratzinger Award personally conferred by Pope Benedict XVI on October 20, 2012. At that time, Pope Benedict commented in his address, "Fr. Daley, with his in-depth study on the Fathers of the Church, has chosen the best school for knowing and loving the one and undivided Church, also in the wealth of her different traditions; for this reason in addition he is carrying out a responsible service in our relations with the Orthodox Churches."[5] But it is the more modest occasion of his

3. Peter W. Martens, ed., *In the Shadow of the Incarnation: Essays on Jesus Christ in the Early Church in Honor of Brian E. Daley, S. J.* (Notre Dame, IN: University of Notre Dame Press, 2008), 1.

4. For new appreciations, see Justin M. Anderson, Matthew Levering, and Aaron Pidel, SJ, eds., *Ignatius of Loyola and Thomas Aquinas: A Jesuit Ressourcement* (Washington, DC: Catholic University of America Press, 2024).

5. Address of His Holiness Benedict XVI, Conferral of the Ratzinger Prize 2012, Clementine Hall, Saturday, October 20, 2012.

receiving the Saint Dominic Medal from the Dominican Province of St. Joseph's pontifical faculty at the Dominican House of Studies on May 14, 2021, that I want to feature. The award's citation recognizes Brian's outstanding service to the Church and the academy, as well as his "immeasurable support to several friars of the Province who have been students and faculty of the Dominican House of Studies." As recipient of the Saint Dominic Medal, Brian was asked to give the commencement address. He did so with characteristic wit and wisdom. Beginning with a *captatio benevolentiae* establishing his connections with Dominicans, and going on to highlight his great-uncle George Ignatius Conlan, a priest of my province who died about twenty years before Brian was born, Brian delivered an address that he titled "On Doing Theology Historically: Reading the Footnotes." It serves as a testimony to his theological methodology or, more simply, his way of understanding and teaching the faith.

Let us now consider Brian's understanding of doing theology historically, drawing amply from that unpublished 2021 commencement address. Afterward, this introduction extols his essays on Jesus Christ in this volume as brilliant exemplifications of that theological approach.

On Doing Theology Historically

In the priory chapel on that Friday evening in May 2021, Brian had his Oxford DPhil gown over his clerical suit to address faculty, students—especially the graduating students—and guests of the Dominican House of Studies. After introductory matters, he explained how he took as his teaching focus the first seven or eight centuries of the Church's theology, termed "patristic studies," and why this approach to theology matters:

> I got into this sub-species of theology partly by historical accident—I was in the class in my high school that studied Latin and Greek, and loved it enough to keep doing it, as a classics major, in college—and partly by obedience, after I became a Jesuit: because my province saw it would need someone to fill that early Christianity slot in our theological faculty a few years down the line. And ever since, I've found this an endlessly rich, engaging—and enjoyable—point of view from which to study our faith![6]

6. Brian attended St. Peter's Preparatory School, Jersey City, New Jersey (1953–1957), before studying at Fordham University as a National Merit Scholar (1957–1961) where he

In contrast to his palpable joy in learning from the Fathers of the Church, which his students experienced from him for several decades, Brian records his dissatisfaction with what the academy typically offers:

> For that very reason, perhaps, I've always been a little puzzled, I have to confess, by the distinction many American theological faculties still tend to make between theology in its "historical" and its "systematic" forms. "Theology," after all, really means "talking about God," thinking and speculating about the mysterious reality of God and—as our ancestors have witnessed to us—about what God has done in our world. Any real Christian theology, I would suggest, needs to be both historical and systematic, if it is to be authentic. We all learn about God not just from our own personal questions and reflections, but from what other people before us have learned and written and preached and shared with us about this divine Mystery—from that ongoing conversation of prayer and witness we call the Church, whose whole history has been taken up, for twenty centuries, with talking to the world, and among ourselves, about God.

Again, theology is "talking about God." But such may not always be the impression that is left by some of its practitioners. Brian stresses that in our Christian theology, it is not simply an awareness that there is a God, but that the First Cause "is aware of us, reaches out to us to gather us in, constantly wills to heal us of our weaknesses and our ills." Moreover, this same God "has chosen to involve himself in our history, and to reveal his thoughts and plans to us through the people Israel, even to become one of us as a human being

---

earned his BA in classics in 1961, *summa cum laude*. He was elected to Phi Beta Kappa and was awarded a Rhodes Scholarship, a Woodrow Wilson Fellowship, and a Danforth Fellowship. As a Rhodes Scholar at Merton College, Oxford, he studied *Literae Humaniores* ("Greats": classics, philosophy, and ancient history), earning First Class honors. He entered the novitiate of the Society of Jesus in 1964 at St. Andrew-on-Hudson, Poughkeepsie, New York. He earned his licentiate in philosophy, graduating *summa cum laude*, from Loyola Seminary, Shrub Oak, New York, before being sent for a licentiate in theology at Hochschule Skt. Georgen, Frankfurt-am-Main, graduating *summa cum laude*. He was ordained a priest on July 25, 1970, and spent 1971–1972 as research assistant to Aloys Grillmeier, SJ. From 1972 to 1978, he resided at Campion Hall, Oxford, for his DPhil, and he was assigned to teach at the Weston School of Theology in Cambridge, Massachusetts, from 1978 until 1996, when he became the Catherine F. Huisking Professor of Theology at the University of Notre Dame. After retiring from Notre Dame, he lived and taught as a senior professor of theology at Georgetown University in 2021 and 2022, and then moved to Murray-Weigel Hall at Fordham University.

in the person of Jesus of Nazareth, an obscure Jewish laborer who lived some twenty centuries ago." Brian underscores the historical dimension of God's revelation:

> The witnesses to God's acts of self-disclosure testify, over and over, to what they have heard and seen, to its truth; ultimately, they form a community living in time, a nation among the other nations, a Church, whose main role among us is to remind the human race that our whole existence is rooted in the reality and the generous love of God, revealed to us as present and active still in human history.

In short, because God reveals himself to us, who have place and time, the very study of God must have historical and communal dimensions in the Church. Brian summarizes this approach:

> The task of theology, then, in the Jewish and Christian way of understanding it, is always radically anchored in its own history: in the ever-changing, ever-growing ways in which people of biblical faith have thought and spoken about God, who remains beyond thought and words. In the process, we learn the rules and content of God's speech to us—and of our speech about God—always from our own forebears. We learn how to speak of God, in other words, first of all from the historical discourse in which biblical faith has, over time, been handed on to us.

Considering this doctrinal tradition of the biblical faith in the Church, Brian communicates an account of a student's interpretation that made his thinking click:

> As puzzled as I was, when I began teaching in a seminary in Boston years ago, about the distinction then being drawn in American schools between "historical" and "systematic" theology, a student of mine—reflecting on the same puzzle—once helped me to clarify the issue by quipping, "As far as I can see, historical theology is just systematic theology with footnotes!"

Following this quip, this Dominican House of Studies commencement address fittingly focuses on Thomas Aquinas: "Who could be more conscious of the whole sweep of Catholic teaching since its beginning than Thomas?" Brian asks, "Yet who has ever surpassed him in the structural arrangement of central theological questions and answering voices—the 'systematic' ordering of all the 'footnotes,' the issues relevant to our understanding of what biblical faith tells us of God and God's work?" Brian continues:

> And just as footnotes by themselves don't add up to a theological argument, but need to be woven tightly into a cohesive, overarching reflection, to which they give texture and depth, so a theological argument that is not anchored—by its footnotes—in the long tradition of human thought about God will seem arbitrary and insubstantial, not representative of the ongoing line of mature Christian reflection. For theology, especially, which is the thoughtful contemplation and arrangement of the things our human community has discovered—thanks to Israel, Jesus and the Church—about the Mystery we refer to as "God," a sense of the continuing development of our categories and our reflections is indispensable.

Brian next interprets Aquinas's *Summa theologiae* I, q. 1, a. 8, ad 2, giving a lesson on Aquinas's use of sources in *sacra doctrina* to show how the witness of the apostles and prophets who have received revelation is paramount for our work, followed by the holy doctors who taught in times after the Bible and then philosophers. For Aquinas, *sacra doctrina* has an inherently historical dimension. The Word was made flesh, after all. Brian argues for certain ramifications to this approach to God:

> If we are to see our faith in God, as revealed through Jesus by the power of the Holy Spirit, as the central truth of our lives, grounded in the central, living truth of all that is, it is vitally important that we understand how the details and implications of that faith have unfolded their meaning to people through human history, and how they continue to unfold it for us. Why do we understand the person and work of Jesus as we do? How does Jesus reveal to us the ultimate truth about the Mystery of God, and about the world, and about ourselves? What do we mean by a *person*? What is the nature and significance of the community of believers, of its acts of worship, of its mission in the world? Where did the world itself originate, what is its role now, where is it headed? These and a whole host of related questions, seen in the context of biblical faith, are questions that have been asked repeatedly, in different forms and idioms, over the course of twenty centuries—questions that all really concern the ultimate meaning of our existence.

From this attentiveness to the perennial questions at the heart of the theological endeavor, the address then names some of those figures from the early Church most significant to the Church and to Brian's own theological work:

> To grasp in some detail how Christian preachers and thinkers—from Ignatius of Antioch and Clement of Rome, at the end of the first century, to Origen and Athanasius, Ephrem and the three great Cappadocians, Ambrose and Augustine, Cyril and Leo, Maximus and John of Damascus, and all the intense debates surrounding the early councils—is to come slowly to realize how our Christian sense of that ultimate meaning of things has gradually taken shape in human society, centered on our understanding of Jesus Christ and his teaching, and how Christ might be calling us to live now and for the future.

Brian then shows how our work in theology, like that of Aquinas and other theologians worthy of the name, must consider the reality of "God with us" amid the fragility of our lives:

> The point—one that major theologians like Thomas Aquinas, through the centuries, have recognized—seems to me to be clear: Christian theology is not just a given, a well-defined, detailed ideology that we simply need to pry open and apply as needed. It is a living thing, discovered in the midst of a living, fragile humanity. How believers have interpreted the message that "Jesus is Lord," and have seen the implications of that Lordship, points to a dizzying variety of questions and answers about the reality we live—and can't avoid living—day by day. So to enter more deeply into the question of "God with us" and its answers—into the reality that centers us and points us beyond ourselves—it is indispensable that we see for ourselves, at least in some degree, the steps by which our common faith in Jesus has evolved, while he remains (as the Letter to the Hebrews reminds us) "the same—yesterday, today and forever" (Heb 13:8).

Following this announcement of the sameness of Christ for all ages, Brian turns directly to the graduates at the commencement:

> The significance of *today* for all of *you*, surely, is not just that another chapter in your lives has reached a conclusion, and that you won't have to write any more papers or take any more exams in theology—at least not for a while. Its real significance, I think, is that all of you, in a variety of ways, are being commissioned—sent out—to be theologians for the Church of the years

> ahead of us: to be "doctors of the Church," to think and talk knowledgeably about the Mystery of God in the midst of God's people and for their sake. It means knowing what representative voices in the long line of the people we call theologians have said and thought about God—some more helpfully than others—through twenty centuries, and trying to put it all together in a way that, if possible, will help the rest of us see it all more clearly, and live from it with more conviction.

Brian concludes in memorable fashion, returning to the "footnotes" that he proposes and, more importantly, the Mystery for our salvation that they reference:

> It means remembering at least a little of what's in those footnotes, but—more importantly—having a growing sense of what it all means for us and for the world: what it means for our lives to say with conviction that God is with us, that Jesus—our own "Emmanuel"—has made him known, and that the Holy Spirit of God still works in us in today's Church, as he did in the Apostles, guiding us ever deeper towards the inexhaustible Truth that God himself is.

The Dominican House of Studies warmly and gratefully received on that May evening this stirring commencement address, which gives an overview of Brian's inspiring approach to faith's study.

The Volume's Essays

Emmanuel, God with us, is at the heart of Brian Daley's theological vision. If you want a monograph on the early Church's thinking about Jesus Christ, you can do no better than Brian's *God Visible: Patristic Christology Reconsidered*.[7] Thanks to the editorial generosity of Phillip Carey, I organized a symposium on that volume in the pages of *Pro Ecclesia*, one of the journals Brian has served in an advisory role. There in *Pro Ecclesia* you will find review essays by three Catholic and three Orthodox theologians, followed by Brian's grateful and faith-filled response.[8] The present volume is not a monograph, but, like

7. Brian E. Daley, SJ, *God Visible: Patristic Christology Reconsidered* (Oxford: Oxford University Press, 2018).

8. Book symposium in *Pro Ecclesia* 28, no. 4 (2019): Andrew Hofer, OP, "The Beginning

the first volume in the present Eerdmans publication, it provides a collection of Brian's previously published essays. This second volume is dedicated to early Christology and falls into five parts. The essays demonstrate Brian's principles of theology communicated at the 2021 Dominican House of Studies commencement, and they provide focused arguments that supplement Brian's monographic treatment in *God Visible*.

The first part gives four synthetic overviews of patristic Christology through particular points of entry. The essay I would like to highlight, which is inspired by Gregory of Nazianzus's *Epistle* 101, to Cledonius,[9] is titled "'One Thing and Another': The Persons in God and the Person of Christ in Patristic Theology." Resisting technical terms, Gregory shows a reciprocity between what is plural and singular, in reverse manner, for the Trinity and Christ by emphasizing the gender of certain nouns in the Greek language. For the Trinity, Gregory uses a plural in the masculine but a singular in the neuter, whereas for Christ, Gregory uses a plural in the neuter but a singular in the masculine. That multiplicity in the neuter for Christ can be translated as "one thing and another." Brian argues that Gregory expresses a truth, sometimes only implicit but nonetheless real, through the early Christian centuries that theologians have developed their thinking about the Trinity and Christ in reversed tandem about what is plural and what is singular regarding the Trinity and Christ. In this argument, "a theology that emphasizes the threeness of persons in God—even a theology that is to some degree 'subordinationist' in conceiving how those three can still be one—tends to stress

---

and the End, and the Stations along the Way" (335–42); Paul L. Gavrilyuk, "Christology beyond Chalcedon: Brian Daley's *God Visible*" (343–46); Khaled Anatolios, "Brian Daley's *God Visible*: End or Beginning?" (347–54); John Behr, "Totus Christus: The Perennial Task of Regaining Wholeness" (355–61); Brian Dunkle, SJ, "Reconsiderations of Chalcedon in *God Visible*" (362–69); Andrew Louth, "Reflections on Brian Daley's *God Visible*" (370–77); Brian E. Daley, SJ, "*God Visible*: A Response to the Responses" (378–84). Referring to the symposium contributors, Brian Daley writes, "The book appeared some 18 months ago, and their comments here have not only been remarkably kind and supportive of the book's intent, but have given me the unusual opportunity now to clarify in my own mind what it was intended to say, perhaps even to recognize what it should have said, or might have said better" (378). He concludes, "My hope for the book is that it will set all believers and disciples reflecting more deeply about what it means to encounter 'the light of the knowledge and the glory of God in the face of Christ' (2 Cor. 4.6), and to join with the early theologians and Councils of the Church in the long, continuing dialogue of reflection we call 'Christology'" (384).

9. See *Ep*. 101.5.18–21. For Brian's thought on Gregory of Nazianzus, see especially his *Gregory of Nazianzus*, Early Church Fathers (London: Routledge, 2006).

the oneness of person in Christ the Savior, occasionally even to the point of seeming to compromise the fullness of his humanity." Brian continues, "On the other hand, a theology with a weak conception of the distinction of persons in God—a theology with a more 'modalist' way of conceiving God's being—tends to stress the twoness of natures or substances in Christ, even to the point of tending to see him as a human person in whom the Word or Wisdom or Spirit of God has come to dwell, as a divine gift extrinsic to himself." Brian illustrates his argument with four chronological test cases, beginning with the contrast of Hippolytus and Tertullian and ending with the variance between the Antiochene theologians and Cyril of Alexandria.

In the volume's second part, we turn in a pair of essays to Brian's focus on the Apollinarian challenge to especially Gregory of Nyssa. For Apollinarius, as Brian stresses, Christ saves us because he is unlike us, whereas for the Cappadocians, Christ saves us because he is like us. Concluding his essay on the "personal identity" of the Savior for Apollinarius and Gregory of Nyssa, for example, Brian articulates four points that show how meditation on Christ proves fruitful for all theology. The first is that Gregory's Christology is a *soteriology*: "The transformation of a complete and normal human nature in Jesus is, for Gregory, the 'first-fruits' of a transformation of all humanity as a race: an active leaven in the 'lump' of our common human dough." Brian next draws out a consequence for *anthropology*: Gregory is more optimistic about our human life than Apollinarius. For his third point, Brian argues that Gregory's depiction of the risen life of Christ affirms an *eschatology* of "the mysterious, unimaginable character of the promised end of history."[10] In the end Brian stresses, "Ultimately, perhaps, Gregory's quarrel with Apollinarius's Christology is really a quarrel about the nature of *God*." For Apollinarius, God the Word seems to be a Mind that is in competition with creation, whereas for Gregory, who stresses the divine transcendence, God never competes with creation.

The volume's third part treats Augustine, the only figure who received a full chapter in Brian's *God Visible*. Brian contributed the entry on Christology in *Augustine through the Ages: An Encyclopedia*, and he has always loved teaching and writing on Augustine.[11] He has never wanted to drive a wedge

10. For his latest volume of translations, see St. Gregory of Nyssa, *On Death and Eternal Life*, trans. Brian E. Daley, SJ, Popular Patristics Series 64 (Yonkers, NY: St. Vladimir's Seminary Press, 2022).

11. Brian E. Daley, SJ, "Christology," in *Augustine through the Ages: An Encyclopedia*, ed. Allan D. Fitzgerald, OSA, foreword by Jaroslav Pelikan (Grand Rapids: Eerdmans, 1999), 164–69.

between Augustine and the Christian East, and I can remember that in a seminar on the Cappadocians he would frequently bring up Augustine to show the complementary nature of Augustine's thinking to what we find in the great Basil, Gregory of Nazianzus, and Gregory of Nyssa. In this part of the volume, we encounter two comparative essays, the first on Origen and Augustine and the next on Ambrose and Augustine. After these marvelous treatments, we find an account of the distinctive elements of Augustine's Christology, with focus on the title "humble mediator." Brian himself comes from an Ignatian spirituality of humility, and we can detect connections between Augustine and Brian's own concentration on this virtue that grounds the Christian life.[12]

The fourth part presents four essays on Christology after Chalcedon. The first essay is a revised form of an address given in 2012 for the Thomistic Institute at the Dominican House of Studies earlier in the month when he received the Ratzinger Award from Pope Benedict XVI. The third gives Brian's argument about the reception of Chalcedon in Leontius of Byzantium, about whom Brian is the world's preeminent authority, and the fourth gives insightful considerations of Christology after Chalcedon regarding nature and the "mode of union." But I would like to turn to the piece that might be considered, frankly, odd: "Apollo as a Chalcedonian: A New Fragment of a Controversial Work from Early Sixth-Century Constantinople." In that essay, Brian analyzes a fragment purported to be an oracle of the god Apollo about Christ and gives a critical edition. Listen to a portion of this Chalcedonian witness in Brian's translation:

> The one who suffers is God, yet the godhead itself does not suffer;
> For he was both mortal and immortal at once,
> Incapable of dying yet capable of it, God's Word and human flesh;
> Yet neither was changed, nor did they come to be separated
> Or exist apart from each other. God himself is also a man,
> Receiving all from his Father and possessing all which was his mother's—
> Possessing life-giving might from his deathless Father,
> And from his mortal mother the cross, burial, contempt and sorrow,
> Seeing into, surveying, and hearing all things at once.

12. See Brian E. Daley, SJ, "'To Be More like Christ': The Background and Implications of 'Three Kinds of Humility,'" *Studies in the Spirituality of Jesuits* 27, no. 1 (1995); and Brian E. Daley, SJ, "The Pursuit of Excellence and the 'Ordinary Manner': Humility and the Jesuit University," in *For That I Came: Virtues and Ideals of Jesuit Education*, ed. William J. O'Brien (Washington, DC: Georgetown University Press, 1997), 11–35.

As Brian shows from his careful work on a rather abstruse text, "Apollo" gives testimony in Chalcedon's faith to Jesus Christ!

The fifth part pairs two essays, one more philosophically based, with attention to different senses of Logos, and the other an exploration in the apocalyptic. One of Brian's greatest scholarly contributions is in eschatology, as seen especially in his monograph *The Hope of the Early Church.*[13] It is appropriate to close this present book of essays on early Christology with his study of early Christian apocalyptic and the person of Christ. That essay begins in dramatic fashion with the first verse of Charles Wesley's "Lo, He Comes with Clouds Descending," a favorite Advent hymn. Attuned to developments in early Christianity, Brian writes:

> What I want to argue here is that even as the drama of Christian apocalyptic narrative lost much of its urgency, as Christian communities came to be more sure of themselves within the wider matrix of late Roman society, the apocalyptic image of the glorified Jesus—"the Lamb who was slain"—as judge to come, victor over the demonic powers of evil, and hidden companion of his church in what was assumed to be the continuing, final age of history, took on a formative, even a determining role for the development of doctrine. Christology, cosmology, ecclesiology—to use the distorting categories of modern academic theology—all became, in the course of the patristic period, East and West, "apocalypticized"; but it was an apocalypticism that had become a vehicle for acknowledging Jesus as Lord of history.

Always attentive to the details of time in writing historical theology, like a master watchmaker at work in precision, Brian narrates in faith how the Church moved over the first Christian centuries to understand the Lord of history—and what that means for us here and now.

In the following pages, we encounter a treasure trove of Brian Daley's studies about the person of the Lord Jesus Christ, which attend to Christ through the different times, figures, and controversies of the early Church in breathtaking fashion. Not exercises in antiquarianism, Brian's works witness to the Mystery of our salvation for consideration today. We find what we heard in his 2021 Dominican House of Studies commencement address: the extraordinary benefit of doing theology historically, reading the footnotes, as the Spirit guides us "ever deeper towards the inexhaustible Truth that God himself is."

13. Brian E. Daley, SJ, *The Hope of the Early Church: A Handbook of Patristic Eschatology* (Cambridge: Cambridge University Press, 1991), 2nd ed. (Peabody, MA: Hendrickson, 2003).

PART 1

Christological Surveys of the Early Church

1 Christ and Christologics

It seems a truism to say that Christology—the interpretation of the person of Jesus in the light of the Christian canon of Scripture, and of the tradition which receives it—is what early Christianity, at its heart, is all about. To recognize in Jesus, on the basis of his crucifixion and resurrection, the unexpected fulfillment of Israel's hopes for a messianic king, a "Christ"; to understand Jesus's language about his "Father in heaven" as expressing his sense of a unique relationship to Israel's single God, and to take him as literally God's "only Son"; to see in him the final revealer of God's secrets and plans, the human embodiment of God's creative Wisdom, God's eternal Word of self-communication now made humanly present in time—all of this was clearly involved in the transformation of memories that led his disciples to proclaim a gospel centered on him: to proclaim that God's kingdom had begun to be real for all humanity in Jesus's death and resurrection. It was because of their understanding of who and what Jesus was (and is) that the first few generations of Christians gradually came to see themselves as forming a distinct body within the religious tradition of Israel; and it was because of their understanding of Jesus, too, that they believed they had a new message of freedom and fulfillment, as well as a new call to moral uprightness and transforming love, to offer to the pagans' world.

Christology, then—to use a term originating in post-Reformation academic theology[1]—lay always at the heart of the developing worship, life,

1. As subjects within the discourse of faith, early Christians tended to distinguish only between *theologia*, "language about God," which came to mean language about God as Trinity, and *oikonomia*, the narrative of God's "management" of history, God's plan of

and thought of the early Church, even as its vocabulary and concepts grew and changed. Our own understanding of that growth, however, has gone through a number of important changes in recent decades. This has been driven less by new archaeological or historical discoveries about late antiquity than by the publication of newly discovered texts from the early Church, on the one hand, and by changes in our commonly accepted assumptions about the history of culture and ideas—including those of religion—on the other. At the same time, the development of new theological perspectives and interests has prompted modern interpreters of the history of Christian faith to ask different questions, and to look for different answers, from those their teachers had proposed in the early decades of the twentieth century.

1. New Perspectives in Christology

Christology, in fact, has moved in the last century from being a theological topic which seemed safe and uncontroversial to an area of bitter controversy and uncertainty. As late as 1954, the Catholic theologian Karl Rahner observed that for theologians of his tradition, at least, Christology was understood to be one of those areas in which all possible problems had been solved by the dense and paradoxical dogmatic formula of the Council of Chalcedon (451), which asserted that "one and the same Lord Jesus Christ, the only begotten Son, must be acknowledged in two natures, without confusion or change, without division or separation" (Neuner and Dupuis 1981: 154, no. 615). In Rahner's view, the Christological complacency of modern Catholic thinkers suggested a surprising unawareness of the far-reaching implications of even the language of Chalcedon itself, and a failure to keep "acquiring anew," at a deeper level of contemplative awareness, an intellectual grasp of the vision of Jesus that the community of faith already possesses (Rahner 1954, trans. 1961: 152–53).

It was precisely the discovery of the need to repossess the content and meaning of classical Christology, it seems, that led, in the middle of the twentieth century, to a questioning of some aspects of what most believers thought had been settled permanently by the Chalcedonian formula. The intrusion of modern historical consciousness—an awareness of the

redemption, which would of course include the story of Jesus. Christian *theologia*, however, clearly found its starting point in the Christian story of the *oikonomia*. See Eusebius of Caesarea, *Hist. eccl.* 1.1.7; Gregory of Nazianzus, *Or.* 38.8.

relativizing influence of context on ideas, a sense that all theories and dogmas are bound to the language and assumptions of a particular time and place—on the understanding of Christian doctrine and Scripture, has led, in the nineteenth and twentieth centuries, to the growing realization, first among "liberal" Protestants but eventually in more traditional branches of Reformed, Anglican, and Catholic theology, that if Jesus is, as Chalcedon proclaims, "complete in divinity and complete in humanity, fully God and fully a human being," then some aspects of the portrait of Jesus traditionally drawn by Christian dogma needed to be seriously questioned.

Rahner, in the same article, alludes to a fundamentally mythical conception of the incarnation, according to which "the 'human' element [in Jesus] is merely the clothing, the livery, of which the god makes use in order to draw attention to his presence here with us," and adds that this conception, which can be met in the Apollinarian and "Monophysite" conceptions of the person of Christ in the patristic period, "probably lives on in the picture which countless Christians have of the 'Incarnation,' whether they give it their faith—or reject it" (Rahner 1954, trans. 1961: 156). The Scottish theologian Donald Baillie, writing in 1947 from a Protestant perspective, also points to an earlier unwillingness on the part of Christians of all the Churches to take the humanity of Christ seriously:

> Theologians shrank from admitting human growth, human ignorance, human mutability, human struggle and temptation, into their conception of the Incarnate Life, and treated it as simply a divine life lived in a human body (and sometimes even this was conceived as essentially different from our bodies) rather than a truly human life lived under the psychical conditions of humanity. (Baillie 1956: 11)

In contrast to this tendency, modern scriptural scholarship, with its emphasis on historical setting and development, had prompted a new engagement on the part of theologians with the historicity of the humanity of Jesus emphasized, in theory at least, by the Chalcedonian dogma. Although Roman Catholic theology, in its officially sponsored form, initially resisted the introduction of historically conditioned thinking to biblical interpretation and the understanding of dogma during the Modernist controversy, by the middle of the twentieth century its perspective had begun to change radically. A gradual dissatisfaction with the deductive, curiously rationalistic character of the scholastic theological manuals used in seminary instruction drew new attention to the patristic and medieval sources of the theological tradition, and to its organic but unpredictable growth. In what came to be known as the *ressourcement* of Catholic theology, context and a sense of coherent development were given primary emphasis (Daley 2005*a*).

In the realm of Christology, this meant paying new attention to the authors and controversies of the early Church, in which the classical Christian understanding of Christ's person, underlying both scholastic theology and most forms of Christian piety, was debated and formed. The object of such renewed historical study was originally to uncover lines of logical development: to see an underlying direction in the apparent twists and turns of early Christological debate, a providentially guided movement towards a final formulation "which like a hidden entelechy had accompanied the wearisome struggles of centuries to interpret the *mysterium Christi*" (Grillmeier 1975: 548). This inner goal, coming gradually and by a kind of common intuition towards full articulation throughout the early debates, was for most students of Christology the formula of the Council of Chalcedon.

The Anglican scholar J. N. D. Kelly, for instance, in his influential handbook *Early Christian Doctrines*, sees "the problem of Christology, in the narrow sense of the word," as "to define the relation of the divine and the human in Christ." Implied in New Testament confessions, and reflected in an unformed way in second- and third-century Christian documents, this issue of Jesus's personal identity as Son of God was brought to the center of debate, Kelly argues, in "the decision, promulgated at Nicaea (325) that the Word shared the same divine nature as the Father"; but the balanced enunciation of the central paradox of Christian faith in Jesus—that he is, as a single subject, both fully divine and fully human—awaited the final "settlement" of the definition of Chalcedon (Kelly 1978: 138; see also pp. 280, 340–42). The much more detailed surveys of early Christology by the German Catholic scholar (later Cardinal) Aloys Grillmeier also begin from the assumption that Chalcedon's formulation is Christianity's most complete expression of the apostolic faith in the person of Christ, the norm by which the adequacy of all earlier or later attempts to express who and what Jesus is must ultimately be judged. Grillmeier writes:

> If we look backwards from the year 451, the definition of the Council doubtless appears as the culmination of the development that had gone before it. If we look ahead to the centuries of Christological controversies which followed, the understanding of the Church's faith in Christ, as expressed in 451, constitutes the firm norm, as well as the great source of discord, which

occupied and divided spirits. In any case, it was at Chalcedon that the decisive formulation of the Church's faith in the person of Jesus was forged. (Grillmeier and Bacht 1952: 5)

2. Developments in Early Christology

2.1. Second and Third Centuries

The way to this Chalcedonian formulation and beyond it—however one evaluates its role as norm for the orthodox understanding of Jesus today—was a long and twisted one. The earliest post–New Testament Christian documents that survive tend to present Jesus as a divine revealer, who had taken on human form. For instance, the Syriac hymns known as the *Odes of Solomon*, which probably date from shortly before or shortly after the year 100, invite the hearer to rejoice in the salvation that God's "Beloved" has brought humanity through becoming like us:

> For there is a Helper for me, the Lord . . .
> He became like me, that I might receive Him.
> In form He was considered like me, that I might put Him on . . .
> Like my nature He became, that I might understand Him.
> And like my form, that I might not turn away from Him.
>
> (Ode 7.3–6)

Ignatius of Antioch (d. *c.* 115), who may have been bishop of the very community for which the *Odes* were composed, also speaks of Jesus unhesitatingly in his letters as "my God" (see, e.g., *Eph.* 18.2; *Rom. Inscr.*; *Rom.* 3.3; *Smyr.* 1.1), but emphasizes even more clearly than the *Odes* do—as a point apparently contested at the time—that his flesh and his human experiences were all real (*Trall.* 9; *Eph.* 18.2; *Smyr.* 2–3.5). For Ignatius, the reality of Jesus's human body is the link between his divine origin and his historical role as healer and savior for fleshly creatures.

The long debate between mainstream Christian leaders and Gnostic teachers, which began in the second century and continued, in various forms, at least through the Middle Ages, was to a large degree focused on a debate about the reality of the Savior's flesh. For Gnostic Christianity, it was axiomatic that the moral and ritual prescriptions of Jewish scripture were given by a lesser god than the God of redemption, and that the created, material world, in which other forms of religion flourished, was in reality hostile and illusory. Understandably, then—at least according to early Christian critics of Gnosticism—the divine Savior, Jesus, who brought to spirits imprisoned in matter a message of redemption and freedom, was thought by most Gnostic sects not to have had a real body, or to have experienced real human need or suffering (Layton 1987: 162, 198, 211, 239, 267, 293–96, 423). For Jesus and for those who believe in him, suggests the Valentinian *Epistle to Rheginus*, "resurrection" does not involve the material human body, even in a transformed state, but is a way of describing the spiritual enlightenment in which the soul lays aside its fleshly concerns like an old garment (see Layton 1987: 320–24).

The most articulate critic of Gnostic forms of Christianity in the second century was Irenaeus of Lyon, a native of Smyrna in Asia Minor, who traveled west and became bishop of that Roman frontier town around 185. In his massive anti-Gnostic elaboration of apostolic tradition, known as *Against Heresies*,[2] Irenaeus makes an elaborate defense of the ordinary ingredients of Christian life in the world, as the place of God's presence and salvation: the Church and its structures of authority; the Jewish scriptures and the Christian writings on which the Church's faith was based; baptism and the eucharist; the fleshly body; the Christian hope of bodily resurrection and judgment; and at the center of all, the person of Jesus the Savior, who can transform human life because he shares at once in God's transcendent reality and in our own. Irenaeus writes:

> Just as through the disobedience of the one human being, who was shaped first from unformed earth, many became sinners and lost life, so it was right that many should be made just and receive salvation through the obedience of one human being, who was born first from a virgin (cf. Rom 5:12–17). . . . But if he had not been made flesh but only appeared as flesh, his work was not truthful. What he appeared to be, then, he also was; God, summing up the ancient formation of humanity in himself in order to put sin to death, made death an empty thing and gave humanity life. Therefore his works are true. . . . For this reason, then, the Word of God became a human being, and the one who is Son of God became Son of Man, so that the human

2. A better translation might be: "Against the Sects." The word *hairesis*, in the Greek of the time, meant first of all a voluntary organization, and thus the set of beliefs or practices that characterized that organization—all taken in contrast with the wider body of the city or world and generally accepted beliefs.

being might receive the Word, and by accepting adoption might become a child of God.[3]

Perhaps the most influential thinker of early Christianity, at least before Augustine, was Origen of Alexandria (c. 185–253), who was also the first Christian to devote his life to scriptural interpretation. Origen's theology and exegesis are always centered on the Church's understanding of the person and work of Jesus (see, e.g., *Princ.* 4.1.6), and his homilies often demonstrate a deep Christocentric piety (Bertrand 1951). He makes it clear that he understands Christ, at the core of his identity, to be the divine Wisdom, the Word of creation and revelation, begotten of the Father "beyond the limits of any beginning that we can speak of or understand" (*Princ.* 1.2.2); it is he who grants to created intellects the share in the life and wisdom of God that is their salvation (*Princ.* 2.6.3). The incarnation of the Word in Jesus, therefore, implies an irreducibly twofold reality in his person (see *Princ.* 1.2.1), even though the agent of salvation is the Word himself—a paradox, as Origen acknowledges, that must strike the contemplative mind with utter amazement (*Princ.* 2.6.2).

2.2. *Arius and Athanasius*

In the fourth century, Athanasius of Alexandria made new and decisive contributions to the articulation of the Church's understanding of Jesus's personal identity. Athanasius is mainly remembered for his defense—beginning in the early 340s—of the credal formula of the Council of Nicaea (325), which he may have helped draft as a young theological advisor to Alexander, then bishop of Alexandria. The issue now was not so much the denial of Christ's flesh as the continuing influence on the conception of Christ's person of Platonic and earlier Christian ideas, which saw God's action in the world as mediated in steps. In this view, God, utterly unknowable and transcendent, created, redeemed, and sanctified his creatures through the Son and the Holy Spirit as intermediaries, who were themselves produced or created in order to accomplish the Father's will. By standing nearer to the Father in the order of creation, by participating in God's qualities and powers and carrying out his purposes, Son and Spirit could themselves be called divine, and were not

3. This translation is based on both the ancient Latin version, which is the only complete text we now have of Irenaeus's work, and a Greek fragment of this passage.

of the same creaturely status as the rest of creation. Yet, according to this position, popularized by the Alexandrian priest Arius and (in a more moderate way) by the scholarly bishop Eusebius of Caesarea, the Son or Word of God, who became enfleshed in Jesus to reveal God's saving mystery, still belonged entirely to the created realm, and had a beginning in some age of time. As Arius himself pointedly observed, "There was a point when he was not."

For Athanasius, by contrast, the universe is brought into being and held in dynamic order by the presence within it of the eternal, transcendent Word of God, who is fully divine, or (in the phrase of Nicaea) "of the same substance" as the one God of Israel. Wholly "other" than the created order because he is God, the Word—as God—is also immediately present to creation, actively involved in forming it and in re-forming it when it becomes destructively alienated from its Creator (Anatolios 1998). In the incarnation, the Word takes on a passible, mortal body, in order to reconstruct and reorder fallen humanity from within, and to communicate the incorruptible life that comes only from contact with God (*Inc.* 9).

For reasons that are probably as much connected to modern perceptions of his authoritarian personality and combative style as to his theological works, Athanasius has been more than a little unpopular with patristic scholars for most of the twentieth century. The main theological objection to his portrait of Christ has been that it represents an extreme form of what Grillmeier has labeled a *logos-sarx* or "Word-flesh" (rather than a "Word–human being") model of Christ's person: like his opponent Arius, like virtually all Greek theologians of the first three quarters of the fourth century—although unlike Origen—Athanasius has almost nothing to say about the soul or the interior human qualities and experiences of Christ, as playing a decisive role in his actions as Savior. R. P. C. Hanson quipped that Christ's relation to the "instrument" of his body is, for Athanasius, "no closer than that of an astronaut to his space-suit" (Hanson 1988: 448; in response, see Anatolios 1997). As Grillmeier more moderately observed, in Athanasius's work "the soul of Christ retreats well into the background, even if it does not disappear completely"; it is certainly not a "theological factor" in his Christology, even if he may regard it as a "physical factor" in Jesus's life and actions (Grillmeier 1975: 308, 325). It is the Word of God, present in the flesh of Jesus and through it to all of humanity, which communicates a vital and transforming energy that leads to the salvation of all his human brothers and sisters.

This critique of Athanasius's understanding of the person of Christ, however, distorts his intentions by judging them in light of fifth-century issues, standards he never intended to meet. His concern throughout his works is to emphasize that Jesus, the Word incarnate, embodies in his person the paradox of a transcendent, immaterial God making his own the limited, unstable realm of matter, in order to communicate to creatures the Creator's healing power and life. Athanasius's language of the Word and his bodily "instrument" seems intended not so much as an ontological analysis of Christ's person as a way of emphasizing the contrast between God and the world of flesh, which provides the background for the astonishing proclamation of the Word's incarnation (Petterson 1995; Anatolios 1998).

2.3. *Apollinarius and His Critics*

In the standard modern narrative of the development of early Christology, however, the debates that swirled around Arius's conception of Christ as creature, and the Nicene assertion that the Son is "of the same substance" as the Father, were essentially theological rather than Christological: arguments about the internal structure of God's transcendent being. It was only in the 360s and 370s, it is usually argued, that the focus of debate shifted from the Person or Persons of God to the personal unity of the incarnate Word—how the eternal Son and the man Jesus can be a single individual—and that the real issues of Christology as such came into focus (Studer 1993: 193–94). The key figure at this new stage of controversy was Apollinarius of Laodicea, a gifted and energetic writer and teacher in the church of Antioch during the second half of the fourth century.

Apollinarius is usually identified with the position that in the person of Christ, the eternal Word of God had simply assumed human flesh—perhaps flesh enlivened by a lower, vegetative soul, or life principle; the Word itself, Apollinarius insisted, took the place occupied in human creatures by the higher, self-determining intellectual soul, or *nous*. This version of what Grillmeier calls *logos-sarx* or Word-flesh Christology is simply a more explicit form of an understanding of Christ's person that had been assumed by most Greek theologians for the preceding century. Apollinarius emerged to prominence in the Antiochene church of the 360s: an enterprising Christian humanist and a leading voice in the Nicene movement, who was also highly critical of the "modalist" form of anti-Arian theology, which minimized any lasting distinction between Father, Son, and Holy Spirit within the mystery of God. This position, represented in the mid-fourth century by Marcellus of Ancyra, interpreted the Nicene confession of "one substance" in God as implying that Trinitarian language refers only to the way in which God has been experienced within salvation history. This position seems to have raised at least as much alarm in orthodox circles as Arius's theology of created mediators. Apollinarius's response was to emphasize the eternal, distinct existence of the person of Christ, and to refer to that existence, in some of his writings at least, not only in terms of the divine Word, but also in Paul's language of "the man from heaven," in whose image we are all being renewed (1 Cor 15:45–49; Greer 1990). Although Apollinarius clearly accepted the material reality of Christ's living body, as the instrument by which the Word acts in the world, he emphasized, in many passages of his works, that "the Lordly human being" is substantially different from the ordinary, fallen human beings he has come to save, in that the Word himself is Christ's sole source of energy, thought, and will.

Persuasive and politically well connected in Syria and Asia Minor, Apollinarius seems at first to have won a number of admirers among Nicene churchmen opposed to a modalist theology. When he began to promote his Christological theories as normative for orthodoxy, however, and even ordained like-minded bishops to make this version of Nicene faith a new basis for ecclesial communion, former friends became increasingly resistant to his views. Another leading bishop-theologian of the Syrian church, Diodore of Tarsus, seems to have raised the alarm against Apollinarius, and Apollinarius was listed among the leaders of heresies at the Council of Constantinople in 381. By the mid-380s, both Gregory of Nyssa and Gregory of Nazianzus had written strong polemics against Apollinarius's understanding of Christ, because it deprived Christ of a human intellectual soul and because it seemed to suggest that even Jesus's flesh was of a different substance from our own. In his first letter to the priest Cledonius, Gregory of Nazianzus quotes an earlier maxim of Origen to sum up his objection:

> That which [Christ] has not assumed he has not healed; but that which is united to his Godhead is also saved.[4] If only half of Adam fell, then that which Christ assumes and saves may be half also; but if the whole of his nature fell, it must be united to the whole nature of Him that was begotten, and so be saved as a whole. (*Ep.* 101)

4. This idea, expressed in slightly different terms, had already been proposed by Origen, *Dialogue with Heraclides* (SC 67.70, ll. 17–19). Gregory's phrase is later quoted by Maximus the Confessor, *Opusculum* 9, "To the Faithful in Sicily" (PG 91.128D–129A). For further references, see A. Grillmeier, "Quod non assumptum—non sanatum," in *LTK* 8. 954–55.

Precisely because the intellectual part of our humanity is what first needs healing, Gregory insisted, the incarnate Word must have a human intellect as well as human flesh. Salvation comes to us by Jesus's identity with us, as God fully sharing in our humanity, not by his merely providing us with an example of moral perfection to imitate.

The Christology developed by the two Cappadocian Gregories, largely in response to Apollinarius, is not, however, simply an affirmation that two wholly different realities coexist in a single agent. Both bishops tend to speak of Christ as a "double" yet radically unified reality in which the flesh, with all its weakness and "through the mediation of a mind," is "mixed together with God" (Gregory of Nazianzus, *Or.* 29.19). Both emphasize that this "blending" of two infinitely unequal ingredients results in the transformation of what is weaker by its assimilation to what is stronger, the "divinization" of the human element in Christ, and through him of all humanity (Gregory of Nazianzus, *Or.* 38.13). God the Word is clearly the agent, the personal center of Christ's actions, the source of his ability to heal our fallen state. To meditate on the person and activities of Jesus, to "walk through" the events of his life as presented in Scripture, enables the believer to "ascend with his Godhead and no longer remain among visible things" (Gregory of Nazianzus, *Or.* 29.18).

For Gregory of Nyssa, the assumption by the infinite and unchangeable Son of God of a full human nature—that is, as a creature always capable of change—brings about in Jesus, and through him in us, a graded transformation of the negative or limiting properties of humanity into divine qualities: the corruptible into the incorruptible, the mortal into the immortal. In the glorified Jesus, one sees the effects of the process begun in the incarnation of the Word, which eventually results in his sharing his divine qualities with us all:

> He who is always in the Father, and who always has the Father in himself and is united with him, is and will be as he was for all ages. . . . But the first-fruits of human nature which he has taken up, absorbed—one might say figuratively—by the omnipotent divinity like a drop of vinegar mingled in the boundless sea, exists in the Godhead, but not in its own proper characteristics. (Gregory of Nyssa, *To Theophilus against the Apollinarists*, GNO 3/1, 126.14–21)

What has only gradually been revealed in Jesus, as his latent divinity, is promised to the rest of humanity through the refashioning of our nature (see also *Eun.* 3.3.68; *Or. catech.* 37).

2.4. *The Nestorian Controversy*

Perhaps the most celebrated stage in the development of early Christology came in the first half of the fifth century, in the controversy between representatives of the so-called Antiochene school of exegesis and theological interpretation, such as Theodore of Mopsuestia, Nestorius of Constantinople, and Theodoret of Cyrrhus, and the Alexandrian school, principally represented by Cyril of Alexandria. The usual way of understanding their differences is to see the Antiochene theologians as maintaining a "Word–human being" (*Logos-anthrōpos*) model of the person of Christ, in which the eternal Word or Son of God, fully divine in nature, has taken up a complete human being to be his "temple" (Theodore, fragments 1–2, 9; Nestorius, *Sermon*; Norris 1980, 113–17, 121, 123–31). So the Word dwells in Jesus and bestows his favor on him in such a unique way that Jesus can be seen as revealing the "face" (*prosōpon*) of the Son in the world, while the Son provides Jesus with a divine "face" (Nestorius, *The Bazaar of Heracleides*, 239–45, 264–68; see Scipioni 1956). The result is that while God the Son and Jesus are never to be confused into a single subject or agent, they reveal each other in a single common form. Along with this approach to understanding Christ, these authors were also known for their distinctive way of interpreting the message of Scripture, in which God is understood to reveal his will and our future through human events but, as God, remains independent of history, transcendent, and uncircumscribed.

The Alexandrian school of the late fourth and fifth centuries, on the other hand, took the inspiration for its Christology from Athanasius, and for its biblical interpretation from Origen. Jesus, in Cyril of Alexandria's understanding, always remained God the Word, subsisting personally in the full humanity that he had made his own—a single divine subject acting and suffering in his own soul and flesh. To those spiritually gifted enough to seek the Bible's deeper meaning, the whole canon of Scripture told his story, as well as that of the people united with him by faith and the sacraments. The active, personal presence of God in the world, which has reached its climax in Christ and the Church, is the central message of the gospel.

Conflict between these two centers of Christian study began simmering in the middle of the fourth century, doubtless from political and ecclesiastical as well as theological motives. It burst into the open, however, in the winter of 428–429, when the newly appointed bishop of Constantinople, Nestorius—a gifted preacher from Antioch, adamantly opposed to any suggestion that the Word was a creature—openly attacked the popular tradition of using the title "God-bearer" (*Theotokos*) for Mary, the mother of Jesus, since it seemed to contradict God's transcendence:

> Mary, my friend, did not give birth to the Godhead, for "what is born of the flesh is flesh" (John 3:6). A creature did not produce him who is uncreatable. The Father has not just recently generated God the Logos from the Virgin. . . . Rather, he formed out of the Virgin a temple for God the Logos, a temple in which he dwelt. (Norris 1980: 124–25)

Cyril of Alexandria, an accomplished and prolific exegete and a subtle theologian, saw in Nestorius's distinctions an implied denial of the direct involvement of God in the world's history. Although the language for distinguishing between *what* God is—God's *substance* or *nature*—and *who* the Savior is—God the Son as an individual (*hypostasis*) or "person" (*prosōpon*)[5]—was still in its early stages of development, and the terminology applied to Father, Son, and Holy Spirit in the Trinity by the Cappadocians was not yet uniformly extended to the complex reality of Christ, Cyril—like Athanasius and Gregory of Nazianzus—stressed the single subject of the acts that have saved us: it is God the Word, God the Son, who is born of a Virgin, who receives the Holy Spirit for us in baptism, who heals the sick and raises the dead by his human touch, who dies in his passible body on the cross and reunites that body with his soul on the morning of resurrection. In an early letter criticizing Nestorius for his rejection of Mary's title *Theotokos*, Cyril sketches out what would be his basic position throughout the debate:

> We do not say that the Logos became flesh by having his nature changed, nor for that matter that he was transformed into a complete human being composed out of soul and body. On the contrary, we say that in an unspeakable and incomprehensible way, the Logos united to himself, in his hypostasis, flesh enlivened by a rational soul, and in this way became a human being and has been designated "Son of man." . . . Furthermore, we say

5. I have put "person" in quotation marks here because the modern understanding of the person, characterized by interior self-awareness, freedom, and the ability to form relationships with other persons, was far from being fully developed in the ancient world. *Prosōpon* (originally "face" or "mask") suggested the role played by an actor on the stage, or by a human individual in the drama of life: an externally perceived form, what we still call a *persona*. *Hypostasis*, the other common word used in the Christological debates for an individual, simply meant a single instance of some universal substance, a logical subject of attribution.

> that while the natures which were brought together into a true unity were different, there is, nevertheless, because of the unspeakable and unutterable convergence into unity, one Christ and one Son out of the two. This is the sense in which it is said that, although he existed and was born from the Father before the ages, he was also born of a woman in his flesh. . . . We assert that this is the way in which he suffered and rose from the dead. It is not that the Logos of God suffered in his own nature, being overcome by stripes or nail-piercing or any of the other injuries; for the divine, since it is incorporeal, is impassible. Since, however, the body that had become his own underwent suffering, he is—once again—said to have suffered these things for our sakes, for the impassible one was within the suffering body. (Norris 1980: 132–33)

Here and throughout his later letters and essays, Cyril is mainly concerned to emphasize that the story of the Gospels, of the birth and death and resurrection of Jesus, is not about the formal relationship of divinity and humanity, but about what the Son of God did in history for our sakes. Cyril is careful to respect the narrative sequence in the story of salvation: "the natures which *were* brought together into a true unity *were* different," yet there *is* now "convergence into unity, one Son out of the two." As he insists here and in later letters, the unity of subject in the story of Jesus is "union in *hypostasis*"—union in the concreteness of an individual existence, which, as the lived-out operation of a single organic being, can also be spoken of as "union in nature," without ever implying by that a blurring of the infinite ontological distinction between God's uncreated being and the being of creatures (*Third Letter to Nestorius* 4–7, trans. Wickham 1983: 18–23).

2.5. *The Controversy around Chalcedon*

The Christological differences between Nestorius and Cyril, and their respective colleagues, grew into a major Church controversy in the late 420s, involving heated discussion among all the major sees. Emperor Theodosius II summoned a council at Ephesus in the early summer of 431, but the representatives of the opposing sides never met to discuss the issues, and the council members dispersed without coming to a common resolution. Only in 433, after Nestorius had been deposed from episcopal power and sent into exile, was agreement reached between the Antiochenes and the Alexandrians: a negotiated statement accepted by both sides and affirmed in a letter from Cyril to John, patriarch of Antioch, carefully crafted to include the positions that each side considered essential.

Less than twenty years later, when the principal participants in that debate had died, controversy broke out again among their followers, most of whom—on both sides—were now less willing to compromise. At issue was the degree to which Cyril's picture of the person of Christ, and some key terms and phrases from Cyril's later letters (characterizing the one Christ as "one nature of the Word, made flesh," or speaking of the union of the divine and human in him as a "union in hypostasis," or as a union "from two natures" rather than "of two natures"), should be regarded as norms for Christian confession. After a series of manifestos and excommunications, and the abortive attempt to resolve the discord at another council at Ephesus in 449, Emperor Marcian eventually succeeded in bringing a synod of bishops together at Chalcedon, across the Bosporus from Constantinople, in the autumn of 451—a gathering at which virtually all the Christian churches were to some degree represented. It was there that the famous statement of the Church's understanding of Christ was formulated—including language from both sides of the dispute, as well as from the joint statement of 433—now appended to the Creeds of Nicaea (325) and Constantinople (381) as a kind of hermeneutical norm for interpreting them in their full Christological implications.

It is important to remember, however, that the dogmatic statement of Chalcedon was not a "settlement" of the Christological controversies that then divided the Church, as historians in the past have suggested. Partisan debate, in fact, was even more heated after the council. Several emperors in the late fifth and sixth centuries sought to downplay or even annul Chalcedon's statement of unity, in the unsuccessful hope of healing the major schisms that followed the council before they became permanent. For a large number of bishops, monks, and lay people in the eastern empire, particularly in Syria, Palestine, and Egypt, the Christology formulated at Chalcedon was an abandonment of centuries of devotion to the person of Christ, as God present in our midst in the full concreteness of a historical human being—an abandonment of the paradoxes sustained so passionately by Athanasius and Cyril, and a victory for the humanistic, overly analytical thinking of Nestorius and his Antiochene supporters. The fact that Pope Leo, and the Latin sources on which he drew, had played an influential part in the council's discussions was also not a positive recommendation to many eastern Christians. As a result, eastern Christians broke communion with the imperially sponsored Church in increasing numbers; in the seventy years after

Chalcedon, a number of major theologians opposed to the council's Christology—among them Philoxenus of Mabbug in Syria, patriarch Timothy "Ailouros" in Egypt, and Severus, a learned monk of Gaza who later became patriarch of Antioch—wrote polemical works arguing that nothing short of the Christological language of Cyril could do justice to the Church's authentic tradition of faith and practice. These writers, and the earlier sources to which they appealed, were to remain the normative "fathers" of the Oriental Orthodox or non-Chalcedonian churches.

2.6. *Late Patristic Developments*

The Second Council of Constantinople (553), sponsored by the emperor Justinian as part of a larger program of rebuilding Church unity, issued a new set of doctrinal canons, reaffirming the formal validity, essential content, and terminology of the Chalcedonian Definition, and seeking to clarify its intent by emphasizing that the "one *hypostasis* . . . acknowledged in two natures" by Christian faith is in fact none other than the eternal *hypostasis* of God the Word (canon 5), "one of the holy Trinity" (canon 10). The council's statement also recognized legitimate and illegitimate ways of understanding the unconfused but united realities in Christ, both as "two natures" and also—in the preferred phrase of Cyril's later letters—as "one nature, made flesh" (canons 7–8).

Despite Justinian's goal of reconciling a fragmented eastern Christendom, the divisions that followed Chalcedon remained largely unaffected by the council of 553. While the Latin West tended to regard these new canons, along with the council's explicit condemnation of the three main doctors of the Antiochene tradition, as an implicit abandonment of the Christological balance of the Chalcedonian Definition, those eastern communities that insisted on the "miaphysite" (one nature, made flesh) model developed by Cyril of Alexandria did not find the council's position unambiguous enough to lure them back into communion with Constantinople, and continued to maintain independent ecclesiastical structures.

In the seventh century, the Christological debate was recast in ostensibly new terms: this time due to the attempt of the patriarch Sergius of Constantinople, and his successor, Pyrrhus, to craft an official interpretation of Chalcedonian terminology in a way more acceptable to dissident eastern Christians, by affirming the single "activity" or "theandric operation" of the two united natures in Christ. This conception could be expressed in psychological terms by speaking of those natures—as Pyrrhus would eventually do—as possessing a single *will*: that of the divine Logos. It was Maximus the Confessor, a learned monk from Constantinople, living for more than two decades as an exile in Latin North Africa, who led the opposition to what he saw here as simply a new form of the Apollinarian hybridization of Christ. In a number of letters and essays written during the 640s, Maximus pointed out some of the further implications of the Chalcedonian picture of a single concrete individual existing in, and fully possessing, two natures—implications intuitively grasped by Augustine two centuries earlier. Every substance or nature, Maximus insisted, operates in a way characteristic of itself; if the human and the divine are distinct natures possessed by the one person of Jesus, as the Church's doctrine teaches they are, then each must have its own distinctive and integral operation, and Jesus must possess, as his own, both a limited human will and the eternal will of God the Son. The marvel of the incarnation, for Maximus, is precisely that Jesus's natures, including their wholly asymmetrical wills, operate distinctly, but in a manner that results not in conflict but in perfect harmony: "He is divine in a human way, and human in a divine way."[6] This further refinement of Chalcedonian Christology was confirmed in Rome at the Lateran Synod of 649, attended by Maximus and presided over by Pope Martin I—both of whom were later imprisoned and fatally mistreated, by order of the emperor Constans II, as a result of their position. It was later confirmed by Pope Agatho in a Roman synod of 680, and officially received in the East by the Third Council of Constantinople (680–681), a gathering now recognized by Orthodox and Western Christians as the Sixth Ecumenical Council of the whole Church.

3. Concluding Reflections

Even this brief survey of the development of early Christology reveals how complex that development actually was, how many issues about God and the world lay beneath the surface of verbal formulations. The Christian understanding of the identity and role of Jesus is not the content of a proposition, which emerged slowly but steadily through a centuries-long process

6. Maximus repeats this maxim several times in his works; see, e.g., *Ep.* 15 to Cosmas (PG 91.573B2–9); *Ep.* 19 to Pyrrhus (PG 91.593A2–9); *Opusculum* 4 to the Higoumen George (PG 91.61B1–C11); *Opusc.* 7 to Marinus (PG 91.84B11–D3); *Dialogue with Pyrrhus* (PG 91.297D13–298A4).

of conflict and debate. It is the glimpse of the central reality of the gospel, a vision of God's healing and transforming presence in the world that yokes together two incommensurables in a single paradox, "God with us." One factor that has led to a change of modern perspective in the understanding of that development, over the past fifty years, has been theology's growing appreciation of the historical reality of the man Jesus: this has made modern theologians more sympathetic to those ancient voices that seem to have articulated a clear sense of the operative human fullness of Jesus's being, and of the cultural and psychological limitations in which, and through which, he acted. In the 1940s and 1950s, for instance, renewed interest in the Antiochene Christology, because of its recognition of Jesus as a complete human being indwelt by the Word, led to new, positive readings of Theodore of Mopsuestia (Greer 1961; Norris 1963) and even of Nestorius (Scipioni 1956; Grillmeier 1975), despite their rejection by Chalcedon and Constantinople II. At the same time, and even through the 1980s, many historical theologians showed questioning, even hostile attitudes towards Athanasius and Cyril of Alexandria, largely because of what was thought to be their over-emphasis on the divine center of Jesus's actions and consciousness. On the other hand, historians of theology also began to recognize, early in the twentieth century, that the Christology actually professed by the "miaphysite" or anti-Chalcedonian theologians of the fifth and sixth centuries, such as Severus and Timothy Ailouros, and by the churches nourished on their works, was much less radical in its picture of the divine unity of Jesus's person than had been previously supposed. Their Christology, seen now as "verbal monophysism," differed from the Chalcedonian model mainly in the unyielding insistence of these authors that orthodox faith could be expressed accurately only in the language of Cyril (Lebon 1909, 1951).

More recently, renewed emphasis on the distinctively scriptural, rather than cultural or philosophical, basis of Christian doctrine has been one of the main factors in a renewed sympathy for the work of Athanasius (Torrance 1995; Petterson 1995; Anatolios 1998) and Cyril of Alexandria (McGuckin 1994; Weinandy and Keating 2003). Interest in Cyril's Christology has probably also been aided by renewed openness among theologians to the idea of God's participation in human suffering (O'Keefe 1997; Smith 2002; Gavrilyuk 2004). Growing interest in the distinctive Christological emphases of Gregory of Nyssa (Daley 1997, 2002), Augustine of Hippo (Geerlings 1978; Drobner 1986; Daley 2005*b*), and Maximus the Confessor (Balthasar 1988; Bathrellos 2004) has also led to a deeper understanding of the symphony of voices interpreting the person of Christ in the early Church. We now realize more clearly than we did fifty years ago that the formula of Chalcedon, its antecedents and its ultimate reception, is only one strand in a much richer and more complex theological fabric. To understand the full range of ancient Christology, we need to listen more attentively to the whole chorus, and to read individual authors not simply in the light of Chalcedon, but as Christological sources in their own right.

Bibliography

Suggested Reading

Primary Sources

The most extensive collection of English translations of early Christian theological texts (second to eighth centuries) remains the nineteenth-century series, Ante-Nicene Fathers and Nicene and Post-Nicene Fathers, which has been reprinted many times by many publishers. For texts specifically representing the Christological controversies, two useful single-volume collections stand out: Edward R. Hardy (ed.), *Christology of the Later Fathers*, LCC (Philadelphia: Westminster Press, 1954); and Richard A. Norris, Jr. (ed. and trans.), *The Christological Controversy*, Sources of Early Christian Thought (Philadelphia: Fortress Press, 1980). For more recent translations of Christological works of important authors, see Frederick Norris and Lionel Williams (trans.), *On God and Christ: St. Gregory of Nazianzus, The Five Theological Orations and Two Letters to Cledonius* (Crestwood, NY: St. Vladimir's Seminary Press, 2002); Brian E. Daley, *Gregory of Nazianzus* (Abingdon: Routledge, 2006) (including Orations 38–39); John A. McGuckin (trans.), *St. Cyril of Alexandria on the Unity of Christ* (Crestwood, NY: St. Vladimir's Seminary Press, 1995); and Paul M. Blowers and Robert L. Wilken (trans.), *On the Cosmic Mystery of Jesus Christ: Selected Writings from St. Maximus the Confessor* (Crestwood, NY: St. Vladimir's Seminary Press, 2003).

Secondary Literature

The most detailed modern history of patristic discussion of the person of Christ remains that of the German Jesuit, later Cardinal, Aloys Grillmeier: first in the three-volume collection of historical studies published for the 1,500th anniversary of the Council of Chalcedon: A. Grillmeier and H. Bacht (eds.), *Das Konzil von Chalkedon: Geschichte und Gegenwart* (Würzburg: Echter, 1951–1954); then in Grillmeier's own unfinished narrative, *Christ in Christian Tradition*, 1 (up to Chalcedon) (London: Mowbray, 1975); 2/1 (review of sources; history of Christology, 451–527) (London: Mowbray, 1986); 2/2 (Church of Constantinople, sixth century) (London: Mowbray, 1995); 2/4 (Church of Alexandria and Ethiopia) (London: Mowbray, 1996). Vol. 2/3, on the Church of Antioch and Syria, is yet to appear. Foundational essays by Grillmeier, mainly on ancient Christology, are also collected in *Mit Ihm und in Ihm* (Freiburg: Herder, 1975) and *Fragmente zur Christologie* (Freiburg: Herder, 1997). A standard, brief, clearly written survey of the development of ancient Christology is Kelly (1978), 109–37, 280–343. Important studies of the development of Christology after Chalcedon include W. H. C. Frend, *The Rise of the Monophysite Movement* (Cambridge: Cambridge University Press, 1972); and Patrick T. R. Gray, *The Defence of Chalcedon in the East* (451–553) (Leiden: E. J. Brill, 1979). A more recent and more detailed history of the growth of early theology, centered on the person of Christ, is John Behr, *The Formation of Christian Theology*; 1: *The Way to Nicaea*; 2: *The Nicene Faith* (Crestwood, NY: St. Vladimir's Seminary Press, 2001, 2004). For an important new theological perspective on the fourth-century debates over God and Christ, see also Lewis Ayres, *Nicaea and Its Legacy: An Approach to Fourth-Century Trinitarian Theology* (Oxford: Oxford University Press, 2004). An excellent general introduction to Christology, which includes discussion of patristic and medieval doctrine, is Gerald O'Collins, *Christology: A Biblical, Historical, and Systematic Study of Jesus* (Oxford: Oxford University Press, 1995).

Important recent studies of particular authors and issues include Roberta C. Chesnut, *Three Monophysite Christologies: Severus of Antioch, Philoxenus of Mabbug, and Jacob of Sarug* (Oxford: Oxford University Press, 1976); Iain R. Torrance, *Christology after Chalcedon: Severus of Antioch and Sergius the Monophysite* (Norwich: Canterbury Press, 1988); Marie-Odile Boulnois, *Le paradoxe Trinitaire chez Cyrille d'Alexandrie* (Paris: L'Institute d'études augustiniennes, 1994); Frederick G. McLeod, SJ, *The Image of God in the Antiochene Tradition* (Washington, DC: Catholic University of America Press, 1999); Uwe Michael Lang, *John Philoponus and the Controversies over Chalcedon in the Sixth Century* (Leuven: Spicilegium Sacrum Lovaniense, 2001); Susan Wessel, *Cyril of Alexandria and the Nestorian Controversy: The Making of a Saint and of a Heretic* (Oxford: Oxford University Press, 2004); and Paul B. Clayton, Jr., *The Christology of Theodoret of Cyrus: Antiochene Christology from the Council of Ephesus (431) to the Council of Chalcedon (451)* (Oxford: Oxford University Press, 2006).

References

Primary Sources

Apollinarius of Laodicea, *Works and Fragments*. H. Lietzmann (ed.), *Apollinaris von Laodicea und seine Schule* (Tübingen: J. C. B. Mohr/Paul Siebeck, 1904; photo-offset of Tübingen ed.: Hildesheim; G. Olms, 1970). Eng. trans. and ed.: Norris (1980).

Athanasius, *On the Incarnation*, SC 199 (Paris: Éditions du Cerf, 1973). Eng. trans.: A. Robertson, *NPNF* 4, 36–67.

Cyril of Alexandria, *Letters 2 and 3 to Nestorius, Letter to John of Antioch*, ed. and trans. L. R. Wickham, in *Cyril of Alexandria: Select Letters* (Oxford: Clarendon Press, 1983), 2–32. Also Eng. trans. and ed.: Norris (1980), 135–45.

Gregory of Nazianzus, *Letter 101*, SC 208 (Paris: Éditions du Cerf, 1974). Eng. trans.: C. G. Browne and J. E. Swallow, *NPNF* 7, 439–43.

—— *Oration 29*, SC 250 (Paris: Éditions du Cerf, 1978). Eng. trans.: L. Wickham, *On God and Christ* (Crestwood, NY: St. Vladimir's Seminary Press, 2002), 69–92.

—— *Oration 38*, SC 358 (Paris: Éditions du Cerf, 1990). Eng. trans.: B. E. Daley, *Gregory of Nazianzus* (Abingdon: Routledge, 2006), 117–27.

Ignatius of Antioch, *Letters*. Eng. trans. and ed.: M. W. Holmes (Grand Rapids: Baker Books, 1992).

Irenaeus of Lyons, *Against Heresies*, SC 100, 152–53, 210–11, 263–64, 293–94 (Paris: Éditions du Cerf, 1965–1982). Eng. trans.: A. Roberts and J. Donaldson, *ANF* 5 and 9.

Nestorius, *The Bazaar of Heracleides* [= *Liber Heraclidis*] (only in Syriac translation, P. Bedjan [ed.], *Livre d'Héraclide de Damas* [Leipzig: O. Harrassowitz, 1910]; Eng. trans.: G. R. Driver and L. Hodgson [Oxford: Oxford University Press, 1925; repr. Eugene, OR: Wipf and Stock, 2002]).

Neuner, J., and Dupuis, J. (1981) (eds.), *The Christian Faith, in the Doctrinal Documents of the Catholic Church* (New York: Alba House).

Odes of Solomon, ed. and trans. J. H. Charlesworth (Missoula, MT: Scholar's Press, 1977); also in J. H. Charlesworth (ed.), *The Old Testament Pseudepigrapha*, 2 (New York: Doubleday, 1985), 725–71.

Origen, *On First Principles*, H. Görgemanns and H. Karpp (eds.), *Vier Bücher von den Prinzipien/Origenes* (Darmstadt: Wissenschaftliche Buchgesellschaft, 1976, 2nd ed. Darmstadt, 1985). Eng. trans.: G. W. Butterworth (New York: Harper & Row, 1966).

Secondary Works

Anatolios, K. (1997), "'The Body as Instrument': A Reevaluation of Athanasius' Logos-Sarx Christology," *Coptic Church Review*, 18: 78–84.

——(1998), *Athanasius: The Coherence of His Thought* (London: Routledge).

Baillie, D. M. (1956), *God Was in Christ: An Essay on Incarnation and Atonement* (London: Faber & Faber).

Balthasar, H. Urs von (1998), *Cosmic Liturgy: The Universe according to Maximus the Con-*

fessor (San Francisco: Ignatius Press). German edition: *Kosmische Liturgie: das Weltbild Maximus' des Bekenners* (Einsiedeln: Johannes Verlag, 1988).

Bathrellos, D. (2004), *The Byzantine Christ: Person, Nature, and Will in the Christology of St. Maximus the Confessor* (Oxford: Oxford University Press).

Behr, J. (2001), *The Formation of Christian Theology*, 1: *The Way to Nicaea* (Crestwood, NY: St. Vladimir's Seminary Press).

Bertrand, F. (1951), *Mystique de Jésus chez Origène* (Paris: Aubier).

Daley, B. E. (1987), "A Humble Mediator: The Distinctive Elements in Saint Augustine's Christology," *Word and Spirit*, 9: 100–17.

——— (1997), "Divine Transcendence and Human Transformation: Gregory of Nyssa's Anti-Apollinarian Christology," *StPatr* 32: 87–95.

——— (2002), "'Heavenly Man' and 'Eternal Christ': Apollinarius and Gregory of Nyssa on the Personal Identity of the Savior," *JECS* 10: 469–88.

——— (2004), "'He Himself Is Our Peace' (Eph 2.14): Early Christian Views of Redemption in Christ," in S. T. Davis, D. Kendall, and G. O'Collins (eds.), *The Redemption: An Interdisciplinary Symposium on Christ as Redeemer* (Oxford: Oxford University Press), 149–76.

——— (2005*a*), "The *Nouvelle Théologie* and the Patristic Revival: Sources, Symbols, and the Science of Theology," *International Journal of Systematic Theology*, 7: 362–82.

——— (2005*b*), "Word, Soul and Flesh: Origen and Augustine on the Person of Christ," *AugStud* 36: 299–326.

——— (2006), "'One Thing and Another': The Persons in God and the Person of Christ in Patristic Theology," *Pro Ecclesia*, 15: 17–46.

Drobner, H. (1986), *Person-Exegese und Christologie bei Augustinus: zur Herkunft der Formel Una Persona* (Leiden: E. J. Brill).

Gavrilyuk, P. L. (2004), *The Suffering of the Impassible God: The Dialectics of Patristic Thought* (Oxford: Oxford University Press).

Geerlings, W. (1978), *Christus Exemplum: Studien zur Christologie und Christusverkündigung Augustins* (Mainz: Grünewald).

Greer, R. A. (1961), *Theodore of Mopsuestia, Exegete and Theologian* (London: Faith Press).

———(1990), "The Man from Heaven: Paul's Last Adam and Apollinaris's Christ," in W. S. Babcock (ed.), *Paul and the Legacies of Paul* (Dallas: Southern Methodist University Press), 165–82.

Grillmeier, A. (1969), "Christology," in K. Rahner et al., *Sacramentum Mundi* (New York: Herder & Herder), 3.186–92.

———(1975), *Christ in Christian Tradition*, 1, rev. ed. (London: Mowbray).

Hanson, R. P. C. (1988), *The Search for the Christian Doctrine of God* (Edinburgh: T & T Clark).

Kelly, J. N. D. (1978), *Early Christian Doctrines* (San Francisco: Harper & Row).

Layton, B. (1987), *The Gnostic Scriptures: Ancient Wisdom for the New Age* (New York: Doubleday).

Lebon, J. (1909), *Le monophysisme sévérien* (Leuven: Van Linthout).

———(1951), "La christologie du monophysisme syrien," in A. Grillmeier and H. Bacht (eds.), *Das Konzil von Chalkedon: Geschichte und Gegenwart* (Würzburg: Echter), 1.423–580.

McGuckin, J. A. (1994), *Saint Cyril of Alexandria and the Christological Controversy* (Leiden: E. J. Brill).

Norris, R. A., Jr. (1963), *Manhood and Christ: A Study in the Christology of Theodore of Mopsuestia* (Oxford: Clarendon Press).

———(1980), *The Christological Controversy*, Sources of Early Christian Thought (Philadelphia: Fortress Press).

O'Keefe, J. J. (1997), "Impassible Suffering? Divine Passion and Fifth-Century Christology," *TS* 58: 39–60.

Petterson, A. (1995), *Athanasius* (Ridgefield, CT: Morehouse).

Rahner, K. (1961), "Current Problems in Christology," trans. C. Ernst, in *Theological Investigations* (Baltimore: Helicon), 1.149–200.

Scipioni, L. (1956), *Ricerche sulla cristologia del 'Libro di Ericlide' di Nestorio*, Par 11 (Fribourg: Edizione universitarie).

Smith, J. W. (2002), "Suffering Impassibly: Christ's Passion in Cyril of Alexandria's Soteriology," *Pro Ecclesia*, 11: 463–83.

Studer, B. (1993), *Trinity and Incarnation*, ed. A. Louth (Edinburgh: T & T Clark).

Torrance, T. F. (1995), "Athanasius: A Study in the Foundations of Classical Theology," in *Divine Meaning: Studies in Patristic Hermeneutics* (Edinburgh: T & T Clark), 179–228.

Weinandy, T. G., and Keating, D. A. (2003) (eds.), *The Theology of St. Cyril of Alexandria* (London: T & T Clark).

2 Seeing God in Flesh

The Range and Implications of Patristic Christology

A little over fifty years ago, in the spring of 1952, an event occurred which, while not great on the stage of history, was surely remarkable within the more intimate theatre of theological scholarship: the appearance of the first volume of a collection of essays on the historical background and the theological consequences of the fifth-century Council of Chalcedon. The collection, entitled *Das Konzil von Chalkedon: Geschichte und Gegenwart*,[1] took three years to be fully published, and eventually ran to three sizeable tomes. Its editors, Aloys Grillmeier and Heinrich Bacht, were two relatively young Jesuit professors of theology at the Hochschule Sankt Georgen in Frankfurt-am-Main. The contributors, all Catholic scholars, were mainly Germans, but also included Austrians, Belgians, French, and even an American; their essays were, for the most part, serious examples of the high scholarship that had flourished in Europe in the first half of the twentieth century: learned, amply argued, fully and meticulously documented, and edited with an accuracy that, in the words of an admiring Oxford reviewer, the late F. L. Cross, "cannot but command the admiration of all, and we suspect, the astonishment of many, of its readers."[2]

Dr. Cross's astonishment was probably due, first of all, to the hard circumstances in which scholarly work of such quality had been done. All of

1. Aloys Grillmeier, SJ, and Heinrich Bacht, SJ, eds., *Das Konzil von Chalkedon. Geschichte und Gegenwart* I (Würzburg: Echter Verlag, 1951 [1952]); II (1952); III (1954).

2. *Journal of Theological Studies* N. S. 4 (1953), 264.

This article was delivered as the Cardinal Pio Laghi lecture at the Pontifical College Josephinum on March 8, 2006.

Europe was still in the grip of the shortages and suspicions that followed the Second World War; Germany was still divided and occupied; academic life was just getting back to its ordinary pace; libraries were often understaffed and inaccessible; paper for printing was scarce. Planning such an ambitious scholarly undertaking in the late 1940s took courage and vision, and bringing it to reality took a resourcefulness that often went beyond the library; while the ever enterprising Fr. Bacht badgered bishops and benefactors across Germany for financial help in the project in the years preceding its publication, the gentle Fr. Grillmeier traveled to Leuven, Brussels, and Paris to encourage contributors, making himself as inconspicuous as possible in railway carriages because his traveling status in those years, as a German national, was never entirely clear. The goal of the project was more than simply an elaborate scholarly *Festschrift* celebrating the fifteenth centenary of the Council of Chalcedon in 451, more than just a learned echo of Pius XII's encyclical on Chalcedon and Christology, *Sempiternus Rex*, produced for the same occasion; the goal was also to celebrate the re-establishment of the German Jesuit theological faculty, now in Frankfurt after fifty years of exile in the Netherlands and the total disruption of the war years, and to get the wheels of Catholic theological scholarship turning again.

Besides the academic and ecumenical effects that the editors seem to have hoped for from their Chalcedon volumes, there was clearly a theological agenda as well. What has been called the *ressourcement*, the rediscovery of the living relevance of the Scriptures and of early Christian tradition for the Church's theology, not simply as footnotes or proof-texts but as actual *sources*, actual witnesses to faith and its reasoned understanding, had begun to give new life to the Roman Catholic Church in the 1930s.[3] Young scholars such as the Jesuits Henri de Lubac, Jean Daniélou, Henri Bouillard, Hugo and Karl Rahner, and Hans Urs von Balthasar, or the Dominicans Marie-Dominique Chenu and Yves Congar, among many others, had found in the Church Fathers and their Latin medieval heirs a richness of theological vision and biblical interpretation that seemed to offer intellectual and spiritual liberation from the abstract dogmatic rationalism of the officially recognized scholastic manuals used in seminaries. The study of major Church doctrines as embodying a historical development in the articulation of faith—what the Germans called *Dogmengeschichte*—had been mainly the preserve of liberal Protestants, especially since the days of Ritschl and Harnack in the

3. See my essay "*La nouvelle théologie* and the Patristic Revival: Sources, Symbols, and the Science of Theology," *International Journal of Systematic Theology* 7 (2005), 362–82.

late nineteenth and early twentieth century; now, for Catholic theologians, that same historical approach seemed to offer possibilities for a new understanding of long-held truths, and for the raising of questions that had found no place in the manualist tradition. Chenu and de Lubac had argued, since the 1930s, for the necessity of this historical perspective in the articulation of faith, because the Word of God had himself become incarnate in human history;[4] but the reaction of Roman theologians and Church authorities had been cautious, at times hostile. Now seemed a good time to propose the importance of history once again.

In one of the most important essays in the third volume of Grillmeier and Bacht's collection, published only in 1954, Karl Rahner makes this very point, cautiously but tellingly:

> Anyone who takes seriously the "historicity" of human truth (in which God's truth too has become incarnate in Revelation) must see that neither the abandonment of a formula nor its preservation in a petrified form does justice to human understanding. For history is precisely *not* an atomized beginning-ever-anew; it is rather (the more spiritual it is) a becoming-new which preserves the old, and preserves it all the more *as* old, the more spiritual this history is.[5]

Rahner goes on to observe something that may seem to us a little startling: that most theologians of his day, as well as most of the faithful, simply assumed that in the area of Christology—reflection in faith on the person of Jesus Christ—all the real problems had been solved by the formula of the Council of Chalcedon in 451, so that raising further questions seemed useless. For Rahner, such complacency clearly weakened Christology:

4. See especially Chenu, "Position de Théologie," *Revue des sciences philosophiques et théologiques* 25 (1935), 232–57 (trans. Denis Hickey, "What Is Theology?" in *Faith and Theology* [New York: Macmillan, 1968], 15–35); *Une École de Théologie: le Saulchoir* (privately published, 1937; repr., with accompanying essays by Giuseppe Alberigo et al.: Paris: Éditions du Cerf, 1985); de Lubac, *Catholicism* (orig. publ. as *Catholicisme. Les Aspects sociaux du dogme* [Paris: Éditions du Cerf, 1937; Eng. trans.: *Catholicism. Christ and the Common Destiny of Man* [San Francisco: Ignatius Press, 1988]), esp. chap. 6; see also his posthumously published essay, "La doctrine du Père Lebreton sur la Révélation et le dogme d'après ses écrits antimodernistes," in *Théologie dans l'histoire* 2 (Paris: Desclée de Brouwer, 1990), 108–56.

5. Karl Rahner, "Chalkedon: Ende oder Anfang?" in Grillmeier and Bacht, *Das Konzil von Chalkedon* III (Würzburg: Echter Verlag, 1954), 4 (whole article: 3–49); English trans. Cornelius Ernst, "Current Problems in Christology," in *Theological Investigations* 1 (London/Baltimore: Darton, Longman and Todd/Helicon, 1961), 150.

> One has only to consider how few really living and passionate controversies there are in Catholic Christology today which engage the existential concern of the faithful (is there a single one?). Unless someone is inclined to regard this fact simply as a mark of superiority, a proof of unruffled orthodoxy and crystal-clear theology, he will listen with patience and good will to the most modest attempt, undertaken with the most inadequate means, to depart from the Chalcedonian formula in order to find the way back to it in truth.[6]

For Rahner, quite clearly, the value of careful historical study of the origins and early consequences of the formula of Chalcedon was that it could release the Church's understanding of Christ from the rigidly metaphysical focus that, in his view, had led to serious distortions in the way both theology and popular devotion understood the person of the Savior—especially his humanity. It is significant, in fact, that this essay first bore the title, in the Grillmeier-Bacht collection, "Chalkedon: Ende oder Anfang?"—"Chalcedon: End or Beginning?"[7] When it appeared in the first volume of Rahner's collected essays that same year, 1954, the article bore a new title, "Probleme der Christologie von heute"—in Cornelius Ernst's English translation, "Current Problems in Christology."[8] To show that the Chalcedonian formula was not simply the end of an ancient controversy, but the beginning of new and deeper questions about the identity and role of Christ, as Rahner felt historical analysis was able to do, was to show that Christology could indeed raise "current problems" and become the center of intense contemporary debate: a prophecy that most of us would probably consider amply fulfilled in the years since 1954!

For Grillmeier, too, and for many of the contributors to these three volumes on Chalcedon, more was at stake than simply historical detail: a whole understanding of theology, especially of the theology of Christ's person, rested on "getting Chalcedon right." Grillmeier himself was particularly concerned, in this work and throughout his later writings, to underline two conclusions he felt we can draw from a study of early Christology. One was the indispensable service philosophical analysis and technical philosophical vocabulary offered to the preservation and clarification of the apostolic mes-

6. Ibid., 152–53.

7. See above, n. 5.

8. Karl Rahner, *Schriften zur Theologie* I (Einsiedeln: Benziger, 1954), 169–222; *Theological Investigations* 1 (above, n. 5), 149–200.

sage of Jesus's Lordship; this was expressly in contrast to Harnack's theory of a gradual alienation of the original, simple Gospel through the introduction of Greek concepts and practices, a "Hellenization," which Harnack saw as coming to an apex in the Chalcedonian formula. Unlike the lines of Christian interpretation which the Church eventually came to reject as "heresies," the mainstream or orthodox use of secular philosophical language, as Grillmeier continually tries to show, is not a syncretistic compromise of Gospel faith, but is "intended to preserve the Christ of the gospels and the apostolic age for the faith of posterity."[9] It is this ability of the Church to use new, secular concepts as a service to the maintenance of a living tradition, Grillmeier believes, which allows for continuity amidst genuine change.[10]

Secondly, Grillmeier is very much concerned to emphasize the "balance," in the Chalcedonian understanding of the person of Christ, between his complete divinity and his complete humanity, both of which are proper to him as a single, unique subject, a single divine "person." Behind this concern, undoubtedly, was a conviction shared by many Catholic theologians of the late 1940s and early 1950s, including several of the contributors to the *Chalkedon* volumes, that modern scholastic theology had not taken the completeness of the humanity of Christ with full seriousness, and that the picture of Christ presented in popular preaching and devotional manuals often steered close to the mythic caricature of "God in a human costume," "God who has put on a body."[11] It was in the 1950s, significantly, that a num-

9. A. Grillmeier, *Christ in Christian Tradition* (2nd ed.; Oxford: Mowbrays, 1975), 555. All subsequent citations of this work, unless otherwise noted, will be taken from this second edition. Cf. Grillmeier's article "Hellenisierung-Judaisierung des Christentums als Deuteprinzipien der Geschichte des kirchlichen Dogmas," in *Mit Ihm und in Ihm* (Freiburg: Herder, 1975), 423–88.

10. See the review of Robert L. Wilken of the first English edition of *Christ in Christian Tradition* (1965), which makes just this point: "In Grillmeier's view the philosophical categories of the fathers and the terms from Greek philosophy actually aided the Church in interpreting and expressing its faith. Grillmeier also wishes to take change, development and diversity with utter seriousness, but he believes one can talk about a developing unity which is more than an arbitrary choosing of one tradition from among many. What emerges as Catholic Christianity in the later Church stands in continuity with the primitive Church" (*Church History* 35 [1966], 362).

11. Karl Rahner makes this same point in the article quoted above: "Looked at from this point of view a single basic conception runs through the Christian heresies from Apollinarism to Monothelitism, sustained by the same basic mythical feeling. The persistence of this idea even in theoretical formulations ought to make us realize that although it may have given up announcing itself in such a theoretical fashion today, the idea probably still

ber of Catholic scholars engaged in controversy over the full meaning of the human consciousness and human freedom of Christ: of the limitations of knowledge inherent in Jesus's human intellect, of the need for him to come to a free human decision to obey his Father's (and his own) divine will.[12] Against this background, one understands better Grillmeier's elaborate efforts to show that theologians of the fourth- and fifth-century Antiochene school, even the hapless Nestorius, were above all concerned to defend the full humanity of Christ, even if they often used somewhat novel biblical and philosophical arguments to do so.[13] Grillmeier tends to read the whole early history of Christology as an evolution from what he calls a "word-flesh" (*logos-sarx*) model of understanding the *person* of Jesus, inspired by a literal understanding of John 1:14, towards what he calls the "word–human being" (*logos-anthrōpos*) model, first fully developed by the school of Antioch and decisively, if more carefully, affirmed by Pope Leo and the Council of

lives on in the picture which countless Christians have of the 'Incarnation,' whether they give it their faith—or reject it" ("Current Problems in Christology," 156).

12. For the Catholic scholastic Christology of the late 19th and early 20th century, it was considered most likely, although not dogmatically certain, that Jesus possessed, for the full length of his human existence, not only the immediate awareness of God proper to the beatific vision, but also "infused knowledge"—knowledge not acquired by the normal empirical process—of all that is humanly knowable. See, for example, Joseph Pohle and Arthur Preuss, *Dogmatic Theology 4: Christology* (St. Louis: B. Herder, 1925): "The human knowledge of Christ is relatively infinite in extent, i.e., it is the highest and most complete knowledge which it is possible for any creature to have in the present economy, and consequently, both with regard to natural and supernatural things, it is the ideal of all knowledge" (267). This became the subject of vigorous debate among Catholic theologians in the *ressourcement* movement that began in the 1930s and was revived after the war. See, for example: Paul Galtier, *L'unité du Christ: Être . . . Personne . . . Conscience* (Paris: Beauchesne, 1939), esp. 237–371; "La conscience humaine du Christ," *Gregorianum* 32 (1951), 525–68; 35 (1954), 225–46; Joseph Ternus, "Das Seelen- und Bewusstseinsleben Jesu," in Grillmeier and Bacht, *Das Konzil von Chalkedon* III, 81–237; Aloys Grillmeier, "Das Christusbild der heutigen katholischen Theologie," in Johannes Feiner, Josef Trutsch, and Franz Böckle, *Fragen der Theologie heute* (Einsiedeln: Benziger, 1957), 265–300, esp. 286–96; Bernard Lonergan, *De constitutione Christi ontologica et psychologica* (Rome: Gregorian University Press, 1964), 83–145; Karl Rahner, "Dogmatic Reflections on the Knowledge and Self-Consciousness of Christ," in *Theological Investigations* 5 (Baltimore/London: Helicon/Darton, Longman and Todd, 1966), 193–215 (bibliography on the discussion, pp. 193–94, 196–97); Jean Galot, "La psychologie du Christ," *Nouvelle revue théologique* 90 (1958), 337–58; *La conscience de Jésus* (Gembloux: Duculot; Paris: Lethielleux, 1971); *Who Is Christ? A Theology of the Incarnation* (Chicago: Franciscan Herald Press, 1981), 319–92.

13. See, for example, Paul Galtier, "Un monument au concile de Chalcédoine—Nestorius mal compris, mal traduit," *Gregorianum* 34 (1953), 427–33.

Chalcedon. In a word-flesh Christology, Jesus's humanity is conceived as the physical, sensible human form in which the Word of God has lived among us; in a word–human being Christology, that "form" is a human being with a soul, with all the interior faculties and qualities that characterize and make possible human knowledge, human freedom, and human love. The question of whether a particular author did or did not take the *soul of Christ* seriously, as a "theological factor" in his reflection on the Savior, is indeed one of the driving questions of Grillmeier's investigation of pre-Chalcedonian Christology; and the reason for his concern seems to have been his desire to show that the fully developed portrait of Christ presented by Christian orthodoxy since Chalcedon cannot dispense with a serious treatment of his inner life as "a human being like us in all things but sin."[14]

It was Robert Wilken, in his 1966 review of the book Grillmeier later developed from his own long chapter in the first *Chalkedon* volume, who first pointed to what seems to be the most serious and abiding flaw in Grillmeier's approach to the early history of Christology: it is really Western scholastic dogma, rather than the early Christian sources themselves, which supplies his narrative with its guiding thread, the lens through which ancient writers and their ideas are interpreted and arranged.[15] This is evident in Grillmeier's organizing focus on the Christological definition of the Council of Chalcedon, as "the formula which like a hidden entelechy had accompanied the wearisome struggles of centuries to interpret the *mysterium Christi*."[16] For Grillmeier, as for virtually all his contemporaries trained in the tradition of scholastic dogmatics—whether Protestant, Anglican, or Catholic—Christology was the "tract" within the discipline of theology which deals with the ontological structure of the person of Christ: the "Mystery" by which the single, divine person of the Son or Word of God now "subsists," within created history, in two complete yet unconfused natures. Christology, as a branch of theology, had come to be understood as the explication of the final paragraph of the dogmatic formula of Chalcedon, which was the first official Church document to present this picture of Christ concisely, in so many words.

Here lies the real difficulty: to see this formula, pregnant with meaning as it is, as in itself the culmination of four centuries of Christian reflection

14. Eucharistic Prayer IV, *Roman Sacramentary*, alluding to Heb 4:15: Jesus, our high priest, is "one who in every respect has been tested as we are, yet without sin."

15. Review (above, n. 10), 363.

16. Grillmeier, *Christ in Christian Tradition*, 548.

on the person of Christ and the central norm of Christological orthodoxy is to say at once too little and too much, to force ancient reflection into a seriously distorting frame by omitting those other themes and details in early Christology that seem to have little to do with the Council's dense structural analysis of Christ's person, and by focusing simply on what did or did not anticipate the central elements of this definition. As Wilken observes,

> Few will be convinced that Chalcedon is really a terminal point in the history of Christology, solely on historical grounds. . . . Too many "accidents" precede Chalcedon, such as the two Ephesine councils in 431, the local councils of 448, 449, and the death of Theodosius and accession of Marcian. The violent reaction after Chalcedon, as well as the growing split in the empire, and the futile attempts at compromise in the century following—all these factors make it difficult to view Chalcedon as the end of a period. Are not the grounds for this view rather more dogmatic than historical?[17]

Grillmeier and his collaborators of the 1950s, as I have said, were not unusual in their view of the crowning importance of the Chalcedonian formula in the history of early Christian theology; textbooks were organized around it, histories of early Christianity tended to make it their final chapter, theological curricula in universities tended to require students to study the history and thought of the Fathers only as far as what was euphemistically—and misleadingly—called "the Chalcedonian settlement." As he continued his project in the decades after 1951, Cardinal Grillmeier himself became increasingly aware that Chalcedon's way of formulating the ontological structure of the person of Christ was not an exhaustive summary of the New Testament witness to Jesus. So at the end of his revised history of pre-Chalcedonian Christology, *Christ in Christian Tradition* 1 (1975), he quotes with approval a sentence of Karl Rahner's from the beginning of his essay on problems in modern Christology: every formal dogmatic statement is a necessary part of the Church's witness to its own tradition, Rahner had written, to "mark the boundary of error. . . . Yet while this formula is an end, an acquisition and a victory, which allows us to enjoy clarity and security as well as ease in instruction, if this victory is to be a true one the end must also be a beginning."[18] Formulas that authoritatively sum up a tradition must always, in other words, be open to further reflection, raise

17. Review (above, n. 10), 363.
18. Rahner, "Current Problems in Christology," 149.

further questions, lead us further into an understanding of the single, inexhaustible Mystery of God's saving presence in history. The question one must ask today, however, as Wilken asked in 1965, is whether a thorough reading of early Christian witnesses to faith in Christ really allows us to call the Council of Chalcedon, on its own, either the end or the beginning of any identifiable period in the history of Christian faith, and so whether its formulation really should be taken, even cautiously, as the high point and summation of ancient Christology.

What was, then, the real achievement of this gathering of Eastern bishops, called by the new emperor Marcian and his long-influential spouse, the empress Pulcheria, in a suburb of Constantinople in the autumn of 451? On the level of Church politics, it was an effort to restore a balance between major centers of influence and the theological traditions with which they had become associated: a balance precariously achieved in 433, after the bitter controversy over Nestorius's views of how to conceive the person of Christ, by the so-called "Formula of Reunion," describing the outlines of traditional faith in the Savior—a formula apparently drafted by Theodoret of Cyrus and proposed by the Church of Antioch, and warmly embraced, for the moment, at least, by Cyril of Alexandria. Cyril had had to labor hard, in the late 430s, to persuade his own sympathizers—bishops like the Armenian Acacius of Melitene, and Succensus of Diocaesaraea, an old admirer of Athanasius—that in agreeing to the carefully balanced phrases in which the Antiochene draft had expressed an understanding of the person of Christ, in confessing an "unconfused union" "of two natures," by which "the same one is coessential with the Father as to his deity and coessential with us as to his humanity," he had not abandoned the Athanasian vision of Jesus as divine Savior.

The principal agents of this peace, however, were dead by the mid-440s: John of Antioch in 442, Cyril in 444, Proclus of Constantinople in 446. Tensions rose again in the imperial capital, as rival groups, doubtless driven by both political ambition and religious traditionalism, accused each other of treachery and extremism. The story of the conflict between the archimandrite Eutyches, an elderly monk of Constantinople well supported by Cyril's successor Dioscorus of Alexandria, and leading clerical figures of the capital, such as Bishop Eusebius of Dorylaeum, is well known. Although the motives for rivalry seem to have been complex, according to ancient witnesses, all the religious reasons given concerned how one conceived the person of Christ. Eutyches, drawing on the older Alexandrian and Apollinarian tradition that emphasized the organic, *dynamic* unity of action and consciousness in the divine Savior of humanity, refused to accept any formula that spoke of two abiding natures or operative realities in the person of the incarnate Word; Eusebius and the rest of the Constantinopolitan establishment held tenaciously to the "two unconfused natures" and "double consubstantiality" language of 433, and excommunicated Eutyches. In the summer of 449, a council of Greek bishops met at Ephesus, with imperial support, to resolve the conflict. Chaired, in the most dictatorial manner, by Dioscorus of Alexandria, and recklessly resistant to the voices of both Antioch and the Latin West, the assembled bishops reinstated Eutyches to his clerical rank, from which two Patriarchal "home synods" in the capital had deposed him, and in turn deposed and excommunicated the leading spokesmen of the Antiochene Church. Supporters of a more "symmetrical" picture of Christ felt they had been the victims of ecclesiastical violence. Hence when the emperor Theodosius II, who had permitted this radicalization to occur, himself died in the summer of 450, it was an obvious time for his successors, Marcian and Pulcheria, to take conciliatory steps, for the unity of both Church and society.

The Council of Chalcedon, convened in September and October of 451, was such a step. The imperial court carefully assured a balanced representation of voices in the seating of delegates, and guaranteed a leading role in the conduct of business to Pope Leo's chief legate, the Greek-speaking Sicilian bishop Paschasius of Lilybaeum. It was easy enough for this new council to reverse the work done at Ephesus in 449 and even to depose Dioscorus of Alexandria, expressly for the contempt he had shown towards Leo of Rome. The *Acta* make it clear, however, that most of the bishops present were very hesitant to try to debate a new "formula of union" on the theology of the person of Christ; they were content to reaffirm "the faith" (or creed) "of Nicaea," which since at least the 370s had been regarded as the touchstone of biblical orthodoxy, along with the creed of the Council of Constantinople of 381, and to take as also normative a few now-classic letters of Cyril and Leo on the Christological issue. It was the emperors, at the urging of Leo's delegates, who finally prevailed on the bishops to allow a drafting commission to finish and propose a statement of common faith—largely by the threat of adjournment, and of calling a new council in the West to deal with the issue, if they continued to resist. The result, reluctantly agreed to ahead of time, enthusiastically acclaimed in the event, is what we know as the Chalcedonian definition.

It is important to look closely at the whole of the Council's statement of faith if one is to realize its intent and its real value. Fr. Grillmeier rightly stressed its "dogmatic," rather than speculative character;[19] it is a formal agreement on the limits of orthodoxy concerning the person of Christ, but clearly not intended to break new theological ground, to solve age-old problems of understanding in creatively crafted new terms, nor even to give unambiguous clarifications of the terms it does use. Probably most of the bishops present would have been hard put to define what "substance" and "nature," "hypostasis" and "prosopon" actually meant when applied to the reality of Christ; as Grillmeier puts it:

> Even if abstract concepts find their way in, the theological method here consists only in "listening to" the proven witnesses of the Christian faith. True, the formulas are carefully developed, but only in connection with an already formed tradition.[20]

The purpose of the statement, quite clearly, is to reaffirm the mainstream tradition of Christian orthodoxy, to rule out the kind of language and thinking about Christ that seemed most seriously in danger of veering away from that tradition, and finally—in the way of a positive delineation of Christ's person—to piece together a patchwork of terms and phrases culled from representative thinkers on both sides of the previous two decades of controversy, in the hope that the document's appearance of forming a seamless conceptual whole might become the basis of real concord in faith, worship, and polity.

The statement begins, accordingly, with a description of the Council's understanding of its mission: to resist the discord sowed in the Church by the Evil One, to build peace by removing falsehood and reaffirming tradition.[21] Significantly, the weight is on liturgically and synodically formulated tradition, rather than on Scripture—perhaps because scriptural texts were capable of so many conflicting interpretations. Expressly following the precedent of the Alexandrian synod that had met at Ephesus in 431, the Council insists that the Creed of Nicaea (325) shall "shine in first place" (*prolampein*)—an acknowledged primacy that now becomes commonplace in ancient conciliar efforts to deal with doctrinal controversy—and that the Creed of Constanti-

19. Grillmeier, *Christ in Christian Tradition*, 545.

20. Ibid.

21. Complete Greek and Latin texts of the decree, with an English translation, can be found in Giuseppe Alberigo et al. and Norman Tanner, eds., *Decrees of the Ecumenical Councils* 1 (London: Sheed and Ward; Washington, DC: Georgetown University Press, 1990), 83–87.

nople (381), a reformulation of the Nicene symbol aimed at ruling out heresies that had become evident after 325, shall also "remain in force" (*kratein*). After quoting both creedal formulas in full—our first documentary evidence, in fact, for the text of the Creed of Constantinople—the formula goes on to assert that these "should have been sufficient for the knowledge and support of true religion,"[22] but that new views of the person of Jesus, obviously deviant from the Apostolic tradition, now call for new responses. Accordingly, the Council declares that it has "received, as in agreement [with this faith], the synodical letters of the blessed Cyril, then shepherd of the Alexandrian church, to Nestorius and the Orientals"[23]—by which it may mean only his "second" letter to Nestorius, not his more challenging "third," along with his affirmation of the formula of agreement with the Antiochenes from 433[24]—and also "has appropriately included, as a support of right teaching," Pope Leo's letter to Bishop Flavian of Constantinople:[25] the famous *Tome*, in which Leo enunciates, in polished but somewhat ambiguous Latin phrases, the more "symmetrical" picture of Christ advocated by Theodoret and the Antiochenes. "Classic" texts, representative of different schools of thought, are thus added as appendices to the two normative, "Nicene" creeds.

Only then, in third place, does the statement of the Council move on to enunciate its own synthetic position, which, like what has gone before, is carefully drafted to be both traditional and even-handed. First, the statement excludes what it regards as extreme positions on the person of Christ: those who "split up the mystery of the dispensation"[26] into *two sons*; those who say that the *divinity can suffer*; those who conceive of a "*confusion or mixture*" of two natures in him; those—presumably Apollinarian sectaries—who think of his human form as itself from heaven; those—like the discredited Eutyches—who insist that the two natures that constitute the person of Jesus have become, at the moment of their union, only one. Only then, in last place, does the statement proceed to express the Council's understanding of the person of Jesus in declaratory terms.

As Grillmeier has observed, the positive Chalcedonian statement itself is a mixture of plain language—"one and the same Son, who is our Lord

22. Ibid., 157.

23. Ibid., 158.

24. The text of the decree leaves it vague just what "synodical letters" of Cyril to Nestorius are included; his letter "to the Orientals," however, clearly refers to the letter of the Alexandrian synod to John of Antioch and his Church, *Laetentur caeli*, of 433.

25. Alberigo and Tanner, *Decrees*, 158.

26. Ibid.

Jesus Christ"[27]—and technical language borrowed from the philosophical traditions of Hellenism and the theological writings of the Cappadocians, Cyril, Proclus of Constantinople, Basil of Seleucia, even Nestorius. So this "one and the same Christ" is "acknowledged to be unconfusedly, unalterably, undividedly, inseparably [four adverbs with a considerable philosophical and theological history] in two natures, since [now borrowing two phrases from Leo's *Tome*] the difference of the natures is not destroyed because of the union, but, on the contrary, the character of each nature is preserved and comes together in one person [*prosōpon*: "persona," role, self-presentation] and one hypostasis [or concrete individual], not divided or torn into two persons but one and the same Son and only begotten God, Logos, Lord Jesus Christ . . ."[28]

All of this is traditional, the statement adds, "just as in earlier times the prophets and also the Lord Jesus Christ himself taught us about him [the statement's only reference to Scripture], and as the symbol of our Fathers [i.e., the Nicene Creed] transmitted to us."[29] Finally, the decree concludes by prohibiting any Christian from writing, thinking, or teaching anything that might contradict the faith witnessed to here.

Read as a whole, the Chalcedonian statement shows that its famous final section is not meant so much to push back the frontier of theological reflection on the person of Jesus, as simply to establish agreed standards for remaining in the tradition of orthodoxy. The emphasis is clearly on the formulation of that tradition in the creeds of Nicaea and Constantinople, with priority given to the former; one might even say, it seems to me, that all of what follows the quoting of that creed is really meant as a set of hermeneutical rules for reading Nicaea correctly, in the context of fifth-century controversy. Those rules are both negative and positive: how one may *not* interpret Nicaea, and how one *may*, even *must* interpret it, in order to remain in the Church's communion of faith and sacrament. But in setting up these rules, in fixing this careful boundary to exclude some positions and leave room for others, great care is taken that the main fears and favorite phrases of both sides of the current controversy be explicitly respected. The five positions excluded, presumably, are meant to represent extremes, caricatures perhaps: lines that no credible, centrist member of either side would want to follow. What positions might be included in the positive part of the statement is less

27. Ibid., 159.
28. Ibid.
29. Ibid.

clear, precisely because phrases from a variety of authors, with a variety of strongly opposed positions on the person of Christ, are here skillfully woven into a single paragraph that is designed to give an appearance of tranquil cohesion. Somewhere in that mix, the statement suggests, lies orthodoxy.

The lasting value of Church documents and synodal statements—their meaning within the continuing life of the community—lies, as we have come to learn, in their *reception*: in the messy, unpredictable process by which the wider Church—its bishops, its writers, its holy people, its "ordinary" faithful—judges such statements and decides, implicitly or explicitly, to recognize them as normative for faith, and to pray and live by them.[30]

The difficulty with regarding the Chalcedonian formula as representing the quintessence of the Church's classical understanding of the person of Christ is precisely that its reception was not unambiguous, not instantaneous, and by no means unanimous, and that—in contrast to the Creed of Nicaea, which also took a good fifty years to be widely accepted as a norm of orthodox faith—its reception at all, at least by Eastern Christianity, depended on further modifications in its Christological formula, further crucial hermeneutical rules for interpreting both its language and the salvation narrative summed up in the creeds: the rules enunciated by what Christians recognize today as the fifth, sixth, and seventh ecumenical councils. Without the canons of Constantinople II, Constantinople III, and even Nicaea II as supplements to its formulations and guides to its proper interpretation, the Chalcedonian formula would probably be regarded as fully orthodox only by Western Christianity.

The full story of the reception of Chalcedon is, of course, too lengthy and complicated to be told here. Attempts by the emperor Marcian, and by his successor Leo I, to install bishops favorable to the Council's union formula in Alexandria, and soon afterwards even in Antioch, ended in violence and

30. On the theological and canonical process of the "reception" of official dogma, against the background of early Christological debates, see Grillmeier, "Konzil und Rezeption: methodische Bemerkungen zu einem Thema der ökumenischen Diskussion der Gegenwart," in *Mit Ihm und in Ihm* (above, n. 9), 303–34; "Die Rezeption des Konzils von Chalkedon in der römisch-katholischen Kirche," in ibid., 335–70. See also Yves Congar, "La 'reception' comme réalité ecclésiastique," *Recherches de science philosophique et théologique* 56 (1972), 369–403; Edward J. Kilmartin, "Reception in History: An Ecclesiological Phenomenon and Its Significance," *Journal of Ecumenical Studies* 21 (1984), 34–54; Jean-Marie Tillard, "Les fondements ecclésiologiques de la 'réception' oecuménique," *Toronto Journal of Theology* 3 (1987), 28–40; Michael J. Himes, "The Ecclesiological Significance of the Reception of Doctrine," *Heythrop Journal* 33 (1992), 146–60.

schism, as more and more monks and pastors in the Greek-speaking world raised irate objections to its representation of the person of the Savior: it was a political solution rather than an authentic articulation of the tradition of faith in which they worshiped and preached; it was a victory for the humanistic, overly analytical thinking of Nestorius and his Antiochene supporters; it was a Western-backed solution, an expression of the dry, neatly balanced categories of Papal bureaucrats rather than of the intense devotion to the Savior, the sense of human transformation by the dynamic personal presence of the divine in Jesus, that had become the core of Greek and Syrian spirituality.[31]

In 482, the emperor Zeno attempted to provide an alternative formula of unity without the help (and the possible divisiveness) of a new council: the so-called *Henōtikon*, drafted by his patriarch Acacius originally as an expression of imperial Church policy for Egypt and later proposed more generally. This document decrees, for the sake of unity and peace, that only the Creed of Nicaea, and its later interpretations at Constantinople and at the Cyrilline synod at Ephesus, along with Cyril's more contested "third" letter to Nestorius, shall be considered normative expressions of Christian faith; "and everyone who has held or holds any other opinion, either at the present or another time, whether at Chalcedon or in any synod whatever, we anathematize."[32] The result was a new schism: this time with the Latin West (the so-called "Acacian" schism), which was not healed until 519, after the elderly Latin-speaking emperor Justin, at the urging of his nephew Justinian, the future emperor and architect of a renewed Mediterranean unity, gave in to the demands of Rome and affirmed the Chalcedonian theology once again.

Two things seem to have become apparent to Justinian during his own early experiences trying to broker a new settlement. One was that as emperor himself from 527, responsible for both the civil and the ecclesiastical peace, he could not simply abandon the Christological statement of Chalcedon, or leave it among documents whose orthodoxy remained undecided, as Zeno's *Henōtikon* attempted to do; if the Empire did not continue to affirm the

31. For a detailed attempt to depict this Eastern attitude to the Chalcedonian formula, see W. H. C. Frend, *The Rise of the Monophysite Movement* (Cambridge: Cambridge University Press, 1972), especially 137–42 (the attitude of Eastern monks towards the person of Christ); 148f. (many in the East saw Chalcedon as a victory for Nestorianism). On the general sympathy for Antiochene thinking in the West at this period, and on the post-Chalcedonian tendency for Popes and Western theologians to identify the Chalcedonian statement with Papal teaching authority, ibid., 131–35, 196–99.

32. See ibid., 174–83, 192; for a full text and translation, ibid., 360–62.

Chalcedonian statement as integral to its vision of Christianity, the Latin West would be lost to the Empire, and important voices in the Greek cultural and political elite would be alienated as well. Justinian's other realization, however, was that he also could not continue to promote Chalcedon in its original, ambiguous form, if he was to have any hope of regaining for the Church and the Empire large regions of Syria and Egypt which were now in schism. The only hope for a single policy on Christian orthodoxy that might be acceptable to at least sizeable portions of both Chalcedonians and non-Chalcedonians lay in a thoroughgoing but subtle revision or expansion of the Chalcedonian statement along lines that made clear its continuity with Cyril's vision of Christ, in both his earlier and his later writings. Although resisted by some controversialists of the 540s—notably Leontius of Byzantium—Justinian's "neo-Chalcedonian" Christology (to use a disputed term coined by modern historians) was eventually canonized at a synod of Greek bishops summoned by the emperor in 553, the synod that has been received by both East and West as the Second Council of Constantinople. After a lengthy introduction condemning the main representatives of the fifth-century school of Antioch—including Theodoret of Cyrus, an influential voice at Chalcedon—especially for their resistance to Cyril's Christology as laid out in his "third" letter to Nestorius, the document's fourteen canons also make it clear that the "one hypostasis or person" in Christ, mentioned at Chalcedon, is in fact none other than the eternal Word of God,[33] and that the Jesus "who was crucified in his human flesh is truly God and the Lord of glory and one of the members of the holy Trinity."[34] It also suggests that there are both orthodox and unorthodox ways of understanding the traditional Cyrillian language about Christ's person—a union "*from* two natures," "one nature of the Word of God, made flesh"—as well as orthodox and unorthodox understandings of the "two-nature" language of Antioch and Chalcedon. Both sides of the Chalcedonian controversy, in other words, stood on equal footing; each had truth on its side, when properly understood, but each stood in danger of exaggeration.[35] After Constantinople II, in consequence, the Chalcedonian formula remained a central part of the recognized tradition of orthodoxy, but had now been qualified in some degree, submitted to

33. Canons 2, 3, and 5: Alberigo and Tanner, *Decrees*, 114–16. This seems to be expressed unambiguously in the concluding phrases of the Chalcedonian formula, but apparently was not unambiguous enough for its critics.

34. Canon 10: Alberigo and Tanner, *Decrees*, 118.

35. Canons 8 and 9: Alberigo and Tanner, *Decrees*, 117–18.

new official norms and ranged alongside other formulas, in order to remain in that tradition.

Even Justinian's efforts of 553 and the years that preceded it did not succeed, however, in mending the Christological breach. Later attempts by seventh-century emperors, too complex to relate here, to reconceive the "hypostatic unity" of Christ articulated at Chalcedon and Constantinople II in terms of a single divine energy that bound the two natures of Christ into an organic, functioning whole—another attempt to make two-nature Christology palatable to the die-hard opponents of Chalcedon—only led to further controversy: this time over whether distinct "energies" and—in psychological terms—distinct "wills" were inherent in Christ's two natures. Thanks to the theological leadership of St. Maximus the Confessor, a Roman synod in 649 rejected both the "monenergist" and "monothelete" positions, essentially as a later form of Apollinarian Christological monism. And when it had become clear to the emperors and Eastern patriarchs that these attempts at revision had come to a dead end, a synod meeting in Constantinople in 680 and 681—recognized by the Churches as the sixth ecumenical council—officially "received" the canons of the Synod of 649 (which were probably written by Maximus himself)[36] and condemned monenergism and monothelitism. The dogmatic statement of Constantinople III is clearly modeled on that of Chalcedon, citing in full not only the Nicene and Constantinopolitan creeds, but the positive statement of Chalcedon. Unlike the theological spirit of Constantinople II, perhaps, the intent of Constantinople III is clearly to amend the Chalcedonian Christology in a "friendly" or affirming, rather than in a restrictive or revisionist, way: but its definition of two energies and wills in Christ is still an amendment, a clarification of precisely how seriously Chalcedon's two-nature language for Christ does need to be taken.

My purpose in this somewhat lengthy narration has not been to give a general history of the early councils of the Church, but simply to argue that in terms of that history—of the history of Christian faith and Christian theology—Chalcedon was neither an end nor a beginning (to use Rahner's phrase), but an important way station: one among several. From the point of view of the next three centuries, certainly, its statement of faith was not a "settlement" in any final sense. It had not caused controversy to abate,

36. See Rudolf Riedinger, "Die Lateransynode von 649 und Maximos der Bekenner," in Felix Heinzer and Christoph Schönborn, eds., *Maximus Confessor* (Fribourg: Editions Universitaires, 1982), 111–22.

but in fact only inflamed it further in many parts of the Christian world; it had not emerged as what Grillmeier called the hidden "entelechy" of earlier attempts at articulating the Mystery of Christ, summarizing the tradition with a fullness that enabled all participants to recognize their chief religious concerns in its mosaic of variously hallowed phrases. The formula of Chalcedon was, in fact, a dividing line: a "scandal" to a large portion of Eastern Christianity, a rallying cry in Egypt and Syria for the agents of schism. Even for those who accepted it as normative, it was not yet the beginning of a discernible new level of certainty about the limits of orthodoxy, or the inspiration—except, perhaps, in the case of Leontius of Byzantium—for serious new theological penetration into that Mystery, until it had been further focused and qualified by the definitions of the later councils. The great virtue of the Chalcedonian definition—its abiding value for theology, and for the Churches today—is surely the breadth and balance with which it yokes together phrases and ideas from competing traditions to be the frame within which a theology of Christ faithful to the biblical narrative, and to the Nicene Creed that sums it up, can continue to be done. But that frame has always needed filling in, and in the Church of late antiquity it also needed a number of added joints and braces, clarifications and definitions, simply to hold together. It is one stage in a much longer process of staking out the course for orthodox Christology.

The real disadvantage for theology in taking the dogmatic statement of Chalcedon as a programmatic theological norm in its own right is that such a practice narrows and distorts reflection on the Mystery of Christ into an exercise in paradoxical metaphysics, an attempt simply to express how the infinite and the finite, the Creator and the creature, the Absolute and the contingent, can be together a single individual, the realms in which a single subject acts. Clearly this paradox is of inescapable importance; but it is not the whole of the Mystery. If Christology is the study in faith of the person of Christ, then it concerns itself in much broader terms with the one whom faith recognizes as Savior and Lord, who reveals to us in fully human terms the way the creating, saving God lives and acts to heal us and draw us to himself. The Mystery of Christ is the bridge between a transcendent, unimaginable God and a world of limited, visible things, forcing us to reconceive the relationship of eternity and time, Creator and created—and in the process, forcing us completely to reconceive God, as Trinity and indivisible Unity, as other and yet with us, including us within the relationships that constitute the divine life. The Mystery of Christ's identity is the mystery of one who transforms our life, even now in the community of faith and worship, anticipating a final, endless transformation that exceeds all our power of imagination: as the First Letter of John reminds us, "All we know is that when he is revealed we shall be like him, because we shall see him as he is" (1 John 3:2). The Mystery of Christ is also the mystery of Israel's relationship to the Church: the mystery by which those who call Jesus "Lord" and "Savior" come to understand him against the background of Israel's long history as the elect of a God who calls from darkness and from fire; the mystery by which non-Jews can call Jewish Scripture their own, and Jews and Gentiles alike find in the early witnesses to him written testimony to a "New Testament," forming with Israel's Scripture a larger canonical whole. The Mystery of Christ, then, is the key to Christian biblical interpretation, as well as to the Christian understanding of God and creation, of grace and the human potential. If one takes Christology to be, in the strict sense, only focused on the unity of his person in the duality of his natures, only the theological "tract" that reflects on the formula of Chalcedon, one runs the risk of leaving most of what Jesus means for Christian faith out of consideration altogether, or at least of impoverishing these other aspects of theology—soteriology, theological anthropology, Trinitarian theology, biblical interpretation—by putting them at an unjustified distance from him.

Let me suggest, then, very briefly, just a few general ways in which what we call ancient Christology seems to have had a wider scope and importance than simply its ability to identify the two natures in the one person of Christ—points which emerge more clearly from our reading of the patristic tradition if we look at its history apart from an exclusive emphasis on the development of Chalcedonian dogma:

1. Christology is really about *God.* It is about God's presence, as Other, as wholly transcendent source of all that is, within the shifting kaleidoscope of our time and space: God revealing his truth and beauty in the person of Jesus, showing us the relationships of Father, Son, and Holy Spirit that constitute the structure and flow of his inner life. How we think about God, as Christians, begins not from philosophical considerations of what must characterize the Divine, but from saying about Jesus, "We have seen his glory, the glory of the Father's only Son, full of grace and truth" (John 1:14). Our notion of God must constantly be readjusted, in the light of our understanding of the Incarnation.

2. The central Mystery of the Incarnation itself is the Mystery of *union*: how God the Word and a historical human being form a single living individual, the subject of two sets of intrinsically incompatible attributions, how these two are here one. To ask even the right questions about this union, we

must keep in mind that the Word and the man, in themselves, are utterly incommensurable beings: not just a "big guy" and a "little guy" trying to occupy the same space, but the God of Mystery embodying himself, personifying himself in a human individual. We are constantly tempted to imagine that the single hypostasis of Christ undergoes a constant tug-of-war, a "turf battle," between the eternal Person of the Word and the historical person Jesus, so that the more he is human, the less he is divine, and the more he is divine, the less he is human. This is due to our forgetting that the Word of God is not a "person" in the same sense that you and I and Jesus are "persons," that the Word does not compete for subjective control with the human Jesus, but constitutes his subject by being the source and center that personifies—makes personal—his very humanity. By contrast, ancient thought about Christ, particularly after Cyril of Alexandria, emphasized more and more that the mingling of divine and human characteristics in his range of attributes revealed an inner dialectic that constituted his identity. As Maximus tells us, "he is divine in a human way, and human in a divine way." In this single individual known to faith, two wholly different kinds of being express themselves in each other. The more fully the Word of God has identified himself with Jesus, in other words, the more fully human Jesus is—and vice versa.

3. For the Church Fathers, what we call Christology can never be thought of as a "tract" separate from what we call *soteriology*. Jesus's first identity for Christian faith is that of *Savior*; reflection on what that salvation requires of him, and leads to in us, produces the growing Christian vision of who and what he is. Part of our modern Western difficulty in appreciating the point of ancient Christologies is that our predominant soteriology, since Anselm, has been centered on the theme of Jesus's substitution or expiatory suffering on our behalf. Although this theme makes an occasional appearance in the New Testament and the Fathers, it is by no means the dominant soteriological model. In the Fathers, in fact, a far more common way of conceiving salvation is that of the transformation of all humanity by the presence of the Word in our flesh: "he became what we are," as Irenaeus (echoed by Hopkins) says, "that we might become what he is."[37] Athanasius, in his treatise *On the Incarnation*, goes so far as to use the transformation of human behavior, and of human hope, as a principal piece of evidence for the complex constitution of Christ's person:

37. Irenaeus, *Adversus haereses* 5, preface.

> If the works of the Word's Godhead had not taken place through the body, humanity would not have been deified; and if the limitations proper to the flesh had not been ascribed to the Word, humanity would not have been completely freed from them. . . . But now since the Word has become human, and has made his own all that pertains to the flesh, these things no longer touch the body . . . and so men and women are no longer sinners, dead according to their proper affections, but having risen according to the *power of the Word*, they remain forever immortal and incorruptible.[38]

4. The question remains, of course, why one must understand God's intervention in human history, God's transformation of humanity from a self-preoccupied and self-destructive mortality to life in union with him, as having taking place through what some later Fathers call the "mode of *union*"—through personal *incarnation.* Why, it is sometimes asked, could God *not* have saved us through a created mediator, a delegate lower than himself but higher than the rest of us—"a perfect creature of God, but not just one of the creatures," as Arius and his followers put it.[39] Despite all their attempts at polemics and apologetics, the answer for early Christian writers seems not to have been so much that God could *only* save us this way, as that God *has* saved us this way: in Jesus we have encountered the living God in a living human being, a *vivens homo*: "We have seen his glory, the glory as of the Father's only Son" (John 1:14). In touching him, we touch the flesh of God.

In the Christmas preface from the old Roman Missal, we hear the Church rejoicing to give God thanks and praise most especially for the person of Christ: "for through the Mystery of the Word's incarnation, the light of your glory has flooded the eyes of our minds anew: that while we know God in visible form, we might be caught up through him—through Christ, the Word now flesh—into a love for things invisible." *Dum visibiliter Deum cognoscimus*: the challenge and the promise of Christian faith, at least as the Fathers knew it, was to recognize in the man Jesus "the visible of the invisible God,"[40] and to grasp, in that vision, the reality at the heart of all things.

38. Athanasius, *Orationes contra Arianos* 3.33.

39. Confession of Faith of Arius and his associates, to Alexander of Alexandria (Urkunde 6, in Hans-Georg Opitz, *Athanasius Werke* 3 [Berlin] 12–13).

40. Irenaeus, *Adversus haereses* 5.6.6.

3 "One Thing and Another"

The Persons in God and the Person of Christ in Patristic Theology

It has become commonplace, in recent years, for theologians to argue that all serious Christian reflection must be, in some way or other, rooted in our understanding that God is a Trinity. Our sense of the Church, for instance, as a communion of persons gathered into one by the Holy Spirit around the eucharistic table, worshiping the God of Mystery as our Father, at the invitation of Jesus our Savior and brother, reveals and deepens our long-held conviction that God is, at the very core of the divine identity, a communion of what we also call—for lack of a better term—"persons." John Zizioulas has argued that even our modern notion of the person itself, which he identifies with "being" at its most intense and authentic level, is revealed in the triune reality of God to be essentially communitarian, relational, ecclesial, eucharistic, since God's own being is eternally constituted as "personal" by the dynamic mutual relations of Father, Son, and Holy Spirit.[1]

Similarly, it has become a theological commonplace to recognize that our awareness of God's triune mode and structure of being is itself rooted in our historical experience of Jesus Christ as Savior and Lord, the single person in whom God's long history of self-revelation and gracious involvement with humanity has reached its universally significant climax. Pope John Paul II, in the apostolic letter announcing his program for the millennial celebrations

1. See John Zizioulas, *Being as Communion: Studies in Personhood and the Church* (Crestwood, NY: St. Vladimir's Seminary Press, 1985), especially chapter 1, "Personhood and Being."

I am grateful to my colleague Prof. Lawrence S. Cunningham for his valuable suggestions on improving this article. Its flaws remain entirely my own.

of 2000, *Tertio Millennio Adveniente*, first called the Church's attention to the significance of this "Great Jubilee" commemorating the incarnation of the Son of God in time, and then remarked, as he turned to the details of his plan: "the thematic structure of this three-year period, centered on Christ, the Son of God made human, must necessarily be theological, and therefore Trinitarian."[2] "Necessarily theological," presumably, because all reflection on the historical career of Jesus must lead the Christian to a confession of the divine Mystery, which Jesus, as Son of the Father and giver of the Spirit, reveals in word and action; and "necessarily Trinitarian," at the same time, because this God whom Jesus has revealed in his whole human history two millennia ago is precisely the single God we call, by a kind of emblematic shorthand, the Holy Trinity of Father, Son, and Spirit. The understanding of God that distinctively characterizes the Christian faith is the inevitable result of the Church's reflection on its historical experience of the immediate, active presence of the divine reality, beginning in the history of Israel and continuing through the life of Jesus and his disciples to the present history and present faith of the Christian community. The now-famous axiom from which Karl Rahner developed his own outline of a Christian understanding of God simply affirms this mutual dependence of our understanding of God acting in history and our mental image of God as he is in himself: "The 'economic' Trinity *is* the 'immanent' Trinity, and vice versa. . . . The doctrine of the Trinity and the doctrine of God's saving plan cannot be adequately distinguished from one another."[3]

In the early centuries of Christian reflection on the Gospel, this paradoxical way of conceiving the divine reality developed concurrently—by a process of curiously intricate mutual influence—with a growing understanding of the personal ontology of Jesus. The distinctive Christian way of understanding both God and Christ, as has often been remarked, is inextricably tied up with the distinctive Christian understanding of the salvation worked by Jesus.[4] The confession of both the triune God and the single person of

2. *Tertio Millennio Adveniente* 39.

3. Karl Rahner, "Der dreifaltige Gott als transzendenter Urgrund der Heilsgeschichte," in *Mysterium Salutis*, vol. 2 (Einsiedeln/Cologne: Benziger, 1967), pp. 328–29.

4. See, for example, the words of Aloys Grillmeier in the very first chapter of his monumental history of Christological dogma in the early Church, *Christ in Christian Tradition*, vol. 1, 2nd ed. (London: Mowbray, 1975), p. 9: "Soteriology remained the actual driving force behind theological inquiry, even—as we shall see especially in the period from the third to the fifth century—behind reflection on the identity of Christ and the Holy Spirit. It will not be possible, nor even necessary, always to demonstrate this connection between soteri-

Jesus, God and man, rests on the recognition that Jesus is the divine Savior, sent into the world to free humanity from the destructive burden of sin and fear; that he must himself be truly divine in order to give our humanity a new beginning, yet that he must also be truly one of us, share our human life and choices, and even our human death, if he is to touch us effectively from within, to heal our humanity from its historic ills.

So Ignatius of Antioch, at the start of the second century, speaks constantly of the risen Jesus as "our God,"[5] yet insists with equal warmth that his flesh and blood, his human birth, and his human suffering and death were real and that he remains "in the flesh" even after his resurrection.[6] "There is only one physician," he writes to the Ephesians, "of flesh yet spiritual, born yet unbegotten, God incarnate, genuine life in the midst of death, sprung from Mary as well as God, first subject to suffering and then beyond it—Jesus Christ our Lord."[7]

Through the course of the next five centuries, amid struggles to understand this set of paradoxes more richly and to affirm them without lessening their power, representatives of the Christian "mainstream" came to be convinced more and more that the mystery of redemption, worked by God's plan in time, is itself the mystery of the person of Christ, understood in all its universal significance. So Maximus Confessor, commenting on Paul's assertion that "the end of the ages has come upon us" (1 Cor. 10:11), sums up the divine plan, or "economy," in the following way:

> That plan [οἰκονομία] was that he [the Creator], without undergoing change, should be contained by human nature through true hypostatic union, and should, without alteration, join human nature to himself, so that he would become a human being, in a way known only to him, and should make the human person divine through union with himself.[8]

My argument here is that there is, throughout the development of early Christian theology, a much closer connection than historians of theology

---

ology and the theology of the Trinity in the same way at every phase of their development. Nevertheless, we must never lose sight of it." Cf. Basil Studer, *Trinity and Incarnation: The Faith of the Early Church* (Edinburgh: T. and T. Clark, 1993), pp. 4–10.

5. E.g., *Eph. Inscr.*; *Eph.* 18:2; *Trall.* 7:1; *Rom. Inscr.*

6. E.g., *Smyrn.* 1.1–3.1.

7. *Eph.* 7:2.

8. *Quaestiones ad Thalassium* 22. *Corpus Christianorum Series Graeca*, vol. 7 (Turnhout: Brepols, 1980), p. 137.

normally suspect between the development of the classically Trinitarian understanding of God—as a single infinite reality or "substance" that *is* three mutually related, eternally self-giving "poles of energy," three concrete individual things or *hypostases*, which the Latin tradition came to call three "persons"[9]—and the development of the classical shape of Christology, by which we confess Jesus Christ to be a single "pole of energy" or hypostasis or person, a single divine subject or agent, who *is* at once fully God in "substance" and fully human in "substance," without causing those human and divine realities to be either confused with each other or distanced from each other. Gregory of Nazianzus's famous formulation of this conceptual reciprocity between theology and Christology, in his *First Letter to Cledonius*, puts this mutual relationship between Trinitarian and Christological language with admirable, if almost untranslatable, simplicity:

> If we must speak concisely, the elements from which the Savior has come to be are one thing and another [ἄλλο μὲν καὶ ἄλλο]—if indeed the visible and the invisible are not the same thing, nor the timeless and the temporal—but not one subject and another [ἄλλος δὲ καὶ ἄλλος]—no way! For both are one by combination, with God becoming human or a human being becoming God, or however one might express it. But I say "one thing and another," the opposite of what is true of the Trinity. For there we speak of "one subject and another" [ἄλλος καὶ ἄλλος], lest we confuse the individuals [ὑπόστασις], but not of "one thing and another," for the three are one and the same in divinity.[10]

The Thesis

My conviction is that this sense of the intrinsic connection between a Trinitarian understanding of the divine Mystery and a balanced but unified conception of the person of Christ, the single Son of God who is at once truly human and truly divine, is, in fact, implicitly present in the growth of Christian theology from at least the second century—long before adequate

9. For a careful and informative account of the development of the language of *hypostasis* and *prosōpon* or *persona* in the Latin and Greek Fathers, see especially André de Halleux, "'Hypostase' et 'Personne' dans la formation du dogme trinitaire (ca. 375–381)," *Revue d'histoire ecclésiastique* 79 (1984), pp. 313–69, 625–70.

10. Ep. 101:20–21 (SC 208:44–16).

terminology was available to give the connection words[11]—and that the development of the one classical scheme in theological language inevitably promoted, conditioned, and even determined the development of the other.[12] More particularly, I believe one can see a kind of implied equation at work in the growth of early Christian understanding of the mysteries of God and of Christ. If one eliminates the extremes that most serious Christian thinkers, from Ignatius on, quickly recognized as absurd—for instance, the notion that God ceases to be God in "emptying himself" to save humanity, or the idea that Jesus's bodily appearance was merely a phantom—then one notices an emergent pattern in the early Christian conceptions of both God and Jesus. The more ancient authors emphasize the complex personal *unity* of Christ as the agent of salvation, the more they are forced to acknowledge the irreducible *threeness* of God, even to the point of having to conceive of Father, Son, and Holy Spirit as in some way ontologically ranked or subordinated, as sharing in the divine reality in differing degrees of fullness. Conversely, the more ancient authors emphasize the radical *unity* of the divine Mystery and see the threeness of Father, Son, and Holy Spirit in what we might call perspectival rather than ontological terms, as a threeness of manifestation in history, corresponding to a threefold human experience of the divine—the more, in other words, they express the Christian sense of God in a "modalist" rather than a Trinitarian direction—the more they are forced to see Jesus, the Savior, as subjectively *double* and to understand his saving role in terms of God's dwelling in a human being or acting in ways parallel to his human actions, rather than in terms of God's personal identity with him. To put it more concisely: one can see in the ancient debates, I believe, that a theology that emphasizes the threeness of persons in God—even a theology that is to some degree "subordinationist" in conceiving how those three can still be one—tends to stress the oneness of person in Christ the Savior, occasionally

11. For helpful reflections on the process of growth in dogmatic terminology and in the "differentiated consciousness" of the Church's continuing faith, see Bernard J. F. Lonergan, *De Deo Trino I: Pars Dogmatica* (Rome: Gregorian University Press, 1964), pp. 17–28, 98–112 (trans. Conn O'Donovan, *The Way to Nicaea: The Dialectical Development of Trinitarian Theology* [Philadelphia: Westminster Press, 1976], pp. 1–17, 118–37).

12. This same connection has been argued for, more tentatively but at much greater length, by Basil Studer in *Trinity and Incarnation* (see note 4). For a careful and suggestive study of the connection between the language of "unconfused union" in patristic debates on the Trinity and that of Christological reflection, see Luise Abramowski, "Συνάφεια und ἀσύγχυτος ἕνωσις als Bezeichnungen für trinitarische und christologische Einheit," in *Drei christologische Untersuchungen* (Berlin: De Gruyter, 1981), pp. 62–109.

even to the point of seeming to compromise the fullness of his humanity. On the other hand, a theology with a weak conception of the distinction of persons in God—a theology with a more "modalist" way of conceiving God's being—tends to stress the twoness of natures or substances in Christ, even to the point of tending to see him as a human person in whom the Word or Wisdom or Spirit of God has come to dwell, as a divine gift extrinsic to himself.

In general, Greek theologians through at least the sixth century tended to be more concerned about the dangers of modalism—usually under the pejorative label of "Sabellianism"—than they were about subordinationism or even tritheism. The reason, I suggest, was that they instinctively saw that a thoroughgoing modalism in one's understanding of the God of biblical history implies reducing Jesus to being simply an inspired and inspiring human person, a Spirit-filled teacher and healer who is really no different in his ontological makeup from the other prophets and saints. The dominant theology in the Latin West, on the other hand, up to the sixth century—joined in the decades after Nicaea by Athanasius and his intellectual followers[13]—tended more to emphasize the transcendence, uniqueness, and singleness of the divine Mystery, and at the same time to give greater emphasis to the distinction and balance, even the relative autonomy, of human and divine in Jesus. Behind all traditions, East and West, lay the real issue of both Trinitarian theology and Christology: how can we understand God as radically one and eternally transcendent with respect to creation and still understand Jesus as a genuinely divine savior, who genuinely acts in our history as a human being like ourselves?

Four Test Cases

To evaluate the validity of the scheme proposed here, one needs to move beyond abstraction and to look more deeply into the arguments proposed by a variety of authors in the ancient controversies over God and Christ. What

13. See the thoughtful warnings against the standard, oversimplified typology of "Eastern" and "Western" approaches to the unity of substance and trinity of persons in God, articulated in the 1890s by Théodore de Régnon, in Michel R. Barnes, "Augustine in Contemporary Trinitarian Theology," *Theological Studies* 56 (1995), pp. 237–50; cf. Barnes, "The Fourth Century as Trinitarian Canon," in *Christian Origins: Theology, Rhetoric and Community*, ed. Lewis Ayres and Gareth Jones (London: Routledge, 1998), pp. 47–67, esp. 61–62. For distinct but largely complementary new attempts to reconceive the entire narrative of fourth-century theological controversy, see Lewis Ayres, *Nicaea and Its Legacy* (Oxford: Oxford University Press, 2004), and John Behr, *The Nicene Faith*, 2 vols. (Crestwood, NY: St. Vladimir's Seminary Press, 2004).

I would like to do here is simply to offer four test cases, in snapshot fashion, from ancient theological debates in which Christological concerns seem to play a determining role in Trinitarian argument, or vice versa. Even though we can only sketch out the details, I hope this may be enough to give at least a certain plausibility to the hypothesis I am proposing and to stimulate further reflection on the degree to which it holds good.

The Monarchian Controversy: Hippolytus and Tertullian

The first test case to consider is that of the so-called monarchian controversy of the late second and early third centuries. At the end of the fifth book of his *Ecclesiastical History*, Eusebius of Caesarea gives several lengthy citations from an anonymous work apparently written early in the third century—known sometimes as "The Little Labyrinth"—which tells of the doctrinal innovations of a number of Roman Christians who had recently been condemned by Popes Victor (189–199) and Zephyrinus (199–217).[14] According to Eusebius's source, these errant Christians were above all concerned to emphasize the radical oneness, the *monarchia*, of the divine power at work in the universe. Their principal deviation from the tradition of Christian faith, as it had developed by then, is said in the document to be their suggestion that since God is simple in being, Jesus was "simply a man" (ψιλὸς ἄνθρωπος), a position that they reportedly reinforced by using both their own corrected version of Scripture in combination with Aristotelian dialectics. A heresiological work ascribed to Tertullian, which may in fact come from Pope Zephyrinus's chancery, adds the detail that some of these Christians also made use of late Jewish speculations about Melchisedek, seeing in him a more exalted mediatorial figure than Christ himself.[15] This line of thought,

14. *Ecclesiastical History* 5.28.

15. Ps.-Tertullian, *Against All Heresies* 8 (CSEL 47.225–226; repr. CCL 2.1410); Eduard Schwartz argued that this work was originally written in Greek by Pope Zephyrinus or one of his clerics and translated into Latin in the early fourth century by Victorinus of Poetovio: *Sitzungsberichte der Bayerischen Akademie der Wissenschaften* 3 (Munich, 1936), pp. 38–45. For Jewish speculations on Melchisedek, see especially the Qumran fragment 11Q13, first published by A. S. van der Woude, "Melchisedek als himmlische Erlösergestalt in den neugefundenen eschatologischen Midraschim aus Qumran Höhle XI," *Oudtestamentische Studiën* 14 (1965), pp. 354–73. For a discussion of this and other texts from Qumran referring to Melchisedek, as well as of the "Melchisedekian" Christians of the late second and early third centuries, see F. W. Horton, *The Melchisedek Tradition: A Critical Examination of the Sources to the Fifth Century A. D. and in the Epistle to the Hebrews* (Cambridge: Cam-

which Adolf von Harnack dubbed "dynamic" or "dynamistic monarchianism,"[16] seems to have been part of a much wider pattern of early Christian argument, ranging in character from popular to highly learned, that set out to place gospel faith within the longer tradition of both Jewish biblical monotheism and its Hellenistic philosophical counterpart. In such thinking, Jesus is seen as the appointed spokesman, the messenger of the one and only God, but not as himself a genuinely divine figure.

Alongside this approach, the same decades around the turn of the third century saw the rise of what Harnack called "modalistic monarchianism," a view of the divine being that seems also to have conceived of God as ontologically one, but as revealing himself in genuinely different ways, under different "faces" (πρόσωπα), through sacred history; those who espoused this position, such as Noetus of Smyrna and his disciples, as well as the mysterious Praxeas refuted by Tertullian, were charged with saying "that the Christ was the Father himself, and that the Father himself was begotten and suffered and died";[17] in other words, they failed to make the necessary distinction between the divine Savior presented in the Gospels and the divine in itself. Both the former "adoptionist" or "dynamic" kind of monarchianism and the latter "modalist" form—different as they may have been in their willingness to call Jesus divine—shared at least a strong sense of the evangelical priority of emphasizing the divine unity, the undivided "monarchy" or rule of God in the world. Manlio Simonetti has argued plausibly that while these two forms of unitive Christian theology may well have been developed in the late second and early third century—in Asia Minor and in Rome, especially—in resistance to the more philosophically self-conscious and speculative Logos-Christology of Justin, Irenaeus, Clement, and Origen, their roots lay in the original Jewish and Christian instinct of rejecting all forms of polytheism.[18] Nev-

bridge University Press, 1976), pp. 60–82 (Qumran), 90–101 (Christian sects); and Claudio Gianotto, *Melchisedek e la sua tipologia. Tradizione giudaiche, cristiane e gnostiche (sec. II A. C.-sec. III* D.C) (Brescia: Paideia, 1984), pp. 61–80 (Qumran), 237–54 (Christian sects).

16. See James Millar, trans., *History of Dogma*, vol. 3 (London: William and Norgate, 1897), pp. 8–50.

17. Hippolytus, *Against Noetus* 1.2; cf. Tertullian, *Against Praxeas* 1: the devil, working through Praxeas, "says that the Father himself came down into the Virgin, himself was born of her, himself suffered, in short himself is Jesus Christ."

18. See Manlio Simonetti, "Il problema dell'unità di Dio a Roma da Clemente a Dionigi," *Rivista di storia e letteratura religiosa* 22 (1986), pp. 439–74 [*Studi sulla cristologia del II e III secolo*, Studia Ephemeridis Augustinianum 44 (Rome, 1993), pp. 183–215]; "Sabellio e

ertheless, both approaches had clear implications for how one understood the person of Jesus.

The two main contemporary responses to the modalist form of "monarchian" theology were Hippolytus's little treatise *Against Noetus*—a work whose authorship has been much disputed in recent years, but which seems to have been written by a Greek in Asia Minor sometime around 200[19]—and Tertullian's work *Against Praxeas*, composed in Carthage probably between 213 and 217. Although the arguments and assumptions of these works are different in important respects, they are also remarkably similar in their insistence that Christian faith demands an understanding of God that makes room, somehow or other, for calling Christ and the Holy Spirit both genuinely distinct from the Father and genuinely divine, all the while preserving the accepted biblical and philosophical principle that the divine power ruling creation is radically one in its being and action.

Hippolytus begins his refutation of Noetus's modalist doctrine by asserting what he calls—in Irenaean fashion—"the answer of the elders":

> We, too, know that there is truly one God.[20] We know Christ. We know that the Son suffered, in the way that he suffered; that he died, in the way that he died; that he rose on the third day and is at the right hand of the Father, and that he is coming to judge living and dead. And we say what we have learned.[21]

Reliable Church tradition, in other words, affirms both the singleness of God and the story of the "economy" of salvation by the death and resurrection of Christ; this twofold tradition must be the guiding norm for any further elaboration of Christian theology. "After all," Hippolytus asks rhetorically a

---

il sabellianismo," *Studi storico religiose* 4 (1980), pp. 7–28 [*Studi sulla cristologia*, pp. 217–38, esp. 236].

19. See M. Simonetti, "Tra Noeta, Ippolito e Melitone," *Rivista di storia e letteratura religiosa* 38 (1995), pp. 393–414, for an argument in favor of this dating and a survey of the long controversy about the authorship of the works ascribed, in ancient or modern times, to Hippolytus of Rome. For an extended consideration of the Christology of the traditional Hippolytan corpus (excluding the *Chroniam*, the *Refutatio omnium haresium*, the *Apostolic Tradition*, and a number of fragments attributed to Hippolytus), see Antonio Zani, *La Cristologia di Ippolito* (Brescia: Morcelliana, 1984).

20. Or, in the translation of Robert Butterworth, *Hippolytus of Rome: Contra Noetum* (London: Heythrop Monographs 2, 1977), p. 44: "We, too, have knowledge of a single God—in the true way."

21. *Against Noetus* 1.7.

few paragraphs later, "would not everyone say that there is only one God? But not everyone would scrap the economy!"[22]

Hippolytus's own approach to explaining how the three "faces" (πρόσωπα) of God encountered in sacred history can be a single divine Mystery is worked out mainly in terms of action and power—in functional terms, one might say. Christ rules over all things, Hippolytus observes in one passage, but is himself—according to 1 Corinthians 15:23–28—also subject to the Father, "so that in all things a single God may be revealed."[23] A little further on, he compares the unity of Christ and the Father, which Jesus claims in John 10:30, to the unity Jesus prays for among his disciples (John 17:22–23): a unity not in substance (οὐσίᾳ) but "in power (δυνάμει), by our disposition towards single-mindedness."[24] Still further on, in a passage Simonetti has characterized as a "pioneering" statement of Trinitarian theology,[25] Hippolytus develops further his understanding of the unity of Father, Son, and Holy Spirit in terms of the single "harmonious economy" (οἰκονομία συμφωνίας), the unified historical work of revelation and salvation, which they achieve together:

> The Father gives orders, the Word performs the work, and is revealed as Son, through whom belief is accorded to the Father. . . . For the one who commands is the Father, the one who obeys is the Son, and the one who brings about understanding is the Holy Spirit. "He who is Father is over all things," he adds, alluding to Ephesians 4:6, "and the Son is through all things, and the Holy Spirit is in all things. We can get no idea of the one God other than by really believing in Father and Son and Holy Spirit."[26]

Although God is always "single" (μόνος), according to Hippolytus, he is also, in his own being, "manifold" (πολύς): a multiplicity that is first revealed when God utters his Word of creation and revelation[27] and when he inspires the prophets by his Spirit;[28] we have come to "see" this manifold reality of

22. *Against Noetus* 3.4 (trans. Butterworth, altered).

23. *Against Noetus* 6.4.

24. *Against Noetus* 7.3 (trans. Butterworth, altered; Butterworth translates δυνάμνει here as "virtually").

25. Simonetti, "Tra Noeto, Ippolito e Melitone," 395.

26. *Against Noetus* 14.4–6 (trans. Butterworth, altered).

27. *Against Noetus* 10.2–11.3.

28. *Against Noetus* 11.4.

God in the incarnate Word.[29] The real issue for Hippolytus, in arguing for a genuine plurality within the single being of God, is clearly to make possible an understanding of the "economy" of salvation in which the Son and the Holy Spirit can be understood as genuinely divine, and yet as genuinely present and acting in the world as the New Testament portrays them, not distanced from the world in the way some ancient philosophical schools imagined divine agency. So the treatise closes with an extended passage in an exalted rhetorical tone, rehearsing the narrative of Jesus's birth, death, and resurrection as the paradoxical story of "God embodied": as one who truly suffered, mentally and physically, while remaining capable of miracles; as one sent into the world by the Father, returning his soul to the Father, raised by the Father from the dead, and finally breathing forth his living Spirit on the disciples.[30] Hippolytus writes at the start of this final meditation,

> So let us in the future believe, blessed brethren, in accordance with the tradition of the Apostles, that God the Word came down from the heavens into the holy virgin Mary, so that once he had taken flesh out of her, and taken a soul of the human kind—a rational one, I mean—and had become everything that a human being is, sin excepted, he might save fallen Adam and procure incorruption for such as believe in his name.[31]

The structure of Hippolytus's rhetoric here suggests that all his earlier speculation about the internal plurality and unity of God is really meant to lay an intelligible foundation for proclaiming this astonishing gospel of the "harmonious economy" of salvation.

Tertullian's treatise *Against Praxeas* is a much more elaborate work, with extended discussion of scriptural passages that bear on the question of the inner unity and plurality of God; Tertullian also makes an original and important attempt to develop philosophical categories for expressing just what, in God, is single and what is threefold.[32] For Tertullian, as for Hippolytus,

29. *Against Noetus* 12.5–13.1.

30. *Against Noetus* 17–18.

31. *Against Noetus* 17.2.

32. See especially chapters 2, 7, 9, 23, 26, and 27. Tertullian's theological vocabulary, and its background in Roman law and Hellenistic philosophy, has been analyzed at length by modern scholars: see especially Joseph Moingt, *La théologie trinitaire de Tertullien*, 4 vols. (Paris: Aubier, 1966–69); René Braun, *Deus Christianorum. Recherches sur le vocabulaire doctrinal de Tertullien*, 2nd ed. (Paris: Etudes Augustiniennes, 1977); and the introduction to the text and translation of the work by Ernest Evans (London: SPCK, 1948). For the con-

what is at stake in the discussion with those who assert a modalist view of God—who say, as his pseudonymous opponent Praxeas is made to say, that "the Father himself came down into the Virgin, himself was born of her, himself suffered, in short himself is Jesus Christ"—is really the Christian narrative of the saving economy. Citing what he calls the "rule of the faith," he insists that

> we believe . . . in one only God, yet subject to this dispensation (which is our word for "economy"), that the one only God has also a Son, his Word, who has proceeded from himself, by whom all things were made . . . ; that this Son was sent by the Father into the virgin and was born of her both human and God . . . ; that he suffered, died, and was buried, according to the scriptures, and having been raised up by the Father and taken back into heaven, sits at the right hand of the Father . . . ; and that thereafter he, according to his promise, sent from the Father the Holy Spirit the Paraclete, the sanctifier of the faith of those who believe in the Father and the Son and the Holy Spirit.[33]

Tertullian makes several attempts to explain how it is that the single divine Mystery or monarchy at the heart of this "economy" can at the same time be permanently and intrinsically manifold: a functional explanation, somewhat like that advanced by Hippolytus, that offers the analogy of an emperor delegating rule to his son to carry out the administration of his empire more effectively;[34] an explanation in terms of differing rank within a single status or sociolegal category, like the various castes of Roman citizens;[35] even an explanation in terms of the process of thought itself, anticipating Augustine's

---

nections between Tertullian's Trinitarian and Christological use of the same terms, see also Abramowski (note 12), pp. 80–86. A good recent survey of Tertullian's theology is Eric F. Osborn, *Tertullian: The First Theologian of the West* (Cambridge: Cambridge University Press, 1997).

33. *Against Praxeas* 2. In citing this work, I use the translation of Ernest Evans (London: SPCK, 1948). In a short but perceptive article, Robert Markus has argued that Tertullian's use of the word οἰκονομία/*dispositio* in the *Adversus Praxean* seems to have a different sense from that in which Hippolytus uses it in *Contra Noetum*. Tertullian seems to be using it, Markus argues, in its "original, secular sense," to mean the ordering or arrangement of the three constituent "elements" of the Godhead; for Hippolytus, on the other hand, as for later writers, it clearly points to the incarnation of God's Word in history. See "Trinitarian Theology and the Economy," *Journal of Theological Studies* 9 (1958), pp. 89–102.

34. *Against Praxeas* 3.

35. *Against Praxeas* 2, 3, 4.

more extended analogy in *De Trinitate* VIII–X, in which the physical uttering of words is always preceded by a kind of mental dialogue between reason (*ratio*) and language (*sermo*).[36] The predominant set of terms Tertullian uses, however, to grapple with the paradox of divine unity and multiplicity is a more material one: the category of substance (*substantia*), which can be one even while it takes on a variety of forms and shapes. So his use of what were to become three common patristic analogies for the Trinity—water flowing from a spring to a river to a drainage canal; light issuing from the sun, first as a beam and then reflected as a bright spot on an object; the stalk of a plant issuing from a root and bearing fruit on its branches—are all, in Tertullian's treatment, essentially images drawn from the material world, reflecting his general assumption (borrowed from Stoic philosophy) that all real things, even the reality we call "spirit," are in some sense *material*, if they are not simply mental or imaginary.[37] In this latter sense, Father, Son, and Spirit all share the one divine "substance" or "stuff" that issues forth from the Father—"not that the Son is other than the Father by diversity, but by distribution. . . . For the Father is the whole substance, while the Son is an outflow [*derivatio*] and assignment [*portio*] of the whole."[38]

Toward the end of title treatise, however, Tertullian makes the same implicit connection that Hippolytus had made between the issue of divine unity and multiplicity and the person of the Savior. As in the *Contra Noetum*, this rhetorical positioning of the Christological argument, at the conclusion of the treatise, gives it particular force. His opponents, Tertullian says—those who assert that in some sense it was the Father, the God of Israel, who was present in the world and who suffered as Christ—attempt to do justice to the New Testament texts by asserting that while the divine Word mentioned in the prologue to John's Gospel is essentially an act of God, a *vox et sonus oris*,[39] the one who audibly speaks of the Father and prays to the Father in the Gospels, the Jesus whom we call Son of God, is in fact simply a man; so the divine suffering that saves us is really only the Father's compassion for him, the sympathetic presence with the man Jesus of a God who is wholly other than he, and who bestows on him a share in the name of "Christ" simply by being a powerful, "anointing" presence within him. Tertullian writes,

36. *Against Praxeas* 5.
37. See, for example, *Against Praxeas* 26.
38. *Against Praxeas* 9.
39. *Against Praxeas* 7.

> Those who contend that the Father and the Son are one and the same, now [in the context of the story of Jesus] begin to divide them rather than to call them one. For if Jesus is one and Christ is another, the Son will be one and the Father another, because Jesus is the Son and Christ is the Father.[40]

Tertullian's own reason for insisting on the personal distinctness of Son and Spirit from the Father, within the divine substance and activity, now becomes clearer: it is to make conceptually possible a real identification of the divine Word with human flesh, in such a way that Jesus can himself be personally "the Christ," "anointed" in his saving role by the gift of the Spirit who belongs uniquely to him, related to the Father as Son and related to the rest of humanity as brother and Lord. If Jesus is a single agent, a single Savior who is both human and divine, he must be a single "person," both over against the Father and over against us. So in a passage that remarkably anticipates both the *Tome* of Leo and the Chalcedonian definition of Christological faith, two and a half centuries later, Tertullian writes,

> Certainly we find him set forth as in every respect Son of God and son of man, since we find him as both God and human, without doubt according to each substance as it is distinct in what itself is. Because neither is the Word anything else but God nor the flesh anything else but human. . . . We observe a double quality [*status*], not confused but combined, Jesus in one person God and human. . . . And to such a degree did there remain unimpaired the proper being of each substance, that in him the spirit carried out its own acts, that is, powers and works and signs, while the flesh accomplished its own passions . . . , and at length it also died.[41]

Tertullian is affirming here the rich and complex texture of the person and activities of Christ, as they appear in the Gospels; but it is only the distinctness of persons within the divine reality that makes conceivable, within some kind of narrative and ontological unity, the genuine divinity and humanity, at once, of him whom the Scriptures call both Son of God and Son of Man.

40. *Against Praxeas* 27; cf. also 29.
41. *Against Praxeas* 27.

The Controversy with Paul of Samosata

The second incident of theological and Christological controversy I would like to examine is the trial and deposition of Paul of Samosata, a civil servant from the Syrian kingdom of Palmyra who became the autocratic and unpopular metropolitan of Antioch, doubtless through political pressure from local rulers, around the year 260. Paul was deposed by a provincial synod in 268, on grounds of both misbehavior and unorthodox teaching, after two earlier attempts to remove him had failed. Once again, our main narrative source is Eusebius of Caesarea, who tells us that Paul was finally deposed for heresy only after a local presbyter named Malchion, who was also a skilled professional rhetorician, had succeeded in unmasking Paul's heterodoxy in a public theological disputation.[42] Paul himself was clearly not a theologian and left no written works of his own; the extant quotations attributed to him all presumably come from the record of the disputation with Malchion, which Eusebius tells us was taken down by stenographers, and most of them are preserved by later sources that are clearly hostile to Paul's memory. Paul became, in fact, for the later patristic centuries a kind of classical theological villain, a poster boy both for unsound doctrine about God and Christ, and for the personal depravity and self-promotion that was thought to be the natural accompaniment of heresy.[43] Controversy still rages among scholars over what Paul actually held and taught, and over the fairness of his trial;[44] despite the bias and the fragmentary, often questionable nature of the sources, however, it seems possible to form at least some opinion of the theological issues at stake between Paul and his episcopal critics at Antioch.

Paul was identified by later heresiology as having effectively denied both the personal, substantial existence of the divine Word or wisdom within the Mystery of God, and the genuine union of any aspect of the divine reality with the man Jesus. The late sixth-century handbook of heresies called *De sectis*—in most cases a work known for its careful and nuanced

42. *Ecclesiastical History* 7.29.

43. See the long description of Paul's arrogant and disedifying behavior in the letter of the Antiochene synod that deposed him, quoted in Eusebius, *Ecclesiastical History* 7.30.

44. For a survey of recent literature on the sources and issues involved, see M. Simonetti, "Per la rivalutazione di alcune testimonianze su Paolo di Samosata," *Rivista di storia e letteratura religiosa* 24 (1988), pp. 177–210 [*Studi sulla cristologia*, pp. 239–71]; Lorenzo Perrone, "L'enigma di Paolo di Samosata. Dogma, chiesa e società nella Siria del III secolo: prospettive di un ventennio di studi," *Cristianesimo netta storia* 13 (1992), pp. 253–327.

treatment of aberrant theologies—describes Paul's approach as that of a simple Unitarian:

> Concerning the nature of God, he spoke of the Father alone; concerning the incarnation, he said that Christ was a mere human being, and that the Word of God came to be in him. . . . Paul of Samosata did not say that the independently subsistent Word came to be in Christ, but he said that the Word was an order and a command: in other words, God commanded what he willed to be done by that man, and he did it. But Paul did not teach the same things as Sabellius concerning the nature of God. For Sabellius said that Father, Son and Holy Spirit are the same person, and said that God is something with three names—not believing at all in a Trinity. But Paul did not say that Father, Son and Holy Spirit are the same person, but he said that the Father is God, who created all things, while the Son is a mere human being, and the Spirit is the grace which came to dwell in the Apostles.[45]

A fourth-century witness, the homoiousian bishop George of Laodicea, writing in the midst of the disputes over the reception of the Nicene formula in the year 359, compares Paul to his own contemporary, Marcellus of Ancyra (of whom more shortly); neither of them, he says, "wanted to say that the Son of God is son in truth, but—taking their start, I think, from the name of Word—they wanted to say that the Son of God is a word from the mouth, an utterance . . . the speech-activity [λεκτικὴ ἐνέργεια] of God."[46] And both Hilary of Poitiers and Athanasius, discussing the acceptability of the Nicene term *homoousios* for describing the relationship of Son to Father, admit that the Antiochene Synod of 268 rejected the term as it was used for God and his Word by Paul of Samosata "on the ground that by attributing this title to God [says Hilary] he had taught that He was single and undifferentiated, and at once Father and Son to himself."[47]

45. *De sectis* 3.3 (PG 86.1213D–1216B).

46. Letter of George of Laodicea, quoted in Epiphanius *Panarion* 73.12.2, 6 (GCS Epiphanius III, 285.1–4, 22).

47. Hilary, *De synodis* 81; cf. Athanasius, *De synodis* 43. In accepting the term *homoousios* into its creed, the Council of Nicaea seems deliberately to have chosen a word with a notorious history of modalist connotations, perhaps in order to shock Arius's sympathizers, such as Eusebius of Nicomedia, with the deliberate extremeness of their affirmation of the Son's unity with the Father. See Hilary, *On the Trinity* 4.4; Ambrose, *On the Faith* 3.125; see also Barnes, "The Fourth Century as Trinitarian Canon," esp. pp. 48–51.

The fragments of text actually attributed to Paul and his opponents in our sources,[48] in fact, do not have much to say about his understanding of the ontological status of the Word within the divine being but deal in a variety of ways with the relation of the Word to the humanity of Christ. Some of them sound almost orthodox by later standards and speak of the Word of God as being "united to the human body which he assumed,"[49] or as existing "in the whole man."[50] Others, however, portray the relation of the Word of God to Jesus in much more extrinsic terms. The letter of the Synod, which deposed him, for instance, quotes him as saying that the divine wisdom dwelt in Jesus as in a temple:

> So that it was, in a sense, one subject within another (*alius in alio*); just as when a garment is wrapped around a human being, although it is something, it is not the same as the person, nor a part of him. In the same way, the Word is himself wrapped up in Jesus Christ, as in someone (or: something) other (*alio*) than the Word himself, but not as if God and the body were united in a substantial way with each of them made into one thing.[51]

It is important to note that the general theological orientation of the bishops who condemned Paul of Samosata in 268 was that of a particular brand of late third- and fourth-century Origenism, which not only strongly affirmed Origen's conception of God as three distinct and hierarchically ranked *hypostases* or concrete beings but believed (in contrast to Origen) that the unity of Christ as a single, divine, and human subject could only be secured if the divine Logos is understood, in him, to be the controlling mind behind his behavior, rather than a purely human *nous*. The Synod's letter asks,

> What does it mean to say that the constitution of Jesus Christ was different from ours? We judge that in this one great respect his constitution was different, that God the Word was in him what the inner man is in us.[52]

48. These fragments can be found most fully, along with thorough commentary and extensive historical study, in the classic work of Gustave Bardy, *Paul de Samosate: Etude historique*, Spicilegium Sacrum Lovaniense: Etudes et Documents 4, 2nd ed. (Paris: E. Champion, 1929).

49. Frag. 20: Bardy, *Paul de Samosate*, p. 50.

50. Frag. 19: Bardy, *Paul de Samosate*, p. 49.

51. Frag. 14: Bardy, *Paul de Samosate*, p. 47.

52. Fragment of the Encyclical Letter of the Synod of Antioch, 268, quoted by Leontius of Byzantium, *Deprehensio et triumphus contra Nestorianos*, florilegium, no. 50.

This vision of the internal unity of Word and humanity in the one subject Christ was, in fact, to be the vision of most of those Greek theologians of the late third and fourth centuries who opposed a modalist or excessively unitary conception of the divine being: it was shared by Arius and most of his followers, who argued that the Son was essentially a divine creature, God by participation rather than by equality with the Father; and its most famous defender was the decidedly anti-Arian Apollinarius of Laodicea. For all of these thinkers, in the tradition of Origen, the personal unity of Word and human in Christ demanded the distinct, personal existence of the Word within the divine substance. For Paul of Samosata, on the other hand, who probably drew on the long Antiochene tradition of Logos Christology but who seems to have wanted to ascribe to the Logos a minimal degree of ontological independence,[53] a strongly unitary view of God implied a view of Jesus in which the human was much more distant, ontologically, from the divine. Denying the Logos personal subsistence within the Mystery of God meant for him attributing independent personal subsistence, over against God, to the human Jesus. On both counts, he was destined to shock pious Origenist ears.

Marcellus of Ancyra and Eusebius of Caesarea

A third controversy from the patristic era, which suggests a strong, if not always clearly expressed, reciprocal influence between the understanding of the persons of the Trinity and that of the person of Christ, was the mid-fourth-century debate over the theology of Marcellus of Ancyra. Like Paul of Samosata, Marcellus is a figure who has attracted a great deal of attention from scholars in recent years; new attributions and identifications of pseud-epigraphical works as his, new analyses of the fragments of his work in the polemical treatises of his opponents (notably Eusebius of Caesarea), as well as a growing new way of reading the actual theological issues of the mid-fourth century have all led to a fuller and more nuanced understanding of Marcellus's complex and subtle theological work than was generally possible twenty-five years ago.[54]

53. See Simonetti, "Per la rivalutazione," pp. 270–71, for a judgment of Paul's likely place in the Antiochene theological tradition.

54. See especially Joseph T. Lienhard, "Marcellus of Ancyra in Modern Research," *Theological Studies* 43 (1982), pp. 486–503; "The 'Arian' Controversy: Some Categories Re-

One of the most controversial and widely hated theologians of his time, Marcellus represented the strongest theological affirmation that was thinkable of the substantial inner unity of God in the decades following the Council of Nicaea. While most Eastern bishops, in the aftermath of Nicaea, were satisfied that the real benefit of the Council had been its rejection of the crude ontological subordinationism popularized by Arius and his supporters, they also seem to have been far less than enthusiastic about the Council's credal formulation of faith, particularly about the term *homoousios*, which had a provocatively overunitive, even modalist, ring.[55] Even Athanasius, who would become an impassioned promoter of the Nicene formula in the late 340s and 350s, as the only possible antidote to the continuing threat of Arianism in its various forms, made little mention of it in the twenty years that immediately followed the Council. The first committed advocate of the Nicene formulation of the divine Mystery whom we know of, perhaps one of its original architects, was Marcellus, bishop of Ancyra in Asia Minor and close associate of Eustathius of Antioch, who was himself one of the leading heirs of the anti-Origenist, strongly unitive theology represented by Paul of Samosata in the late third century.[56] As is well known, Marcellus emphasized in his writings that God is radically one and utterly inconceivable: one substance or οὐσία, one concrete being or ὑπόστασις, one source of action or *persona* (πρόσωπον).[57] When we consider the economy of salvation, we can say that this divine monad has "expanded" for our sake into a plurality of *personae*, but biblical faith must continue to affirm that all of these forms—the God of creation and the God of Sinai, Father, Son, and Holy Spirit—are fundamentally "one and the same." God's Logos or Word is eternally present in God as a power or potentiality (δύναμις), which becomes actual when God "speaks the word" of creation, revelation, or salvation. It is only in the event of the Incarnation, Marcellus holds—echoing a tradition

considered," *Theological Studies* 48 (1987), pp. 415–37; Gerhard Feige, *Die Lehre Markells von Ankyra in der Darstellung seiner Gegner* (Leipzig: Benno, 1991); Klaus Seibt, *Die Theologie des Markell von Ankyra* (Berlin: De Gruyter, 1994); and Joseph T. Lienhard, *Contra Marcellum: Marcellus of Ancyra and Fourth-Century Theology* (Washington, DC: Catholic University of America Press, 1999).

55. See Barnes, "The Fourth Century as Trinitarian Canon," pp. 50–51.

56. See A. H. B. Logan, "Marcellus of Ancyra and the Councils of AD 325: Antioch, Ancyra, and Nicaea," *Journal of Theological Studies* 43 (1992), pp. 428–46.

57. For a brief summary of Marcellus's theology, see Lienhard, "The 'Arian' Controversy," pp. 426–27; see also the other works mentioned in note 54.

reaching back to Hippolytus—that the Word can be said to be "begotten" or can be called "Son"; for this reason, Marcellus seems to conceive of Jesus, the distinct individual whom we call Son of God, not as himself the divine Word but as "the human flesh, which God's word took up."[58] In another fragment, Marcellus makes it clear that the Incarnation does not imply any real duality of persons within God:

> For if spirit [which he uses as a generic term for the divine substance] is considered in its own right, the Logos rightly is understood as one and the same with God; but if the fleshly addition, which the Savior [i.e., the one God] took on himself, is considered, the divinity appears simply to have expanded, in this regard, as an active power, so that the Monad remains, as we would expect, really undivided.[59]

In "taking up" the human Jesus, Son of Man, Marcellus asserts in another passage, the Logos has "prepared the Man"—and it is unclear whether he is using ἄνθρωπος here in an individual or a universal sense—"to become, by adoption, Son of God, so that when all this is achieved it might once again, as Logos, be united with God,"[60] and become again simply what the Logos has always been: the Word of God. As a result, the presence of the Logos in the human Jesus always remains, in Marcellus's view, the presence of a transcendent power that is totally other in substance and agency from Jesus the man; the story of Jesus's agony in the garden, for instance, makes it clear not only that Christ possesses two wills, but that these wills, in turn, reveal two willing subjects, two ontological sources of action:

> For that the Father has so willed is clear from the fact that what he willed came to pass; but that the Son did not so will is clear from what he asks for. After all, he says in another place, "I seek not my own will, but the will of the Father who sent me."[61]

One of Marcellus's most outspoken opponents throughout the 330s was Eusebius of Caesarea: the heir of Origen's exegetical and theological legacy

58. Frag. 63 in E. Klostermann and G. C. Hansen, eds., *Eusebius Werke*, vol. 4 (GCS 3rd ed.; Berlin: Akademie-Verlag, 1991), p. 196f.

59. Frag. 71 (ibid., p. 198).

60. Frag. 41 (ibid., p. 192).

61. Frag. 73 (ibid., p. 198f).

at Caesarea and the most articulate exponent of a nuanced, if still clearly subordinationist, Origenist view of God as a Trinity of distinct *personae.* Eusebius criticizes Marcellus not only for his denial of eternal reality to these divine "persons" but for all that this denial implies for Christology. Like most fourth-century theologians, from the bishops gathered at Antioch in 268 until Apollinarius of Laodicea a century later, Eusebius assumed that a true Christian confession of the divinity of Christ meant an affirmation that the eternal divine reason or Logos has become the subjective center of Jesus the man, taking the place in him of a human intelligence or *nous.* So Eusebius asks rhetorically, in his anti-Marcellan work, *The Church's Theology*,

> If Marcellus says that the Word, while in the flesh, spoke these phrases [Eusebius is referring to John 6:48, "I am the bread of life," and 6:51, "I am the living bread, which has come down from heaven"], still why should we affirm this as grounds for confessing that he is not Son, but only Word? How did he exist in the flesh when he spoke these things? Surely as one who was alive, who subsisted, whose existence was "outside" [ἐκτός] the Father! And what was the Father at that time, if he did not have his own Word within him but existed without a Word? But when the Word dwelt in the flesh, when he engaged in his earthly activities, if he was "outside" the Father—alive and subsistent and giving motion to the flesh in the way a soul does—surely he was another alongside the Father; and two hypostases existed, he himself and the Father.[62]

Kelley McCarthy Spoerl has argued that in fact one of the driving forces behind the theological and Christological work of Apollinarius of Laodicea, in the 360s and 370s, was his own equally fierce opposition to both Arius and Marcellus.[63] This is especially clear in his short synthetic work, Ἡ κατὰ μέρος πίστις (*The Faith*—or *The Creed—in Detail*). The first twelve chapters of this treatise, in Hans Lietzmann's modern edition,[64] are devoted to rejecting the "Arian" assertion that the Word of God and the Spirit of God are creatures, sent to do God's work in the world; the Christian understanding of salvation requires instead, Apollinarius insists, the recognizably Athanasian

62. Eusebius, *The Church's Theology* 1.20.39–41.

63. Kelley McCarthy Spoerl, "Apollinarian Christology and the Anti-Marcellan Tradition," *Journal of Theological Studies* 45 (1994), pp. 545–68. See also Abramowski (note 12), pp. 103–5.

64. Hans Lietzmann, *Apollinaris von Laodicea und seine Schule: Texte und Untersuchungen* (Tübingen: J. C. B. Mohr, 1904; repr. Hildesheim: Georg Olms, 1970), pp. 167–71.

confession that even "while the word of God conducted himself like a man, carrying out his appointed tasks while uniquely joined to the flesh, still he preserved the divine presence to all things."[65] The second, longer, part of the treatise, however, is directed against those who deny that there are three persons in God and "say that the Father and the Son are really the same"[66]—Marcellus and his followers, in other words. After an elaborate investigation of the scriptural basis for speaking of three distinct and eternal "persons" (πρόσωπα) or sources of activity in God, Apollinarius shows that this very conception of God is the basis for what he understands to be an orthodox view of the person of Christ:

> We believe that God became incarnate in human flesh; that nevertheless he possesses his own proper activity unadulterated, since his mind is untrammeled by the sufferings of spirit and flesh; that he directs the flesh and its fleshly motions in a divine and sinless way. . . . He is true God, who, though not Himself flesh, has appeared in the flesh, perfect with a true and divine perfection, neither two persons nor two natures. After all, we do not say that we worship four—God, and the Son of God, and a human being, and the Holy Spirit. . . . But we say that the Word of God became human for our salvation, in order that we might receive the likeness of the heavenly man and that we might be divinized in the likeness of him who is by nature the true Son of God, and in his flesh the Son of Man, our Lord Jesus Christ.[67]

A little further on, Apollinarius sums up his integrated view of the Son of God, as central to the Christian confession both of God and of the person of the Savior:

> There is one Son, the same before and after the incarnation, God and human, one and the same in each state. The divine Word is not another person alongside the man Jesus; but rather he, the pre-existent Son, came to unite himself to flesh taken from Mary, and established himself as a perfect and holy and sinless man; and thus he worked the renewal of humanity and the salvation of the whole world.[68]

65. Apollinarius, *The Faith in Detail*, p. 12 (Lietzmann, *Apollinaris*, p. 171); cf. Athanasius, *Against the Pagans*, pp. 41–45; *On the Incarnation* 8, 41–42.

66. Apollinarius, *The Faith in Detail*, p. 13 (Lietzmann, *Apollinaris*, pp. 171–72).

67. Apollinarius, *The Faith in Detail*, pp. 30–31 (Lietzmann, *Apollinaris*, pp. 178–79).

68. Apollinarius, *The Faith in Detail* (Lietzmann, *Apollinaris*, p. 181).

Whatever questions would later be raised about the adequacy of Apollinarius's conception of the humanity of Christ, in which the divine Logos or wisdom took the place of a human *logos* or *nous*—a conception, as I have said, that he shared with more than a century of predominantly Origenist theologians before him (although not with Origen himself), including the opponents of Paul of Samosata, Arius, Eusebius of Caesarea, and possibly even Athanasius—his insistence here on the intrinsic connection between the real existence of the Son in the Trinitarian Mystery and his real existence as a single Savior, who is necessarily both divine and human if he is really to bring humanity face to face with God, is itself a classical expression of what would become orthodox Christology.

The Antiochene Theologians and Cyril of Alexandria

As a final tableau in this rogues' gallery of ancient Trinitarian and Christological disputes, let us look briefly at the fifth-century controversy over the constitution of Christ's person, especially as it involved the Antiochene approach to theology and Scripture, represented by Diodore of Tarsus, Theodore of Mopsuestia, Nestorius of Constantinople, and Theodoret of Cyrrhus, over against what is commonly called the Alexandrian tradition, represented above all by the archbishop Cyril.[69] By the third decade of the fifth century,

69. Theological scholarship has undoubtedly oversimplified the process of Christological debate and exegetical practice in the fourth and fifth centuries by speaking of the "schools" of Antioch and Alexandria as if they were parallel phenomena, mutually shaping each other by their polemics. It would be more accurate to say that the work of a century of scriptural interpreters based in Antioch—beginning with Diodore of Tarsus and continuing especially in Theodore of Mopsuestia and Theodoret of Cyrrhus—grew up as a reaction against the exegesis of late fourth-century Origenist scholars based in Egypt, especially Didymus the Blind and Evagrius of Pontus. The difference between these two approaches was theological, rather than "methodological" in a modern sense; it involved varying conceptions of the shape and significance of sacred history and differing ideas of how God is related to the world. But it is important to remember that the approach to both the Bible and God's presence in history represented by Didymus and later by Cyril of Alexandria was much more representative of the "mainstream" position of early Christian writers than was that of their Antiochene critics. For contemporary scholarly analysis of the relationships of these two schools, see especially Frances Young, *Biblical Exegesis and the Formation of Christian Culture* (Cambridge: Cambridge University Press, 1997), esp. pp. 161–212; and John J. O'Keefe, "Impassible Suffering? Divine Passion and Fifth-Century Christology," *Theological Studies* 58 (1997), pp. 39–60; O'Keefe, "Theodoret's Line in the Sand: Saying 'No' to Diodore," forthcoming.

of course, when this tempest had reached gale force, open debate in the Greek-speaking church over the oneness and threeness of God had, to a large extent, subsided. While the Council of Constantinople in 381 had made no attempt to define formally the ways in which the divine Mystery is one and is three, or to specify the relationship of the unity of God to the person of Christ, still the Cappadocian conception of a God one in root being and in all activity, yet eternally and irreducibly three concrete *things*, three hypostases, because of the distinctive ways in which Father, Son, and Spirit share and realize the divine being, was clearly the unspoken background both for the Council's new, extended version of the Nicene formula of faith and for its anathemas against Arians, modalists, and Apollinarians alike. For Eastern bishops and theologians who wished to remain in the "mainstream" imperial Church, the controversy over the substance and persons of God had essentially been settled, by consensus, in Cappadocian terms.

Yet it can be argued that the real distinction in thought between the Antiochene and Alexandrian "schools" of theology in the late fourth and fifth centuries was not simply a quarrel about the structure of Christ's person as an isolated issue; their debate, rather, revealed fundamentally different conceptions of how God is involved in creation and history. In the theology of Theodore of Mopsuestia and his pupils, and perhaps even in that of Theodore's teacher Diodore of Tarsus, sound theology and sound exegesis were both thought to rest on their ability to preserve the transcendence of God—even of a God conceived as eternally Trinitarian—from the compromise of a too-direct involvement in the categories and events of history, especially from the compromises of circumscription and passibility. Alongside this concern to emphasize God's otherness, God's distance from the limitations of the created order, the early Antiochenes showed a concern to protect, in their account of God's acts in history, the autonomy and narrative causality of the created order itself. God beckons to us, they argued, through the typological events of history, guides us providentially by his grace and by the influence of the Holy Spirit in us, reveals to us in the resurrection of Jesus the eschatological salvation to come. But to speak of God acting directly, personally, in human history, in such a way that God can be personally encountered in human events by human beings, was, for them, to introduce a confusion of the divine and the human that was potentially destructive of a right understanding of both.[70]

70. For a fuller discussion of the predominant understanding of the relationship of God to creation in the Antiochene writers, see G. Koch, *Die Heilsverwirklichung bei Theodor*

Because of this overall concern to protect the Christian understanding of God's transcendence and inner unity—the unity of all three πρόσωπα or *personae* who share the divine substance—all the representatives of the "school" of Antioch were bitter opponents of both the Arian and the Apollinarian theologies. Theodore of Mopsuestia, for instance, in the third of his *Catechetical Homilies*, seems to continue to use *hypostasis* language[71] for the divine substance, in pre-Cappadocian style, as a synonym for οὐσία[72] and emphasizes, in the following homily, both the "unbridgeable gulf" in being between God and creation and the identity of "substance" between God the Father and the Son who "took on" the human being, Jesus of Nazareth.[73] The historian Socrates tells us that when Theodore's pupil Nestorius came to Constantinople as the new patriarch in April of 428, he immediately attacked the remnants of the Arian community there with a reformer's zeal;[74] he later defended his campaign against the Marian title *Theotokos* as essentially a way of protecting the "coessential Godhead" from the "Arian" suggestion that any one of the three "persons" in God is subject to passibility or limitation.[75] And Silke-Petra Bergjan has shown, in her study of Theodoret of Cyrus's Trinitarian theology, that that last, most centrist representative of the fourth- and fifth-century school of Antioch also weighted his presentation of the Trinity "auf die Einheit Gottes hin" and put particular stress on the infinite ontologi-

von Mopsuestia (Munich: Hueber, 1965); Koch, *Strukturen und Geschichte des Heils in der Theologie des Theodoret von Kyros: Eine dogmen- und theologiegeschichtliche Untersuchung* (Frankfurt: Knecht, 1974); Joanne McWilliam Dewart, *The Theology of Grace of Theodore of Mopsuestia* (Washington, DC: Catholic University of America Press, 1971); G. Hellemo, *Adventus Domini: Eschatological Thought in Fourth-Century Apses and Catecheses* (Leiden: Brill, 1989), pp. 208–31.

71. In the extant Syriac translation, *qnomā*, which is normally the equivalent of Greek ὑπόστασις. See also Greek fragments 7 and 8 of Theodore's work *On the Incarnation*, where the separate divine and human realities in Christ are referred to as ὑποστάσεις.

72. At the beginning of the chapter, Theodore says of the Logos, "To indicate that he was with God—not from outside, as a stranger, but of the very nature (*qyana*) of the substance (*'ithutha*)—he was called Word." *Catechetical Homily* 3.14, in *Les Homélies catéchétiques de Théodore de Mopsueste*, ed. R. Tonneau and R. Devreesse, Studi e Testi 145 (Vatican City: Libreria Editrice Vaticana, 1949), p. 73. For Theodore's use of the word *hypostasis* (*qnomā*) in the same sense in the same chapter, see p. 74.

73. See *Catechetical Homily* 4.6–13, in Tonneau and Devreesse, *Les Homélies*, pp. 83–91.

74. *Ecclesiastical History* 7.29.

75. See especially his "second letter" to Cyril of Alexandria, *Collectio Vaticana* 5.4–7: ACO 1, 1.1.30.5–32.4; also his *Book of Heracleides* II/1, trans. S. R. Driver and L. Hodgson (Oxford: Oxford University Press, 1925), pp. 162, 174–75.

cal distance between God and creation.[76] Theodoret's discussion of the unity of God, Bergjan convincingly argues, is mainly developed in terms of the divine attributes recognized by Greek philosophy, buttressed by biblical texts but not primarily derived from the biblical narrative or conceived in biblical categories.[77] Although Theodoret accepts the now-canonical Cappadocian language of one οὐσία and three ὑποστάσεις when speaking directly of the Trinitarian Mystery, he is generally unwilling to apply that same terminology to the complex being and simple subjective center of Christ. Both terms, presumably, still suggested too much metaphysical density, so that Theodoret speaks of Christ almost exclusively in the more dynamic, behavioral terms of two irreducibly different "natures" (φύσεις) united in the common self-presentation or role of a single *persona* (πρόσωπον).[78]

Cyril of Alexandria, the prime opponent of these Antiochene theologians in the second quarter of the fifth century, also habitually uses the Cappadocian terminology in speaking of the unity and Trinity of God;[79] like the Antiochenes, he uses this terminology also in speaking of the unity and difference in the person of Christ, without ever explicitly clarifying the connection between the two fields of discussion.[80] Even more than the Antiochenes, however, Cyril's voluminous treatises on the Trinity stress the permanent threeness of Father, Son, and Holy Spirit within the single, simple being of God.[81] Although Father and Son cannot be thought of

76. Silke-Petra Bergjan, *Theodoret von Cyrus und der Neunizänismus* (Berlin: De Gruyter, 1993), pp. 192–93.

77. Bergjan, *Theodoret von Cyrus*, pp. 192, 195.

78. For references in the works of Theodoret, see Bergjan, *Theodoret von Cyrus*, pp. 195, 203–5, 207–10. Bergjan acknowledges her indebtedness to K. McNamara, "Theodoret of Cyrus and the Unity of Person in Christ," *Irish Theological Quarterly* 24 (1957), pp. 313–28. On the development of Theodoret's terminology and conception of the unity of substances in the person of Christ, see Grillmeier, *Christ in Christian Tradition* 1, pp. 488–95. Grillmeier observes (p. 489) that although, in some works written after the Council of Chalcedon, Theodoret seems to have been willing to speak of the one Christ as a single hypostasis, his earlier writings suggest that he, like Cyril, continued—in spite of the Cappadocian attempt to regulate the use of these terms—to take ὑπόστασις as a synonym for φύσις or nature: the reality that something is and according to which it operates.

79. See, for example, Cyril's letter *De recta fide ad Pulcheriam et Eudociam*, ed. Philip E. Pusey (Oxford: Parker, 1877), 7.321.11–322.7, where he carefully summarizes the Cappadocian picture of a God one in substance and activity, but three in hypostases because of the relationships of origin among them; cf. *Adversus Nestorium* 4.1 (Pusey, 6.179.17–27); 4.2 (Pusey, 6.185.24–186.1; 187.1–18).

80. See Bergjan, *Theodoret von Cyrus*, pp. 190–91.

81. See, for example, *Dialogues on the Trinity* 7 (641.6–17: SC 246.171); *Adv. Nest.* 4.1

apart from each other, he argues in his second *Dialogue on the Trinity*,[82] still the Son is constituted a distinct hypostasis—a real, individual, concrete "thing"—by the Father's causal relationship to him.[83] Even though the first chapter of the book of Hebrews speaks of the Son as the "stamp" (χαρακτήρ) of the Father's hypostasis (Heb 1:3), Cyril insists this must not be taken to suggest the Son is simply an accident, an ἀνυπόστατος χαρακτήρ, of some unitary divine substance.[84] Cyril's sense of the urgency of affirming the distinctness of persons within the Mystery of God seems to be inherently linked to his Christological concern to emphasize that the Savior is a *single* Son, a single acting subject, even though Cyril never reflects on the link explicitly. So he readily makes use of the phrase "union in hypostasis" (ἕνωσις καθ' ὑπόστασιν) in his earlier controversial writings—a phrase that to Theodoret seemed to compromise the Son's transcendence as a hypostasis within the being of God, and even to suggest a return to Arianism.[85] For Cyril, only language such as this, with its unmistakably Trinitarian overtones, can convey the full reality of who it is that we encounter, who it is that is acting among us, in Christ. So he writes, in his *Apology for the Twelve Anathemas, against Theodoret*,

> The phrase "in hypostasis" signifies nothing else than simply that the nature or hypostasis of the Logos—that is, the Logos himself—joined in truth to a human nature without any kind of change or confusion . . . , is recognized and is in fact one Christ, the same both God and a human being.[86]

It is this single hypostasis, whose primordial *nature* or principle of activity is that of the divine substance, whom Cyril—even in his writings before the Nestorian crisis—recognized as the ontological center of the person of Jesus, the source of the divine gifts and energies manifested in him. He writes in his dialogue *On the Incarnation*,

---

(Pusey, 6.179.17–27); 4.2 (Pusey, 6.185.24–186.1). See Bergjan, *Theodoret von Cyrus*, p. 181 n. 58.

82. *Dialogues on the Trinity* 2 (449.31–38: SC 231.318); see Bergjan, *Theodoret von Cyrus*, p. 178.

83. *Dialogues on the Trinity* 2 (431.29–39: SC 231.264–66).

84. *Dialogues on the Trinity* 5 (557.32–40: SC 237.298; 558.30–43: SC 237.302).

85. See Cyril, *Apologia for the Twelve Anathemas, against Theodoret* 4 (ACO I, 1, 6.121.2–4); 2 (114.10–12).

86. Cyril, *Apologia* 2 (ACO I, 1, 6.115.12–16).

> We must attribute priority [τό πρεσβύτατον], then, to him, even when united to flesh: to God, that is, naturally united to flesh and accustomed to share with his own body the riches of his proper nature.[87]

Much more than either the Christology or the theology of any of the Antiochenes, Cyril's understanding of the person of the Son—both within the divine Mystery and as he is encountered in history—is in fact derived from the New Testament: from the narrative of the preaching and miracles of Christ; from his suffering, which Christians confess as redemptive; from his resurrection, which revealed the full meaning of his Sonship and the full power and promise of his Holy Spirit. In his tract *On the True Faith, to the Princesses Pulcheria and Eudokia*, for instance, from the year 430, Cyril explains St. Paul's reference to God the Father as "the one who raised our Lord Jesus from the dead" (Rom 4:24) by giving a detailed reflection on the rhythmic flow of life among the persons of the Trinity.[88] He immediately goes on to consider Paul's treatment of our own baptism "into the death of Christ" in Romans 6:3–8 and insists that if this baptism is done "in the name of the Father and of the Son and of the Holy Spirit," then the mortal, passible Son whose death gives us life in baptism must be identical with the eternal Son of the Father and the giver of the eternal Spirit:

> It is necessary to recognize, then, that the Word of God, having come to be as we are, willingly suffered in the flesh. For these are the conditions under which we are baptized into his death: that he is one Son, impassible in the nature of Godhead, but passible in the flesh. How, then, could anyone doubt that Christ shapes us anew, by his resurrection, into newness of life? For he presents us to himself and to the Father "as if we had come alive from the dead" (Rom. 6:13), as Scripture says: dead to sin, but alive in righteousness (cf. Rom. 6:10–11).[89]

For Cyril, the identification of the eternal Son of God as the one who has offered for us the sacrifice of his own human death, and who continues to intercede for us with the Father as our priest, "vested in the robes of divinity

87. *On the Incarnation of the Only-begotten* (SC 97.292.13–15). On the dating of this dialogue, see the introduction by G. M. de Durand, ibid., 52.

88. *On the True Faith, to Pulcheria and Eudokia*, 35 (Pusey 7.321.11–322.17).

89. *On the True Faith*, 36 (Pusey 7.324.1–9).

as God and offering priestly service as a man [λειτουργῶν ἀνθρωπίνως],"[90] is precisely the reason it is so essential to maintain a clear understanding of the abiding distinction of persons within the divine Mystery. Otherwise we are left with the absurd alternatives of either imagining the risen Jesus, the eternal priest of the book of Hebrews, as a human "Son" who has now become an honorary fourth member of the Trinity,[91] or of ruling out the continuing role of the Son in the historical sanctification of humanity.

Concluding Conjectures: Unity and Distinction in God and Christ

At the end of this somewhat sketchy survey of early Trinitarian and Christological debate, let us attempt to draw a few more general conclusions.

First, the reason there seems to be so strong a link—a kind of reverse proportion—between the way we understand unity and distinction in God and the way we understand unity and distinction in the person of Christ is that these are not merely independent theological ideas, separate areas on the dogmatic map, or separate chapters in the catechism. "Trinitarian theology" and "Christology" are modern terms, not ancient ones, and represent tracts in the theological curriculum of the modern Western university rather than categories of patristic discussion. Both of them are really *about* one thing: the distinctively Christian understanding of how God is related to the world and to history; how God can be both transcendent Mystery—ultimate, infinite, free of creaturely limitations, uncircumscribed by human thought—and also "Emmanuel," God-with-us, God personally encountered in Jesus, God speaking today in the Scriptures and in the Church. The doctrine of the Trinity is really a narrative creed in miniature, a formulaic way of speaking about a God who is active in history, who reveals himself genuinely in the "economy" of salvation witnessed to by the Bible, while remaining beyond history, beyond all human knowing. For Christian faith, Jesus reveals this God to us in his own person as Son and draws us into this God's inner life,

90. *On the True Faith*, 28 (Pusey 7.313).

91. Theodoret too, in several of his letters from the period of the most intense Christological controversy in the late 440s, insists that he does not hold Christ to be "two Sons," and that the notion of adding a fourth person to the Trinity is blasphemy: e.g., Ep. 126, 143, 144, 146. As Bergjan rightly observes, however, "Wie sich . . . trinitarische Differenz und christologische Einheit zueinander verhalten, bleibt völlig offen. Theodoret formuliert, dass der Menschgewordene kein anderer als die zweite trintarische Person sei, ohne aber auszuformulieren, was die Einheit der Person meint" (*Theodoret von Cyrus*, p. 204).

in which his existence as Son is rooted. That is the ultimate reason we call Jesus Savior and Lord.

Second, there seem to be, throughout the history of Christian reflection, two basic casts of mind, two predogmatic perspectives, that set the stage for the differing approaches to the Trinity and to Christ that we have been discussing here. One tends to place the strongest emphasis on God's *otherness*, God's absoluteness and simplicity as the source and goal of all being; it draws on the biblical narrative, and biblical categories for support, of course, but its driving engine seems to be critical reason applied to faith, a philosophical assumption of what God must be like if faith is to be credible. The other mind-set tends to place the strongest emphasis on God's *activity within history*, on God's personal, concrete presence and accessibility in the world and in religious language and action; it makes use of philosophical language and argument, of course, but its driving engine is religious response to the biblical proclamation. The first mind-set—which is clearly that of a minority in the early Church, even if it was at times an influential minority—shows itself in monarchian and modalist forms of theology and in the Antiochene tradition of Christology and exegesis; its strength is clearly its reasonableness, but when exaggerated it can become a bloodless and pedantic rationalism. The second, more widespread, mind-set shows itself in the Origenist tradition of Trinitarian thought, in Apollinarianism, and in Alexandrian Christology and exegesis; its strength, surely, is its existential character, its sacramental and ecclesial implications, and its spiritual intensity, but when it becomes exaggerated—as in the massive, often violent rejection of the Chalcedonian formula that swept the Greek East in the late fifth century—it can be the root of pious fanaticism. And there were clearly some extraordinary thinkers in the early centuries of theological reflection—Athanasius, the three great Cappadocian Fathers, and Maximus Confessor in the East, as well as Augustine in the West—who are more difficult to identify, precisely because they seem to have avoided both extremes and to have reached out for a carefully constructed theological and Christological equilibrium.

Third, it seems to me at least possible that these two casts of mind with respect to God and the world may also be most typically at home with two rather different perspectives on the role of the Church in the world—perhaps even fostered by two different kinds of Church community. Let me advance this further, more tentative, suggestion in the form of questions: Is it plausible that the more unitive approach to theology, which emphasizes both God's distance from the world and the human completeness of Jesus, in distinction from the divine Logos, tends to be more congenial to those with a more robust view of human authority and a more favorable attitude toward secular institutions and secular forms of behavior? Is it likely that the more Trinitarian approach to theology, with its more integrated and Logos-centered view of the person of Christ, tends to appeal more to Christians who are intensely concerned with maintaining the boundaries between Church and world, who are more willing to challenge human authority, learning, and reason?

Clearly such identifications are conjectural and run the risk of sociological reductionism. Clearly too, many questions can be raised about the application of such a scheme to the historical evidence we have. But a few aspects of the patristic cases we have been considering might give this further suggestion some credibility:

(a) Despite their condemnation of some of the more extreme representatives of monarchian theology, the bishops of Rome, from the time of Pope Victor until at least the mid-third century, seem strongly to have favored a monarchian or unitive brand of theology; they were also, by and large, strong Church leaders during that period, willing to exercise their own authority in reconciling the *lapsi* and other public sinners to communion at home, and eager to affirm their leadership in churches outside Rome's immediate geographic area. Their Trinitarian critics—Hippolytus,[92] Tertullian, Novatian—on the other hand, tended to be "rigorists" on the question of the reconciliation of sinners, skeptical about the degree to which human authority may be relied on in determining the boundaries of the community of grace. The communities around them were generally regarded as schismatic churches and were especially critical of the Roman bishops.

(b) Paul of Samosata, deposed from his episcopal dignity for holding a Unitarian view of God and for teaching that Christ was a "mere man," was repeatedly accused of being authoritarian and of taking an overly secular approach to the exercise of power.

(c) Klaus Seibt, in his recent massive study of the theology of Marcellus of Ancyra, argues at length that Marcellus's way of viewing the theological tradition before him was strongly influenced by his close relationship to

92. This is especially true if we identify the Hippolytus assumed to be the author of *Against Noetus*, which we have discussed above, with the author of the *Refutation of All Heresies* often associated with him. In any case, the author of the second work is sharply critical of both the theology and the reconciliation policy of Pope Callistus: see *Refutation* 9.12.15–26.

the emperor Constantine. Seibt views Marcellus's work as an attempt to develop, in the early years of imperial patronage of the Church, a theology suited to an *ecclesia triumphans*: a Christology "borne by a concern for the exaltation and self-confidence of the Church as it became part of the world, as well as for a positive evaluation of humanity in general."[93] Although a similarly triumphalistic tendency has often been noted in the historical and apologetic work of Eusebius of Caesarea, Marcellus's Origenist contemporary and his archenemy in things theological,[94] Eusebius's reasons for celebrating Constantine seem to have been quite different. For him, the emperor represents the conclusion of God's saving work, which began in the history of Israel; the emergence of Christianity from the shadows of persecution for him was the fulfillment of God's promise to his faithful ones, rather than the glorification of the human in the person of Jesus. There is, in other words, a more biblical and eschatological dimension to Eusebius's affirmation of the value of imperial structures than to that of Marcellus. The center of Eusebius's enthusiasm, in fact, is not the empire at all, but the Church, which prefigures the kingdom of heaven.[95] This is a point of comparison, however, that clearly calls for further study.

(d) In the Christological disputes of the fifth century, it was principally the Antiochene writers, with their emphasis on the internal unity of God

93. Klaus Seibt, *Die Theologie des Markell von Ankyra* (Berlin: De Gruyter, 1994), p. 517; for an extended argument toward interpreting Marcellus in this direction, see pp. 460–520.

94. See, for example, Erik Peterson's famous essay, *Der Monotheismus als politisches Problem: Ein Beitrag zur Geschichte der politischen Theologie im Imperium Romanum* (Leipzig: Hegner, 1935), in which he argues that the Christian theological defense of monotheism in terms of a single divine μοναρχία had, almost inevitably, political overtones supportive of universal imperial government, until the Cappadocians developed a viable model of God as both three and one, in a way without parallel in the created world (see esp. 97–99). George Huntston Williams attempted to draw the same parallel between "the conception one has of Christ and his several offices" and imperial claims to authority in Church and world: "Christology and Church-State Relations in the Fourth Century," *Church History* 20 (1951), pp. 3.3–33, 4.3–26. Both these positions, along with the similar approach of Hendrik Berkhof, have been elaborately contested by Jean-Marie Sansterre, "Eusèbe de Césarée et la naissance de la théorie 'césaropapiste,'" *Byzantion* 42 (1972), pp. 131–95, 532–93; nevertheless, Sansterre argues that Eusebius's "political theology" of exalting Constantine was a strategy to persuade him to take a more active role in Church affairs, and specifically to annul the Nicene credal formula.

95. See, for example, *Laus Constantini* 5.2–5, 16.6; *In Psalmos* 86.2–4. For a discussion of Eusebius's theological understanding of the Kingdoms of God and the world, see F. Edward Cranz, "Kingdom and Polity in Eusebius of Caesarea," *Harvard Theological Review* 45 (1952), pp. 47–66.

> and the irreducible distinction of divine and human in Jesus, who expressed, on occasion, strong support for the providential role of the Christian emperors.[96] After the Council of Chalcedon, on the other hand, the strongest advocates of Cyril's theology and Christology separated themselves quickly from the imperial Church, and eventually, in large part, from the Christian empire as well, setting up their own episcopates, which continued to subdivide, as controversy over confessional details continued, into new and more exclusive communities. In Rome and the West during the fifth and sixth centuries, where relations with the empire varied in warmth but where papal authority, even outside of Italy, grew steadily stronger to fill the vacuum left by the shrinking of imperial authority, theological sympathy remained strongly pointed in the pro-Chalcedonian (and pro-Antiochene) direction.

These are tentative identifications, all of which invite further reflection. What is clear is that amid all the hypotheses we may care to form or choose to reject, neither our way of conceiving and talking about God nor our way of conceiving and talking about Christ can be isolated from each other, or treated as distinct, self-contained "fields" of Christian reflection, and that both of them are inseparably connected with our way of understanding the Church and the world.

In the year 375, Basil of Caesarea wrote a letter "to the learned [λογιωτάτοις] in Neocaesaraea" in Polemonian Pontus—to Christians, in other words, in that city of eastern Asia Minor, whose education seemed to make them both more vulnerable to deception by fads and more capable of intellectual leadership. One of the subversive movements of which Basil warns them is "the evil of Sabellius": the ontological modalism of Marcellus and his followers that, in Basil's view, leads to a kind of spiritual "drunkenness"—intoxicating, but ultimately destructive.

> For the person who says that Father, Son and Holy Spirit are one thing with many faces [ἓν πρᾶγμα πολυπρόσωπον], and who proposes a single concrete reality [μίαν ὑπόστασιν] for all three—what else is he or she doing but denying the existence of the Only-begotten before all ages? That per-

96. See, for example, Diodore's comments on Rom 13:1 (K. Staab, *Pauluskommentare aus der griechischen Kirche*, Neutestamentliche Abhandlungen 15 [Münster: Aschendorff, 1933], p. 107); Theodoret, *Commentary on Daniel* 2 (PG 81.1308). See Peterson, *Der Monotheismus*, pp. 82–83, for further references.

> son denies, too, his presence among men and women, in realization of the divine plan, his descent into Hades, his resurrection, his judgment; and he denies the characteristic activities of the Spirit.[97]

Rejecting that God is inherently and eternally a Trinity, in Basil's view, implies a rejection of the economy of salvation narrated in the Christian Bible, because it denies the real existence of the Son and the Holy Spirit as agents capable of making God personally present in history.

As people who profess to "see the glory of God in the face of Christ" (2 Cor 4:6), we can only imagine and describe that divine glory, in this present life, in terms of what we have encountered in him. Our theology and our Christology implicitly contain each other and offer us together—but never separately—the intelligible framework for Christian meaning and Christian hope. Our God is the God of the economy revealed in the Church's Scriptures; but this God, whom we have encountered and encounter still in Scripture and Church, is, we believe, God as he truly is.

97. Epistle 210.

4 The Word and His Flesh

Human Weakness and the Identity of Jesus in Patristic Christology

"But you—who do you say that I am?" (Mark 8:29). Jesus's blunt question to the disciples, it is often said, remains one of the driving questions of Christian faith: the question, for all those who desire to follow him, of how we understand his identity. For the Church of the first several centuries, this question was, to a large degree, raised and focused by the scandal of his human weakness: his suffering and death, of course, but also his human growth and his human needs, as witnessed by the New Testament, as well as the limits his finite human nature imposed on his actions and knowledge. If he is truly the Messiah of Israel and the eschatological giver of God's Holy Spirit, as early Christians were generally ready to confess, what sense can one make of his human ordinariness and obscurity, his human vulnerability and mortality? And if those limiting qualities are taken to be essential to the narrative of how he has actually become humanity's Savior and Lord—if his death, as Jesus himself suggests on the road to Emmaus (Luke 24:26), is in fact the divinely ordained prelude to his resurrection and entry into messianic glory—how must one conceive of *him* as the subject of that narrative?

The classical understanding of Christian orthodoxy, formed in the early Church over seven or eight centuries of preaching and controversy and expressed in a growing stream of biblical commentary, theological argument, creedal confessions, and conciliar formulas, was and continues to be that Jesus is himself the Son of God: the eternal Word "by whom all things were made," who in time has become a human among humans, in order to transform and liberate the humanity he has made his own, even to offer humanity a share in the life of God. Classical Christian orthodoxy confesses that the Jesus who revealed God's will and God's love in works and words of power is "one and the same" as the Jesus who slept in the boat, who wept for Lazarus, and who suffered on the cross: God the Son, humanly "personalizing" the transcendent fullness of the divine Mystery in the body and mind, the relationships and limitations, of his own fully human life. The Second Council of Constantinople (553) expresses this central, irreducible paradox of Christian orthodoxy in the clear, if confrontational, terms of a canonical ultimatum:

> If anyone says that the Word of God who performed miracles was someone other than the Christ who suffered, or says that God the Word was *with* the Christ "born of a woman" (Gal 4:4) or was *in* him as one in another, but does not confess that our Lord Jesus Christ, the Word of God made flesh and made human, is *one and the same*, and that both the miracles and the sufferings which he voluntarily endured in the flesh belong to the same one, let that person be anathema.[1]

What I would like to suggest in this essay is that this classical understanding of the single, paradoxical identity of Jesus developed precisely as part of an ongoing struggle in the early Church to grasp and express the saving meaning of his real human limitations and human sufferings, assuming that they are proper to a subject who is not simply and exclusively a human being. Taking these limitations seriously—limitations that include his human passivities, his ability to experience grief and to suffer and die—was always a challenge for early believers, because such passivities seemed to conflict both with his role as God's herald and Savior and with the paradigmatic character of his human behavior. Yet the alternative was to disregard the contents of the Gospel narrative, and to depreciate his humanity in a serious way.

Through the process of protracted, often sharply polemical reflection on the implications of this paradox, early Christian theologians developed a grammar for language about Jesus that staked out the conditions for *identifying* him in the fullness of apostolic faith—for saying, as far as human and Christian speech can say, just who and what Jesus is, how the reality of God is involved through him in the history of the world, and what God has done for us in him. Only in knowing his identity, patristic Christology suggests—only in being able to name Jesus for who and what he is—do we begin to understand our own human identity and our ultimate vocation.

1. Second Council of Constantinople, canon 3, trans. J. Neuner and J. Dupuis, *The Christian Faith in the Doctrinal Documents of the Catholic Church* (New York: Alba House, 1982), p. 159, alt.; emphasis mine.

Clearly, it is impossible here to offer a full summary of the growing sense of both the complexity and the simplicity of the identity of Jesus in the writings of those Fathers considered to represent the mainstream of early Christian orthodoxy. What I would like to do is to offer four "snapshots," four brief and impressionistic characterizations, of the ways four Greek theologians from the second to the seventh century—Irenaeus, Athanasius, Cyril of Alexandria, and Maximus the Confessor—invite us to conceive of the identity of Jesus. My hope is that this will provide us with a sense of developing consistency within the early classical tradition of Christology, one that builds on the New Testament witness yet moves well beyond it philosophically and theologically, and that it will provoke us to deeper reflection for ourselves.

Irenaeus of Lyons

Writing from the frontier region of Gaul around the year 185, Irenaeus tried, in his massive work *Against Heresies* (*Adversus haereses*), to confront the recurrent "Gnostic" tendency in religious thought, which had already made its presence felt in the small circle of Christian believers, and which continues, in various ways, to have its appeal: the tendency to deconstruct the continuity and credibility of the public world, including the institutions and religious traditions we live in; to look on matter and the body, as well the responsibilities we bear toward the material and bodily world, as part of an illusory realm, the creation of a lesser god, the fruit of a superhuman conspiracy or a cosmic mistake; to see human freedom, the redemption of the human spirit from illusion and enslavement to history, as possible only through a radically revisionist narrative of our origins, which calls us to disregard the accepted realities of daily life and find our meaning within ourselves, in the secret "enlightenment" communicated to an elect few. For Christian Gnostics of the second century, such as the Valentinians, the source of this redeeming knowledge was thought to be the Savior Jesus: not the earthy Jewish prophet of the four Gospels but the representative of an archetypal *plērōma* of heavenly actors, whose doings long antedate the history of the material world and who engage in this present history only to rescue from it those few who can see the illusion of matter, flesh, and human institutions for what it is.

Irenaeus's concern, through all the twists and turns of his proclaimed "unmasking and refutation" of Gnostic teaching, is to argue for the unity and religious relevance of what ordinary Christians regard as the real world—the unity of God as Creator and Savior; the unity of the biblical narrative, of the created universe, of the human person, of the worldwide Church and its message—and to insist that it is in *this* world, in *this* history, in *this* body, for all their limitations, that the gospel of redemption through Christ is already on the way to fulfillment. Only in such a unified framework of time and space is there an intelligible form to the story of human alienation and hope, a convincing proclamation of good news. And in this unified narrative, the identity of Jesus as both divine Word and fleshly human being is clearly the paradoxical heart of the story of salvation, the link between source and goal, promise and fulfillment.

So Irenaeus criticizes the Gnostics, in book 3 of *Against Heresies*, for being unaware

> that [God's] only-begotten Word, who is always present with the human race, united to and mingled with the work of his hands,[2] according to the Father's pleasure, and who became flesh, is himself Jesus Christ our Lord, who did also suffer for us, and rose again on our behalf.[3]

By experiencing in himself every stage and aspect of human growth, while communicating to his own body and to the human family in solidarity with him God's own incorruptible life, Irenaeus's Word made flesh becomes the unique Mediator, the only one capable of restoring friendship and *communio* between humanity and its Creator.

In explaining Jesus's work of mediation in book 4 of *Against Heresies*, Irenaeus lays special emphasis on the revelation of God's glory—of God's life-restoring presence to the human mind and senses—which only Jesus, as Word and Son in human form, can achieve. For Irenaeus, it is the revelation of God in the historical, fleshly Jesus that is the heart of redemption:

> For the manifestation of the Son is the knowledge of the Father; for all things are manifested through the Word. . . . For the Lord taught us that no one is capable of knowing God, unless he be taught of God—that is, that God cannot be known without God—but that this is the express will of the Father, that God should be known. . . . For by means of the creation itself, the Word reveals God the Creator; and by means of the world, the Lord as maker of the world; and by means of the formation [of the human creature],

2. The Greek word here is *plasma*: that which is shaped by God's hands, thus "creation" in its most palpable sense.

3. Irenaeus, *Against Heresies* 3.16.6, ed. A. Robertson and J. Donaldson, *ANF* 1:442, alt.

> the craftsman who formed him; and by the Son, that Father who begot the Son.... And through the Word himself who had been made visible and palpable, the Father was shown forth; and although all did not equally believe in him, still all did see the Father in the Son: for the Father is the invisible of the Son, but the Son is the visible of the Father.[4]

By revealing his splendor in the incarnate Word, God communicates life to mortal creatures, draws them into the vital *communio* of his own radiance.

In identifying the saving work of Christ with his presence on earth as incarnate Word, God made real flesh, Irenaeus looks even beyond Christ's revelatory role to connect his person with the continuing sacramental life of the Church. So in book 5 of *Against Heresies*, he emphasizes the importance of the Eucharist, taken in this life to be our bodily nourishment, as a pledge of the fullness of the redemption that will be achieved for us in the resurrection of our own material, mortal bodies. It is only because the Word of God has actually become flesh and blood himself, he insists, that the Eucharist, the food that conveys his flesh and blood to us in liturgical signs, can be for us a promise of everlasting life. Here, as before, Irenaeus emphasizes the complex identity of Jesus, God's eternal Word who has made our limited, visible, material nature his own, as itself the key to the Church's present faith in him as Savior, and to her hope that our flesh will share in the salvation he offers.

For Gnostic Christians, the passible, limited body and the whole visible, bodily order of fragile human relationships and limiting human institutions constituted the world from which Christ came to save us by secret knowledge. Irenaeus, by contrast, and with him the growing consensus of Christian tradition, proclaims the body, the Church, and the world as forming together the locus of salvation, precisely because in the person of Jesus the life-giving Word has made all of these things his own.

Athanasius of Alexandria

It is no exaggeration to say that Athanasius's whole long career as bishop and theologian was occupied with the Church's fourth-century struggle to identify who and what Jesus is. Born in the closing years of the third century, Athanasius was elected bishop of Alexandria in 328, three years after the

4. *Against Heresies* 4.6.3–6 (*ANF* 1:468–69, alt.).

presbyter Arius had been excommunicated by the Council of Nicaea, essentially for his insistence that the Son of God is himself the first and noblest of creatures. But the issues raised by Arius and his followers were not resolved by Nicaea's creed and canons; until his death in 373, Athanasius continued to fight for a strong conception of Jesus's identity as fully divine—from the early 340s, by an increasingly explicit emphasis on the importance of the Nicene Creed's formulation that the Son is "of the same substance as the Father."

Undoubtedly, both "Arian" and "Nicene" approaches to Jesus's identity were the agenda of theological families rather than organically developed theological systems; undoubtedly, too, the way Nicaea's "substance" language was accepted, understood, and eventually extended to include the Holy Spirit's relationship to the Father grew slowly throughout the fourth century and found different expressions among different authors.[5] Still, the thinking opposed by Athanasius throughout his career had a relatively consistent pattern: the well-established tradition of Platonic and earlier Christian thought that saw God's activity in the world as communicated in steps, and that conceived of the Son and the Holy Spirit, God's mediating agents in creation, as themselves produced, even "created" by a wholly transcendent Father, as God's first steps in self-communication. As such, Son and Spirit were understood to participate in the Father's being and operations to such a preeminent extent that they might legitimately be called "divine," even "like the Father in all things"; but they were seen as less than the Father in their being, simply because the Father alone is the primordial source of all that is.

Part of the Arian argument, it seems, came from scriptural references to the limitations of knowledge professed by Jesus, the Word made flesh, in passages such as Matthew 24:36, as well as from the New Testament witness to Jesus's ability to grow and change (e.g., Luke 2:52)—both seen as features not of divine substance but of the world of "becoming."[6] Similarly, the suffering of Christ was seen as a crucial part of the limitation and vulnerability that prove the creaturely status of the Son.

Against this "Arian" view, Athanasius argued with increasing energy throughout his life for a view of the Word—and in his later works, also of the Spirit—as fully equal with the Father in being and life, fully one reality

5. On the fourth-century controversies surrounding Arius and Nicaea, see, most recently, John Behr, *The Nicene Faith* (Crestwood, NY: St. Vladimir's Seminary Press, 2004); Lewis Ayres, *Nicaea and Its Legacy* (Oxford: Oxford University Press, 2004).

6. The most penetrating analysis of Arius's theological position and its philosophical and cultural roots remains Rowan Williams, *Arius: Heresy and Tradition* (London: Darton, Longman & Todd, 1987; rev. ed., Grand Rapids: Eerdmans, 2002).

with the Father, precisely because both Word and Spirit accomplish within creation what only God, and not a creature, can do. For Athanasius, the transcendent Logos, or active Reason, of God, eternally generated by the Father within the divine Mystery itself, is commissioned to be the Father's active and ordering presence in the world. God, as God, is totally "other" than creation; nothing that belongs to the created realm (which for Athanasius means brought into being from nothing) can be called "divine" in the strict sense. So God the Word and God the Spirit, whom baptismal faith instinctively recognizes as divine because they impart to creatures a share in divine life, must be seen as *other* than creation, but not *distant* from it: not part of creation, yet so actively involved in it, so present to it for its good, that they can direct, order, and heal it from within. This presence to creation of the Word who is not a creature is realized most fully, Athanasius argues, in his incarnation.[7]

In Athanasius's decades-long campaign to refute the Arian position in all its many shades and to promote a strong sense of the Son's full status as God, even after he has made a human form, or "body," his own, the scandal of Jesus's limitations and sufferings, as well as their crucial importance to his identity as Savior, play a critical, if complex, role. This is made clear in what may be his earliest works: the pair of apologetic treatises, written probably in the early 330s, known as *Against the Pagans* (*Contra gentes*) and *On the Incarnation* (*De incarnatione*). These essays offer an elaborate argument for the plausibility of the Christian conception of an incarnate, saving, crucified Logos by telling the story of how humanity, originally created to participate in the ordered rationality of the divine Logos, and so to share in the divine quality of incorruptibility by knowing God, lost that gift by fatal choices. Humanity therefore needed to be redeemed, reshaped in God's image, endowed again with unending life, by the Word's coming to share in our world, our wounded physicality, and even our death.

After poignantly describing the effects of human sin on the descendants of Adam and Eve in the early chapters of *On the Incarnation*, depicting sin as a growing epidemic that has robbed humanity of its rationality and vitality and reduced it to being dominated by greed and violence, Athanasius points out the only remedy left to the Logos, as just and compassionate Creator: to take on human corruptibility and mortality himself and to overcome death in his own person, through his identity as incarnate Word:

7. For helpful synthetic presentations of Athanasius's theology, see Alvyn Pettersen, *Athanasius* (London: Geoffrey Chapman, 1995); Khaled Anatolios, *Athanasius: The Coherence of His Thought* (London: Routledge, 1998).

> To this end [the Word] took to himself a body capable of death, that it, by partaking of the Word who is above all, might be worthy to die in the place of all, and might, because of the Word which had come to dwell in it, remain incorruptible, and that from then on corruption might be kept from all by the grace of the resurrection.[8]

In this treatise, Athanasius identifies the saving effect of the Word's incarnation in two principal ways: as his restoration of vital energy within the vulnerable human community "in putting away death from us and renewing us again"; but equally as his revelation to fallen human minds of the Word's power and presence, restoring to them the similarity to himself that makes them rational and holy.[9] Like Irenaeus, Athanasius is convinced that the Word's self-revelation in human terms itself opens up the new possibility of human participation in God's immortality.[10] Even Jesus's death on the cross—for ancient minds, the principal obstacle to belief in his divine identity—Athanasius describes as a moment of revelation: only a real death, a death inflicted by the violence of others, a death in public view, could qualify as the prelude to definitive resurrection and victory:

> He accepted on the cross, and endured, a death inflicted by others, and above all by his enemies, which they thought dreadful and ignominious and not to be faced; so that when this also was destroyed, both he himself might be believed to be the life, and the power of death might be brought utterly to nought.[11]

Jesus's passion reveals most forcefully, for Athanasius, the cost to God of his decision to restore humanity by taking our weakness to himself, but also its effect on faith.

Athanasius returns to the troubling issue of the weakness of the incarnate Word in his *Third Oration against the Arians*, written probably in Rome toward the end of his second exile, in 345–346. In this somewhat rambling treatise, he deals in detail with the scriptural arguments advanced by the opponents of Nicaea against the notion that the Word, generated by the Father and capable of incarnation, even of suffering, could be "of the

8. Athanasius, *On the Incarnation* 9, trans. A. Robertson, *NPNF*² 4:40–41, alt.
9. *On the Incarnation* 16 (*NPNF*² 4:45).
10. See, e.g., *On the Incarnation* 54 (*NPNF*² 4:65).
11. *On the Incarnation* 24 (*NPNF*² 4:49, alt.).

same substance" as the Father. Athanasius's refutation of Arian exegesis follows a single form: the one Mystery proclaimed in the Gospels is that indeed "the Word has become flesh," the divine Son has taken on a body such as ours, to communicate through that human body a new revelation of God and new vitality; therefore, those passages in Scripture that ascribe to the Son vulnerability or ignorance, or even a creaturely dependence on God, are to be taken as referring to his acquired humanity, his "flesh," and not to his core identity as God the Word. The Gospel narrative presents us with a Jesus whose identity is complex, paradoxical; yet that identity is itself both the key to right interpretation of Scripture, for Athanasius, and its central message of salvation.

Athanasius goes on to apply this principle to Jesus's physical and mental suffering, in Gethsemane and on the cross:

> Wherefore of necessity when he was in a passible body, weeping and toiling, these things which are proper to the flesh are ascribed to him, together with the body. . . . And as to his saying, "If it be possible, let the cup pass" (Matt 26:39), observe how, though he thus spoke, he rebuked Peter, saying "You are not thinking the things that are of God, but those that are human" (Matt 16:23). For he willed what he deprecated—and that was why he had come; but *his* was the willing (for this was why he came!), but the terror belonged to the flesh. Therefore as a human being he utters this speech also; and yet again, both were said by the same one, to show that he was God, willing this himself, but that having become human, he had a flesh that was in terror. For the sake of this flesh he combined his own will with human weakness, that by destroying this he might, in turn, make humans undaunted in face of death.[12]

Athanasius is not yet ready—as Augustine and later Maximus the Confessor would be—to acknowledge explicitly in the incarnate Word two naturally distinct wills, two fully operative (if utterly incommensurate) levels of psychological and cognitive activity. For him, the decisive, conscious agent in the life and works of Christ, even in his moments of most abject suffering, is the Word who is divine. Fear, pain, ignorance, mortality are all proper to "flesh"—*our* flesh, humanity in its fallen state, deprived of the clarity of vision and incorruptibility of life that God intended for us when he originally shaped us in the image of the Son. Yet Athanasius argues repeatedly that

12. Athanasius, *Oration 3 against the Arians* 56–57 (*NPNF*[2] 4:424, alt.).

the Word, by making these weaknesses of "the flesh" his own, has begun to transform and heal them. So he sees in Gethsemane and Calvary the testing place of the saving identity of Jesus: Jesus experiences there, as his own, a true human terror, a sense of abandonment in the face of death, yet remains willing to carry out the eternal plan of sacrificial love, which is both his own and his Father's.[13]

Cyril of Alexandria

Athanasius's learned and strong-minded successor in the first half of the fifth century, Cyril of Alexandria, exerted perhaps the most formative influence on what have become the classic Christian language rules for speaking of the complex identity of Jesus the Savior. Taking "body" and "flesh" in the fullest sense of their biblical usage, to signify not only biological materiality but mind, feelings, and will, Cyril speaks of the human Jesus not as an "assumed man," as some of his Antiochene contemporaries would do, but as "one Christ along with his flesh, the same at once God and a human being."[14] Cyril's emphasis on the radical unity of Christ as subject of all that is predicated of him, and on the divine Word as the basis and central focus of that unity, is rich with implications for his portrait of Jesus. In his celebrated *Third Letter to Nestorius* (of Constantinople), written in the autumn of 430—a manifesto on the orthodox understanding of the Savior as the basis for continuing communion in faith and sacrament between the two prelates and their churches—Cyril insists that this sense of Jesus's unity as subject is the warrant for our worship of him, "without separating and parting the human and God as though they were mutually connected [only] by unity of rank and sovereignty."[15] An awareness of this unity enables the participant in a eucharistic liturgy to recognize in the sacramental gifts "not mere flesh (God forbid!) or the flesh of a man hallowed by connection with the Word . . . , but the truly life-giving flesh belonging properly to God the Word himself."[16] It presents Christ's priestly sacrifice on the cross, identified as such typologically in the letter to the Hebrews, as the Son's offering of his

13. This is emphasized also throughout *On the Incarnation*; see especially 27–32, 46–55.

14. Cyril, *Third Letter to Nestorius* 12, anathema 2, trans. Lionel R. Wickham, *Select Letters* (Oxford: Clarendon, 1983), p. 29, alt.

15. *Third Letter to Nestorius* 4 (Wickham, p. 19, alt.).

16. *Third Letter to Nestorius* 7 (Wickham, p. 23, alt.).

own body to the Father, "for us and not for himself."[17] And it provides the real justification for Cyril's insistence, throughout his quarrel with Nestorius, on the importance to orthodoxy of Mary's traditional title, "God-bearer" (*Theotokos*), since the Church believes that the eternal Word of God "united what is human to himself in his own concrete individuality [*kath' hypostasin*] and underwent fleshly birth from her womb."[18]

The dispute between Cyril and the representatives of the Antiochene exegetical and theological tradition—Nestorius, Theodoret of Cyrus, and their teachers Diodore of Tarsus and Theodore of Mopsuestia—was not primarily a dispute about the fullness of Christ's humanity, as has sometimes been suggested, a dispute in which the Antiochenes were primarily concerned with emphasizing that humanity, while the Alexandrians offered it only lip service. Rather, the main differences seem to lie in different senses of the relevance of history and time to salvation, and of the ontological and existential boundaries between God and the world. For Antiochenes such as Theodore or Theodoret, the saving and transforming encounter of humanity with God, with all the freedom from corruptibility, passion, and sin that it promises, is a gift reserved in its fullness for the eschatological future, a new "state" (*katastasis*) that at present is realized only by the risen Christ, and pointed to by Scripture and the symbols of the Church's worship. The world we presently live in is separated by an unbridgeable gulf from God and his eternity, in the Antiochene view, and the main task of theology is to keep its language about God pure from anything that might confuse these realms, or imply some limitation or circumscription of God's being. For Cyril and his followers, by contrast, the news of the incarnation of the Word is precisely that the God who is ontologically "other" than creation has now become personally present within it, has made a human creature his own embodiment, united it to his own concrete existence, or *hypostasis*, identified himself with the full individual nature of a man, so that the creative and healing energies proper to God are now accessible in time, in the person of Christ and in the Church that is his body. As a result, while Theodoret lays strong emphasis, in his polemical treatises against Cyril, on the importance of keeping the Word free from any suggestion of sharing in human suffering, Cyril insists with equal force that the Christian message of salvation rests on the paradoxical but literal ascription of human suffering—acquired through incarnation—to God the Word.

17. *Third Letter to Nestorius* 9 (Wickham, p. 25).
18. *Third Letter to Nestorius* 11 (Wickham, p. 29, alt.).

Cyril's reason for insisting on this living paradox of a divine Word who suffers, not as God, but still truly suffers in his own flesh,[19] is not simply to head off the Antiochene criticism that his portrait of Christ compromises the divine attribute of impassibility. Rather, it is central to his soteriology that the Word made flesh should indeed suffer what we humans suffer, but in a way free from the elements of compulsion, self-preoccupation, and fear that normally accompany our own suffering.[20] He is fully human, yet human in a freer, more virtuous way than we can be—in a way that offers us both a model and an unattainable norm—because he is himself God the Son. As Cyril remarks in his *Scholia on the Incarnation*, "He has reserved to his [human] nature that it should be superior to all."[21]

In an interesting fragment of book 7 of his *Commentary on John* (written before the controversy with Nestorius began), Cyril makes this same point with reference to human grief, with which Jesus is said to have struggled at the death of his friend Lazarus (John 11:33–34). The Fourth Gospel tells us that Jesus "was indignant and was troubled" as he stood before Lazarus's tomb. Cyril writes:

> Since Christ was not only God by nature, but also a human being, he suffers in a human way along with everyone else. But when grief begins to be stirred up in him, and the holy flesh is inclined to shed tears, he does not allow it to suffer this in an unrestrained way, as usually happens with us. "He was indignant[22] in the Spirit" (John 11:33): that is, in the power of the Holy

19. See J. Warren Smith, "Suffering Impassibly: Christ's Passion in Cyril of Alexandria's Soteriology," *Pro Ecclesia* 11 (2002): 463–83.

20. See Cyril, *Second Oration to the Royal Ladies* (PG 76:1393B); cf. Smith, "Suffering Impassibly," pp. 463–64.

21. Cyril, *Scholia on the Incarnation of the Only-Begotten* 37, ed. Philip E. Pusey, *Cyrilli Archiepiscopi Alexandrini Opera* 6 (1875; reprint, Brussels: Culture et Civilisation, 1965), pp. 574–75; trans. Pusey, *St. Cyril, Archbishop of Alexandria, Five Tomes against Nestorius*, etc. (Oxford: J. Parker, 1881), pp. 232–33.

22. The Greek word in John 11:33, ἐμβριμάται (*embrimatai*), is usually translated as indicating deep emotion: "he was deeply moved" (RSV), "he was greatly disturbed" (NRSV), "[he was in] great distress" (JB). The original meaning of the verb is "to snort" and is used for horses, but in its (fairly infrequent) application to human beings it appears to mean "to express anger," "to rebuke indignantly" (cf. Dan 11:30 LXX; Matt 9:30; Mark 1:43). Cyril clearly understands the verb to mean that Jesus "rebuked" his own flesh, in the power of the Holy Spirit, for its tendency to be undone by grief. It is in response to this inner, divine rebuke that his human nature is then said to be visibly "troubled" but ultimately healed of this weakness.

> Spirit he rebukes his own flesh, so to speak. . . . For this is the reason the Word of God, powerful in every way, came to be in flesh—or rather, came to *be* flesh: that by the activities of his own Spirit he might strengthen the weaknesses of the flesh, and set this nature free from an earth-bound way of thinking, and might re-shape it to be concerned only with what pleases God. For surely it is an illness of human nature to be tyrannized by grief; but this, too, has been abolished first in Christ, along with our other illnesses, that it might come over from him to us.[23]

In the complex subjective identity of the Word made flesh, the inner dialogue between these two complete and wholly different realms of being leads to a new subordination of what is human to God, and to new human freedom from the tyranny of our passions—a freedom now accessible to us all through Jesus's own person.

Maximus the Confessor

The immediate solution to the bitter fifth-century dispute between Cyril of Alexandria and the Antiochene theologians over how to conceive and express the identity of Jesus—although by no means a final, comprehensive solution—was the formulation of Christian faith in his person hammered out by the Council of Chalcedon in 451 and appended to the normative creeds of Nicaea and Constantinople I as a kind of hermeneutical key. Rejecting any formulation that might suggest a permanent separation or an indiscriminate confusion of the human and the divine in Jesus, insisting on the full reality of both levels of his existence as a single person, the language agreed on at Chalcedon confesses him to be

> one and the same Son, our Lord Jesus Christ: the same one perfect in divinity and perfect in humanity, truly God and truly human . . . recognized in two natures without confusion, without change, without division, without separation, with the difference between the natures in no way removed through the union; rather, the distinctive property of both natures is preserved and comes together in a single *persona* and a single concrete individual (*hypostasis*).[24]

23. Cyril, Fragment on John 11:33–34 (ed. Pusey, 4:279–80).

24. Text in Giuseppe Alberigo et al., ed. and trans. Norman P. Tanner, *Decrees of the*

The language of the Chalcedonian formula was carefully woven together from a variety of earlier conciliar and theological texts, representing both sides of the debate as well as earlier stages of agreement between them.[25] Yet the formula offered a divided Eastern Christendom little respite from the bitter disputes of the 430s and 440s. For theologians sympathetic to the Antiochene tradition, for ecclesiastical politicians looking for consensus, and for most Western theologians, it seemed a welcome and evenhanded compromise; but for the great majority of monks, clergy, and faithful outside the main cities of the Eastern Empire, as well as for a number of Eastern Christian intellectuals of the late fifth century, it was an equivocation, a failure to acknowledge the centrally divine identity of the Savior as the core of even his human experiences and acts. For those who rejected the Chalcedonian formula, in the fifth century and afterward, only the terminology of Cyril's later letters, centered on the formula "one nature of the Word, made flesh," captured the vital, mutually expressive unity of the human and the divine elements that determined the identity of Jesus.

In the second quarter of the seventh century, the emperor Heraclius's efforts to reunify the Eastern Empire led to new efforts on the part of his court bishops to find a way of construing the official Chalcedonian Christology that might be acceptable to dissident Christians. Patriarch Sergius of Constantinople (in office 610–638), borrowing a phrase from Pseudo-Dionysius's *Letter 4*, cautiously advanced the theory that all the human activities of Christ, mental and bodily, were manifestations of "a single theandric operation" (*mia theandrikē energeia*), flowing forth from God's power and using his human nature as a created instrument. Sergius seems quickly to have refined this position in a somewhat more psychological direction, arguing in letters from the late 620s onward that the human experiences and actions of Jesus all express the single *will* and operation of the second person of the Trinity, even though they do so through the instrumentality of the complete human nature that God the Son has made his own. It was in response to this attempt to reread Chalcedon yet again that Maximus the Confessor was to make his name, and bear final witness with his life.

A well-educated native of Constantinople, born about 580, who had spent some years as a bureaucrat at the imperial court, Maximus became

Ecumenical Councils, vol. 1 (London: Sheed & Ward; Washington, DC: Georgetown University Press, 1990), p. 86, alt.

25. For an analysis of the text, see Aloys Grillmeier, *Christ in Christian Tradition*, vol. 1, 2nd ed. (London: Mowbray, 1975), pp. 543–54, and the literature cited there.

a monk about 613 and eventually moved west with other Byzantines to escape the Persian invasion of western Asia Minor, settling around 628–629 in Carthage, where he kept up a lively theological correspondence throughout the Greek-speaking world. For Maximus, Sergius's new interpretation of the Chalcedonian formula amounted to a tacit denial of its central affirmation about the identity of Jesus: the completeness of his two utterly incommensurate, fully functioning realities—that of God and that of a human being—yoked together in the unique historical particularity of a single individual. Every nature, Maximus argued, to be completely itself, must be completely operational; a nature, after all, in classical Aristotelian terminology, is a substance (i.e., a definable kind of being, a "what") considered as a principle of operation. And since willing and desiring are integral to all intellectual natures, and form part of what we mean by consciousness, to deny that Jesus possesses a full human will (*thelēma physikon*), which by natural impulse seeks its own human welfare, is to deny the fullness of his human nature, affirmed by the tradition of faith and canonized at Chalcedon.

For Maximus, as for Athanasius three centuries earlier, the test case of Jesus's identity in the Gospels, in terms of consciousness and will, is the scene of his agony in Gethsemane. But while Athanasius construed that story in terms of a tension between the Word and his "flesh," Maximus sees at play simply an instance of what is implied more broadly by the Christology of Chalcedon: Jesus's two natures, with all their faculties and operations, remain intact and distinct, but his single hypostasis—his unique individual *way* (*tropos*) of being God and being human—gives a different modality to both his eternal existence as Son of God and his historical existence as son of Mary. Jesus is, as Maximus remarks in several places, "divine in a human way and human in a divine way."[26] For the human will and the other human faculties of Jesus, this divine modality, communicated by the divine hypostasis whose nature it is, brings that human nature to its own creaturely perfection. So he writes of the Gethsemane scene, in *Opusculum 7*, that Jesus's prayer for deliverance was a clear expression of his humanity's natural dynamism toward self-preservation.

> On the other hand, that it [Jesus's human will] was completely deified and in agreement with the divine will, that it was always moved and formed by it and remained in accord with it, is clear from the fact that he always carried

26. See, e.g., Maximus, *Letter 15* (PG 91:573B); *Letter 19* (PG 91:593A2–B1); *Opusculum 4* (PG 91:61BC); *Opusculum 7* (PG 91:84B–D); *Disputation with Pyrrhus* (PG 91:297D–299A).

> out perfectly the decision of his Father's will, and that alone. So, as a human being, he said, "Not my will, but your will be done" (Luke 22:42). In this he offered himself to us as a model and norm for putting away our own wills to fulfill God's will perfectly, even if we should see death threatening us as a result. . . . He had, then, a human will. . . . Constantly and completely divinized by its assent to, and its union with, the Father's will, it was, to put it precisely, divine by union, not divine by nature; so it truly became, and so it should be called. But it never departed from its natural constitution by being divinized.[27]

In a number of his writings, Maximus stresses that it is precisely the unique structure of Jesus's person that contains and reveals the promised eschatological structure of human salvation.[28] In the identity of Jesus, Maximus discovers the full reality of grace, laid open to us in the divine modality of Jesus's humanity, and sees there at the same time the full realization of human nature as it was created to be. "Divinization," a hallowed term in the Greek patristic tradition for the goal of God's gracious work in redeemed humanity, is thus for him both a gift beyond the resources of human nature and the full realization of what God intended that nature to become. It has first been achieved, Maximus argues, in the person of Christ.

Concluding Reflections

In the four Greek Fathers whose treatment of Christ we have briefly surveyed, it is his human weakness—the limitation of his energy, strength, and intellect, his ability to suffer and die—that both raises the greatest challenge to the Church's proclamation of his lordship and stimulates the most profound theological reflection on what it might mean to say, with the centurion at Calvary, "This person truly was Son of God" (Mark 15:39). Irenaeus's opposition to Gnostic portraits of Christ clearly rests on an affirmation of the central importance of Jesus's innerworldly materiality—a realm that for Gnostic thought was irreducibly alien to God—for the full message of salvation. Athanasius, two centuries later, sees in the suffering of Jesus the full proof that God's Word has taken on the complex, damaged human reality Athanasius calls "flesh," and has begun to transform it by making it the

27. *Opusculum 7* (PG 91:80D, 81D).
28. See *To Thalassius*, question 60 (CCSG 22:73.10–19).

vehicle of revelation and renewed life. Cyril of Alexandria, along with his fifth-century contemporaries, develops a more nuanced technical vocabulary for speaking of the identity of Jesus—of what is single and what is twofold in his identity, and how they are related—and argues that in the very act of making our human weakness his own, the Son of God has begun to transform us, to give us virtue and life in place of sin and death, simply by being both God and fully human at once. Maximus the Confessor, in the seventh century, continues to reflect on the structure of Christ's person, using the vocabulary of Cyril and the Council of Chalcedon; for Maximus, Christ's will is especially the place in which human freedom begins to share in the transcendent freedom of God, and to choose, by the grace Christ communicates, the destiny for which God created humanity in the beginning.

All of these portraits of the person of Christ are way stations in a continuing process of Christian reflection on who Jesus really is and what he means for us: reflection that is rooted in the narrative of the Gospels and the apostolic witness and returns constantly to the New Testament for judgment and verification. These patristic readings of the Gospels are framed, certainly, by particular New Testament affirmations about Jesus that set the hermeneutical conditions for reading the longer narratives of his life and work: by the schema in Philippians 2:5–11 of the self-emptying and glorification of one who in the beginning is "equal to God"; by the portrait in Hebrews 4:14–5:10 of Jesus, Son of God and high priest, who "learned obedience through what he suffered"; and above all, perhaps, by the affirmation in the opening verses of the Fourth Gospel that the Word "who was in the beginning with God . . . became flesh and dwelt among us" (John 1:2, 14). Yet patristic reflection on the person of Christ clearly expresses a tradition of faith and understanding that moves into realms of discourse and conceptuality the New Testament writers could never have imagined or understood, a tradition that continues to evolve wherever Christians receive and think about the gospel. As Athanasius argues in defense of the creedal language of Nicaea, the fact that both the supporters and the opponents of Arius could use similar scriptural texts and phrases to undergird their opposed positions made it necessary for the Council to employ "strange" terms—terms taken from philosophy and science rather than Scripture—as interpretative norms for ensuring that the Scriptures themselves would be understood in the way the Christian tradition had always taken them, and the New Testament's apostolic authors had intended them.[29]

29. See Athanasius, *Defense of the Nicene Definition* 5.18–24, esp. 21; cf. Origen, *On First Principles* preface 2.

If we are to make sense, ourselves, of the classical Christian understanding of Jesus's identity that emerges in these and other early Christian writers, we must keep several cautions in mind. The two distinct "substances" or "natures" early theology sees in the person of Christ are, of course, two wholly incommensurable realities—not two parallel species of being competing for center stage. The one does not rule the other out. And the one "person" the Church recognizes as "owning" these two substances or natures is not classically understood in the way modern Westerners conceive of a person, defined by being a unique, self-contained pole of consciousness and free decisions, capable of forming relationships with other, equally distinct persons. In the classical understanding of both the triune God and Jesus Christ, "persons," or hypostases, are irreducible individual subjects of predication and attribution; yet the heart of both these Mysteries, for Christian faith, is that the three related "persons" in God share a single consciousness and will, a single substance, and that the one "person" of the incarnate Word possesses both an infinite divine mind and will and a complete human mind and will like our own. For the post-Chalcedonian understanding of the person of Christ, the Mystery of the gospel is that God the Son—"one of the Holy Trinity"—is "selved" in the full human knowledge and freedom of the son of Mary, and expresses in Jesus's human life and actions what it is to be Son of the Father and giver of the Spirit. The one who is "God from God, light from light," in Nicene language, has lived out in a human life, in a human body and mind, with all their inherent vulnerability and promise, what eternal Sonship means, so that we too who call Jesus "Lord" might also dare to call God "Father" and to live in his Spirit as God's sons and daughters.

In a famous passage in its Pastoral Constitution on the Church in the Modern World, *Gaudium et Spes*, the Second Vatican Council makes this same link between the identity of Jesus and the identity to which all of us are called, in grace:

> In reality it is only in the Mystery of the Word made flesh that the mystery of humanity truly becomes clear. For Adam, the first human being, was a type of him who was to come, Christ the Lord. Christ, the new Adam, in the very revelation of the Mystery of the Father and of his love, fully reveals humanity to itself, and brings to light its very high calling.[30]

30. *Gaudium et Spes*, §22, trans. Paul Lennon, in *Vatican Council II*, ed. Austin Flannery (Northport, NY: Costello, 1996), p. 185.

In the Greek Fathers we have surveyed here, that same Christian intuition is expressed with increasing clarity and wonder. In the person of Jesus—a human being who, at the moment of his most abject human weakness, is recognized as "truly Son of God"—the ancient faith of Christians finds both the pledge of God's indomitable love and the form of our human vocation. The identity of Jesus, however we parse it, is meant to be the pattern and promise of our own.

5 Antioch and Alexandria

Christology as Reflection on God's Presence in History

Every beginning student of theology knows at least something of the opposition between "Antiochene" and "Alexandrian" approaches to Christology and to biblical interpretation in the decades leading up to the councils of Ephesus and Chalcedon. The usual way of characterizing their differences is to say, in Grillmeier's terminology, that the theologians of the "school of Antioch" who flourished in the late fourth and early fifth centuries—Diodore of Tarsus, Theodore of Mopsuestia, Nestorius of Constantinople, Theodoret of Cyrus—represented, with a variety of modulations, the classic "Word–human being" (λόγος-ἄνθρωπος) approach to conceiving of the person of the Savior: God's divine Logos, who shares fully in the divine substance, has "taken up" a full human being to be his "temple," his dwelling place, and bestows his favor on this human being to such a unique degree that the man represents him in the world, reveals the "face" (πρόσωπον) of the Word as his own, shares even in divine honor and status; yet this indwelling of the Word in the man does not reduce or substantially alter the full operation of the man's human faculties, and never blurs the natural boundaries between the Creator and the creature, God and the human. Along with this approach to Christology, it is usually said, scholars from the "school of Antioch" were known for their skills in interpreting Scripture, and especially for their aversion to the allegorical or figural style of exegesis—seeing every incident and every phrase as a cipher for the human person's salvation in Christ or for spiritual growth—which had dominated ancient Scripture scholarship since Origen. Antiochene exegetes are seen as showing a greater respect for the "historical" or "literal" meaning of the biblical text, an interest that corresponded with their emphasis on the humanity of Jesus. The "school of Alexandria" on the other hand—drawing on the powerful legacy of Athanasius, influenced by the Origenist tradition of biblical scholarship, as represented by the late fourth-century exegete Didymus the Blind, and nourished by the Christology of Apollinarius of Laodicea and his loyal followers—were dominated by the towering ecclesiastical, exegetical, and theological figure of Cyril of Alexandria. Their biblical interpretation remained in the allegorical camp, which reached the heights of baroque fantasy at Didymus's hands; and their picture of Christ was unworldly, representing him as God the Word owning, transforming, and irradiating human flesh and even a human mind, to such an extent that Jesus could no longer be called a human being on his own, but formed "one nature," one living organism with the Word, who was the source and master of all his human acts.

Like all caricatures, this picture has a good deal of truth to it, but it is not the whole story, and so can be misleading. Recent studies of the work of Antiochene and Alexandrian exegetes in the period have tended to conclude that it is hard to speak of differences in "method" or even in hermeneutical principles between scholars in the two "schools," although interpreters from Antioch were deliberately less ingenious in finding spiritual significance in every passage of the Bible than their Alexandrian contemporaries were. They were also committed to the early Christian assumption that the Bible, as a continuous narrative of God's history with the world, finds its climactic and unifying meaning in the saving acts of Jesus Christ, and recognized the need for ἀναγωγία, the quest for a "higher meaning" in a text, when such interpretation seemed warranted (see Diodore, *Commentary on the Psalms*, Prologue, CCSG 6, 7.123–8.162; cf. Young 2002). For Diodore and his pupils, the key to good exegesis was never to let the interpretation of individual texts slip out of their context in the story of salvation history, as they understood it. While they did not share our modern understanding of historical investigation, they did begin their interpretations of texts with an overarching narrative of the history of God's promises as they move towards fulfillment, in Israel and the Church, and insisted that every scriptural passage be interpreted in the context of its presumed original location within that narrative. Influenced, perhaps, by the tradition of rhetorical training at Antioch, they were on the lookout for practical, moral applications of the texts they studied—a tendency most obvious in the exegesis of John Chrysostom. Exegetes in Alexandria, on the other hand, such as Didymus and Cyril, although interested in the events of Israel's past, seem to have taken greater interest in finding the ways in which a given text might nourish their readers' spiritual and theological growth, or deepen their grasp of the full meaning of the Mystery of Christ. They tended to be grammarians rather than rhetoricians—seekers for meaning, rather than for moving examples—and to read the Scripture contemplatively rather than kerygmatically (cf. Wessel 2004: 183–252).

As far as their respective understandings of the person of Christ are concerned, however, it is an over-simplification to suggest that the Antiochene theologians of the fourth and fifth centuries were primarily concerned with promoting a sense of the full humanity of Jesus, or that the Alexandrians gave that full humanity only lip service; it is here, perhaps, that Grillmeier's typology of word-flesh and word–human being Christology loses its usefulness and becomes misleading, under the influence of mid-twentieth-century concerns (see McGuckin 1994: 205–7). Diodore himself, for instance, occasionally uses the traditional terminology of "the Logos and his flesh," without suggesting thereby any diminution of Jesus's humanity (see Greer 1966); and Cyril is insistent, throughout his increasingly bitter controversy with Nestorius, that the "flesh" which he speaks of as forming "one nature" with the Word, in the Incarnation, included a complete and functioning rational human soul. Even if he made use of terms and formulas popularized by Apollinarius and his followers, Cyril was no Apollinarian in his understanding of the humanity of Christ. Neither "school" was interested in seeking to recover a "historical Jesus" who was thought to be more real, more foundational to faith, more like ourselves, than the Jesus presented in the Gospel narrative; and neither "school" understood the "person" of Christ to be identified in any privileged way with his human consciousness (see McGuckin 1994: 134, 207). These are modern concerns, remote from the general world of ancient philosophical and theological discourse.

Two things separated the theological thought-patterns of the theologians we label as "Antiochenes" and "Alexandrians." One is a different sense of the relevance of *time* to human salvation in Christ. The Antiochenes seem to have thought of the fullness of human salvation as an eschatological state, characterized by the gift of unchangeability and stability, by freedom from sin and passion, and by the incorruptibility and immortality of the risen body; these graces are fully realized now only in the risen Jesus, who lives eschatologically already, in a different "state" (κατάστασις) or world than the world of space and time we inhabit. Theodore of Mopsuestia and Theodoret emphasize that salvation is given to us at present only as a promise, in the "pledge" of the Holy Spirit and in the "types" or anticipatory symbols of the Church's sacraments; when we move on from this κατάστασις to the next, at the end of history, we will share in the state of transformation now revealed in the glorified human Christ (see Koch 1965: 141–79; Dewart 1971: 30–48;

Koch 1974; Daley 1991). Secondly, the Antiochene theologians emphasize the *boundaries* between God and creation, between God's sphere of being and activity and that of the concrete, historical world we inhabit.

> It is well known that the one who is eternal and the one whose existence has a beginning are greatly separated from each other, and the gulf found between them is unbridgeable. (Theodore of Mopsuestia, *On the Nicene Creed*, Catechetical Homily 4; Mingana 1932: 45)

Unlike Athanasius, who also emphasized God's otherness than creation but who laid an equal, coordinate emphasis on the divine Logos's personal, substantial presence within creation, the Antiochenes were concerned to maintain only God's distance—out of an underlying concern not to promote any idea of creation or salvation that might compromise the transcendent qualities of the three divine Persons. "Divinization" of the fallen human being is rarely mentioned by either Theodore or Theodoret (see Koch 1965: 150; Koch 1974: 235–38). In contrast to their interest in biblical "history," perhaps, Antiochene theologians tend to begin their treatments of theological issues, including salvation in Christ, by discussing God's being in the more general terms of the unity of the divine substance and its common attributes, as understood from the Greek philosophical tradition, rather than in terms of the scriptural narrative (see Koch 1974: 235; Theodoret, Ep. 145; cf. Bergjan 1993: 192–95). So in his so-called Sermon "against the Theotokos," which opened his controversy with Cyril of Alexandria, Nestorius treats the person and saving work of Jesus within the context of God's general providence: because God, who transcends the world, never ceases to care for the world he has created—because God is "untouched by change," yet "benevolent and just"—he finally has "dignified it with a gift which was furthest away and yet nearest to hand," and has taken up a human being, Jesus, to "bring about the revival of the human race" (Nestorius's *First Sermon Against the Theotokos* in Norris 1980: 124, 126; also see 123–31). These ideas were heavy with implications for their understanding of the person of Christ.

Apart from his commentary on the Psalms, Diodore's work survives mainly in small fragments, mostly preserved by hostile sources. Diodore was a prolific writer of vast learning; he is supposed to have produced commentaries on the entire Old Testament, as well as works on natural science and polemical treatises directed against the Jews, Neoplatonist philosophy, and a number of Christian sects. Many of the fragments dealing with the person of Christ are taken from his work *Against the Synousiasts*, which was apparently an anti-Apollinarian treatise, attacking the portrait of Christ as "the man from heaven," an organic unity of the divine Logos with living human flesh, which the Apollinarians had popularized (see Greer 1990). It is understandable that Diodore should have emphasized the distinctness of the Logos from the human being in which he has revealed himself in our midst (Diodore of Tarsus, Fragment 36; Abramowski 1949: 51–53). What worried his later critics was that Diodore, in his anti-Apollinarian work, seems to have insisted on the distinction of "two Sons" in Christ: the son of Mary, who, as "temple" of God the Word, can be called "Son of God" by *grace*, and the one who is Son of God by *nature*, ὁμοούσιος with the Father, and who is God the Logos. With the subsequent Antiochene tradition, Diodore was very concerned with theological precision; so he writes:

> If anyone, speaking inexactly, also wants to call the Son of God, God the Word, son of David because of the temple of God the Word that was taken from David, let him call him so. And let him call the one descended from David's seed Son of God, by grace but not by nature—as long as he is not unaware of his natural ancestors and does not reverse the order, or say that the one who is incorporeal and before the ages *is* both from God and from David, both passible and impassible. (Diodore of Tarsus, *Against the Synousiasts*, Frag. 4, as in Leontius of Byzantium, *Deprehensio et Triumphus super Nestorianos* [*DTN*])

Diodore is willing to apply the title "Son of God" to Jesus as a conventional, non-literal way of pointing out that he was the bearer or dwelling-place of the eternal Son of God, but he insists on the abiding distinction between what Jesus and the Word are in themselves, and what Jesus has become, by God's gracious action, in the divine economy. In another fragment, he denies preaching "two sons" in any way that would be harmful to Trinitarian or Christological doctrine:

> We urge you to be safe in being precise about doctrine. The Son, perfect before the ages, assumed a perfect descendant of David: the Son of God took the Son of David. You say to me, "Then you are proclaiming two sons?" I do not speak of two sons of David; for I did not say that God the Word is David's son, did I? Nor do I say there are two Sons of God in essence; for I do not say there are two produced from God's essence, do I? I say that God the eternal Word dwelt in him who is from the seed of David. (Diodore of Tarsus, *Against the Synousiasts*, Frag. 1, in Leontius of Byzantium, *DTN*)

The point seems almost a pedantic one, but one can see here the sense of the boundary between the divine nature and the historical order in which God has worked salvation, the sense that God's transcendence must be protected from pious imprecision, which would characterize both Diodore and his heirs.

Perhaps the most gifted and influential of those heirs was Theodore of Mopsuestia. Diodore's pupil spent ten years as a presbyter and scriptural commentator in Antioch, in the 380s, before becoming bishop of Mopsuestia, sixty miles north of the city, in 392. His exegesis, which has earned him the title "the Interpreter" in the Assyrian Church of the East, follows the same analytical, sparingly figural approach Diodore had developed; it also seeks—as Diodore's did—to situate biblical passages in their place within the longer narrative of God's people, as they are drawn towards eschatological salvation. Theodore has also left catechetical and doctrinal works of great interest, such as fragments of a large treatise *On the Incarnation*, directed against Arian and Apollinarian conceptions of Christ as Diodore's work had been.

Theodore is deeply concerned to draw a sharp, bright line between the transcendent, triune God—separated from creation by an "unbridgeable gulf" of being—and the "human nature," the "form of a human being," which God the Son "put on" to reveal himself in the human world (Theodore of Mopsuestia, *Cat. Hom.* 5; Mingana 1932: 50–51; cf. *Cat. Hom.* 5; Mingana 1932: 36ff.). Theodore's usual way of speaking about the relation of the divine Son to the man Jesus is in terms of "indwelling," of presence as in a temple (alluding to Jesus's words in John 2:19), or of the Son's "clothing" himself in the "form of a servant" (as suggested by Phil 2:7). More important for him seems to have been the precise *mode* of the Son's presence in a visible, created human being. In a fragment of his treatise *On the Incarnation*, Theodore distinguishes between God's presence in essence (οὐσία), in operation or activity (ἐνέργεια), and in "good pleasure" or "favor" (εὐδοκία). As the transcendent ground and source of all created being, and the provident guide of the universe in its continued functioning, God must be present to all creatures equally in essence and in operation; so Theodore argues that the only way in which he can be particularly present or absent to individuals must be in the third way of "good pleasure," of love and grace. The Word's indwelling in Jesus, then, must be conceived along these lines, as representing a unique degree of divine election and good pleasure, a unique identification of this man with the Word, by God's prior choice and action, which has enabled Jesus to reveal the Word uniquely to the world and to share uniquely in God's glory and work as judge and savior of human history. Theodore concludes:

> The indwelling took place in [Jesus] as in a son; it was in this sense that [God] took pleasure in him and indwelt him. But what does it mean to say "as in a son"? It means that having indwelt him, he united the one assumed as a whole to himself and equipped him to share with himself in all the honor in which he, being Son by nature, participates, so as to be counted one person (πρόσωπον) in virtue of the union with him and share with him all his dominion, and in this way to accomplish everything in him, so that even the examination and judgment of the world shall be fulfilled through him and his advent. Of course, in all this the difference in natural characteristics is kept in mind. (*On the Incarnation VII*, Frag. 2; Norris 1980: 117)

Theodore is willing to accept the Church's traditional language of "incarnation" to describe the presence of the Word in Jesus, provided one understands it as meaning the Word became actually visible in human terms, and "assumed a complete man, who was a man not only in appearance but a man in a true human nature" (*Cat. Hom.* 5; Mingana 1932: 60; cf. 54). To take incarnation any more literally than this—to identify "the Son of the seed of David according to the flesh," of Romans 1:3, with the eternal Son—is incorrect: "Indeed it is not God who became flesh, nor was it God who was formed from the seed of David, but the man who was assumed for us" (*Cat. Hom.* 8; Mingana 1932: 91). Theodore's favorite way of speaking about this "assumption," it seems, is in terms of *union*: it is a "close union" or "precise union" (ἄκρα ἕνωσις; e.g., *Cat. Hom.* 3, 6, 8; Mingana 1932: 36ff.; 66ff.; 84; 91), an "ineffable union" (ἄρρητος ἕνωσις; e.g., *Cat. Hom.* 8; Mingana 1932: 86ff.), a "perfect union (τελεία ἕνωσις) between the one who was assumed and the one who assumed" (*Cat. Hom.* 6; Mingana 1932: 64). Theodore insists that this union between Word and man is not transitory: "the human form can never and under no circumstances be separated from the divine nature which put it on" (*Cat. Hom.* 8; Mingana 1932: 89). Jesus the man has always been "precisely united" with God the Word. But Theodore is reluctant to speak of what it is that binds the divine Son and the man Jesus together in other than functional terms: the man was so led by the Holy Spirit that "he had the Logos of God working within him and throughout him in a perfect way, so as to be inseparable from the Logos in his every motion" (*On the Incarnation* VII, Frag. 3l; Norris 1980: 117); and they are unified, most strikingly and most visibly, in the honor they receive, both from God the Father and from the rest of creation, as the man Jesus is glorified (e.g. *Cat. Hom.* 6, 7; Mingana 1932: 65, 78, 80). Seizing on the biblical axiom that a husband and wife are "no longer two, but one flesh" (Gen 2:24; Matt 19:6), Theodore observes that a married couple clearly are not impeded from this unity by their being two people (*Cat. Hom.* 8; Mingana 1932: 90; cf. *On the Incarnation* VIII, Frag. 7; Norris 1980: 120).

Theodore's careful picture of the "perfect union" of two different acting beings in Christ the Savior affects his way of theologically interpreting the activities of Christ, as they are reported in the Gospels. In "assuming the fashion of a human being" and dwelling in him, the Logos "hid himself at the time in which he was in the world, and conducted himself with the human race in such a way that those who beheld him in a human way, and did not understand anything more, believed him to be simply human" (*Cat. Hom.* 6; Mingana 1932: 65). All the events of Jesus's life, guided by the indwelling Word, were intended by God to be saving Mysteries, Theodore goes on to suggest, that is, models of the growth towards immortality which we also hope to share.

> It was easy and not difficult for God to have made him at once immortal, incorruptible and immutable as he became after his resurrection, but because it was not he alone whom [God] wished to make immortal and immutable, but us also who are partakers of his nature, he rightly, and on account of this association, did not so make the first-fruits of us all, in order that, as the blessed Paul said, "He might have the pre-eminence in all things" (Col. 1.18). In this way, because of the communion that we have with him in this world, we will, with justice, be partakers with him of the future good things. (*Cat. Hom.* 6; Mingana 1932: 69, 70)

In such reflections, Theodore sounds like Gregory of Nyssa. Yet he emphasizes, too, that Jesus the man had to pursue virtue himself, even though

> he fulfilled virtue more exactly and more easily than was possible for other people, since God the Logos . . . had united Jesus with himself in his very conception and furnished him with a fuller cooperation for the accomplishment of what was necessary. (*On the Incarnation* VII, Frag. 5; Norris 1980: 119)

Theodore also emphasizes the reality of the sufferings and death of Jesus: a natural death whose public character served to emphasize the physical reality of his resurrection, "by which death was abolished" (*Cat. Hom.* 7; Mingana 1932: 74). Jesus's passion and death raise the ultimate difficulties to our accepting a literal understanding of the Word's incarnation. Alluding to a version of Hebrews 2:9, which was known by Origen—"Apart from God [χωρὶς θεοῦ] he tasted death for everyone"—Theodore emphasizes that Jesus was only able to die because the Godhead kept himself "cautiously remote" from him in that time, "yet also near enough to do the needful and necessary things for the nature he had assumed." He continues:

> He himself [i.e., the Word] was not tried with the trial of death, but he was near to him and doing to him the things that were congruous to his nature as the maker who is the cause of everything. That is, he brought him to perfection through sufferings and made him forever immortal, impassible, incorruptible, and immutable for the salvation of the multitudes who would be receiving communion [κοινωνία] with him. (*Cat. Hom.* 8; Mingana 1932: 87)

In all of his reflections on the experiences of Jesus and their significance in the economy of salvation in the *Catecheses*, at any rate, Theodore tends to speak of the Logos and the man in whom he dwelt, or even of the "natures" of divinity and humanity, as two agents, two "he's," without much precision on the way in which they can be thought of as one. Occasionally, he uses the terminology of *person* (πρόσωπον)—the dynamic concept of a "speaker" or dramatic "role" associated with a theatrical "mask" or "face" (πρόσωπον)—to suggest that it is in their permanent association of action and appearance that the Word and the man Jesus find their inseparable unity. So Theodore writes, in a fragment of *On the Incarnation*:

> When we try to distinguish the natures, we say that the "person" of the human being is complete and that that of the Godhead is complete. But when we consider the union, then we proclaim that both natures are one "person," since the humanity receives from the divinity honor surpassing that which belongs to a creature, and the divinity brings to perfection in the human being everything that is fitting. (*On the Incarnation* VIII, Frag. 8; Norris 1980: 120–21)

Theodore's most famous pupil, undoubtedly, was the monk Nestorius. Nestorius was brought to Constantinople as bishop in the spring of 428. The contemporary ecclesiastical historian Socrates characterizes him as vain, quarrelsome, and intolerant of other opinions (*Ecclesiastical History* 7.29), and hazards the judgment that Nestorius was "disgracefully illiterate" in the theological tradition (*Ecclesiastical History* 32). In the sermon which provoked the outbreak of hostilities between himself and Cyril of Alexandria, Nestorius gives voice to a more rigid version of Theodore's conception of Christ than we find in Theodore's own works. Nestorius is mainly concerned here to draw clear distinctions between the divine Logos, who has saved us all in Christ, and the human Jesus, the Son of Mary, who was his "temple," "the instrument of his godhead" (*First Sermon "against the Theotokos"*; Norris 1980: 125). God cannot be born, God cannot die, he insists: but God, who is above all change, is also active in the world, benevolent towards his creatures (*First Sermon "against the Theotokos"*; Norris 1980: 125–26). So the Son, in Paul's words, "emptied himself, taking the form of a slave" (Phil 2:7); he "assumed a person (πρόσωπον), of the same nature [as ours]" (*First Sermon "against the Theotokos"*; Norris 1980: 127) in order to pay to God the debt our nature had incurred through sin (*First Sermon "against the Theotokos"*; Norris 1980: 126f.). In this human "person," which now belongs to the Son of God, our nature or common reality, Nestorius argues, was able to plead its case before God against the devil, who brought charges against it going back to Adam. Pointing to the innocence of Jesus, the new Adam, human nature itself calls out for release from the punishment of corruption and mortality:

> Our nature, having been put on by Christ like a garment, intervenes on our behalf. . . . This was the opportunity which belonged to the assumed man, as a human being: to dissolve, by means of the flesh, that corruption which arose by means of the flesh. (*First Sermon "against the Theotokos"*; Norris 1980: 128)

Human nature can make this claim on God because it now belongs to "the Christ, who is at once God and man" (*First Sermon "against the Theotokos"*; Norris 1980: 129). The human being, who is the created instrument of the Word, is honored and worshiped and followed by the faithful because the Word is "within" him and has "assumed" him as his "instrument" (*First Sermon "against the Theotokos"*; Norris 1980: 129, 130). The very difference between the deity and humanity that have come together in Christ is what makes possible his uniquely exalted position as Savior.

Later on in the 430s and 440s, the exiled Nestorius labored to defend his own orthodoxy in a series of tracts and letters, some of which have come down to us in a collection known as the *Book of Heracleides*. There Nestorius attempts to develop a whole Christology based on the idea of "union by *persona* (or πρόσωπον)," in order to clear himself from the reputation of having taught that the Word and Jesus were "two Sons." The conception behind Nestorius's argument seems to be based on the familiar text Philippians 2:6–7, where Christ is said to have put aside the "form of God" (μορφὴ θεοῦ) and have taken up the "likeness of a slave" (μορφὴ δούλου), so that he "came to be in human likeness [ὁμοιώματι], and was found, in shape, as a human being [σχήματι ὡς ἄνθρωπος]." Probably drawing on Neoplatonic theory as well as on earlier Antiochene usage, Nestorius speaks of these various "forms" or "appearances" as πρόσωπα: "faces" or "*personae*." Every natural substance, he suggests in the *Book of Heracleides*, has its own πρόσωπον, its external form or self-presentation, formed from its intrinsic natural properties, which allows it to be known by others. Since the Word of God and the historical man Jesus are irreducibly distinct in their own fundamental realities, and since any suggestion of a blending of the two inevitably would imply compromising either the transcendence of the Word or the humanity of Jesus—making him into an Arian or an Apollinarian Son of God—what the Incarnation really means, in Nestorius's scheme, is that each of these two realities in Christ has conferred its own "face" on the other, forming a single, externally perceptible whole, which acts and appears as one. Nestorius insists this exchange of πρόσωπα is more than a matter of simple behavior, of "acting as if"; by conferring their "faces" on each other, the Word and the man actually "form" each other into something new. So he writes, alluding to Philippians 2:

> For he [the Word] exists in his hypostasis and has made it [the flesh?] the likeness of his likeness, neither by command nor by honor nor simply by the equality of grace, but he has made it his likeness in its natural likeness [= form], in such a way that it is none other than that very thing which he has taken for his own πρόσωπον, so that the one might be the other and the other the one, one and the same in the two substances: a πρόσωπον fashioned by the flesh and fashioning the flesh in the likeness of its own Sonship in the two natures, and one in the two natures—the one fashioned by the other and the other by the one, the same unique likeness of the πρόσωπον. (Nestorius, *Book of Heracleides*; Driver and Hodgson 2002: 159, trans. modified)

Nestorius wants to affirm a genuine and lasting unity between the eternal Word and the human Jesus; but he insists on conceiving it in terms of an exchange of perceptible forms, the Word shaping the human Jesus into someone who reveals God, and Jesus giving the Word of God human words and a human face. He is opposed to any way of conceiving the unity of Christ in terms of "substance." To see Christ's unity as substantial or natural unity implies for Nestorius inevitably that either the Word is himself capable of change and suffering, and therefore less than fully God, or the humanity of Jesus is incomplete, simply a matter of appearance. Nestorius writes:

> We shun those who speak of the Incarnation apart from this union: either by a change only in likeness, which is the view of the pagans, or in hallucinations, or in a form [σχῆμα] without hypostasis which "suffers impassibly" [Nestorius's caricature of Cyril's view]; or in predicating natural sufferings of God the Word, as being either hypostatically united to the flesh or in the flesh as a rational or irrational soul [text uncertain]; or, finally, in asserting that the union resulted in a natural hypostasis and not a voluntary πρόσωπον. For we may not make the union of God the Word corruptible and changeable, nor call it passible and necessary, but it is a voluntary union in πρόσωπον and not in nature. (Nestorius, *Book of Heracleides*; Driver and Hodgson 2002: 181, trans. modified)

For Nestorius as for Theodore, what was most to be feared in speaking of the Incarnation as substantial or natural, or as the hypostatic or concretely realized union of the Word and a man, was that it compromised the transcendent qualities of God: his impassibility, his unchangeability, his freedom. God reveals himself in Christ, but not as being himself part of our world.

Theodoret of Cyrus was a contemporary and a defender of Nestorius, a bitter critic of Cyril of Alexandria, yet also the most moderate of the Antiochenes in his understanding of the unity of Christ, the most ready to work towards a conciliatory position. In his late work, the *Eranistēs*, Theodoret mounts an elaborate refutation of what he understands to be the weakness of the Alexandrian approach to Christ: that it so emphasizes the identity of God and the human in him, that it takes John 1:14, "The Word *became* flesh and dwelt among us," so literally, that it inevitably suggests the Word, as God, underwent change, rather than simply being the saving agent of change in humanity—for Theodoret, such an assertion would contradict "the incorporeal, illimitable character of the divine nature" (*Eranistēs*, Dialogue 1; Ettlinger 1975: 66.4–68.12).

Theodoret insists, throughout this work, that an accurate theology, faithful to the Christian tradition, must distinguish between the human Jesus, who underwent change and suffering and who received the gift of incorruptibility in his resurrection, and the divine Word who had made the human Jesus his own. Theodoret constantly stresses that it was the man and not "the divine nature" that suffered on the Cross, and that the two sets of properties are united only in the πρόσωπον, the one acting figure formed by the two utterly different individuals, the two ὑποστάσεις, of the Word and Jesus, indivisibly united now in their saving actions as the Christ (*Eranistēs*, Dial. 3; Ettlinger 1975: 209.26–30). So Theodoret affirms, through the mouth of his "Orthodox" speaker:

> It behooves us to say that the flesh was nailed to the tree, but to hold that the divine nature even on the cross and in the tomb was inseparable from this flesh, though from it derived no sense of suffering, since the divine nature is naturally incapable of undergoing both suffering and death and its substance is immortal and impassible. . . . And when we are told of passion and of the cross, we must recognize the nature which submitted to the passion; we must avoid attributing it to the impassible one, and must attribute it to that nature which was assumed for the distinct purpose of suffering. (Ettlinger 1975: 227.2–6; 228.23–25; trans. Blomfield Jackson, *NPNF* II, 3.233–34)

The task of orthodox theological language, Theodoret assumes, is to keep this distinction of the divine and the human constantly before the Church's eyes, along with their wonderful unity in the economy of salvation.

The main opponent of Nestorius and Theodoret, from the late 420s until his death in 444, was Cyril of Alexandria, the most thoughtful and prolific spokesman for the Alexandrian tradition. Cyril's opposition rested on a different way of conceiving and speaking about the Mystery of Christ and about salvation: different terminology, different priorities, a different rhetoric. The non-negotiable axiom of Cyril's Christology is not the *otherness* of the divine nature with respect to circumscribed, mutable, passible creatures, but the *involvement* of God the Son, the second hypostasis of the divine Trinity, in the historical process of salvation we call God's "management" of things—his "economy" (McGuckin 1994: 184; see also O'Keefe, 1997: esp. 58). So Cyril underlines the continuity in the narrative of the Scriptures and the Creeds, by emphasizing the singleness of the subject of the acts that have saved us: it is God the Word, God the Son, who is born of a Virgin, who receives his own Holy Spirit in baptism for our sakes, who heals the sick and raises the dead by his human touch, who dies in his own body on the Cross and reunites that body with his own soul on the morning of the resurrection. Cyril is careful to distinguish his own understanding of the person of Christ from that of Apollinarius: the "one nature" or real, living agent, the Word, who has "been made flesh" in time, includes in that biblically named "flesh" a complete human mind, a "rational soul." Cyril agrees with his Antiochene critics that the Logos, as God, does not undergo change or limitation or suffering in his own divine nature, even while he insists that it is this very Logos as agent, as subject, who experiences precisely these things in what has become, by incarnation, his own passible, changeable human flesh.

In his first statement of this Christological approach within a context of controversy—his so-called "second letter" to Nestorius, in which he takes the Constantinopolitan bishop to task for the deficiencies in his formulation of the Mystery—Cyril expresses his position concisely yet completely; citing the Nicene Creed as the guide for what must be said of Christ, and for how one must say it, he explains:

> We do not say that the Logos became flesh by having his nature changed, nor for that matter that he was transformed into a complete human being composed out of soul and body. On the contrary, we say that in an unspeakable and incomprehensible way, the Logos united to himself, in his hypostasis, flesh enlivened by a rational soul, and in this way became a human being and has been designated "Son of man." He did not become a human being simply by an act of will or "good pleasure" (εὐδοκία), any more than he did so by merely taking on a "person" (πρόσωπον).
>
> Furthermore, we say that while the natures which were brought together into a true unity were different, there is, nevertheless, because of the unspeakable and unutterable convergence into unity, one Christ and one Son out of the two. This is the sense in which it is said that, although he existed and was born from the Father before the ages, he was also born of a woman in his flesh. . . . It is not the case that first of all an ordinary human being was born of the holy Virgin and that the Logos descended upon him subsequently. On the contrary, since the union took place in the very womb, he is said to have undergone a fleshly birth by making his own the birth of the flesh which belonged to him. We assert that this is the way in which he suffered and rose from the dead. It is not that the Logos of God suffered in his own nature, being overcome by stripes or nail-piercing or any of the other injuries; for the divine, since it is incorporeal, is impassible. Since, however, the body that had become his own underwent suffering, he is—once again—said to have suffered these things for our sakes, for the impassible one was within the suffering body. (Cyril of Alexandria, *Second Letter to Nestorius*; Norris 1980: 132–33)

In reading this text, it is important to attend to the particular terms and expressions Cyril chooses to signify the personal unity of Christ. As in the

Nicene Creed, the subject of the narrative is God the Logos; *he* is the one who became a human being, experienced true birth from a human mother, suffered in the way only humans can suffer. Christology is not about "divinity" and "humanity," first of all, but about what the Son of God did for our sakes. Secondly, the verbs reveal a sense of the importance of time, of narrative sequence: "the natures he brought together *were* different, yet there *is* now convergence . . . one Son out of the two"; what *were* different *are* now, in a new sense altogether, "one and the same." And thirdly, Cyril speaks here and elsewhere of this new unity in Christ as "union in hypostasis" (ἕνωσις καθ' ὑπόστασιν), in the concreteness of an individual existence, and later even as "union in nature" (ἕνωσις κατὰ φύσιν), understanding "nature," too, as the living actuality of an organic individual being (*Third Letter to Nestorius*, §4, 5, and anathema 3; Wickham 1983: 19, 29). The Word can be said to have "made fleshly birth his own" (οἰκειοῦσθαι), so that the flesh, its sufferings, and even its death are now "his" (see also *First Letter to Succensus* 6).

The implications of this picture of Christ are both linguistic and substantive. Linguistically, Cyril delights in using the somewhat shocking turns of phrase that we usually classify as "the communication of properties," predicating human experiences directly of God the Word and divine qualities directly of the man Jesus. In his celebrated "Third Letter to Nestorius," for instance—a piece meant to stake out the boundaries between his own approach and that of the Antiochenes as confrontationally as possible—he refers to the Eucharistic species as "the personal, truly vitalizing flesh of God the Word himself" (*Third Letter to Nestorius*, 7; Wickham 1983: 23; cf. anathema 11), and later goes on to anathematize those who "do not acknowledge God's Word as having suffered in flesh, been crucified in flesh, tasted death in flesh and been made first-born from the dead, because as God he is Life and life-giving" (*Third Letter to Nestorius*, anathema 12; Wickham 1983: 33; also see Chadwick 1951; Gebremedhin 1977). Just like the title θεοτόκος for Mary, which first moved Nestorius to impose some distinctions in the interest of Nicene orthodoxy, phrases like these are deliberately meant as "limit-cases," hard sayings that test the extent to which we are willing to affirm that God the Word is really the one who has saved us in the person and works of Jesus, that God the Word is really the one we encounter in Jesus's humanity and even in his sacramental presence in the Church. But the Christological debate, for Cyril, is clearly not simply a debate over how we think and talk about the Savior; it is also a consideration of what we actually understand God to have done for us, with us, in Christ.

For Cyril and his Antiochene interlocutors, the most challenging substantive aspect of the paradox of Christ's person was his suffering: must

Christians affirm that God the Son is the one who suffered, in his own flesh, on the Cross, or must one make a strict distinction between the suffering one and the one who raised him? Cyril insists most emphatically, in many of his later works, that the first of these statements is in fact a central affirmation of Christian faith. So he asks, in his third *Tome against Nestorius*, "By faith in whom, then, are we justified? Is it not in him who suffered death according to the flesh for our sake? Is it not in one Lord Jesus Christ? Have we not been redeemed by proclaiming his death and confessing his resurrection?" (*Against Nestorius* 3.2, in ACO I, 1, 6.61; Russell 2000: 165). Cyril is willing to concede, by the mid-430s, that the humanity and the divinity that belong to Christ can be distinguished as two separate natures during his earthly life, by a kind of exercise in thought "at the merely speculative level" (κατὰ μονὴν τὴν θεωρίαν), as long as one recognizes that in fact "they belong to one individual, so that the two are two no more, but one living being is brought to its full realization through both" (*Second Letter to Succensus*, 5, trans. mine; cf. Wickham 1983: 92–93). And it is this "one living being"—God the Word, who has taken on our "flesh" in time—who is the subject of his flesh's passion:

> The passion therefore will belong to the economy, God the Word esteeming as his own the things which pertain to his own flesh, by reason of the ineffable union, and remaining external to suffering as far as pertains to his own nature, for God is impassible. (Scholia on the Incarnation 36; Pusey 1881: 225)

Cyril repeatedly affirms that Christ, as the Word with his "flesh," "suffered impassibly"—a paradox that excited the amazement and scorn of his Antiochene opponents, and even some modern scholars (Cyril, *To the Royal Ladies, on Right Faith* 2.164; PG 76.1393B; *On the Creed*, 24; *That Christ is One*; McGuckin 1995: 117; see Theodoret, *Eranistēs*, 3; Ettlinger 1975: 218.29–34; see also Cyril, *Second Letter to Succensus*, 4–5; cf. Hallman 1991).

In some of these passages Cyril suggests that the "impassible suffering" of Christ is more than simply a paradox that tests our grasp of the Mystery of his person; Cyril also presents it as "an example [ὑποτύπωσις] for us in human fashion . . . so that we might follow in his steps" (*To the Royal Ladies, on Right Faith* 2.164; see Smith 2002). If one remembers that suffering, like all human "passions" or passivities, was understood in the Hellenistic world as an experience that normally destroyed the harmony and integrity of a natural organism, Jesus's "impassible suffering," seen as human vulnerability freely taken on and "owned" by the life-giving Word of God in his human body and soul, becomes the means by which he heals *our* passions and destructive weaknesses in his own humanity, and turns our suffering into a means of growth. So Cyril writes of the death of Christ, the climax of his sufferings, in his *Letter to the Monks*, during the summer of 431:

> As one of us, though he knew not death, he went down into death through his own flesh, in order that we might also go up with him to life. For he came to life again, having despoiled the nether world, not as a human like us but as God in flesh, among us and above us. Our nature was greatly enriched with immortality in him first, and death was crushed when it assaulted the body of life as an enemy. For just as it conquered in Adam, so it was defeated in Christ. (*Letter to the Monks of Egypt* 38; McInery 1987: 33)

What was really at stake for Cyril, however, in the question of the suffering of the incarnate Word and in all the other issues surrounding that of the unity of subject in Christ, was the economy itself; to attribute the acts and words and even the sufferings of Christ to anyone but God the Son, to anything but the Word's own flesh, is for him to lessen the message of the Gospel. Quoting John 3:16—"God so loved the world that he gave his only-begotten Son"—Cyril asks plaintively:

> When God the Father so exalts his love for the world, explaining how immensely great and vast it is, then why do our opponents so belittle it, saying that it was not the true Son who was given for us? They introduce in place of the natural Son someone else who is like us, and has the sonship as a grace; but it really was the Only-begotten who was given for our sake. . . . What will then be left of the great and admirable love of the Father, if he only gave up a part of the world for its sake, and a small part at that? Perhaps it would not even be wrong to say that the world was redeemed without God's help, since it was served in this respect from within its own resources? (*That Christ Is One*; McGuckin 1995: 120–21)

If it is God who has redeemed the world, and if he has done it in Christ, who is God's own Son, then Cyril insists we must see the story of Christ as nothing less than a story about God himself.

Perhaps the real issues that divided the theologians of Antioch and Alexandria in the fourth and fifth centuries could be expressed in broader questions such as these:

(1) *What is theological language really about?* For Nestorius and Theodoret, at least, its purpose was to prevent us from making dangerous mistakes about God: it needed to be precise, self-conscious, and technically sophisticated if it was to avoid the pitfalls of Arianism, Apollinarianism, or pagan myth. For Cyril, its purpose was to express and elicit reverence and wonder at the great things God has done for us; it was evocative, deliberately paradoxical, redolent of the atmosphere of liturgical prayer; and the great danger to be avoided was speaking of Christ in overly secular terms.

(2) *How should one read the Scriptures?* Both the Antiochene and the Alexandrian traditions of theology were rooted in highly developed cultures of scholarly biblical interpretation; both "schools" recognized in the Christian Bible a single witness to a single story of salvation that culminated in the person and work of Christ, a story summed up in Creeds like that of Nicaea (cf. Wessel 2004: 268–69). But the Antiochenes insisted on the need for a certain degree of hermeneutical sophistication if one were to read the Bible in a way worthy of God—a hermeneutic based on the Greek philosophical tradition about what the divine nature is and is not. Cyril was aware of these philosophical traditions, too, and was willing to use them to the degree that they did not obscure the shocking originality of the biblical message; but Scripture itself, not philosophy, for him had to be the starting point of Christian theology. So on the question of the suffering of the Word in his flesh, he concludes his argument by saying: "Inspired Scripture tells us he suffered in 'flesh,' and we would do better to use those terms than to talk of his suffering 'in a human nature'" (*Second Letter to Succensus*, 5; Wickham 1983: 93). Philosophical language always brought with it the subtle tendency to place human reasoning about what God must be like above the Gospel message about who and what God is.

(3) *How does God save us?* The Antiochene theologians tend to understand salvation in terms similar to Gregory of Nyssa's: as growth in moral virtue and stability, coupled with freedom from physical corruptibility, both of which are presently visible in the risen Christ but are promised to us only in the age to come. They speak a good deal of the work of grace and of the presence of the Holy Spirit in the Church, but are noticeably reluctant to use the language of "divinization." In fact, the Antiochenes tend to conceive of grace, to use Augustine's terminology, more in cooperative than in operative terms, more as assistance than as the creation of new freedom: God clearly has begun the work of redemption among us, but—as in Jesus—God clearly expects us to "grow in grace by pursuing the virtue which is attendant upon understanding and

knowledge" (Theodore of Mopsuestia, *On the Incarnation* VII, Frag. 5; Norris 1980: 119; also see Dewart 1971: 49–73). For Cyril, on the other hand, grace is God's work, just as the story of salvation is the story of God's action, not ours. Nestorius, in fact, criticizes Cyril by saying, "You take as the starting point of your narrative the maker of the natures [in Christ], and not the πρόσωπον of union" (*Book of Heracleides*; Driver and Hodgson 2002: 153): Cyril begins with God, he suggests, not with the Christ who is a balanced union of what is divine and what is human. And while tacitly accepting this criticism, Cyril also sees God as the end of the narrative, frequently drawing on 2 Peter 1:4 to remind his readers that salvation in Christ implies we are to become "sharers in the divine nature." In his *Commentary on John*, for instance—a work that antedates the Nestorian controversy by as much as five years—Cyril reflects on the Mystery of Christ's person as the foundation of the Church's unity:

> He came to be at once God and a human being, so that by joining together in himself things that are widely separate in nature and have diverged from all kinship with each other, he might reveal humanity as a participant and "sharer in the divine nature." . . . So the Mystery of Christ has come into being as a kind of beginning, a way for us to share in the Holy Spirit and in unity with God: all of us are made holy in that Mystery. (*Commentary on John*, 11:11; Pusey 1872: 998a–1000a)

(4) *How is God related to this created order?* How *real* is God's presence in this world of space and time? The Antiochenes were concerned to emphasize God's *otherness* with regard to creation, God's freedom from all the limitations and vulnerabilities that classical philosophy saw as part of contingent existence; they feared that a Christology that one-sidedly emphasized the single subject of Christ's person and acts might lead to the "confusion" of God and a creature, might lose its sense of God's transcendence. Cyril, and the Alexandrian tradition since Athanasius, on the other hand, while also aware of the otherness of God, were even more concerned to emphasize God's intimate presence in and to creation: this was in their view the paradox on which biblical faith turned. Cyril's fear was of losing a sense of the divine authorship of salvation. The Antiochenes saw God and creation as for now related synchronically, dialectically; the most interesting part of the narrative of salvation, for them, lay in the eschatological future, when the promise present in the Gospel, and in the symbolic "types" of the Church's liturgy, would come to fulfillment for humanity. Their Christology made room for a created

> order that possesses real autonomy, for real independence in human action; but the danger was of driving a wedge between God and the created order that would eventually make God remote from, even irrelevant to, everyday life. Cyril saw God's role in creation and redemption rather in diachronic, dramatic terms (see, e.g., *On the Creed*, 7–15); the turning point in the history of salvation lay already in the past, in the Word's taking on our human flesh and our human experiences to be his own. The fulfillment of the promise was available to the believer, in Jesus's gift of the Holy Spirit to the disciples, and through them to the Church; in the Church's unity, centered on the personal, substantial Eucharistic presence of Christ; in the incipient realization, even now, of our human participation in the life of God. Cyril's Christology took God's reality in Christ, and so in the life of the Christian disciple, with the utmost seriousness; the risk was that this reality might so overshadow ordinary, mundane reality—in Jesus and in our day-to-day religious life—that the Gospel might lose its credibility altogether and become a Gnostic myth.

Christology is always the affirmation of paradox. The theologians of both Antioch and Alexandria recognized that both sides of the paradox of Christ, as "Emmanuel," had to be maintained if the Gospel message of his coming was to be proclaimed fully. The fact that subtle differences in their terminology, their rhetorical emphasis, their imagery and argument concerning the person of Christ, were able to grow into different theological, exegetical, and spiritual traditions, and ultimately to lead to ruptures within the Christian body that still exist today, ought to remind us just how deep the paradox of his person runs, and how urgent it is for all of us still to engage it faithfully.

Suggested Reading

Grillmeier (1988); McInery (1987); Norris (1980).

Bibliography

Primary Sources

Diodorus Tarsensis (1980), *Commentarii in Psalmos* I, ed. J.-M. Olivier, Corpus Christianorum Series Graeca, vol. 6 (Turnhout: Brepols).

Driver, G. R., and L. Hodgson (trans.) (2002), *Nestorius: The Bazaar of Heracleides* (reprint, Eugene, OR: Wipf and Stock; previously printed by Oxford University Press, 1925).

Ettlinger, G. H. (trans. and ed.) (1975), *Eranistes (English and Greek Edition)* (Oxford: Oxford University Press).

Leontius of Byzantium, "Deprehensio et Triumphus super Nestorianos," in J.-P. Migne (ed.), *Patrologia Graeca*, vol. 86 (Paris: Migne), 1357B–1385B.

McGuckin, J. (trans.) (1995), *On the Unity of Christ* (Crestwood, NY: St. Vladimir's Seminary Press).

McInery, J. L. (trans.) (1987), *St. Cyril of Alexandria: Letters 1–50*, Fathers of the Church 76 (Washington, DC: Catholic University of America Press).

Mingana, A. (trans.) (1932), Theodore of Mopsuestia, *On the Nicene Creed*, Woodbrooke Studies 5 (Cambridge: W. Heffer & Sons).

Norris, R. A., Jr. (trans. and ed.) (1980), *The Christological Controversy* (Minneapolis: Fortress).

Pusey, P. E. (ed.) (1872), *Sancti patris nostri Cyrilli archiepiscopi Alexandrini in D. Joannis evangelium*, 3 vols. (Oxford: Clarendon Press).

Pusey, P. E. (trans.) (1881), *Scholia on the Incarnation* (London and Oxford: Parker and Rivingtons).

Schwartz, E. (ed.) (1927), *Acta Conciliorum Oecumenicorum* [ACO] (Berlin and Leipzig: De Gruyter).

Theodoret (1892), *Dialogues*, trans. B. Jackson, in P. Schaff and H. Wace (eds.), *Nicene and Post-Nicene Fathers* [*NPNF*] Series II, vol. 3 (Grand Rapids: Eerdmans; reprint, Peabody, MA: Hendrickson Publishers, 1995).

Secondary Sources

Abramowski, R. (1949), "Der theologische Nachlass des Diodor von Tarsus," *Zeitschrift für die neutestamentliche Wissenschaft* 42: 51–53.

Bergjan, S.-P. (1993), *Theodoret von Cyrus und der Neunizänismus* (Berlin: De Gruyter).

Chadwick, H. (1951), "Eucharist and Christology in the Nestorian Controversy," *Journal of Theological Studies* 2: 145–64.

Daley, B. E. (1991), *The Hope of the Early Church: A Handbook of Patristic Eschatology* (Cambridge: Cambridge University Press).

Dewart, J. M. (1971), *The Theology of Grace of Theodore of Mopsuestia* (Washington, DC: Catholic University of America Press).

Gebremedhin, E. (1977), *Life-giving Blessing: An Inquiry into the Eucharistic Doctrine of Cyril of Alexandria* (Uppsala: Uppsala University Press).

Greer, R. A. (1966), "The Antiochene Christology of Diodore of Tarsus," *Journal of Theological Studies* 17: 327–41.

Greer, R. A. (1990), "The Man from Heaven: Paul's Last Adam and Apollinaris' Christ," in W. S. Babcock (ed.), *Paul and the Legacies of Paul* (Dallas: Southern Methodist University Press), 165–82.

Grillmeier, A. (1988), *Christ in Christian Tradition: From the Apostolic Age to Chalcedon (451)*, 2nd ed. (Louisville: Westminster/John Knox).

Hallman, J. M. (1991), *The Descent of God: Divine Suffering in History and Theology* (Minneapolis: Fortress).

Koch, G. (1965), *Die Heilsverwirklichung bei Theodor von Mopsuestia*, Münchener theologische Studien 31 (Munich: Max Hueber Verlag).

Koch, G. (1974), *Strukturen und Geschichte des Heils in der Theologie des Theodoret von Kyros. Eine dogmen- und theologiegeschichtliche Untersuchung*, Frankfurter theologische Studien 17 (Frankfurt: Knecht Verlag).

McGuckin, J. (1994), *St. Cyril of Alexandria: The Christological Controversy* (Leiden: Brill).

O'Keefe, J. J. (1997), "Impassible Suffering? Divine Passion and Fifth-Century Christology," *Theological Studies* 58: 39–60.

Russell, N. (2000), *Cyril of Alexandria* (London: Routledge).

Smith, J. W. (2002), "'Suffering Impassibly': Christ's Passion in Cyril of Alexandria's Soteriology," *Pro Ecclesia* 11: 463–83.

Wessel, S. (2004), *Cyril of Alexandria and the Nestorian Controversy: The Making of a Saint and a Heretic* (Oxford: Oxford University Press).

Wickham, L. R. (1983), *Cyril of Alexandria: Select Letters* (Oxford: Clarendon Press).

Young, F. M. (2002), *Biblical Exegesis and the Formation of Christian Culture* (Grand Rapids: Baker).

PART 2

Cappadocian Christology and the Apollinarian Challenge

6 Divine Transcendence and Human Transformation

Gregory of Nyssa's Anti-Apollinarian Christology

It is something of a commonplace among historians of early Christian doctrine to say that Gregory of Nyssa's portrait of the person of Christ is both puzzling and unsatisfactory. Puzzling, because it does not easily fit into the taxonomy of fifth-century controversy, or take a clear position within the categories of nature and person—οὐσία and φύσις, ὑπόστασις and πρόσωπον—which Gregory himself helped define for the Trinitarian mystery, and which were to be canonized for Christology during the debate around Chalcedon. Unsatisfactory, because Gregory seems—sometimes even in the same sentence—to combine the features of both a fundamentally unitive and a fundamentally divisive Christology, the specters of Nestorianism and Eutychianism, in a single rather unsophisticated vision. Tixeront, writing early this century, speaks for many since his time when he writes:

> In several passages [Gregory] . . . seems to distinguish two persons in Jesus: the man, in the Savior, is a tabernacle where the Word dwells; the divinity is in Him who suffers (*Contra Eunomium* III, 3, 51 [GNO II/2 (Leiden, 1960), p. 126]; *ibid.* 62 (130); *Antirrheticus adversus Apollinarium* 54 (GNO III/I [Leiden, 1958) 222f.]). However, the contrary tendency—the Monophysite tendency—is more striking and at times makes us feel somewhat uneasy.[1]

1. J. Tixeront, *Histoire des dogmes dans l'antiquité chrétienne* II (Paris, 1912), p. 128 (Eng. trans.: *History of Dogmas* II [St. Louis, 1914], p. 127). Here, as elsewhere in this paper, I have

This essay was originally published in *Studia Patristica* 32 (1997), pp. 87–95, and is reprinted here by kind permission.

Tixeront goes on to explain that this uneasiness is mainly inspired by Gregory's frequent use of the terminology of *mixture* to describe the relation of the divine and the human in Christ, and by his insistence that the humanity of Jesus was gradually transformed by the dominant power of the divine nature, so that in the end—like a drop of vinegar in a boundless ocean—it is virtually unrecognizable, swallowed up in the greatness of God.[2] For Tixeront, such conflicting tendencies are typical of the "obscurities" of fourth-century Greek Christological language, which had still not reached the level of professional precision needed to "bring the Christological problem to a perfectly satisfactory and definite solution"—a consummation, presumably, that in his view would begin with Leo's *Tome*, and reach its full development in Western scholasticism.[3]

It is my contention here that if one considers Gregory of Nyssa's theological portrait of Christ in its own terms—within the characteristic features of his thought and style, and within the context of the controversies that exercised him in his own day—one will find it remarkably powerful and also remarkably consistent, both in itself and with the rest of his thought on God, creation, and the mystery of salvation. Gregory never treats of the person and being of Christ in a single, thematically focused treatise, comparable to

cited Gregory of Nyssa's works by referring to the critical edition, *Gregorii Nysseni Opera* (GNO) (Leiden, 1958–).

2. Ibid.; Tixeront cites *C. Eun.* 3.3.34 (GNO 2/2, 119), 44 (123), 63 (130), 67 (131); *Antirrh.* 42 (GNO 3/1, 201). Tixeront might also have cited, as evidence for Gregory's paradoxical Christological language, a passage in *Antirrhētikos* 48, in which Gregory is discussing Apollinarius's tendency to speak of Christ, the "heavenly man," as composed of the three irreducible elements of body, soul, and spirit. "To some degree," Gregory writes, "we do not disagree with him; for in saying that all the elements comprising our nature are also found in that man, one would not be wrong. 'But the heavenly man, too,' he says of the Lord, 'is also a life-giving spirit.' This, too, we accept. . . . For the one mingled with the heavenly man, who transformed his earthly element through blending it with what is superior to it, is no longer called earthly but heavenly." For an interpretation stressing rather the similarity of Gregory's Christology to that of the Antiochene school, see J. N. D. Kelly, *Early Christian Doctrines* (5th ed.: San Francisco, 1976), pp. 298–300.

3. Ibid., p. 130 (Eng. trans. 129f.); cf. 126 (Eng. trans. 126): "The terminology of our authors [in the fourth century] was not sufficiently accurate, nor their conception of the doctrine sufficiently precise, to enable them to bring to a successful issue that work which was to be the work, not of mere witnesses of the tradition, but of professional and well-trained theologians, working on the data of tradition." For a more nuanced judgment on Gregory's Christology, which nevertheless still judges it confused and inadequate, precisely in judging it by Chalcedonian standards, see A. Grillmeier, *Christ in Christian Tradition* 1 (London and Oxford, 1975), pp. 371f., 376.

his *opuscula* on the Trinity; most of his Christological writing appears either in a polemical context—in works against Eunomian Arianism or the "new" heresy of the Apollinarians—or in works dealing with the interior, spiritual fulfillment of the individual, such as *On Perfection* or the *Commentary on the Song of Songs*. Surprisingly, perhaps, he rarely uses the vocabulary he and his fellow Cappadocians had so carefully honed for Trinitarian discussions to express what is one and what is manifold in Christ, but speaks instead in a variety of scriptural and philosophical images which were richly suggestive for him, but which were used for different purposes by both sides of the Christological conflicts a half-century later.

Perhaps the simplest way to characterize what is distinctive in Gregory's Christology in a brief paper such as this is to consider the main lines of the conception of Christ's person and work that he developed in controversy with the Apollinarians, a group he charged with being even more wrong-headed and dangerous than Eunomius and the later Arians.[4] Gregory's first work directed against this ambitious and theologically creative new ecclesiastical party was probably his letter addressed to Theophilus, bishop of Alexandria, shortly after the latter's election in 385. In it, Gregory asks for the help of Theophilus and his clergy in resisting the missionary activities of the Apollinarians. Their position, he says somewhat over-simply, is to "represent the Word and creator of the ages, the Son of Man, as fleshly, and divinity of the Son as mortal"—a summary of Apollinarian Christology that also characterizes his interpretation of it in the longer *Antirrhētikos*.[5] But his main effort in this brief letter is to refute the main Apollinarian charge against him and his colleagues: that by insisting on the completeness of Jesus's humanity, including a human consciousness or νοῦς, they are teaching "two Sons . . . , one who is so by nature, the other who has become so later by appointment."[6]

In reply, Gregory presents the Incarnation of the Word as the culmination of the theophanies of sacred history—all acts of self-revelation by a single divine Son. Since the previous appearances of the Son had not had the desired effect of communicating the fullness of the divine reality for the healing of a fallen, ever-more-fleshly humanity, "he emptied himself, so that nature might receive as much of him as it could hold."[7] As in the treatise

4. *Antirrh.* 44 (GNO 3/1, 205.21–206.9).

5. *Ad Theophilum adversus Apollinaristas* (GNO 3/1, 120.14f). For this same interpretation of Apollinarian Christology in Gregory's contemporaries, see below, n. 22.

6. Ibid. (120.17f.).

7. Ibid. (123.7–14).

On Perfection, where human salvation and fulfillment are conceived as the process of coming to be like Christ, sharing all his moral and spiritual characteristics, through a combination of intimate, contemplative knowledge and disciplined imitation,[8] Gregory assumes here that the saving process begins in the revelation of the glory of God, and that the Son has achieved this in a new and unparalleled way in his life, death and resurrection, by the moral and physical transformation of weak human flesh. The real news of the Gospel, Gregory suggests here, is that the Word, who remains transcendent and unchanging, has taken on human nature in the man Jesus and made it his own, so that "everything that was weak and perishable in our nature, mingled with the Godhead, has become that which the Godhead is."[9]

The point of the Incarnation, in other words, is that the human nature of Jesus, as the "first fruits" of a redeemed humanity, should gradually lose the distinguishing characteristics (ἰδιώματα) of our fallen race—corruptibility, mortality, the capacity to change for the worse—and take on the characteristics of the divine nature, "absorbed by the omnipotent divinity like a drop of vinegar mingled in the boundless sea."[10] Gregory clearly has in mind the manifestations of the risen Lord, who has passed through the trials of weakness and death and has received, in and for his humanity, "the name above every name" (Phil 2.9), his own eternal titles of "Lord" and "Christ" (Acts 2:36).[11]

> For a duality of Sons might consistently be presumed, if a nature of a different kind could be recognized by its own proper signs within the ineffable

8. GNO 8/1, 173–214, esp. 205.22–206.14.

9. Ibid. (126.10f.).

10. Ibid. (126.19f.).

11. Ibid. (127.12f.). These two texts are part of a small group of New Testament passages Gregory repeatedly uses, throughout his writings, to construct his theory of the continuing identity of the Word within the saving transformation of the human being he assumed. Besides the full text of the "hymn to Christ" in Phil 2:5–11, they include John 20:17 (the risen Christ telling his disciples, through Mary Magdalene, "I am ascending to my Father and to your Father, to my God and to your God"); the parable of the lost sheep (Luke 15:4f.), in which humanity is seen as the strayed sheep "taken up" by the word; and the combination of the images of humanity as "mass" of dough (Matt 13:33) and the risen Christ as the "first-fruits" of a new humanity (1 Cor 15:23). See the thorough discussions of Lucas F. Mateo-Seco, *Estudios sobre la cristologìa de san Gregorio de Nisa* (Pamplona, 1978), esp. pp. 30–74 (Phil 2:5–11); and Reinhard M. Hübner, *Die Einheit des Leibes Christi bei Gregor von Nyssa. Untersuchungen zum Ursprung der "physischen" Erlösungslehre* (Leiden, 1974), esp. pp. 104–45.

> Godhead of the Son. . . . But since all the traits we recognize in the mortal [Jesus] we see transformed by the characteristics of the Godhead, and no difference of any kind can be perceived—for whatever one sees in the Son is Godhead: wisdom, power, holiness, freedom from passivity—how could one divide what is single . . . ?[12]

There is no danger, in other words, of the kind of Christological dualism the Apollinarians fear, provided one sees that the man Jesus, "taken up" by the eternal Son, is constantly being transformed in role and character to reveal the Son ever more fully in himself.

This same approach to the relationship of Christ's humanity and divinity underlies the more elaborate argument in Gregory's longer anti-Apollinarian polemic, the *Antirrhētikos.* This tract, which seems to have been written somewhat later than the *Letter to Theophilus,*[13] is a phrase-by-phrase analysis and rebuttal of Apollinarius's *Demonstration of the Divine Incarnation in Human Likeness (Apodeixis),* a work for which Gregory's quotations are now virtually our only source. Here Apollinarius apparently accuses his opponents of holding that Christ is simply a divinely inspired human being, an ἄνθρωπος ἔνθεος,[14] and that the crucified savior had "nothing divine in his own nature."[15] By rejecting his party's conception of Christ as the divine mind enfleshed in an animated body, Apollinarius argues, his opponents' only alternative is to conceive of him as a graced human being:

12. Ibid. (126.21–127.9).

13. So G. May, "Die Chronologie des Lebens und des Werkes Gregors von Nyssa," in M. Harl (ed), *Ecriture et culture philosophique dans la pensée de Grégoire de Nysse* (Colloquium of Chevetogne, 1969) (Leiden, 1971), p. 61, following H. Lietzmann, *Apollinaris von Laodicea und seine Schule I* (Tübingen, 1904), p. 83f. and E. Mühlenberg, *Apollinaris von Laodicea* (Göttingen, 1969), p. 90. The main arguments for putting the *Antirrhētikos* later than the letter to Theophilus are the letter's total lack of reference to the arguments of the longer work and the fact that Gregory of Nazianzus does not seem to have known about Apollinarius's *Apodeixis* before the mid-380s. J. Daniélou, "La chronologie des œuvres de Grégoire de Nysse," *Studia Patristica* 7 (TU 92: Berlin, 1966), p. 163f., suggests the *Antirrhētikos* was composed in the winter of 382–383, on the basis of the work's treatment of the relation of the Logos to Jesus's soul and body in death; in this dating he follows J. Lebourlier, "A propos de l'état du Christ dans la mort, II," *Revue des sciences philosophiques et théologiques* 47 (1963), p. 180, and is joined by Hübner, *Die Einheit des Leibes Christi*, p. 135f., n. 166. The chronology of Gregory's works is a notoriously speculative business.

14. *Antirrh.* 4 (GNO 3/1, 135.17–24); cf. 25 (169.21ff.).

15. Ibid., 27 (172.16ff.).

> If the Lord is not enfleshed mind [νοῦς ἔνσαρκος], he must be wisdom enlightening the mind of a human being; but that is in all people. And if that is so, then the coming of Christ was not the presence of God [ἐπιδημία θεοῦ], but the birth of a human being.[16]

For Apollinarius, the elements of the Savior can only be the eternal divine Mind or Spirit and the animal body of "flesh" he assumed: "He is God in virtue of the enfleshed Spirit, and human in virtue of the flesh taken on by God."[17] And since his fleshly component is not "foreign" to the divine Spirit—as it would be if it "belonged" to a human mind as part of a complete human being[18]—it is accurate, in Apollinarius's view, even to say that "Christ the human being" is heavenly and eternal:

> The human being Christ pre-exists, not in that the Spirit—that is, God—is another alongside him, but in that the Lord in the nature of the God-man is the Divine Spirit.[19]

When one looks beneath the conventional rhetorical surface of his response, Gregory's critique of Apollinarius is based on a distinctively different understanding of both the being of God and the nature of salvation.

> "Who does not know," he asks scornfully, "that the God revealed to us in flesh, according to the word of pious tradition, is immaterial and invisible and uncompounded, and that he was and is infinite and uncircumscribed, existing everywhere and penetrating all creation, but that he has been seen, as far as appearance goes, in human circumscription?"[20]

16. Ibid., 36 (188.23–27).

17. Ibid., 7 (140.3ff.). It is interesting to note the frequent echoes, in the passages of Apollinarius's *Apodeixis* quoted by Gregory, of the "Spirit-Christology" of the second and third centuries: drawing on 1 Cor 15:45 ("the second Adam is a life-giving spirit"), Gregory notes, Apollinarius "says he is called '(the man) from heaven' for this reason, that the heavenly spirit is made flesh in him" (ibid., 12 [146.27f.]). See also Apollinarius's epistle to Jovianus 1 (Lietzmann 250.7, 251.15). On "Spirit-Christology" in the patristic period, see M. Simonetti, "Note di cristologia pneumatica," *Augustinianum* 12 (1972), pp. 210–32; G. W. H. Lampe, *God as Spirit* (Oxford, 1977), pp. 210–27.

18. Ibid., 22 (162.17–19).

19. Ibid., 12 (147.12ff.).

20. Ibid., 18 (156.14–18).

Apollinarius's conception of Christ not only limits the Logos by making him the rational soul or "spirit" guiding a human body;[21] it implies that this one governing soul, at least, is eternal, σύμφυλον θεοῦ.[22] Secondly, Gregory insists, to replace the human mind of Christ with the eternal Logos is to make his humanity simply into a lower form of animal life, a "beast of burden";[23] to have a right to be called human and to be the revealer of human ἀρετή, Christ needed a human mind, human needs and limitations, and especially a human will.[24]

This last point is of central importance for Gregory's own understanding of the person and work of Christ. The message of Scripture about

21. Ibid. (156.26–157.9); 35 (185.7–10). Cf. 50 (227.23–26): "If human nature receives either a mind like ours or God in place of a mind, these two must be of the same magnitude and status as each other—if indeed the place where mind is contained is also the place where divinity is received."

22. Ibid., 28 (174.14–19). It is in the context of his insistence that the identification of the divine Logos with a νοῦς capable of governing a human composite is a violation of the divine transcendence that one should probably understand Gregory's oft-repeated point—exaggerated, surely, for rhetorical purposes—that Apollinarius holds even the "flesh" of Christ to be eternal (e.g., 13 [147.16–148.4]; 15 [150.10ff.]; 18 [155.25–156.1]). Apollinarius himself seems rather to have suggested simply that the heavenly origin of the Word implies the heavenly character of the whole Christ (see *De unione* 1f. [Lietzmann 185f.]), stressing the biblical image of Christ as "the Son of Man who came down from heaven" (*Antirrh.* 6 [138.18–21, 25–29]), and thus to have asserted no more than that the *whole* Christ, as θεὸς ἔνσαρκος, entered into the world through the Virgin's womb as through a "channel" (ibid., 24 [166.14–28]). In other places, Apollinarius insists that the Word took the "created garment" of his flesh from the Virgin, even though it was divinely generated in her and was never a distinct organism apart from the Word: see, e.g., *De unione* 6, 9, 13 (Leitzmann 187f., 188f., 191). The Cappadocians, however, seem to have shared their contemporaries' sense that Apollinarius really held the very flesh of Christ pre-existed in heaven: see Athanasius, *Ep. to Epictetus* 2–9 (PG 26.1052C–1065B), a passage which seems to have the Apollinarians, among others, in mind but does not mention them by name; Basil of Caesarea, Ep. 261.2 (PG 32.969B13–972A1); Gregory Nazianzen, Ep. 101.16 (ed. P. Gallay, SC 208.42), 30 (ibid., 48); Ep. 202.10–13 (ibid., 90–92); cf. Ep. 102.14f. (ibid., 79), where Gregory suggests the Apollinarian Christ has only the appearance of human flesh.

23. *Antirrh.* 23 (165.9–28). Cf. Gregory of Nazianzus, Ep. 101.34f. (SC 208.51): "If [Jesus] is endowed with a soul, but not with a mind, how is he human? For a human being is not an animal without intelligence. Of necessity, the outward form and tabernacle would then be human, but the soul would be that of some horse or ox or some other unintelligent being; and this will be what is saved . . ."

24. Ibid., 31f. (179.8–182.5). In other passages, too, Apollinarius explicitly rejected the notion of two wills or operations in Christ: see, e.g., Frags. 108f., from *On the Incarnate Appearance of God* (Leitzmann 232f.); Frag. 117, from the *Syllogistic Treatise against Diodore [of Tarsus] to Heraclius* (Leitzmann 235f.).

Jesus, Gregory says, is that "the divine being, changeless and unvarying in essence, has come to be in a changeable and alterable nature, so that by his own unchangeability he might heal our tendency to change for the worse."[25] So it is essential for him to conceive of Christ the Savior as possessing all that is vulnerable and variable in our nature, including our mind, precisely so that all of what is natural and changeable in each of us may, beginning in Christ, be transformed and exalted.[26] The κένωσις of the Son, spoken of in Philippians 2:7, is not simply another revelation of the eternal God in our changeable world, Gregory argues, but the concrete act of God, at a definite point in our history, taking on a human being as something new, but thoroughly his own.[27] So Gregory insists quite simply that the eternal "Christ" and "Lord" in the course of time "took up a man"[28]—"not purely and simply a common man,"[29] since he was born by a divine mode of conception, yet certainly a man in the full sense;[30] and the salvation he has worked for all humanity is nothing less than to have transformed the passible, corruptible characteristics (ἰδιώματα) of that man into the divine characteristics of the Son, so that in his exaltation the man can now share the "name that is above every name"—the eternal, unnameable reality of God.[31] As a result, the believer always *knows* Jesus Christ in two ways, both as a human being and as God—"human in what is seen, God in what is known to the mind."[32]

25. Ibid., 2 (133.6–9).

26. Ibid., 5 (138.7–9): ". . . What is passible receives death, but what is beyond the reach of passion works freedom from passibility in that which is passible"; cf. 21 (160.6–161.5).

27. Ibid., 15 (151.10–21).

28. Gregory uses various forms of this expression: see, e.g., ibid., 7 (140.23–25: ὅλον συνάπτει τὸν ἄνθρωπον); 34 (184.1–15; ἀνθρώπου πρόσληψις); 38f. (193.6–18: ἀνάληψις and πρόσληψις); 49 (215.17–21: the very word πρόσληψις implies a difference in nature).

29. Ibid., 21 (160.3–11).

30. Ibid., 22 (203.16–29); 49f. (214.19–215.25).

31. Ibid., 21 (161.13–26): "And since the man in Christ was called by a name, in the usual way, according to what is consistent with humanity, through the mysterious instruction given to the Virgin by Gabriel, and that human element was named Jesus, as we are told, but (since) the divine nature is not graspable in a name, the two have become one by mixture [διὰ τῆς ἀνακράσεως]. Therefore God is called by a human name, for 'at the name of Jesus every knee shall bow,' and the man comes to be beyond all naming—something characteristic of godhead, which cannot be signified by any verbal sign—so that as the exalted being comes to exist in what is lowly, the lowly takes on exalted characteristics; for just as the godhead receives the name of the man, so that which is joined, from lowliness, to the godhead comes to be above every name."

32. Ibid., 37 (191.24ff.); cf. 27 (173.10–14).

Towards the end of the *Antirrhētikos*, in a passage of striking clarity, Gregory sums up the relationship between the eternal Son—who is himself always called "Christ" and "Lord" because he is always anointed by the Spirit and ruler over all creation[33]—and the human being he has assumed:

> We say that he is always the Christ, both before the economy and after it; but he is human neither before it nor after it, but only during the time of the economy. For the flesh, in its own proper characteristics [ἰδιώματα] did not exist before the Virgin, nor after his ascent into heaven. "For even if we once knew Christ according to the flesh," Scripture says, "we no longer know him thus" (2 Cor 5:16). . . . But since humanity is changeable, but the divine unchangeable, the divinity is not moveable by alteration, either towards the better or towards the worse (since it does not receive what is worse and there is nothing which is better); but the human nature in Christ does possess the ability to change for the better, being transformed from corruption to incorruption, from what is perishable to what is imperishable, from what is short-lived to what is eternal, from what is bodily and of perceptible shape to what is bodiless and without shape.[34]

The importance of this transformation in Christ, for Gregory, is of course that it marks the beginning of the transformation in which each of us is called to participate: a transformation of the human into the divine which does not seem to involve, in his view, an annihilation of human nature, so much as the suffusion of all its naturally changeable, "fleshly" characteristics with the stability and luminous vigor of God. Both ἕνωσις, after all, and the various terms for "mixture" which Gregory habitually employs for the union in Christ (μίξις, κρᾶσις, and their cognates) mean in his vocabulary the close unification of elements that still remain naturally or numerically *different*: a relationship (σχέσις) rather than a total absorption.[35] Unlike Aristotle, who uses the image of a drop of wine in ten thousand gallons of water as an example of the kind of mixture that annihilates the smaller element altogether,[36] Gregory seems to see even the lesser, human partner in the "mixture" of the

33. Ibid., 52f. (220.2–221.20).

34. Ibid., 53 (222.25–223.10).

35. See esp. ibid., 22 (161.26f.); 34 (184.27–30). For a thorough and penetrating analysis of Gregory's terminology for the union of natures in Christ, including its background in classical philosophy, see J.-R. Bouchet, "Le vocabulaire de l'union et du rapport des natures chez saint Grégoire de Nysse," *Revue thomiste* 68 (1968), pp. 533–82.

36. *De gen. et corr.* 1.10 (328a27–29).

Incarnation—though absorbed now like the proverbial drop of vinegar in the ocean of divinity and no longer perceptible, through any of its own peculiar qualities, to mind or sense[37]—as continuing to exist and even to undergo further change. And as the "first-fruits" of a new humanity, endlessly undergoing transformation into the qualities that reflect the stable glory of God, the risen and transfigured human Christ is the one means by which the rest of the race can also participate in that same process of "divinization": not, be it said, through some connection conceived of in purely physical terms, or through sharing in some Platonic universal,[38] but through human involvement with Christ in salvation history, especially through faith, baptism, and a disciple's imitation.[39]

Gregory's anti-Apollinarian Christology, as we have briefly sketched it out here, is certainly strange, even a little shocking, by post-Chalcedonian standards. The reason, I would suggest, is first of all terminological. The language of φύσις and ὑπόστασις, οὐσία and πρόσωπον, which were to frame the debates of the fifth and sixth centuries and which had been given stable definition for Trinitarian discussion by the Cappadocians themselves, is strikingly absent, as I have already said, from Gregory's discussion of Christ; both ὑπόστασις and πρόσωπον, in fact, when they are used in these works, are applied to the man Jesus alone, not to the incarnate Christ.[40] The reason, presumably, is that Gregory is afraid to support the Apollinarian conception of the man Jesus as ἓν πρόσωπον and ἓν ζῶον with the eternal hypostasis of the Son; such terms are too multivalent within the theological realm of discourse, too analogous, to be used safely in the same context of both the "persons" of the Trinity and a human person, of both the "substance" of God and our human reality.

37. *Antirrh.* 42 (GNO 3/1, 201.10–16); cf. the passages cited in nn. 2 and 10 above, and *C. Eun.* 3.3.68f. (GNO 2/2, 133.1–4).

38. For a careful discussion and refutation of the overly literal interpretation of Gregory's idea of human solidarity and "physical" redemption found in many histories of dogma, see especially Hübner, *Die Einheit des Leibes Christi* (above, n. 11), esp. pp. 1–25 and 95–198; cf. Mateo-Seco, *Estudios* (above, n. 11), p. 53; Bouchet, "Le vocabulaire" (above, n. 35), p. 538; and A. Lieske, "Zur Theologie der Christusmystik Gregors von Nyssa," *Scholastik* 14 (1939), p. 510.

39. So, e.g., *Antirrh.* 55 (GNO 3/1, 226.17–227.9: baptism as imitation of Jesus's saving and voluntary death); cf. *On Perfection* (GNO 8/1, esp. 210.4–214.6: imitation of Christ's ἀρεταί).

40. *Antirrh.* 54 (GNO 3/1, 223.11–224.5); *C. Eun.* 3.3.42 (122.25–29). For a thorough discussion of the Christology of Gregory's works *Contra Eunomium*, see now B. Pottier, *Dieu et le Christ selon Grégoire de Nysse* (Brussels, 1994).

In any case, Gregory's Christology differs from that of the fifth-century debates also in that his main interest is *not* to identify precisely what is one and what is manifold in Christ, but to explore the conditions of possibility for our sharing in his triumph over death and human corruption. Not only is the modern category of "person," as autonomous and reflective subject, far from his mind, as it was from that of all the Greek Fathers; his real interest is in our salvation: in what happens to human *nature*—to τὸ ἀνθρώπινον, the common reality all of us concretely share—when it is brought into contact with τὸ θεῖον, the transcendent reality of God, through the one historical individual who is, in an unconfused and inseparable way, both God and a human being. Nonetheless, it is clear that for him, as for the classical Christology of the fifth, sixth, and seventh centuries, the Mystery of Christ is also one of unconfused and undivided union: God the Word making a complete human being his own instrument of revelation and healing for the world, while at the same time enabling that human being to be, most perfectly, what all humans are created to be—fully itself, and fully, though always increasingly, a participant in the life and even the qualities of God.

In a recent, thoughtful article comparing Origen's *De principiis* and Gregory's *Catechetical Oration* as synthetic constructions of Christian theology, Anthony Meredith remarks: "By and large, Origen's thought is largely theocentric, Gregory's is Christocentric."[41] The reason, Meredith suggests, is Gregory's preoccupation with Apollinarianism. While I would certainly agree on the central place given to the person and work of Christ in all Gregory's thought, I suggest that he is not concerned with *Christology* in the same sense or to the same degree as Nestorius, Cyril, Theodoret, and Leo would be, let alone Severus, Leontius of Byzantium, and Maximus Confessor. He is concerned above all with Jesus Christ as the man in whom and through whom the infinite and saving reality of God touches us all: with preserving the transcendence of the God who is present in him, and with emphasizing the transformation of that human reality which God, in the man Jesus, has made his own.

41. Anthony Meredith, "Origen's *De Principiis* and Gregory of Nyssa's *Oratio Catechetica*," *Heythrop Journal* 36 (1995), p. 8.

7 "Heavenly Man" and "Eternal Christ"

Apollinarius and Gregory of Nyssa on the Personal Identity of the Savior

Reading the documents of the controversy between Apollinarius of Laodicea and the Cappadocian Fathers over the identity and internal structure of Christ's person is, for someone schooled in the standard modern accounts of early Christology, likely to puzzle at first, rather than to enlighten. The fragments and the whole treatises of Apollinarius that still exist, on the one hand, offer a portrait of Christ that is less bizarre, less classically docetic in its representation of his humanity, more coherent and persuasive in strictly theological terms, than modern *Dogmengeschichte* may lead us to suppose. Kelly McCarthy Spoerl has amply demonstrated, in a series of articles published since 1993, that Apollinarius's conception of Christ is inseparably connected to his unwaveringly Nicene, Athanasian approach to the being of God, as well as to his controlling desire to resist the modalism, embodied in the specter of Marcellus of Ancyra, that haunted most mid-fourth-century Greek theologians.[1] Rowan Greer has pointed out similarities between Apollinarius's understanding of Christ and that of Irenaeus, and has shown the roots of both to lie in Paul's presentation of Christ as "the human being from heaven," in the words of 1 Corinthians 15:47f.: "Both [Irenaeus and Apollinarius] read the same texts," Greer writes, "both saw Christ as the new Adam; both treated the new humanity as transcendent of the old."[2] In the view of

1. See Kelly McCarthy Spoerl, "Apollinarius and the Response to Early Arian Christology," *SP* 26 (1993): 421–27; "Apollinarian Christology and the Anti-Marcellan Tradition," *JTS* n.s. 43 (1994): 545–68; "The Liturgical Argument in Apollinarius: Help and Hindrance on the Way to Orthodoxy," *HTR* (1998): 127–52.

2. Rowan A. Greer, "The Man from Heaven: Paul's Last Adam and Apollinarius's

both Spoerl and Greer, Apollinarius's Christology may have carried within it anthropological and theological assumptions that would prove disastrous for an understanding of Christ's solidarity with the rest of humanity, but its scriptural arguments and fundamental theological concerns were themselves neither strange nor particularly extreme, in the context of late fourth-century Greek debate over the status and work of the Savior.

Gregory of Nyssa's treatment of the person of Christ, on the other hand, is also difficult to fit into what modern writers usually take—with the Chalcedonian formula as their norm—as the terms of classical patristic Christology, even in their early stages of evolution. Gregory rarely speaks of one hypostasis or two natures in Christ, for instance;[3] he generally avoids using the title *Theotokos* for Mary;[4] prefers to speak of the human reality of Christ as a human being, an ἄνθρωπος, who is "taken up" or "appropriated" by God the Logos;[5] and even identifies two πρόσωπα or speaking roles among the biblical sayings of Christ;[6] yet, like Gregory Nazianzen, he also frequently

Christ," in *Paul and the Legacies of Paul*, ed. William S. Babcock (Dallas: Southern Methodist University Press, 1990), 165–82, here 165–66.

3. Although Gregory follows Basil and Gregory Nazianzen in speaking of Father, Son, and Holy Spirit as hypostases within the single substance (οὐσία) of God, he rarely uses this same vocabulary for Christ as a single subject, even though he strongly affirms that the Logos and the human Jesus are not two agents (e.g., *Or. cat.* 79.3–12), and strongly denies the charge of proposing "two Sons" (e.g., *C. Eun.* 3.3.57–69; *Ad Theophilum* [GNO 3.1:120.16–121.2; 126.14–127.10; *Antirrhētikos adv. Apollinarium* 39 [GNO 3.1:194.3–27]). For a thoughtful and balanced survey of the main features of Gregory's Christology, still one of the most useful despite its age, see Karl Holl, *Amphilochius von Ikonium in seinem Verhältnis zu den grossen Kappadoziern* (Tübingen: J. C. B. Mohr, 1904; repr. Darmstadt: Wissenschaftliche Buchgesellschaft, 1969), esp. 220–35. A more general survey of Gregory's Christology, in the context of his understanding of salvation, is Jaroslav Pelikan, "The Mortality of God and the Immortality of Man in Gregory of Nyssa," in *The Scope of Grace: Essays on Nature and Grace in Honor of Joseph Sittler*, ed. Philip J. Hefner (Philadelphia: Fortress, 1964), 79–97. On Gregory's christological terminology, see Jean-René Bouchet, "Le vocabulaire de l'union et du rapport des natures chez saint Grégoire de Nysse," *Revue Thomiste* 68 (1968): 533–82.

4. An exceptional passage is *Ep.* 3.24, where Gregory insists, apparently against Apollinarian charges, that it is not *his* party who call "the holy Virgin, the Theotokos, also ἀνθρωποτόκος, as we hear that some of their party readily do." Gregory's other uses of the Theotokos-title are in his early treatise *De virginitate* 14.1.24 and 19.6.

5. See, for instance, *Antirrh.* 1197C (GNO 3.1:184.5–15): "What, after all, is the difference between 'union with flesh' and 'the assumption of a human being'?"; also 1200A (GNO 3.1:184.20, 27, 30), 1212A (GNO 3.1:193.11) [ἀνθρώπου πρόσληψις]; *C. Eun.* 3.4 (GNO 2:139.17; 140.15); *Antirrh.* 1212A (GNO 3.1:193.11) (ἀνάληψις); *C. Eun.* 3.10 (GNO 2:294.8); *Ep.* 3.15 (προσοικειοῦσθαι). For language of "indwelling," see also *Ep.* 3.19–20.

6. See, for example, *Ref. c. Eun.* 83 (GNO 2:346.14–16: the speaker in biblical passages);

uses the language of "mixture" to describe the union of divine and human,[7] and his portrait of the risen, glorified Christ, in at least three oft-cited passages, represents his entire humanity as swallowed up in the eternal reality of the glorified Son, like a drop of vinegar lost in a boundless ocean.[8] So twentieth-century historians of doctrine have tended to ask themselves anxiously whether Gregory is basically Antiochene or basically Alexandrian in his christological orientation,[9] or whether—if we assume those *are* the unchanging alternatives—his Christology is not simply immature, confused, and inconsistent.[10] As an opponent of Apollinarius, Gregory seems too similar to the enemy, at some moments, and too much like Diodore of Tarsus, at others, to carry the torch for classical orthodoxy.

I have already attempted, in an earlier essay, to argue that once one abandons the attempt to measure Gregory's Christology by the conceptual or methodological norms of Chalcedon, or of the fifth-century controversies that led up to it, it is easier to see that Christology as forming a consistent and powerfully convincing whole with the rest of his thought about God and human salvation.[11] The very difficulty of fitting his Christology into either of the usual stereotypes of fifth-century Antiochene and Alexandrian thought

---

Antirrh. 1128A (GNO 3.1:133.12; 1181C (GNO 3.1:173.13) [in both of which τὸ δουλικὸν πρόσωπον is equated with "the form of a servant"].

7. Gregory uses various forms of μίξις: e.g., *C. Eun.* 3.4 (GNO 2:158.26); *Antirrh.* (GNO 3.1:217.20); *Cat. or.* (GNO 3.4:48.4; 79.6); various forms of κρᾶσις: *C. Eun.* 3.1.45 (GNO 2:19.12); 3.4 (GNO 2:139.27); *Antirrh.* (GNO 3.1:161.18; 225.12); *Ep.* 3.15.

8. *Ad Theoph.* (GNO 3.1:126.17–21); *Antirrh.* (GNO 3.1:201.10–17); *C. Eun.* 3.3.68 (GNO 2.125.28–126.3). For an interpretation of this image against the background of earlier Greek theories of fluid mixture and pharmacology, see Jean-René Bouchet, "À propos d'une image christologique de Grégoire de Nysse," *Revue Thomiste* 67 (1967): 584–88.

9. See, for example, Holl, *Amphilochius von Ikonium*, 235 (closer to Antiochene position); J. Tixeront, *Histoire des dogmes dans l'antiquité chrétienne* (Paris: Lecoffre, 1912), 2:128 (tendencies of both schools, more often "monophysite"); J. N. D. Kelly, *Early Christian Doctrines* (San Francisco: Harper and Row, 1976), 298–300 (closer to Antiochene). Elias Moutsoulas has argued that Gregory and the other Cappadocians stand somewhere between the main aims and emphases of Alexandria and Antioch, even though some of Gregory's "bolder images" have an obviously "monophysite" color: Παρατηρήσεις ἐπὶ τῆς Χριστολογίας Γρηγορίου τοῦ Νύσσης, Θεολογία, 40 (1969): 252, citing Moutsoulas's earlier work, Ἡ σάρκωσις τοῦ Λόγου καὶ ἡ θέωσις τοῦ ἀνθρώπου κατὰ τὴν διδασκαλίαν Γρηγορίου τοῦ Νύσσης (Athens: [Organismos Panepistemiou Athenon,] 1965), 219.

10. See, for example, Tixeront, *Histoire des dogmes*, 130; also Aloys Grillmeier, *Christ in Christian Tradition* (London: Mowbray, 1975), 1:371f., 376.

11. See "Divine Transcendence and Human Transformation: Gregory of Nyssa's Anti-Apollinarian Christology," *SP* 32 (Leuven: Peters, 1997), 87–95.

seems, in fact, to reinforce a growing sense of unease in contemporary scholarship with the relevance of these hoary categories.[12] My purpose here, however, is rather to ask, in the context of the controversy between the three great Cappadocians and Apollinarius and his followers, which apparently began in the late 360s and had reached epic proportions by the mid-380s, just what the real difference between them was: more specifically, to ask what there was in Apollinarius's own well-integrated and strongly Nicene understanding of the person of Christ that seemed so theologically dangerous to the bishop of Nyssa, and how Gregory's presentation of the Savior really differed from his.

On the surface, at least, they had much in common. Like all three Cappadocians, Apollinarius had been, all his adult life, an outspoken admirer of the great Athanasius, and a defender of the Nicene language of consubstantiality as the proper way to identify the godliness of the Son; he had been an equally determined opponent of the "economic modalism" of Marcellus of Ancyra, which seemed to imply a flattening-out of the real economy of salvation by making a personal incarnation of the Word, a personal presence of the Son in flesh, impossible.[13] With regard to the person of Christ, Apollinarius and Gregory of Nyssa—both formidable verbal artists—use astonishingly similar language in places to speak of what is unified and what is distinct in the Savior.[14] Both tend to use the simple term ἕνωσις as the most basic category for describing the unique composition of Christ as a union of two real and irreducibly distinct elements;[15] both speak of Jesus, the incarnate Word, as the "Lordly human being" (κυριακὸς ἄνθρωπος),[16] a "man" taken up or

12. See, for instance, John McGuckin's sharp criticism of this terminology in *St. Cyril of Alexandria: The Christological Controversy* (Leiden: Brill, 1994), 205.

13. For a thorough discussion of Apollinarius's trinitarian theology, see the three articles of Kelly McCarthy Spoerl mentioned in n. 1.

14. For Gregory of Nyssa's christological terminology, see Bouchet, "Le vocabulaire."

15. See Apollinarius, *Contra Diodorum*, frags. 140–42 (ed. H. Lietzmann, *Apollinaris von Laodicea und seine Schule* [Tübingen: J. C. B. Mohr, 1904], 241.3–26); frag. 147 (Lietzmann 246.20–28); frags. 160–61 (Lietzmann 254.5–26): it is the union of Jesus's flesh to the Word, not the nature of the flesh itself, that allows us to call his flesh divine. See also Gregory of Nyssa, *Antirrh.* (GNO 3.1:184.27–30): "union [of the Word] with flesh [σαρκὸς ἕνωσις]" means the same thing as "assumption of a human being [ἀνθρώπου πρόσληψις]"; *Or. cat.* (GNO 3.4:39.13–22); frag. of *Letter to the Monk Philip*, quoted in John of Damascus, *Contra Jacobitas* 112 (ed. B. Kotter, *Die Schriften des Johannes von Damaskos* [Berlin: De Gruyter, 1981], 4:149.3–6).

16. Gregory Nazianzen, *Ep.* 101.12 (SC 208:40), testifies to the characteristic use of this christological slogan by the Apollinarians. For a history of the use of this striking phrase, probably coined by Apollinarius but used by a variety of later writers with very different

dwelt in by the divine Logos,[17] yet both are willing to apply strict limits to the sense in which we can speak of even the visible Christ simply as "human" (ἄνθρωπος);[18] both affirm that "Christ" and "Lord" are proper titles of the eternal Son, and express his relationship, respectively, to his Father and to creation;[19] both speak of the human flesh of Christ as thoroughly divinized by its union with God the Word, as we shall see below—in Gregory's case, so much so that although Christ's humanity eternally remains, its fleshly characteristics and psychological and moral limitations are, for all practical purposes, abrogated by his ascent into glory.[20] Both Apollinarius and Gregory of Nyssa, too, presuppose a direct connection between our present moral struggle, our enduring lack of virtue, and the weakness and corruptibility of

---

approaches to the mystery of Christ, see Aloys Grillmeier, "Κυριακὸς ἄνθρωπος. Eine Studie zu einer christologischen Bezeichnung der Väterzeit," *Traditio* 33 (1979): 1–63 [= *Fragmente zur Christologie* (Freiburg: Herder, 1997), 152–214].

17. See Apollinarius's *Anakephalaiōsis*, beginning with a provocative chain of syllogisms designed to lead repeatedly to the conclusion, "Christ is not a human being [ἄνθρωπος]": Lietzmann, 242.24–243.28. The work then goes on, in the same syllogistic style, to prove that Christ is *not* "a human being in whom God dwells," but that he *is* "God and a human being [θεὸς καὶ ἄνθρωπος]" (244.6–16), and *not* simply, as we aspire to be through grace, "a human being joined to God [ἄνθρωπος θεῷ παραζευχθείς]" (245.30). Apollinarius's point, clearly, is not to deny altogether that Christ is a human individual, but to define just what kind of human he can be understood to be. Gregory of Nyssa, on the other hand, insists that while the Son is eternally "Christ" and "Lord," he can only be called "human" for the limited period of his life on earth—not before his conception in Mary's womb, nor after his ascension into glory: *Antirrh.* (GNO 3.1:222.25–29).

18. According to Gregory of Nyssa's *Antirrhetikos*, Apollinarius distinguished between an ἀνάληψις τοῦ νοῦ καὶ ὅλου ἀνθρώπου by the Word, which he rejected, and a πρόσληψις σαρκός, which he affirmed; Gregory considers this simply playing with words (GNO 3.1:193.6–18). Apollinarius also refers to Christ's humanity as "the human being from Mary": *Ep. ad Jovianum* (Lietzmann, 251.4–5); cf. the pseudo-Athanasian *Sermo maior de fide* 30 (ed. Eduard Schwartz, *Sitzungsberichte der bayerischen Akademie der Wissenschaften* 1924 [6]: 27; PG 26:1285A): this is generally thought to be a work of the Apollinarian school.

19. Gregory, in fact, defends himself at some length against Apollinarius's charge that he and his allies deny that Christ, as the Christ, is eternal: *Antirrh.* (GNO 3.1:219.14–223.10). Because "the glory before the ages surrounding God the only-begotten is understood to be the Holy Spirit," he can be called "Christ"—the one "anointed" by the Holy Spirit—simply in terms of his trinitarian relationships (GNO 3.1:222.15–21).

20. In debate with Apollinarius, Gregory is even willing to say, "He is always the Christ, both before the course of his earthly life [οἰκονομία] and after it; but he is human neither before it nor after it, but only during the time of his earthly life." He immediately qualifies this, however, by suggesting that after the ascension he is simply not a human being in "fleshly" terms: "For the human being did not exist before [conception in] the Virgin, nor is the flesh in its own proper characteristics after his ascent into heaven" (GNO 3.1:222.25–29).

our bodies.[21] And for both of them, the healing of our moral and physical corruptibility is only available through contact with the eternal, incorruptible Christ: a contact realized through faith in him, through careful imitation and ascetical self-discipline, and through the more physical encounter of the sacraments, especially the Eucharist.[22]

How, then, can we understand the intense, often bitter, opposition that evidently existed between Apollinarius and his followers and the Cappadocians and theirs, during the 370s and 380s? Some of it, clearly, was rooted in ecclesiastical and political issues. Apollinarius and Basil of Caesarea had been mutually admiring correspondents during the late 350s; but when Apollinarius began gathering his hard-line Nicene followers in western Syria into what resembled more and more a dissident church, and was—like Paulinus of Antioch—uncanonically ordained their bishop, possibly during Julian's reign, his relationship with Basil seems to have changed, despite the fact that Basil himself occasionally pursued the same uncanonical tactics himself as metropolitan of Caesarea.[23] During the late 370s, when Apollinarius was ordaining likeminded bishops for other cities, even his former supporters in Rome and Alexandria seem to have broken communion with him, and by the early 380s the Apollinarians of Asia Minor and Syria were engaged in intense, polemical competition with the imperially sponsored form of the Nicene Church, in which the Cappadocians were key players.[24] Despite

21. See, for instance, Gregory of Nyssa, *Or. cat.* (GNO 3.4:26.3–12; 35.16–36.16); Apollinarius, frags. 74–76 (Lietzmann, 222.6–24: the mind as changeable, inconstant); frags. 150–51 (Lietzmann, 247.22–248.7: the mind as self-determining but inconstant); *Letter to the Bishops of Diocaesaraea* 2 (Lietzmann, 256.5–6); *Anakephalaiōsis* 30 (Lietzmann, 246.13–17: the mind wars against the flesh).

22. For Apollinarius's conception of the ways in which we make contact with the saving and healing presence of the incarnate Christ, see frag. 165 (Lietzmann, 262.28–263.14: by faith, by following him and imitating his behavior); frag. 116 (Lietzmann, 235.8–17: by being nourished by his life-giving flesh); cf. Gregory of Nyssa, *Or. cat.* (GNO 3.4:93.1–98.7): nourishment of the Eucharist; ibid. (GNO 3.4:98.8–105.9): moral reform and imitation of Christ.

23. For a plausible reconstruction of Apollinarius's career at this point, and of his changing relations with Basil, see G. L. Prestige, *St. Basil the Great and Apollinarius of Laodicaea*, ed. Henry Chadwick (London: SPCK, 1956), 14–16. John McGuckin suggests that it was Diodore of Tarsus, one of the chief supporters of Bishop Meletius of Antioch, who first persuaded Gregory of Nazianzus, and perhaps through him Gregory of Nyssa, of the theological and ecclesiastical dangers raised by Apollinarius and his associates: see *Saint Gregory of Nazianzus: An Intellectual Biography* (Crestwood: St. Vladimir's Seminary Press, 2001), 231–32.

24. See Gregory of Nazianzus, *Ep.* 101.6–9 (SC 208:38–40); 202.4–7 (ibid. 88–90): they are a worse danger to the Church than the Eunomians or the Macedonians; Gregory of

his intense commitment to the cause of Nicaea, Apollinarius had become a sectarian leader.

The core of the Apollinarian challenge to the established church, and the heart of orthodox arguments against the Apollinarians, however, was clearly felt by both sides of the debate to be theological rather than simply political: each side was convinced that the other took a distorted view of the person of Christ. In one sense, Apollinarius's basic conception of Christ, as the enfleshed divine Logos, was nothing new: the Antiochene synod that condemned Paul of Samosata in 268, and in the fourth century Arius, Athanasius, and even Origen's great admirer Eusebius of Caesarea,[25] had all simply assumed that the Logos, as the divine spiritual mind governing the universe, was also the mind of the Savior, bringing to realization in him, as a single human composite, what it constantly achieved on a cosmic scale for the preservation of creation. But some drew unacceptable conclusions. Arius had taken this organic internal unity of Christ to be a proof that the Logos must himself be a creature; Apollinarius, affirming the consubstantiality of the Logos with the eternal Father but also insisting—against Marcellus—that the Logos's distinct, filial relationship to the Father is part of the eternal structure of the mystery of God, naturally tended to conceive of the whole person of Christ as divine, and thus in some sense as eternal, building his argument on scriptural texts that spoke of Jesus as "the man from heaven."[26]

Gregory Nazianzen's portrayal of Apollinarius's Christology, in his letter to Nectarius of Constantinople, surely oversimplifies the Apollinarian understanding of the "divine flesh" of Christ, but it probably gives us—despite Gregory's attempts to reduce the Apollinarian position to absurdity—an accurate picture of the way the sect's approach to the person of Christ was generally understood:

> He asserts that the flesh which the only-begotten Son assumed in the incarnation for the remodeling of our nature was no new acquisition, but that that carnal nature was in the Son from the beginning. And he puts forward as a witness to this monstrous assertion a garbled quotation from the Gospels, namely, "no man has ascended up into heaven save the one

Nyssa, *Ad Theoph.* (GNO 3.1:120.12–121.10): their charges against the Orthodox; *Antirrh.* (GNO 3.1:132.15–25): they are "false prophets," and their teaching must be tested.

25. On Eusebius's "*logos-sarx*" Christology—surprising in view of his general adherence to Origen's theology—see Grillmeier, *Christ in Christian Tradition*, 1:178–79.

26. For a thoughtful analysis of Apollinarius's use of Scripture to support his picture of Christ, see Greer, "Man from Heaven," esp. 166–74.

> who came down from heaven, the Son of Man who is in heaven" [John 3:13]. As though even before he came down he was the Son of Man, and when he came down he brought with him that flesh, which it appears he had in heaven, as though it had existed before the ages and been joined with his essence. For he alleges another saying of an apostle, which he cuts off from the whole body of its context, that the second man is the Lord from heaven [1 Cor 15:47]. Then he assumes that that man who came down from above is without a mind, but that the Godhead of the only-begotten fulfills the function of mind, and is the third part of this human composite, inasmuch as soul and body are in it on its human side, but not mind, the place of which is taken by God the Word.[27]

The abundant remains of Apollinarius's own writings reveal that while his Christology is not always consistent in all its details, it does lay central stress on the living, organic unity of the Logos, the divine Mind, with the soul and flesh of Jesus as "one person" (ἓν πρόσωπον) and "one living being" (ἓν ζῶον), so that "nothing should be adored like the flesh of Christ."[28] Gregory of Nyssa paraphrases Apollinarius's portrait of the unified, centrally divine person of Christ—based on sayings of Jesus in texts like John 17:5, "Glorify me . . . with the glory I had with you before the world was made"—in the following terms:

> He says that the Son, who is enfleshed mind, was "born of a woman" [Gal 4:4], not having become flesh in the Virgin but coming forth from her as through a passage [παροδικῶς]; just as he was before the ages, he appeared at that time in visible form, being God in the flesh [σάρκινον θεόν], or—as he himself calls him—enfleshed mind.[29]

In several extant fragments of his works, Apollinarius himself strenuously denies holding that the actual flesh of the man Jesus is heavenly or eter-

27. *Ep.* 202, to Nectarius, 10–14 (SC 208:90–92; trans. Charles Gordon Browne and James Edward Swallow, repr. in *Christology of the Later Fathers*, ed. Edward Rochie Hardy, LCC 3 [Philadelphia: Westminster, 1954], 231 [alt.]).

28. *Apodeixis*, cited in Gregory of Nyssa, *Antirrh.* (GNO 3.1:204.31–205.1, 204.17–18).

29. *Antirrh.* (GNO 3.1:166.24–28). Gregory of Nazianzus also criticizes the Apollinarians, in his celebrated *First Letter to Cledonius*, for suggesting that the Word, in becoming flesh, "passed through the Virgin as through a conduit, but was not completely formed in her, in a way at once divine and human" (*Ep.* 101.16: SC 208:42).

nal, even though we adore it as "God's flesh."[30] Yet there are other passages where he does speak of Christ's body simply as "God's flesh"[31] and insists that the Word exists "in the singleness of the mingled, incarnate divine nature";[32] for this reason, his body, although "consubstantial with us," shares both in the name and the reality of his divine consubstantiality.[33] As Rowan Greer has pointed out, such language seems intended to assert the same mutual predicability of divine and human attributes in Christ that would later be called the "communication of idioms"; but it does so in language that was easily misunderstood, and perhaps not always fully under control.[34] One main reason for this, Greer perceptively observes, is that Apollinarius apparently lacks a sense of the importance of *time* or *history* in conceiving of the composite person of Christ: for him, "to speak of Christ is to speak of a timeless reality."[35] Christ, in Apollinarius's rather vaguely formulated soteriology, renews fallen human beings, whose unstable minds are held captive by fleshly passions, precisely because he is the perfect divine mind, ruling his flesh in sovereign freedom: unlike the flesh of a graced human being, who is simply "joined to God,"

> the flesh of God is an instrument of life, conformed to our passibilities for the sake of achieving God's plans; the thoughts and actions of the flesh are not proper to it, but being subjected to our passibilities in a way that befits flesh, it is strong against those passions, because it is God's flesh. In this way, it leads the way towards impassibility for those bodies which are not like it, but which live in a similar way.[36]

For Apollinarius, Christ's role as savior rests primarily on the fact that he is *unlike* us; he is unique and sovereign because although he shares our tripartite structure, he is by nature God. As such, he becomes a "new Adam"

30. *Ep. ad Dionysium* 7 (Lietzmann, 259.5–9): the Apollinarians confess to saying that Christ is "the Son of Man from heaven," not that his flesh is from heaven; *Tomus synodalis* (Lietzmann, 262.27–263.4): the Logos took "flesh consubstantial with our flesh" and is united to it as the human spirit is united to our flesh. This latter passage comes from a brief declaration by "Apollinarius and those with me," presumably intended to present their Christology in a light more acceptable to the wider Church.

31. E.g., *Anakephalaiōsis* 29 (Lietzmann, 246.2–7): for a quotation, see text below.

32. Frag. 9 (Lietzmann, 206.27–28).

33. *De unione* 8 (Lietzmann, 188.14–18).

34. Greer, "Man from Heaven," 170–71.

35. Ibid., 171.

36. *Anakephalaiōsis* 29 (Lietzmann, 246.2–7).

for us by taking on flesh similar to ours, and offers us a new model for imitation, a new form for living our own lives now, as enfleshed minds, in a divine way: in Apollinarius's words, Christ "gives a share in pure virtue to every mind that is subject to him, to all who are made like Christ in mind and who are not unlike him in flesh."[37] It is, above all, through obedience to and imitation of this Christ who is radically different from ourselves in his dominant energies, and yet who shares the same composite structure of mind, soul, and flesh that we possess, that Apollinarius believes we may come to share in his moral and physical incorruption.

A good deal of the polemical response of the two Gregories to Apollinarius's theology consists in their denial of his charge that any other approach to the mystery of Christ apart from his own ends in the worship of two Sons, or in the introduction of a fourth person—the divinely inspired, yet human person of the Savior—into the Trinity of the Church's traditional faith. Yet clearly both Gregories go further than simple rebuttal; drawn by Apollinarius's challenge, as well as that of the radically subordinationist Eunomians, both attempt to develop a vision of the person of Christ that is intrinsically connected to their own understanding of salvation, of the human person, of eschatological hope, and of the very being of God. What I hope to show here, in fact, is that their real objection to Apollinarius's portrait of Christ is not simply the absence there of a human soul; it is, rather, his failure to see in Christ the source and type of God's project of reshaping all of humanity together, and every human person individually, in God's image, through the inner communication of divine life to a complete and normal human being. For them, on the other hand, such a soteriological Christology is a central, determining feature of any sound and thorough understanding of the Christian gospel.

In many ways, the celebrated phrase in Gregory of Nazianzus's first letter to Cledonius puts the whole Cappadocian position in a nutshell: "That which he has not assumed he has not healed; but that which is united to his Godhead is also saved."[38] We are saved from sin and death not simply by

37. Quoted by Gregory of Nyssa, *Antirrh.* (GNO 3.1:199.5–7, 14–15). Cf. another quotation in the same work: "The self-moved mind in each of us shares in redemption, to the degree that it allows itself to belong to Christ" (GNO 3.1:192.17–18).

38. Gregory of Nazianzus, *Ep.* 101.32 (SC 208:50; Hardy, 218). Gregory summarizes, in this famous aphorism, a principle important in patristic Christology since the late second century: see, for instance, Irenaeus, *Haer.* 5.14.1–2 (SC 153:182–88), who argues on these grounds that Jesus's humanity "recapitulates" the flesh and blood of the whole race; cf. Tertullian, *Carn. Chr.* 10 (SC 216:256). The closest early parallel to Gregory's formulation

remodeling our humanity after the enfleshed divine mind, but through a real union of God with humanity that begins in the united person of Christ. As a result, the person of Christ must be a union of God the Word, in his full divine substance and personal presence, with a complete human being; God's "assumption"—his ἀνάληψις or πρόσληψις—not simply of σάρξ but of an ἄνθρωπος is the central action of God's historical work of salvation.

In Gregory of Nyssa's version, this "assumption of a human being" to form the incarnate person of Christ is worked out in the distinctive terms of Gregory's own comprehensive theological and spiritual synthesis, in what one might call a "Christology of transformation."[39] Gregory summarizes this Christology in a passage in his *Antirrhētikos* against Apollinarius, marked by the use of some favorite terminology and scriptural allusions:

> The Logos, who "is in the beginning and is with God" [John 1:1], has "become flesh" [John 1:14] in these last days [Heb 1:2] out of love for humanity, by sharing in the humble reality of our nature; by this means, he mingled with what is human [τῷ ἀνθρώπῳ ἀνακραθείς] and received our entire nature within himself, so that the human [τὸ ἀνθρώπινον] might mingle with what is divine and be divinized with it, and that the whole mass [φύραμα] of our nature might be made holy through that first-fruit [ἀπαρχή: Rom 11:16].[40]

The striking feature of Gregory's account of salvation and the Savior here is its *narrative* structure: unlike Apollinarius, who focuses on the distinctive ontological characteristics of the incarnate Word and suggests they are held in a timeless, even eternal balance of mind and flesh, Gregory puts the accent on the incarnation as *event*, as the beginning of decisive and life-giving change within changeable human history and the ever-changing human person.[41] To put it more precisely: in Gregory's terms, the point of

---

is found in Origen's *Dialogus cum Heraclides*: "For the whole human being would not have been saved, if [Christ] had not taken on a whole human being" (SC 67:70). For the use of this principle by other theologians in the fourth century and later, see the excellent summary article by Aloys Grillmeier, "Quod assumptum non est, sanatum non est," *Lexikon für Theologie und Kirche* (Freiburg: Herder, 1963), 8:954–56.

39. See my article "Divine Transcendence and Human Transformation" (above, n. 11).

40. *Antirrh.* (GNO 3.1:151.14–20).

41. For Gregory's frequently asserted conviction that "everything that depends upon creation for existence has an innate tendency to change," see *Or. cat.* (GNO 3.4:24.3–6); cf. *Vit. Moys.* 2.2–3 (GNO 7.1:33.19–34,14); *De perfectione* (GNO 8.1:213.1–214.6). On the

the Nicene Creed is not simply to proclaim that the Son is "of one substance with the Father," but also to confess that "he came down from heaven and *became* flesh, so that his flesh is understood not to have existed before his descent."[42] The point, similarly, of the "hymn" of Philippians 2:6–11 is, for Gregory, its affirmation that the one who, as "equal to God," had no perceptible form at all, *took on* that form which we can see and understand, only when he "emptied himself" in time: "*at that point* he came to be in a form, when he took up form and wrapped himself in it."[43] Gregory's conclusion may seem at first sight rather startling: we can only call the Lord a "human being" during the time of his earthly life,[44] even though as divine Son he is always "the Christ," because he is always "anointed" by the glory of God, which is poured out in the Holy Spirit. As a result, what *changes* in the narrative of God's "self-emptying" is not God, nor even Christ as an eternal divine person, but the "human being" in which he "formed himself" to meet the capacities of our senses:

> Since the human is changeable, while the divine is unchangeable, the divinity is unmovable with respect to change, neither varying for the better nor for the worse (for it cannot take into itself what is worse, and there is nothing better); but human nature, in Christ, undergoes change towards the better, being altered from corruption to incorruption, from the perishable to the imperishable, from the short-lived to the eternal, from the bodily and the formed to what is without either body or form.[45]

At the end of part 3 of *Contra Eunomium* 3, Gregory deals with the neo-Arian charge that scriptural witness to the elevation and glorification of Christ, in such passages as Acts 2:36 ("God has made both Lord and Christ this Jesus, whom you crucified"), suggests that the Son, who is "*made* Lord and Christ," is changeable and therefore a creature. Here Gregory again makes the argument that it is the full human being, the ἄνθρωπος "assumed"

---

importance of physical change in Gregory's thought, see Jean Daniélou, *L'Être et le temps chez Grégoire de Nysse* (Leiden: Brill, 1970), 95–115.

42. *Antirrh.* (GNO 3.1:143.7–9; emphasis mine).

43. *Antirrh.* (GNO 3.1:160.1–2; emphasis mine).

44. Gregory may well be thinking here of the passage in Apollinarius's *Anakephalaiōsis* described in n. 17. The final section of the argument is a similar set of syllogisms arguing that Christ is, in any case, not what each of us is: "a human being joined to God [ἄνθρωπος Θεῷ παραζευχθείς]." For text, see Lietzmann, 242.24–245.30.

45. *Antirrh.* (GNO 3.1:223.2–10); cf. Athanasius, *Or. III c. Arianos* 34, 53.

by the Logos, rather than the Logos as such, who is changed by receiving divine glory: in a telling Greek pun, Gregory asserts that "the Godhead is emptied [κενοῦται], so that it might become receivable by human nature; the human being is renewed [ἀνακαινοῦται], becoming divine by being mingled with the divine."[46] Gregory's point is that the process of transformation which the Gospels show to have taken place in Christ—the change from humility to glory, from growth in "wisdom, age and grace" to the mysterious splendor of the resurrection—although it is a change only in his humanity, reveals precisely whose humanity this has been from the beginning.[47] Appealing, as he so often does, to the natural science of his time for a likely metaphor, Gregory compares the personal divinity of the man Jesus to the element of fire which always lies hidden within a piece of wood, only to be revealed when the wood is set ablaze; so

> he who thought little of human shame, because he is Lord of glory, concealed, as it were, the flame of life within his bodily nature in the course of events [οἰκονομίᾳ] that led to death, but he enkindled it and fanned it into flame again by the power of his own divinity, warming the body that had died and so infusing that meager first-fruit of our nature with the infinity of divine life, and made that, too, into the thing he himself was . . . , making everything that is piously understood to be in God the Word also to be in the one assumed by the Word. As a result, these no longer [i.e., after his resurrection] seem to exist separately on their own, according to some kind of distinction, but the mortal nature, mingled with the divine in a way that overwhelms it, is made new, and shares in the divine nature—just as if, let us say, the process of mixture were to make a drop of vinegar, mingled in the sea, into sea itself, simply by the fact that the natural quality of that liquid no longer remained perceptible within the infinite mass that overwhelmed it.[48]

Gregory thus comes to speak of progress, of a process of change, within the humanity of Jesus, which both represents and opens the way for a sim-

46. *C. Eun.* 3.3.67 (GNO 2:131.19–22).

47. Cf. Gregory's *Ep.* 3.16–22 (SC 363:136–42), where Gregory insists that one must not understand this progressive transformation of Christ's human nature in the sense that Jesus the man only gradually became God; it is rather to be understood as "a true theophany" (*Ep.* 3.16), in which the presence of God is more and more luminously revealed within creatures—in Christ's case, most dramatically revealed in the manner of his entering the world and in his ascension into glory (ibid., 22).

48. *C. Eun.* 3.3.68–69 (GNO 2:132.14–21, 24–133.4).

ilar process in us. If his humanity has been, in the end, overmastered and absorbed, as far as its perceptible natural characteristics went, by the divinity to which it is united, the theological promise in this transformation rests on the fact that his humanity was, and in a paradoxical way still is, completely normal, completely similar to ours. Although as Word he is Wisdom itself, "we do not doubt that that part of our flesh that was united to the divine Wisdom received a share in the good thing that Wisdom is";[49] so, too, he struggled to remain "obedient unto death [Phil 2:8], for since death entered in because of the disobedience of the first human being, for that reason it is driven away through the obedience of the second human being."[50] Jesus's prayer in Gethsemane reveals that the Word has taken on, as part of God's deliberate strategy of salvation (ἐξ οἰκονομίας), a human will and human vulnerability (πάθος);[51] it is this human will, with its natural freedom to determine action, that enables Jesus to share in "pure virtue."[52] And just as the result of the "first man's" disobedience was death (Rom 5:19), the divine reward for the "second man's" obedience unto death is resurrection and entry into glory, a transformation not only of his own individual humanity but of humanity itself:

> For this reason he became "obedient unto death" [Phil 2:8], that through his obedience the wound of disobedience might be healed, and through his resurrection from the dead he might make death vanish, which entered along with disobedience. For the resurrection of the human [Jesus] from the dead is the point at which death disappears.[53]

In the resurrection and ascension of Jesus into glory, Gregory argues, the glory which belongs to the Word from all eternity as God, the glory in which he is "anointed" by the Holy Spirit and which is the foundation of his title "Christ," comes to belong also, "at the end of the ages, to the one united to Christ"[54]—namely, or at least primarily and prototypically, to Jesus. And the effect of this glorification on the humanity of Christ is nothing less than its total transformation; as Gregory writes to Theophilus of Alexandria,

49. *Antirrh.* (GNO 3.1:175.10–12).
50. *Antirrh.* (GNO 3.1:160.27–29).
51. *Antirrh.* (GNO 3.1:181.14–22).
52. *Antirrh.* (GNO 3.1:198.1–7; cf. 199.6–11).
53. *Antirrh.* (GNO 3.1:161.1–5).
54. *Antirrh.* (GNO 3.1:222.4–21).

> Everything that was weak and perishable in our nature, mingled with the Godhead, has become that which the Godhead is. . . . The first-fruits of the human nature which he has taken up—absorbed (one might say figuratively) by the omnipotent divinity like a drop of vinegar mingled in the boundless sea, exists *in* the Godhead, but not in its own proper characteristics. For a duality of Sons might consistently be presumed, if a nature of a different kind could be recognized by its own proper signs within the ineffable Godhead of the Son. . . . But since all the traits we recognize in the mortal [Jesus] we see transformed by the characteristics of the Godhead, and since no difference of any kind can be perceived—for whatever one sees in the Son *is* Godhead: wisdom, power, holiness, freedom from passion—how could one divide what is one into double significance, since no difference divides him numerically?[55]

Along with this strong affirmation of the transformation of human nature by its taking on the characteristics (ἰδιώματα) of the divine, Gregory does—less frequently—also affirm that the human structure assumed by God is not simply lost in the process, since God remains ever faithful to the commitment implied in the incarnation:

> For the divine nature, as we have said, when it is mutually and naturally united with body and soul and has become one with both of them by mixture, is never separated from either of them—"for God's gifts," scripture says, "are irrevocable" [Rom 11:29]—but they remain forever. For there is nothing that can separate anyone from union with God except sin; and in one whose life is free from sin, surely union with God is inseparable.[56]

The nature of this unequal union of God and the human in Christ, however, and the transformation of the human element that it brings about, result, in Gregory's view, in a state of integrated existence in which the human, as such, is so dominated by the present reality of God that it is scarcely recognizable to our present understanding. It has itself become, in a participatory way, divine.

55. *Ad Theoph.* (GNO 3.1:126.17–127.10). Other passages sounding this theme of the transformation of human nature in the person of Christ include: *Antirrh.* (GNO 3.1:169.24–170.14): the assumption of Elijah to heaven in a chariot of fire as a type of the transformation of Christ's humanity; *C. Eun.* 3.3.34 (GNO 2:119.2127); 3.43 (GNO 2:123.5–10); 3.62 (GNO 2:130.2–5); 4.43 (GNO 2:150.21–27).

56. *Antirrh.* (GNO 3.1:224.17–24).

What are the implications, within Gregory's remarkably coherent theology, of this way of understanding the relationship of the human nature and the human experiences of Christ to his own proper divinity?

1. First of all, as others have remarked,[57] this Christology really is a *soteriology.* The transformation of a complete and normal human nature in Jesus is, for Gregory, the "first-fruits" of a transformation of all of humanity as a race: an active leaven in the "lump" of our common human dough.[58] Even his celebrated image of the "drop of vinegar in the ocean" may well be a hint at the "medicinal" effect on the rest of humanity of the resurrection of Christ, since vinegar in water was prescribed as a cure in some of the Hippocratic writings Gregory seems to have known.[59] For each of us, in Gregory's view, salvation from the corrupting, deadly disease of sin can only come about through a transformation of our human nature similar to that which we see in Christ, which draws its healing energy from him: a transformation that begins in our growth in virtue, a created reflection of the divine light[60] which is the true human glory,[61] and which reaches its perfection, as far as the material side of our nature is concerned, in the resurrection of the body. So in the *Life of Moses*, his treatise on the dynamic process of human perfection, Gregory interweaves his discussion of the life of virtue, and of our human hope to share in the Paschal mystery, into an interpretation of the sweetening of the water of Marah in the book of Exodus:

> For to the one who has left the pleasures of Egypt, to which he was enslaved before he crossed the sea, life seems at first hard to bear and unpleasant, because it is deprived of pleasures. But if the wood is cast into the water—that is, if one makes one's own [παραλάβοι] the mystery of the resurrection, which takes its beginning through wood (and when you hear "wood," surely you will think of the cross!)—then the life shaped by virtue is sweeter, more

57. E.g., Bouchet, "À propos d'une image," 588; Moutsoulas, "Παρατηρήσεις," 265–70.

58. See, for instance, *Or. cat.* (GNO 3.4:77.24–78.17).

59. See Bouchet, "À propos d'une image," for the argument and for references. For Gregory's knowledge of and interest in Greek medicine, see Mary Emily Keenan, "St. Gregory of Nyssa and the Medical Profession," *Bulletin of the History of Medicine* 15 (1944): 150–61.

60. See *Hom. in Cant.* 9 (GNO 6:285.17): "Virtue is not outside the divinity"; *De an. et res.* (Roth, 86): "The divine nature is the source of all virtue." At the end of part 7 of *Contra Eunomium* 3, Gregory even says, "The Lord is virtue," just as he, Christ, is the supreme Good, "the fount of light and truth and of every good thing": *C. Eun.* 3.7.60–64 (GNO 2:236.10–237.18). See also *De Beatitudinibus* 4 (GNO 3.1:122).

61. *Antirrh.* (GNO 3.1:164.21–24): "The glory of a human person is true glory: the life, that is, which is lived according to virtue."

> refreshing, than any confection that delights the senses with pleasure, for its pleasure comes from the hope of what is to come.[62]

It is in the life of virtue, then, seen as part of a life of faith and of discipleship in the Church,[63] a life marked out and nourished by the sacraments of baptism[64] and the Eucharist,[65] that the transformation begins in each of us which also will end, like that of Christ's "assumed ἄνθρωπος," in complete divinization.

2. As Rowan Greer has remarked, the *anthropology* implied in Gregory's understanding of the person of the Savior is clearly more optimistic than that of Apollinarius, who saw the human mind as naturally unstable and irreparably ensnared in the contaminating passions of the flesh, unless a new model should be given it in a "heavenly man."[66] In many of his works, by contrast, Gregory sees the changeability of creatures not only as morally neutral in itself, but as the ontological foundation for that endless progress towards the Good which is his definition of created perfection.[67] "Sin is a failure of nature," Gregory writes to three ascetic women in *Epistle* 3, "not a proper characteristic of it, just as sickness and deformity were not naturally ours from the beginning, but occur contrary to nature."[68] What is most natural in us, Gregory argues at eloquent length in his dialogue *On the Soul and Resurrection*, is our "original form," the image of God as created in Adam:[69] this form, now overlaid with "garments of skin"—for Gregory, passibility and mortality—as a result of the fall, will gradually be restored in each human being through the healing of the passions and growth in virtue, either in this life or in the purgation which follows,[70] and will take on bodily form, in a way yet unknown to us, through our own resurrection.[71] The final state of

62. *Vit. Moys.* 2.132 (GNO 7.1.74.24–75.9).

63. *Or. cat.* (GNO 3.4, 98.8–106.18).

64. *Or. cat.* (GNO 3.4:82.1–92.25); *Antirrh.* (GNO 3.1:226.26–227.9): in baptism we voluntarily die along with Christ, are buried with him, and imitate his resurrection.

65. *Or. cat.* (GNO 3.1:93.1–95.23).

66. Greer, "Man from Heaven," 172, with references.

67. For references, see above, n. 39.

68. *Ep.* 3.17 (SC 363:136.142–45).

69. *De an. et res.* (Roth, 119); see also *De hom. opif.* 16–18. For a recent reinterpretation of the latter passage, and of Gregory's understanding of the role of gender in that "original form," see John Behr, "The Rational Animal: A Rereading of Gregory of Nyssa's *De hominis opificio*," *JECS* 7 (1999): 219–47.

70. *De an. et res.* (Roth, 119–20).

71. *De an. et res.* (Roth, 115).

the human person, which is a restoration of our original state, "is nothing else, according to my judgment, but to be in God himself."[72] And it is precisely this moral and bodily transformation by union with God, brought to its fulfillment in resurrection from death, that Christian faith sees achieved in the person of Christ: Gregory's anthropology of growth towards God, in other words, finds its paradigm in his "Christology of transformation."

3. Gregory's christological dispute with Apollinarius seems even to have had its implications for their understanding of Christian *eschatology.* Gregory quotes a passage from the *Apodeixis* in which Apollinarius seems himself to be criticizing Gregory's notion of resurrection as a thoroughgoing divinization of the human: "If after the resurrection he becomes God and is no longer human," Apollinarius asks, "how will the Son of Man send out his angels? And how shall we see the Son of Man coming on the clouds of heaven [Matt 24:30–31]?"[73] Apollinarius's "timeless" Christology seems to imply for him that the "heavenly man" will remain forever in the form in which he walked the earth, complete (as Gregory distastefully observes) with hair and nails—that God and the Logos and bodily nature are permanently fixed in their present relationships of need and grace. This understanding, indeed, may be part of the reason that the Apollinarians were accused, in a number of contemporary sources, of having millenarian expectations:[74] Paradise must be a bodily place, if Christ and his Church are to find their fulfillment there! Gregory, on the other hand, dismisses such difficulties contemptuously: it is promised that we will see Christ come again "in the glory of his Father" (Matt 16:27), and the glory of God is "purified of all form that can be contemplated visually,"[75] for "the divine lies beyond every bodily conception."[76] For Gregory, the mystery of Christ's resurrection reveals to us the mysterious, unimaginable character of the promised end of history—the mystery of Christ's own form, as well as of our own fulfillment.

4. Ultimately, perhaps, Gregory's quarrel with Apollinarius's Christology is really a quarrel about the nature of *God.* Towards the end of

72. *De an. et res.* (Roth, 116).

73. *Antirrh.* (GNO 3.1:228.18–22).

74. See, for example, Gregory of Nyssa, *Ep.* 3.24 (SC 363:142–44); Gregory of Nazianzus, *Ep.* 101.63–64 (SC 208:64); *Ep.* 102.14 (ibid., 76); Basil of Caesarea, *Ep.* 263.4; 265.2; Epiphanius of Salamis, *Panarion* 77.36–38 (GCS 37:448–451: not Apollinarius but his followers). For further references, see Brian E. Daley, *The Hope of the Early Church* (Cambridge: Cambridge University Press, 1991), 80.

75. *Antirrh.* (GNO 3.1:230.9).

76. *Antirrh.* (GNO 3.1:230.23).

his *Antirrhētikos*, he quietly criticizes Apollinarius for what may be his underlying error: he thinks of God the Word simply as mind, and so sets the stage for inevitable competition and conflict between the powerful and holy divine mind and its poor human counterpart. "For if the Godhead takes the place of the mind [in Christ]," Gregory remarks, "one could not say that the Godhead is superior in comparison to mind, since it, too, like mind, would be given its place [in the incarnate Word] by nature." In Gregory's view, as is well known, God's substance and nature are beyond all creaturely comprehension:

> Who does not know that the God who has appeared to us in flesh is, according to what reverent tradition tells us, immaterial and invisible and uncomposed; he was and is indefinable and uncircumscribed, he exists everywhere and penetrates all creation, but in perceptible mode he is seen in the circumscribed form of a human being?[77]

The central paradox of the incarnation of the Word, Gregory realized, is simply the paradox of personal—and, in that sense, ontological—union between the formed and what is beyond form, between the infinite, transcendent God and a perfect but limited human creature in time and space. God can "assume" this creature, Gregory knew, can make him his own—and in "assuming" him can "heal" all those who share the same human ancestry and structure—simply because God is utterly *different* from the human creature in every aspect of God's being. God can assume and heal every aspect of humanity in Christ, because God can never be a competitor with any aspect of Christ's humanity; his presence *within* that humanity as God, as Maximus Confessor would later make more explicit, is what allows it to be most fully and most freely itself.[78] Gregory puts the point

77. *Antirrh.* (GNO 3.1:156.14–18).

78. Maximus's insistence on the two undiminished natural "operations" of the incarnate Word, and thus on his two "natural wills," rests on the conviction, which Maximus often expresses in his christological writings, that the very union of divine and human elements in the mystery of Christ both relies on and guarantees the continuing distinctness and integrity of both. See, for example, *Opusculum* 8, to Nicandros: "The one [nature] is preserved by preserving the other, the one maintained by maintaining the other. For clearly it [i.e., the Incarnation] is a union of things only insofar as the natural distinction of those things is preserved. For when the one [i.e., the union] ceases, clearly the other [i.e., distinction] ceases, too, being made completely to disappear in the confusion of the two" (PG 91:97A1–5). Cf. also *Opusc.* 7, to Marinus (PG 91:73D–80C); *Ambigua* 4 (PG 91:1056C–1060D); *Ep.* 12, to John the Chamberlain (PG 91:408A–D); *Dialogue*

more simply: "That which always remains the same cannot, by its nature, become anything other than what it is; it can come to be *in* another, surely, but it cannot *become* that other."[79] Humanity changes, and there lies its hope; God never changes, because God's nature lies beyond all limit and definition. It is a principle destined to be misunderstood and even misused in the christological debates of the century that was to follow; but in the context of Gregory's theology, and of his "Christology of transformation," it seems to be both indispensable and true.

with Pyrrhus (PG 91:309A–B: the Word possesses the full human nature "in a divine way [θεϊκῶς]"). And see Hans Urs von Balthasar, *Kosmische Liturgie. Das Weltbild Maximus' des Bekenners* (Einsiedeln: Johannes Verlag, 1961), 253–56. Here, as elsewhere, Maximus is clearly influenced by the Cappadocian tradition.

79. *Antirrh.* (GNO 3.1:227.14–16).

PART 3

Augustine's Christology

8 Word, Soul, and Flesh

Origen and Augustine on the Person of Christ

If we were asked to name the two Christian thinkers of the first five, or even the first ten, centuries of the Church's history who had the most profound and lasting influence on the later course of Christian thought, most of us would probably settle on Origen and Augustine. In many ways, they were very different people. Origen lived and worked in the cosmopolitan Greek culture of the third century: born around 185; brought up in Alexandria, the center of literary, scientific, and philosophical studies of the ancient Mediterranean world, a melting-pot of ethnic and religious traditions; trained in Homer and the Greek tragedians, in dialectics, in the handbook philosophy distilled from Plato; yet an intensely committed Christian from birth, an ascetic, a *philoponos* or "hard-core" believer, always ready to give the ultimate witness of blood for his faith. Origen eventually moved from Alexandria, around 231, to the smaller city of Caesarea on the Palestinian coast, and established there what amounted to the first Christian faculty of biblical studies, an intellectual center devoted to the study and interpretation of Scripture for Christians of every level of education and interest. A lifelong member of the Church, and probably always a layman, Origen was by profession a scholar, a relentlessly learned and speculative mind in an age when Christian theology was still a new and almost undefined enterprise, a game with few rules. As his treatise *On First Principles* shows, Origen himself believed that the only key to understanding Scripture in the endlessly rich, life-giving ways God intended it to be read was to read it within the framework of the Church's traditional

This paper was delivered at the Saint Augustine Lecture on September 30, 2004, at Villanova University, the Institute for the Study of Augustine and Augustinian Traditions.

"rule," professed by Christians in baptism;[1] but the process of elaborating that rule into a dogmatic structure was only beginning, and Origen's mind delighted in playing with a variety of alternative plans for its construction.

Augustine was a century and a half younger, born in Thagaste, in rural North Africa in 354. He was a Latin in language and culture, who, by his own admission, knew little Greek; a professional rhetorician, a world-class teacher of persuasive speech, an artist and theoretician with words; a first-class product of the educational system of his age, he always retained the dramatic, Rome-centered view of human history and society that years of reading Vergil and Cicero had distilled in his soul. Unlike Origen, Augustine came to the full practice of his Christianity only gradually and with great struggle. Yet when he did take the step of presenting himself for baptism, at the age of thirty-three, Augustine knew it was a commitment that would change every aspect of his life. After four years attempting to form a community of celibate, educated friends bound by prayer and contemplation, as well as by common possessions and a common table, Augustine was called to a life of ordained ministry: first (in 391) as presbyter and preacher in the coastal African city of Hippo Regius, then four years later as its bishop. Until his death in 430, Augustine led an extraordinarily busy life: administering the spiritual and temporal affairs of his Church, filling the bishop's customary role of local magistrate and mediator, constantly involved in the problems of the whole African Church, constantly in demand as preacher, constantly being consulted by letter and by passing visitors on every conceivable aspect of Christian faith and practice, yet still living with his priests in a kind of proto-monastic community, still grasping at every opportunity for quiet reflection on the larger mysteries of faith. Writing a century and a half after Origen, acutely aware of the disputes over doctrine that had wracked the Christian community since Origen's time, and of the normative guidelines that had begun to emerge, after the end of persecution, in the canons and creedal formulas of Nicaea and later councils, local and general, of the fourth and early fifth centuries, Augustine carried out the theologian's tasks with an evident sense of responsibility. Although the Christian vision of God, for instance, raises all kinds of theoretical questions that challenge the human

1. *De principiis* preface 2. For an argument that the purpose of this treatise is in fact to develop a detailed understanding of the "rule of faith," as the basis for an authentic interpretation of Scripture free from Gnostic or Marcionite distortion, see my article "Origen's *De Principiis*: A Guide to the 'Principles' of Christian Scriptural Interpretation," in John Petruccione (ed.), *Nova et Vetera: Patristic Studies in Honor of Thomas Patrick Halton* (Washington, DC: Catholic University of America Press, 1998) 3–21.

mind to its limits, Augustine makes it clear, at the start of his great work *On the Trinity*, that his project is not one of unfettered philosophical speculation, but one of searching the Scriptures, in the light of the Church's articulated tradition, for some deeper understanding of the faith Christians professed; in doing so, he hopes to provide "the talkative reason-mongers" of his day with a reasoned account of what is already accepted as the *fides Catholica*, so that they may return to the beginning and right order of faith, realizing at least what a wholesome regimen is provided for the faithful in holy Church, whereby the due observance of piety makes the ailing mind well for the perception of unchanging truth.[2]

Origen would have said the same, surely; but by Augustine's time the boundaries between Catholic faith and heresy had become, on several issues, considerably clearer.

Different as they were in time, language, and profession, however, Origen and Augustine appear to most of us, from our present vantage-point in the ongoing tradition of Christian thought, as remarkably similar. Both of them were figures of controversy in their own day, and even more after their death; Origen, until the end of late antiquity, and Augustine, in our own day, have become the "theologians you love to hate" par excellence—the theologians most widely blamed, especially by those who have not read much of their work, for all that seems wrong about the Church's presentation of the Gospel. Both, on the other hand, have remained enormously influential on the way Christians—even Christians who deeply disagree with them—have framed theological discourse. In a very real sense, Origen and Augustine set the agenda for later patristic and medieval theological discussion, in East and West respectively, on such key issues as God's Trinitarian being, the single yet complex person of Christ, human freedom in relation to God's saving action in the world, the principles of scriptural interpretation, Christian hope for eternal life, and—especially in Augustine's case—the sacramental nature and structures of the Church.

Origen's thoughtful triple analysis of the coherence of the Christian rule of faith, in his treatise *On First Principles*, stands alongside Augustine's brilliant syntheses of the same confession in Book I of *On Christian Learning*, or in the opening sections of *On Primary Catechesis*, as landmarks in the systematization of the Church's teaching. Yet neither was what one might call, in the wake of the theological textbooks used in the medieval and modern university, a systematic thinker. Both were occasional writers, who responded

2. *De Trinitate* 1.4 (trans. Edmund Hill; Brooklyn: New City, 1990) 67.

to requests or perceived needs by writing treatises on particular theological subjects; both were exegetes, commentators on Scripture, hugely prolific pastoral preachers who spent a great deal of time expounding the biblical Word—without notes—to congregations of "ordinary" Christians, as the most fundamental nourishment of their faith; both were thoroughgoing public intellectuals, critical of dominant thought-patterns in their own cultures, yet undaunted champions of the value of traditional education for deepening and solidifying individual Christians' grasp of the apostolic teaching.[3] Both, too, although radically biblical in their approach to the task of theology, had been decisively influenced by the philosophical tradition of ancient Platonism: that aesthetic, value-centered approach to philosophy that moderns also "love to hate," but which the ancients generally regarded as the system of thought most capable of speaking meaningfully about transcendence. For both Origen and Augustine, it was the Platonic philosophical tradition, with its conception of ultimate reality as a non-material, timeless, benevolent, and active divine substance constantly present in material and historical things, that provided the one plausible intellectual alternative to the radical dualism of the Valentinians or the Manichees.

It was the *libri Platonicorum*, Augustine tells us, which finally led him to "turn within" in his restless search for a God who would satisfy his critical intellect, the "immutable light" supplying the mind with the criteria for making judgments, the Truth which simply "is," and is present, though often unrecognized, to each of us.[4] And it was the dialogic, probing form of Platonic thought, immortalized in the whole tradition from the early Socratic dialogues to the lecture-notes of Plotinus, that left an indelible stamp on both the controversial style and the preaching of these early Christian thinkers.[5] Although the content of their thought was the Christian biblical

3. It is interesting to compare Augustine's discussion of the relevance of traditional learning—especially the literary and rhetorical arts, but also mathematics, geography and history, natural science and dialectics—in *De doctrina Christiana* with the description of Origen's curriculum for would-be exegetes in the *Prosphōnētikos* ascribed to his pupil, Gregory the Wonder-Worker. Joseph Trigg remarks: "Origen is the only early theologian comparable to Augustine in sheer intellectual energy and power" ("Origen," in Allan D. Fitzgerald, O. S. A. [ed.], *Augustine through the Ages: An Encyclopedia* [Grand Rapids: Eerdmans, 1999] 604).

4. *Confessiones* 7.9.16.

5. For a discussion of Augustine's adoption of the classical philosophical tradition of "psychagogy," or spiritual and intellectual formation, through question, hypothesis, and discussion, especially in his preaching, see the dissertation of Paul R. Kolbet, "The Cure of

message, its intellectual idiom and its metaphysical framework owed more to Platonism than to any other philosophical system.

Given even these external similarities, one might expect that Augustine would have shown a lively interest in Origen's thought, which was the center of swirling, bitter controversy in the Church of his day. In fact, Augustine did show signs of growing interest in Origen from the 390s on, but apparently had difficulty getting reliable information on Origen's teachings; it is hard to say with certainty just which of Origen's works, if any, Augustine had himself read.[6]

Although Origen had been criticized by contemporaries as a theological risktaker, probably because of the exuberantly allegorical style of his biblical

---

Souls: St. Augustine's Reception and Transformation of Classical Psychagogy" (University of Notre Dame, 2002).

6. There is a fair amount of scholarly literature on the question of Augustine's actual knowledge of Origen. Berthold Altaner, "Augustinus und Origenes," *Historisches Jahrbuch* 70 (1951) 15–41 [= *Kleine Patristische Schriften* (Texte und Untersuchungen 83; Berlin: Akademieverlag, 1967) 224–52], argued from the appearance of similar arguments and exegetical interpretations that Augustine probably had access to a number of his works, at least by 411–412 (date of Ep. 140), and possibly as early as 388–389 (*De Genesi contra Manichaeos*). Many of these similarities, however, are less than conclusive evidence of textual dependence. Less helpful is Willy Theiler, "Augustin und Origenes," *Augustinus* 13 (1968) 423–32. Henry Chadwick's survey, "Christian Platonism in Origen and Augustine," in Henri Crouzel and Richard Hanson (eds.), *Origeniana Tertia* (Rome: Pontificio Istituto Orientale, 1985) 217–30, is largely dependent on Altaner's list. For further possible parallels, see Gerard Bartelink, "Die Beeinflussung Augustins durch die griechischen Patres," in J. den Boeft and Johannes van Oort (eds.), *Augustiniana Traiectina* (Paris: Etudes Augustiniennes, 1987) 14–18. Giulia Sfameni Gasparro, "Agostino di fronte alla 'eterodossia' di Origene," *Augustiniana* 40 (Mélanges Tarsicius van Bavel; 1990) 219–43, offers a balanced assessment of these parallels, in a judicious overview of Augustine's knowledge of Origen. Takeshi Kato offers an unusual Husserlian perspective in comparing Origen's and Augustine's conception of "voice," in "La Voix chez Origène et Saint Augustin," ibid. 245–58. Caroline P. Hammond Bammel has argued, on the basis of several close textual parallels, that Augustine had read and was using Origen's Commentary on Romans, probably in Rufinus's abbreviated translation, when he wrote *De peccatorum meritis et remissione*, his first work against the Pelagians, in 411: "Augustine, Origen and the Exegesis of St. Paul," *Augustinianum* 32 (1992) 341–68 [= *Tradition and Exegesis in Early Christian Writers* (Aldershot/Brookfield, VT: Variorum, 1995) XVII]; "Rufinus' Translation of Origen's Commentary on Romans and the Pelagian Controversy," in Antonio Scottà, *Storia ed esegesi in Rufino di Concordia* (= *Antichità Altoadriatiche* 39; Udine: Arti Grafische Friulane, 1992) 131–42 [= *Tradition and Exegesis* XVIII]. Most recently, György Heidl has offered an extended argument for Augustine's use of Origen in his very earliest works: *Origen's Influence on the Young Augustine: A Chapter of the History of Origenism* (Piscataway, NJ: Gorgias Press, 2003). At the time of writing, I have not yet been able to consult this work.

interpretation and his alleged hope for the ultimate salvation of all rational creatures, including the demons,[7] it was not until the very end of the fourth century that criticism of his thought hardened into open dispute. Epiphanius of Salamis, in 374, had drawn on earlier critics of Origen, in his *Panarion* or handbook of heresies, to expound the "heretical" nature of Origen's doctrine of the Trinity, his theory that the material world, along with our material bodies, was created as God's response to a pre-incarnate "fall" of souls, and his overly spiritualized conception of the resurrection body. As sympathy for Origen's speculations, and for the bold intellectual thrust of his speculative style, grew within some learned monastic circles, opposition grew as well; Epiphanius attempted unsuccessfully to persuade John, bishop of Jerusalem, to condemn Origen's writings in the mid-390s, and at least succeeded in recruiting Saint Jerome as a cantankerous and somewhat mercurial ally. The controversy took flight, apparently spurred by a dispute among certain Egyptian ascetics over whether God should be imagined as having a luminous human form—as some ancient rabbinic and Syriac Christian sources had suggested—or was rather to be thought of as radically transcending visible shape, as Origen and his contemporary disciple Evagrius insisted.[8] This "anthropomorphite" controversy in Egypt reached a peak in the formal condemnation of Origen's notions of God and of the body (as both being too spiritual, too ethereal) by Theophilus, bishop of Alexandria, in his festal letters of 400 and 401, but not before it had swept into the Latin-speaking world

7. See his apologetic "Letter to Friends in Alexandria," written at the time of his expulsion from that Church by Bishop Demetrius in 231, as discussed by Jerome, *Apologia adversus Rufinum* 2.18–19, and Rufinus, *De adulteratione librorum Origenis* (PG 17.624A2–625A2). For modern discussions of his condemnation, see C. C. Richardson, "The Condemnation of Origen," *Church History* 6 (1937) 50–64; Henri Crouzel, "A Letter from Origen 'to Friends in Alexandria,'" in David Neiman and Margaret Schatkin (eds.), *The Heritage of the Early Church* (Festschrift for George Florovsky; *Orientalia Christiana Analecta* 195: Rome, 1973) 135–50.

8. For an illuminating discussion of the background and implications of this "anthropomorphite controversy" in the 390s, and its roots in Semitic Jewish and Christian speculation, see Alexander Golitzin, "Recovering the 'Glory of Adam': 'Divine Light' Traditions in the Dead Sea Scrolls and the Christian Ascetical Literature of Fourth-Century Syro-Mesopotamia," in *Dead Sea Scrolls as Background to Postbiblical Judaism and Early Christianity* (Leiden: Brill, 2003) 275–308; "The Vision of God and the Form of Glory: More Reflections of the Anthropomorphite Controversy of A. D. 399," in John Behr (ed.), *Abba* (Crestwood, NY: St. Vladimir's Seminary Press, 2003) 273–97; see also Andrei Orlov and Alexander Golitzin, "'Many Lamps Are Lighted from the One': Paradigms of the Transformational Vision in Macarian Homilies," *Vigiliae Christianae* 55 (2001) 281–98.

as well, shattering the friendship of Jerome and his long-time colleague, Rufinus of Aquileia, and stirring up spirits throughout the Western Church.[9]

Just what Augustine knew of this controversy, and just when he knew it, is not entirely clear, nor is it clear how much of Origen's actual work Augustine ever read, even in the Latin translations that began to appear in fair abundance in the 390s. Ambrose, his spiritual mentor in Milan in the months before his baptism, was an avid reader of Origen and borrowed many of Origen's ideas and strategies in his own sermons and treatises; Hilary of Poitiers, whose work Augustine read and admired, was also influenced by Origen. So the fact that Augustine speculates, in some of his works of the late 380s and early 390s, on the possibility of a pre-mundane existence and fall of created intelligent souls—one of the ideas most closely associated with the Origenist tradition—does not necessarily prove direct familiarity on his part with Origen's writings.[10] In a letter to Jerome written in 394 or 395, Augustine encourages the scholar of Bethlehem to continue translating "the books of those who have so excellently commented on our Scriptures in Greek," especially "the one whom you preferably cite in your writings," which clearly means Origen.[11] Probably in 397, he wrote again to Jerome asking, among other things, for a clear description of the theological errors for

9. The fullest discussion of the Origenist controversy of the 390s, in all its Eastern and Western ramifications, is Elizabeth A. Clark, *The Origenist Controversy: The Cultural Construction of an Early Christian Debate* (Princeton: Princeton University Press, 1992). For a wider discussion of the controversies over various forms of Origenism in Christian antiquity, see Antoine Guillaumont, *Les 'Kephalaia Gnostica' d'Evagre le Pontique et l'histoire de l'Origénisme chez les Grecs et chez les Syriens* (Paris: Éditions du Seuil, 1962). For the development of interest in Origenism in the West, see Basil Studer, "Zur Frage des westlichen Origenismus," *Studia Patristica* 9 (= *Texte und Untersuchungen* 94; Berlin: Akademieverlag, 1966) 270–87.

10. Robert J. O'Connell has argued in a number of works that Augustine remained continually, if cautiously, interested in this possibility through much of his career, at least up to the second decade of the fifth century; see Robert J. O'Connell, *Augustine's Early Theory of Man* (Cambridge, MA: Harvard University Press, 1968); "Pre-existence in the Early Augustine," *Revue des Études Augustiniennes* 26 (1980) 176–88; *The Origin of the Soul in Augustine's Later Works* (New York: Fordham University Press, 1994). O'Connell connects this with Augustine's attitude to what he had learned of Origenism, in "St. Augustine's Criticism of Origen in the *Ad Orosium*," *Revue des Études Augustiniennes* 30 (1984) 84–99. For a representative example of the contrary opinion, see Gerard P. O'Daly, "Did St. Augustine Ever Believe in the Soul's Preexistence?" *Augustinian Studies* 5 (1974) 227–35.

11. Ep. 28.2 (trans. Roland Teske: *The Works of Saint Augustine: The Letters* [New York: New City, 2001] 92).

which Origen was then being attacked in the East;[12] in 404 or 405, he confessed in another letter to Jerome that he had not read any of the six or seven authors—including Origen and his Alexandrian admirer Didymus—whom Jerome now considers heretical, and seems ironically puzzled by Jerome's own change of position.[13] Caroline Bammel has made a persuasive, if not conclusive, case that Augustine had read Rufinus's abridged Latin translation of Origen's *Commentary on Romans* by the time he wrote his first anti-Pelagian work, *On the Deserts and Punishment of Sinners and the Baptism of Infants*, in 411.[14] But even after that date, Augustine remained dependent on the reports of others, mainly of critics of Origen, for information as to the doctrinal content of his works. So his little treatise *To Orosius, against the Priscillianists and the Origenists*, written in 415, is a careful analysis and critique of those positions the Spanish priest Orosius had summarized for him, in a written memorandum or *Commonitorium*, and probably at greater length orally.[15] Augustine here offers a measured refutation of what he understands to be those Origenist positions that clash with the received faith of the Church: that the punishment of fallen angels and sinners in Hell is not genuinely eternal; that Christ's final "subjection" of himself and his Kingdom to the Father, mentioned in 1 Corinthians 15:28, will mean the dissolution of creation in a featureless union with God; that the "place" of rational creatures, in this world of very unequal destinies, is due to their fall from union with God through a pre-cosmic sin; that creation is co-eternal with God; that all spiritual creatures, including the angels, need to go through a process of purgation before reaching full beatitude; that the purpose of the "new heaven and new earth" promised in Scripture (Isa 66:22; Rev 21:1) is only to be a place of purgation for souls; and that the sun and stars are animated bodies.

Throughout his remarks on what Orosius had represented to him as Origen's theories, it is important to note that Augustine remains cautious and low-keyed, commenting only that some of those propositions seem to him to be alien to a "sound Christian faith"[16] or that it would be "better" to take a different position.[17] After observing that even the authors of the books of Scripture occasionally make false or misleading statements about these

12. Ep. 40.6.9 (trans. Teske, 151).

13. Ep. 82.3.23.

14. Bammel, "Augustine, Origen and the Exegesis of St. Paul" (above, n. 6).

15. For both works, see CCL 49.157–178.

16. *Contra Priscillianistas et Origenistas*, CCL 49.170.161–162.

17. Ibid. 172.204.

things, he concludes with an affirmation of the normativity of Scripture, "which God has set up as a kind of sky over all human hearts,"[18] and suggests:

> Perhaps learned scholars [like Origen?] will teach you these things, if you apply to them as much of a knowledge of how to learn as you do a concern for knowing, so that you don't form opinions about the unknown as if it were known, or either believe what should not be believed, or not believe what should be.[19]

Augustine does not comment, interestingly, on several other points Orosius had identified as dangerous Origenist theories: that the "eternal fire" mentioned in the Gospel is a metaphor for the internal suffering of guilt, or that all intellectual creatures will eventually be restored to God's friendship—two points Augustine would later soundly reject in *City of God* XXI—or that the human body of Christ changed radically in its character in the course of sacred history, and that its materiality is now "diminished," although not totally vanished, in his uncircumscribed, glorious state at the right hand of the Father. One wonders if he was less sure than Orosius, in 415, that these ideas were errors, or if he simply neglected to deal with them.

Augustine continues his attitude of cautious criticism in the occasional remarks on Origen that appear in his later works. In Book XI of *The City of God* [written in 417] he expresses his "astonishment that a man so erudite and well versed in the Church's literature" as Origen could have been so wrong in suggesting, in his work *On First Principles*, that God created the material world as a place for the purgation of sin, rather than as a rich and variegated expression of his own goodness.[20] In Book XXI of the same work [from 426], Augustine spends a number of chapters criticizing the view of "tender-hearted Christians" who believe that no one, not even the evil spirits, will be punished eternally for their sins, and clearly has upholders of the Origenist tradition of universal salvation in mind. In his little treatise *On Heresies* [428], heavily based on an abbreviated version of Epiphanius's Greek handbook, Augustine is again explicitly cautious about condemning Origen for doctrines that may not be his, but says that any Catholic would be "violently shocked" by his doctrine of universal salvation, and by the apparent corollary that since no judgments are final, those ultimately

18. Ibid. 178.380.
19. Ibid. 178.382–385.
20. *De civitate Dei* 11.23.

converted from evil may again slip into sin, in an endless cycle of fall and redemption.[21] In two passages of his late *Unfinished Work against Julian* (of Aeclanum) [429–430], Augustine again brands as the "error of Origen" the notion that the devil will someday undergo conversion of heart and be saved.[22] Vittorino Grossi has made the fascinating suggestion that Augustine's real purpose in rejecting these putatively Origenist positions in these and other late works—the "watermark" or subtext involving Origen in the late Augustine—was his concern to reject the possible charge, from the followers of Pelagius and from others troubled by his own position on divine election, that he was simply offering another form of what was thought to be Origen's conception of an inexorably victorious divine will, overriding rather than mysteriously inhabiting creaturely choices.[23] As Caroline Bammel has remarked, the theses ascribed to Origen in these works, in the bald, assertive form in which Augustine rejects them, are in fact distorted, "a travesty of Origen constructed by anti-Origenists" like Jerome and Epiphanius;[24] the important thing for us to notice is that it is these putative Origenist *theses*, rather than any text of Origen himself, that Augustine criticizes, and that he always does so in a context of respect for Origen's continuing reputation as a scholar. One gets the sense that even when Augustine feels he must criticize Origen, his restraint is a sign he was aware of the risk involved in making polemical statements based on second-hand information.

In any case, as I have already suggested, it is difficult to know precisely just how much of Origen's work Augustine ever read, or what he would have thought of it had he studied it with care. More interesting, I think, and more fruitful than the question of Augustine's possible dependency on texts or passages of Origen, is a simple comparison of their ideas and their interpretive instincts, reflecting on the similarities and differences between the theological and exegetical visions of these two trail-blazers of Christian

21. *De haeresibus* 43 (CCL 46.310.14–311.26).

22. *Contra Iulianum opus imperfectum* 5.47 (PL 45.1484); 6.10 (PL 45.1518).

23. Vittorino Grossi, "La presenza in filigrana di Origene nell' ultimo Agostino (426–430)," *Augustinianum* 30 (1990) 423–40, esp. 430. The main scriptural text at issue in these late debates over divine election was 1 Tim 2:4: God "desires all people to be saved and to come to the knowledge of the truth." Augustine insists, in his later works on grace, that while God's mysterious choice of those on whom he will have mercy is not defeated by human freedom, the effect of grace is not to override human freedom but to restore and preserve it in its ability to choose the good. See, for example, *De correptione et gratia* 7.14; 8.17 [426–427].

24. Bammel, "Augustine, Origen, and the Exegesis of St. Paul" (see n. 6 above) 346, n. 26.

thought. How Augustine came to articulate positions that resemble those of Origen can be explained by indirect as well as direct influence; ideas have their day, and themes circulate in the bloodstream of religious as well as secular culture. What is more helpful to our own theological formation is to see ways in which these two powerful thinkers, whose influence was so determinative for the later course of Christian doctrinal development, actually agreed or disagreed in their approach to the central issues of intelligently articulating the faith.

As Henry Chadwick perceptively observed two decades ago—without much further elaboration—"perhaps the most striking parallels [between Origen and Augustine] occur in Christology."[25] What I propose to do here is to elaborate Dr. Chadwick's statement: to look, in a necessarily brief and summary way, at what seem to me to be the main similarities and differences between the understanding of the person of Christ, and of the mystery of our salvation through and in Christ, that appears in the works of these two great early Christian thinkers.

I. Similarities

1. Christ and Scripture

For both Origen and Augustine, it is so clear as almost to go without saying that the meaning of the whole Christian scriptural canon, Old Testament and New, is revealed and summed up in the Church's understanding of the person and the work of Christ. Origen begins his great elaboration of the rule of faith, *On First Principles*, by stating simply:

> All who believe, and who are sure that "grace and truth have come through Jesus Christ" (John 1:17) and realize that Christ is the truth—just as he said, "I am the Truth" (John 14:6)—receive the knowledge which leads humanity towards good living and happiness from no other source than the very words and teaching of Christ. By "the words of Christ" we mean not only those which expressed his teaching while he was made human and involved in flesh; for even before that, Christ, the Word of God, was in Moses and the prophets.[26]

25. Chadwick, "Christian Platonism in Origen and Augustine" (see above, n. 6) 229.
26. *De principiis* preface 1. For classic surveys of Origen's Christology, see Henri Crou-

For Augustine, too, the whole story of canonical Scripture is the story of the involvement of divine Truth, the Wisdom of God, in the world of creatures, to reveal the love that is God's sole motive for creating, and for redeeming those creatures who had fallen away from him;[27] the Word made flesh embodies that love concretely, in his person and the deeds of his life.[28]

> The whole of holy Scripture which was written before him was written to proclaim in advance the coming of the Lord, and whatever was committed to writing and sealed with divine authority after his coming tells of Christ, and urges us towards love. . . . Therefore there is, in the Old Testament, a hidden presence of the New, and in the New Testament a revelation of the Old.[29]

The starting point, Augustine argues, for grasping even the mystery of God's own being, which the Scriptures lead Christians to conceive as a Trinity of persons in a single reality or substance, is nothing else than the New Testament's presentation of Jesus, as the one who "emptied himself" from being "in the form of God" to take the "form of a servant" (Phil 2:7),[30] and who asked his Father to send on his disciples "the Spirit of Truth, whom the world cannot receive" (John 14:15–17). Christ himself is the summation of Christian faith and preaching, the only Word universally expressed in the Bible.

---

zel, *Théologie de l'Image de Dieu chez Origène* (Paris: Aubier, 1955); Marguérite Harl, *Origène et la fonction révélatrice du Verbe incarné* (Paris: Éditions du Seuil, 1958); Michel Fédou, *La Sagesse et le monde. Essai sur la christologie d'Origène* (Paris: Desclée, 1994).

27. *De doctrina Christiana* 1.35: "The whole temporal economy of our salvation, therefore, was shaped by the providence of God that we might know this truth and be able to act on it." Cf. ibid. 1.38.

28. The best survey of Augustine's Christology is still Tarsicius J. Van Bavel, *Recherches sur la Christologie de saint Augustin* (Fribourg: Éditions Universitaires, 1954). For briefer surveys, with more recent bibliography, see Brian E. Daley, "A Humble Mediator: The Distinctive Elements in Saint Augustine's Christology," *Word and Spirit* 9 (1987) 100–117; "Christology," in Allan D. Fitzgerald, O. S. A. (ed.), *Augustine through the Ages* (Grand Rapids: Eerdmans, 1999) 164–69.

29. *De catechizandis rudibus* 4.8 (CCL 46.128).

30. Origen, too, tends to refer back constantly to this text as the guiding framework for his understanding of the person and work of Christ, and of what it means to follow Christ: see, for example, *De principiis* 2.6.1; 4.4.5; *Contra Celsum* 4.15, 18; 6.15; *Commentary on John* 1.32. For a discussion of Origen's emphasis on the "self-emptying" of the Word of God, see Fédou, *La Sagesse et le monde*, 311–31.

2. *Jesus as Mystery*

Both authors prefer to speak of the mystery of Christ in concrete, personal, pastoral terms rather than in the analytic categories of formal ontology. The first and most striking thing about Jesus, as the Gospel presents him and faith understands him, is the paradox of God present in fully human form, God living our life. Origen sums up his own sense of the challenge to human faith Jesus embodies in a passage of *On First Principles*, Book 2:

> Of all the marvelous and splendid things about him, there is one that utterly transcends the limits of human wonder and is beyond the capacity of our weak mortal intelligence to think of or understand: namely how this mighty power of the divine majesty, the very Word of the Father and the very Wisdom of God, in which were created "all things visible and invisible," can be believed to have existed within the compass of that man who appeared in Judaea; yes and how the Wisdom of God can have entered into a woman's womb and been born as a little child. . . . The human understanding, with its narrow limits, is baffled and struck with amazement at so mighty a wonder; it knows not which way to turn, what to hold on to, or where to go. If it thinks of God, it sees a man; if it thinks of a man, it beholds one returning from the dead.[31]

Although Augustine, in some works written after 411, begins to use more technical, ontological categories to characterize the personal paradox of the Word made flesh, he tends to avoid this as well, and to use more concrete rhetorical tactics to invoke the inconceivable reality of what the Church professes about Christ. A passage from one of his early homilies, on Psalm 56, may serve as an example of Augustine's characteristic way of presenting the Mystery of Jesus:

> A whole human being is with the word, and the Word with a human being, and the human being and the Word are one human being, and the Word and the human being are one God.[32]

31. *De principiis* 2.6.2 (trans. George Butterworth [New York: Harper, 1966] 109 [altered]).

32. *Enarratio in Psalmum* 56.5 [393–394] (CCL 39.698). Compare this passage from one of his homilies on the Gospel of John, from 413: "Christ is the Word, and Christ is the Word of God, and Christ the Word is God; but Christ is not only the Word, since 'the Word

In the first book of his treatise *On the Trinity*, a section probably dating from the early 400s, Augustine reflects on the theological implications of Paul's language in Philippians 2:

> Because the form of God took on the form of a servant, each is God and each is human, but each is God because of God taking on, and each is human because of the human being taken on. Neither of them was turned or changed into the other by that "takeover"; neither godhead changed into creature and ceasing to be godhead, nor creature changed into godhead and ceasing to be creature.[33]

Augustine seems here to be deliberately straining the capacities of ordinary human language, in order to confront the believer with the mind-straining mystery at the heart of Christian faith—something that more technical categories such as "person" and "nature" might well be too weak to capture.

3. *Christ's Human Soul*

Nevertheless, both Origen and Augustine unequivocally portray Christ as the eternal Word or Wisdom of God, acting in and through a human being—a human soul and body—as his created instrument. Both writers simply assume a model of the human person that had become more or less standard in late antique philosophy, in which the core of a person's identity, the center of a person's activity and the subject of all qualities predicated of the person, is the self-determining consciousness or *soul*. In this anthropology, the soul plays a role in the human individual, the "little world" or microcosm, analogous to that played by the divine Logos in the "big world" of creation: of its own nature free from the vulnerabilities of matter, yet present to matter and spiritually experiencing its needs, maintaining the order and mutual support of all the parts of the material world as a functioning whole.[34] Augustine observes, for instance, in his early treatise contrasting the practices of the Catholic Church

became flesh and dwelt among us.' Therefore Christ is both Word and flesh" (*In Joannis Evangelium tractatus* 23.6 [CCL 36.235–236]).

33. *De Trinitate* 1.14 (trans. Edmund Hill [New York: New City, 1991] 75).

34. For examples of this analogy in the Church Fathers, see Athanasius, *Contra gentes* 30–33, 41–44; Gregory of Nyssa, *De anima et resurrectione* [*NPNF* 433–436 (integrative role of soul), 439–440 (soul and passions)]. For this same conception in Augustine's work, see his important letter to Volusianus (Ep. 137) [411–412] [trans. 122–125].

with those of the Manichaean community, "The human person is a rational soul using a mortal and earthly body."[35] For both authors, this conception of the soul as a person's active center or subject and the body as the soul's instrument offers the most obvious way of understanding the incarnation of God's eternal, transcendent Word in the world of human action. Origen offers a hypothetical narrative framework to integrate this conception of spiritual and mental action within a material universe with the biblical story of creation and redemption. "In the beginning," he suggests in *On First Principles*, the created universe consisted simply of a limited number of rational souls, enjoying blessedness by being united with God in loving contemplation, yet free in determining their own actions and relationships and so capable of turning away from God in rebellious self-affirmation.[36] After souls had fallen, in the great and ultimately inexplicable event of sin, and God had created the present material world as a place of medicinal exile and conversion, one still remained faithful—the soul which was to become Jesus in human history; by clinging to the Logos, he became inseparably one with him in spirit, as a lump of iron plunged in fire becomes fiery through and through.[37]

> Because this soul-substance acted as a mediator between God and flesh—for it was not possible that God's nature be mixed with a body without some mediator—the God-man, as we call him, was born; this substance took up an intermediary position, since it was not against its nature to take up a body. But, on the other hand, as a rational substance, it did not find it contrary to its nature to participate in God,[38] to whom it had, as we said before, totally yielded itself, as Word and Wisdom and Truth.[39]

For Origen, it is clearly the divine Logos, the agent of creation, who acts in and through Jesus to communicate saving knowledge and power to fallen,

35. *De moribus ecclesiae Catholicae et de moribus Manichaeorum* 1.27.52 (PL 32.1332) [387–388]; for a similar conception, see *De quantitate animae* (PL 32.1035–1080) [387–388]; *Confessiones* 10.6.9. For a discussion of this largely Neoplatonic conception of the soul, see Ernest Fortin, *Christianisme et culture philosophique au cinquième siècle. La querelle de l'âme en Occident* (Paris: Études Augustiniennes, 1959).

36. See especially *De principiis* 1.4–8; 2.9. Although Origen offers this theory as an explanatory hypothesis rather than as Church doctrine, it is a scheme that implicitly underlies much of his exegesis and theological argument.

37. *De principiis* 2.6.6.

38. In Rufinus's Latin translation, *capere deum*: a phrase found also in the Latin translation of Irenaeus, *Adversus haereses* 5.32.1.

39. *De principiis* 2.6.3.

embodied intellects; he is the moving and expressive force in the soul of Jesus, just as that soul is the moving and expressive force in Jesus's body—as Lothar Lies has phrased it, the "actual underlying subject" and "the ultimate foundation of all Christological statements" for Origen.[40] Drawing, somewhat fancifully, on a text in Lamentations, "The breath of our countenance is Christ the Lord, of whom we said that we shall live under his shadow among the nations,"[41] Origen suggests in this same passage that Christ, the eternal Son and Word of God "anointed" with his Spirit, is the inner breath of Jesus's soul and body, which follow his intellectual movements as our own shadow follows our physical gestures.[42] Without adopting Origen's framework narrative of the pre-incarnate life of Jesus (although, as we have said, he did at least consider the idea of the pre-existence of human souls as one way of articulating original sin), Augustine also identifies the soul of Jesus as the dynamic link between the transcendent Logos and the world of physical bodies:

> The Son of Man has a soul [he writes in an early Tractate on John's Gospel], and has a body. The Son of God, that is, the Word of God, has a human being, consisting of a soul and a body. Just as a soul having a body does not make two persons, but one human being, so the Word having a human being does not make two persons, but one Christ.[43]

And the place of contact between these two infinitely disparate beings is Jesus's soul, which—as a spiritual substance—is innately capable of participation in the spiritual life of God; so Augustine writes to his pagan correspondent Volusianus in 411,

> Unless the soul is mistaken in its understanding of its own nature, it is immaterial; much more immaterial is God's Word. Therefore the combining

40. "Das eigentliche tragende Subject [Christi] ist der Logos. Seine Persönlichkeit als der eine letzte Grund aller christologischen Aussagen kommt in seiner Fürsorglichkeit zum Vorschein." Lothar Lies, "Vom Christentum zu Christus nach Origenes' Contra Celsum," *Zeitschrift für katholische Theologie* 112 (1990) 176.

41. Lam 4:20.

42. *De principiis* 2.6.7. See also *Contra Celsum* 3.41, where Origen affirms: "He, whom we think and have believed to be God and Son of God from the beginning, is the very Logos and wisdom and truth itself. We affirm that his mortal body and the human soul in him received the greatest elevation not only by communion, but by union and intermingling, so that by sharing in his divinity he was transformed into God" (trans. Henry Chadwick [corrected edition: Cambridge: Cambridge University Press, 1965] 156).

43. *In Joannis Evangelium tractatus* 19.15 [413].

of God's Word with a human soul ought to be more believable than the combining of a soul and a body.[44]

One implication of this model for understanding the person of Christ is that the conscious freedom of Jesus's soul to determine his own actions is a key element in the unity of his person.

Augustine anticipates later developments in classic Christological doctrine by clearly affirming the unconfused presence in the whole Christ of both a human and a divine will.[45] Although Origen does not, as far as I know, reflect directly on the importance of Christ's two natural wills for our understanding of the Christian message, as Maximus Confessor would do four centuries later, this is clearly the implication of his portrait of Christ. It is because "the soul which belongs to Christ so chose to love righteousness as to cling to it unchangeably and inseparably, in accord with the immensity of its love," that it became one with the Word by quasi-natural bonds;[46] yet the Son's own will, Origen argues in his *Commentary on John*, is "unchanging from the will of the Father, so that there are no longer two wills but one will; thus, because there is one will, the Son says, 'I and the Father are one.'"[47] The personal unity of Word with human being in Christ, in the eyes of both writers, does not result in a mutilation of his humanity, but in its perfection and free transformation.

4. Christ as Mediator

Both Origen and Augustine like to characterize the central role of Christ in sacred history in the phrase of 1 Timothy 2:5, as that of "*mediator* between God and humans": the one who restores God and intelligent creatures to

44. Ep. 137 [trans. 128].

45. See, for instance, *Enarratio in Psalmum* 93.19 [summer, 414]; *Contra sermonem Arianorum* 6.7 [419].

46. *De principiis* 2.6.5.

47. *Commentary on John* 13.36. For a discussion of Origen's treatment of the human and divine wills in Christ and their role in determining his personal unity, see Rebecca Lyman, *Christology and Cosmology: Models of Divine Activity in Origen, Eusebius and Athanasius* (Oxford: Oxford University Press, 1993) 74–80. Origen's own reflections on the scene of Jesus's agony in Gethsemane, the classic New Testament text presenting the relationship of his human will and the divine will, are in the *Exhortation to Martyrdom* 29 and the *Commentary on John* 13.249.

a harmonious and loving relationship with each other, such as God had planned in creating them. There are differences, clearly, in the way they tend to understand this mediation. For Origen, it is mainly identified with the status of the Logos himself, even apart from his incarnation, as "image of the invisible God" and "firstborn of all creation" (Col 1:15); it is the Logos's role to communicate to creatures knowledge of the inaccessible Father, in a way that enables them to participate in wisdom and life.[48] Although Augustine also tends to speak of Christ's mediatorship primarily in terms of revelation, he usually emphasizes that this is due to his incarnation:

> Therefore he is the mediator between God and humanity [he explains in a sermon preached sometime between 409 and 411], because he is God with the Father, because he is human among human beings. Divinity without humanity is not a mediator; humanity without divinity is not a mediator. But between divinity alone and humanity alone the mediating link is the human divinity and the divine humanity of Christ.[49]

For both writers, the mediating work of the Son of God in the course of created history involves movement, often described as a "journey" and usually linked with the pattern of his humiliation and glorification summed up in Philippians 2:5–11, that key Pauline passage we have mentioned already. For Origen, the real content of every human journey is growth in knowledge of the truth, and in the holiness that is born of real knowledge. So, in a famous passage of his *Seventeenth Homily on Numbers*, Origen sees the book's long list of Israel's camping-spots in the desert, on their way to the Promised Land, as figural language for the soul's growth in knowledge of spiritual things, guided by God's hand; we, too, need always to be ready to "fold the tents" of our own particular stage of understanding and move close to our permanent place of rest with God.[50] In his own human life, the incarnate Word mirrored this journey of growth for us by first "emptying himself" of the sublime knowledge that was his, and in taking on a human soul and body took on our human need to grow, to learn, to question. Applying to Jesus Jeremiah's words, "I do not know how to speak—I am only a youth!" (Jer 1:6), Origen writes:

48. See *De principiis* 2.6.1; *Contra Celsum* 6.17; 7.43.

49. Sermon 47.12.21; on humanity's need for a mediator in order to find God, see also *Confessiones* 7.18.24–21.27; 10.42.67–43.70; 11.2.4.

50. *Homily 17 on Numbers*, 4 (SC 29.348–49).

He learns, then, and in a certain way acquires knowledge—not of great things, but knowledge of lower, smaller things; just as when I speak with small children, I force myself to stammer in baby-talk, so the Savior, as long as he is in the Father and remains in the majesty of divine glory, does not speak human language, does not know how to talk to those below, but then, when he comes in a human body, he says, "I do not know how to speak, for I am too young"—young in terms of his bodily birth, but ancient as the first-born of all creation.[51]

Jesus, for Origen, teaches us humility through a wide range of his human actions, revealing for the first time that humility is a God-given virtue.[52]

For Augustine, too—and still more emphatically—the "way" marked out for us by Jesus in his own history is the way of humility, which heals us from the "swelling tumor" of pride.[53] The point of Jesus's mediation, in fact, is in Augustine's view his role as *way*; so he writes, in Book 11 of *The City of God*:

It is as a human being that [Christ] is mediator, and through this, too, that he is the way. If there is a way between the one walking and the point towards which one is walking, one has a hope of reaching one's goal; but if there is none, or if one is unaware of how to get there, of what use is it to know where one wants to go? There is only one way that is assured against all error: that the very same person should be God and a human being—God, as the goal to which we are going, and a human being, as the way by which we go.[54]

Yet the very difficulty Augustine tells us he found himself in, as a young Manichee learning to read the world anew through Platonist lenses, was that he had not yet "embraced the Mediator" to walk on that way. And the reason was that he had still not grasped the central direction of that way:

As yet I was not humble enough to hold the humble Jesus; nor did I understand what lesson his weakness was meant to teach us. For your Word, the eternal Truth, far exalted above even the higher parts of your creation,

51. *Homily 1 on Jeremiah* 8 (SC 232.212–14).

52. *Contra Celsum* 6.15.

53. A familiar metaphor; see, for example, *Confessiones* 7.7.12.

54. *De civitate Dei* 11.2 [417]. For the same idea, see *De doctrina Christiana* 1.34.38.

> lifts his subjects up towards himself. But in this lower world, he built for himself a humble habitation of our own clay, so that he might pull down from themselves and win over to himself those whom he is to make subject to him; lowering their pride and heightening their love, so that they might go on no farther in self-confidence, but rather should become weak, seeing at their feet the Deity made weak by sharing our coats of skin, so that they might cast themselves, exhausted, upon him and be uplifted by his rising.[55]

To follow the way of the Mediator is to see in him the "mercy" of a "humble God,"[56] and to conform one's mind and one's heart to that humility.[57]

5. *The Goal of Faith*

For both Origen and Augustine, too, the long-term shape of Jesus's saving effect on the life of the disciple is to lead him or her more and more deeply into the knowledge of divine Truth that enables created minds to participate in God's life. Origen tends to identify this with a growing ability to read Scripture not just "according to the flesh," but "according to the Spirit" (see 2 Cor 5:16), to be more and more aware of Christ's presence, as divine Word and Wisdom, in or beneath the surface-meaning of any given text. In the introduction to his great *Commentary on John*, where he is talking about the Christian's ability to hear in all of Scripture the "good news" of God's promise fulfilled, Origen remarks:

> One must be a Christian both in a spiritual way and in a bodily way. And when it is required to proclaim the "bodily" Gospel, saying among fleshly people that one "knows nothing except Jesus Christ and him crucified" (1 Cor 2:2), one must do that. But when they are found to be equipped with the Spirit and to be bearing fruit in him, in love with heavenly Wisdom,

55. *Confessiones* 7.18.24 (trans. Albert C. Outler [Philadelphia: Westminster, 1955] 152) (altered).

56. *De catechizandis rudibus* 4.8; cf. *De Trinitate* 4.4; *De peccatorum meritis et de remissione* 2.17.27.

57. The notion that humility is the condition for genuine knowledge of God and growth towards union with him is a theme that runs through Augustine's works; see, for example, *Contra academicos* 3.19.42 [386]; *In Joannis Evangelium tractatus* 25.11 [413]; *De Trinitate* 13.18.23 [416]; *De praedestinatione sanctorum* 15.31 [429].

> then one must give them a share in the Word that ascends upwards from the Incarnation, towards what he "was in the beginning with God" (John 1:2).[58]

Significantly, Origen sees in the incident of Jesus's transfiguration an invitation to that same process of growth: one must "ascend" with him from one's worldly preoccupations and modes of knowing, after passing through the "six days" of the present creation, to see him no longer in the "form of a servant" but in the "form of God," his divine identity shining like dazzling light through the "garments" of the scriptural text.[59] For Augustine, too, the "way" laid out for us by the Mediator—the way of humility—is precisely a way that leads beyond darkness to light, beyond faith to knowledge, beyond the weighty mortality of flesh to participation in God's endless life.[60] This is the process that he describes in Books 12–14 of *De Trinitate* as the mind's growth from the level of knowledge—which includes faith and characterizes our mental process in this present life—to the level of wisdom, which is nothing less than "the mind attaining to a share of [God's] nature, truth and happiness," "cleaving to God" and seeing unchangeably everything that God sees.[61] So Augustine remarks, in a homily for Ascension Day, 410, "Through

58. *Commentary on John* 1.7.43.

59. *Commentary on Matthew* 12.36–39. Frédéric Bertrand, in his now classic work *Mystique de Jésus chez Origène* (Paris: Aubier, 1951), analyzes in much greater detail the ways in which Origen presents this growth in knowledge of Jesus and personal relationship with him, through scriptural interpretation and through moral and spiritual growth. He classifies this progress in terms of five images Origen himself uses in his scriptural commentaries: looking for Jesus (like Mary and Joseph at the end of Luke 2); approaching Jesus (like the crowds and the sick, and like the disciples who "went into the house with him" in Matt 13:36); welcoming Jesus (like Peter in Mark 1:29, or Zacchaeus in Luke 19:6); following Jesus (like the disciples ascending the mountain of the Transfiguration in Matt 17:1–8); and touching Jesus (the hem of his garment: Mark 6:56; his feet, with penitential tears: Luke 7:38; his head, with ointment: John 12:3; his breast, like the Beloved Disciple at the Last Supper: John 13:23–25).

60. Although not explicitly described in terms of growth in and even beyond knowledge, Augustine presents this progress as the purpose of the Incarnation in *De Trinitate* 13: "For surely if the Son of God by nature became son of man by mercy for the sake of the sons of men (that is the meaning of 'The Word became flesh and dwelt amongst us' [John 1:14]), how much easier it is to believe that the sons of men by nature can become sons of God by grace and dwell in God; for it is in him alone and thanks to him alone that they can be happy, by sharing in his immortality; it was to persuade us of this that the Son of God came to share in our mortality" (13.12; trans. Hill 353).

61. *De Trinitate* 14.20. This final state of participative consciousness or wisdom, which will only be attained, by God's free gift, after this present life, brings to perfection the image of God in the created mind: ibid. 23–26.

Christ as human being, you find your way to Christ as God. . . . It is the same Christ, by which you go and to which you are going"[62]—but the goal, he suggests, is to know him not in the *forma servi*, but in the *forma Dei*. Or as he puts it in *City of God* 11, "Humanity's journey is to humanity's God through the God who became human."[63] As Henry Chadwick writes, "Both Origen and Augustine see the historical Christ as a concession to our weakness, through whom we may rise to the vision of the eternal."[64] And the reason is that for both of them human salvation is ultimately nothing less than the loving, endlessly unifying contemplation of God.

II. Differences

In a strikingly broad range of ways, then, I suggest, these two great theological pioneers offer us a similar understanding of the role of Christ as Incarnate Word and savior of a fallen creation. Clearly, however, there are major differences between them, in emphasis, tone, and actual theological content, which we must keep in mind in order to grasp their understanding of the person of Christ. In the brief space that remains for me here, let me simply sketch out a few of these differences.

1. The Stability of Christ's Bodily Nature and Appearance

One of Origen's most distinctive Christological themes is the variability or fluidity of Jesus's bodily form. In a famous passage of his *Contra Celsum*, for instance, Origen replies to the pagan Platonist's suggestion that Jesus's failure to reveal himself as divine to all his contemporaries shows a lack of power:

> Although Jesus was one, he had several aspects; and to those who saw him he did not appear alike to all. That he had many aspects is clear from the saying, "I am the way, the truth, and the life" (John 14:6), and "I am the bread" (John 6:35), and "I am the door" (John 10:9), and countless other such sayings. Moreover, that his appearance was not just the same to those

62. Sermon 261.7 (PL 38.1206).

63. *De civitate Dei* 11.2 [417].

64. Chadwick, "Christian Platonism in Origen and Augustine" (above, n. 6) 230.

> who saw him, but varied according to their individual capacity, will be clear to people who carefully consider why, when about to be transfigured on the high mountain, he did not take all the apostles, but only Peter, James, and John. For they alone had the capacity to see his glory at that time. . . . I think that at the time before he ascended the mountain when his disciples alone came to him and he taught them the beatitudes, even here when he was somewhere lower down the mountain, when it was late and he healed those brought to him, delivering them from all illness and disease, he did not appear the same to those who were ill and needed his healing as he did to those who were able to ascend the mountain with him and were in good health.[65]

Origen goes on to say that Jesus was generally visible to his contemporaries only before he had conquered the powers of sin and death; "but after he had 'put off the principalities and powers' (Col 2:15), all those who formerly saw him could not look upon him, as he no longer had anything about him that could be seen by the multitude."[66]

Origen gives at least three explanations for what may seem to us a very peculiar conception of Christ's human form. One is to draw the analogy with the Greek philosophical idea of "prime matter": of itself, simple matter—the metaphysical principle of continuity within change—is classically understood as capable of receiving any form and quality, but as having no proper form of its own; rather, "it is clothed with qualities such as the Creator wishes to give it, and often it puts aside its former qualities and receives better and different ones."[67] So the human body of Christ, he suggests, and in fact all human bodies, should be understood as capable of transfiguration. Secondly, Origen emphasizes that the Logos is the real subject, the controlling center, of the personal form and actions of the human Christ, even though he has a complete human soul and body. The human soul of Jesus freely chose to "cling" to the Logos, Origen insists, and in the process was so transformed that it was no longer susceptible to committing sin: "what formerly depended upon the will was by the influence of long custom changed into nature."[68] Thirdly, Origen sees the changing form of Christ's appearance as an integral part of the pedagogical process by which the Word leads fallen souls

65. *Contra Celsum* 2.64 (trans. Chadwick 115).
66. Ibid. (trans. Chadwick 115–16).
67. Ibid. 3.41 (trans. Chadwick 156).
68. *De principiis* 2.6.5 (trans. George Butterworth [New York: Harper, 1966] 112).

back to contemplative union with God. Origen writes, for instance, of Jesus's transfiguration:

> If you wish to understand the transfiguration of Jesus before those who "ascend the high mountain privately with him," you should realize that the Jesus of the Gospels is understood more simply, and known, as one might say, "according to the flesh" by those who have not ascended, through elevating works and thoughts, the "high mountain" of wisdom; but that he is no longer known according to the flesh to those who have ascended, but is understood as God throughout the Gospels, and is contemplated, by their way of knowing, in the "form of God."[69]

Coming to know Jesus as God, as the Word with his human soul and body, is the heart of the conversion process, in Origen's view; and he seems to have assumed that this could affect the very way Jesus's contemporaries actually saw him, just as it also determines the spiritual progress of the contemporary believer.

Augustine, on the other hand, offers no such speculations about Jesus's physical form, and shows surprisingly little interest in the Transfiguration episode in the Gospels. For him, the great contrast in Jesus's redemptive "way" remains that between the *forma Dei*, Jesus's inner identity as eternal Word, which is known only to the purified mind, and the *forma servi*, which the Word took on to reveal to us his way of humility. Certainly, he assumes that the Logos remained free with respect to creaturely necessity even when incarnate, and therefore in some sense not bound by the laws of his human nature in the same way that we are; but in fact, he assumed, the Logos did *choose* to make these necessities his own, and to live under them.[70] Whether even the eyes of our risen bodies will be able literally to "see" God in heaven, too, is something Augustine discusses at length in the last book of *The City of God*; at best, he suggests there, we will see him indirectly, in the renewed physical forms of a new creation: "God will be so known by us, and shall be so much before us, that we shall see Him by the spirit in ourselves, in one another, in Himself, in the new heavens and the new earth, in every created thing."[71] But Augustine never applies this notion of altered corporeality to the Jesus of the Gospels, or to our knowledge of Jesus in the present life.

69. *Commentary on Matthew* 12.37.
70. See Van Bavel, *Recherches sur la Christologie*, 124–27.
71. *De civitate Dei* 22.29.

2. *Grace, Freedom, and Christ*

One obvious difference in theological emphasis between Origen and Augustine is in their understanding of the present condition of human freedom, and its dependence on the healing grace of God to be effective. In the face of philosophical and Gnostic determinism, Origen staunchly defends the continuing ability of created intellects to determine their own moral choices,[72] even though he also affirms our need for God's gracious presence to be entirely successful in choosing the good;[73] in Augustine's day, Jerome accused Pelagius and his followers of being Origenists in their affirmation of the human ability to pursue perfection.[74] Augustine, on the other hand, as his theological career progressed, emphasized ever more strongly the impotence of the human will to steer any of us to perfection, or even to take the first steps in turning to God as savior.

This difference in perspective on the relationship of divine grace and human freedom left traces in the ways Origen and Augustine understand the incarnate Word. For Origen, the very union of Jesus's rational soul with the Logos is rooted in that soul's unswerving, pre-incarnate choice "to 'love righteousness' (Ps 44:8 LXX [45:7]), so that, because of its immense love, it clung unchangeably and inseparably" to the Word[75] and "by yielding itself to the Word's light and brilliance became with him, from the beginning, one spirit."[76] For Augustine, on the other hand, the Incarnation of God's Word served as the ultimate model of God's redemptive, utterly unmerited gift of himself, a gift that stands at the origin of human freedom and choice rather than responding to it. So in his late work *On the Predestination of the Saints* [428–429]—perhaps with a critical glance at what he has heard of Origen's Christology—Augustine remarks that "the most illustrious light of predestination and grace is the Savior himself—'the mediator himself between God

72. See especially *De principiis* 3.1.

73. See, for example, *Commentary on John*, Greek fragment 45 (ed. A. E. Brooke, vol. 2 [Cambridge: Cambridge University Press 1896] 259–61: good works are generated by Christ and the Church together, as bridegroom and bride); *Commentary on Matthew* 10.19 (both human faith and divine power are needed, if our lives are to bear fruit); *Contra Celsum* 7.83 (we need God's help if our conscience is to be completely pure).

74. Ep. 133.3. On the connection between the Pelagian party and the Origenist tradition, see Clark, *The Origenist Controversy* (above, n. 9) 194–44.

75. *De principiis* 2.6.5.

76. Ibid. 2.6.3.

and humanity, the human being Christ Jesus' (1 Tim 2:5)."[77] The identification of God's Son with the human Jesus is the cause of his full humanity, including his ability to choose the good and bring it to realization; it is by being taken up into the life and being of God the Son that the humanity of Jesus, with all its faculties, comes into being—*ipsa assumptione creatur*![78] "Surely that gracious gift of his birth," he writes in another late work, "joined man with God, flesh with the Word, in the unity of a person. Good works followed on that birth—good works did not merit it!"[79] In us, too, it is our "new birth" as God's children by grace that enables us to be free for doing good.

3. *The Body of Christ*

In addition to differing understandings of the depth and radicality of our human need for healing grace, Origen and Augustine had different assumptions about the extent of salvation. Origen famously believed that at the end of cosmic history, however distant that might be, God's will to "reconcile the world to himself" (2 Cor 5:19) would be fully triumphant: evil will come to an end, Christ will destroy all forces hostile to God, and all intellectual creatures would be saved.[80] Augustine, on the other hand, remained convinced that God's final judgment of humanity would result in the eternal damnation of those who remained hardened in the alienation of sin; in many later works, he points out emphatically that the whole of humanity might justly be

77. *De praedestinatione sanctorum* 15.30 (trans. R. E. Wallis, in Whitney J. Oates [ed.], *The Basic Writings of Saint Augustine* 1 [New York: Random House, 1948] 804) (altered). Augustine goes on: "The human being [Jesus], how did he deserve this—to be assumed by the Word co-eternal with the Father into unity of person, and to be the only-begotten Son of God? Was it because any kind of goodness in Him went before [Incarnation]? What did he do before this? What did he believe? What did he ask, that he should attain to this unspeakable excellence? Was it not by the act and the assumption of the Word that that man, from the time he began to be, began to be the only Son of God?" (ibid.). See also ibid. 31; Sermon 174.2 [413]: "The Word of God, God's unique Son, took up a human soul and flesh, not because it had first deserved this or labored through its own virtue to receive this exalted station, but utterly *gratis*."

78. *Contra sermonem Arianorum* 6.8 [419].

79. *De correptione et gratia* 11.30 [426].

80. See *De principiis* 2.3.7; 3.6.1, 3; *Commentary on John* 1.16.91; *Homilies on Joshua* 8.5; *Commentary on Romans* 8.9. For a discussion of his theory of *apokatastasis* or universal salvation, and further literature, see my *The Hope of the Early Church* (2nd edition: Peabody, MA: Hendrickson, 2003) 58–59.

damned because of its participation in Adam's sin, and that the gratuitous nature of God's mercy is revealed precisely in that it is bestowed only on some individuals.[81] This difference in soteriological optimism leaves its traces in how Origen and Augustine use the term "body of Christ" in its corporate or social sense. For Augustine, the "whole Christ" (*totus Christus*), a term that often appears in his sermons as a key to understanding biblical images, clearly refers to the Church in its final perfection. Who is to be included in the Church, Christ's eschatological Body, is not yet fully clear, but certainly faith, baptism, the transforming gift of the Holy Spirit, and perseverance in grace are conditions for inclusion.[82] Origen, on the other hand, does not shy away from including all humanity, even all creation, in that eschatological Body, which the Son will "hand over to the Father" (1 Cor 15:28) in an act of final submission; so he writes, in a homily on Psalm 36:

> The Apostle says that we are the body of Christ, and each of us individually his members (1 Cor 12:27). Christ, therefore, is the one of whom the whole human race, perhaps even the totality of creation, is the body, and each of us individually are his members.... When, then, he has healed all who are called his body and his members, so that they no longer struggle in the sickness of disobedience, and all the members are healthy and subject to God, he rightly says that he will be subject to God, since we, his members, will be obedient to God in all things.[83]

This conception of who is to be saved, who will be included in Christ's Body and who is affected, even now, by his grace, leaves its mark, in turn, on the different approaches Origen and Augustine usually take to scriptural

81. See Ep. 186.4.12 [417]; Ep. 190.3.9–12 [418]; Ep. 194.2.4–5 [418]; Serm. 26.12.13 [418]; *Enchiridion* 25.99 [423–424]; *De civitate Dei* 21.12 [425–426]; *De correptione et gratia* 10.28 [426]; *De praedestinatione sanctorum* 8.16 [429]; *De dono perseverantiae* 14.35 [429].

82. See, for example, *De peccatorum meritis et de remissione* 1.31.60–33.62 [411]. In his *Homilies on the First Letter of John*, Augustine uses the image of Christ's Body, united by love and mutual communion, as the boundary between the true (Catholic) Church and the false Church (of the Donatists): see, for example, Hom. 10.3. For the concept of "Christ, head and members" as a hermeneutical principle, see, for example, Serm. 341.1; *Enar. in Ps.* 58.2; and see Michael Cameron, "Augustine's Construction of Figurative Exegesis against the Donatists in the *Enarrationes in Psalmos*" (diss., University of Chicago, 1996); Michael Fiedrowicz, *Psalmus Vox Totius Christi. Studien zu Augustins Enarrationes in Psalmos* (Freiburg: Herder, 1997); see also Fiedrowicz's introduction to Augustine, *Expositions of the Psalms* 1 (trans. Maria Boulding: Hyde Park, NY: New City, 2000) 43–60.

83. Origen, *Homily II on Psalm 36*.1 (SC 411.96).

exegesis. Both of them, as we have said, regard the whole canon of Scripture as containing a single message of salvation in Christ; but Origen's usual approach is to read this message, this Gospel, as good news for the individual seeking God, for the soul whose only ultimate fulfillment is in union with God through his Word, while Augustine's common assumption is that the Gospel is for the Church, and for those individuals whom God empowers to remain in the Church by the grace of perseverance.

One example, of many possible ones, must suffice for us here. In the eleventh book of his *Commentary on Matthew*, Origen offers an interpretation of the scene in Matthew 14:22–33, in which Jesus comes to his disciples across the waves as they are being tossed by a storm on the Sea of Galilee. Jesus allowed his disciples to sail alone and to fall into danger, Origen says, to teach them

> that the one who arrives at the other side reaches it because Jesus sails along with him. But what is the boat into which Jesus caused the disciples to enter? Is it perhaps the conflict of temptations and difficulties in which anyone may be constrained by the Logos, into which one goes unwillingly, as it were, when the Savior wishes to train his disciples. . . . The Savior then compels the disciples to enter into the boat of temptations and to go before him to the other side, and through victory over them to go beyond critical difficulties; but when they had come into the midst of the sea and the waves in these temptations . . . they were not able, struggling as they were without Jesus, to overcome the waves and the contrary wind and reach the other side. And so the Word, taking compassion on them who had done all that they could do to reach the other side, came to them walking upon the sea.[84]

For Origen, the familiar scene is a parable of human struggle with temptation, which providentially teaches us our need for the presence and instruction of the Logos in our lives.

Augustine, on the other hand, in a sermon to his congregation on the same text from about 400, sees in the passage a clear reminder of our need to be in the Church. All of us are "foreign travelers," he says, even though not all of us are particularly eager to go home.[85] Every voyage exposes one to storms:

84. *Commentary on Matthew* 11.5 (trans. John Patrick: *Ante-Nicene Fathers* 10 [repr., Grand Rapids: Eerdmans, 1980] 434–35) (altered).

85. Sermon 75.2; for this same idea, see *De doctrina Christiana* 1.4, from about the same time.

> So it's essential we should stay in the boat, that is, that we should be carried on the wood, to be enabled to cross this sea. Now this wood, on which our feebleness is carried, is the Lord's cross, with which we are stamped and reclaimed from submersion in this world. . . . [Jesus goes off to pray alone.] Meanwhile the vessel carrying the disciples—that is, the Church—is being tossed about and battered by the storms of temptations and trials; and there's no easing up of the contrary wind, that is, of the devil's opposition to her. But the one who is interceding for us is greater than he is. For in this turbulent situation in which we find ourselves struggling, he gives us confidence by coming to us and reassuring us. The one thing he has to do is stop us from shaking ourselves loose in our agitation in the boat, and hurling ourselves into the sea. Because even if the boat is being agitated and tossed about, still it is a boat. It alone carries the disciples, and receives Christ on board. Sure, it's in distress and danger in the sea, but without it we all perish immediately. So keep yourself in the ship, and turn to God with your requests. . . . If God enables seafarers to come safely to port, is he going to leave his Church to her fate, and not bring her through to the final haven of rest?[86]

The Church is our boat, our place of safety even when it appears to be going down; the Church is where the frightened disciple can expect to encounter the absent Christ; the Church is what Christ will ultimately save, and so will save all those still on board her. Christ's Body, for Augustine, is a very particular group of chosen individuals, sealed and nourished by the sacraments and enabled by grace to remain faithful, and it is in them that his power is felt and his presence realized.

One could say many other things, obviously, about the understanding of the person and work of Christ that runs through the work of these two seminally influential Fathers of the Church. Despite differences in language and theological culture, and despite Augustine's own uneasiness about Origen's orthodoxy, based on the conflicting estimates of his own contemporaries, they clearly share a great deal in their approach to understanding Jesus. Both were unrelentingly Christocentric in their approach to understanding the story of the world and the Mystery of God; both read Scripture as a single proclamation of Christ, a single Gospel; both understood Christ as God the Son, present in our world in the fullness of our human nature and sharing

86. Sermon 75.2–4 (trans. Edmund Hill; *St. Augustine: Sermons III* [Brooklyn: New City, 1991] 304–5).

our human experience, yet in his central identity divine; both identified the way of salvation as a journey with Christ, a journey through humility to participation in the life of God that can be best understood in terms of the knowledge that is also love—knowing Christ crucified, and moving through his death and resurrection, Good Friday and Easter, towards knowing him in glory, knowing him, the Son of God, as he is.

Towards the end of *The City of God*, Augustine asks what Paul means in saying, "No other foundation can anyone lay than that which is laid: Jesus Christ" (1 Cor 3:11).

> In a building, the foundation comes first. Whoever, then, has Christ in his heart, so that no earthly or temporal things—not even those that are legitimate and allowed—are preferred to him, has Christ as a foundation.[87]

Surely Origen would say the same thing—as would countless later voices in the Christian spiritual tradition. As disciples today, we still turn to Origen and Augustine, still engage their thought and puzzle over its oddities, because they have become for us a means of drawing closer to that foundation: because they teach us, as they have taught Christians for over seventeen centuries, to build our lives on the Mystery and the Person of Christ.

87. *De civitate Dei* 21.26 [426] (trans. Marcus Dods; in Oates [ed.] [above, n. 77] 600) (altered).

9 The Giant's Twin Substances

Ambrose and the Christology of Augustine's Contra sermonem Arianorum

St. Augustine's Christology has not been the object of a great deal of study. Three or four serious books,[1] it is true, and several weighty articles[2] have appeared over the last three and a half decades, discussing Augustine's understanding of the person and work of Christ and adding substantially to the handful of earlier works on the subject.[3] Yet in comparison with the abundance of scholarly works on other aspects of the Bishop of Hippo's thought, the attention paid to his Christology by modern scholarship has been strikingly small.

1. The most thorough and important study of Augustine's Christology remains that of T. J. Van Bavel, *Recherches sur la Christologie de saint Augustin* (Paradosis 10; Fribourg: Editions universitaires, 1954). Also important are W. Geerlings, *Christus Exemplum. Studien zur Christologie und Christusverkündigung Augustins* (Mainz: Grünewald, 1978); G. Remy, *Le Christ médiateur dans l'oeuvre de S. Augustin*, 2 vols. (Paris: Champion, 1979); H. Drobner, *Persons-Exegese und Christologie bei Augustinus* (Leiden: Brill, 1986).

2. Among recent articles on Augustine's Christology, see especially J. T. Newton, "The Importance of Augustine's Use of the Neoplatonic Doctrine of Hypostatic Union for the Development of Christology," *AS* 2 (1971) 1–16; B. Studer, "Le Christ, notre justice, selon S. Augustin," *Recherches Augustiniennes* 15 (1980) 99–143, and "'Una Persona in Christo.' Ein augustinisches Thema bei Leo dem Grossen," *Augustinianum* 25 (1985) 453–87; G. Bonner, "Christ, God and Man in the Thought of St. Augustine," *Angelicum* 61 (1984) 268–94. See also my survey, "A Humble Mediator: The Distinctive Elements in St. Augustine's Christology," *Word and Spirit* 9 (1987) 100–117.

3. Aside from brief treatments in standard works on the history of dogma, the main earlier study is the controversial book of Otto Scheel, *Die Anschauung Augustins über Christi Person und Werk* (Tübingen: J. C. B. Mohr, 1901).

The reason, undoubtedly, lies to a large extent in the subject itself. Although Augustine's theology and spirituality, taken as a whole, can justly be characterized as Christocentric, technical questions about the identity and achievement of Christ were not subjects of controversy or prolonged investigation for him, in the way that sin and grace, or the reality of the Church, or "the Trinity, which is God" surely were. So aside from several fine Christmas sermons,[4] a short, early refutation of Apollinarian Christology in the *Eighty-Three Various Questions*,[5] and the eloquent apologetic for the notion of an incarnate God that he sent to the senator Volusianus in 412,[6] Augustine generally deals with Christological issues warmly and movingly, but in passing. And while the centrality of Christ's role as mediator between God and the human race, as the "way" of humility leading us to "the humble God,"[7] remains clear from his earliest works, most of what Augustine has to say about the person of Christ is couched in fairly untechnical terms, and seems not to offer a ready analytical hand-hold for the modern interpreter.

The one set of works that offer an exception to this general observation—curiously neglected by scholars, yet an important part of Augustine's later theological development—are his works against the Arians. Not usually regarded as one of his major disputes, Augustine's public controversy with Arian Christians may have begun as early as 406, in a discussion held by the bishop and his friend Alypius with Count Pascentius, an imperial fiscal official[8] who was also an enthusiastic but somewhat confused Arian. After a single meeting, the dialogue was interrupted, and sputtered out in a series of increasingly petulant letters from both sides.[9] Towards the end of his life, Augustine took

4. *Sermones 184–196:* PL 33, 995–1021. Sermons 190 and 196 seem to date from the 390s; the rest were probably delivered between 410 and 416. In citing works of Augustine, I will give the date, when known, in square brackets immediately after the chapter numbers.

5. *De diuersis quaestionibus LXXXIII*, q. 80 [c. 395]: CC 44/A, 232–38. Several other of these questions deal with the relation of Jesus to the Father, in terms that suggest Augustine is thinking of the Arian controversy, although he nowhere mentions the Arians by name: see Qq. 16, 23, 37, 50, 60, and 69: CC 44/A, 21, 27f., 59, 77, 184–96 (esp. 185.53f.; 193.204–11; 194f.230–41).

6. *Epistula 137* [412]: CSEL 44, 96–125.

7. See, for example, *Confessiones* 7.18.24 [397–401]: CC 27, 108; *De catechizandis rudibus* 4.8 [399]: CC 46, 129; *Sermo 261*, 7 [Ascension, 410]: PL 38, 1206; *De ciuitate dei* 11.2 [417]: CC 48, 322.

8. Possidius, *Vita Augustini* 17, tells us that Pascentius was *comes domus regiae* and a *fisci vehementissimus exactor* (PL 32, 47.14ff.). For a discussion of what actual office Pascentius may have held, see J. R. Martindale, *The Prosopography of the Later Roman Empire* II (Cambridge: Cambridge University Press, 1980), pp. 834f.

9. *Epistulae 238–241*: CSEL 57, 533–62.

part in a more professional public disputation with the bishop Maximinus, the accomplished Arian preacher and apologist who seems to have come to Africa, perhaps from Illyria, with the imperial army commanded by the Gothic general Sigisvult in 427.[10] The transcript of their debate, together with the two books Augustine later wrote to refute Maximinus's position, provide us with his most complete treatment of the issues and scriptural *loci* at stake in the later Arian controversy in the West. But Augustine mounted substantial arguments against the Arian position in a number of other places, too: a letter, of unknown date, to a certain Elpidius, who had sent him an Arian treatise;[11] several of the later *Tractates on John*;[12] Books 5–7 of *De Trinitate*; and a number of explicitly anti-Arian sermons, none of them, as far as we can tell, delivered earlier than 416.[13] The key work for interpreting and dating all of these efforts, however, is a modest treatise that has not often been studied—an occasional piece, which bears signs of having been hastily written, yet a work that seems to mark both a turning point in his Christological thought and a new assimilation of the anti-Arian polemic of his old mentor, Ambrose of Milan: his little essay *Contra sermonem Arianorum*.[14]

In the second book of his *Retractationes*,[15] Augustine explains the context of this treatise: he has been sent a copy of an anonymous tract setting

10. For Maximinus's career, see M. Meslin, *Les ariens d'occident* (Paris: Editions du Seuil, 1967), pp. 92–96; M. Hanssens, "Massimino il Visigoto," *La Scuola Cattolica* 102 (1974) 474–514. For a general discussion of Augustine's controversies with Arians, see M. Simonetti, "Agostino e gli Ariani," *REA* (1967) 55–84; W. A. Sumruld, "Augustine's Theological Opposition to the Gothic Arians, AD 418–430" (diss., Southwestern Baptist Theological Seminary, 1985).

11. *Epistula 242*: CSEL 57, 563–67.

12. The most important anti-Arian passages in the *Tractates on John* are Tractates 18; 20 (both on John 5:19); 26.5–10 (on John 6:41–59); and 71 (on John 14:10–14). The first three of these are usually dated in 413, the last 418: see S. Zarb, "Chronologia operum Sancti Augustini," *Angelicum* 10 (1933) 50–110; 359–96; 478–512; 11 (1934) 78–91. Because of similarities of argument in some passages to the *Contra sermonem Arianorum*, Anne-Marie La Bonnardière dates all the *Tractates* from 24 on after 418: *Recherches de chronologie Augustinienne* (Paris: Études Augustiniennes, 1965), pp. 72–118. However, if the newly discovered Epistle 23* A is, as seems likely, referring to the *Contra sermonem Arianorum* as one of the works Augustine wrote in the autumn of 419 (see below), La Bonnardière's *terminus a quo* will have to be moved back a further year.

13. *Sermo 117*, 6–17 [418]; *Sermo 135*, 2–5 [417]; *Sermo 139* [416–418]; *Sermo 140* against Maximinus [Christmas 427 or 428]; *Sermo 183* [after 416]; *Sermo 226* [416–417]; *Sermo 341* [December 12, 418]; *Sermo 380*, 3–6 [June 24, 417]; *Sermo Guelferbytanus 17* [421–423]. See La Bonnardière, *Recherches*, 96f., 111.

14. PL 42, 683–708.

15. *Retractationes* 2.52 [426/427]: CSEL 36, 188f.

forth the principles of Arian theology, and has been urgently asked to reply. One of the letters of Augustine recently discovered by Johannes Divjak—*Epistle* 23* A—allows us to specify these circumstances, with cautious certainty, even more closely. Writing to an unnamed correspondent—perhaps his biographer, Possidius of Calama—in December of 419, Augustine there lists the works he has dictated since their return together from Carthage the previous September: an output of some 6,000 lines, he says, including "something against the Arians, in reply to what our friend Dionysius sent me from Vicus Juliani."[16] Among Augustine's extant anti-Arian works, only the *Contra sermonem Arianorum* is a direct reply to a document sent to him by a correspondent, so it seems plausible to identify it with the work mentioned in this letter. Although this means dating the *Contra sermonem Arianorum* about a year later than is usually supposed,[17] such a chronology fits smoothly into the general sequence of works given in the *Retractationes*, and sets this treatise, along with *Epistles* 190 and 202A, the first book of *De natura et origine animae*, and some of the *Tractates on John*, in the busy period between September 11 and December 1, 419.[18]

The Arian treatise Dionysius sent Augustine is apparently not so much a discourse or an organically developed tract as a set of propositions or theses, arranged in the general order of the ancient baptismal creeds and explaining in patient detail the anti-homoousian understanding of the relationship of the Son and the Spirit to each other and to the eternal Father. The Arian theology it presents is not the radical, dialectically grounded "anomoean" variety, against which the Cappadocians had aimed their efforts, but the older, more moderate "homoean" strain current among the Goths and represented in Latin, in the late fourth century, by the writings of Palladius of Ratiaria and Maximinus: a theology that recognized both Son and Spirit as truly divine, truly *like* the Father in deserving our worship, but that saw in their missions and their hierarchically ordered relationships, to each other and to the Father, proof that each is different (*alius*) from

16. *Epistula XXIII*A* (ed. Divjak): CSEL 88, 122.12f: ". . . dictaui contra Arrianos ad illud quod mihi Dionysius noster de Vico Iuliani miserat." Dionysius is otherwise unknown; Vicus Iuliani is about 25 miles from Hippo.

17. See, for example, Meslin, *Les ariens d'occident*, pp. 132ff.; La Bonnardière, *Recherches*, pp. 96ff.

18. For this chronology, as well as the identification of references in the letter, see the notes of Robert B. Eno in *Saint Augustine, Letters VI (1*–29*)*, FC 81 (Washington, DC: Catholic University of America Press, 1989), 165–67. I am grateful to Fr. George Lawless, OSA, for directing me to this passage in Epistle 23*A.

the others "in nature and rank, position and condition, dignity and power, ability and action."[19]

Augustine's point-by-point, thesis-by-thesis reply to the document's conception of God is brief, but consistent with the position he expounded at such length in the *De Trinitate*, the last parts of which he seems to have written shortly after *Contra sermonem Arianorum*.[20] God is radically, indivisibly one, he argues, in nature and operation, even though Father, Son, and Spirit may never be confused with one another.[21] "The whole [Trinity], whatever it is, is the ultimate, true, unchangeable God."[22] The distinction of the persons, then, rests not in their works—which they perform as one[23]—but in their relationships of origin;[24] even taking flesh, which is proper to the Son alone, is not a sign of a lesser nature, and is done with the active cooperation of the Father and the Spirit.[25] So Augustine's argument in the treatise moves quickly and inevitably from a consideration of the Arian understanding of God's trinity and unity to the issue of the unity and distinction within the person of Christ. Recognizing that the Arian position, probably since Arius himself, had been largely based on the assumption that a God capable of direct contact with the world—capable of creation and providence, of incarnation and suffering—must be God in a lesser sense than the God of transcendent mystery, Augustine articulates here a portrait of Christ that distinguishes, with a technical precision and a concentration of phrasing

19. *Sermo Arianorum* 31: PL 42, 681f: "Alium esse [Spiritum] a Filio, et natura et ordine, gradu et affectu, dignitate et potestate, virtute et operatione, sicut et Filius natura et ordine, gradu et affectu, divina dignitate et potestate, unigenitus Deus alius est ab ingenito Deo." On the theology of the Western Arians in the late fourth and early fifth century, see the works of Meslin and Simonetti, and R. P. C. Hanson, "The Arian Doctrine of the Incarnation," in R. C. Gregg (ed.), *Arianism: Historical and Theological Reassessments* (Patristic Monograph Series 11; Cambridge, MA: Philadelphia Patristic Foundation, 1985), pp. 181–211. For a careful portrait of Homoean Arianism, Western and Eastern, see R. P. C. Hanson, *The Search for the Christian Doctrine of God* (Edinburgh: T. and T. Clark, 1988), pp. 557–97.

20. See La Bonnardière, *Recherches*, 75, 111, 166f., where she argues that at least *De Trinitate* 2.3.5 and 15.20.38 reflect arguments already set forth in *Contra sermonem Arianorum*.

21. *Contra sermonem Arianorum* 15.9: PL 42, 694.53–695.2.

22. *Contra sermonem Arianorum* 27.23: PL 42, 702.33f: "Totum quidquid illud est, summum, verum, immutabilem Deum."

23. *Contra sermonem Arianorum* 15–16, 9: PL 42, 694.4–696.3.

24. See, for instance, *Contra sermonem Arianorum* 14.9; 15.9; 23.19: PL 42, 693.19–25; 694.4–695.2; 700.9–21.

25. *Contra sermonem Arianorum* 15.9: PL 42, 695.4–24.

infrequent in his earlier works, between a complete human reality and the complete reality of God, both within the unity of a single, acting person.

Augustine begins the section of his treatise that deals directly with the person of Christ—chapters 5 through 14—with the observation that what the Arian document in his hands says about the Son assumes "that Christ took up human flesh without a human soul."[26] This is, he says, "the particular heresy of the Apollinarians," but it has always been characteristic of Arian theology as well.[27] In his *De haeresibus*, written in 428, Augustine repeats this point, and says he found it to be true in his own reading and discussions, though he has not found it said against the Arians by any other Catholic writers except Epiphanius.[28] The point is well taken; a strong *logos-sarx* model of the person of Jesus had, in fact, been characteristic of Arian theology since the beginning, and had formed an essential element in their portrait of the Lord as a mediating figure between the transcendent God and the world of fallen creatures.[29] What is curious here is Augustine's apparent surprise at his discovery, since Ambrose had made the same point fairly clearly in his *De incarnationis dominicae sacramento*.[30] And this fact becomes even stranger when one realizes, in reading on in Augustine's treatise, how similar his own terminology and line of argument are to those used by Ambrose himself in his anti-Arian treatises. In the six chapters that follow, Augustine proceeds to refute the propositions in his Arian tract that deal specifically with the human experiences and behavior of Jesus, and does so by insisting over and over that the biblical evidence shows us not a soulless hybrid, superior to humans in his godlike internal constitution but always subordinate in being to the ultimate God, as the Arian Christ is, but rather that Christ "has joined to the only-begotten Word not only flesh, but also a human soul,"[31] and "that there is one

26. *Contra sermonem Arianorum* 5.5: PL 42, 686.54ff: ". . . hoc volunt intellegi, quod humanam carnem sine humana anima Christus assumpserit."

27. *Contra sermonem Arianorum* 5.5: PL 42, 686.56–687.1: ". . . quae propria haeresis Apollinaristarum est: sed etiam istos, id est, Arianos, in eorum disputationibus, non solum Trinitatis diversas esse naturas, sed etiam hoc sentire deprehendimus, quod animam non habeat Christus humanam."

28. *De haeresibus* 49: CC 46, 321.6–11; for Epiphanius's treatment of the same point, see *Ancoratus* 35: CCS 1.44; *Panarion* 69.60.1f.: GCS 3.208f.

29. For a thorough discussion of the role of this Christological model in the development of Arian theology in East and West, see especially Hanson, "The Arian Doctrine of the Incarnation" (above, note 19).

30. *De incarnationis dominicae sacramento* 6.49: CSEL 79, 249.

31. *Contra sermonem Arianorum* 9.7: PL 42, 690.16ff.: ". . . fateanturque Christum non tantum carnem, sed animam quoque humanam Verbo unigenito coaptasse."

person in both natures—that is, the nature of God and of a human person."[32] The emphasis on the soul of Christ is, of course, not new for Augustine; in *Confessions* 7, for instance, he recalls that while his friend Alypius, in their pre-conversion days, thought all Catholics had an effectively Apollinarian notion of Christ, the two of them already saw clearly that the New Testament presented him as a complete human being.[33] Augustine continued to stress the importance of Christ's human soul throughout his works, especially as the point of contact between the Word and his humanity.[34] What is new here is his explicit, metaphysically precise reflection on the continuing, functional completeness of Christ's human nature, within the unity of a single subject, as a way of showing the continuity between the New Testament evidence and the faith of Nicaea. In doing this, Augustine seems unmistakably to echo, in ways he has not done since his very earliest Catholic writings, the categories and arguments of Ambrose, especially of several passages in his *De fide* and *De incarnationis dominicae sacramento.*

The most obvious clue to a link with Ambrose here is Augustine's reference to Christ as a "twin-substanced giant," *geminae gigas substantiae*,[35] a striking phrase from Ambrose's Christmas hymn, *Veni, redemptor gentium*, which Augustine and later Latin writers delighted in quoting.[36] Giants, to the classical mind, were "sons of the earth," often referred to in Latin poetry,

32. *Contra sermonem Arianorum* 7.6: PL 42, 688.16ff.: "Unam quippe ostendit esse personam in utraque natura, hoc est, Dei et hominis. . . ."

33. *Confessiones* 7.19.25: CC 27, 108.7–109.30.

34. For references, see Van Bavel, *Recherches sur la Christologie*, pp. 51–54; Daley, "A Humble Mediator," 102ff.

35. *Contra sermonem Arianorum* 8.6: PL 42, 689.27.

36. The fifth strophe of the hymn is as follows:

Procedat e thalamo suo,
pudoris aula regia,
geminae gigans substantiae;
alacris occurrat viam.

For the text of the hymn and a full discussion of the literary questions surrounding it, see A. S. Walpole, *Early Latin Hymns* (Cambridge: Cambridge University Press, 1922), pp. 50–57; M. Simonetti, *Studi sull' innologia popolare cristiana dei primi secoli* (Atti dell'accademia nazionale dei Lincei 8.4.6: Rome, 1952), pp. 382–87. Both Simonetti and Walpole regard this hymn as certainly by Ambrose; Simonetti dates it around 385–387, because of its anti-Arian content (see Paulinus, *Vita Ambrosii* 13; Augustine, *Confessiones* 9.7.15 on the origin of Ambrose's composition of hymns). For the later use of the phrase *geminae gigas substantiae*, see J. De Ghellinck, "Note sur l'expression 'Geminae Gigas substantiae,'" *Recherches de science religieuse* 5 (1914) 416–21.

with other mythic monsters, as "composite" (*gemini*) or even "two-bodied" (*bicorpores*), because they combined various characteristics of humans and beasts.[37] Philo saw in the giants of Genesis 6:4 a figurative allusion to souls who had left their "better situation" to dwell in an inferior place, by abandoning the path of reason and transforming themselves "into the lifeless and inert nature of flesh," thus becoming "sons of the earth" in a negative sense.[38] So when Psalm 18:6, in the old Latin version, referred to the sun's course with the phrase,

> He has come forth like a bridegroom leaving his chamber,
> He has rejoiced, like a giant, to run his way,[39]

the application to Christ, the "sun of justice" who became flesh for us, lay close at hand, particularly since this psalm appears to have been used in the liturgy for the key Christological feasts of Christmas and the Ascension since the late fourth century.[40]

In the mind of Ambrose (who knew both his Latin literature and his Philo), and later of Augustine, it was the Incarnation, the conjunction of the two realities of God and a human being in the intimacy of a single womb and the strenuous course of a single life, that made Christ both "bridegroom" and joyful "giant," Son of God and "son of the earth." Ambrose writes:

37. See, for instance, the reference to Runcus and Purpureus, "sons of the earth," as *bicorpores gigantes* in Naevius, *De Bello Punico* I, Frag. 19 (20): ed. W. Morel, *Fragmenta Poetarum Latinorum Epicorum et Lyricorum* (Stuttgart: Teubner, 1963), p. 20. For references to centaurs, Triton the merman, and the Minotaur (half bull, half man) as *gemini*, see, e.g., Ovid, *Metamorphoses* 12.449; Manilius, *Astronomica* 2.552; 4.785; Seneca, *Medea* 641; Statius, *Thebaid* 5.707; *Silvae* 1.4.98.

38. Philo, *De gigantibus* 15.65; cf. 13.60.

39. "Et ipse tamquam sponsus procedens de thalamo suo; / exultavit sicut gigas (gigans) ad currendam viam. . . ."

40. For the use of Ps 18:6 in the liturgy of both feasts, see Augustine, *Sermones 372*, 2 (Christmas) and *377* (Ascension): PL 39, 1662 and 1672. Both sermons are listed among the *sermones dubii* of Augustine, but are probably from the early fifth century; *Sermo 372*, 3 alludes to the fact that the congregation has just sung the Ambrosian hymn containing this expression (PL 39, 1663.25–31). In the pre-Vatican II Latin liturgy, Ps 18:6 appeared in both the Gradual and the Communion antiphon for the Ember Saturday in Advent, in antiphons for both Matins and Second Vespers of Christmas Day, in a responsory for the feast of the Visitation, and in an antiphon for Matins on the feast of the Ascension: see C. Marbach, *Carmina Scripturarum* (Strassburg, 1907), ad loc.

> The holy prophet David described him as a giant, because he is one in a double, composite nature, and shares both in divinity and in humanity; "coming forth like a bridegroom from his chamber, he has rejoiced like a giant to run his way": the bridegroom of the soul, according to the phrase, and a giant of the earth, who, passing through all the duties of our way of life, even though he was always the eternal God, took on himself the mysteries of the Incarnation—not divided, but one, because each element is one person and one person is in both elements, namely divinity and the body.[41]

The one who had "joined himself to our human nature" like a spouse in his bridal chamber, Augustine later remarked, then "rejoiced to run the way": "he was born, he grew, he taught, he suffered, he rose, he ascended—he *ran* the way, he did not *cling* to the way!"[42] The psalm-verse clearly spoke to both authors of the mystery of the Incarnation, of the earthy vitality of the Lord; yet for Augustine in the *Contra sermonem Arianorum*, it is not merely the psalm-verse that comes to mind, apparently, but Ambrose's use of it: not only does he quote Ambrose's poetic phrase in full, but twice more, in this same section of the work, he refers to Christ as *gemina substantia . . . sed una persona*, language otherwise rare in Augustine's Christological terminology.[43]

41. *De incarnationis dominicae sacramento* 5.35: CSEL 79, 240f.10–19: "Quem quasi gigantem sanctus David propheta describit, eo quod biformis geminaeque naturae unus sit, consors divinitatis et corporis, qui 'tamquam sponsus procedens de thalamo suo exultavit tamquam gigans ad currendam viam,' sponsus animae secundum verbum, gigans terrae, quia usus nostri officia percurrens, cum deus semper esset aeternus, incarnationis sacramenta suscepit, non divisus, sed unus, quia utrumque unus et unus in utroque, hoc est vel divinitate vel corpore." For Augustine's similar interpretation of the verse, see *Enarratio in Psalmum 18, Sermo 1*, 6 [392]: CC 38, 103.9–12; *Enarratio in Psalmum 18, Sermo* 2, 6 [411/412]: CC 38, 109.27–110.34; *Enarratio in Psalmum XLIV* 3 [403]: CC 38, 495.14–17; *Enarratio in Psalmum 87*, 10 [414/416]: CC 39, 1215.36–40; *Confessiones* 4.2.19 [397–401]: CC 27, 50.22–25; *De consensu evangelistarum* 1.3.46 [400]: CSEL 43, 47.7–11; *In Ioannis Epistulam ad Parthos tractatus* 1.2 [407?]: PL 35, 1979.28–40. Following the Psalm, Augustine usually emphasizes the strength implied in the image of the giant, rather than his earthiness.

42. *Enarratio in Psalmum 18, Sermo* 2, 6 [411–12]: CC 38, 110.31–34: "Hoc est enim 'gigas exultauit ad currendam uiam': natus est, creuit, docuit, passus est, resurrexit, ascendit; cucurrit uiam, non haesit in uia." Compare his interpretation in the "dubious" Christmas sermon mentioned above: *Sermo 372*, 2: PL 39, 1662: "'Processus ut sponsus,' 'exultavit ut gigas.' Pulcher et fortis: pulcher ut sponsus, fortis ut gigas. Pulcher, ut ametur; fortis, ut timeatur; pulcher ut placeret, fortis ut vinceret. . . ."

43. *Contra sermonem Arianorum* 7.6: PL 42, 688.19f: "Quoniam itaque gemina quidem substantia, sed una persona est . . ."; ibid. 9.7: PL 42, 690.16–22: "fateanturque Christum non tantum carnem sed animam quoque humanam Verbo unigenito coaptasse, ut esset

This Christological part of his treatise has other similarities, too, to arguments of Ambrose in the *De incarnationis dominicae sacramento*: each of them fairly insignificant in itself, but all significant in their convergence. In chapter 7, for instance, just before his first reference to the *gemina substantia* in the one person of Christ, Augustine argues: "He revealed that there is indeed one person in both natures—that is, the natures of God and the human being—lest, if he should make two [persons], there should begin to be a quaternity, not a trinity."[44] Ambrose, too, in his argument against the Apollinarian Christology of both Arians and Nicenes, had made the same point negatively:

> Nor am I afraid of seeming to introduce a tetrad [i.e., instead of a triad or trinity]. For we, who make this profession [of a human soul in Christ], worship only a trinity. I do not divide Christ, when I distinguish the substance of his flesh from his divinity, but I preach one Christ with the Father and the Spirit of God. . . . For he is not one person [*unus*], because he shares the same substance, but one thing [*unum*].[45]

Ambrose turns his point in a slightly different direction from Augustine's, arguing that it is the Apollinarians who, by making the flesh of Christ "one substance" with God, alongside the Word, seem to be introducing a *quartum increatum* into the divine Mystery.[46] But it is nonetheless striking that

una persona; quod Christus est Verbum et homo, sed ipse homo anima et caro, ac per hoc Christus Verbum, anima et caro. Et ideo sic intelligendus geminae substantiae, divinae scilicet et humanae. . . ." On Augustine's use of *substantia* for speaking of the underlying divine and human realities in Christ, a term going back to Tertullian, see Van Bavel, *Recherches sur la Christologie*, p. 45; V. Bourke, *Augustine's View of Reality* (Villanova, PA: Villanova University Press, 1964); for the background and implications of this and related terms, see A. de Halleux, "'Hypostase' et 'Personne' dans la formation du dogme Trinitaire (ca. 375–81)," *Revue d'histoire ecclésiastique* 79 (1984) 313–69, 625–70.

44. *Contra sermonem Arianorum* 7.6: PL 42, 688.16–19: "Unam quippe ostendit esse personam in utraque natura, hoc est, Dei et hominis, ne si duas faciat, quatemitas incipiat esse, non trinitas." For a similar argument, also in the context of "two-substance" language about Christ, see Augustine, *Sermo 130*, 3: PL 28, 727.10–12 (see below, n. 61).

45. *De incarnationis dominicae sacramento* 7.77: CSEL 79, 263.140–48: "Nec timeo, ne 'tetrada' videar inducere. Nos enim vere solam, qui hoc adserimus, colimus trinitatem. Non enim Christum divido, cum carnis eius divinitatisque distinguo substantiam, sed unum Christum cum patre et spiritu dei praedico. . . . Non enim, quod eiusdem substantiae est, unus, sed unum est."

46. Ibid. 77f.

Augustine's echo of his "twin-substance" language should also echo concern to show that such a conception of Christ does not endanger the Church's Trinitarian confession.

A few paragraphs later, Augustine quotes from the Arian document a curious passage depicting Christ entering the glory of the Father "with his very body, like a shepherd with his sheep and a priest with his offering and a king with his purple garment."[47] He asks, ironically, what kind of sheep this might be. "If it is flesh without a soul that [Christ] brought back [to the Father], what is that sheep but senseless earth, which cannot give thanks? What can flesh do without a soul?"[48] Ambrose, in the same seventh chapter of *De incarnationis dominicae sacramento* that I have just cited, asks a similar question of those who propose a Christ made up of Word and flesh:

> What use would it be to take up flesh without a soul, since after all senseless flesh and an irrational soul are neither susceptible of sin nor worthy of reward? He took up, then, for my sake, what was more seriously endangered in us. What good is it to me, after all, if he did not redeem all of me?[49]

Although Augustine, characteristically, focuses on the ability to give thanks to God as the fulfillment of salvation, the soteriological uselessness of a Christ with human flesh but no human soul is the point of his question as it had been of Ambrose's.

A few paragraphs later, Augustine is replying to the Arian contention that God's command to his Son, "Sit at my right hand," implies—in the very glorification of Christ—obedient subordination. Augustine points out that words such as this, spoken within the Trinity, are always to be taken as metaphors for eternal relationships:

47. *Contra sermonem Arianorum* 10.8: PL 42, 690.50ff.: ". . . cum ipso corpore, ut pastor cum ove, et sacerdos cum oblatione, et rex cum purpura."

48. *Contra sermonem Arianorum* 10.8: PL 42, 690.52–57: "Quaerendum est ab eis qui ista dicunt, qualem ovem pastor reportaverit Patri. Si enim caro sine anima est quam reportavit, quid est ovis ista nisi terra sine sensu, quae nec agere gratias potest? Quia sine anima caro quid potest?"

49. *De incarnationis dominicae sacramento* 7.68: CSEL 79, 259.63–67: "Quid autem opus fuit carnem suscipere sine anima, cum utique insensibilis caro et inrationabilis anima nec peccato sit obnoxia nec digna praemio? Illud ergo pro nobis suscepit, quod in nobis amplius periclitabatur. Quid autem mihi prode est, si totum me non redemit?"

> How, after all, does the Son hear the Father? How are many words said by the Father to the one and only Word? How does he speak in a passing way to the one to whom he speaks everlastingly? How does he say something in a temporal way to the one, coeternal with himself, in whom all things were already present which he says at their proper times?[50]

Ambrose, too, in an earlier passage in the *De incarnationis dominicae sacramento*, insists that the Word of God is not to be understood as too closely analogous to temporal, human speech:

> The Son is not such a Word, because the Father of the Word is not such a Father. We must be careful, then, not to seem to raise in his case a question taken from corporeal speaking: God is incorporeal; he does not, then, as incorporeal, have corporeal speech. If there is no corporeal speech in the Father, the Son is not a corporeal word. If there is no body in the Father, there is no time in the Father; if there is no time in the Father, surely there is none in the Son.[51]

This theme of the difference between temporal speech and the wholly internal, bodiless, and timeless utterance of the Word of God is, of course, a familiar one in Augustine's works, and need not, of itself, show that he is thinking of Ambrose here.[52] Still, it is worth noting that this argument appears in both treatises in the context of arguments for the equality of Son to Father, and for the necessity of distinguishing between his humanity and his divinity as two complete substances.

Besides these Ambrosian resonances in the specifically Christological part of Augustine's treatise, there are also echoes in the same section, less verbal than structural, but at least as striking, of another anti-Arian work of Ambrose: the second book of his *De fide*, addressed to the emperor Gratian.

50. *Contra sermonem Arianorum* 12.9: PL 42, 692.20–26: "Quomodo autem Filius audit Patrem? quomodo dicuntur a Patre multa verba unico Verbo? quomodo transeunter loquitur ei quem stabiliter loquitur? quomodo aliquid temporaliter ei dicit in quo sibi coaeterno jam erant omnia quae congruis quibusque temporibus dicit?"

51. *De incarnationis dominicae sacramento* 3.19f.: CSEL 79, 233.63–69: ". . . non tale verbum filius, quia non talis est pater verbi. Cavendum ergo, ne et illi quaestionem vocis corporalis videamur inferre: incorporeus est deus; vocem utique incorporeus corporalem non habet. Si vox corporalis non est in patre, nec filius verbum est corporale. Si corpus in patre non est, nec tempus in patre est; si tempus in patre non est, utique nec in verbo est. . . ."

52. See, e.g., *Sermo 119*, 7: PL 38, 675f. [date uncertain].

The Arian treatise Augustine is refuting has begun its own Christological section by asserting that the Incarnation of "the Lord Jesus" is proof of the honor in which God holds his human creatures, whom he has made "a little less than the angels."[53] So God sent the Son to carry out his will and redeem humanity by his death; but the very obedience of Jesus, according to the treatise, also shows his subordination, as divine Son, to the Father. Further, the treatise interprets his death as a separation of his body from the mediating divine Word that took the place, in him, of a human soul. Augustine responds, as we have already said, by a long and complicated argument for the equality of Son and Father based on the distinction of two complete and functioning substances—the divine and the human—within the single subject, Jesus. But the point of his argument, and the scriptural passages on which he bases it, also resemble closely the argument of Ambrose for the completeness and mutual harmony of two wills in Christ, and for the paradoxical unity of the divine and the human in Christ's single person, which Ambrose developed in *De fide* 2.5.41–2.9.73.

Although Augustine here is replying to a specific Arian document, with its own scriptural proof texts and its own particular assumptions used in interpreting them, it seems striking that he himself relies, to a large extent, on texts of his own, and that the texts on which he rests most of his argument are in most cases texts Ambrose used in this section of his *De fide*. Similarly, the main Christological points developed here by Augustine are the points Ambrose labors to establish in the passage I have cited: the implications of the two complete natures of Christ for the internal struggles of his will, as revealed in Scripture, and the paradoxical liberty a two-nature Christology gives us to predicate divine attributes of the man Jesus and human experiences of God the Son—the structural character of the person of Jesus known by later Christological writers as the "communication of idioms."

One may well ask just what these similarities prove. The scriptural texts Augustine draws into the argument here were doubtless familiar from a century of controversy over the relation of Jesus to God, and some—like John 10:30 and John 14:28—had been classic *testimonia*, evidence that had to be either welcomed or explained away, since the days of Tertullian and Hippolytus. Some of the likeness between Ambrose's thought and Augustine's on the issues at hand is also inevitably due to the likeness of their opposition: the Arians Augustine criticized in Africa, in 419 and afterwards, were the successors of the same Latin-speaking homoeans Ambrose had

53. *Contra sermonem Arianorum* 5.5: PL 42, 686.43–54.

opposed at Sirmium and Aquileia and Rome in the years between 375 and 382, and against whom he directed his earlier polemical tracts; Palladius was their ablest spokesman, and Maximinus, who later debated with Augustine, Palladius's leading defender. Inevitably, then, the anti-Arian arguments of Ambrose and Augustine could be expected to show similarities.

Nevertheless, risky though it always is to speculate on the influence of one ancient theologian upon another, I want to suggest that Augustine probably had at least these two works of Ambrose—the *De incarnationis dominicae sacramento* and the first two books of the *De fide*—in mind, and perhaps even in hand, as he dictated his critique of the Arian manifesto sent to him in the autumn of 419. In subtle but important ways, the Christology of this brief treatise marks a change of emphasis from the Christology of his earlier mature works. Augustine had emphasized, certainly, since the early 390s, the completeness both of the humanity of Jesus—internally and externally, soul and body—and of his divinity as Word; he saw these two realities as functional, active, yet united in the eternal *persona* of the Wisdom of God.[54] Yet in his works written between the mid-390s and about 412, Augustine usually stresses the transformation and elevation of the human nature of Christ in its assumption by the Word,[55] and sees the human acts of Christ essentially as accomplishing instrumentally, and revealing sacramentally, the divine acts of the Word,[56] much as the body, in Neoplatonic anthropology, acts fundamentally as revealer and instrument of the human being's personal center, the soul.[57]

54. See, for instance, *Expositio epistulae ad Galatas* 27 [394/395]: PL 35, 2125.3–9; *De agone Christiano* 20.22 [396]: CSEL 41, 122f.; *De consensu evangelistarum* 1.35.53 [c. 400]: CSEL 43, 59. On Augustine's use of the terms "nature" and "person" to express the union of the divine and the human in Christ, see Van Bavel, *Recherches sur la Christologie*, pp. 13–23, 47–57.

55. For references, see Van Bavel, *Recherches sur la Christologie*, p. 53; referring to this elevation and perfection of the human nature assumed by the Word, Van Bavel asserts: "Plus que n'importe quel Père avant lui, saint Augustin insiste sur ce point" (ibid.).

56. See, e.g., *De diuersis quaestionibus LXXXIII*, q. 73.2: CC 44/A, 211.45–212.67; for further references, see Van Bavel, *Recherches sur la Christologie*, p. 64f.

57. For his instrumental conception of the body in his earlier writings, see, e.g., *De moribus ecclesiae catholicae et de moribus Manichaeorum* 1.27.52 [387/389]: PL 32, 1332.46f.; *De quantitate animae* 13.22 [387/388]: CSEL 89, 158.6ff. Augustine continued, throughout his life, to conceive of the union of Word and human being in the Incarnation on the analogy of the union of soul with body: see, e.g., *Epistula 137* [411/412]: CSEL 44, 96–125. The purpose of the Incarnation is to help our human weakness "see" the divine Word (*Sermo 341*, 3, *contra Arianos* [418/19]: PL 39, 1495.7–10); Jesus's humanity is the "ass" on which the Word, like

Concern with the Arian question, however, began to be a real issue for Augustine around 413, if not before,[58] and this seems to have brought with it a clearer understanding that the human experiences and human reality of Christ had to be distinguished more unambiguously, more metaphysically, from his divine nature, as somehow coordinate and mutually complementary within the subjective unity of his person, if one were not to be drawn into the Arian error of conceiving the Word as limited by the created bounds of the human being he assumed, as made less than God by his very identity with a human soul and body. So it is in the *Enarratio* on Psalm 93, delivered at Thagaste in the summer of 414, that Augustine—without referring to the Arians—elaborates seriously for the first time on the two complete wills in Christ, revealed in his struggle at Gethsemane;[59] and it is in these same years that he comes to speak more reflectively on the paradox of the reciprocal predication of divine and human attributes for the two natures in Christ—what has come to be known as the *communicatio idiomatum*—a procedure that presupposes a structural symmetry in the constitution of the Incarnate Word.[60]

With the *Contra sermonem Arianorum*, we find the first full-scale articulation, in precise language, of this new Christological perspective. Not only does Augustine use here—three times—Ambrose's picturesque phrase *gemina substantia* for the two realities in Christ: a formula echoing the older Latin tradition of Tertullian's *Adversus Praxean* but not found, to my knowledge, in Augustine's earlier works.[61] He also insists here, more clearly than

the Good Samaritan, lays the wounded body of humanity (e.g., *Sermo 119*, 7: PL 38, 676.1–3; *Sermo 341*, 3 [418/19]: PL 39, 1495.12–15). See also Geerlings, *Christus Exemplum*, pp. 110–14.

58. See Tractates 18 and 20 on the Gospel of John, usually dated about 413, which deal directly with the Arian interpretation of the relation of the Son to the Father, in connection with John 5:19.

59. *Enarratio in Psalmum 93*, 19: CC 39, 1319–21.

60. See, for instance, *De peccatorum mentis et remissione* 1.31.60 [411]: CSEL 60, 61.1–8; *Epistula 187*, 3.9 [417]: CSEL 57, 88; *Tractatus in Euangelium Ioannis* 27.4; 111.2 [after 418?]: CC 36, 271.11–30; 629.11–14; *Contra Maximinum* 2.20.3: PL 42, 789f. See Van Bavel, *Recherches sur la Christologie*, p. 57.

61. *Sermo 130*, 3: PL 38, 727.8–10, speaks of *duae substantiae, sed una persona* in Christ, but the date of this sermon is uncertain. Augustine uses the phrase *gemina substantia* in *Tractatus in Euangelium Ioannis* 59.3 (an anti-Arian passage, using Ambrose's phrase directly), and *Tractatus* 78.3, both passages presumably from after 418, and in the late anti-Arian work, *Contra Maximinum* 2.10.2: PL 42, 765. For his reservations about the use of *substantia*-language for the persons in God, because of its suggestion of the possibility of accidents and its identification both with universal reality (= Greek *ousia*) and with con-

before, on the reality of Christ's two wills and the propriety of *communicatio idiomatum* language as concrete, existential implications of these two natures or substances.[62] The "one person," who is Christ, is now presented unabashedly as "Word and human being; but that human being is soul and flesh, and for this reason Christ is Word, soul and flesh."[63] True, this same way of expressing the mystery of Christ's person appears in one of Augustine's earliest sermons: *Sermon* 214, *In traditione symboli*, delivered at Easter 391, shortly after his ordination as a presbyter. There, too, the principle of the *communicatio idiomatum* is both enunciated and applied.[64] But the earliest works of Augustine, in their presentation of the doctrines of the Trinity and the person of Christ, show similarities to the thought of Ambrose that would not emerge again with such clarity until Arianism became for him, as it had been for Ambrose, a matter of direct concern.[65]

---

crete individuals (= Greek *hypostasis*), see *De Trinitate* 5.2.3–3.4; 5.8–9.10; 7.4.7–6.11: CCL 50, 207ff., 216f., 255–65; La Bonnardière suggests these books also, which deal directly with Arian arguments, may have been composed as late as 418.

62. See *Contra sermonem Arianorum* 7.6–8.6: PL 42, 687.38–689.35. For a formulation of the principle of the "communication of idioms," note the following: "Hanc unitatem personae Christi Jesu Domini nostri, sic ex natura utraque constantem, divina scilicet atque humana, ut quaelibet earum vocabulum etiam alteri impertiat, et divina humanae, et humana divinae, beatus ostendit Apostolus. . . . Ergo et illa divinitas hujus humanitatis nomen accepit . . . et ista humanitas illius divinitatis nomen accepit. Apparet tamen idem ipse Christus, geminae gigas substantiae, secundum quid obediens, secundum quid aequalis Deo; secundum quid Filius hominis, secundum quid Filius Dei. . . ." Ambrose's phrase seems to be, for Augustine here, the picturesque summary of the principle of reciprocal predication.

63. *Contra sermonem Arianorum* 9.7: PL 42, 690.16–21 (repunctuated): "Fateanturque [sc. Ariani] Christum non tantum carnem, sed animam quoque humanam Verbo unigenito coaptasse, ut esset una persona; quod Christus est Verbum et homo, sed ipse homo anima et caro, ac per hoc Christus Verbum anima et caro." For further argument that Augustine's conception of the *una persona* in Christ takes on a new, more metaphysically precise connotation in his anti-Arian works after 418, see Basil Studer, "Una Persona in Christo. Ein augustinisches Thema bei Leo dem Grossen," *Augustinianum* 25 (1985) 453–87.

64. "Cum enim sit totus Filius Dei unicus Dominus noster Iesus Christus Verbum et homo, atque ut expressius dicam, Verbum, anima, et caro; ad totum refertur quod in sola anima tristis fuit usque ad mortem (Mt 26:38); quia Filius Dei unicus Iesus Christus tristis fuit, ad totum refertur quod in solo homine crucifixus est . . .": PL 38, 1068. This same formula, that the person of Christ is *Verbum, anima et caro*, appears later in the *Tractates on the Gospel of John*, which seem to have been written after the *Contra sermonem Arianorum*: see, e.g., *Tractatus in Euangelium Ioannis* 27.4; 47.10–11: CC 36, 271, 410.

65. For a discussion of the similarity to Ambrose's Christology in the earliest works of Augustine, up to *De fide et symbolo* [393], see C. Basevi, "Alle fonti della dottrina agostin-

The balance and metaphysical clarity of Augustine's picture of Christ in the *Contra sermonem Arianorum*, a balance that continues in his later *Sermons* and *Tractates on John*, seem perhaps less "Augustinian" than the strongly integrated, explicitly Word-centered Christ of his works from the mid-390s on; yet this model of Christ anticipates more clearly than those earlier writings do the Christological symmetry of Leo and Chalcedon, a point that may explain Leo's direct use of the work in his *Tome to Flavian*.[66] And while Augustine makes no explicit mention of Ambrose in this treatise—he seldom does acknowledge his theological debts publicly, after all—still the clearest inspiration for such a symmetrical portrait of Christ, a portrait that stressed the parallel completeness of his substances or natures rather than the central dominance of the Word, was to be found in the early writings of the great bishop of Milan, developed and perhaps even invented by him as a weapon against the Arians.[67] As Augustine struggled to meet the challenge posed by the specious attractiveness of an Arian Christ, it seems more than likely that he turned again to a Christological model he had used in the early years of his ministry, and reached for the treatises, as well as the familiar hymn, of the anti-Arian bishop of Milan, whose faith had reshaped his own at the time of his conversion. It was Ambrose's giant now, not simply the self-emptying Word and the humble mediator of Augustine's earlier mature writings, who was to "run the way" of fifth-century Western Christology.

iana dell'incarnazione: l'influenza della cristologia di Sant'Ambrogio," *Scripta Theologica* 7 (1975) 499–529.

66. Without mentioning his source, Leo cites *Contra sermonem Arianorum* 8.6: PL 42, 688.37–51 in the *Tome*, Ep. 28.5 (PL 54, 771 A9–B5). There are also echoes of *Contra sermonem Arianorum* 7.6: PL 42, 688.6–25 in chapter 3 of the *Tome* (PL 54, 763 A12–B8).

67. For the suggestion that Ambrose is the first writer to use a clear two-nature/one-person conception of Christ specifically as a polemical weapon against the Arians, see L. Herrmann, "Ambrosius von Mailand als Trinitätstheologe," *Zeitschrift für Kirchengeschichte* 69 (1958) 212.

10 A Humble Mediator

The Distinctive Elements in Saint Augustine's Christology

Perhaps the most remarkable thing about St. Augustine's Christology is that it seems, on the surface at least, so unremarkable. One reason, surely, is that the meaning and reality of Jesus was one of the few theological subjects on which Augustine never became embroiled in controversy. The origin of evil and of sin, the meaning of history, the normative characteristics of the Church, the relation of God's grace and our freedom, the tension between Christian life and secular culture—all these were subjects that engaged Augustine's energies and drew from him positions and arguments that became classical in the Christian West. The reason, undoubtedly, was that they were points of dispute in his own time, questions on which his contemporaries had urgently asked for his help.

Augustine's career as a theologian, however, lay precisely between crucial turning points in ancient Christological debate. Apollinarianism, which had seemed so unscriptural to him and his friend Alypius, even before their baptism,[1] had been rejected by the body of the Church's bishops at Constantinople in 381; the controversy raised by Nestorius's attack on Mary's title *Theotokos* was just reaching its crest at Augustine's death in the summer of 430. Apart from a few controversial works against Arians, and from his role in correcting the "pre-Nestorian" views of the Gallic monk Leporius,[2]

1. *Conf.* 7.19.25 [397–401] (*Corpus Christianorum, Series Latina* [= CCL] [Turnhout: Brepols, 1981] 109). Although the dating of Augustine's works is often disputed, I will here give the most likely date for each work mentioned, if it is known, in square brackets after the textual reference.

2. See his Ep. 219, *Ad episcopos Galliae* [418–421], in which he assures the bishops who had excommunicated Leporius for his Christological views that the monk had corrected

Augustine seems never to have been drawn into serious debate about the person of Christ. So, except for a few outstanding sermons, a brief tract against the Apollinarians,[3] and the eloquent little apology for the idea of an incarnate God that he sent the pagan senator Volusianus,[4] he left us no works that specifically deal with Christological issues.

Even so, it is strikingly clear to anyone who reads even a few pages of Augustine's writings that the mystery of Christ's person and work is never far from his mind. His theology of grace, his view of the Church and of the relation of time to eternity, his reflections on "the Trinity, which is God," all find their center and anchor in a sophisticated, astonishingly balanced Christology—a Christology that is all the more striking for being developed, as it seems, in passing. Its very balance, in fact, along with its freedom from open controversy, seems to have made Augustine's Christology go relatively unnoticed by modern scholarship.[5] Augustine's portrait of the Redeemer seems so classical, so complete, so fully in accord with crucial later documents like Leo's *Tome to Flavian*[6] and the dogmatic definitions of Chalcedon and Constantinople II and III, that it seems to have no characteristic profile of its own.

In general, Augustine avoids technical speculation on the unity and inner constitution of Jesus's person, preferring to speak of the mystery of Christ in concrete, rhetorically challenging phrases that let the believer savor the inherent paradox of preaching an incarnate God.[7] So he identifies

---

his "careless error." Both this letter and Leporius's accompanying *Libellus Emendationis* or "profession of corrected faith" represent many of Augustine's own Christological concerns; see the convenient edition of P. Glorieux, *Prénestorianisme en occident* (Monumenta Christiana Selecta 6; Tournai and New York: Desclée, 1959).

3. *De div. quaest.* 83, q. 80 [c. 395] (CCL 44A [1975] 232–38).

4. Ep. 137 [412] (CSEL 44 [1904] 96–125).

5. Apart from brief and dutiful expositions in the standard works on the history of dogma, Augustine's Christology has been little studied in the last century. An exception is the controversial work of Otto Scheel, *Die Anschauung Augustins über Christi Person und Werk* (Tübingen, 1901), which argued that Augustine never managed to synthesize his Neoplatonic conception of the Logos with the biblical picture of Jesus. The most useful modern work on the subject is Tarcisius J. Van Bavel, *Recherches sur la Christologie de saint Augustin* (Paradosis 10; Fribourg: Editions universitaires, 1954). See now also Hubertus Drobner, *Persons-Exegese und Christologie bei Augustinus* (Leiden: Brill, 1986).

6. In language and thought, the *Tome* has a thoroughly Augustinian ring—probably because Leo's secretary, Prosper Tiro of Aquitaine, was a friend and lifelong defender of Augustine.

7. For a list of such phrases, or paraphrases, for the Incarnation, see Van Bavel, *Recherches sur la Christologie*, 41–44.

Jesus, in some of his earlier works, simply as "the God-man"—*homo Deus*[8] or *Deus homo*.[9] In an early explanation of one of the psalms, he uses this technique of Christological paradox more elaborately, in a powerful sentence that defies elegant translation: "A whole human being is with the Word, and the Word with a human being, and the human being and the Word are one human being, and the Word and the human being are one God."[10] A homily on part of John's Gospel, delivered some twenty years later, puts the paradox more pointedly still: "That very one is human who is God, because God has become a human being."[11] Here and in countless passages like them, Augustine seems deliberately to be using a simple vocabulary to underline the complexity and inner tensions of the Christian message.

In addition to this "rhetorical Christology," however, he also speaks of the mystery of Christ in more technical terms. Many passages in his works show a deep, reflective understanding of what is implied in the news that God's Word has become flesh, an understanding that anticipates with surprising fullness the main features of classical, post-Chalcedonian Christology. Without ever embarking on a full metaphysical consideration of the meanings of "person" and "nature" and their mutual relationship, for instance, Augustine frequently uses this terminology to insist that Jesus, the Mediator between God and humanity, has "joined both natures in a unity of person."[12] Christ is the "twin-substanced giant," he asserts in a bold, oft-borrowed allusion to Psalm 19:5.[13] Because of God's unique relation, as transcendent Creator, to his creatures, he observes in Book 13 of the *De Trinitate*, such a combination is at least conceivable: "A human nature can be so joined to God that one person comes into being from two substances."[14] Augustine insists, too, throughout his career, that the

8. E.g., Serm. Denis 4.2 [Easter 396–397] (MA 1 [Rome 1930] 22); *C. Faust.* 13.8 [397–398] (*Corpus Scriptorum Ecclesiasticorum Latinorum* [= CSEL] 25.1 [Vienna: Tempsky and Freytag, 1891] 388); see Van Bavel, *Recherches sur la Christologie*, 19, n. 21.

9. E.g., *De cat. rud.* 4.8 [399] (CCL 46 [1969] 128f.); Van Bavel, *Recherches sur la Christologie*, 19, n. 21.

10. *Enar. in Ps.* 56.5 [393–394] (CCL 39 [1956] 698).

11. *In Jo. Ev. tr.* 21.7 [Summer, 412] (CCL 36 [1954] 216).

12. Ep. 137.9: ". . . in unitate personae copulans utramque naturam" (CSEL 44 [1904] 108).

13. *C. serm. Arian.* 6.8 [419]: "geminae gigas substantiae" (PL 42.689); the phrase is adopted by Leporius in his *Libellus* (Glorieux 19). For a list and analysis of the passages in which Augustine expressed the unity of Christ as that of one person in two natures or substances, see Van Bavel, *Recherches sur la Christologie*, 21–24.

14. *De Trin.* 13.17.22: "Sic Deo coniungi potuit humana natura ut ex duabus substantiis fieret una persona . . ." (CCL 50A [1968] 412).

humanity of Jesus was and remains complete, undiminished both corporeally and psychologically by its union with the Word.[15] As his struggle in Gethsemane to accept his God-given "cup" reveals, Jesus even possessed two complete wills.[16] Only in his sinlessness is the humanity of Jesus unlike ours, since it was conceived without the influence of uncontrolled desire, purely by the grace of the Holy Spirit.[17]

At the same time—although he does not put it in these terms—Augustine clearly understands the Logos to be the active subject of the Incarnation, the personal center which shapes and gives identity to Jesus the man. It is faith in Jesus Christ *as God*, he insists, which is the true foundation of the heavenly city;[18] the reason Scripture sometimes gives stronger emphasis to his humanity is to emphasize the full, saving reality of God's coming into the world.[19] The human nature of Jesus is therefore "in God,"[20] nor does the Word of God cease to be present in power to all creation, as giver and shaper of participated being, simply because it has been made flesh in Jesus.[21] So Augustine sees the Incarnation of the Word—the Word's human "coming" into the world—as the radical transformation of a human individual which it creates by its very act of possession, but not as a change on the part of God. "A human being draws near to God and becomes one person (with him)";[22] "the Son of God becomes Son of Man by the assumption of what

15. E.g., Ep. 137.8 [412] (CSEL 44.107); Ep. 187.4 [417] (CSEL 57 [1911] 83f.); Ep. 187.10 (CSEL 57.89): the Word will *always* have his full humanity. On the genuine emotions and psychological suffering of Jesus, see *Enar. in Ps.* 93.19 (CCL 39.1320f.); *In Jo. Ev. tr.* 60.2 [418] (CCL 36.478f.); *De civ. Dei* 10.27 [417] (CCL 47 [1955] 302); 14.9 [419] (CCL 48 [1955] 427f.). Augustine insists that he was always convinced by the Gospels of the full humanity of Jesus, even before his final conversion: *Conf.* 7.19.25 (CCL 27.109).

16. See, e.g., *Enar. in Ps.* 93.19 (CCL 39 [1956] 1319–21); *C. serm. Arian.* 6.7 (PL 42.688).

17. This idea reappears with some frequency throughout Augustine's career: e.g., *De Trin.* 4.4 [c. 401] (CCL 50 [1968] 164); *De Gen. litt.* 10.18 [c. 415] (CSEL 28.1 [1894] 319f.); *Enchir.* 10.34 [423–424] (CCL 46 [1969] 68).

18. *De civ. Dei* 22.6 [426] (CCL 48 [1955] 813).

19. Serm. 174.1 [413]: "Venit enim per quod homo erat. Nam per quod Deus erat, semper hic erat. . . . Quia ergo venit per infirmitatem humanam, ideo praedicans adventum eius (Paulus) dixit: 'Humanus sermo' (1 Tim. 1:15). Non liberaretur humanum genus, nisi sermo Dei dignaretur esse humanus" (PL 38.940).

20. See, e.g., Ep. 187.10 [417] (CSEL 57.89), where he also speaks of Jesus as "Deus in homine." The man Jesus did not pre-exist as a creature, before being "taken up" by the Word, Augustine insists in another famous passage; "he was created in the very act of being assumed" (*ipsa assumptione creatur*): *C. serm. Arian.* 6.8 (PL 42.688).

21. See, e.g., *In Jo. Ev. tr.* 2.8, 12.8, 30.1, 31.9 [413] (CCL 36.15, 125, 289, 298).

22. Serm. 293.7 [June 24, 413] (PL 38.1332).

is lower, not by a change of what is higher."[23] As a result, the sufferings of Jesus, though they belong to the Incarnate Word personally, are undergone by him freely and not by any natural necessity, as our sufferings are.[24] Yet the reality of both a full range of human experiences and the full mystery of God, possessed by a single subject, allows an "exchange of names," a cross-attribution of titles, between the Word and Jesus the man.[25] However one attempts to analyze the cause and the implications of the Incarnation, the fact of it remains that God has not only *taken on* a human being, but *is* one: "the same one is a man, who is God."[26]

This picture of the person and the reality of Christ—a picture whose details could be elaborated at great length—may sound, in fact, so balanced, so classical as to be virtually indistinguishable from the later tradition of Latin Christology. Clearly both Augustine's piety and his theology find their center in the person of Jesus.[27] Yet the lack of direct Christological controversy in his career, and the absence of the technical, metaphysically honed Christological vocabulary that would come to be developed in the debates of the two and a half centuries after his death, often leave his allusions to Jesus's person and to his role in our salvation as vague as they are powerful. It is difficult,

23. Serm. 186.2 [Christmas, 411–412]: "Qui erat Dei Filius, factus est hominis filius assumptione inferioris, non conversione potioris" (PL 38.1000). Understanding this point seems to have been Leporius's main problem; see Ep. 219 and the *Libellus* (Glorieux 11, 16f.).

24. See, e.g., *De div. quaest.* 83, q. 80.4 [c. 395] (CCL 44A. 237f.); *De Trin. 4.16.* [c. 401] (CCL 50.181f.); *In Jo. Ev. tr.* 60.5 [418] (CCL 36.479f.).

25. See, e.g., Serm. 214.6 [391] (PL 38.1068f.); *De Trin.* 1.13.28 [c. 400] (CCL 50.69f.); Ep. 187.9 [417] (CSEL 57 [1911] 88f.). See Van Bavel, *Recherches sur la Christologie*, 61f.

26. *In Jo. Ev. tr.* 21.7 [413]: "Ipse est tamen homo qui Deus . . ." (CCL 36.216). With a characteristically intense use of Johannine language, Augustine puts the same point more simply in another passage in his discourses on John: "Christ is the Word, and Christ is the Word of God, and Christ the Word is God; but Christ is not only the Word, since 'the Word became flesh and dwelt among us.' Therefore Christ is both Word and flesh" (*In Jo. Ev. tr.* 23.6: CCL 36.235f.). It is this identity of Word and flesh at the heart of the person of Jesus that makes possible the dearest hope of Christians: to share in the very substance of God (*In Jo. Ev. tr.* 23.5f.).

27. Christ is "the proper foundation of the Catholic faith": *Enchir.* 1.5 [423–424] (CCL 46.50). The whole content of Christian faith is centered on the "case" (*causa*) between Christ and Adam: *De grat. Chr.* 2.24.28 [418] (CSEL 42 [1902] 186f.). Only by the grace of Christ, by faith in his mediatorship and his resurrection, can any human being, in any age, be saved from destruction: ibid.; cf. *De civ. Dei* 22.22, 24 [426] (CCL 48.845, 851f.). So we will all be judged on whether we have "made Christ our foundation" (1 Cor. 3:11), which Augustine interprets as the decision not to put any temporal creature before Christ: *De civ. Dei* 21.26 [426] (CCL 48.796f.).

therefore, to identify a peculiarly Augustinian approach to understanding the mystery of Christ, or to determine a clear line of development within his own Christological thought.[28] Nonetheless, I believe that there are signs, in Augustine's works, of both a characteristic viewpoint in his presentation of Jesus and of some moderate, if significant, changes in emphasis. What I hope to do here is to sketch the outlines of a few of these characteristic, developing features.

I. Augustine's Model of Incarnation: Christ as Word and Soul

A first point to consider in any search for a distinctively Augustinian Christology is the model, the underlying mental image or class of metaphors, he prefers to use in conceiving of Jesus as both fully human and fully divine. Drawing on the Neoplatonic philosophical tradition—the tradition that was for him the key to making intellectual sense of the Christian Gospel—Augustine understood the human soul to be a complete spiritual substance, independent of the body it vivifies, in control of the body, yet existing sufficient to itself. The soul, he assumed, is incorporeal, always engaged in knowledge and desire, immune to death and dissolution; more important, perhaps, it is the soul that is the real "self" of a person, a person's subjective and unifying center.[29] Throughout his career, then, Augustine seems to have seen it as metaphysically necessary—as Origen had done before him[30]—that the human soul of Christ should be the connecting link, the point of contact, between the divine Logos, the creative "mind" of God, and Jesus the man. That the Logos, who is infinite Spirit, should "mingle" with the human spirit of Jesus is really less baffling, Augustine writes to Volusianus, than that *our* human spirits should "mingle" with our bodies, a substance far more alien

28. For the thesis that Augustine's Christology changed little in substance during his career, see Scheel, *Die Anschauung Augustins*, 391; also Eugene Portalie, *A Guide to the Thought of St. Augustine* (Chicago: Regnery, 1960) 153, who essentially agrees with Scheel.

29. For a discussion of the Neoplatonic doctrine of the soul, as inherited and used by Augustine, see especially Ernest Fortin, *Christianisme et culture philosophique au cinquième siècle. La querelle de l' âme en Occident* (Paris: Etudes Augustiniennes, 1959). For Augustine's version of this conception of the soul, see especially *De quant. an.* [387–388] (PL 32.1035–80); cf. *De mor. eccl. et de mor. Manich.* 1.27.52 [387–89]: "The human person is a rational soul using a mortal and earthly body" (PL 32.1332); *Conf.* 10.6.9 [397–401] (CCL 27.160).

30. See especially Origen, *De principiis* 2.6.3–6. It is significant, perhaps, that Origen was a pupil of the Middle Platonist Ammonius Sakkas in Alexandria at roughly the same time as Plotinus, whose works exercised such a strong influence on Augustine.

to their nature than God is to a soul.[31] So the Manichaean charge that genuine incarnation would contaminate the divine substance is groundless, he argues; the Word is not directly united to a material body at all, but forms a living unity with Jesus's soul.[32] So, too, Augustine conceived the death of Christ, throughout his career, as the separation of both the Logos and the human soul of Jesus—still inseparably united—from his body. "What more could his passion and death do," he asks, "than separate the body from the soul? It did not separate the soul from the Word."[33]

As a result of this conception of *how* the Word is united to Jesus the man, perhaps, the later Augustine also uses the relationship of soul and body more and more as a Christological analogy, to illustrate the organic yet unconfused unity of the Incarnation—an analogy that would become commonplace in the works of Cyril of Alexandria and the later Greek tradition as well. "The Son of Man has soul and body," he explains in a lecture on John's Gospel; "the Son of God, who is the Word of God, has a human being as the soul has a body. And just as a soul having a body does not make two persons but one human being, so the Word having a human being makes not two persons but one Christ."[34] God acts in the created universe, he suggests in *Confessions* 7, in something of the way the human "heart" exercises its life-giving and integrating role throughout the human body.[35] But more literally than God is the "life" of every creature, even of every soul that longs for him; the divinity of the Word, united to Jesus's human soul, is his *vera vita*.[36]

31. Ep. 137.11 [412]; cf. Ep. 137.8 (CSEL 44.109ff.; 106f.). See also Serm. Denis 5.4 (MA 1.26); *De div. quaest.* 83, q. 80.1 [c. 395] (CCL 44A.233).

32. *De fid. symb.* 4.10 [393] (CSEL 41.13f.).

33. *In Jo. Ev. tr.* 47.10 [413]; cf. *In Jo. Ev. tr.* 47.11–13 (CCL 36.409–12). For this same assumption, see Serm. Denis 5.4 (MA 1.26); *C. Faust.* 12.35 [397–398] (CSEL 25.1 [1891] 362); Ep. 164.5.14 [c. 414] (CSEL 44.5134). It is also affirmed without question by Leporius at the end of his *Libellus emendationis* (Glorieux 22f.). For a full discussion of this understanding of the death of Jesus, and its Christological implications, in patristic literature, see Aloys Grillmeier, "Der Gottessohn im Totenreich," in *Mit ihm und in ihm* (Freiburg: Herder, 1975) 76–174.

34. *In Jo. Ev. tr.* 19.15 [413]: "Filius hominis habet animam, habet corpus. Filius Dei, quod est Verbum Dei, habet hominem, tamquam anima corpus. Sicut anima habens corpus non facit duas personas, sed unum hominem; sic Verbum habens hominem non facit duas personas, sed unum Christum" (CCL 36.199).

35. *Conf.* 7.1.2 (CCL 27.93).

36. Serm. Denis 5.7 (MA 1.28). On God as the "life" of the human person, see, e.g., *De lib.* 2.16.41.162 [388–395] (CCL 29 [1970] 265); *Conf.* 7.1.2; 10.6.10; 10.17.26 (CCL 27.93, 160, 168); *De civ. Dei* 19.26 [425] (CCL 48.696).

This parallel between the constitution of the Incarnate Word and that of every human being, although not articulated in so many words by Augustine before 411, makes clearer some other images that he uses for the Incarnation throughout his life: his speaking of the Word, for instance, as "bearing" (*gerere, portare, agere*) a human being,[37] or—more frequently—having "put on" a human body like a garment.[38] For the Neoplatonists, too, such images seemed naturally suited to express the soul's relationship to the material body it sustained and governed. Although Stoics and Platonists alike denied that the body is merely a garment or instrument, to which the soul has only an extrinsic relationship, their very concern to stress the point reflects at least the sense that the body is distinct from the heart of the human substance; it is the soul that "bears" the body and "holds it together" in existence.[39] The phrase used by the Neoplatonist tradition to express this relationship of soul and body was frequently "unconfused union": a union that was a "mixture" of two radically different substances in a single subject, which did not produce a new hybrid but allowed both matter and spirit to retain their integrity and distinct existence.[40] For Augustine, as later for the Greek interpreters of the formula of Chalcedon (and probably even for its drafters), it was the analogy between the Word's relationship to the human Jesus and this understanding of the human soul's relationship to its body that enabled them to see the Incarnation as an intimate, living unity of two irreducibly distinct realities. The root of the analogy seems to lie, for Augustine at least, in his

37. E.g., *De ord.* 2.9.27 [386]: "ipsum hominem agens" (CCL 29 [1970] 122); *De serm. Dom.* 1.7.18 [394]: "homo quem portabat Dominus" (CCL 35 [1967] 19); *De Trin.* 13.18.23 [416]: "Deus humiliter, non quomodo alios sanctos regebat illum hominem [= Jesum], sed gerebat" (CCL 50A [1968] 414). This image is to be distinguished from a similar usage, in which the man Jesus is said to be "carrying the *persona* of divine Wisdom": i.e., playing Wisdom's functional role; see *Exp. Ep. in Gal.* 27 [394–395] (CSEL 84 [1971] 92); *De agon.* 20.22 [396] (CSEL 41 [1900] 122).

38. E.g., Serm. 263.3 [396–397]: the body of Christ is the *habitus* of the Word, who descended from heaven "naked" but ascended "clothed with our flesh" (PL 38.1211). Cf. *De div. quaest.* 83, q. 73.2 [388–395]: like a garment, Jesus's humanity took its shape from the Word who "wore" it, "that it might be changed for the better" (CCL 44A.211f.).

39. See Plotinus's famous image of the net borne by the sea, used to illustrate how the material world is "carried" by soul: *Enneads* 4.3.9; cf. Claudianus Mamertus, *De statu animae* 3.3 (CSEL 11.158). For a full discussion of this theme in Neoplatonism, see Fortin, *Christianisme*, 111–37.

40. See the Christian Neoplatonist, Nemesius of Emesa, *De natura hominis* 3 (PG 40.601); cf. Proclus, *In Timaeum* 32C (ed. E. Diehl 2 [Leipzig: Teubner, 1904] 53.15). See Fortin, *Christianisme*, 114–19.

insight into the kinship between the Word and the human spirit, a kinship that is the place and the foundation of their union in Jesus.

II. Revelation and Humility: Christ as Mediator

A second point that received distinctive, if subtly shifting, emphasis in Augustine's Christology was Jesus's role as "Mediator between God and humanity" (1 Tim 2:5). The conception of the Incarnate Word as mediator was, of course, not new, but it was a favorite term for Augustine: perhaps the one title, after "Christ," which he applies most frequently to Jesus. It probably appealed to him both because of its biblical origin and because it helped him integrate the Church's faith in Jesus with his undeniably Neoplatonic conception of the universe. In general, he uses the title "mediator" more often to suggest Christ's position between the transcendent being of God and this created universe—Christ's status in the hierarchy of beings—than to refer to his active role in reconciling God with the human race. "Therefore he is the mediator between God and humanity," Augustine explains in a sermon from the years 409–411, "because he is God with the Father, because he is a human being among human beings. . . . Divinity without humanity is not a mediator; humanity without divinity is not a mediator. But between divinity alone and humanity alone the mediating link is the human divinity and the divine humanity of Christ."[41]

Most of the time, too, Augustine presents the primary purpose of this intermediate or synthetic position of the Word as *revelation*. So, in an early letter to his friend Nebridius, he tries to explain the thorny question of why only God the Son, not the whole divine Trinity, has become incarnate. As every substance, he argues, is characterized by three metaphysical functions—its root being, its *species* or identifiable structure, and its dynamism of continued existence—so an analogous triad can be found in God; and the role of intelligibility, of self-revelation, of mediation between God and intelligent creatures, is thus not simply characteristic of God, but of the second person in God.[42]

This strikingly Neoplatonist reading of Christian Trinitarian faith, in which the mediatorship of Christ is modeled on the ontological and episte-

41. Serm. 47.12.21: "Inde est mediator Dei et hominum; quia Deus cum Patre, quia homo cum hominibus. . . . Divinitas sine humanitate non est mediatrix, humanitas sine divinitate non est mediatrix; sed inter divinitatem solam et humanitatem solam mediatrix est humana divinitas et divina humanitas Christi" (PL 38.310). Cf. *Conf.* 7.18.24–21.27; 10.42.67–43.70; 11.2.4 (CCL 27.108–12; 191ff.; 196).

42. Ep. 11.2–4 [c. 389] (CSEL 34 [1895] 25–28).

mological role of the Plotinian *nous*, is also reflected in the way Augustine speaks of the "person" (*persona*) of Christ in his earlier works. Like most of the Fathers, he means by *persona* less the subjective center of conscious individual existence—as we modern Westerners might understand it—than "the revelatory form of some other thing,"[43] the role played by an individual, which displays his or her character, defines his or her meaning in the drama of history. So Augustine refers to Jesus's distinctive position among his brothers and sisters, in his early "Explanation" of Galatians [394–395], as that of "naturally having and performing the role [*personam*] of Wisdom," by being "made one with Wisdom itself, which took him up without any other intermediary."[44] Though he was unaware of it in the days before his final conversion, Augustine came to realize that Jesus is distinguished from other human beings not just by having a greater share in divine Wisdom, but by having the very "person of Truth."[45] So he distinguishes, in an Ascension Day sermon of 396 or 397, between the "person" of the Word and the "clothing of the person" (*personae habitus*), which was his human nature; if, without losing his identity, the Word has made us members of his body, "then it is all the more impossible that that body, which he took from the Virgin, could have in him any other person."[46] Conversely, Augustine describes the Incarnation in a still earlier work as the Word's "taking on the person of a lower nature, namely a human one."[47] However one conceives the "role" played in sacred history by the Word made flesh, the "person" of the Mediator, in such passages, is not so much the center of his being as the way he communicates to us the full reality of his "mediating" position in creation, a position uniting our world with God.

In later works, Augustine continues to emphasize this "metaphysical" mediatorship of Jesus's person: his role as the connecting link between the eternal reality of God and our human nature.[48] But he couples this with an in-

43. "Forme révélatrice d'une autre chose": Van Bavel, *Recherches sur la Christologie*, 18.

44. *Exp. Ep. in Gal.* 27: "Omnes fiunt filii: non natura, sicut unicus Filius, qui etiam Sapientia Dei est; neque praepotentia et singularitate susceptionis ad habendam naturaliter et agendam personam Sapientiae, sicut ipse Mediator unum cum ipsa Sapientia sine interpositione alicuius mediatoris effectus . . ." (PL 35.12125).

45. *Conf.* 7.19.25 [397–401] (CCL 27.109).

46. Serm 263.3: "Nam si nos sibimet tamquam sua membra ita coaptavit, ut etiam nobis conjunctis idem ipse sit, quanto magis illud corpus, quod de virgine assumpsit, aliam non potest in illo habere personam" (PL 38.1211). Cf. *De Trin.* 2.6.11 (CCL 50.93f.).

47. *De Gen. Man.* 2.24.37 [388–389] (PL 34.215).

48. E.g., Ep. 137.9 [412] (CSEL 44.108): Jesus is mediator between God and humanity because he joins *in unitate personae utramque naturam*—a phrase that suggests an under-

creasing emphasis on the Incarnation of the mediating Word as the concrete, exhaustive revelation of God's healing love and mercy. To be sure, this soteriological aspect of the Incarnation is also suggested by the early Augustine;[49] but the revelation of a healing, mediating love becomes, in *De Trinitate* 13.13 [c. 417], Augustine's explanation of why God chose to save humanity in such a costly way as the passion of Jesus, and the Incarnation is presented in many of the anti-Pelagian writings as "the brightest example of predestination and grace."[50] "The Word was made flesh that we can see," he observes in his first homily on the First Epistle of John, "so that that by which we see the Word [i.e., the heart] might be healed within us."[51] At the same time, the humanity of the Word is presented in Augustine's middle and later works not simply as the means by which God has touched humanity to heal it, but as the "way" by which humanity can itself draw near to God. "Through Christ as human being, you find your way to Christ as God," he remarks in his Ascension Day homily of 410.[52] "The way to humanity's God," he asserts in a memorable passage of the *City of God*, "is, for the human being, the human God. This is 'the mediator between God and humanity, the man Christ Jesus.' For it is as a human being that he is mediator, and through this too, that he is the way. If there is a way between the one walking and the point towards which one is walking, one has a hope of reaching one's goal; but if there is none, or if one is unaware of how to get there, of what use is it to know where one wants to go? There is only one way that is assured against all error; that the very same person should be God and a human being—God, as the goal to which we are going, and a human being, as the way by which we go."[53]

---

standing of *persona* now drawing closer to the Cappadocian use of *hypostasis*, as meaning the concrete individual.

49. E.g., *De util. cred.* 15.33 [392], where the purpose of the Incarnation is seen as the revelation of God's mercy, in order to "win back our love" and "drive away our fears" (CSEL 25 [1891] 41 f.); cf. *De cat. rud.* 4.8 [399] (CCL 46.128).

50. See below, n. 61.

51. *In Jo. Ep. tr.* 1.1 [413?]: "Factum est Verbum caro, quam videre possumus, ut sanaretur in nobis unde Verbum videremus" (SC 75 [1961] 112).

52. Serm. 261.7: "Per hominem tendis ad Deum Christum. . . . Idem ipse Christus, et qua eas et quo eas" (PL 38.1206).

53. *De civ. Dei* 11.2 [417]: ". . . ut ad hominis Deum iter esset homini per hominem Deum. Hic est enim mediator Dei et hominum, homo Christus Jesus. Per hoc enim mediator, per quod homo, per hoc et via. Quoniam si inter eum qui tendit et illud quo tendit via media est, spes est perveniendi; si autem desit aut ignoretur qua eundum sit, quid prodest nosse quo eundum sit? Sola est autem adversus omnes errores via munitissima, ut idem ipse sit Deus et homo; quo itur Deus, qua itur homo" (CCL 48.322).

Augustine had made this same point almost twenty years earlier, in Book 7 of his *Confessions*. Neoplatonism, he insists, had given him clarity on the fundamental qualities of the divine mystery, and on its relationship to the created world, yet he remained "too weak to enjoy" God, because he was still infected with the intellectual's pride, still lacking in love.[54] To be healed, he no longer needed theological knowledge, but simply the grace of Christ experienced firsthand, the joyful consciousness of sins forgiven, the love that "builds on the foundation of humility";[55] "for I was not yet humble enough to embrace the humble Christ Jesus as my Lord, nor did I understand the lesson that his weakness is meant to teach."[56] It is, in fact, the *humility* of Christ, the human self-emptying of the eternal Word of God for the sake of sinners, that was, for both the early and the late Augustine, the distinctive element of the Christian Gospel—the truth that lies beyond the reach of the philosophical mind, but that is the first condition for anyone's movement towards God.[57] To heal the disease of pride communicated to our race by Satan, the "proud mediator," a "humble mediator" was needed.[58] The humility of the Incarnate Word is, for Augustine, the most fundamental truth in the Gospel of salvation: "a proud humanity is a great misfortune, but a still greater mercy is a humble God!"[59]

III. The Paradigm of Grace: Christ as Savior

The distinctive message of the Christian Gospel, then, for Augustine, was not so much its vision of God and the world as its revelation of grace: God's love for sinners, God's humble self-emptying for their sakes, God's gentle but powerful intervention in human hearts to heal the "tumor" of pride and point them homeward to him. Although this view is evident in his earliest

54. *Conf.* 7.20.26 [397–401] (CCL 27.109).

55. *Conf.* 7.20.26; cf. 7.21.27 (CCL 27.110ff.).

56. *Conf.* 7.18.24: "non enim tenebam Deum meum Jesum humilis humilem, nec cuius rei magistra esset eius infirmitas noveram" (CCL 27.108).

57. See, e.g., *Contra academicos* 3.19.42 [386] (CCL 29 [1970] 60); *In Jo. Ev. tr.* 25.11 [413] (CCL 36.253); *De Trin.* 13.18.23 [416] (CCL 50A.414); *De praed. sanct.* 15.31 [429] (PL 44.983).

58. *Exp. Ep. ad Gal.* 24 [394–395]: "Restat ergo ut qui mediatore superbo diabolo superbiam persuadente dejectus est, mediatore humili Christo humilitatem persuadente erigatur" (CSEL 84.86f.).

59. *De cat. rud.* 4.8 [399]: "Magna est enim miseria superbus homo, sed maior misericordia humilis deus" (CCL 46.129). For the notion of a "humble God," cf. *De Trin.* 4.4 [c. 401] (CCL 50.163f.); *De pecc. merit.* 2.17.27 [411] (PL 44.168).

works, it took on new focus in his long debate with the Pelagian party about the precise implications of the Gospel of grace, and it left, in his later writings, a new and distinctive stamp on his Christology.[60] "The most shining example of predestination and grace," he writes a year or so before his death, "is the Savior himself, the very Mediator between God and humanity: the human being Jesus Christ."[61] The "grace of the Mediator" is, at its heart, nothing else but the event of Incarnation: the fact "that while human nature does not belong to the nature of God, yet such human nature does belong, by grace, to the person of the only-begotten Son of God—and that by a grace so great that there is none greater, none even approaching equality!"[62]

It is this "grace of Incarnation," in fact, the grace of his truly singular union with God, that makes Jesus unique, and uniquely able to save: "Take away this grace, and what is Christ but a human being?"[63] If grace is essentially God's gift of the Holy Spirit, the "mystical and invisible anointing" of Jesus by the Spirit that is the root grace of his being occurred not at his baptism, when the dove descended, but "at the moment when the Word of God was made flesh."[64] So Augustine describes the result for Jesus's humanity of union with the Word in terms of grace as well: the grace of freedom from sin,[65] and the grace of sanctification.[66]

Augustine's reason for speaking of the personal union of the Word with the humanity of Jesus as the model and source of grace seems, in these later works, to have been dictated largely by his need for a Christological grounding in his criticism of the Pelagian view of human self-sufficiency. Jesus the man did not *merit* the supreme grace that was his—the grace of personal identity with God the Son. "Surely he did not first live as Son of Man," he asks rhetorically in a sermon from the early years of the controversy, "so that he might be made Son of God because he had lived well? He began from there—

60. This Christological nuance is clearly enunciated, for instance, in Augustine's first work on the doctrine of grace, *De pecc. merit.* [411]: see previous note.

61. *De praedest. sanct.* 15.30 [429]: "Est etiam praeclarissimum lumen praedestinationis et gratiae, ipse Salvator, ipse Mediator Dei et hominum, homo Christus Jesus" (PL 44.981).

62. *In Jo. Ev. tr.* 82.4 [418]: "Quod cum ad naturam Dei non pertinet humana natura, ad personam tamen unigeniti Filii Dei per gratiam pertinet humana natura; et tantam gratiam ut nulla sit maior, nulla prorsus aequalis" (CCL 36.534).

63. Serm. 67.4.7: "Tolle gratiam istam; quid Christus, nisi homo? quid, nisi quod tu?" (PL 38.436).

64. *De Trin.* 15.26.46 [418–419] (CCL 50A.526f.).

65. E.g., *Enchir.* 12.40 [423–424] (CCL 46.72); *De corrept. et grat.* 11.30 [426] (PL 44.934f.).

66. *In Jo. Ev. tr.* 108.5 (418) (CCL 36.618).

that was his origin: he was created by being taken up by God. . . . The Word of God, the only Son of God, assumed soul and flesh: not those of a human being who had deserved this beforehand, or who had labored to receive this exalted state by his own virtue, but as sheer gift."[67] "That utterly gratuitous birth," he writes in another anti-Pelagian work, "joined a human being in unity of person with God, flesh with the Word. Good works followed on that birth, but good works did not earn it."[68]

It is this unmerited elevation of a human being to union with God that reveals the reality of grace, the mystery of predestination for glory, in each of us; what we see in the Incarnation is the pattern of what we hope for, in a limited way, for ourselves. "By that same grace, by which that human being was made from his first moment the Christ, anyone at all is made a Christian from the first moment of his faith; the Christian is reborn from the same Spirit from whom he [Christ] was born; our sins are forgiven by the same Spirit who brought it about that he [Christ] had no sin at all. God surely foreknew that he would do these things. This, then, is the predestination of the saints, which appeared most fully in the Saint of saints."[69] The mystery of Christ, as Augustine realized throughout his life, is essentially the mystery of our salvation, of our transformation; it is the mystery by which we, "who are by nature" sinful "sons of men, might by grace become, through him, sons of God."[70]

67. Serm. 174.2 (413): "Numquid et ille prius vixit filius hominis, et bene vivendo factus est Filius Dei? Inde coepit, et inde incoepit, et susceptione factus est. . . . Verbum Dei, unicus Dei Filius, assumpsit animam et carnem hominis, non autem se promerentis, nec ad illam percipiendam sublimitatem virtute proprie laborantis, sed omnino gratis" (PL 38.941). It is probably because of the implications of the point for his doctrine of grace that Augustine stresses, in his later works, that the creation of Jesus's humanity took place in the same act by which the Word made that humanity his own: "ipsa assumptione creatur" (*C. serm. Arian.* 6.8 [419] [PL 42.683]; *Enchir.* 11.36 [423–424] [CCL 46.69]).

68. *De corrept. et grat.* 11.30 [426]: "Ista nativitas profecto gratuita coniunxit in unitate personae hominem Deo, carnem Verbo. Istam nativitatem bona opera secuta sunt, non bona opera meruerunt" (PL 44.934). For further references, see Van Bavel, *Recherches sur la Christologie*, 38f.

69. *De praed. sanct.* 15.31 [429]: "Ea gratia fit ab initio fidei suae homo quicumque Christianus, qua gratia homo ille ab initio factus est Christus; de ipso Spiritu et hic renatus, de quo est ille natus; eodem Spiritu fit in nobis remissio peccatorum, quo Spiritu factum est ut nullum haberet ille peccatum. Haec se Deus esse facturus profecto praescivit. Ipsa est igitur praedestinatio sanctorum, quae in Sancto sanctorum maxime claruit" (PL 44.982).

70. *De civ. Dei* 21.15 (426): "Unicus enim natura, Dei Filius propter nos misericordia factus est hominis filius, ut nos, natura filii hominis, filii Dei per illum gratia fieremus" (CCL 48.781).

In the end, then, the distinctive elements in St. Augustine's Christology seem, above all, to be points on which he came more and more to see the intimate and unique relevance of Jesus to our salvation. In recognizing that the union of the transcendent Word to a human soul and its flesh is at least analogous to our own integrity as incarnate spirit; in seeing in Jesus the Mediator the revelation of the divine humility and self-emptying that lovingly "mediates" between God and his creation, that brings God to us and us to God; and in finding in Jesus the source and model of that life of grace in which we, his members, share through the gift of his Spirit—in all three of these developing Christological insights, Augustine the Neoplatonist grew more and more securely into Augustine the Catholic preacher, Augustine the biblical theologian.

In the thirteenth book of his *De Trinitate*, Augustine lists what he sees as the distinctive lessons the Incarnation of the Word has to teach us. The points he selects are all notions that would have been foreign, even shocking, to the "Platonists" whose books first eased his difficulties with biblical Christianity.[71] One learns from Christ, he says, the unexpected place the human race holds in God's creation, superior even to angelic spirits, who—unlike Christ and us—"have no flesh." One learns, too, the reality of unmerited grace, which in Jesus meant personal union with God's Word. One learns the manner in which God overcomes our pride—the greatest obstacle between us and him—with "such great humility" of his own. One learns to perceive, in the sufferings of Christ, the distance we have fallen from God, and the value of Jesus's suffering as a way of sharing and healing our human weakness. One learns, too, the meaning and reward of true obedience, in which our ultimate welfare stands. Finally, one learns to see, in one sweeping vision, the goodness and justice of God, who has brought it about that the devil should be overcome by the very humanity he had once defeated.[72]

These are not lessons one might learn from philosophers. They are, rather, lessons full of paradox and mystery, difficult to express in any but the most dramatic, biblical terms—lessons Augustine, in his own life, took many years to absorb. But perhaps they are, as he here suggests, the only distinctive lessons Christian theology has to teach us: the news that the Lord Jesus, our humble Mediator and our God of grace, has made us his own.

71. See *Conf.* 7.9.13–10.16; 18.24–21.27 [397–401] (CCL 27.101–4; 108–12).

72. *De Trin.* 13.17.22 [417] (CCL 50A.412f.). See also a similar list of "lessons" to be drawn from the Incarnation in *Enchir.* 28.108 [423–424] (CCL 46.107f.)

PART 4

Christology after Chalcedon

11 Unpacking the Chalcedonian Formula

From Studied Ambiguity to Saving Mystery

One of the central questions Christian theologians continue to ask themselves, as they confront the mystery of the person of Christ, is, what is the significance for us today of the Council of Chalcedon? For generations of modern scholars, especially those in the West, the dense and rather technical phrases forged at that fifth-century gathering of Christian bishops and appended to a restatement of what we know as the "Nicene Creed" represented a major milestone in the Churches' ongoing clarification of how disciples are to understand the person of Jesus the Savior.

In J. N. D. Kelly's widely used survey, *Early Christian Doctrines*,[1] for instance, Chalcedon's "settlement" of the twenty-four-year dispute between Nestorius and his Antiochene supporters and Cyril of Alexandria and the Church of Alexandria was the culmination of "the decisive period for Christology"[2] in the early Church, an attempt to define an understanding of Christ that could be accepted by all Christians throughout the Empire, but which nevertheless—surprisingly, perhaps—"failed to bring permanent peace."[3] Aloys Grillmeier, in his foundational study of the growth of early Christian understandings of Jesus, speaks of the years up to Chalcedon as temporally defining "the development of belief in Christ from its beginning to its first climax in a council of the Church."[4] In an influential study of the theology of

1. J. N. D. Kelly, *Early Christian Doctrines* (rev. ed.; San Francisco: Harper and Row, 1978), 310–43.

2. Ibid., 310.

3. Ibid., 342.

4. Aloys Grillmeier, *Christ in Christian Tradition*, vol. 1, trans. J. S. Bowden (Oxford: Mowbray, 1975), 555.

the seventh-century monk and theologian Maximus the Confessor, Hans Urs von Balthasar emphasizes the centrality of Chalcedon's formulaic, classically dialectical picture of the person of Christ as central to Maximus's whole approach to God, the world, and the human spirit. The reason, Balthasar argues, lies in Chalcedon's ability to affirm both unity and abiding difference in Christ as the dominant pattern of God's relationship to creation:

> From the moment that Chalcedon, in its sober and holy wisdom, elevated the adverbs "indivisibly" (ἀδιαιρέτως) and "unconfusedly" (ἀσυγχύτως) to a dogmatic formula, the image of a reciprocal indwelling of two distinct poles of being replaced the image of mixture. This mutual ontological presence (περιχώρησις) not only preserves the being particular to each element, to the divine and the human natures, but also brings each of them to its perfection in their very difference, even enhancing that difference. Love, which is the highest level of union, only takes root in the growing independence of the lovers; the union between God and the world reveals, in the very nearness it creates between these two poles of being, the ever-greater difference between created being and the essentially incomparable God.[5]

With a little help from German Romantic philosophy, and perhaps from his Jesuit confrère Erich Przywara, Balthasar here sees in the Chalcedonian picture of Christ not only Maximus's central inspiration, but the early Church's final paradigm for conceiving how the transcendent God can be present and crucially active in the world.

One might multiply examples. But does this understanding of Chalcedon's portrait of Christ really represent its intent or its lasting meaning? What led to its articulation? What was, one may ask, the real achievement of this gathering of over five hundred Eastern bishops, mainly from the Greek-speaking East, called by the new emperor Marcian and his long-influential spouse, the empress Pulcheria, in a port suburb across the Bosporus from Constantinople, in October of 451? On the level of Church politics, at least, it was a step towards restoring a balance, however briefly, between major centers of influence in the Church of the mid-fifth century, and the theological traditions with which they had become associated: a balance precariously achieved in 433, after the bitter controversy over Nestorius's views on how to conceive the person of Christ, by what is often called the "Formula of

5. Hans Urs von Balthasar, *Cosmic Liturgy*, trans. Brian E. Daley, SJ (San Francisco: Ignatius Press, 2003), 63–64.

Reunion," which sketched the outlines of traditional faith in the Savior—a formula apparently drafted at that time by Theodoret of Cyrus and proposed by the Church of Antioch, but which was also warmly embraced by Theodoret's principal rival, Cyril of Alexandria. After heated debates between the bishop of Constantinople, the Antioch-trained exegete Nestorius, and Cyril of Alexandria, Church leaders in 433 had agreed—at least on paper—on a document they could live with.

The principal agents of this peace of 433, however, were dead by the mid-440s: John of Antioch in 442, Cyril himself in 444, Proclus of Constantinople in 446. Tensions began to rise again in the imperial capital, as rival groups, doubtless driven by both political ambition and religious traditionalism, accused each other of treachery and extremism. The story of the conflict in the mid-440s between the archimandrite Eutyches, well supported at the imperial court and by Cyril's successor Dioscorus of Alexandria, and leading clerical figures of the capital who opposed Eutyches, such as Eusebius of Dorylaeum, is well known. Although the motives for tension and rivalry between Constantinople, Antioch, and Alexandria seem to have been complex, according to ancient witnesses, the religious reasons that were given all had to do with how one conceived the person of Christ. Eutyches, drawing on the older Alexandrian and Apollinarian tradition that emphasized the organic, dynamic unity of action and consciousness in the divine Savior of humanity, refused to accept any formula that spoke of two abiding natures, or operative substantial realities, present in the person of the incarnate Word. Christ is a single agent, called by the Letter to the Hebrews "the pioneer of our salvation."[6] To number the realities in Christ was to divide him. Yet most of the Constantinopolitan establishment, by contrast, held tenaciously to the "two unconfused natures" and "double consubstantiality" language of the Formula of 433: God and created humanity, after all, must never be fused into one—God remains God, not a piece of the living world!

In response to his aggressive promotion of a highly unitive, God-centered picture of Christ, Eutyches was deposed by the patriarch and resident bishops in Constantinople—the "Home Synod"—late in 448. An outcry ensued. In the summer of 449, a council of Greek bishops met, with imperial support, at Ephesus, to deal with the conflict. Chaired, reportedly in a highly dictatorial manner, by Archbishop Dioscorus of Alexandria, and recklessly resistant to the voices of both the Church of Antioch and the Latin West, the assembled bishops reinstated Eutyches to his clerical rank, and in turn

6. Heb 2:10; 12:2.

deposed and excommunicated the leading spokesmen of the Antiochene Church, who were thought still to have a dominant voice in the Church of the capital. Supporters of a more "symmetrical" picture of Christ's divinity and humanity felt that now *they* had been the victims of political violence. Hence when the emperor Theodosius II, who had permitted this polarization of positions to occur, himself died in the summer of 450, it was time for his successors, Marcian and Pulcheria, to take conciliatory steps, for the unity of Church and society.

The Council of Chalcedon, convened in September and October of 451, was intended to be such a step. This time the imperial court carefully assured a balanced representation of voices in the seating of delegates and guaranteed a leading role in the conduct of business not only to the main Eastern sees, but also to the Roman bishop Leo's chief legate, the Greek-speaking Sicilian bishop Paschasius of Lilybaeum. It was easy enough for this new council to reverse the work done at Ephesus in 449, to reinstate the losers there, and even to depose Dioscorus of Alexandria—notably for the contempt he had shown at Ephesus towards Leo of Rome. The *Acta* make it clear, however, that most of the bishops present at Chalcedon were hesitant to go beyond that, or even to try to debate a new "formula of union" on the theology of the person of Christ; they were content to reaffirm "the faith of Nicaea," regarded since the 370s as the touchstone of biblical orthodoxy, as expressed in its creed—the reformulated Nicene Creed produced by the Council of Constantinople of 381—and were apparently ready to take as also normative a few now-classic letters of Cyril and Leo on the Christological issue. It was the emperors, in fact, at the urging of Leo's delegates, who finally prevailed on the bishops at Chalcedon to go a step farther, and to allow a small drafting commission, huddled for a few hours in a side-chapel of the basilica of St. Euphemia, where the council was meeting, to stitch together, in addition to the Nicene text, a new statement of common faith—driven largely by the emperors' threat of adjournment, and of calling a new council in the West, if the Eastern delegations continued to resist. The resultant statement of faith, reluctantly agreed to in advance, enthusiastically acclaimed in the event, is what we know as "the Chalcedonian definition."

It is important to look closely at the whole of the council's statement of faith if one is to realize its intent and its real value. Cardinal Grillmeier rightly stressed its "dogmatic" rather than speculative character.[7] It was, in other words, a "ballpark" definition, a formal agreement on the boundaries

7. Grillmeier, *Christ in Christian Tradition*, 1:545.

of orthodox Christian faith concerning the person of Christ, but clearly not intended to break new theological ground, to solve age-old problems of understanding who Jesus is in creatively crafted new terms, or even to give unambiguous clarifications of the terms it does use. Some of its language was technical, and drew on the philosophical parlance of the day; some appears to have simply been taken from the works of writers who had been part of the controversy on both sides. Probably most of the more than five hundred bishops present would have been hard put to explain what "substance" and "nature" (universal reality) and *hypostasis* and *prosōpon* (reality as individual and concrete) actually mean, when applied to Christ, and what the difference among them is. The purpose of the statement seems rather to have been to reaffirm the main lines of the tradition of Christian orthodoxy, and to rule out the kind of language and thinking about Christ that seemed most seriously to present a danger of veering away from that tradition. It is a composite document, clearly intended to be inclusive. To the degree that it offers a positive delineation of Christ's person, the Chalcedonian formula sets out to piece together a patchwork of terms and phrases from various sources, perhaps in the hope that the appearance of a seamless conceptual whole might in time—if not questioned too closely—become the basis of real concord in faith, worship, and polity.

The statement begins, accordingly, with a description of the council's understanding of its mission: to resist the discord sowed in the Church, it says, by the Evil One, to build peace by removing falsehood, and reaffirming normative, centrist tradition.[8] Significantly, the weight is on liturgically and synodically formulated phrases, rather than on Scripture—perhaps because scriptural texts were capable of so many conflicting interpretations. Expressly following the precedent of the Alexandrian synod that had met at Ephesus in 431 (the ecumenical council that never was) the bishops of Chalcedon insist that the Creed of Nicaea (325) shall "shine in first place" (*prolampein*)—an acknowledged primacy in understanding the mystery of God that from this time on became standard procedure in ancient conciliar efforts to deal with doctrinal controversy—and add that the Creed of Constantinople (381), a reformulation of the Nicene symbol aimed at ruling

8. Complete Greek and Latin texts of the decree, with an English translation, can be found in Giuseppe Alberigo et al. and Norman Tanner, eds., *Decrees of the Ecumenical Councils*, vol. 1 (London: Sheed and Ward; Washington, DC: Georgetown University Press, 1990), 83–87. For another excellent English translation, with notes and ample introductions, see Richard Price and Michael Gaddis, *The Acts of the Council of Chalcedon*, 3 vols., Translated Texts for Historians 45 (Liverpool: Liverpool University Press, 2007), 2:201–5.

out heresies that had become evident after 325, shall also "remain in force" (*kratein*). After quoting both creedal formulas in full—our first documentary evidence, in fact, for the now-familiar text of the Creed of Constantinople—the formula goes on to assert that these "should have been sufficient for the knowledge and support of true religion,"[9] but that new views of the person of Jesus, obviously deviant from apostolic teaching, now call for new responses consistent with this Nicene tradition. Accordingly, the council declares that it has "received, as in agreement [with this faith], the synodical letters of the blessed Cyril, then shepherd of the Alexandrian church, to Nestorius and the Orientals"[10]—by which it seems to mean only Cyril's "second" letter to Nestorius from 430, not his later and more challenging "third," along with his affirmation of the Formula of Reunion from 433.[11] It adds that it has also "appropriately included, as a support of right teaching," Pope Leo's letter to bishop Flavian of Constantinople:[12] the famous *Tome* in which Leo enunciates, in polished, if somewhat ambiguous, Latin phrases, the more "symmetrical" picture of Christ advocated in the Greek world principally by Theodoret and the Antiochenes. "Classic" texts, representative of different schools of thought, are here being cited, in other words, as normatively echoing the two more formal "Nicene" creeds.

Only then, in third place, does the statement of Chalcedon move on (apparently at the emperors' insistence) to enunciate its own synthetic position, which, like what has gone before, seems carefully crafted to be both traditional and even-handed. First, the statement excludes what it regards as extreme and unacceptable positions on the person of Christ: those who "split up the mystery of the dispensation"[13] into regarding Christ as *two sons*; those who say that the *divinity can suffer*; those who conceive of a "*confusion or*

9. Alberigo and Tanner, *Decrees*, 1:84.

10. Ibid., 158.

11. The text of the decree does not specify just what "synodical letters" of Cyril to Nestorius are included, although it is his "second" letter to Nestorius in the spring of 429, not the stern ultimatum sent to Nestorius by Cyril and his local synod in the fall of 430, which was read at the first session of Chalcedon. Cyril's letter "to the Orientals," also read in the first session, clearly is the letter of the Alexandrian synod to John of Antioch and his Church, *Laetentur caeli*, of 433. See the *Acta* of Chalcedon, Session 1, no. 240 (*Acta Conciliorum Oecumenicorum*, ed. E. Schwarz [Berlin, 1914–1940], J. Straub [Berlin, 1971–1984], and R. Riedinger [Berlin, 1984–1995], II, 1, 1 [pp. 104.13–106.29]) and 246 (*ACO* II, 1, 1 [pp. 107.20–111.8]); and Session 5, no. 34 (*ACO* II, 1, 2 [p. 129.8–10]); Alberigo and Tanner, *Decrees*, 1:83–87.

12. Alberigo and Tanner, *Decrees*, 1:85.

13. Ibid.

mixture" of these two natures in him; those—presumably Apollinarian sectaries—who think of his human form as itself coming from heaven; those—like the now-discredited Eutyches—who insist that the once-two natures that constitute the person of Jesus have become, since the moment of their union, only one. Only then, in last place, does the statement express the council's understanding of Jesus in positive, declaratory terms.

As Grillmeier observed over sixty years ago, this positive statement itself is a mixture of plain language—"one and the same Son, who *is* our Lord Jesus Christ"[14]—and technical language borrowed from the philosophical traditions of Hellenism and the theological writings of earlier well-known Fathers: from the Cappadocians, Cyril, Proclus of Constantinople, Basil of Seleucia, even apparently from Nestorius himself. So this "one and the same Christ" is

> acknowledged to be unconfusedly, unalterably, undividedly, inseparably [four adverbs with a considerable philosophical and theological history[15]] *in* two natures, since [now borrowing two phrases from Leo's *Tome*] the difference of the natures is not destroyed because of the union, but, on the contrary, the character of each nature is preserved and comes together in one person [πρόσωπον: "persona," role, self-presentation] and one hypostasis [or concrete individual], not divided or torn into two persons but one and the same Son and only begotten God, Logos, Lord Jesus Christ . . .[16]

All of this is traditional, the statement adds, "just as in earlier times the prophets and also the Lord Jesus Christ himself taught us about him [the statement's only reference to Scripture], and as the symbol of our Fathers [i.e., the Nicene Creed] transmitted to us."[17] Finally, the decree prohibits any Christian from writing, thinking, or teaching anything that might contradict the basic shape of the faith witnessed to here.

Read as a whole, the Chalcedonian statement makes it clear that this famous final section is not meant to push back the frontier of theological reflection on the person of Jesus, but simply to establish agreed conceptual

14. Grillmeier, *Christ in Christian Tradition*, 1:159.

15. For the Neoplatonic background to the way the union of distinct natures in Christ is conceived in the language of Chalcedon, see Luise Abramowski, "Συνάφεια und ἀσύγχυτος ἕνωσις als Bezeichnung für trinitarische und christologische Einheit," in *Drei christologische Untersuchungen* (Berlin: De Gruyter, 1981), 63–109.

16. Alberigo and Tanner, *Decrees*, 1:86; Grillmeier, *Christ in Christian Tradition*, 1:159.

17. Alberigo and Tanner, *Decrees*, 1:86–87.

standards for remaining within the tradition of orthodoxy for the future. The emphasis is on the earlier formulation of that tradition, in the creeds of Nicaea and Constantinople, with priority given to the former; one might even say that all of what follows the quoting of those creeds is really meant as a set of hermeneutical rules for reading the Christological vision of Nicaea correctly, in the context of fifth-century controversy. Those rules are both negative and positive: how one may *not* interpret Nicaea; and how one *may*, even *must* interpret it, in order to remain in the Church's communion of faith and sacrament. But in setting up these rules, in carefully fixing this boundary to exclude some positions and leave room for others, great care is taken that the main fears and favorite phrases of both sides of the current controversy be explicitly respected. The five positions excluded are, presumably, meant to represent extremes—caricatures perhaps, of what groups at the time actually held, lines that no credible, centrist member of either side would want to follow. What positions might be included under the positive part of the statement is less clear, precisely because phrases from a variety of authors, with a variety of contrasting positions on the person of Christ, are here skillfully woven into a single paragraph that is designed to give an appearance of tranquil cohesion. Somewhere in that mix, the statement suggests, lies orthodoxy.

The lasting value of Church documents and synodal statements—their meaning within the continuing life of the community—lies, as we have come to learn, in their *reception*: in the messy, unpredictable process by which the wider Church—its bishops, its writers, its holy people, its "ordinary" faithful—judges and uses such statements and over time decides, implicitly or explicitly, to recognize them as normative for faith, to pray and live by them.[18] And the difficulty with regarding the Chalcedonian formula as representing the quintessence of the Church's classical understanding of the person of Christ, as modern theologians often take it to be, is precisely that its reception was not unambiguous, not instantaneous, and by no means unanimous, and that—in contrast to the Creed of Nicaea, which also took a good fifty years to be widely accepted as a norm of orthodox faith—its reception at all by Eastern Christianity depended, in the end, on further modifications and nuanced qualifications that also became canonical for

18. On the theological and canonical process of the "reception" of official dogma, see A. Grillmeier, "Konzil und Rezeption. Methodische Bemerkungen zu einem Thema der ökumenischen Diskussion der Gegenwart," in *Mit Ihm und in Ihm: Christologische Forschungen und Perspektiven* (Freiburg: Herder, 1975), 303–34.

orthodox Christians over the next two centuries: on further, crucial hermeneutical rules for interpreting both *its* language and the Nicene salvation narrative it summed up. These are the rules enunciated in the decrees of what most Christians today recognize as the fifth, sixth, and seventh ecumenical councils. Without the canons of Constantinople II (further emphasizing the unique personal union of Christ's two natures in a single divine, eternal subject), Constantinople III (insisting that the two natures in Christ still remain sufficiently distinct to include two complete and functioning wills), and even Nicaea II (arguing that if Jesus is truly God with a human face, it is wholly appropriate to venerate the image of that face as something holy), as supplements to its formulations and guides to its proper interpretation, the Chalcedonian decree would probably be regarded today as fully orthodox only by Western Christianity.

The full story of the reception of Chalcedon is, of course, too lengthy and complicated to be told at any length here. Attempts by the emperor Marcian (d. 457), and by his successor Leo I (d. 474), to install bishops favorable to the council's union formula in Alexandria, and soon afterwards even in Antioch, ended in violence and schism, as more and more monks and pastors in the Greek-speaking world raised irate objections to Chalcedon's even-handed representation of the person of the Savior: it was a political solution, opponents charged, rather than an authentic articulation of the tradition of faith in which these Churches worshiped and preached; it was a victory for the humanistic, overly analytical thinking of Nestorius and his Antiochene supporters; it was a Western solution, an expression of the dry, neatly balanced categories of papal bureaucrats, rather than of the intense devotion to the Savior, or of the sense of human transformation by the dynamic personal presence of the divine in Jesus, which had already become the core of much Greek, Egyptian, and Syrian spirituality.[19]

For Eastern bishops who had attended the council in 451, the choice of whether or not to abandon Chalcedon's statement of faith in the years that followed, and to join in the call for a new gathering, seems to have been a difficult one; most of them were not schooled in the niceties of the disputed

19. For a detailed attempt to depict this Eastern attitude to the Chalcedonian formula, see W. H. C. Frend, *The Rise of the Monophysite Movement* (Cambridge: Cambridge University Press, 1972), especially 137–42 (the attitude of Eastern monks towards the person of Christ) and 148f. (many in the East saw Chalcedon as a victory for Nestorianism). On the general sympathy for Antiochene thinking in the West at this period, and on the post-Chalcedonian tendency for popes and Western theologians to identify the Chalcedonian statement with papal teaching authority, see ibid., 131–35, 196–99.

terminology, yet they realized the pastoral dangers both in continuing to maintain the council's position as normative and in returning to the ideological conflicts of the 440s by simply abandoning Chalcedon. One bishop from the coast of Polemonian Pontus in northern Asia Minor, Euippius of Neocaesaraea, when canvassed for his advice by the emperor Leo a few years later, wrote back that he and his local colleagues had come to the conclusion that they should not abandon the Chalcedonian position: because so many wise and holy bishops had been present there, and because (more importantly) those bishops at Chalcedon had so strenuously endorsed the faith of Nicaea. Borrowing a famous phrase, however, from Gregory of Nazianzus,[20] the rhetorical genius of the fourth-century Church, Euippius assured the emperor that he and his colleagues were expressing this view "as fishermen, not as philosophers [ἁλιευτικῶς, οὐκ ἀριστοτελικῶς]"; all the technical complexities of person and nature, "unconfused" and "inseparable," it seems, were a little beyond them.[21]

In 482, the emperor Zeno attempted to provide an alternative formulation of the unity of Christ without the help (and possible divisiveness) of calling a new council: the so-called *Henōtikon*, drafted by his patriarch Acacius originally as an expression of imperial Church policy for Egypt, and later proposed more generally, it seems, for the whole empire. This document decrees, for the sake of unity and peace, that only the Creed of Nicaea, and its later interpretations at Constantinople and at the Cyrilline synod at Ephesus (431), along with Cyril's more contested "third" letter to Nestorius, shall be considered normative expressions of Christian faith; "and everyone who has held or holds any other opinion, either at the present or another time, whether at Chalcedon or in any synod whatever, we anathematize."[22] The result of this implied slight of the council, as being at least possibly heretical, was a new schism: this time a break in communion from the side of Rome and the Latin West (the so-called Acacian schism), which was not healed until 519, after the elderly Latin-speaking emperor Justin, at the urging of his nephew Justinian, the future emperor and architect of a renewed Medi-

20. See *Orat.* 23.12 (an oration entitled "On Philosophy, and the Selection of Bishops").

21. For this reply and a number of others, gathered—in Latin translation—in a collection known as the *Codex Encyclius*, see the text in *ACO* II [pp. 9–98], esp. no. 40 (*ACO* II [p. 84.2–3]); for a discussion of the collection and its importance for the reception of Chalcedon, see Grillmeier, "*Piscatorie—Aristotelice*," in *Mit Ihm und in Ihm*, 283–300; Frend, *Rise of the Monophysite Movement*, 161–63.

22. See Frend, *Rise of the Monophysite Movement*, 174–83, 192; for a full text and translation, see ibid., 360–62.

terranean unity, gave in to the demands of Rome and affirmed an explicitly Chalcedonian theology as the norm once again.

Justinian himself, a learned theologian as well as a masterly politician, spent the first decade after his own accession, in 527, trying to bring the opponents and the defenders of Chalcedon together by promoting patient dialogue on the theological issues. By that time, however—eighty contentious years after the council—positions had hardened into immovable fronts, and the issues dividing the main parties were less substantial differences over how to understand the person of Christ than differences in how one identified and privileged the voices of authentic tradition. If Cyril of Alexandria was to be the touchstone of orthodoxy, as most sixth-century parties to the discussion now seemed to agree, how was the Church to evaluate the contribution of Pope Leo, and of Leo's friendly Antiochene correspondents such as Theodoret? Which of Cyril's writings best represented his normative position? Was Cyril's approach to Christ compatible with the formula of Chalcedon, and with the Christology of those who now defended Chalcedon as orthodox?[23] Or was Chalcedonian Christology, in fact, a disguised form of the Nestorianism, the divisive conception of Christ, that Cyril had so adamantly opposed?

Two things seem to have become apparent to Justinian during his own early experiences trying to broker a new settlement. One was that, as emperor himself after 527, responsible for both the civil and the ecclesiastical peace, he could not simply abandon the Christological statement of Chalcedon, or leave it among documents whose orthodoxy remained undecided, as Zeno's *Henōtikon* had diplomatically tried to do. If the empire did not continue to affirm the Chalcedonian statement, formed under imperial leadership, as integral to its official vision of Christianity as the state religion—as binding law—the Latin West would be lost to the empire, and important

23. In the late fifth and early sixth centuries, representatives of both sides of the controversy over Chalcedon produced anthologies or florilegia of excerpts from Cyril's voluminous works, designed to show the compatibility or incompatibility of the Chalcedonian formula with his thought. Severus of Antioch composed a treatise, the *Philalēthēs*, attacking the reliability of such a pro-Chalcedonian florilegium of texts from Cyril; see R. Hespel, *Le florilège de Cyrille refuté par Sévère d'Antioche*, Bibl. du Muséon, 37 (Louvain, 1955). On the increasing use of these anthologies in sixth- and seventh-century controversial theology, see Marcel Richard, "Notes sur les florilèges dogmatiques du Ve et du VIe siècle," in *Actes du VIe Congrès international d'Études byzantines* I (Paris, 1950), 307–18 (= *Opera Minora*, 3 vols. [Turnhout: Brepols, 1976–1977] vol. 1, no. 2); and especially "Les florilèges diphysites du Ve et du VIe siècle," in Aloys Grillmeier and Heinrich Bacht, eds., *Das Konzil von Chalkedon*, 3 vols. (Würzburg: Echter, 1951–1954), 1:721–48 (= *Opera Minora* vol. 1, no. 3).

voices in the Greek cultural and political elite would be alienated as well. Equally important, perhaps, a monument of imperial religious policy that had been formulated at the behest of his predecessor Marcian, and officially defended for decades, would now be abandoned. Justinian's other realization, however, was that he also could not continue to promote Chalcedon in its original, carefully balanced but verbally ambiguous form, if he was to have any hope of regaining for the Church and the empire large regions of Syria and Egypt that were now in schism. The language of Chalcedon, by itself, was simply too open to what many in the East regarded as a "Nestorian" reading. The only hope for a single policy on Christian orthodoxy that might be acceptable to at least sizeable portions of both the Chalcedonian and the non-Chalcedonian public lay in a thoroughgoing but subtle rephrasing or expansion of the council's statement, along lines that made fully clear its compatibility with Cyril's Word-centered vision of Christ, in both his earlier and his later writings. Although resisted by some pro-Chalcedonian controversialists of the 540s—notably Leontius of Byzantium—Justinian's "neo-Chalcedonian" approach to Christology (to use a disputed term coined by modern Western historians) was eventually canonized as binding Church doctrine at a synod of Greek bishops summoned by the emperor to his palace in the capital in 553. This is the synod that has been received by the principal Churches of both East and West as the Second Council of Constantinople.

After a lengthy theological introduction, condemning by name three of the main figures honored in the fifth-century "school of Antioch"—Theodore of Mopsuestia, from the late fourth century, who remained the best-known Antiochene exegete and theoretician; Theodoret of Cyrus, an outspoken critic of Cyril and an influential voice at Chalcedon; and a letter attacking Cyril by the fifth-century Syrian bishop Ibas of Edessa—precisely for their resistance to the most uncompromising form of Cyril's Christology, the fourteen canons of Constantinople II also make it clear that the "one hypostasis or person" in Christ, mentioned at Chalcedon, *is* in fact none other than the eternal Word of God,[24] and that the Jesus "who was crucified in his human flesh *is* truly God and the Lord of glory, and one of the members of the holy Trinity."[25] It also suggests that there are both orthodox and unorthodox ways of understanding traditional Cyrillian characterizations

24. Canons 2, 3, and 5 (Alberigo and Tanner, *Decrees*, 1:114–16). This seems to be expressed clearly in the concluding phrases of the Chalcedonian formula, but apparently was not unambiguous enough for its critics.

25. Canon 10 (ibid., 1:118).

of Christ's person—a union of the divine and human realized "*from* two natures"; "*one nature* of the Word of God, made flesh"—as well as orthodox and unorthodox understandings of the "two-nature" language of the theologians of Antioch and of Chalcedon itself. Both sides of the controversy, in other words, were now seen as being on equal footing; each had truth on its side, when properly understood, but the language of each side stood in danger of heresy through one-sided readings or exaggeration.[26] After Constantinople II, in consequence, the Chalcedonian formula, as such, remained a central part of the recognized tradition of imperially sponsored orthodoxy, but its official interpretation had now been qualified in some degree, submitted to new official norms and ranged alongside other, competing Christological formulas, precisely in order to be acknowledged with them as part of the longer orthodox tradition.

The conclusion seems clear. Without in any way detracting from its importance as a formulation of what is central to the Christian tradition, the Chalcedonian definition itself can better be understood as a mid-fifth-century way station, a brilliant but largely unsuccessful attempt to reconcile competing traditions of language and thinking about the person of Christ, than as a settlement, let alone as the climax, of patristic debates about Christ, or as itself an adequate foundation for lasting ecumenical agreement. Despite the efforts of imperial policy in the second half of the fifth century to set the formula of Chalcedon quietly aside (as in the period of the "Acacian schism," between 478 and 518) or later to enforce it as settled imperial law (as generally after 518 under Justin), public argument over the structure and activities of Christ's person, as one who is both God and human, continued unabated after the council. Fronts hardened, political and theological rivalries now became the foundations of Christian bodies that no longer shared ecclesial communion (many of which still exist, as the "Oriental Orthodox" Churches). In the process, imperially sponsored efforts to recast the council's statement of faith in language acceptable to all the disagreeing parties—including the official formulations of Constantinople II and III—also never succeeded in establishing the reconciliation of these Churches with the wider Chalcedonian communion, despite their eventual acceptance in the Orthodox and Catholic traditions as ecumenical conciliar statements.[27]

26. Canons 8 and 9 (ibid., 1:117–18).

27. See Frend, *Rise of the Monophysite Movement*; Christian Lange, *Mia Energeia: Untersuchungen zur Einigungspolitik des Kaiser Heraclius und des Patriarchen Sergius von Constantinopel* (Tübingen: Mohr Siebeck, 2012).

One reason, surely, for this mixed reception was the perceived ambiguity of the Chalcedonian formula itself. Its carefully crafted phrases excluded positions which most informed Christian thinkers of the mid-fifth century would immediately have recognized as extremes, and which few would have directly affirmed for themselves: thinking of Christ as "two sons," thinking the Godhead by itself can suffer, thinking that humanity and divinity have been "confused" in Christ into some new, hybrid entity which is neither divine nor human because it is both at once. But Chalcedon's *positive* formulation of how the Church must interpret Nicene theology and confess the person of Christ, for all its even-handedness, still seems to have struck many—probably a majority—of Greek-speaking Christians as *too* symmetrical, too dialectical, too ready to affirm the continuing, even independent, functioning of the two utterly different realities or "natures" united in Christ's one "person," to count as an unambiguous affirmation of the Church's ancient faith that it was truly God the Son who spoke and healed, died and rose, as the Jesus of the Gospels. The echoes of Antiochene phrases in the formula, the prominent place in it of carefully balanced phrases taken from Pope Leo's "Tome" to Flavian of Constantinople (449), all continued to call forth an allergic reaction in the many Eastern monks and faithful who had come, in the controversies of the mid-fifth century, to regard Cyril of Alexandria, and Cyril alone, as the most articulate and reliable spokesman for Christian piety. The Chalcedonian statement, despite its anchoring in the Nicene and Constantinopolitan creeds, and its final assertion that the "one *persona* (*prosōpon*) and individual (*hypostasis*)" formed by the two continuing, countable realities (οὐσίαι, φύσεις) in Christ *is* "one and the same only-begotten Son, God, Word, Lord Jesus Christ," apparently did not seem, in the eyes of many, to insist clearly enough that it was *God* who was the agent of the saving work of Jesus, God the Son who is the actual referent when we speak of the earthly actions and sufferings of the Son of Man.

So the Christological controversies of the century that followed the Council of Chalcedon, within the sphere of influence of the imperial Church—controversies that grew even more intense, in both language and spirit, than those of the three decades that preceded the council—came to be centered on whether or not the terminology of the Chalcedonian statement could be reconciled with the conception of the person of Christ found in the older, more universally recognized representatives of the orthodox tradition: especially in Athanasius, Gregory of Nazianzus, and Cyril of Alexandria. In this process of the "reception" of Chalcedon, a new style of theology, which had haltingly begun in the late fourth-century controversies with the "Eunomian" Arians over how to conceive of God as both radically one and irreducibly three—a style I would characterize as "scholastic" or academic—now almost completely replaced the more exegetical and homiletic forms of theological discourse that had predominated in earlier centuries. Whereas previously theological controversies had been conducted largely in oratorical style—in works shaped by the rhetorical canons of epideictic and forensic speech—Christological argument from the mid-fifth century on came to be couched almost exclusively in the style of the classroom, the scholastic disputation, the philosophical lecture. The exact definition of terms, the analysis of traditional formulas, the development of complex chains of argument in syllogisms and theses, formed an increasingly large part in the development of theological ideas. Technical concepts and strategies, drawn especially from the ideologically Neoplatonic commentators on the Hellenistic philosophical "scriptures" of Plato and Aristotle, now came to play a decisive, if unacknowledged, role on all sides in reflection on the unity of the person of Christ. Learned monks and educated laypeople (often called σχολαστικοί), rather than bishops, more and more dominated theological discussion. In the process, for that very reason, it became increasingly important to establish one's credentials by showing that the orthodox "Fathers," from Athanasius to Cyril, supported one's position—a task usually accomplished by appending a sizeable anthology of authoritative excerpts from these classical authors to one's own attempts at Christological argument.[28] As a result, controversy over Christ's person, from the mid-fifth to the mid-ninth century, turned into a series of technical, subtle, philosophically sophisticated debates over the logical consistency of the Chalcedonian formula, and over who now represented the true legacy of Cyril. What Westerners since the Middle Ages would call Scholastic theology began, I believe, in the thought-world of these later Greek Fathers.

What I would like to argue here, too, is that even in this new style of argument current in the sixth and seventh centuries, much more came to be at stake than simply the attempt to justify Chalcedon's orthodoxy, a quarrel over dry, technical theological terminology or over arcane details of the ontology of the human subject. Among those who defended the orthodoxy and the indispensable importance of Chalcedon's "symmetrical" picture of Christ in this philosophical fashion, the central issue was not so much the

28. For further details of this new "scholastic" style of theological argument, see my article "Boethius's Theological Tracts and Early Byzantine Scholasticism," *Mediaeval Studies* 46 (1984): 158–91.

full humanity of Christ, or the parallel survival of what modern scholars like Grillmeier call "word-flesh" and "word–human being" models of conceiving Christ's unity, as it was a wider perspective that probably had never crossed the minds of the drafters of the Chalcedonian formula itself: a new sense of the *paradigmatic* importance of the person of Christ, in its very structure, for revealing *God's way of saving and transforming humanity* through non-destructive union, as the goal of creation itself. For Leontius of Byzantium in the mid-sixth century, as for Maximus the Confessor in the mid-seventh and John of Damascus in the mid-eighth, the Chalcedonian formula becomes, to an increasing degree, more than just a summary of the varying terms and models used to speak of Christ; it develops into the concrete, living model of how God acts to save and "divinize" humanity, by establishing a relationship with the world and with each of us, which—analogous to the person of Christ itself—makes us one with God in our concrete mode of being who we are, without compromising either the natural distinctiveness of what we are as creatures, or the inconceivable fullness of what God is.

For Leontius—to take him simply as an early but representative example—it was the Chalcedonian formula, properly and deeply understood, which offered the Churches the most reliable guide for avoiding possibly misleading ways of understanding the person and work of Christ. This was not simply a battle about words, Leontius insisted:

> What is at issue for us is not a matter of phrasing, but the *manner* in which the whole mystery of Christ exists [περὶ τοῦ τρόπου τοῦ ὅλου κατὰ Χριστὸν μυστηρίου]. So we cannot make judgments or decisions here simply on the basis of this or that expression or of certain phrases, but on the basis of its fundamental principles [ἐκ τῶν πρώτων ἀρχῶν].[29]

Yet the most fundamental of those principles behind the Chalcedonian portrait of Christ, in Leontius's view, is (significantly) not some biblical or traditional theological assertion, but the distinction between universal being and particular being—οὐσία or φύσις, on the one hand, and ὑπόστασις or πρόσωπον, on the other—which I have mentioned already. This is a terminological rule developed in the 360s or 370s by the Cappadocian Fathers for expressing the unity and distinction of Father, Son, and Holy Spirit within the one God, but (curiously) not applied with any consistency to the mystery of Christ during the bitter fifth-century debates leading up to Chalcedon. So

29. *Deprehensio et triumphus super Nestorianos* 42 (PG 86:1380B).

"substance" or "nature," in Leontius's terminology—terminology that resonates constantly with the discourse-world of the Neoplatonic commentaries on Aristotle contemporary to his work—refers to the kind of universal reality in which many individuals participate, the kind of reality—like "horse," "cow," or "human being"—that defines what any individual thing is. The language of "hypostasis," on the other hand—and in the case of human beings, "person" (πρόσωπον)—refers to a concrete individual within such a universal class, something or someone existing uniquely "by itself" (καθ' ἑαυτό), able to be counted, to be labeled with a proper name. And while, as Leontius readily admits, "there is no such thing as a non-hypostatic nature"[30]—while universal natures or substances (such as "divinity" or "humanity") have no independent existence as universals, either in this present realm of being or in some separate, ideal world of forms—still individual things or hypostases are also unintelligible, and to that degree unreal, apart from their structural relationship to universal reality—apart, in other words, from being *what* they are.[31] So the ontological structure of particular things, in Leontius's view, consists of a kind of dialectic, a reciprocal shaping, that takes place between universal substances or natures and concrete individuals.[32]

What distinguishes a being—universal or individual—from all others, Leontius and his contemporaries assume, are that being's "characteristics" or ἰδιώματα: universals or generic "natures" are marked off from other natures by "essential qualities" (οὐσιοποιοὶ ἰδιώτητες), concrete individuals by individual qualities or "accidents." In each case, it is these particular qualities or characteristics that mark a thing off as what it is, and not something else.[33]

30. *Contra Nestorianos et Eutychianos* 1 (PG 86:1277D–1280A).

31. For a discussion of the question of the status of universals and their relation to individual things in fifth- and sixth-century philosophy, and of the influence of these discussions on Leontius and his contemporaries, see my article "'A Richer Union': Leontius of Byzantium and the Relationship of Human and Divine in Christ," *Studia Patristica* 24 (1993): 239–65, esp. 246–53.

32. See *Contra Nestorianos et Eutychianos* 1 (PG 86:1280A): "Nature admits of the predication of being, but hypostasis also of being-by-oneself. The former presents the character of genus, the latter expresses individual identity. The one brings out what is peculiar to something universal, the other distinguishes the particular from the general. To put it concisely, things sharing the same essence and things whose structure [λόγος] of being is common are properly said to be of one nature; but we can define as a 'hypostasis' either things which share a nature but differ in number, or things which are put together from different natures, but which share reciprocally in a common being."

33. Leontius, like many Platonically oriented Aristotelians of his time, seems simply to assume that the characteristics that allow us to tell universals or individuals from one

The importance of all of this for Christology is that it is precisely in this interplay of universal and individual qualities—of essential characteristics and particular, historical features or "accidents"—that things and persons become what and who they are; and it is this that makes it possible for a single, concrete thing to share at once in two distinct, unconfused natures. What distinguishes spirit from matter, soul from body, for instance, on the level of substance or nature—being without extension, intelligent and free, on the one hand, and being solid or colored on the other—is precisely the set of specific characteristics that unite all souls or all bodies with each other in the same universal class. But what distinguishes *this* soul from all other souls—its conscious relationship or σχέσις to a particular bodily frame, in a particular corner of time and space—is precisely what unites it ontologically to *this* body, enables them both to form *this* particular person: not just a "soul" or a "body" or even a "human being" in general, but Peter or John.

It is this set of defining relationships (these σχέσεις, in the technical vocabulary of Aristotle's *Categories* and Porphyry's *Eisagōgē*)[34] which in turn make understandable the Chalcedonian portrait of the unique person of Christ, in Leontius's view. Christ, as Son of God and Son of Mary, is naturally set off from all other beings in heaven and on earth by the transcendent characteristics of God's essence, on the one hand, insofar as we (for the most part negatively) understand them, and by the universal characteristics of humanity (itself a composite of the generic characteristics of soul and body), on the other. What makes him *God* is not what makes him *human*, and vice versa: these characteristics, and the universal natures or substances they identify, are "unconfused." At the same time, the characteristics that mark the *Son* off, within the divine nature, from Father and Holy Spirit, that identify him as a divine *hypostasis*—his generation from the Father's being, his filial obedience, his role as receiver and sender of the Spirit—are precisely the characteristics which, when mingled with the unique *human* accidents of his historical existence—being a Jew from the early Roman Empire, the son of Mary, the carpenter from Nazareth, a man of determined appearance and height and weight—make him a single, unique, historical hypostasis who is *both* God and human, or in Leontius's words, give him "coherence and unity with himself."[35]

another are, in themselves, constitutive of the reality of those universal or individual entities. The epistemological and gnoseological levels are not carefully or consistently distinguished.

34. See esp. *Contra Nestorianos et Eutychianos* 4 (PG 86:1288A–1289A); Daley, "A Richer Union," 252–53.

35. *Epilyseis* 1 (PG 86:1917D); see also *Epaporemata* 25 (PG 86:1909CD).

And it is the relationship of mutual interchange and completion, "the common share in being" (κοινωνία τοῦ εἶναι),[36] which exists concretely between these two natures themselves in the person of Christ—God the Word forming Jesus for himself as his way of existing in the world, the human Jesus fully expressing in human terms what it is to be Son of God—that results in their "mutually inherent life" (ἡ ἀλληλοῦχος ζωή).[37] Yet while Christ's personal existence is based on these relationships, the unity at the core of his person is not simply extrinsic or accidental, not simply a matter of moral harmony between two wholly different conscious subjects, as the Antiochene theologians seemed (to their critics, at least) to suggest. It is a "substantial" union, in which the concrete individual, Jesus, is constituted in his being by the very confluence, the mutual shaping, of these two analogous, incommensurable, yet still radically personal realities—his being Son of God and son of Mary—through the shared characteristics that mark them off from other divine or other human persons.[38]

Although all this analysis may seem to some like the driest form of metaphysical speculation, Leontius insists that comprehending its meaning is, in fact, central to a proper understanding of the orthodox tradition of faith. The Chalcedonian picture of Christ—as *one* hypostasis, one individual, one Christ Jesus, who exists as subject *in two* unconfused and undivided natures, both of which continue to be fully intact and operative as what they are while being joined inseparably with each other in a way that mutually defines both—is not only logically coherent, in Leontius's view, but theologically necessary to a Christian understanding of the world. "The mode of union, rather than the structure [λόγος] of nature, contains the great mys-

36. *Contra Nestorianos et Eutychianos* 1 (PG 86:1280A); *Epilyseis* 1 (PG 86:1917D).

37. *Contra Nestorianos et Eutychianos* 4 (PG 86:1288D).

38. *Epilyseis* 4 (PG 86:1925C); *Epilyseis* 8 (PG 86:1940D); *Contra Aphthartodocetas* (PG 86:1353A); *Deprehensio et triumphus super Nestorianos* 42 (PG 86:1380D). Although Aristotle and his earlier commentators had seen "relationship" (*to pros ti, schesis*)—spatial relationships, for instance, such as "near this tree," or temporal relationships such as "before the flood"—as the most extrinsic kind of accident, Plotinus and the Neoplatonist commentators of the fifth century had begun to argue that some kinds of relationship, at least, can represent a sharing of, and even a constitutive basis for, being: see Plotinus, *Enneades* 6.1.6; Simplicius, *In Aristotelis Categorias commentaria* 7 (ed. C. Kalbfleisch [Berlin, 1907], 169.1–173.32). For further discussion, see my essay "Nature and the 'Mode of Union': Late Patristic Models for the Personal Unity of Christ," in Stephen Davis, Daniel Kendall, SJ, and Gerald O'Collins, SJ, eds., *The Incarnation: An Interdisciplinary Symposium on the Incarnation of the Son of God* (Oxford: Oxford University Press, 2002), 164–96.

tery of religion," he writes.[39] The gospel is not simply the communication of a deeper understanding of what God is, or what humanity is, although we come to understand both God and humanity in a new way because of our faith in Christ. Rather, the gospel is the proclamation of the union of God and humanity in a particular person: the news that God's eternal Son and a finite human being have in fact become a single individual within history, without thereby ceasing to be what God the Son and what that particular human being are, in and by themselves.

Somewhere, Leontius insists, between "the way of confusion," identified with the approach of Eutyches, and "the way of division," identified with that of Nestorius, lies the reality that the Church—doubtless without fully realizing it at the time—proclaims of Christ at Chalcedon: "the middle way of unconfused and inseparable union." He explains:

> This is the kind of *union* we are speaking of: more unitive than the kind that completely divides, but richer than the kind that completely confuses, so that it neither makes the things united completely the same as each other, nor wholly other. If, then, a union of this kind shows its product to be neither wholly the same nor wholly different, we must investigate *how* it is the same, and *how* different. True belief recognizes the sameness to be in the hypostasis, the difference in the natures.[40]

Chalcedon, in Leontius's reading, sets before the later Church this paradox that lies at the heart of the biblical message, and that Balthasar rightly saw as central to Maximus's theological vision in the seventh century. The "organic union" (συμφυὴς ἕνωσις) of the Son's divine nature with a full human nature in the single person of Jesus of Nazareth, the Christ, results not in a kind of mythic hero, whose every act and thought is miraculous because his humanity is permanently changed by belonging to God, but in something much more astonishing: in a God who is "with us" and makes our weaknesses, even our mortality, his own, while remaining utterly divine; and in a man who always acts humanly, even though his "nature and his name" (to paraphrase Charles Wesley) is "Son of God."

My argument here has been simply this: although modern Western theologians have tended to see Chalcedon's paradoxical formulation of who and what Christ is as the climax and lasting settlement of several centuries

39. *Epilyseis* 8 (PG 86:1940C).
40. Ibid. (PG 86:1941AB).

of ancient controversy, in fact by itself it settled very little, but led only to more bitter and lasting disputes. What Christians since the Middle Ages understand as "Chalcedonian" Christology is, in fact, Chalcedon as "received" in the following four centuries: a reading of the council's cautious formulation through the modifying lenses of several later ancient councils, as well as through the hermeneutical contributions of late antique philosophy and the interpretation of a number of influential ancient and medieval theologians. Beginning with the intensely pro-Chalcedonian apologetics of Leontius of Byzantium, in the mid-sixth century—whom I have cited at some length here—but continuing in the writings of others like the more critical Emperor Justinian, the philosophical politician Boethius, and (in the following centuries) Sophronius of Jerusalem, Maximus Confessor, and John of Damascus, to name a few, it was the reception of Chalcedon's paradoxical vision of Christ's person as suggesting something *more than originally intended*—as holding out nothing less than a model for God's saving relationship with the world he created—that seems to have assured the definition itself its continuing place at the center of Christian reflection. For Leontius, as later for Maximus and John of Damascus, both of whom build on his terminology and arguments, only the language and thought of Chalcedon, as interpreted and received, can give adequate expression to the "mystery of union," the recognized reality of "God with us," that is, in the end, the heart of the world's salvation.

12 Apollo as a Chalcedonian

A New Fragment of a Controversial Work from Early Sixth-Century Constantinople

It seems to have been something of a Christian commonplace, at the turn of the fifth century, to taunt the ancient pagan oracles for being unable to predict their own demise. "Where are the frightening and shadowy spectres of Hecate," asked Gregory of Nazianzus in his Epiphany sermon of 380 or 381, "and the subterranean tricks and prophecies of Trophonius, or the mutterings of the oak of Dodona, or the sophistries of the Delphic tripod, or the prophetic drink of Castalia? The only thing they could not prophesy was this: their own falling into silence."[1] Commenting, some thirty years later, on the stinging challenge to the prophetic powers of the pagan gods in Isaiah 41:22, Jerome observed "that after the coming of Christ all the idols have fallen silent. Where is Delphic Apollo and Loxias, Delian and Clarian [Apollo], and the other idols that promised knowledge of the future and deceived mighty kings? Why were they able to foretell nothing about Christ, nothing about his apostles, nothing about the ruin and abandonment of their temples? If, then, they were not able to foretell their own downfall, how could they foretell the good or bad fortunes of others?"[2]

Although some Christian parts of the *Oracula Sibyllina* probably go back to the second century,[3] Christian writers seem to have been less interested in

1. *Oration 39 (On the Holy Lights)* 5 (ed. C. Moreschini; trans. P. Gallay, SC 358 [Paris, 1990], 156–58).

2. *Commentarium in Isaiam Prophetam* 12 [written 408–410] (PL 24:434, A3–11).

3. On the dating of the various parts of the Sibylline collection, see the foundational work of J. Geffcken, *Komposition und Entstehungszeit der Oracula Sibyllina*, Texte und Untersuchungen NF 8/1 (Leipzig, 1902), and the introductions and annotations to the translation of J. J. Collins in J. H. Charlesworth, ed., *The Old Testament Pseudepigrapha*, vol. 1 (New York, 1983), 317–472.

disputing—or co-opting—the powers of the other Hellenistic oracles until the age of Constantine. Clement of Alexandria, it is true, had insisted on the uselessness and obsolescence of the famous oracles of antiquity in his *Exhortation to the Pagans*[4] and even cited from Herodotus a brief oracle of Pythian Apollo in the course of a much larger anthology of pagan "plagiarisms" from the Bible;[5] but it was only Constantine's Christian admirers Lactantius and Eusebius of Caesarea, drawing mainly on the critically annotated dossier of their contemporary Porphyry, the *Philosophy Obtained from Oracles*, who first made a point of citing oracular texts in support of their own apologetic ends.[6] The challenge raised by Gregory of Nazianzus and Jerome may be a witness not only to the continuing popularity of Porphyry's work, but also to the memory of Julian's fruitless attempts to revive oracular activity at the major ancient shrines.[7] If the oracles of the gods were actually able to see and speak the truth, these Christian writers retort, they should have been able to recognize both the real divinity of Christ and the passing of their own age.[8]

This late fourth-century critique seems also to have suggested the program for a new, if limited, form of Christian literary activity: composing

4. *Protreptikos logos* 2.1–3.

5. *Strom.* 5.14.

6. See Lactantius, *Inst.* 7.13.6, quoting the Greek text of an oracle of Apollo of Miletus to argue for the indestructability of the soul—even though the same oracle, "ut divinae religionis inimicus," had counseled Diocletian to persecute the Christians (*De mort. persecut.* 11.7). Cf. Eusebius, *Praep. evang.* 3.14–4.9; 4.20; 5.5–10; 6.7 (from Oenomaeus); 9.10.

7. According to the Christian historian Sozomen, writing in the 440s, Apollo himself replied to Julian, when the emperor asked about restoring the oracle at his shrine at Daphne, near Antioch, that "the place was filled with dead bodies, and this prevented the oracle from speaking" (*Hist. eccl.* 5.19.19). Julian understood this as a reference to the relics of the Antiochene Christian martyr-bishop Babylas, which had been transferred to the site by Julian's own brother Gallus. The relics were solemnly removed at the emperor's order, but the shrine mysteriously burned down a few days later: see Sozomen, *Hist. eccl.* 5.19.10–5.20; Ammianus Marcellinus, *Hist.* 22.12.8–13.3. Julian admitted the failure of his efforts to restore the oracle at Daphne: *Misopōgōn* 346B, 361BC. The eleventh- and twelfth-century Byzantine chronographer George Kedrenos says that Julian also sent his physician Oribasius to Delphi, to revive the oracle there, and received the oracular information that the god no longer had the power of speech (304A [ed. I. Bekker; *Corpus Scriptorum Historiae Byzantinae*, 33 (Bonn, 1838); 532.4–10]).

8. For the revival of interest in oracles with an eschatological flavor among both pagans and Christians in the late fourth century, see Henry Chadwick, "Oracles of the End in the Conflict of Paganism and Christianity in the Fourth Century," in E. Lucchesi and H. D. Saffrey, eds., *Mémorial André-Jean Festugière: Antiquité païenne et chrétienne*, Cahiers d'Orientalisme, 10 (Geneva, 1984), 125–29.

or rewriting "pagan" oracles, in the classical Hellenic style (including the Ionic dialect) of the genuine oracles and the Homeric hymns rather than the more speculative and apocalyptic form of the Sibyllines, to bear witness to the Christian faith. A number of examples survive, suggesting by their Trinitarian theology and their less than subtle allusions to the triumph of Christianity a date in the last third of the fourth century.[9] Karl Buresch made a first attempt at publishing the extant examples of these Christianized oracles in 1889, as an appendix to his study of the oracle of Apollo at Claros,[10] and in 1941 Hartmut Erbse accomplished with distinction the complicated task of editing these works critically, arranged in the various collections and forms in which they have survived.[11] According to Erbse, the collection on which the tradition after 500 is mainly based was a huge work simply called the *Theosophia*—a word used by both Porphyry and Eusebius for statements of religious revelation.[12] This work seems to have been compiled, with an apologetic purpose, by an Alexandrian Christian during the reign of the emperor Zeno (474–491), in eleven books: seven books "on right faith" (περὶ τῆς ὀρθῆς πίστεως)[13] and four containing oracles of both pagan and Christian origin, sayings of Greek philosophers, verses of the Sibyls, and a final summary of world history. This last book seems to have included prophecies of the imminent end, attributed to "Hystaspes, king of the Persians or Chaldeans."[14] Although the whole *Theosophia* is lost, a collection of ninety-one excerpts from its oracular books is preserved in a manuscript

9. See Pierre Batiffol, "Oracula Hellenica," *Revue biblique* 13 (1916): 177–99, for a good survey of the genre.

10. Karl Buresch, *Klaros. Untersuchungen zum Orakelwesen des späteren Altertums* (Leipzig, 1889), 89ff.

11. Hartmut Erbse, *Fragmente griechischer Theosophien*, Hamburger Arbeiten zur Altertumswissenschaft, 4 (Hamburg, 1941)—a work which is unfortunately, if understandably, rare today in North America. Hereafter cited as Erbse.

12. See, e.g., Porphyry, *De abstinentia* 4.9; Eusebius, *Praep. evang.* 1.5 (16D) [Christian revelation], 4.9 (147C) [Greek oracles, based on Porphyry].

13. No fragments remain to give us a clue of what the content of this doctrinal summary may have contained. If the collection originated in Alexandria, however, as Erbse and earlier scholars argue, it is more than likely that it reflected an anti-Chalcedonian Christology, since Alexandria was the stronghold of resistance to that Council from the late 450s onwards.

14. Echoing an expectation found among Christian authors since at least the third century, the document seems to have set the end of the world, six thousand years after creation, at either AD 501 or 507–508: see Erbse, 1–3. For another "oracular" prophecy of the nearing end, from the first decade of the sixth century, see Paul J. Alexander, *The Oracle of Baalbek: The Tiburtine Sibyl in Greek Dress*, Dumbarton Oaks Studies, 10 (Washington, 1967); on the relation of this work to the *Theosophia* tradition, ibid., 118–20.

now in Tübingen,[15] hence the title by which the corpus is usually known: the "Tübinger Theosophie." It is the epitomator's introduction to this collection that provides us with virtually all the information we have about the extent and origin of the *Theosophia*.

There are other oracles as well, generally imitative of the tradition represented by the *Theosophia* and sometimes expanding on shorter fragments within that collection, which survive in verse and prose in a variety of sources. It is one of these "expanded" Christian oracles that I present here in a new edition: an improved text of a known oracular poem, in a newly discovered apologetic context that claims to form the final section of a hitherto-unknown work of Chalcedonian Christological polemic, apparently composed in connection with the struggles in Constantinople that led to the deposition of Patriarch Macedonius II in the summer of 511. The oracle itself was originally composed, it seems, in shorter form—perhaps as early as the fourth century—simply to express the "surrender" of the god of Delphi to the sovereign claims of the God of Christian revelation, and was embedded in the apocalyptic and apologetic matrix of the *Theosophia*—perhaps by an Alexandrian compiler of anti-Chalcedonian sentiment—some quarter century before 511. In the present text it appears in an extended version, apparently as the final rhetorical flourish of a work arguing for the orthodoxy of the Chalcedonian conception of the person of Christ, and pleading for the restoration of Church unity on the basis of that Christology. It is a long trajectory for a short poem to have traveled in little more than a century.

I. The Crisis of 511

In order to point out the significance of this extended oracle and its surrounding exhortation, it is important for us to summarize briefly the conflicts that racked the Eastern Churches during the later years of the reign of Emperor Anastasius (491–518), and especially the crisis reached in the exile of Patriarch Macedonius.

15. This manuscript, Tübingen 27, is a copy made by the humanist Bernhard Haus, in 1580, of a famous thirteenth- to fourteenth-century manuscript of Greek apologetic works, mainly from the second century, which found its way to Strasbourg in the eighteenth century (as Codex Argentoratensis 9) and was destroyed in the burning of the library during the Franco-Prussian war in 1870.

The century between the Council of Chalcedon (451) and the Second Council of Constantinople (553), which reaffirmed and significantly reinterpreted the Chalcedonian formulation of the identity and characteristics of Christ, was a century of unremitting dispute, in the Eastern empire, over Christology and Church authority. Chalcedon's celebrated dogmatic statement that "one and the same Christ, Son, Lord, Only-begotten, must be acknowledged in two natures, without confusion or change, without division or separation," a union of the utterly different realities of God and humanity in which "the character proper to each of the two natures was preserved as they came together in one person [πρόσωπον] and one individual [ὑπόστασις],"[16] was a carefully crafted formula of compromise. It was designed to include not only the concerns and the language of Cyril of Alexandria and his followers—with their strong emphasis on Jesus's single, operative identity as divine savior—but also terms reflecting the insistence of Antiochene theologians like Theodore of Mopsuestia and Theodoret of Cyrrhus, as well as Pope Leo of Rome, that humanity and divinity can never be wholly blended, and remain distinct and functionally unconfused in Jesus's actions and person. Despite the intentions of its drafters, however, the formula of Chalcedon was almost immediately rejected by the vast majority of Eastern monks and faithful as falling far short of Christian faith and piety. They considered it a politically motivated sell-out to the secular spirit of Antioch and the West, a practical denial that Jesus is God present in our flesh.[17]

In July 482, Emperor Zeno promulgated a formula of faith drafted by Acacius, his patriarch, hopefully called the *Henōtikon* or "statement of union." In that document the extreme positions of both Christological parties before Chalcedon are rejected, and the position of Cyril of Alexandria held up as normative. The status of Chalcedon itself, however, is left unmentioned, except for the deliberately vague statement, "Everyone who has held or holds any other opinion, either at the present or another time, whether at Chalcedon or in any synod whatever, we anathematize."[18] For the public and the

16. Greek text in E. Schwartz, *Acta Conciliorum Oecumenicorum* 2:1.1.128–130; translation in J. Neuner and J. Dupuis, *The Christian Faith in the Doctrinal Documents of the Catholic Church* (New York, 1982), 154–55 (slightly altered). For both original text and translation, see also Norman P. Tanner, ed., *Decrees of the Ecumenical Councils* (London/Washington, 1990), 1:86.

17. For a survey of the theological, ecclesiastical, and political controversies that followed Chalcedon, see especially W. H. C. Frend, *The Rise of the Monophysite Movement* (Cambridge, 1972); P. T. R. Gray, *The Defense of Chalcedon in the East (451–553)* (Leiden, 1979).

18. Text in Evagrius Scholasticus, *Hist. eccl.* 3.14; translation in Frend, *The Rise*, 361.

Church officials of Constantinople, a city whose position of ecclesiastical supremacy in the East as the "New Rome" had been confirmed irrevocably by the celebrated canon 28 of Chalcedon,[19] to disown Chalcedon was tantamount to abandoning both Church order and orthodox faith. Yet in the rest of the Christian East—especially in the Churches of Syria, Palestine, and Egypt, which stood under the hegemony of the ancient patriarchates of Antioch and Alexandria and the recently elevated patriarchate of Jerusalem—Chalcedon remained, in the eyes of most people, unredeemable. Even a statement as broad as Zeno's *Henōtikon* was doomed to fail as a formula of unity.

The reigns of Zeno (475–491) and his successor Anastasius I (491–518) were a time of intense theological activity, as well as of bitter conflict. Polemicists on both sides of the Christological divide assembled massive chains of argument, and equally massive dossiers of documentation, to prove that the Christology of their opponents was not in harmony with the longer orthodox tradition, especially as that tradition was represented by the great Alexandrian bishops Athanasius and Cyril.[20] For the opponents of Chalcedon, like the patriarch of Alexandria Timothy "Ailouros" (d. 477), any talk of "two natures" continuing to operate in a discernible way in the historical Jesus was Nestorianism, a denial of Jesus's integral divine identity as savior. In their view, only the Christological formulas urged by Cyril in his later letters—"one nature of the Word, made flesh," and "from two natures, one"—were able to do justice to the unity of Christ's person and his ability to act with transcendent power in his human deeds and encounters. Chalcedon's defenders, on the other hand, began assembling collections of passages from Cyril and the earlier orthodox Fathers to show that the Council's "two-nature" language about Christ also had an acceptable pedigree.[21] By the first

19. On this canon, see my article "Position and Patronage in the Early Church: The Original Meaning of 'Primacy of Honour,'" *Journal of Theological Studies* 44 (1993): 529–53, esp. 539–49, and the bibliography cited there.

20. In addition to the works of Frend and Gray cited above (n. 17), see now the detailed analysis of post-Chalcedonian Christology in Aloys Grillmeier, *Christ in Christian Tradition*, vol. 2/1 (Atlanta: John Knox, 1987) and *Jesus der Christus im Glauben der Kirche*, vol. 2/2 (original German ed.: Freiburg, 1989); vol. 2/4 (Freiburg, 1990). On the distinctive theological methods used in these debates, see also my "Boethius' Theological Tracts and Early Byzantine Scholasticism," *Mediaeval Studies* 46 (1984): 158–91, esp. 167–74.

21. See, for instance, the pro-Chalcedonian florilegium of passages from Cyril, probably assembled in Alexandria around 482, published by R. Hespel, *Le florilège Cyrillien réfuté par Sévère d'Antioche*, Bibliothèque du Muséon, 37 (Leuven, 1955). For a survey of Chalcedonian documentary activity in this period, see Marcel Richard, "Les florilèges diphysites du Ve et VIe siècle," *Das Konzil von Chalkedon* (Würzburg, 1951), 1:721–48 (= *Opera Minora* I, 3).

decade of the sixth century, Chalcedonian polemicists like Nephalius and John "the Grammarian" of Caesarea had begun to develop a new line of argument. They insisted, on the one hand, that the "two-nature" Christological formula of Leo and Chalcedon had been necessary to withstand the "confusion" of the divine and the human implied in the Christology of the extreme Cyrillian Eutyches; on the other hand, they conceded that one must speak of the one hypostasis of Christ existing both "in two natures" and "from two natures" if one is to avoid all danger of heresy. This "neo-Chalcedonian" position began gradually to incorporate other strongly unitive phrases from the arsenal of Chalcedon's opponents into its defense of the Council's orthodoxy, speaking of a "union by hypostasis" (καθ' ὑπόστασιν) in Christ, or a union "by composition" (κατὰ σύνθεσιν) of two natures into one, and affirming that the Christ who spoke and acted in a naturally human way, who suffered and died in his human nature on the cross, was himself indeed "one of the holy Trinity."[22] By the Council of Constantinople in 553, with the support of the theologian-emperor Justinian, this way of expressing the identity of Jesus was to become the officially received orthodox interpretation of the Chalcedonian formula.

Although personally a committed opponent of Chalcedonian Christology, Emperor Anastasius I never officially disowned the Council of 451, but continued to support his predecessor's *Henōtikon* as the foundation of official imperial policy. In fact, at the insistence of Patriarch Euphemius, he signed a confession of faith in accord with the *Henōtikon* before being crowned in 491, and the document was kept—to the emperor's growing discomfort—in the patriarchal files until the summer of 511. Euphemius's successor Macedonius II—an elderly and respected former bureaucrat, and a nephew of the Chalcedonian patriarch Gennadius (458–471)—was himself

22. For standard modern surveys of this "neo-Chalcedonian" approach to Christology, see Charles Moeller, "Le chalcédonisme et le néo-Chalcédonisme," *Das Konzil von Chalkedon*, 1:637–720; S. Helmer, *Der Neuchalkedonismus. Geschichte, Berechtigung und Bedeutung eines dogmengeschichtlichen Begriffes* (diss., Bonn, 1962); A. Grillmeier, "Der Neuchalkedonismus," *Historisches Jahrbuch der Görresgesellschaft* 77 (1958): 151–66 (= *Mit Ihm und in Ihm* [Freiburg, 1978], 371–85); *Jesus der Christus*, 2/2:48–82; P. T. R. Gray, "Neo-Chalcedonianism and the Transition from Patristic to Byzantine Theology," *Byzantinische Forschungen* 8 (1982): 61–70. On the emergence of the "theopaschite" formula, "One of the Holy Trinity has been crucified," as a point of controversy in the early decades of the sixth century, see especially Aloys Grillmeier, "Vorbereitung des Mittelalters. Eine Studie über das Verhältnis von Chalkedonismus und Neu-Chalkedonismus in der lateinischen Theologie von Boethius bis zu Gregor dem Grossen," *Chalkedon* 2 (Würzburg, 1952), 2:791–839; *Jesus der Christus*, 2/2:333–59.

a Chalcedonian. Macedonius, however, was eager to restore communion with both anti-Chalcedonian Alexandria and the pro-Chalcedonian Latin Church, and seems to have seen continuing allegiance to the *Henōtikon* as the best hope for bringing the disputing parties of Christendom together.[23] His policy was to bring about a détente founded upon a low-keyed but continuing recognition of Chalcedon as a norm for orthodox doctrine. His local supporters included the "Sleepless Monks" of Constantinople, a large community known for its round-the-clock liturgical prayer and its outspoken adherence to Chalcedonian Christology.[24]

Macedonius's approach remained generally successful until 507, when the Syrian bishop Philoxenus of Mabbug, the most articulate and violent anti-Chalcedonian leader of his time, arrived in the capital to lobby for his campaign against Flavian, the patriarch of Antioch, and all past and present defenders of a "two-nature" Christology. In the following year, a younger and still more astute opponent of Chalcedon arrived to join Philoxenus's efforts: Severus, monk of the monastery of Maiouma in Palestine and future patriarch of Antioch. He came with a body of some two hundred fiercely anti-Chalcedonian monks to defend their interests against repressive measures in the Jerusalem patriarchate and to launch a new campaign of theological controversy and ecclesiastical diplomacy against the Chalcedonian party. Appointed by the emperor as mediator in the worsening controversy between Philoxenus and Flavian, Severus drafted a "formula of assurance" (τόμος τῆς πληροφορίας) for them in 509 or 510. This document called the two disputing parties to recognize only the Councils of Nicaea and Constantinople as normative for Christian faith and anathematized both the *Tome* of Leo and the dogmatic formula of Chalcedon for suggesting there are two persons in Christ, while endorsing Chalcedon's rejection of the "extreme" Christologies of Nestorius and Eutyches.[25] The Chalcedonian star was declining, and with it the credibility and effectiveness of the *Henōtikon*.

Patriarch Macedonius was not prepared to accept the "formula of assurance" himself, nor to condemn the Christological writings of the fifth-century Antiochene school by name, as Philoxenus and Severus continued

23. For a portrait of Macedonius and a detailed analysis of his fall from power, see W. H. C. Frend, "The Fall of Macedonius in 511—a Suggestion," in A. M. Ritter, ed., *Kerygma und Logos. Beiträge zu den geistesgeschichtlichen Beziehungen zwischen Antike und Christentum*, Festschrift Carl Andresen (Göttingen, 1979), 183–95.

24. Ps.-Zacharias Rhetor, *Hist. eccl.* 7.7.

25. See Grillmeier, *Christ in Christian Tradition*, 2/1:275–76, for the extant text of this document and further discussion and bibliography.

to demand.[26] The anti-Chalcedonian party in the capital, now fortified by a large and highly vocal contingent of monks from Syria and Palestine, began a new strategy for increasing pressure on the patriarch sometime in 510: they began to sing during the liturgy in the "Great Church" of Hagia Sophia a version of the *Trisagion* hymn long in use in Antioch, but regarded in Constantinople as a direct challenge to Chalcedonian Christology, in which the words "crucified for us" were added to the familiar refrain, "Holy God, holy mighty one, holy immortal one, have mercy on us."[27] A riot followed; monks from the anti-Chalcedonian party claimed injury, and Macedonius was loudly accused of being responsible. According to the contemporary historian Theodore Anagnostes (Theodorus Lector), Macedonius was summoned into the emperor's presence and forced to sign a document reaffirming his acceptance of the *Henōtikon* and of the faith of the Councils of Nicaea and Constantinople, but making no allusion to either Ephesus or Chalcedon.[28]

Severus's biographers, John of Beit Aphthonia and Zachary the "Scholastic" or "Rhetorician," report more focused doctrinal challenges from the controversial monk. According to John, Severus prompted one of the imperial advisors, the patrician Celer, to ask the patriarch directly whether he confessed as one individual the hypostasis of the Holy Trinity who had become human, without change, and had been born of Mary; Macedonius—doubtless seeing in such language an abandonment of the more symmetrical

26. See Ps.-Zacharias Rhetor, *Hist. eccl.* 7.7 (on Philoxenus). According to Ps.-Zacharias (ibid.), Macedonius was regarded by the Severan party as an unabashed admirer of the Antiochenes, and was said both to have commemorated Nestorius in the liturgy and to have compiled a florilegium of texts from Diodore of Tarsus, Theodore of Mopsuestia, and Theodoret of Cyrrhus, the arch-enemies of Cyrillian Christology. Another Syriac fragment preserves the statement of Severus and the fourteen non-Chalcedonian bishops who ordained him patriarch of Antioch in 512, accepting Nicaea, Constantinople, Ephesus, and the *Henōtikon*, but anathematizing Leo's *Tome*, Chalcedon, and a long list of Antiochene theologians (PO 2:322–25).

27. For the background of the use of this hymn and its versions, and further bibliography, see Eduard Schwartz, *Publizistische Sammlungen zum acacianischen Schisma* (Munich, 1934), 241–43; Grillmeier, *Jesus der Christus*, 2/2:268–77. The crux of the misunderstanding was apparently that the three invocations of the hymn had always been taken, in the capital, to refer to the three Persons of the Holy Trinity, while the Antiochene Church—its original home—had traditionally understood them all to refer to Christ. Thus a fairly minor addition to the text, officially authorized in Antioch at the time of the anti-Chalcedonian patriarch Peter the Fuller (471–479), sounded in pro-Chalcedonian Constantinople, forty years later, like a blatant confusion of divine and human realities, a step even beyond Eutyches's "confusion of natures" to include the entire Trinity in the suffering of Jesus.

28. Theodore Anagnostes, *Epitome* 487M (ed. Günther C. Hansen, GCS [Berlin, 1971], 138).

Christology of Chalcedon—replied that he would never make such a confession, even if his tongue should be cut out as a result.[29] Zachary reports a debate on doctrinal issues (δόγματα) between Severus and the patriarch, held before judges appointed by the emperor—probably in the spring or early summer of 511.[30] The North African writer Liberatus adds the information that one of the principal accusations against Macedonius at this time was that he had falsified the text of the Gospels and of Paul, a charge that seems to reflect a consistent concern of Severus to challenge the authenticity of scriptural texts habitually used by his Chalcedonian opponents in what he perceived as a "Nestorian" sense.[31]

Macedonius's downfall followed quickly. The anti-Chalcedonian chronicle ascribed to Zachary the Rhetor reproduces a letter written by a Syrian presbyter, Simeon of Amida, to a leading priest of the party, Archimandrite Samuel, which narrates the events with a journalistic flair; other details can be found in the eighth-century chronographer Theophanes and other historians. On Wednesday, 20 July, Macedonius was compelled to repudiate the Council of Chalcedon and its "two-nature" Christology publicly.[32] When he celebrated the liturgy two days later, neither the emperor nor his wife, the empress Ariadne (who was sympathetic to the Chalcedonian cause), communicated with him.[33] Realizing the gravity of the situation, Macedonius withdrew to the monastery of Dalmatou in the western quarter of Psamathia—a long-established religious community known for its unimpeachably orthodox faith. There he wrote an appeal to the emperor, "saying he accepted Chalcedon and considered all who did not do so to be heretics; and the monks concelebrated with him."[34] During the two weeks that followed, Macedonius seems to have remained at Dalmatou, even though the emperor ordered the monastery's food subsidy and water

29. *Vita Severi* (ed. M. A. Kugener, PO 2.3:236–37). Cf. Frend, "The Fall of Macedonius," 191.

30. See *Vita Severi* (ed. Kugener, PO 2.1:109); Frend, "The Fall of Macedonius," 192; Grillmeier (*Christ in Christian Tradition*, 2/1:278) identifies this debate with the occasion on 20 July 511, when Macedonius was forced publicly to curse the Council of Chalcedon (Ps.-Zacharias, *Hist. eccl.* 7.8).

31. See Liberatus, *Breviarium* 19 (ed. E. Schwartz, ACO 2.5.133.8–13); cf. Schwartz, *Publizistische Sammlungen*, 243–44, n. 3; Frend ("The Fall of Macedonius," 192–94) emphasizes the importance of scriptural discussion in the controversy, especially insofar as it concerned the divine and life-giving character of the dead body of Christ.

32. Letter of Simeon of Amida, Ps.-Zacharias Rhetor, *Hist. eccl.* 7.8.

33. Ibid.

34. Theophanes, *Chronographia* 6004 (ed. C. De Boor [Leipzig, 1883], 1.155.3–4).

supply to be cut off.[35] The anti-Chalcedonian forces pressed their charges, adding to their complaints of violence during the *Trisagion* riot new accusations of corruption, conspiracy, and even pedophilia against the patriarch; but the main charge remained that Macedonius was at heart a Nestorian.[36] Fearing a popular reaction, Anastasius gave liberal bonuses to his officers and the troops in the city on 29 and 30 July, and required his officers to renew their oath of loyalty. On Sunday the 31st, he professed his own orthodox faith publicly—with tears—but also ordered the gates and harbors of the city to be guarded.[37] On 1 August, the police began arresting leading members of the clergy and confiscating Church documents—including, it seems, the profession of faith the emperor had signed twenty years earlier at his coronation.[38] The following Saturday, 6 August, the emperor held a palace audience (σιλέντιον κομβέντον), at which both pro- and anti-Chalcedonians gave testimony. Anastasius again personally criticized Macedonius for relying on theological sources that taught a Sabellian view of God and a "two-nature" conception of Christ, and roundly anathematized all the followers of Chalcedon as "Jews." Macedonius, who had not been present, replied from his monastic retreat by anathematizing as heretics all who rejected the Council's teaching.[39]

Reconciliation was no longer possible. On Sunday, 7 August, in Macedonius's absence, the clergy and people assembled for the liturgy at Hagia Sophia cried out against him, and his name was no longer commemorated in the diptychs; the chief of police grimly assured the crowd that their desires for orthodox unity would be taken seriously. Later in the day the patriarch was arrested along with a number of his clergy by Celer, the *magister officiorum* or head of the Senate, as they attempted to take refuge in a church. Ordered by Celer to hand over the *acta* of Chalcedon in symbolic surrender,

35. Ps.-Zacharias, *Hist. eccl.* 7.8.

36. Ibid. 7.7–8; Theophanes *Chron.* 6004 (ed. De Boor, 1.155.9–11); Evagrius Scholasticus, *Hist. eccl.* 3.32.

37. Ps.-Zacharias, *Hist. eccl.* 7.8. Simeon's letter quotes the emperor as saying on this occasion: "Whoever sets out to make common cause with Macedonius, or has communication with him, is opposed to my majesty."

38. Theodore Anagnostes, *Epitome* 488M (ed. Hansen [n. 28 above] 139); Evagrius Scholasticus, *Hist. eccl.* 3.32.

39. Ps.-Zacharias, *Hist. eccl.* 7.8. It is a striking fact that since the late fourth century a strongly unitive view of God was generally coupled with a view of Christ that strongly distinguishes between his two natures, while a more unitive Christology is associated with a clearer emphasis on God as a Trinity of persons. This identification is clear in the emperor's remarks, as cited in Simeon's letter (n. 32 above).

Macedonius laid them instead, with his own seal, on the altar.[40] That same evening, the patriarch was escorted out of the city under guard, and sent to exile in Euchaïta, a remote monastery in the mountains of Hellenopontus, where his predecessor Euphemius had also ended his days. Fearing, apparently, to appoint such a fierce anti-Chalcedonian as Severus patriarch in the capital, the emperor had a priest named Timothy elected Macedonius's successor—a man willing, at least, to resume communion with the non-Chalcedonian Church of Alexandria. Severus himself was consecrated patriarch of Antioch in November 512, and became the dominant theological voice of the Eastern Church until Anastasius's death in 518.

Anastasius's troubles at Constantinople continued, however, through the next several years, and their repercussions were felt throughout the Christian East. In 513 or 514, a pro-Chalcedonian military officer in the Balkan peninsula named Vitalian—himself a Scythian, but possibly a relative of Macedonius—led an insurrection in the army and forced the emperor to name him commander of the imperial troops in Thrace. Central to Vitalian's policy was the demand that Macedonius be recalled and that the emperor summon a new ecumenical council for 515, to be presided over by Pope Hormisdas of Rome, an uncompromising Chalcedonian. Vitalian's campaign was ultimately unsuccessful, and the council was never held. Yet his program doubtless found strong support among the clergy and citizens of the capital and western Asia Minor in the years 513–515; in any case, it forced Anastasius to carry on long negotiations with Chalcedon's supporters, and to stop short of abandoning the *Henōtikon* as imperial policy.[41] The last years of his reign were years of unresolved polarization in theology and Church life, awaiting the theological and political genius of a Justinian.

II. The Present Text

The little text that I have edited here is an unusual echo of those troubled years in the Church of Constantinople. Unnoticed until now, as far as I

40. Ps.-Zacharias Rhetor, *Hist. Eccl.* 7.8. According to Theophanes (*Chron.* 6004: De Boor, 1.155.12–20), Celer brought the copy of the *acta* to Macedonius so that he could publicly tear them up, but the patriarch responded by laying them on the altar.

41. See Grillmeier, *Christ in Christian Tradition*, 3/1:310–17; cf. Viktor Schurr, *Die Trinitatslehre des Boethius im Lichte der "skythischen Kontroversen"* (Paderborn, 1935), 127–37; Hans-Georg Beck, "The Early Byzantine Church," in Karl Baus et al., *The Imperial Church from Constantine to the Early Middle Ages*, ed. H. Jedin, *History of the Church*, vol. 2 (New York, 1980), 432–36.

am aware, it is part of a collection of orthodox Christological and anti-iconoclast works and florilegia in a tenth-century manuscript now in the Bibliotheca Marciana in Venice.[42] Its title, as it appears in the manuscript, suggests something at once more predictable and more ambitious: "A Harmony (*Symphōnia*) of What Was Said by Blessed Cyril, Bishop of Alexandria, and by the Holy Scripture, with What Was Taught About the Faith by the Holy Synod in Chalcedon" (lines 1–4). One imagines that the original work that bore this title may have been a large florilegium of scriptural texts and passages from Cyril designed to show the orthodoxy of Chalcedonian Christology, much like the anonymous florilegium of the same kind and purpose attacked by Severus in his *Philalēthēs*, a major polemical tract put together in Constantinople between 508 and 511.[43] A marginal gloss in the Venice manuscript, in the same hand as the text itself, notes: "This passage is written towards the end of the *Symphōnia*," and the opening sentence of the text identifies it as an excerpt from a larger document—a curious but confirmatory appendix, presumably, to a work of a more scholastic kind:

> Eager to lend support to right faith, and wishing to enjoy a share in the abundance of victory, I have thought it necessary—to provide a still greater refutation of "spurious knowledge" [1 Tim 6:20] and still deeper shame for its partisans—to enter into this book also the oracle, which the spurious Greek god Apollo is said to have given to one of his priests who consulted him about Christ. The oracle was found at Delphi in Thessalonica, in the twenty-first year of the reign of Anastasius, in the month of August, on the eighteenth day, in the fourth indiction, on the fifth day of the week [i.e., on Thursday, 18 August 511], after a severe rainstorm, with the force of a flood, had occurred; it is engraved on a tablet buried next to the foundation of the temple of that very idol. (5–16)

42. Cod. Marc. Gr. 573 (coll. 415), fols. 26v–30r. This beautifully preserved manuscript, in the fine early minuscule hand of a single scribe, once belonged to Jacopo Contarini and is one of seventeen manuscripts left by him to the Marciana in 1714. See A. M. Zanetti and A. Bongiovanni, *Graeca D. Marci bibliotheca codicum manuscriptorum per titulos digesta* (Venice, 1740), 300; Elpidio Mioni, *Codices Graeci manuscripti Bibliothecae Divi Marci Venetiarum: Thesaurus Antiquus II* (Rome, 1985), 478. Mioni does not attempt to identify this text further, and lists the part after the verse "oracle" (lines 61–end) as a separate work.

43. The original florilegium has been edited by R. Hespel, *Le florilège Cyrillien* (n. 21 above); Severus's refutation of it, as a patchwork of quotations taken out of their contexts, is entitled *Philalēthēs*: ed. R. Hespel, CSCO 133 (text), 134 (translation) (Leuven, 1952). For a discussion of both works, see Grillmeier, *Jesus der Christus*, 2/2:20–48.

The author feels constrained to explain why he includes a pagan oracle in a work of Christian controversy: it is not that Chalcedon needs further witnesses for its orthodoxy, beyond the Bible and the written and lived witness of the Fathers (16–24),

> but, as I said before, [I have done this] in the attempt to persuade unbelievers by even this proof. In the august and venerable Gospel, after all, for this reason and no other, after the Father's witness [to Jesus] from heaven and the assurance of passages from Scripture and of the Apostles and even of the elements, the demons themselves—albeit unwilling—are found proclaiming, for the refutation of the unbelieving Jews, the power of the only-begotten God the Word, who has come to us, as one of us, for our sakes. (25–33)

There follows the text of the putative oracle itself (35–60), a twenty-six-line poem in the characteristic dialect and vocabulary of the oracular tradition. The first eight lines, in which the god announces his own imminent departure from the cultic stage, are, as I have mentioned, already familiar from the *Theosophia*, and may well have been composed, along with other Christian oracular literature, as early as the end of the fourth century:

> You should not have consulted me this very last time,
> My ill-fated minister, about the sublime God,
> The Spirit who holds all things clustered together—
> Heavenly signs, light, rivers, earth, Tartarus, air and fire—
> And who drives me, though unwilling, from this dwelling.
> This dawn is all that is left for my tripods.
> Alas, my tripods, groan! Apollo is leaving,
> Leaving because heavenly light, in mortal form, has overcome me.
> (35–42)[44]

With the following line (43), however, the poem makes a sharp change in thematic focus. Apollo is still the presumed speaker, yet the rest of the oracle, despite its Homeric echoes,[45] is a little lecture on Chalcedonian Christology.

44. The version of these lines contained in the *Theosophia* differs sharply in some places; it contains two additional lines (after lines 36 and 39), and omits line 40. See Erbse (n. 11 above), 170–71.

45. Compare, for instance, the depiction of Jesus shedding "hot tears" for his dead friend Lazarus (52–53) with *Iliad* 16.3.

It deals with the themes of the suffering and death of Christ (43–45), his "double consubstantiality" with his divine Father and his human mother (48–49), and the continued "operation" of his two natures through the interweaving of his human emotions with acts of divine power, as revealed in events like the raising of Lazarus (52–56). The focus on the "theopaschite" question and the emphasis on the unambiguous divine identity of Christ ("Christ is my God") are characteristic of the growing "neo-Chalcedonian" interpretation of the Council. Yet, the stress on the balance between his divinity and humanity, and the insistence that both exist together without change or separation (46–47), is almost a direct paraphrase of Chalcedon's formula of faith. The text is worth translating in full:

> The one who suffers is God, yet the godhead itself does not suffer;
> For he was both mortal and immortal at once,
> Incapable of dying yet capable of it, God's Word and human flesh;
> Yet neither was changed, nor did they come to be separated
> Or exist apart from each other. God himself is also a man,
> Receiving all from his Father and possessing all which was his mother's—
> Possessing life-giving might from his deathless Father,
> And from his mortal mother the cross, burial, contempt and sorrow,
> Seeing into, surveying, and hearing all things at once.
> Hot tears once flowed from his eyes,
> When the sad news about his friend reached him;
> And he destroyed the reason for grieving, and brought out of Hades
> The man whom he had grieved for, who rushed forth again into the light.
> As a mortal he grieved, and as God he saved.
> He fed five thousand from five loaves,
> On the lofty hills; for such was the will of his immortal might.
> Christ is my God, who was stretched out on the tree,
> Who died, who went into the tomb, who was raised from the tomb
> into heaven.
>
> (43–60)

This long form of the oracle, like the short form in the *Theosophia* collection, is also known from other sources. Buresch published a somewhat less satisfactory version of it, which he had found in a thirteenth-century manuscript in Athens;[46] the first fifteen lines (35–49) also appear in a twelfth-

46. Atheniensis Graecus 1070, fols. 186r–v; the text is re-edited by Erbse, 214–15.

century Paris manuscript.[47] In both of these manuscripts, the text of the oracle is followed by a shorter version of the explanation of its finding and its significance, with which our own text begins:

> It was found in Delphi in Italy [*sic*!], in the twenty-first year of the emperor Anastasius [511], when a great thunderstorm, with the force of a flood, had occurred; it is engraved on a tablet, and is buried next to the foundation of the idol's temple.[48]

In the Paris manuscript, this digest of the explanatory information contained in our text continues somewhat further:

> [It was found] when someone put this god to the test. For in the Gospels, too, after the Father's witness from heaven and the assurance of scriptural passages and of the elements, even the demons themselves are found proclaiming the power of the only-begotten God the Word.[49]

There are additional indications that this poem, in its long, Chalcedonian version, was known and considered significant in late Christian antiquity. Two elaborate, pre-metaphrastic accounts of martyrdoms—the "Passion of St. Artemius" attributed to the otherwise unknown John of Rhodes,[50] and the "Passion of St. Catherine," both of which show dependence on the mid-sixth-century chronicler John Malalas[51]—put verses from it into the mouths

47. Parisinus Graecus 690, fols. 248v–249r; see Erbse, ibid.

48. Erbse, 215.

49. Ibid., apparatus.

50. Text in Angelo Mai, *Spicilegium Romanum*, 4 (Rome, 1840), 340–97; oracle: 376. It is reproduced in *Acta Sanctorum* 56, Octobris VIII [for 20 October] (Paris/Rome, 1866): 856–85; oracle: 873. Portions of the *vita* are also edited by J. Bidez, as appendices I and II to his edition of Philostorgius's *Church History:* GCS (2nd ed.; Berlin, 1972), 150–65; oracle: 164. It may be significant that St. Artemius, although reputedly an Alexandrian, was venerated primarily in Constantinople, where his relics were preserved in the Church of St. John the Baptist (Prodromos).

51. The text of this *vita* is edited by J. Viteau, *Passions des Saints Écaterine et Pierre d'Alexandrie* (Paris, 1897); for a re-edition of the text and a thorough discussion of its sources, see E. Klostermann and E. Seeberg, "Die Apologie der heiligen Katharina," *Schriften der Königsberger Gelehrten Gesellschaft* 1/2 (1924): 31–87. For the relationship of this life to the work of Malalas, see J. Bidez, "Sur diverses citations, et notamment sur trois passages de Malalas retrouvés dans un texte hagiographique," *Byzantinische Zeitschrift* 11 (1902): 388–94.

of their respective saints as part of long apologetic speeches.[52] There also exist two small collections of Christian pseudo-oracles, in abbreviated prose paraphrases, which seem to be related to each other and which each include a version of this piece. One of these collections, entitled "Oracles and Sayings of the Greek Philosophers," was first studied and commented on in 1691 by the English philologist Richard Bentley in his letter to the Oxford New Testament scholar John Mill.[53] The other, containing a less truncated paraphrase of the work, is found only in the celebrated late eighth-century manuscript Vaticanus Graecus 2200—chiefly known both for its early cursive minuscule hand and for its long Chalcedonian Christological florilegium, published by Franz Diekamp under the title *Doctrina Patrum de Incarnatione Verbi*.[54] In that manuscript, the *Doctrina Patrum* is followed by a small collection of pagan oracles and passages from Greek philosophers, combined with passages from the New Testament and from Cyril of Alexandria's apologetic treatise *Contra Julianum*; all are arranged to bring out supposed parallels in pagan religious thought to orthodox Christian doctrines of the Trinity, the Incarnation, and the saving passion and death of Jesus.[55] A prose version of our oracle, containing lines 41–60 in a less radically paraphrased form than that of Bentley's collection, appears as a key witness to the Greek gods' understanding of the crucifixion. Equally striking, perhaps, as a possible parallel to our own text is the rather baroque title of this little florilegium: "A Harmony (*Symphōnia*), Moving from the Ancient Greek Philosophers to the Holy, Inspired New Scripture; or: a Demonstration and Defense, by Means of Them, of the Holy, Consubstantial and Super-essential, Undivided,

52. The *Passio Artemii* has vv. 35–43 of the present text [i.e., the short "oracle" contained in the *Theosophia* plus the first line of its continuation]: AS 873; the *Passio Catharinae* includes a more complicated patchwork: lines 42b–44, 47b–48a, 50b, 52, 57, 58b–60: see Klostermann and Seeberg, "Die Apologie," 40 and 54–56.

53. This letter is reproduced in PG 97:722–25; for the paraphrase of this oracle, see 724CD; Erbse, 211–12. For a discussion of the text, and of the wider tradition of collections of putative sayings from pagan wise men, see Anton von Premerstein, "Griechisch-heidnische Weise als Verkünder christlicher Lehre in Handschriften und Kirchenmalereien," *Festschrift der Nationalbibliothek in Wien* (Vienna, 1926), 647–66, esp. 649–50 and 656. This paraphrase, which still contains some of the Ionic vocabulary of the original "oracle" but is written as prose, contains, in abbreviated form, lines 42 (the end of the first part of the oracle), 45–47, 51, and 53–56.

54. Münster, 1907.

55. For the text of this little collection, see J. Pitra, *Analecta Sacra*, 5 (Paris/Rome, 1888), 305–8; Erbse, 202–8. The paraphrase of the present oracle is found in Pitra (308) and Erbse (206–7).

Creative, Life-Giving and Adorable Trinity—I Refer to Father, Son and Holy Spirit; and Concerning the Excellent and Beneficent Economy, in the Flesh, of One of that very All-Holy and All-Praiseworthy Blessed Trinity, God the Word."[56] Although the verbal similarity between this title and the title of the text in Marcianus Graecus 573 is limited to the single word *Symphōnia*, this term is rare enough in the polemical literature of the sixth through eighth centuries,[57] and the neo-Chalcedonian orientation of both florilegia clear enough, to make it at least conceivable that the compiler of the collection in Vaticanus Graecus 2200 had access to the lost florilegium—otherwise containing (as far as we know) only passages from Cyril and the Scriptures—of which our text forms the conclusion.

The text in the Venice manuscript extends, however, beyond the presentation of the oracle in its "normal" poetic form. First of all, it offers a complete paraphrase of the oracle in colloquial early Byzantine Greek prose, on the grounds that some readers may not understand its epic idiom. So the text continues:

> The language of the oracle is clear. But to let the significance of what is contained in it be more clearly understood—since not everyone has been trained by an education in secular literature—it is interpreted as follows . . . (61–63)

This paraphrase (64–97) concludes the oracle as such. The text in Marcianus Graecus 573 then ends with both a warning and an appeal, addressed to a hostile body of readers. The warning suggests quite clearly, in language rich in biblical echoes,[58] that the opponents of the author(s) enjoy considerable political power:

> Now be shamed with a great shame, be confused with overwhelming confusion, all you who rest your hope on human power: I mean either dialectical

56. Pitra, *Analecta*, 305; Erbse, 202.

57. In the pro-Chalcedonian florilegium of passages from Cyril that Severus attacked in his *Philalēthēs*, for instance, the word used to characterize the purpose of the first section, where the chief terms of the Chalcedonian definition are put in parallel with similar terms from Cyril's writings, is "comparison," ἀντιπαράθεσις (Hespel, *Le florilège Cyrillien* [n. 21 above])—in the Syriac translation, *pechmā* (Severus *Philalēthēs* [n. 43 above]).

58. Although it is not a direct quotation from the Old Testament, the reference to the "shame and confusion" that is sure to come on those who rely on human power suggests such Septuagint passages as Ps 43:16, Isa 45:16–17, and Dan 3:44.

> cleverness or great excess of wealth, or whatever other thing is thought to be something, but in reality is nothing! (98–103)

There follow three Old Testament quotations (103–114), all urging trust in God rather than in human beings: again, sentiments appropriate for a party that senses itself severely under pressure.[59]

The final lines of the text are an impassioned profession of orthodox Chalcedonian faith in Christ, and an equally impassioned appeal for unity in the Church.

> We have believed, and still believe, not in an ordinary human being or in one like us, but in the Son of God the Father and in God the Word, who even when he became human remained, although in this nature like ours, that which he was and is and will be: namely God. (115–119)

The *person* in whom the author professes his faith, in other words, is the divine Person of the Son, whom the Church recognizes as "one of the Holy Trinity"; the doctrine of the Incarnation, for the author, means that the Son came to exist "in" a human nature such as ours, but this does not diminish Christian assurance that his continuing identity—*who* he "was and is and will be"—is simply "God." Such language is clearly meant as a defense of the Chalcedonian confession of Christ as "one hypostasis or person *in two natures*," but the details and direction of its explanation are closer to those of Constantinople II (553) than of the Chalcedonian formula itself.

If his opponents continue to reject such a confession, the author continues, thus contradicting even the demons who speak through pagan oracles, they themselves deserve eternal punishment more than the demons (119–126). He then concludes:

59. It is interesting that all three quotations are given in variant forms of the usual Septuagint text. The first, Ps 118:8–9, corresponds to the pre-correction reading of the Codex Alexandrinus, and may simply represent a minor variation in the sixth-century text of the Greek Bible. The second, however, from Sir 2:10–11, by substituting ἤλπισεν for ἐπίστευσεν, and the third, by omitting the whole middle section of Jer 17:5, give readings found in Chrysostom but not in the standard Septuagint manuscripts. If differences in biblical text-form were an important part of the debates between Severus and Macedonius, as Frend argues ("The Fall of Macedonius," 192–95), these citations—which suggest a biblical source of an Antiochene-Constantinopolitan type—again identify this text squarely with the camp of Macedonius.

> Therefore tremble, tremble, I beg you, and putting an end to discord, become one with us, just as the Lord himself, who became human, asks of his Father, saying, "Holy Father, keep them in your name, which you gave to me, so that they may be one as we are one." [John 17:11] (126–131)[60]

An honest recognition of the sources of faith in Christ leaves one no choice, he seems to suggest, but to find Church unity based on the dogmatic formula of Chalcedon.

* * *

What can one say, in conclusion, about the nature, date, and authorship of this unusual little text?

1. While its interest, as a new witness to a Christian pseudo-oracle already known from other sources, may be limited, its literary and historical importance as the only fragment of an otherwise unknown work of Chalcedonian apologetic, the *Symphōnia*, is considerable. From the title and from other indications within the text itself, one can conclude that this work must have been a sizeable florilegium, containing not only passages from Cyril of Alexandria, like the collection criticized by Severus in the years immediately preceding the crisis of 511, but also biblical testimonia. This is the first trace we possess of what must have been an important piece of early sixth-century controversial theology.

2. The author or authors of the text remain unknown, but the contents clearly indicate someone who considered himself both a defender of the orthodoxy of Chalcedon and a member of a beleaguered minority. The text's insistence on a precise date for the supposed rediscovery of an old oracle at Delphi that corroborated its argument—Thursday, 18 August 511, just eleven days after the patriarch Macedonius had been sent into exile—only makes sense if the work was composed in the heat of that same controversy, shortly after the patriarch's downfall. We know from the *Church History* ascribed to Zachary the Rhetor that when a synod of mainly Syrian and Palestinian bishops gathered at Sidon the following October, at the emperor's command,

60. It is worth noting that the text of John 17:11 quoted here follows the "Alexandrian" reading in opposition to the version quoted by John Chrysostom, which omits the second half of the verse. As Severus himself recognized in his famous letter to Thomas of Germanicaea on biblical variants, the issue of finding a reliable Bible text was more complex than a simple opposition between Alexandrian and Antiochene traditions; see Ep. 108 (PO 14:266–70).

to consider ways of restoring unity, a group of Antiochene monks opposed to the *Henōtikon* and to Flavian, their patriarch—led by one Cosmas of Qennešrin—submitted a document in seventy-seven chapters, with an extensive florilegium of patristic authorities, attacking the orthodoxy of Leo's *Tome* and the Chalcedonian formula.[61] Flavian was able to withstand the attack for the moment, and the synod made no further specifications for uniformity in doctrine beyond the *Henōtikon*.[62] Although there is no evidence in our text directly linking the *Symphōnia* to this synod, it is certainly plausible to suppose that it, too, may have been hastily composed for the occasion, as documentation for the Chalcedonian side. If that is true, its argument and even the appeal of its "oracle" will have had a short-lived success.

In any case, the sense of crisis that our fragment conveys, and its allusions to the influence and "dialectical cleverness" of the opponents, best fit the years between the summer of 511 and the death of Anastasius in July 518—years when Philoxenus and Severus were at the height of their intellectual and ecclesiastical powers, and the defenders of Chalcedon found themselves increasingly isolated. The place of its composition and principal circulation seems most likely to have been Constantinople, both because of its Chalcedonian character and its explicit connection with the events of the summer of 511, and also because of its later use in the life of St. Artemius, a martyr whose cult was centered in the capital. Yet the possibility that its oracle was also used by the Antiochene chronographer John Malalas, writing in the middle decades of the sixth century, suggests that the oracle and perhaps the whole of the *Symphōnia* may have been known in Syria as well. It lends at least some further plausibility to our suggestion that the *Symphōnia* may have been prepared by scholarly Chalcedonians—probably in the capital—for the Synod of Sidon in the autumn of 511.

61. Ps.-Zacharias Scholasticus, *Hist. eccl.* 7.10; cf. the *Chronicon miscellaneum ad a.d. 724 pertinens* (ed. E. W. Brooks; trans. I. B. Chabot, CSCO 3:221 [text], 4:168 [trans.]). For further details of the Synod of Sidon, see L. Duchesne, *L'Église au VIe siècle* (Paris, 1925), 27–29; Schwartz, *Publizistische Sammlungen* (n. 27 above), 245; Grillmeier, *Christ in Christian Tradition* (n. 20 above), 2/1:279–81.

62. According to Ps.-Zachary (ibid.), Flavian's response to the proposal of Cosmas and his associates was to say, "It is enough for us to anathematize the books of the school of Diodore [of Tarsus] and the charges made by some people against the Twelve Chapters of Cyril [i.e., Theodoret's *Refutation of Cyril's Twelve Anathemas*], and Nestorius—lest we stir up the sleeping snake and corrupt many with his poison!" For Flavian, the main task was still damage control.

3. The oracle itself, which occupies most of our present fragment, was evidently included in the original text of the *Symphōnia* as a kind of postscript, adding dramatic force to what was otherwise probably a rather technical argument. Comparison with the *Theosophia* shows that this is an expanded version of an earlier composition, tailored to the Christological issues of the first two decades of the sixth century. Whether the oracle, with the narrative of its putative discovery and its vernacular prose paraphrase, first circulated independently, as a kind of Chalcedonian broadside, in the weeks after Macedonius's downfall, or whether (as seems less likely) it was composed by the author or authors of the *Symphōnia* directly, as a coda to their dossier of biblical and theological texts, it clearly gained a currency of its own within a short time and remained popular with later hagiographers. The notion of a fading but eloquent Greek god, one of the chief "demons" who had held the pagan mind in thrall, bearing a precocious witness to the balance and paradox of classical Chalcedonian Christology, understandably never ceased to fascinate the Greek Christian imagination.

Possible Evolution of the Oracle μὴ ὄφελες

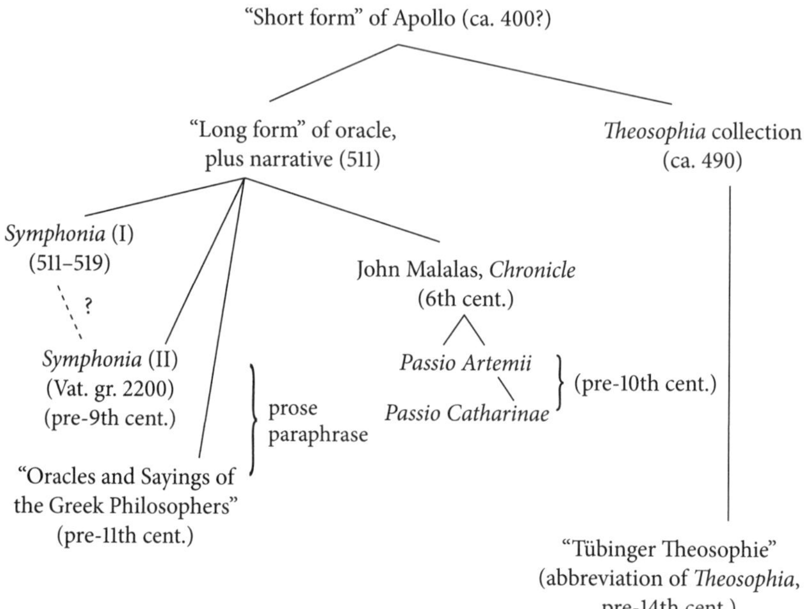

THE TEXT

Witness to the whole text:

M: Marcianus Graecus 573 (x cent.), fols. 26r–30r

Witnesses to the oracle:

F: Atheniensis Graecus 1070 (xiii cent.), fol. 186r–v
P: Parisinus Graecus 690 (xii cent.), fols. 248v–249r (lines 35–49 only)
θ: Tübingensis Mb 27 (xvi cent.): "Tübinger Theosophie," ed. H. Erbse, 170–71 (lines 31–38 only)
Art: Passio Artemii: AS Oct. VIII, 873 (lines 31–39 only)
Cath: Passio Catharinae, Version C: ed. E. Klostermann and E. Seeberg, *Die Apologie der heiligen Katharina:* Schriften der Königsberger gelehrten Gesellschaft 1.2 (1924), 40 (lines 42b–44, 47b–48a, 50b, 52, 57, 58b–60)

fol. 26r

ΣΥΜΦΩΝΙΑ ΤΩΝ ΠΑΡΑ ΤΟΥ ΜΑΚΑΡΙΟΥ ΚΥΡΙΛΛΟΥ ΤΟΥ ἈΛΕΧΑΝΔΡΕΙΑΣ ἘΠΙΣΚΟΠΟΥ ἘΙΡΗΜΕΝΩΝ ΚΑΙ ΤΩΝ ΠΑΡΑ ΤΗΣ ΘΕΙΑΣ ΓΡΑΦΗΣ ΠΡΟΣ ΤΑ ΠΑΡΑ ΤΗΣ ἘΝ ΧΑΛΚΗΔΟΝΙ ἉΓΙΑΣ ΣΥΝΟΔΟΥ ΔΟΓΜΑΤΙΣΘΕΝΤΑ ΠΕΡΙ ΤΗΣ ΠΙΣΤΕΩΣ.[63]

Τῇ ὀρθῇ πίστει συνασπίσαι σπουδάζων καὶ νίκης περιουσίᾳ χρήσασθαι βουλόμενος, εἰς μείζονα μὲν ἔλεγχον τῆς ψευδωνύμου γνώσεως, πλείονα δὲ αἰσχύνην τῶν ταύτης | fol. 26v ὑπασπιστῶν, ἀναγκαῖον ἡγησάμην καὶ τὸν χρησμὸν ἐγχαράξαι τῷδε τῷ βιβλίῳ ὃν λέγεται πεποιηκέναι πρός τινα τῶν αὐτοῦ ἱερέων, πυνθανόμενον αὐτοῦ περὶ τοῦ Χριστοῦ, ὁ ψευδώνυμος τῶν Ἑλλήνων θεὸς Ἀπόλλων, ὅστις εὕρηται ἐν Δελφοῖς τῆς Θεσσαλονίκης, εἰκοστῷ πρώτῳ ἔτει τῆς βασιλείας Ἀναστασίου, μηνὶ Αὐγούστῳ ιη´, ἰνδικτιῶνος δ´, ἡμέρᾳ πέμπτῃ, γενομένης ἐπομβρίας μεγάλης, κατακλυσμοῦ δύναμιν ἐχούσης, ἐγγεγραμμένος ἐν πλακὶ καὶ ἀποκείμενος εἰς τὰ θεμέλια τοῦ ναοῦ τοῦ αὐτοῦ εἰδωλίου. Τοῦτο δὲ πέπραχα οὐχ ὡς ἐκ τούτου τὴν ὀρθότητα τῶν ἐγκριθέντων δογμάτων παρὰ τῶν ἐν Χαλκηδόνι ὁσίων καὶ μακαρίων πατέρων παραστῆσαι βουλόμενος — «ἔλαιον γὰρ ἁμαρτωλοῦ μὴ λιπανάτω τὴν κεφαλήν μου» [Ps. 140:5 (LXX)] — ἐχούσης <ταύτης τῆς πίστεως> μάλιστα τὴν μαρτυρίαν ἀξιόπιστον καὶ περιφανῆ, ἔκ τε παλαιᾶς καὶ καινῆς διαθήκης, ἔτι δὲ καὶ τῶν ὀρθοδόξων πατέρων, ὧν οἱ μὲν σεμνότητι βίου | fol. 27r διαπρέποντες, οἱ δὲ καὶ μέχρις αἵματος τὴν τούτων ὁμολογίαν ποιησάμενοι, τοῦδε τοῦ βίου διεξῆλθον τὸ στάδιον· ἀλλ' ὅπερ ἤδη προφθάσας ἔφην, ἐντρέψαι καὶ ἐκ τούτου πειρώμενος τοὺς ἀπειθεῖς. Καὶ γὰρ καὶ ἐν τῷ σεπτῷ καὶ προσκυνουμένῳ εὐαγγελίῳ, ταύτης καὶ οὐχ ἑτέρας ἕνεκα τῆς αἰτίας, μετὰ τὴν τοῦ Πατρὸς ἐξ οὐρανοῦ μαρτυρίαν, καὶ τῶν γραφικῶν κεφαλαίων τὴν πίστιν καὶ τῶν ἀποστόλων, ἔτι δὲ καὶ τῶν στοιχείων, καὶ αὐτοὶ οἱ δαίμονες εἰς ἔλεγχον τῶν ἀπίστων Ἰουδαίων, εἰ καὶ ἄκοντες, ἀλλ' ὁμῶς εὑρίσκονται ἀνακηρύτ-

63 Scholion ad ll. 4–5 (eodem manu): ΠΡΟΣ ΤΑ ΤΕΛΗ ΤΗΣ ΣΥΜΦΩ<ΝΙΑΣ> ἘΠΕΓΕΓΡΑΠΤΟ ὉΥΤΟΣ Ὁ ΛΟΓΟΣ

3 καλχιδόνι **M** 4 συνώδου **M** 6 ψευδονύμου **M** 9 ἱερέων] μιαιρέων **M** 10 πυνθανόμενον αὐτοῦ] ποιθομένου αὐτὸν **M**; ψευδόνυμος **M** 12 ἔτι **M** 14 ἔχουσα **M** 15 πλακεῖ **M** 17 καλχιδῶνι **M** 20 ταύτης τῆς πίστεως supplevi 24 διέξηλθεν **M**

τοντες τὴν δύναμιν τοῦ δι᾽ ἡμᾶς καθ᾽ ἡμᾶς ἐληλυθότος πρὸς ἡμᾶς μονογενοῦς Θεοῦ Λόγου.

Ἔχει δὲ ὁ χρησμὸς οὕτως·
μὴ ὄφελες πύματόν με καὶ ὕστατον ἐξερεέσθαι,
δύσμορ᾽ ἐμῶν προπόλων, περὶ θεσπεσιοίο θεοῖο
καὶ πνοιῆς τῆς πάντα περὶξ βοτρύδον ἐχούσης,
τείρεα, φώς, ποταμούς, χθόνα, τάρταρον, ἠέρα καὶ πῦρ,
fol. 27v ἥ μὲ καὶ οὐκ ἐθέλοντα δόμων | ἀπὸ τῶνδε διώκει·
ἥδε ἐμοὶ τριπόδων ἔτι λείπεται ἠριγένεια.
αἴ, αἴ, ἐμοὶ τρίποδες, στοναχήσατε· οἴχετ᾽ Ἀπόλλων·
οἴχετ᾽, ἐπεὶ βροτόεις με βιάζεται οὐράνιος φώς.
καὶ ὁ παθῶν θεός ἐστι, καὶ οὐ θεότης πάθεν αὐτή·
ἄμφω γὰρ βροτὸς ἦεν ὁμῶς καὶ ἄμβροτος αὐτός,
ἀθάνατος θνητός τε, Θεοῦ Λόγος, ἀνδρομέη σάρξ,
οὔτε ἀμειβομένων οὔτ᾽ ἐς χύσιν ἄμφω ἰόντων,
οὔτ᾽ ἑκὰς ἀλλήλων· αὐτὸς θεὸς ἠδὲ καὶ ἀνήρ,
πάντα φέρων παρὰ Πατρός, ἔχων δέ τε μητρὸς ἅπαντα,
ἀθανάτου παρὰ Πατρὸς ἔχων φυσιζοὸν ἀλκὴν,
μητρὸς δ᾽ ἐκ θνητῆς σταῦρον, τάφον, ὕβριν, ἀνίην,
πάνθ᾽ ἅμα εἰσορόων τε καὶ ἀμφιθέων καὶ ἀκούων.
τοῦ καὶ ἀπὸ βλεφάρων ποτ᾽ἐχεύσατο δάκρυα θερμά,
εὖτέ μιν ἀγγελίη λυγρὴ μόλεν οἷο φίλοιο·
αὐτὸς καὶ θρήνων πρόφασιν λύσεν, ἐκ τ<οῦ> ᾅδου
ἀνέρα τὸν θρήνησε παλίσσυτον εἰς φάος ἕλκει·
ὡς βροτός ἐθρήνησε καὶ ὡς θεὸς ἐξεσάωσεν.
fol. 28r πέντε τε | χιλιάδας πυρῶν ἐκ πέντ᾽ ἐκόρεσσεν,
οὔρεσιν ἐν ταναοῖσι· τὸ γὰρ θέλεν ἄμβροτος ἀλκή.

---

32 ἐληλυθότι **M** 35 ante ὄφελες add. μ᾽ **FP; με]** τε **FP** 36 δύσμορ᾽ ἐμῶν] δύστηνε **θ;** θεσπεσιοίο θεοῖο] θεσπεσίου γενετῆρος **θ;** post lin. hanc add.: ἀμφί τε τηλυγέτοιο πανομφαίου βασιλῆος **θ** 37 πνοῆς **P;** τῆς] ἣ **θ;** βοτρυῆδον **M** Art; ἐχούσης] εἴσχει **θ** 38 τείρεα] οὔρεα **θ;** φώς] γῆν **θ;** χθόνα] ἅλα **θ;** καὶ **FP** Art 39 διώξει **θ;** post lin. hanc add.: αὐτίκ᾽ ἐρμαῖος δὲ λελείψεται οὐδὸς ἀφήτωρ **θ** 40 om. **θ;** ἥδε] οἱ δὲ **M;** ἐμοὶ] ἐμὴ **FP** Art; λείπετε **M;** λείπετο **FP** Art 41 αἴ αἴ] οἴμοι **θ;** ἐμοὶ] με **FP** Art; οἴχεται Mac 42 βροτόεις] φλογόεις **θ;** βροτόεις με] με βροτός **FP;** βροτός με Art; γε βροτός με conj. Erbse 43 καὶ ὁ] ὁ δὲ Cath 44 βροτὸς ἦεν ὁμῶς] βροτόσωμος Cath; ἄβροτος **M** 45 ἀνδρομένη **MacP** 46 χύσιν] σχίσιν Cath (σχέσιν conj. Klostermann-Seeberg 55, n. 45) 47 ἠδὲ] ἠὲ **P** 49 ἀθάνατος **FP;** φυσιζωὸν **M**ac 50 δ᾽ ἐκ] δὲ **F;** θνητοῖς Cath (versio Metaphrastica); τάφον ὕβριν ἀνίην] ὕβριν ταφήν Cath 51 ἅμ᾽ **P** 52 τοῦ] ὃς Cath 54 τοῦ ᾅδου] τᾴδου **M**corr 54–56 damnavit Erbse in **FP** 55 εἰς] ες **F;** ἕλκων **F** 56 ἐξεσαώσε **F** 57 πέντε τε] ὅς πέντε Cath; ἐκ πεντ᾽ om. Cath; τε om. Mac; κόρεσεν Cath

Χριστὸς ἐμὸς θεός ἐστιν, ὃς ἐς ξύλον ἐξετανύσθη,
ὃς θάνεν, ὃς τάφον ἦλθεν, ὃς ἐκ τάφου ἐς πόλον ὦρτο.

Σαφὴς μὲν καὶ ἡ τοῦ χρησμοῦ διαλαλία· πρὸς εἴδεσιν δὲ σαφέστερον τῶν ἐν αὐτῷ ἐμφερομένων, διὰ τὸ μὴ πάντας τῇ τοῦ ἔξω λόγου παιδείᾳ γεγυμνᾶσθαι, ἑρμηνεύεται ὡς ὑποτέτακται·

οὐκ ὤφελές με τελευταῖον τοῦτο καὶ ἔσχατον ἐρωτῆσαι,
δυσθάνατε τῶν ἐμων ἱερέων, περὶ θεῖου καὶ φυβεροῦ Θεοῦ
καὶ πνοῆς τῆς ἐν τάξει βότρυος πάντα περισφιγγούσης·
τὰ ἄστρα, τὸ φώς, τοὺς ποταμούς, τὴν γῆν, τὸν τάρταρον,
 τὸν ἀέρα καὶ τὸ πῦρ·
ἥτις πνοή, καὶ μὴ βουλόμενον, μὲ τούτων ἀπελαύνει τῶν
 οἴκων,
καὶ μία μοι μόνη ἐπὶ ταῖς μαντίαις ἡμέρα περιλέλειπται·
στενάξατε, ὦ τρίποδες· ἀναχωρεῖ ὁ Ἀπόλλων,
ἀναχωρεῖ βιαζόμενος ὑπὸ ἀνθρώπου καὶ θεοῦ.
fol. 28v καὶ ὁ παθῶν θεός ἐστιν, καὶ ἡ θεότης ἔμεινεν ἀπαθής· |
ὁ γὰρ αὐτὸς ἄνθρωπός ἐστι καὶ θεός,
ἀθάνατος καὶ θνητός, Λόγος Θεοῦ καὶ ἀνθρωπίνη σάρξ·
οὔτε ἐναλλαγὴν ἐχόντων αὐτῶν πρὸς ἄλληλα, οὔτε συγχεο-
 μένων·
οὔτε ὑποβαλλομένων χωρισμῷ· ὁ γὰρ αὐτὸς καὶ θεός ἐστι
 καὶ ἄνθρωπος,
φερὼν ἐν ἑαυτῷ πάντα τὰ τοῦ Πατρὸς καὶ πάντα ἔχων τὰ
 τῆς μητρός·
ἀπὸ μὲν τοῦ ἀθανάτου Πατρὸς τὴν ζωοποιὸν δύναμιν ἔχων·
ἀπὸ δὲ τῆς θνήτης μητρὸς τὸν σταῦρον, τὸν τάφον, τὴν
 ὕβριν καὶ τὴν λύπην,
ἐν ταὐτῷ πάντα καὶ ὁρῶν καὶ περιέπων καὶ ἀκούων.
τούτου ποτὲ ἀπὸ τῶν βλεφάρων ἠνέχθη δάκρυα,
ἡνίκα τῆς χαλεπῆς ἤκουσεν ἀγγελίας τοῦ φίλου·
αὐτὸς καὶ τῶν θρήνων ἔλυσεν τὴν πρόφασιν,
καὶ ἀπὸ τοῦ ᾅδου τὸν παρ'αὐτοῦ θρηνηθέντα πάλιν εἰς φῶς
 ἀνήγαγεν·
ὡς ἄνθρωπος ἐθρήνησεν, καὶ ὡς θεὸς ἔσωσεν.
πέντε χιλιάδας ἀπὸ πέντε ἄρτων ἐχόρτασεν
ἐν τοῖς μακροῖς ὄρεσιν· τοῦτο γὰρ ἡ θεῖα δύναμις ἐβουλήθη.

---

59 θεὸς ἐμός **F;** ἐν ξύλῳ Cath 60 ὃς τάφον ἦλθεν om. Cath; τάφου] ταφῆς Cath; ἐς] εἰς Cath 61–63 uncialibus, ut titulus operis, scribuntur in **M** 61 ἴδεσιν **M** 63 ἑρμηνεύται **M** 64 ὠφιλές **M**; τελευτέον **M** 71 περιλέλιπται **M** 88 χαλαμπῆς **M**

fol. 29r ἐμός ἐστι θεὸς ὁ Χριστός, ὁ ἐπὶ | ξύλου ταθείς,
ὁ ἀποθανών, ὁ ταφείς, καὶ πάλιν ἐκ τάφου εἰς οὔρανον ἀνελθών.

Και ταῦτα μὲν ὁ χρησμός· ἀλλ' αἰσχύνθητε λοιπὸν αἰσχύνῃ μεγάλῃ, καὶ ἐντράπητε ἐντροπῇ ὑπερβαλλούσῃ, πάντες οἱ ἐπὶ ἀνθρωπίνῃ δυναστείᾳ ἐπερειδόντες τὴν ἑαυτῶν ἐλπίδα, εἴτε ἐπὶ διαλεκτικῇ λέγω δεινότητι, εἴτε ἐπὶ πλούτου πολλῇ περιουσίᾳ, εἴτε δὲ καὶ επ' οἵᾳ δήποτ' οὖν ἑτέρᾳ νομιζομένῃ μὲν, μὴ οὔσῃ δέ· καὶ μὴ θελήσετε τῆς τοῦ προφήτου παραινέσεως μικρὰ φροντίσαι, ἐν ᾗ, ἄριστα συμβουλεύων, ταῦτα διεξέρχεται καὶ φησίν· «ἀγαθὸν πεποιθέναι ἐπὶ Κύριον ἢ πεποιθέναι ἐπ᾽ἄνθρωπον· ἀγαθὸν ἐλπίζειν ἐπὶ Κύριον ἢ ἐλπίζειν ἐπ' ἄρχουσιν» [Ps. 117:8–9 (LXX var.)]. καὶ πάλιν ἕτερος σοφὸς οὕτω λέγει· «ἆρά τε τοὺς ὀφθαλμοὺς ὑμῶν εἰς ἀρχαίας γενεὰς καὶ ἴδετε· τίς ἤλπισεν ἐπὶ Κύριον καὶ κατῃσχύνθη, ἢ τίς ἐνέμεινεν τῷ φόβῳ αὐτοῦ, καὶ ὑπερεῖδεν αὐτόν; διότι ἐλεήμων καὶ οἰκτίρμων ὁ
fol. 29v Κύριος, καὶ ἀφίησιν ἁμαρτίας καὶ σῴ|ζει ἐν καιρῷ θλίψεως» [Sir. 2:10–11 (LXX var.)]. ἕτερος δὲ καὶ ἄρα τε τοὺς τοιούτους οὑτωσὶ λέγων· «ἐπικατάρατος ὃς πέποιθεν ἐπ' ἄνθρωπον καὶ ἀπὸ Κυρίου ἀποστῇ ἡ καρδία αὐτοῦ» [Jer. 17:5 (LXX var.)].

Ἡμεῖς δὲ οὐκ ἐπὶ κοινὸν ἄνθρωπον καὶ τῶν καθ' ἡμᾶς ἕνα, ἀλλ' ἐπὶ τὸν τοῦ Θεοῦ καὶ Πατρὸς Υἵον καὶ θεὸν Λόγον, καὶ ὅτε γέγονεν ἄνθρωπος ἀπομείναντα δηλονότι, καὶ ἐν τῇ καθ' ἡμᾶς φύσει, τοῦτ' ὅπερ ἦν καὶ ἔστιν καὶ ἔσται, τουτέστιν θεόν, καὶ πεπιστεύκαμεν καὶ πιστεύομεν· ὑμεῖς δὲ αὐτοὶ φόβῳ καὶ δέει ὑποκείσθαι ἂν εἴητε δίκαιοι, εἴπερ, ὡς αὐτοὶ οἱ δαίμονες εὖ ἔχειν καθομολογοῦσιν, κακίζειν ἐπιχειροῖτε, δυσσεβέστεροι ἤδη καὶ αὐτῶν γεγονότες, καὶ κατὰ τοῦτο δικαίως σφοδρότερον καὶ αἰώνιον ὄλεθρον τίσετε ἀπὸ προσώπου Κυρίου, ὅτ' ἂν ἔλθῃ ἐνδοξασθῆναι ἐν τοῖς ἁγίοις αὐτοῦ καὶ θαυμασθῆναι ἐν πᾶσιν τοῖς φυλάξεσιν τὰς ἐντολὰς αὐτοῦ μέχρι τέλους, καὶ τὴν εἰς αὐτον πίστιν ἀνόθευτον καὶ ἀπαρεγχείρητον. διὸ φοβήθητε,
fol. 30r φοβήθητε, παρακαλῶ, καὶ καταλύ|σαντες τὴν ἔριν, γένεσθε μεθ' ἡμῶν ἕν, καθὼς καὶ αὐτὸς ὁ Κύριος, ἄνθρωπος γεγονώς, τὸν ἑαυτοῦ Πατέρα παρεκάλει, λέγων· «Πάτερ ἅγιε, τήρησον αὐτοὺς ἐν τῷ ὀνόματί σου, ᾧ δέδωκάς μοι, ἵνα ὦσιν ἕν, καθὼς ἡμεῖς» [John 17:11].

---

100 ἐπερίδοντες **M** 103 θελήσηται **M** 108 εἴδετε **M** 110 ὑπερῖδεν **M** 111 ἀφείησιν **M** 120 εἴηται **M** 121 ἐπιχειριοῖτε **M** 122 γεγονῶτες **M** 123 τίσηται **M** 126 ἀπαρεγχείριτον **M** 129 τήρισον **M**

13 Leontius of Byzantium and the Reception of the Chalcedonian Definition

One of the central questions Christian theologians continue to ask themselves, as they confront the Mystery of the person of Christ, is: what is the significance for us today of the formula produced by the Council of Chalcedon? For generations of modern scholars, especially those in the West, the dense and rather technical phrases forged at that fifth-century gathering of Christian bishops, and appended to a restatement of what we know as the Nicene Creed, represented a major milestone in the Churches' ongoing clarification of how we are to understand the person of Jesus the Savior. In J. N. D. Kelly's widely used survey, *Early Christian Doctrines*,[1] for instance, Chalcedon's "settlement" of the twenty-four-year dispute between Nestorius and his Antiochene supporters and Cyril of Alexandria and his local church was the culmination of "the decisive period for Christology"[2] in early Christianity, an attempt to define an understanding of Christ that could be accepted by all believers throughout the Empire, but which nevertheless—surprisingly, perhaps—"failed to bring permanent peace."[3] Our own centenarian, Fr. Aloys Grillmeier, in his foundational study of the growth of early Christian understandings of Jesus, *Christ in Christian Tradition*, speaks of the decades leading up to Chalcedon as progressively defining "the development of belief in Christ, from its beginning to its first climax in a council of the church."[4] In his influential study of the theology of the

1. J. N. D. Kelly, *Early Christian Doctrines* (San Francisco 1978, rev. ed.) 310–43.
2. Ibid. 310.
3. Ibid. 342.
4. A. Grillmeier, *Christ in Christian Tradition* 1 (Oxford 1975, 2nd ed.) 555.

seventh-century monk and theologian Maximus the Confessor, Hans Urs von Balthasar emphasizes the centrality of Chalcedon's formulaic, classically dialectical picture of the person of Christ as central to Maximus's whole approach to God, the world, and the human spirit. The reason for Chalcedon's abiding importance, Balthasar there argues, lies in the Council's ability to affirm both unity and abiding difference in Christ as the dominant pattern of God's relationship to creation:

> From the moment that Chalcedon, in its sober and holy wisdom, elevated the adverbs "indivisibly" (ἀδιαιρέτως) and "unconfusedly" (ἀσυγχύτως) to a dogmatic formula, the image of a reciprocal indwelling of two distinct poles of being replaced the image of mixture. This mutual ontological presence (περιχώρησις) not only preserves the being particular to each element, to the divine and the human natures, but also brings each of them to its perfection in their very difference, even enhancing that difference. Love, which is the highest level of union, only takes root in the growing independence of the lovers; the union between God and the world reveals, in the very nearness it creates between these two poles of being, the ever-greater difference between created being and the essentially incomparable God.[5]

With a little help from Romantic philosophy—and perhaps from the musings of his Jesuit confrère Erich Przywara—Balthasar here sees in the dialectical, balanced Chalcedonian picture of Christ not only Maximus's central inspiration, but the early Church's final, authoritative paradigm for conceiving how the transcendent God can be present and crucially active in the world.

I. Definition of Chalcedon

Yet, as often happens when one looks at Church doctrine in the context of history, one soon discovers that Chalcedon's contemporaries and near contemporaries did not all see its doctrinal statement in quite such clear and simple terms, or as leading so unequivocally to resolution. The council had been summoned, in the late summer of 450, by the new emperor Marcian and his theologically astute spouse, Pulcheria, in response to widespread concern among the churches in the Mediterranean area over the synod that

5. H. U. von Balthasar, *Cosmic Liturgy* (Einsiedeln 1988; Eng. trans. San Francisco 2003) 63–64. German original: *Kosmische Liturgie* (Einsiedeln 1961, 2nd ed.) 55.

had met at Ephesus in 449, particularly over its strong affirmation of the teachings of the archimandrite Eutyches in the imperial capital. Eutyches had challenged the orthodoxy of the episcopal leadership in the churches of Constantinople and Antioch, citing for support passages from the later letters of Cyril of Alexandria backing his own insistence that the one Jesus, Son of God, was formed "from two natures," the divine and the human, but that "after the union and the incarnation, they [namely, Cyril, Athanasius] no longer affirmed two natures but one."[6] This radical expression of the concrete, dynamically functioning "natural" unity of the divine and the human in Christ, a unity that from the incarnation on must exclude every Christian reference to duality in him, had been proposed before. But with Eutyches's dogged advocacy—strongly supported by Dioscorus, Cyril's successor as bishop of Alexandria and so spokesperson for the Church of Egypt—it became not only a theological and devotional position, but an ecclesial and political emblem: Christ was one; Christ was God in human flesh; and Cyril of Alexandria—ultimately Cyril alone—was the norm for orthodox faith.

In the eyes of his critics, Eutyches's conception of Christ's single reality implied an Apollinarian, even a Gnostic tendency towards a "mixture and confusion" of Christ's complex way of being. The determined support of Dioscorus and the Church of Egypt for Eutyches's critique of Church leadership meant that a struggle was brewing, which would involve churches and regions and their cherished leaders, past and present, as much as it involved language and ideas. Alarmed by what he had heard of the growing dispute in Constantinople over Eutyches's formulation of the Mystery of Christ, Pope Leo of Rome wrote his famous dogmatic letter or "Tome" to Patriarch Flavian of Constantinople on June 13, 449: also drawing on Cyril's classic formulations of Christ's subjective unity, but emphasizing that the major elements in Christ—divinity and humanity, God the Son and the son of Mary—each remain distinguishable and operative within that unity. "The distinctive character of each nature and substance remaining . . . unimpaired," Leo wrote, "and coming together into one Person, . . . an inviolable nature was united to a nature capable of suffering. . . . Thus, in the whole and perfect nature of true humanity, true God was born—complete in what belonged to him, complete in what belonged to us . . ."[7]

6. See the summary account of the questioning and critique of Eutyches at Ephesus, in 449, later read into the minutes of session 1 of Chalcedon: trans. Richard Price and Michael Gaddis, *The Acts of the Council of Chalcedon* I (Liverpool 2007), 223–24.

7. Leo, *Tome* 3 (cf. J. Stevenson and W. H. C. Frend, *Creeds, Councils and Controversies* [London 1989] 338–39).

Humanity and divinity, both in Cyril's view and in Leo's, remain radically other than each other; Jesus exhibits both of them complete in his single person; yet how they combine—and whether either, in the end, is operatively distinguishable in Jesus's actions—is now the question. More important, how we answer this—what authorities in the tradition we draw on—largely determines how we understand and relate to Jesus.

When Marcian and Pulcheria acceded to the reins of the Eastern Empire in August, 450, one of their first acts was to summon another council of bishops, designed to be ecumenical, for the following fall: specifically to extinguish the growing flames of conflict over Eutyches and his critics. The bishops who gathered in the city of Chalcedon, across the Bosporus from the capital, were willing to disown both Eutyches and Dioscorus, even to the point of removing them both from clerical office. But for the first several sessions, a majority of them balked at putting together a new, common formula of faith, beyond reaffirming as foundational the "faith of Nicaea." Under pressure from the emperor, however, and in light of his threat to dissolve the Council if they continued to resist, and to meet again in a year or so at some site in the Latin West, the Council eventually charged a committee with drawing up a statement that promised to represent the understanding of a strong majority of them—a text, now lost, that seems to have been the basis for most of the Chalcedonian decree that we know. That original draft, most scholars assume, was probably deliberately constructed by the committee to distance itself from the extreme positions the Church's faith in Christ had faced in the previous three decades, and represented a kind of patchwork summary of the principles of orthodoxy: it was apparently formed, like the Chalcedonian definition we know, from classic phrases borrowed from Cyril's Letter to John of Antioch of 433, from his Second (less provocative) Letter to Nestorius from 429, and from some of the Antiochene Theodoret of Cyrus's more centrist pronouncements. The assembled bishops seem to have heard this compromise formula with a good deal of relief, when it was read, and pressed the imperial commissioners to let it be signed. Yet something still seemed missing to Leo's three Western delegates, and to the emperor, his wife, and the imperial commissioners: an explicit endorsement of the language not only of Cyril, but of Leo.[8] And when the bishops, ever reluctant

8. So *Acts of Chalcedon*, Session 5, cc. 15–17 (trans. Price and Gaddis 2.198): "The most glorious officials said [to the assembled bishops], 'Do you accept the letter of Archbishop Leo?'

"The most devout bishops exclaimed, 'Yes, we have accepted and signed it.'

"The most glorious officials said: 'Then its contents must be inserted in the definition.'"

to add anything controversial to an official text, protested that such an endorsement was unnecessary, the imperial response was to repeat the threat of adjourning the Council and calling another one in the Latin West. According to the *Acta*, the bishops present then quickly agreed, and the document was sent back to the drafting committee for presumably minor revision.

The Chalcedonian definition of orthodox faith in Christ, as we know it, is the result of this collaborative authorship. Presumably, the few phrases from Leo's *Tome* that were added, and the tacit recognition thereby of Leo as an authority on a par with Cyril, simply expressed as Church-wide consensus the continuing integrity and efficacy of Christ's two natures or levels of acting, which everyone—including Cyril, in his later letters—acknowledged to be central to the constitution of Christ. The main difference of the final text from its previous draft, beyond the addition of phrases from Leo's *Tome to Flavian*, apparently, was that the council now clearly affirmed that the single Christ of history subsists "in" (not simply "from") "two natures," and that "the character of each nature" in which he exists—radically different as these are by themselves—are "preserved and come together into one person and hypostasis." The two radically different active realities in Christ—his "natures," as the word was then understood—continue to be functional and real within their own identities, even though they now permanently exist and operate together.[9]

II. Immediate Aftermath: Reception and Contradiction to Chalcedon

As is well known, this final form of the definition of Chalcedon, although intended as a unifying text, proved almost immediately to be highly divisive.

9. So the key new part of the definition, in phrases taken from Leo's *Tome* which became the chief target of future rejection, seems to have been the affirmation of "one and the same Christ, Son, Lord, Only-begotten, acknowledged in two natures [originally "*from* two natures"], the difference of the natures being in no way destroyed by the union [from: Cyril 2nd letter to Nestorius], but rather the distinctive character of each nature being preserved and coming together into one person and one hypostasis, not parted or divided into two persons . . ." (*Acts of Chalcedon* Session 5, c. 34 [trans. Price and Gaddis 2.204]). Cf. analysis of A. de Halleux, "La definition christologique à Chalcédoine," *RTL* 7 (1976) 3–23 (first part) and 155–70 (second part) (summarized by A. Grillmeier, SJ, in his *Jesus der Christus im Glauben der Kirche*, vol. 1: *Von der apostolischen Zeit bis zum Konzil von Chalcedon (451)* [Freiburg 1979] 755–59).

Its portrait of Jesus seemed to many Christians in the Eastern part of the Empire—especially to monks and their devout followers in Egypt, Syria, and eastern Asia Minor, who wanted above all to underline the transcendent power and holiness of Jesus's person—to be substituting philosophical hair-splitting for the Christian confession of faith, and, moreover, to be doing this in a way that implicitly put the Latin-speaking Leo on a level of authority parallel to the great Cyril. One of Cyril's outspoken advocates at the Council, Bishop Eustathius of Beirut, made the point in the First Session that Cyril had sufficiently affirmed the permanent distinction between the divine and the human in Christ's person, by coining the phrase "one nature of the Word of God, made flesh"; so, Eustathius concluded, "Anathema to whoever says 'one nature' in such a way as to abolish Christ's flesh that is consubstantial with us—and anathema to whoever says 'two natures' in such a way as to divide the Son of God."[10] As Paul Galtier pointed out, in a celebrated article on the influence of Cyril and Leo at Chalcedon, Cyril used the biblical image of the gold plating on the acacia wood of the Ark of the Covenant to suggest that "human nature is enveloped by the divinity in Christ, without being changed."[11] "Basically," Galtier continued, on the fundamental understanding of the complex reality of Christ "there is full agreement among the Council, St. Leo and St. Cyril. But the way in which the latter of these habitually expresses his thought is incontestably different."[12] Cyril, for instance, "avoids considering [the two natures] by themselves (ἰδικῶς); to him this would seem to divide them, to separate them from each other, and so to introduce into Christ a human being [simply] associated with God."[13] For someone deeply imbued with the traditional piety, and the theological and exegetical vision, of the Alexandrian church, this would be an abandonment of several centuries of inherited, passionate faith: to see Jesus as someone other than the Son of God, present and acting in his human form, and to turn away from the powerful thought and language of Alexandria's great spokesman, Cyril. On the other hand, most representatives of Antioch, Constantinople, and the West saw the origin of a "Eutychian" hybridization and confusion of God and a human being in some of Cyril's later formulations. Leo and

10. *Acts of Chalcedon*, Session 1, c. 267 (trans. Price and Gaddis 1.185).

11. Cyril of Alexandria, *Scholia on the Incarnation* 11, cited by P. Galtier, "Saint Cyrille d'Alexandrie et Saint Léon le Grand à Chalcédoine," in A. Grillmeier and H. Bacht (eds.), *Das Konzil von Chalkedon. Geschichte und Gegenwart* I (Würzburg 1951) (345–87) 366.

12. Galtier, "Saint Cyrille d'Alexandrie," 367.

13. Ibid.

Cyril represented mutually exclusive emphases, if not totally incompatible visions of Christ.

The final formula produced at Chalcedon was itself a blending of differing traditions, a summary born out of compromise. As we know, the compromise had little lasting power in much of the Eastern Empire. In Alexandria, where devotion to Cyril and his thought was predictably strong, a large anti-Chalcedonian party resisted Proterius, the imperially designated successor to Dioscorus, whom the Council had deposed, and chose instead the presbyter Timothy, nicknamed "the Cat" (*Ailouros*), as their bishop. When Proterius was murdered by an angry crowd, in 457, the anti-Chalcedonian Timothy was for almost three years the only bishop in the city, even though he was never officially recognized as such by the imperial government. A learned theologian and writer, Timothy became in time one of the leading voices—along with Severus, the monk of Gaza who had studied in Alexandria and Beirut, and who became bishop of Antioch in 512—in the moderate, learned theological opposition to any Christology that was not solely based on Cyril, particularly on his Third Letter to Nestorius and his later letters. In an attempt to broker a reconciliation that avoided confronting neuralgic issues head-on, the emperor Zeno, in 482, issued his own decree (drafted by Acacius, his patriarch in Constantinople) known as the *Henōtikon* or "Formula of Union," proclaiming the Creed of Nicaea, and its later interpretation by Cyril of Alexandria, to be the only binding summary of the Empire's Christian faith, and declaring, with studied vagueness, that "everyone who has held another opinion, either at present or at another time, whether at Chalcedon or in any synod whatsoever, we anathematize."[14] It was an unmistakable imperial disavowal of the Chalcedonian formula.

The edict's effect, predictably, was further division: a break in communion between the imperially sponsored churches of the Eastern Empire and the churches in communion with Rome, today called the "Acacian schism," which lasted until 519. Local churches in Egypt and northeast Africa, Syria, Palestine, and what today are Iraq and Jordan also progressively distanced themselves from the imperial Church: by the turn of the sixth century most monks and ordinary Christians in these regions had recognized non-Chalcedonian bishops as their leaders, and new ecclesial communions

14. Cf. W. H. C. Frend, *The Rise of the Monophysite Movement* (Cambridge 1972) 174–83; translation of complete decree: ibid. 360–62. Cf. the analysis of A. Grillmeier, *Christ in Christian Tradition* 2/1 (London: Mowbray, 1987) 247–56 with English text of the Henoticon, pp. 256–57.

had begun to be formed, which still exist today as the "Oriental Orthodox" Churches. As a result, religious, political, and social fragmentation increasingly characterized the Eastern half of the Christian Roman Empire, despite repeated attempts by the emperors and their theological advisors in the sixth, seventh, and eighth centuries to find concepts and language that would build unity on the common ground of the "faith of Nicaea." What has come to be called "neo-Chalcedonian" Christology by many twentieth-century scholars[15] is one of the results: a portrait of Christ, put forward by a number of sixth- and seventh-century theologians, that varies in detail, but that agrees at least in continuing to affirm the formula of Chalcedon as binding; in its self-consciously academic method and style; and in its affirmation of the Christology of Cyril of Alexandria as its prime inspiration. This approach to Christology, actively sponsored by the emperor Justinian, eventually found full official expression in the canons of the Second Council of Constantinople in 553.

III. Christology after Chalcedon until 553

Let us consider, then, in more detail the complex Christological landscape in the two centuries after Chalcedon. There were still, presumably, active defenders and followers of Theodore of Mopsuestia and the fifth-century

15. The term seems to have been coined by the Louvain Syriac scholar Joseph Lebon, in *Le Monophysisme sévérien* (Louvain 1909); see also: J. Lebon, *Ephrem d'Amid, patriarche d'Antioche, Mélanges d'histoire offerts à Charles Moeller* (Louvain/Paris 1914) 197–214; Lebon, "Restitutions à Théodoret de Cyr," *RHE* 26 (1930) 523–60; Lebon, "La Christologie du monophysisme syrien," in Grillmeier-Bacht, *Chalkedon* I, 425–580; Ch. Moeller, "Un Représentant de la christologie néochalcédonienne, Nephalius," *RHE* 40 (1944–1945) 73–140; Moeller, "Le Chalcédonisme et le néo-chalcédonisme de 451 jusqu'à la fin du VIe siècle," in Grillmeier-Bacht, *Chalkedon* I, 637–720; M. Richard, "Le Néo-chalcédonisme," *MSR* 3 (1946) 156–61 = *Opera Minora* II, no. 56; S. Helmer, "Der Neuchalkedonismus. Geschichte, Berechtigung und Bedeutung eines dogmengeschichtlichen Begriffes" (diss., Bonn 1962); A. Grillmeier, "Der Neu-Chalkedonismus. Um die Berechtigung eines neuen Kapitels in der Dogmengeschichte," in Grillmeier, *Mit Ihm und in Ihm* (Freiburg 1975) 371–85; P. T. R. Gray, "Neo-Chalcedonianism and the Tradition: from Patristic to Byzantine Theology," *ByF* 16 (1982) 61–70; K.-H. Uthemann, "Das anthropologische Modell der hypostatischen Union," Κληρονομία 14 (1982) 215–37; Uthemann, "Der Neuchalkedonismus als Vorbereitung des Monotheletismus," *StPatr* 29 (Oxford 1995) 373–413; Uthemann, "Definitionen und Paradigmen in der Rezeption des Dogmas von Chalkedon bis in die Zeit Kaiser Justinians," in J. van Oort and J. Roldanus (eds.), *Chalkedon: Geschichte und Aktualität* (Leuven 1997) 54–122.

"school of Antioch," whose writings have mainly disappeared: theologians such as Basil of Cilicia, whose works are summarized by the ninth-century patriarch Photius in his description of the contents of his own library.[16] According to Photius, Basil—a priest of Antioch at the turn of the fifth and sixth centuries, still called Diodore and Theodore "Church Fathers," defended the orthodoxy of the Chalcedonian formula as it stood, and attacked those who, in the decades after the Council, were busy reinterpreting its decrees in a more Cyrillian direction. There were also writers whose main purpose seems to have been to defend the formula of Chalcedon simply by defining its terms more closely and by using them more consistently: the bishop Hypatius of Ephesus[17] (preserved only in fragments), the monk Leontius of Byzantium, and probably Ephraim of Amida, a successful bureaucrat who became patriarch of Antioch in 527, but who subsequently became a supporter of Justinian's policy of reconceiving and re-expressing Chalcedonian Christology.

Leontius, of whose Christology we will speak more in a moment, significantly claims in his works to have been an admirer of Diodore and Theodore himself, in his younger days, and was apparently also a friend of Basil of Cilicia. In his six surviving works, however, he focuses his energies on arguing that anyone who—with the help of late antique philosophy and the Cappadocians' language for speaking of the Trinity—can grasp the ontological distinction between the universal realities "essence" (*ousia*) or "nature" (*physis*), on the one hand, and the concrete realities we call "individual" (*hypostasis*) or "person (*persona*)" (*prosōpon*), on the other, will see that the language of Chalcedon is the only way to express accurately the two wholly different levels of reality in which the single subject, Jesus Christ, lives and acts.

There were, of course, the hard opponents of the Chalcedonian formulation as well: Timothy "Ailouros" of Alexandria, Severus of Antioch, and two important Syriac writers, Severus's friend Philoxenos, bishop of Mabbug, and the poet and preacher Jacob of Sarug. All of these opponents of the Council's formula regarded the two-nature language of Chalcedon as essentially a heretical departure from the Church's faith in the divinity of Christ—as

16. Photius, *Bibliotheca*, Cod. 107. Basil is said here to have dedicated one of his writings, a refutation of the work of the neo-Chalcedonian John of Scythopolis, to a certain Leontius, "most holy and dear to God," whom he addresses as "father." It is possible that this was the monk we know as Leontius of Byzantium; see the introduction to *Leontius of Byzantium: Complete Works* (ed. B. E. Daley, Oxford 2018) 23–24.

17. An analysis of his position in the *Collatio cum Severianis* in A. Grillmeier (with T. Hainthaler), *Christ in Christian Tradition* II/2 (London 1995) 230–48.

simply "Nestorianism light"; yet all of them, in reverent adherence to Cyril, strongly affirmed the full humanity of Christ in body and soul, rejected Apollinarianism, and simply argued that everything in that humanity now belonged to a single divine subject, the Son and Word of God. So Christ's human characteristics could now only be spoken of as centered in the Logos, owned by him—as part of the single, functioning reality, the one concrete "nature," that the Son of God always is.

It is in the midst of this pattern of conflicting interpretations of the Council's decree and language that what has been called, in the last century, a "neo-Chalcedonian" understanding of Christ must be situated. A series of writers from the late fifth and early sixth centuries seem to have tried to perform the controversial task of maintaining Chalcedon's balanced picture of Christ as normative, and acknowledging its recognized place in the canon of ecumenical councils, while emphasizing its authentic continuity with the language and thought of Cyril. This consciously mediating approach seems to have begun with the Egyptian monk Nephalius, in the first decade of the sixth century; and to have been taken up by the Palestinian John of Caesarea (Severus's opponent, called the "Impious Grammarian" in Severus's polemic against Chalcedon) and by Bishop John of Scythopolis, who was also the first commentator on the works of the Ps.-Dionysius. It was also developed more at length, with considerable analytical depth and complexity, by the otherwise unknown Leontius of Jerusalem, who seems to have written in the 530s and 540s. Perhaps the dominant figure in this approach to reflection of Christ, though, at least in terms of its public effect, was the emperor Justinian (519–565)—a well-read and acutely subtle theologian in his own right—who incorporated the "neo-Chalcedonian" movement's intellectually synthetic tactics into his imperial policy, as a path to rebuilding the Empire's cultural and religious unity.

Justinian's approach was to apply heavy pressure on the official Church to distance itself from what he and his advisors saw as the heretical currents of his day, whether overly divisive or overly unitive in their conception of Christ, while at the same time encouraging a healthy pluralism in the interpretation of mainstream doctrine, as formulated at Chalcedon. So in 543 he issued a decree condemning "Origenism"[18]—apparently a hybridized form of ascetical Origenism, cultivated in some Eastern monastic communities of

18. See B. E. Daley, "What Did 'Origenism' Mean in the Sixth Century?," in G. Dorival, A. Le Boulluec (eds.), *Origène et la Bible. Actes du Colloquium Origenianum Sextum*, Chantilly, 30 août–3 septembre 1993 = BEThL 118 (Leuven 1995) 627–38.

the time, which was thought to suggest permanent division between the immaterial divine Logos and Jesus the man—and another decree the following year, condemning the "three chapters"—three notorious fifth-century cases (Theodore of Mopsuestia with his teaching and as a person, Theodoret's anti-Cyrillian writings, and the letter of Ibas to the Persian Mari) of what was thought to be divisive Antiochene speculation on the person of Christ.

Eventually, the emperor summoned another council at Constantinople, in May, 553, which set about canonizing his carefully pluralist agenda. Its canons, originally resisted but eventually "received" by the main Churches of East and West as the pronouncements of the Fifth Ecumenical Council, recognize "four holy synods"—presumably Nicaea, Constantinople I, Ephesus, and Chalcedon—as normative for faith (can. 11; cf. cans. 5 and 6, citing "the holy synod in Chalcedon"), but also explicitly recognize that the classical formulas associated with Cyril and Leo can be taken in both orthodox and unorthodox ways. The Word of God is both eternally born of the Father and born in time as Son of Mary (can. 2), yet is "one and the same," the single subject to whom we ascribe both miracles and suffering (can. 3). The union of the divine Word with the human Jesus takes place "by synthesis, in hypostasis": in the concrete individuality of a single subject, who personally embodies these two realities or natures, without confusing or dividing them (can. 4). So it is a mistake to take the statement of "the holy synod in Chalcedon" as presenting a divisive (read: "Antiochene") portrait of Christ, through a merely extrinsic union of two individuals (cans. 5 and 6). Rather, one must understand that one concrete individual (*hypostasis*) has been formed of two utterly different natural realities, so that the difference between them remains undiminished "for the mind considering them"[19]; yet they are not separated into two acting individuals, "for one [subject: εἷς] is from both [natures], and both realities [ἀμφότερα] exist through one" (can. 7). So Cyril's reference to "one nature of God the Word, made flesh," is to be understood, as "the holy Fathers took it," to signify two natural realities forming one unique Christ as a concrete individual (καθ' ὑπόστασιν), not the formation of a new, hybrid kind of reality (can. 8). We must, then, worship a single, yet complex, Christ, who is "God the Word made flesh" (can. 9), recognizing the fundamental paradox of faith that "our Lord Jesus Christ, who was crucified in the flesh, is true God and Lord of glory and one

19. In the Greek: τῇ θεωρίᾳ μόνῃ τὴν διαφορὰν τούτων λαμβάνει. The phrase originally is used by Cyril in his *Letter to Eulogius* (*Ep*. 44) 1, probably written—to the priest Eulogius, his agent in Constantinople—between 433 and 435.

of the holy Trinity" (can. 10). All the statements in these canons, one could say, are meant to reassure those who reject Chalcedon's language, as overly beholden to the "divisive" agenda of Antioch and Leo, that Chalcedon's intent was really to affirm the complex Mystery of Christ's personal unity. They are also intended to call Chalcedon's diphysite defenders to recognize that the cherished phrases of Cyril's "miaphysite" portrait of Christ can themselves be understood in a Chalcedonian way.

The canons of Constantinople II, then, tersely articulate both a reaffirmation of the Christological portrait of Chalcedon, and a measured interpretation of its language in an Alexandrian direction: they express a phase of the repeated sixth-century attempt to distance the language of 451 from its connections with the earlier Antiochene tradition, while also condemning outright Theodore of Mopsuestia, the anti-Cyrillian writings of Theodoret of Cyrus, and an anti-Cyrillian letter of bishop Ibas of Edessa (the so-called "three chapters" or *kephalaia*). The implications are clear: Chalcedon's portrait of Christ, while still the linguistic norm of the imperial Church, is to be read in the light of Cyril's writings if it is to be considered orthodox, even if its two-nature language is formally at variance with much of Cyril's later terminology; Leo's *Tome*, on the other hand, is itself no longer mentioned; and the subject—the hypostasis or "person"—to whom the attributes and actions of Christ are all to be ascribed, is unequivocally identified now as divine: as God the Word, "one of the holy Trinity." This attempt to reread the more dialectical language of Chalcedon in the light of Cyril's thought, while still reaffirming that Council's formula as the accepted norm of the Empire's faith, is really the fullest expression we have of what has understandably been called "neo-Chalcedonianism": a reception of Chalcedon that both extends and carefully re-interprets the foundation it builds on.

IV. Leontius of Byzantium

It is in the context of these debates surrounding and expressing the reception of the Chalcedonian definition that we must also situate the works of the sixth-century theologian we have mentioned: Leontius of Byzantium, a logically disciplined, philosophically oriented writer who seems to have flourished mainly in the 530s and 540s, and who has been characterized—correctly, I believe—in recent decades as a "strict Chalcedonian."[20] Leontius's

20. See M. Richard, "Léonce de Jérusalem et Léonce de Byzance," *MSR* 1 (1944) 35–88

main aim was to argue that if one understands the terms of the Chalcedonian definition correctly, in the light of the earlier (especially Cappadocian) tradition of language about God, then the formula of the Council is, in fact, the only possible way to summarize correctly biblical and ecclesiastical tradition about the person of Jesus. In this position, and in his attempt to construct a whole understanding of Christ on the basis of Chalcedon's balanced affirmation of the mutual reciprocity of divine and human realities in Christ, Leontius stands virtually alone in patristic literature. Since Friedrich Loofs's 1887 monograph on Leontius,[21] he has been recognized as a major contributor to the reception of Chalcedon's language and conceptuality; as I have argued elsewhere, however,[22] Loofs's misreading of a celebrated paragraph in the first question of his treatise *Against the Nestorians and Eutychians*, with its reference to "enhypostatic natures," has led to a long tradition of misunderstanding Leontius's whole Christological argument, and to seeing him as the patristic ancestor of modern theories of the unity of Christ that are really quite distant from his much more modest, more terminologically oriented, intentions.

In this treatise, probably produced in the late 530s, Leontius introduces his treatment of the Chalcedonian definition by arguing that both sides in the Christological standoff that preceded the council shared the same misconception, that "nature" and "hypostasis" really point to the same thing: the living, concrete realization of some intelligible reality, in which alone the universal designation of what it is can be encountered. All sides to the discussion seem to agree, he says, that, strictly speaking, "there is no such thing as an anhypostatic nature" (οὐκ ἔστι φύσις ἀνυπόστατος). This was apparently a common axiom of Alexandrian philosophy in the sixth century; enough of Aristotelian realism had embedded itself in the eclectic thought and vocabulary of later Greek philosophy to produce a consensus that natures or essences cannot be properly said to exist, to be substantial, on their own, separately from the concrete, historical, individual things or hypostases in which they are realized. If, then, one confesses two natures in Christ, as

= Richard, *Opera Minora* III, no. 59; Grillmeier (with Hainthaler), *Christ in Christian Tradition* II/2, 181–270. See also B. E. Daley, *Leontius of Byzantium: Complete Works* (Oxford 2017) 75–76.

21. F. Loofs, *Leontius von Byzanz und die gleichnamigen Schriftsteller der griechischen Kirche* = TU III, 1–2 (Leipzig 1887).

22. See my forthcoming article "Leontius of Byzantium and the 'Enhypostatic Humanity' of Jesus," in the *T&T Clark Handbook of Christology*, edited by Darren Sumner and Chris Tilling. Parts of this article are also closely paralleled in that essay.

the Chalcedonian formula does, it seemed to Chalcedon's critics on both sides that one must also confess in him two hypostases or individual beings: a conclusion that implied for miaphysites the necessity of abandoning Chalcedon's talk of "two unmixed natures," and for diphysites the necessity of abandoning its language of "one hypostasis or person."

Leontius, too, is ready to acknowledge the principle that natures or essences are only real when encountered in hypostases or concrete individuals; but in a celebrated passage he goes on to argue that this implies nothing more than that every nature, if it is real and not simply theoretical, exists in a hypostatized state (ἐνυπόστατος); it does *not* imply that every real nature in itself is a distinct hypostasis. So he writes:

> Hypostasis, gentlemen, and the hypostatic are not the same thing, just as essence and the essential are different. For "the hypostasis" signifies the individual, but "the hypostatic" the essence; and "the hypostasis" defines the person by means of peculiar characteristics, while "the hypostatic" signifies that something is not an accident, although it has its being in another and is not perceived by itself. Such are all qualities. . . . There could never, then, be an anhypostatic nature—that is, essence. But the nature is not a hypostasis, because it is not a reversible attribution; for a hypostasis is also a nature, but a nature is not also a hypostasis: for nature admits of the predication of being, but hypostasis also of being-by-oneself; and the former presents a generic character, the latter expresses individual identity. And the one brings out what is peculiar to something universal, the other distinguishes the particular from the general. To put it concisely, things sharing the same essence are properly said to be of one nature, and things whose structure of being is common; but we can define as "hypostasis" either things which share a nature but differ in number, or things which are put together from different natures, but which share reciprocally in a common being. I mean that they share being, not as if they completed one another's essence, as happens with essences and with things that are essentially predicated of them—which are called qualities—but insofar as the nature and essence of each is not considered by itself but with the other, to which it is joined and assimilated. One finds this in various things, not least in the case of soul and body, whose hypostasis is common but each of whose natures is individual, with a different way of being.[23]

23. Cf. Leontius of Byzantium, *Contra Nestorianos et Eutychianos* 1 (ed. Daley 132.10–135.20).

The passage, as understood here, says nothing about a process of ontological or anthropological assimilation, in which a nature is absorbed into the existence of something which already exists, and which already has a nature of another kind. The prefix ἐν-, in adjectival forms such as this, has no locative significance—no suggestion that one reality is "in" another; nor is there any hint that what is ἐνυπόστατον is in some kind of halfway stage between subsistent and accidental being, as Loofs and many modern scholars influenced by him assume. In fact, Leontius is apparently suggesting—along with the philosophical and theological tradition in which he writes—that what is ἐνυπόστατον is precisely *not* an accident, does not have its being *in* another thing at all, but exists "for itself" (καθ' ἑαυτό). As an existing natural thing, a "what," possessing an identifiable essence, every nature confronts our experience as a concrete individual object or hypostasis.

What, then, is the main point Leontius is trying to make—here and in the rest of his six extant treatises? His Christological achievement, I suggest, is perhaps more modest, at first sight, than what many twentieth-century historians of early theology have supposed it to be. He is not a Cyrillian, nor a "neo-Chalcedonian" trying to interpret the Chalcedonian definition in Cyrillian terms. Nor is he, as Adolf von Harnack suggested,[24] a neo-Apollinarian, let alone—as the philosopher Stefan Otto has more recently theorized[25]—a precocious forebear of modern personalist philosophy. He is simply a cautious, sensitive, and persistent defender of the conceptual correctness, even inevitability, of the formula of Chalcedon. An Alexandrian in his philosophy if not in his Christology, he makes liberal use of the terminology, the logic, and the anthropological analysis of the sixth-century Neoplatonic Alexandrian commentators on Aristotle—the "school" of Ammonius Hermeiou, especially—to demonstrate both the plausibility of the Chalcedonian formula and the implausibility of its alternatives. Leontius is not a neo-Chalcedonian or a proto-personalist; he is a dialectician. The six works of his that we possess tell us next to nothing about the inner life of Christ, let alone anything new or particularly profound in the field of philosophical anthropology. Leontius is not even "the first scholastic," as

24. A. Harnack, *History of Dogma* IV (trans. E. B. Speirs and James Millar, London 1898) 233–34; see 232–40 for Harnack's whole somewhat confused discussion of Leontius. (German original: *Lehrbuch der Dogmengeschichte*, 2. *Die Entwicklung des kirchlichen Dogmas*, Freiburg 1894, 3rd ed., 382–83, resp. 381–85.)

25. S. Otto, *Person und Subsistenz. Die philosophische Anthropologie des Leontios von Byzanz. Ein Beitrag zur spätantiken Geistesgeschichte* (Munich 1968).

Harnack calls him[26]—that is a title that John of Caesarea, writing some twenty years before him, or perhaps even Gregory of Nyssa, in the 380s, might more justly claim. Writing, rather, in a generally "scholastic" age of definition and technical debate, represented in a variety of forms of philosophical discourse, he sets out to use the tools of his time to protect the Chalcedonian portrait of Christ from compromise.

To be more precise: Leontius made it his first concern to clarify philosophically the terms being used in the Christological debates of his day. Insisting on univocality and consistency in theological language—against the contention of Severus and his anti-Chalcedonian followers, that the "newness" of the Incarnation requires of Christian writers a "new" use of terms, not bound by earlier philosophical or theological precedents—Leontius demands that Christology use the same definitions of nature and person, *physis* and *ousia*, *hypostasis* and *prosōpon*, that Athanasius and the Cappadocians had used, and had ultimately canonized, in their discussion of God as Trinity. In this increasingly technical terminology, the *hypostasis* or *prosōpon* (role, external form) of a being we encounter—most often a human being—is the concrete individual, the immediately given substance or reality we experience in our world, in which we recognize wider, abstract levels of reality.[27] Nature, on the other hand, or essence—*physis* or *ousia* in Greek philosophical language—denotes the intelligible class or genus to which an individual is known to belong, when we identify it as what it is, and in which it realizes its identifiable existence.[28] So *ousia* and *physis* denote genuine realities, in the Platonist-Aristotelian understanding of late antiquity: an *ousia* is something real (a πρᾶγμα), possessing being (τὸ εἶναι), and so in its

26. Harnack, *History of Dogma* 4.234. (German original: *Lehrbuch der Dogmengeschichte* 2, 381–82).

27. ὑπόστασις was originally not a word used in philosophical discourse, but in medical treatises and other discussions of natural phenomena; it suggests "sediment," the concrete, indeterminate material one encounters in analyzing known fluids. It seems best to translate it as "concrete individual": a "thing." Πρόσωπον, a word originally found in discussions of literature, and also in legal treatises, is, by contrast, an active human or quasi-human individual, such as a character in a play or a human or corporate agent in a legal proceeding. Its original meaning was "face," and came to be used to describe the masks worn by actors in an ancient drama to identify their roles, then the role itself. It might be best translated by our English term "persona." Neither term carries the connotations of interior experience and relationship suggested by the modern Western language of "person."

28. Both terms are found in Aristotle's treatises. Οὐσία answers the question "What is it?" and is one of Aristotle's ten "categories" of reference; φύσις refers to how an object identified as having that essence can be expected to function and behave.

own way complete (τέλειον); but they have no existence independent of the concrete things that embody it, as the Platonic forms had once been thought to do. A universal essence or nature really exists, as a universal and intelligible thing, but—taking "exists" in a somewhat different sense—only exists in the concrete reality where we experience it, when it is "instanced" in an individual or "hypostatized." So Leontius can take it as a generally assumed principle, in the passage quoted above, that "a non-hypostatic nature does not exist" in the full sense.

More important for Christology, in Leontius's understanding, a hypostatized nature is not necessarily exclusive or univocal in its ontological identity. A hypostasis can realize, can instance or share in, more than one complete, universally real nature at a time, can unite two or more identifiable classes of being in itself: either by hybridizing them into a new, composite nature, or by existing on both levels simultaneously, without mingling them. An example of this latter kind of union of natures, for Leontius and his contemporaries, is that of soul and body in the complete human person. It is crucial to remember, in any case, that for ancient philosophical anthropology, such "levels" of universal being or *ousia* are still realities, even if of a different metaphysical kind from the reality of the concrete things we encounter in day-to-day experience. They are not just abstract classes, ways of speaking; as objects of our knowing, they determine our experience of the world.

Applying these terms to Christ, Leontius makes it his chief concern to show the logical consistency of the Chalcedonian conception of him as one hypostasis—one concrete, individual agent or subject—uniting two complete and recognizable natures, God and the human, that in themselves remain simply what they are, intact and unmixed. To sum up briefly the argument he develops at length in his three anti-miaphysite works: we perceive in the Christ of the Gospels two contrasting realities, two utterly different ways of being and behaving—the human and the divine. If each of them is real—if we are to avoid Docetism, on the one hand, and secular naturalism, on the other—we must acknowledge the continuing operation in Christ of two complete essences, two natures. Yet Christ is himself clearly one agent, one subject of predication, one concrete, numerable, and nameable individual: one hypostasis and one *prosōpon*, in the terms of fifth-century philosophical analysis. So the union of his two living elements is not just a union of willing or a coincidence of accidental qualities; it is a union in one acting individual of two complete and distinct natures, two essences, both of which the individual inhabits and "uses" as his own.

Leontius's favorite formulation of the union is not, as one might expect, that of ἕνωσις καθ' ὑπόστασιν—union with respect to the hypostasis, which would be favored by the Second Council of Constantinople and later—but ἕνωσις κατ' οὐσίαν or ἕνωσις οὐσιωδής. It is not, he seems to imply, simply a union in appearance or behavior, nor is it the kind of organic union that fuses two previously distinct beings into a new, single, amalgamated agent, with its own composite definition. It is rather the real, mutually engaging unity of two ways of being, which remain distinct yet inseparable, mutually complementary, in the life of a single individual. Leontius writes, in his *Solutions to the Arguments of Severus*:

> The middle way between these [namely, between a union merely by relationship and a union by substantial mixture]—unconfused and inseparable union—recognizes that each element in the union remains undiminished in its own individual character, because it is unchangeable; but it holds them both to be common, and to belong to one subject, because of that very union of essences. So that what is properly characteristic of each is common to the whole, and what belongs to the whole is common to each, because of the unconfused particularity of the same whole in each. For there would not be an exchange of characteristics, if the peculiar character of each did not remain undisturbed, even in their union.
>
> This, then, is the kind of union [we are speaking of]: more unitive than the kind that completely divides, but richer than the kind that completely confuses, so that it neither makes the elements that are united completely the same as each other, nor leaves them wholly other. If, then, a union of this kind shows its product to be neither wholly the same nor wholly different, we must investigate how it is the same, and how different. True belief recognizes the sameness [to be] in the hypostasis, the difference in the nature; for "it is the opposite of [the way it is] in the Trinity," according to St Gregory [of Nazianzus].[29]

The ontological paradox Leontius is trying to capture here—in all its emphasis on the real unity of the natures in Christ, and on the "richness" of their uneven integration—belongs, he seems to be arguing, to the heart of orthodox Christology, as proclaimed at Chalcedon.

* * *

29. Cf. Leontius of Byzantium, *Epilyseis* 8 (ed. Daley 302.15–304.10).

In any theoretical writing, but particularly in the writing of such a careful and subtle thinker as Leontius, what one does not say—what one apparently avoids saying—is often as important for later understanding of the argument as what one says. So we must notice, I suggest, that while Leontius spends a great deal of time and argument showing how Christ exists both as one hypostasis and as two distinct, utterly incomparable natures, he nowhere explicitly and in his own name identifies that one hypostasis with the Logos, as John of Damascus and the later orthodox tradition would do. He also seems, as we have suggested, not to be primarily concerned with the consciousness or the subjectivity of Christ. The hypostasis of the incarnate Word, as earlier scholars have observed,[30] is conceived by Leontius and most of his contemporaries as a logical rather than an anthropological entity: the bearer of predicates, the countable unit, rather than God's intelligence embodied in a human mind and human flesh. Leontius hardly ever goes beyond questions of the one and the many, of individuals and classes, to look "inside" Christ and reflect on who he is. Perhaps this was simply the discreet silence of diplomacy; still, it is important to realize that while he does not expand his thoughts on the inner human experience of Christ, as Theodore of Mopsuestia had done,[31] or as Maximus later would do, he also avoids identifying that inner experience in quasi-Apollinarian fashion, simply as the operation of "the mind of God." His description of the person of Christ is, in the end, as symmetrical, as inexplicit, as cautious as the formula of Chalcedon itself.

Perhaps the clearest indication of where Leontius really stands comes in Question 2 of the *Contra Nestorianos et Eutychianos*, where—reflecting on the use of the human soul-body composite as an analogy for the ontological union of two complete natures in Christ—he writes:

30. See, for instance, V. Grumel, "Léonce de Byzance," in DTC 9/1 (Paris 1926), 400–426, especially cols. 406–407; Grillmeier (with Hainthaler), *Christ in Christian Tradition* II/2 (above, n. 17), 192.

31. It is worth remembering that Leontius reserves his most vituperative polemics for Theodore, in his treatise *Deprehensio et Triumphus super Nestorianos*, even though his own emphasis on the metaphysical balance of the person of Christ seems closer to the Antiochene than to the Cyrillian way of conceiving him. Perhaps, as Marcel Richard once suggested, that treatise was more a defensive smokescreen than an exposition of Leontius's real conception of Christ; see M. Richard, "Léonce de Byzance était-il origéniste?," *REByz* 5 (1947) 31–66, esp. 43–44 (= *Opera Minora* II, no. 57).

> The Logos is complete and perfect, and beyond all perfection; so, too, the human soul is complete, as far as the definition of its existence[32] goes [i.e., in what we understand as its substance or nature]. But even though he is complete as God, the Logos is not the complete Christ, unless the humanity is joined together with him; nor is the soul a complete human being, even though it has a complete essence, unless the body is understood to be in conjunction with it.[33]

Here and throughout his works, Leontius distinguishes himself by beginning his Christological reflections not with God, with the eternal Logos and the story of his gracious intervention in human history, but with the divine *fait accompli* of Jesus Christ, whom we know, through the Gospels, to be "with us" as both God and a human being. It is almost as if Leontius were saying: the concrete hypostasis we see acting in the Gospels, what we call today the person Jesus Christ, is at his core neither simply divine nor simply human, even though he exists and acts fully as God, eternally, and now fully as a man; being human or divine, after all, is in itself a matter of nature, of substance, not of person or hypostasis. The "one hypostasis" we see—the unit, the subject of attributes, and also the acting, conscious, individual whom we call the "Christ"—is both God and human, both Jesus of Nazareth" and "Logos" by name. The purpose of Chalcedonian Christology, and of all our human philosophizing about him, is first of all to keep us from over-simplifying, and so lessening, the "richness" of that complex, saving union.

32. Πρὸς τὸν ὅρον τῆς ὑπάρξεως (ed. Daley 138.13).

33. Cf. Leontius of Byzantium, *Contra Nestorianos et Eutychianos* 2 (ed. Daley 138.12–16). See also his *Deprehensio et Triumphus super Nestorianos* 42, where he describes the "manner of the union" in Christ as "having come to be essentially (οὐσιωδῶς) but not relationally (οὐ σχετικῶς)—in such a way that the Logos should be in the perfect humanity [of Christ] what 'the inner human' is in us, to use the words of the Apostle (Rom 7.22; Eph 3.16): subsistent along with it, and contributing to the definition of the whole [Christ] after the union" (ed. Daley 442.13–445.3).

14 Nature and the "Mode of Union"

Late Patristic Models for the Personal Unity of Christ

One of the older colleges of the University of Oxford—the one which still, more than six centuries after its foundation, characteristically goes by the name of "New College"—bears on its coat of arms a medieval English proverb which apparently was the motto of its fourteenth-century founder, Bishop William of Wykeham: "Maners Makyth Man." The bishop was surely not trying to remind future generations of undergraduates of the importance of writing thank-you notes promptly and passing the port to the left; "manners," in this somewhat archaic usage, clearly means something closer to "virtue" or "good character," something akin to the Latin word *mores*—in the words of the *Oxford English Dictionary*, "a person's habitual behaviour or conduct, especially in reference to its moral aspect." It may not be too much of an exaggeration to say that behind this phrase lies a whole anthropology, a whole metaphysics of what it is to be human: as free and intelligent beings, we are not simply the products of instinct or of the mechanical forces of our nature, not fully definable by dispassionate observation or philosophical analysis; we are formed, made human, made *persons* in the fullest sense by our choices and habits, and by the patterns in our relationships to others that define moral character.

We have gathered in this "summit" conference to reflect on the significance, for the Church and for human thought, of the Christian doctrine of the incarnation: the fundamental conviction of Christian faith that in Jesus

---

Parts of this chapter, in earlier versions, were given as a paper to the North American Patristic Society (Chicago: May, 1996), and to the Thirteenth International Conference on Patristic Studies (Oxford: August, 1999).

of Nazareth God's eternal, personally substantial Word "became flesh and dwelt among us, and we have seen his glory . . ." (John 1:14). What I propose to consider here, as a student of early Christian theology, is thus not so much anthropology as Christology. More specifically, I want to call attention to a continuing pattern of reflection on the ontological makeup and identity of Christ, which developed in Greek theology during the four centuries after the Council of Nicaea and which seems to have rested on the assumption that the concrete being of any individual subject—what was called the *hypostasis*—is primarily to be defined not by nouns and verbs, but by adverbs: not in terms of the universal concept that identified its substance, in other words, or of the range of possible functioning that was called its "nature," but rather in terms of its "manner" or "mode" of being, of the way it realized its natural potential, the source and style of its origin, the web of relationships it formed with others, and all the other particular, historically contingent characteristics that identified that individual unmistakably as itself. My point here is that as the mainstream Greek Fathers, from the Cappadocians to John of Damascus, came more and more to describe the mystery of the person of Christ, at once divine and human, in the same terms they had come to use to describe the three persons who comprise the divine Mystery itself—οὐσία and φύσις, ὑπόστασις and πρόσωπον—they came to realize that the characteristics that were seen to be the key for distinguishing the persons of the Trinity—not their nature as God, but their origin, their "mode of existing" or of coming-to-be (τρόπος τῆς ὑπάρξεως), their relationships to each other—could also usefully be employed for giving an account of the uniqueness and inner coherence of the person of Christ, in the "mode of union" by which the reality of God and the human reality shaped, expressed, and conditioned each other in the life and work, the concrete existence, of Jesus.

Admittedly, the technicalities of the ancient vocabulary for the Mystery of God's being, and of God's presence in the world through Jesus, can strike us today as impenetrably arcane. Still, a closer look at the formation and use of this ancient terminology can help us understand better, I think, that what these terms were meant to convey about Christ was less rigidly abstract, less schematic, and less far removed from our own experience of historical existence than is often supposed. To put this chapter's thesis simply: for at least a central strand in Greek patristic tradition, just as *who* Father, Son, and Holy Spirit are is grounded in *how* they take their origin from each other and are related to each other, so it was the "how" of Jesus—how he came to be, how he acted—that revealed and even grounded the reality of who he was and what he was, and that serves for us as an efficacious model of how we are called to live and what we are called to be. Let us try, in broad strokes at least, to sketch out the meaning and development of this family of words and phrases that came to assume a growing importance in the development of classical Christology.

I. Leontius and the Mode of Union

"The mode of union," writes Leontius of Byzantium about the person of Christ, shortly before the middle of the sixth century, "rather than the intelligible structure [λόγος] of nature, contains the great mystery of our religion." Here and in several other places throughout his six extant controversial treatises, Leontius insists that "union and nature are not the same thing,"[1] and says that he will focus his own reflections not on the two natures or substances themselves, which Christian faith confesses to be joined in Christ, but on their "mode of union" (τρόπος τῆς ἑνώσεως).[2] Although his reflections on that union may seem, to a modern reader, to be immersed to the point of unintelligibility in technical detail, Leontius himself is passionately convinced that this is one of the crucial, overarching issues in the christological disputes of his day. "What is under discussion," he writes, "is not simply a matter of phrasing, but the modality of the whole mystery revealed in Christ: a mode of union, namely, that has come into being in a substantial, and not simply a relational, way, so that the Word is, within a complete humanity, what 'the inner person,' in the Apostle's words, is in each of us—co-existing, and contributing after the union to the definition of the whole person . . ."[3] The chief issue in Christology during that embattled century after Chalcedon, in other words, is for Leontius not the nature of the God who has appeared in Christ, nor the natural constitution of the human person as *capax Dei*, but the manner in which those utterly distinct realities, joined in the one we confess to be Son of God, work together to form a single, concrete, contingent, historical individual: "Let us, then," he writes, "investigate the mode of union and the product [ἀποτέλεσμα] of it."[4]

1. *Contra Nestorianos et Eutychianos* (henceforth *CNE*), 5 (1293A): "That which is said to be one by union is not the same as that which is one by nature . . ."; *Epaporemata* (henceforth *Epap*), 26 (1909 D): ". . . union and nature are not the same."

2. *CNE* 7 (1297C); *Epil.* 8 (1940A, D; 1944D); *Deprehensio et triumphus super Nestorianos* (henceforth *DTN*), 42 (1380C).

3. *DTN* 42 (1380BC).

4. *Epil.* 8 (1940C). For a similar insistence that readers focus their attention not

Leontius's method of christological inquiry, reduced to its elements, is to begin not with a consideration of divinity in itself and humanity in itself, or with the related problem of how divine being and divine generation might differ from their human analogues; rather, he insists, we must begin from the concrete, historical Christ, the product of the incarnation, and ask how one can conceive the "mode of union" that brings to reality Christ's complex existence as a person.[5] In Leontius's view, the Chalcedonian formulation of the person of Christ as one hypostasis, one concrete individual, existing simultaneously in two real and fully operational natures, is the only way to avoid "the way of division" and "the way of confusion," and to follow instead "the middle [and therefore correct!] way . . . [of] unconfused and inseparable union."[6] "This kind of union," he remarks a few lines later—in an unacknowledged paraphrase of a remark of Gregory Nazianzen's on the Trinity—"is more unitive than one of completely divided things, yet richer than one of completely confused things; it does not make the elements united completely the same as each other, nor completely different."[7] In the very difference of the elements united in Christ, in fact—in the paradoxical and unique heterogeneity of Christ's single person—Leontius sees something central to the saving mystery of the incarnation; if there were not "something incommunicable in the union, rooted in the very greatness of the divine nature," he writes, "there would be no condescension in the divine love for humanity, but only a natural joining of what is lofty with what is humble."[8] To be good news, in other words, our language and our thoughts about Christ must convey the miraculous character, the wonder, of the *way* God has chosen to meet us in human terms.

simply on the language used for Christ, but on Christ as a "thing" (πρᾶγμα), see his anti-Chalcedonian contemporary, John Philoponus, *Diaetetes*, frag. 2, in Nicetas Choniates, *Panoplia dogmatica* (PG 140.56B).

5. See esp. *Epil.* 8 (1940C, 1941B).

6. *Epil.* 8 (1941A).

7. *Epil.* 8 (1941B); cf. Gregory Nazianzen, *Or.* 34. 8 (SC 308, 213, lines 14–15): the reality of God "is more united than beings which are totally divisible, but richer than things that are completely unitary."

8. *Epil.* 8 (1940A). An ancient scholion in a 10th-cent. MS of Leontius's works at this point underscores the importance accorded to this assertion by Byzantine scholars: "We speak the truth when we say that the mode of union is not realized by the principle of natural necessity, but solely by the principle of [God's] love for humanity." The fact that neither the nature of God nor the nature of humanity, taken in themselves, can give us a satisfactory explanation of how we are saved in Christ confirms the fact that it is not something "natural," but is a free gift of divine love.

Leontius's own approach to explaining the Chalcedonian paradox is to develop more fully the Cappadocian terminology of substance and individual, which had been designed to facilitate discourse on the Trinity: substance (οὐσία) and nature (φύσις) refer, he insists, to the being and operation of things at their universal or general level, to the intelligible perfection or form in which many individuals normally participate; "hypostasis" and "person" (πρόσωπον) refer to the being and perceptible role of a concrete, historically identifiable individual, who participates—in order to be intelligible and real—in one or more universal substances, but who is marked off as a particular being, made eligible for a proper name, by his or her (or even its) unique pattern of accidental characteristics.[9] In a painstaking exposition of the interlocking relationships that bind concrete individuals together within a generic substance, or link generic substances within a single individual, Leontius recasts the traditional use of the soul-body relationship in the human person as an analogy for the incarnation of the Word by suggesting, in effect, that *every* human being is a remarkable "hypostatic union" of two irreducibly different natures,[10] joined by an act of divine power into a single historic, existential unity that allows its different levels of being to remain intact and operative in themselves.[11]

Leontius draws help here from the Neoplatonic understanding of the Aristotelian category of relationship (τὸ πρός τι, σχέσις), especially as it is used by Porphyry and Nemesius of Emesa to explain how a soul can be dynamically and ontologically united with a body without loss of its own transcendence.[12] In doing so, he takes pains to insist that the union of natures or substances in Christ is something "substantial" and not merely "relational,"[13]

9. See esp. *CNE* 1 (1280A). In the first seven testimonia of the florilegium appended to this treatise, Leontius offers as his sources various well-known passages of the works of Basil and Gregory Nazianzen that defined these terms for use in talking about God from a Nicene perspective.

10. See esp. *CNE* 4 (1285C–9B); *CNE* 7 (1301C–4C). It is interesting, if puzzling, to note that Leontius generally avoids the term "hypostatic union" (ἕνωσις καθ' ὑπόστασιν, ἕνωσις ὑποστατική), perhaps simply because it was favored by the anti-Chalcedonian and "neo-Chalcedonian" parties of his time. He only uses the phrase twice on his own (*CNE*, preface to florilegium [1308C]; *Contra Aphthartodocetas* [henceforth *CA*; 1384 D]), and prefers to speak of the union in Christ as "substantial" (οὐσιωδής) or a "union according to substance" (ἕνωσις κατ' οὐσίαν): see, e.g., *CNE* 7 (1300A).

11. *Epil.* 8 (1940A).

12. See my article "A Richer Union: Leontius of Byzantium and the Relationship of Human and Divine in Christ," *Studia Patristica* 24 (1992), 239–65.

13. *Epil.* 4 (1925C); *Epil.* 8 (1940D). At the end of *CA* (1353A), he refers to the "organic [συμφυσῆς] union" of the Word with the full humanity of Jesus; in *DTN* 42 (1380D), he

even though it is itself, ultimately, an ontological relationship between substances that are complete in themselves and incapable of confusion. The concept of *relationship* had generally been understood, in the Aristotelian tradition, as the most extrinsic kind of accident,[14] and was doubtless still freighted with overtones of metaphysical "distance" in the minds of many, despite the efforts of some of the Neoplatonists to see in certain kinds of relationship, at least, a real sharing of being.[15] For Leontius, the "substantial relationship" of union between the divine Logos and the human nature of Christ is precisely *not* a "relationship that divides," like a union simply in grace or in will, or a mere expression of divine benevolence towards the man Jesus.[16] Hence the crucial importance for him, when explaining the Chalcedonian conception of Christ, to stress that a union of two different substances in one hypostasis, although not "natural" in that it is not automatically produced by those substances' natural functioning, is nevertheless a union of real ontological value, resulting in a real personal identity. In such a composite hypostasis, the two separate natures "receive/together, in one another, a common share in being [κοινωνία τοῦ εἶναι],"[17] since the hypostasis is itself created by "their mutually inherent life" (ἡ ἀλληλοῦχος ζωή).[18]

---

insists that "the Fathers" taught that the union "came to be in a substantial way, but you [the Nestorians] speak of one that is relative and moral [σχετικὴν καὶ γνωμικήν]."

14. See Aristotle, *Categories* 7; Alexander of Aphrodisias, *Quaestiones naturales et morales*, 2.9 (ed. I. Bruns, *Supplementum Aristotelicum*, 2/7 (Berlin: G. Reimer, 1892), 54.20–31); Olympiodorus, *In Cat.* 4: *Commentatores in Aristotelem Graeci* (henceforth *CAG*), 12/1 (ed. A. Busse; Berlin, G. Reimer, 1902) 54.4–26; Elias, *Prolegomena* 11: *CAG* 18/1 (ed. A. Busse; Berlin: G. Reimer, 1900), 29.8–18.

15. See esp. Simplicius, *In Cat.* 7: *CAG* 8 (ed. C. Kalbfleisch: Berlin, G. Reimer, 1907), 169.1–173.32. See also Plotinus, *Ennead* 6.1.6. Perhaps with this shift of meaning in mind, the Cappadocians were prepared to speak of the defining relationships between Father, Son, and Holy Spirit as σχέσεις, too: e.g., Gregory of Nazianzus, *Or.* 29.16; *Or.* 31.9; Gregory of Nyssa, *Ref. Conf. Eun.* (Werner Jaeger et al., *Gregorii Nysseni Opera*, 10 vols. (Leiden: Brill, 1960–1990), 2.319.1–3, hereafter *GNO*); cf. Ps.-Athanasius, *Dialogue on the Trinity* 1.25 (PG 28.1156A). For a brief discussion, see F. Heinzer, *Gottes Sohn als Mensch*, Paradosis 26 (Fribourg: Universitätsverlag, 1980), 47–48.

16. *CNE* 7 (1305C).

17. *CNE* 1 (1280A); cf. *Epil.* 1 (1917D). Late antique philosophers occasionally used κοινωνία, "participation," "communion," as a synonym for ἕνωσις: see Simplicius, *In Cat.* 7: *CAG* 8 (ed. Kalbfleisch), 169.19–20; John Philoponus, *In de anima*: *CAG* 15 (ed. M. Hayduck: Berlin: G. Reimer, 1897), 471.28–29. Origen, however, in his *Contra Celsum*, contrasts the terms, saying that the soul of Christ was united to God "not just by κοινωνία, but by union (ἕνωσις) and intermingling (ἀνάκρασις)": 3.41 (SC 136, 96.9).

18. *CNE* 4 (1288D). Neoplatonic philosophers often used the word ἀλληλουχία, "mu-

The twenty-sixth of Leontius's *Hypothetical Propositions* (*Epaporemata*) against Severus of Antioch and other early sixth-century opponents of Chalcedon puts his conception of the distinctive ontological structure of composite hypostases clearly:

> If all consubstantial beings [ὁμοούσια] are joined together by the category of nature, and therefore are called "one nature," while beings of different substance [ἑτερούσια] are habitually joined by union and *not* by nature, and if union and nature are not the same, then the product coming from both is not the same. But if what nature joins together is called "one nature," what is joined together by union will be said to be one in hypostasis, but *not* in nature and substance.[19]

In the person of Christ, in other words, as in all composite hypostases, it is precisely "union, not nature," that serves as the foundation of the subject's inner identity.

II. Mode of Union: Its Philosophical and Theological Background

Given the emphasis this sixth-century defender of the Chalcedonian definition places, then, on the distinction between union and nature and the importance of the "mode of union" in the ontology of the person and in the constitution of Christ, as well as the continuing use of this phrase by such later orthodox figures as Maximus Confessor and John of Damascus, it seems reasonable to ask what background and context, if any, such language might have in earlier philosophical and theological discussion. *Tropos*, which at its most general simply means "manner," "mode," or "way," is used by Aristotle and Stoic writers to refer to the "forms" or figures of syllogisms, and more generally to indicate the various possible types of demonstration.[20]

---

tual inherence," to express intense organic unity. See Iamblichus, *In Nicomachi arithmeticam introductionem* (ed. Klein; Leipzig: Teubner, 1975), 7.6–7; *Theologoumena arithmeticae* (ed. de Falco; Leipzig: Teubner, 1922), 20. 16–17; Dexippus, *In Aristotelis Categorias commentarium*: *CAG* 4/2 (ed. A. Busse; Berlin; G. Reimer, 1888), 66.25–26; Simplicius, *In Cat.* 8: *CAG* 8 (ed. Kalbfleisch) 127.19–21.

19. *Epap* 26 (1909D).

20. See, e.g., Aristotle, *Pr. anal.* $43^{a}10$; $45^{a}4$; $65^{a}18$; *Post. anal.* $82^{b}15$; *De an.* $402^{a}19$; Chrysippus: H. von Arnim, *Stoicorum Veterum Fragmenta*, 2. 81.19–25; 82.20–83.10; the school of Crinis: ibid., 3. 269.12–23.

Aristotle also uses the word more widely, to refer to the "circumstances" of the natural behavior of living things, "the how and where and when,"[21] as well as to character or habit, "the condition of a soul brought about by custom."[22] It seems to have been in the works of the fifth- and sixth-century Athenian Neoplatonist Damascius that *tropos* first acquired a more ontological shading for the philosophers, signifying the attributes of the ultimate principles of being or transcendent hypostases, such as the "mode" of eternity or even the "mode" of substance itself.[23] *Henōsis* or "union" was also not a term of major metaphysical or anthropological interest for most Hellenistic philosophers. Neoplatonic Aristotle-commentators like the fourth-century Dexippus[24] or the fifth-century Syrianus[25] occasionally spoke of union as a kind of substantial relationship distinct from simple homogeneity, but it was only in the later fifth and sixth centuries that it became a major term in the metaphysical vocabulary. Damascius uses *henōsis* in a variety of senses, ranging from the formal unity of a universal class or form to higher levels of metaphysical unity, which ground both sameness and distinction in the world of experience that is, in his system, contained within Being-as-One, "the substance of all substances."[26] For his pupil Simplicius, *henōsis* always implies both a real, intelligible, single being shared by a number of elements, and an abiding distinction among them; to be recognized as such, a union must always bind together distinct realities.[27] This holds all the more true if the things united belong to wholly different levels of being; so in discussing

21. *De gen. anim.* 740^{b}22–23.

22. *De an.* 361^{b}. Damascius, in his *Life of Isidore*, frequently uses the word to denote a person's public "style" or personality: e.g., 69.3; 99.5; 109.17; 261.15.

23. *De principiis* 1.115.9; *In Parmenidem* 32.5; 177.18; 316.8–11; *In Phaedonem* 8.6; 123.7.

24. *In Cat.* 3, 1.1 = *CAG* 4/2, 65.25.

25. *In Met.* B 4 = *CAG* 6/1 (ed. G. Kroll; Berlin: G. Reimer, 1902), 43.18. See also *In Met.* B 2: *CAG* 6/1, 24.12–14, where Syrianus says that the intellectual life of the stars enjoys an "unconfused union" and a "ceaseless sharing" with other intelligible substances.

26. *De principiis* 1.299 (ed. L. G. Westerink and J. Combès [Paris: Les Belles Lettres, 1989], 3. 17). For Damascius, the whole realm of actuality consists of entities formed by a constant tension between the opposed principles of the One and the Many (ibid. 1.128: Westerink-Combès 2. 66): it is a "mixed" realm, where unity and multiplicity form together a kind of descending metaphysical scale of reality, reaching from the relative unity of intelligible forms to a kind of unity "which opens itself up, as it were, to distinction" (ibid. 1.206: Westerink-Combès 2. 191).

27. See, e.g., his commentary on Epictetus's *Enchiridion* (ed. F. Dübner, *Theophrasti Characteres*, Paris: Firmin Didot, 1840, 2. 100), lines 33–34: a unity comes to be "not by way of contact nor continuity nor bodily mixture, but by the joining into one of separate and indivisible forms; while their distinction remains unmixed, the whole contains each part."

Aristotle's category of "relationship," Simplicius observes that the communion (κοινωνία) of what he calls "primary" real substances with "secondary" real substances—the soul with the body, for example, or God with the mind—must be understood as something real itself, even as "hypostatic," yet not as bringing about the kind of union that exists between beings that share the same substance or nature (ὁμοούσια, ὁμοφυῆ).[28]

It was in Christian discussion of what we call the "persons" of the Trinity and the person of Christ, beginning in the second half of the fourth century, that both these terms—*tropos* and *henōsis*—took on a range of ontological meanings that eventually made them both classical and problematic. Origen, it is true, in one fragment, already uses the phrase "mode of union" to designate the ineffable mystery of "the way God took on a human body,"[29] and in the *Contra Celsum* he insists that Christ's soul and body were united with the Logos not merely by participation (κοινωνίᾳ), but by union and mingling (ἑνώσει καὶ ἀνακράσει).[30] But the widespread, reflective theological use of these terms, separately and together, began only in the later stages of the fourth-century trinitarian debates, which were also the opening stages of debate over the unity of the person of Christ. It seems, in fact, to have been Apollinarius of Laodicea, that brilliant and innovative opponent of the idea of a human soul in Christ, who coined the phrase "supreme union" (ἄκρα ἕνωσις)—later a standard christological term—to refer to the organic integrity of the Incarnate Word;[31] his disciple Timothy of Berytus further

28. *In Cat.* 7 (8, 169.16–23). Simplicius believes that the life of the mind includes a constant, undivided union between the act of knowing and the intelligible object (*In de anima*: *CAG* 11 (ed. M. Hayduck), 11.31–32; 191.12–23; 237.15–29; 243.19–20); this means that contemplation, the highest kind of knowing, is a union of the mind with the unitive basis of intelligible *reality* itself that is only a step short of complete identity (ibid. 29.2–3; 47.20–21; 67.3–7; 235.17–21; 311.36–38).

29. This is a fragment dealing with John 1:23–24, found in the catenae: E. Preuschen, GCS Origenes 4 (Leipzig: J. C. Hinrichs, 1903), 498.23–24.

30. *Contra Celsum* 3.41.8–10 (SC 136, 96).

31. See, e.g., frags. 140–42, from his *Contra Diodorum* in H. Lietzmann (ed.), *Apollinaris von Laodicea und seine Schule: Texte und Untersuchungen* (Tübingen: J. C. B. Mohr, 1904), 241, lines 3–26; also his *Professio fidei cum Jovio Episcopo* (ed. Lietzmann, 286.16–287.9: flesh of Christ is ἀκρῶς ἑνωμένη with the Word); frag. 147 (ed. Lietzmann, 246.20–28: τελειωτάτη ἕνωσις of God with his body). All these fragments are contained in Leontius of Byzantium's florilegium of passages from the Apollinarian school, *Adversus fraudes Apollinaristarum* (henceforth *AFA*)! The phrase is also used by Proclus of Constantinople—a christological "moderate"—in his *Tomus ad Antiochenos* 14 (*ACO* 4/2, 190.8), to refer to the indivisible identity of Word and human "flesh" signified by ἐγένετο in John 1:14. It reappears frequently in controversial works of the 6th and 7th centuries.

defined the phrase as meaning that the Logos and his flesh shared each other's titles and characteristics, while remaining unchanged within their own natures.[32] Apollinarius insists, in several passages of his work *Against Diodore*, that it was the union of Jesus's flesh to the Word, not the nature of his flesh itself, that allows us truly to call that flesh divine.[33] Because it is divine through union, and not itself consubstantial with the Word, the flesh of Christ can retain its own distinctive nature while joined to the Word, in Apollinarius's view,[34] since—as his disciple Valentinus insisted—"union does not mean consubstantiality, and if something is consubstantial there is no union; nothing is united or joined with itself, but one thing is united or joined with *another*."[35]

It was doubtless the use of this terminology by Gregory of Nyssa, however, that gave it both a clearer range of meaning and lasting influence on the orthodox tradition. Gregory, as has often been pointed out, in his attempt to refute the neo-Arian or "Eunomian" notion that the "unbegottenness" of the Father and the "begottenness" of the Son indicate two radically different beings, argued that the different "modes" or "forms of generation" predicated of the Son and the Spirit, and so implicitly of the ingenerateness of the Father, are simply three distinct "modes of existing" (τρόποι τῆς ὑπάρξεως), and do not imply ontological separation or division of activity within the single infinite, unknowable divine substance. In the first book of his *Against Eunomius*, Gregory draws on the analogy between human generation and divine generation, arguing that even among humans, different modes of coming into concrete existence—that of Adam, for instance, who was formed from the earth, and that of his son Abel, who was born in the normal way—do not mean the two individuals in question possess different substances or natures:

> The first human being and the one begotten from him each had their being in different ways—the one from the coupling of parents, the other from the formation of earth—and they are thought to be two; yet they are not separated from each other in the structure of their substance. . . . For the one and the other is each a human being, the structure of substance is common to the two of them: each is mortal, each also rational, each shares in mind

32. Timothy of Berytus, *Ad Homonium*, in Leontius, *AFA* 2 (1960 D).

33. Frag. 160 (ed. Lietzmann, 254.5–6); frag. 161 (ed. Lietzmann, 254.19–26); this is echoed by his disciple Valentinus in his *Apologia* (ed. Lietzmann, 287, 289; cited in Leontius, *AFA* [1953BC, 1956B]).

34. Frag. 161 (ed. Lietzmann, 254.25–26); frag. 112 (ed. Lietzmann, 233.30–234.10).

35. Valentinus, *Apologia*: ed. Lietzmann, 288.

> and knowledge in the same way. But if the structure of humanity, in the case of Adam and Abel, is not changed by the variation in their begetting—since neither the sequence nor the mode of their coming-to-exist introduces any alteration to their nature, but it is affirmed to be the same by the common agreement of sober people, and no one would contradict it who is not badly in need of an anti-hallucinatory drug [lit.: hellebore]—why must this unreasonable notion be artificially forced onto the divine nature?[36]

The very names of "Father" and "Son," Gregory adds, which are used by Jesus, "teach us of the unity of nature in the two subjects, with the relationship of the one to other signified both by the natural meaning of the names and by the very language of the Lord."[37]

In all his discussion of the "relationships" and "modes of existence" implied by Father-Son language, in fact, Gregory of Nyssa seems clearly to be thinking in terms of *origination*: of the particular characteristics given to a person by the conditions of his or her historical begetting. For Gregory, it seems, both "existence" and "hypostasis," as terms marking the particularity of individual humans—and so applicable, by analogy, to the persons in the Trinity—refer to the distinctive character that is rooted in the particular *origin* of each individual: in a person's ancestry and family relationships.[38] In a passage in his *Antirrhetikos against Apollinarius*, in fact, Gregory confirms the fact that he conceives of "hypostatic" or individual being, in the case of humans, at least, primarily as being determined by one's origin; after reflecting on the unique way in which Jesus was conceived, by divine power in the womb of the Virgin, he concludes:

> In this way the truly "new human being" was created, the first and only one to reveal such a mode of hypostasis [τὸν τοιτοῦτον τρόπον τῆς ὑποστάσεως] in his own case: created according to God and not in the human way, with the divine power pervading the whole nature of the mixture on an

36. *Contra Eunomium* 1.496–97 = *GNO* 1, 169.20–170.12. For references to the different "modes of begetting" in the Trinity, see *C. Eun.* 3.32 (*GNO* 2, 197.7); *Refutatio confessionis Eunomii* 91 (*GNO* 2, 349.18); "forms of begetting": *C. Eun.* 3.37 (*GNO* 2, 199.11); *Ref. conf. Eun.* 94 (*GNO* 2, 351.5).

37. *C. Eun.* 1.498 (*GNO* 1, 170.13–17).

38. See *C. Eun.* 3.36 (*GNO* 2, 198.16–17). On the notion of ὕπαρξις in Stoic philosophy, as suggesting not simply "existence" but *caused* existence, "the actuality of an effect," see P. Hadot, "Zur Vorgeschichte des Begriffs 'Existenz,' ὑπάρχειν bei den Stoikern," *Archiv für Begriffsgeschichte* 13 (1969), 115–27; cf. F. Heinzer, *Gottes Sohn als Mensch*, 33–39.

> equal basis [with the human], so that neither part (I mean, soul and body) lacks a share in divinity, but it is, in all likelihood, present in both in the way that is suitable and appropriate.[39]

Each of us is a unique person in human history, Gregory seems to be saying, because we have each come into existence in a unique way; in Christ's case, that mode of origin—birth from a virgin, by the power of the Holy Spirit—is both human and divine. As for union, *henōsis*, Gregory of Nyssa shows a tendency similar to that of the authors we have already discussed, taking it always to signify both oneness and abiding distinction. Defending his own tendency, in speaking of the Mystery of Christ, to equate the two phrases "union [of the Word] with flesh" and "assumption of a human being," Gregory argues: "'Union,' after all, is *with* something, and 'assumption,' surely, is *of* something; each signifies a relation [*schesis*] to something else—the one who assumes is united to what is assumed, and that which is united is united by the act of assumption."[40] In a fragment of a lost letter, Gregory even anticipates Leontius's analysis of the difference between the unity of a natural or universal essence, an οὐσία, and the existential unity of a concrete individual who may be composed of more than one such essence: "Things which are of the same substance [*homoousia*] have achieved identity, but it is the opposite with things of different substances. For if both are one by an ineffable union, still they are not so by nature, for they remain unchanged. Christ, then, who exists as two natures, is truly recognized in them, but possesses a single *persona* of sonship."[41]

In one passage of his *Catechetical Discourse*, Gregory actually anticipates Leontius's phrase, "mode of union" (τρόπος τῆς ἑνώσεως), when trying to explain the constitution of the person of Christ. It is no more absurd, he argues, to think of the transcendent spiritual substance of God being naturally united to a limited, circumscribed creature who is both spirit and matter than it is to consider the union of the human soul with its body. He writes:

39. *Antirrh. adv. Apol.*: *GNO* 3/1, 223.20–224.5. This is precisely a line of approach to the distinctive character of the person of Christ that Leontius later argues we must avoid. See pp. 307–8, above.

40. *Antirrh. adv. Apol.*: *GNO* 3/1, 184.27–30. For other statements of a similar nature, see *C. Eun.* 3.63 (*GNO* 2, 130.11–18); 3.69 (= *GNO* 2, 133.5–7).

41. *Letter to the Monk Philip*, quoted by John of Damascus, *Contra Jacobitas* 112 (ed. B. Kotter, *Die Schriften des Johannes von Damaskos* [Berlin: De Gruyter, 1981], 4. 149.3–6). One might even translate the final phrase, "plays a single role of Sonship."

> If the manner in which your soul is joined to your body is a mystery, you must certainly not imagine this former question is within your grasp. In the one case, while we believe the soul to be something different from the body because on leaving the flesh it renders it dead and inactive, we are ignorant of the manner of the union. Similarly, in the other case we realize that the divine nature, by its greater majesty, differs from that which is mortal and perishable; but we are unable to detect the manner of the mixture.[42]

Gregory's description, in this passage, of the soul's union with the body yields unmistakable resonances with contemporary Neoplatonic accounts of the human composite, particularly that in Porphyry's *Sentences*.[43] The comparison of this union of spiritual and material to the "manner of union" in the incarnation, however, was also explicitly made by Gregory's Christian contemporary, Nemesius of Emesa—whom Gregory may have known personally—in his treatise *On Human Nature*.[44] In an oft-cited passage in the third chapter of this work, Nemesius develops his description of the soul's union with the body much more fully than Gregory had needed to do, yet along similar lines. Rejecting all the forms of physical "mixture," previously classified by the Stoics, as inadequate models for conceiving how the spiritual soul and the material body can organically comprise a single person, Nemesius argues that the two are united

42. *Oratio Catechetica* 11 = *GNO* 3/4, 39.13–22; trans. Cyril G. Richardson, in E. R. Hardy (ed.), *The Christology of the Later Fathers*, Library of Christian Classics 2 (London: SCM Press, 1954), 288 (trans. corrected). Later on in the work, Gregory uses the language of physical "mixture" to contrast the unique unity of God with the humanity of Christ, on the one hand, and God's general, sustaining presence in us and in all creation, on the other. Different as they are, both kinds of presence are real. "For even if the manner of God's presence in us is not the same as this [the incarnation], it is at any rate admitted that he is equally present with us in both cases. In the one, he is united to us insofar as he sustains nature in being; in the other, he is mixed with what is ours, so that what is ours may become divine by being mixed in with the divine . . ." (ibid. 25 = *GNO* 3/4, 64.3–9; trans. mine).

43. See *Sententiae ad intelligibilia ducentes* 27–29 (ed. E. Lamberz [Leipzig: Teubner, 1975], 16–20).

44. On possible contacts between Nemesius and Gregory Nazianzen, see L. Le Nain de Tillemont, *Mémoires pour servir à l'histoire ecclésiastique des six premiers siècles* (2nd ed.; Paris: Charles Robustel, 1714), 9. 541, 607. In fact, chs. 2–3 of his *De natura hominis* were at times attributed to Gregory of Nyssa in the early Byzantine period: see J. Dräseke, "Ein Testimonium Ignatianum," *Zeitschrift für wissenschaftliche Theologie* 46 (1903), 505–12, esp. 506–8. For a description of the Neoplatonic theory of the transcendent union of spiritual and material substances in a single subject, as represented in the works of Porphyry and Nemesius, see Daley, "A Richer Union," 254–56.

> in a kind of relationship, and by presence, as God is said to be present in us. For we say that the soul is bound by the body in a kind of relationship, and by a relative inclination and attitude, just as we say the lover is bound by the beloved: not in a bodily or spatial way, but by way of relationship [κατὰ σχέσιν].[45]

This model of body-soul unity, Nemesius goes on to say, can be seen "in a purer form" in the relationship of the divine Word to the human being Jesus—"purer," perhaps, because while the soul is enhanced in its powers, yet also made to suffer new limitations and passions, through its union with the body, the Word in the incarnation remains unchanged and unlimited, giving the man Jesus a share in its divinity but itself remaining untouched by his bodily variability weaknesses.[46] So "this mode of mixture or union is something new," Nemesius observes; yet it is not simply a matter of God's "good pleasure, as some respected people believe, but *nature* is its cause," since the fact that the two substances preserve their integrity as they do is due to the "proper nature of God."[47]

Nemesius's way of conceiving the "manner of union" of the incarnation in terms of relationship and causal operation, rather than physical presence or spatial mixture, seems itself to have played a role, as we have already mentioned, in shaping Leontius's explanation of how two different natures can be united without amalgamation or hybridization in a single hypostasis; in this way, this explanation entered the later tradition of orthodox Christology.[48] Leontius's explicit insistence, however, against Nemesius, that

45. *De natura hominis* 3. I have used here the edition of B. Einarson, which is to appear in the *Corpus medicorum Graecorum*, as it is presently available in the databank *Thesaurus linguae Graecae*. See also the annotated and corrected text of this chapter in R. Arnou, *De "Platonismo" Patrum*, Textus et documenta, ser. theol. xxi (Rome: Gregorian University Press, 1935), 54–55; trans W. Telfer, *Cyril of Jerusalem and Nemesius of Emesa*, Library of Christian Classics 4 (Philadelphia: Westminster Press, 1955), 299. See also Alberto Siclari, *L'Antropologia di Nemesio di Emesa* (Padua: La Garangola, 1974), 115–37.

46. Nemesius of Emesa, *De natura hominis* 3.

47. Ibid.

48. For Leontius's use of an argument of Porphyry's, summarized in this chapter of Nemesius's work, see A. Grillmeier, "Die anthropologische-christologische Sprache des Leontius von Byzanz und ihre Beziehung zu den *Symmikta Zetemata* des Neuplatonikers Porphyrius," in H. Eisenberger (ed.), *Hermeneumata: Festschrift für Hadwig Hörner zum sechszigten Geburtstag* (Heidelberg: Winter, 1990), 61–72 (= Grillmeier, *Fragmente zur Christologie* [Freiburg: Herder, 1997], 264–76); see also Grillmeier, *Jesus der Christus* (Freiburg im Breisgau, Basel, Vienna: Herder, 1979), 2/2. 211–12. For the parallelism between Nemesius's

"union and nature are *not* the same thing," and that the internal cohesion of the person of Christ is due to union *rather than* to nature, seems to have been more directly influenced by the controversies between the Antiochene theologians and Cyril of Alexandria that surrounded the great synods of the early fifth century.

In his *Eighth Catechetical Homily*, for instance, Theodore of Mopsuestia takes great pains to distinguish in Christ between the natures of the "assuming" divine Son and of the "assumed man," the "form of a servant" in which the Son worked our salvation. Theodore continues:

> The distinction between the natures does not annul the exact conjunction[49] nor does the exact conjunction destroy the distinction between the natures, but the natures remain in their respective existence while separated, and the conjunction remains intact because the one who was assumed is united in honour and glory with the one who assumed, according to the will of the one who assumed him. . . . The fact that a husband and wife are "one flesh" does not impede them from being two. Indeed, they will remain two because they are two, but they are one because they are also one and not two. In this same way here [in the incarnation] they are two by nature and one by conjunction: two by nature, because there is a great difference between the natures, and one by conjunction because the adoration offered to the one who has been assumed is not divided from that offered to the one who assumed him, since he [the one assumed] is the temple, from which it is not possible for the one who dwells in it to depart.[50]

Anyone familiar with the christological controversies of the early fifth century will easily hear in the passage the tinkling of the Antiochene bells that were to alarm Cyril of Alexandria, with his more organic and integrated

---

christological argument and the definition of Chalcedon, see E. Fortin, "The *Definitio Fidei* of Chalcedon and Its Philosophical Sources," *Studia Patristica* 5 (Berlin: Akademie-Verlag, 1962), 489–98, esp. 493; and L. Abramowski, "Συνάφεια und ἀσύγχυτος ἕνωσις als Bezeichnung für trinitarische und christologische Einheit," *Drei christologische Untersuchungen* (Berlin and New York: De Gruyter, 1981), 63–109, esp. 63–70.

49. In the Syriac text, *naqiputha hatittha*; this was a standard expression used in the later "Nestorian" tradition to express the union of natures in Christ, and probably translates the Greek ἄκρα συνάφεια, a self-consciously diphysite alternative to Apollinarius's ἄκρα ἕνωσις.

50. Theodore of Mopsuestia, *Catechetical Homily* 8.13–14 (ed. Raymond Tonneau and Robert Devreesse, Studi e Testi [Vatican City: Vatican Apostolic Library, 1949], 204–7; trans. A. Mingana, *Woodbrooke Studies* [Cambridge: Heffer, 1933], 5. 89–90 [altered]).

understanding of Christ: the seemingly weak term "conjunction" (συνάφεια); union explained primarily in terms of will; union attested simply by our common honor and adoration; the analogy of the union of husband and wife. So Cyril's famous "Third Letter" to the patriarch Nestorius, written in the autumn of 430, explicitly rejects terminology that presents the union of God and humanity in Christ primarily in terms of dignity, authority, or an extrinsically conceived "indwelling," parallel to the way in which Christ or the Spirit dwells in the hearts of the saints.[51] Nothing short of "union by nature" (ἕνωσις φυσική, ἕνωσις κατὰ φύσιν) can express for Cyril the inner bond between the Word and his own humanity.

> For equality of honor does not unite the natures. Peter and John, for instance, are of equal honor with each other, as both apostles and holy disciples, but the two are not made into one. Nor do we think of the mode of conjunction as being by association, for this is not enough for a natural union, nor as being by a relationship of participation, in the way that we, being "joined to the Lord," as it is written, are "one spirit" with him (1 Cor 6:17). Indeed, we reject the term "conjunction" [συνάφειαν] altogether, as not sufficiently indicating the union.[52]

In the third of the celebrated anathemas which end this forceful letter, Cyril makes this point more emphatically: "If anyone divides the hypostases in the one Christ after the union, joining them only by a conjunction in dignity, or authority or power, and not rather by a coming-together in a natural union, let him be anathema."[53] A "*natural* union," in the terms of this letter and of many of Cyril's writings that poured out during the years of controversy that followed Nestorius's deposition in 431, seems to signify above all a *true* union, a union realized in ontological terms, in contrast with a merely "relational conjunction," such as each of us enjoys with God by the grace of adoptive sonship.[54] Cyril is clearly groping for terms to mark off the metaphysical uniqueness of the incarnation.

51. Ep. 17.5 (ed. Eduard Schwartz, *ACO* 1/1. 1.36.15–20).

52. Ibid.; trans. adapted from that of Hardy, *Christology of the Later Fathers*, 351.

53. Ibid., anathema, 3; Hardy, 353.

54. See *Apol. adv. Theodoretum* 3 in Philip E. Pusey (ed.), *Sancti Patris Nostri Cyrilii Archiepiscopi Alexandriae Epistolae Tres Oecumenicae* (Oxford: Clarendon Press, 1975), 4. 412.23–414.2; cf. ibid. 414.4: ἕνωσις κατὰ φύσιν means ἕνωσις οὐ σχετική, ἀλλὰ κατὰ ἀλήθειαν: also ibid. 416.16–17, 24–25; 418.3–7. See also *Expl. XII Cap.* (ed. Pusey, 246.16–17); *Apol. adv. Orientales* 3 (ed. Pusey, 286.23–24; 287.21–22; 288.3–5).

Yet it is crucial to recognize that Theodore of Mopsuestia also saw the united natures in Christ as in some way genuinely forming one reality, and that Cyril, too, remained far from asserting that union, in the case of the incarnation, means either a confusion of godhead and humanity without distinction, or the hybridization of two transcendentally different beings by some natural mechanism proper to either or both of them. In the eighth of his *Scholia on the Incarnation*, Cyril muses on the utterly mysterious nature of the union of God and an individual humanity in Emmanuel, and concludes that although "the mode of the union" is beyond our understanding, still it is not entirely "off the mark" to conceive of it in terms analogous to the union of body and soul in each of us, by which the soul "owns" the body and experiences its physical sensations and its suffering, without itself becoming body in the process.[55] In his second letter to Succensus, written perhaps somewhat earlier, between 433 and 435, Cyril affirms the dialectical character of this mode of unified being more simply:

> Understanding, then, as I said, the manner of his becoming human, we see that two natures come together with each other, without confusion and without separation, in the way of an indivisible union. For the flesh is flesh and not divinity, even though it became God's flesh. Similarly, the Word is God and not flesh, even though, in a way fitting the economy, he made the flesh his own.[56]

In his attacks on Cyril, Theodoret of Cyrus generally ignored passages such as these, and focused instead on the strongly unitive Christology of Cyril's third letter to Nestorius and its anathemas, in giving voice to all the misgivings the Antiochene tradition felt about the Alexandrian approach to the Mystery of Christ. The natural union (ἕνωσις κατὰ φύσιν) of two different things, such as the union of soul and body, which Cyril and his followers offer as a model for the incarnation, Theodoret argues in his doggedly anti-Cyrillian dialogue, *Eranistēs*, is a mutual fusion of equal ingredients, which may leave the characteristics of both elements still recognizable, but

55. *Scholia de incarnatione Unigeniti* 8 (ed. Pusey, 6. 510–14, esp. 512.3–15). Cyril explains the analogy in terms that, if anything, emphasize the distinction of the elements: "Just as the body is naturally different with regard to the soul, but one human being is formed from both, and is called such, so from the perfect hypostasis of God the Word, and from a humanity that is also perfect, according to its own structure, there is one Christ, himself existing at the same time as God and a human being" (ibid. 514.2–8).

56. Ep. 45.6 (Ep. 1 to Succensus): *ACO* 1/1. 6.153.12–20.

which by definition allows neither the guiding role.[57] Theodoret even has his Cyrillian character assert, in the course of the discussion, that the "supreme union" realized in the incarnation is what the philosophers call a "complete mixture" (κρᾶσις δι' ὅλων), the Stoic term for an irreversible physical compound.[58] Theodoret is willing to allow the continued use of the body-soul analogy in discussions of the incarnation, insofar as it represents a real unity in the midst of abiding distinction,[59] but he stresses (as Cyril himself did) that the union of natures found in Christ is also significantly different from that of body and soul, in that it is *not* a union of equal elements and is *not* forced into reality by the nature of either element (as our human union is),[60] but is rather due solely to divine grace and favor.[61] Clearly, he argues, the incarnation is a "conjunction" (συνάφεια),[62] a "union of natures" (ἕνωσις τῶν φύσεων);[63] but while it produces a single, indivisible, dynamic external form or *prosōpon*,[64] it leaves the natures of divinity and humanity in Christ "unmixed" and "unconfused."[65] Interestingly, Theodoret does not take up the more relational understanding of *hypostasis* developed by Gregory of Nyssa, as a useful point of departure for talking about the person of Christ. At times he seems to assume *hypostasis* is a synonym for "nature"; at other times he uses it—without further explanation—as the apparent equivalent of *prosōpon*, his preferred term for speaking about Christ as a single agent.[66] In the *Eranistēs*, his main contribution to christological controversy, Theodoret himself uses hypostasis-language only with reference to the persons of the Trinity.[67] And even in his discussions of the Trinity, while he uses the Cappadocian language of one *ousia* and three *hypostaseis* unreflectively, as something already canonized by use, his interest is less in the characteristics and relationships of origin that distinguish the persons in God, than in a

57. *Eranistēs* 2 (ed. G. Ettlinger; Oxford: Clarendon Press, 1975), 116.11–13; 137.31–138.3.

58. Ibid. 2 (144.35–36; 145.19); 3 (200.1–2).

59. Ibid. 2 (137.31–138.3).

60. Cyril presents this as Theodoret's critique of his own third anathema, in *Apologia contra Theodoretum* 3 (ed. Pusey, 6. 408–12).

61. *Eranistēs* 2 (137.31–138.3).

62. Ibid. 3 (190.21).

63. Ibid. 2 (122.10; 133.11–24).

64. Ibid. 3 (209.26–30).

65. Ibid. 3, syllogism 2 (257.18–28); syllogism 12 (261.1–2).

66. For a discussion of Theodoret's use of "hypostasis" language, see A. Grillmeier, *Christ in Christian Tradition* (Oxford: Mowbray, 1975), 1.489–91.

67. See *Eranistēs* 1 (64.11–13; 65.11–16, 23–24; 66.3–5); 2 (116.23–24; 117.7–10).

philosophical discussion of the attributes that mark God, as a single Mystery, off from creation.[68]

During his long years of exile, the embattled Nestorius himself struggled to give systematic form and argument to a christological position not radically different from that of his more moderate Antiochene colleagues, such as Theodoret. Although the collection of his late essays, in what is now known as the *Book of Heracleides*, remains, for literary as well as philosophical reasons, confusing and difficult to interpret, it is clear that Nestorius, too, rejected the language of "natural union" for the person of Christ as failing to do justice to the full richness of the divine initiative in the mystery of redemption. The key to Cyril's mistakes, Nestorius observes, is that his approach to the constitution of Christ's person is narrative or diachronic—"economic," a modern theologian might say—rather than analytical; it is focused on the divine initiative in salvation and on the origins and operations of the radically different components of the "person" in which God the Son historically carries out his work, rather than on the paradoxical structure of Christ's being—what Leontius would later call the *apotelesma* or "end-product" of the incarnation:[69] "You take as the starting-point of your narrative the Maker of the natures and not the *prosōpon* of union."[70] For Nestorius, as for Theodoret, what is *one* in the actual, concrete Christ is not the substance of God or the substance of humanity, let alone the natural functioning of either, but the concrete, intelligible, visible *form* in which Christ meets us: in Christ, God the Son, whose substance radiates its own set of identifying divine characteristics—exhibits its own *prosōpon* or *persona*—has "taken up" the human characteristics, qualities, and behavioral potentialities of the man Jesus by freely identifying himself with him, freely assuming through Jesus "the form of a servant." The result is a new, combined "*prosōpon* of union," which leaves the underlying substances intact and distinct, while permanently creating a new, unified, divine and human face for God.[71]

68. See esp. S.-P. Bergjan, *Theodoret von Cyrus und der Neunizänismus* (Berlin: De Gruyter, 1993), 192–95.

69. *CNE* 7 (1297C–1305C); *Epil.* 8 (1937A–1945C).

70. *Book of Heraclides* 2.1 (ed. P. Bedjan; Paris and Leipzig: Letouzey et Ané, 1910), 225; trans. G. R. Driver and L. Hodgson, *The Bazaar of Heracleides* (Oxford: Clarendon Press, 1925), 153 (modernized). For a description of Nestorius's understanding of the "natural union" of the human person, and for parallels in Stoic texts, see L. I. Scipioni, *Ricerche sulla Christologia del "Libro di Eraclide" di Nestorio*, Paradosis 11 (Fribourg: Edizioni Universitarie, 1956), 25–31.

71. See Scipioni, *Ricerche*, 80–88 for texts and interpretation.

III. Maximus the Confessor and John of Damascus

Writing in defense of the christological formula of Chalcedon in the 530s and 540s, Leontius of Byzantium, of course, faced a somewhat different situation from that of Gregory of Nyssa and Cyril of Alexandria, Theodoret of Cyrus, and Nestorius—a situation in which the fluid, often ambiguous terms of the previous century's polemics had become hardened by caricature and by repeated use as slogans of battle. The mood of the Byzantine Church during Justinian's reign was certainly in favor of reinterpreting, or at least clarifying, the language of the definition of Chalcedon in terms less ambivalent in themselves, and more congenial to Cyril's Christology. The canons of the Second Council of Constantinople in 553, while reaffirming the Chalcedonian definition as a binding codicil to the Nicene faith, were aimed primarily at excluding any interpretation of Chalcedon that seemed sympathetic to the language or concerns of Theodore, Nestorius, or even the more centrist Theodoret. So Constantinople II rejected the idea of a "relational union" (ἕνωσις σχετική) in Christ as Nestorian, even though its conceptual roots really lay with Gregory of Nyssa, and it condemned explicitly those who say that the union of natures in the incarnation is achieved by grace, combined operation, equality of honor, relationship, power, unity of name or divine good pleasure—who formulate the Mystery of Christ, in other words, in any terms other than that of a union "by synthesis or by hypostasis."[72] In this strongly unitive climate, it was the supreme achievement of Leontius of Byzantium to have upheld some of the more complex nuances of what such a "hypostatic" union actually implied, and to have argued—however modestly and abstractly—for a more relational understanding of the Chalcedonian Christology, an approach which more fully represented all the interests and voices in the debates of the previous two centuries, yet carried rich theological and anthropological implications of its own.

As one who had studied and excerpted the writings of the Apollinarian school firsthand, Leontius emphasized once again, without mentioning Apollinarius's name, the important insight of that controversial writer: it is union, *henōsis*, and *not* the nature of either God or Jesus's humanity that allows us to call his flesh divine. Speaking again of Christ, as Gregory

72. Second Council of Constantinople, Anathema 4: in G. Alberigo et al. (eds.), *Conciliorum Oecumenicorum Decreta* (Bologna: Istituto per le scienze religiose, 1973), 114–15; trans. N. P. Tanner (ed.), *Decrees of the Ecumenical Councils* (Washington, DC: Georgetown University Press, 1990), 114–15.

of Nyssa and Nemesius had done, as *one* in "the mode of union" rather than by the "principle of nature," Leontius revived the metaphysical distinction between *tropos* and *logos*, mode of origin and structure of being, that had been forged in Gregory's trinitarian theology; and he preserved it, in the christological context, for the use of later synthetic thinkers like Maximus the Confessor and John of Damascus. Remaining sympathetic to Cyril's concern that the personal unity of Christ be understood in real, intrinsic terms as forming a single ontological whole, Leontius treated the traditional analogy of the human body and soul for the incarnation in a positive way, while recognizing its limitations, and sharply criticized the "proponents of division" in the Antiochene tradition for rejecting it.[73] Yet his constant concern to emphasize the continuing, substantial, and natural distinction between God and humanity in Christ, and to stress the historical, contingent, unpredictably providential character of the "mode of union" that forms Christ's unique hypostasis, was itself a serious re-espousal of one of the Antiochenes' underlying christological concerns: that God's presence and saving action in Christ not be reduced to a part of the world's natural process.

Our considerations up to now have pointed to Leontius's role, in the middle of the contentious sixth century, as preserver and systematizer of crucial elements in earlier Greek philosophical and theological vocabulary that seemed to open promising ways of seeing the Church's mainstream doctrines of the Trinity of God and the Mystery of Christ, the dogmas of Nicaea and Constantinople and Chalcedon, as a continuous whole. What remains for us is to cast a brief, summary glance at two of the dominant figures in Greek theology in the centuries after the Council of 553—Maximus the Confessor and John of Damascus—to see how their own use of this vocabulary of the "mode of union" in Christ deepened and enriched, in significant and promising ways, earlier patristic reflection on God, Christ, and salvation.

Writing a hundred years after the sixth-century struggles over the reception of Chalcedonian Christology, Maximus the Confessor remains deeply indebted to Leontius's analysis of the language and concepts of trinitarian and christological debate. His *Epistle* 15, especially, written in his "middle period" of activity sometime between 634 and 640, is a masterful and synthetic summary of the issues of substance and nature, hypostasis and persona, with regard to the Triune God and to Christ, that without a doubt draws heavily and directly on Leontius's anti-Severan writings, even if Maximus never

73. *CNE* 2 (1280C–1284A).

mentions the earlier monk by name.[74] Maximus's use of the terminology of nature, union, and modality in a trinitarian context is evident in many of his works; in the *Mystagōgia*, for example, written early in his career (probably around 630),[75] Maximus summarizes the classical Christian understanding of God as being

> one substance, three hypostases; a tri-hypostatic singleness of substance and a consubstantial triad of hypostases; a monad in a triad and a triad in a monad; . . . a monad by its structure of substance [κατὰ τὸν τῆς οὐσίας λόγον] or being, but not by synthesis or conflation or confusion of any kind; a triad by the structure of how it exists and concretely comes to be, but not by separation or alienation or any kind of division. For the monad is not divided up by the hypostases, nor is it in them by relation and seen in them by contemplative thought, nor are the hypostases compounded into the monad, nor do they fill it out by a process of combination; rather, it is identical with itself, yet in different ways.[76]

In other early works, also dating from the late 620s or early 630s, Maximus applies this same language of sameness of substance and difference in manner of subsisting to the unity of Christ's person, with a clarity and thoroughness seldom found in the earlier tradition we have been examining. In the brief *Difficulty 36*, for instance, Maximus comments on a remark

74. On the structure of the person of Christ, as analyzed in this letter, see esp. PG 91, 557A–560D. The best recent survey of Maximus's use of the terms "nature" and "hypostasis" is Nicholas Madden, "Composite Hypostasis in Maximus Confessor," *Studia Patristica* 27 (1993), 175–97.

75. See P. Sherwood, *An Annotated Date-List of the Works of Maximus the Confessor*, Studia Anselmiana 30 (Rome: Orbis Catholicus, Herder, 1952), 32; I.-H. Dalmais, "Mystère liturgique et divinisation dans la 'Mystagogie' de saint Maxime le Confesseur," in C. Kannengiesser and J. Fontaine (eds.), *Epektasis*, Mélanges Daniélou (Paris: Beauchesne, 1972), 55; cf. the introduction to the critical edition of the *Mystagogia* by C. Sotiropoulos (Athens: s.n., 1978), 87. For a discussion of Maximus's use of the λόγος–τρόπος distinction in trinitarian theology and Christology, see P. Sherwood, *The Earlier Ambigua of St. Maximus the Confessor*, Studia Anselmiana 36 (Rome: Orbis Catholicus, Herder, 1955), 154–64; A. Riou, *Le Monde et l'église selon Maxime le Confesseur*, Théologie Historique 22 (Paris: Beauchesne, 1973), 80–91; Heinzer, *Gottes Sohn als Mensch*, 117–45. Riou observes (p. 80) that he has not found a thorough study of the patristic use of the word τρόπος in connection with the incarnation—a gap that the present study is intended, in some degree, to fill.

76. *Mystagogia* 25 (ed. Sotiropoulos, 239.57–240.72).

in Gregory Nazianzen's celebrated *Christmas Oration*,[77] that "the second communion" of God with humanity, in the incarnation, is "more amazing" than the original communion enjoyed by an unspoiled creation before the fall. Maximus writes:

> Formerly nature possessed no union with God in any mode or structure [τρόπον ἢ λόγον] of substance or hypostasis, those categories in which all beings are generally understood; but now it has received a union in hypostasis with him, through the ineffable union, preserving unchanged its own different structure of substance in relation to the divine substance, towards which it is hypostatically one and yet different, through the union. As a result, in the structure of its being [τῷ τοῦ εἶναι λόγῳ], according to which it has come into existence and continues to be, it [Christ's humanity] remains in unquestionable possession of its own being, preserving it undiminished in every way; but in the structure of *how* it is [τῷ τοῦ πως εἶναι λόγῳ], it receives existence in a divine way, and neither knows nor accepts at all the urge towards movement centered on any other thing. In this fashion, then, the Logos has brought into being a communion with human nature that is much more wonderful than the first one was, uniting the very nature to himself hypostatically, in a substantial way.[78]

In this thicket of technical terms and interlocking grammatical connections, Maximus lays out what will be a main theme of his Christology throughout his career: the point that in the person of Christ, a complete and fully functioning humanity has been brought into existence, which realizes and even goes beyond God's original design in creating the human person, precisely because the union of Jesus the man with the divine Logos is a union that preserves the substantial and natural differences of God and the human completely, and yet totally alters (at least as far as created history is concerned) the "how" of their relationship and their common action—the kind of "how" that makes concrete individuals or hypostases just what they are.[79] Jesus is Jesus by being, in every respect and at every moment, Son of God, Word made flesh; yet the intimacy and ontological absoluteness of this identification of the man from Nazareth with the second hypostasis of the

77. *Or.* 38.13.

78. *Ambigua* 36 (PG 91, 1289C3–D5).

79. Nicholas Madden remarks, à propos Maximus's *Opusculum* 25 (PG 91, 272B): "The *ousia* exists as 'what,' the *hypostasis* as 'how' or 'who'" ("Composite Hypostasis," 190).

Trinity do not make Jesus in any way less human than any other member of Adam's race. Rather, it changes the "manner" of his being human, in a way that sets out before us the new "manner of being" that is the pattern of our redemption.

Another important passage developing this terminology in the context of both Christology and theological anthropology is Maximus's long *Difficulty* 42, commenting on a passage in Gregory Nazianzen's oration *On Holy Baptism* that speaks of the three "births" of the redeemed—birth of the flesh, rebirth in baptism, and the coming new birth of the resurrection.[80] Towards the end of the discussion, Maximus makes the point that *renewal* (καινοτομία), which is what the Gospel of salvation really proclaims to us, is primarily a renewal of the "mode" of our being, rather than of the formal structure or *logos* of its nature,

> because if the *structure* [of Christ's humanity] is renewed, that would destroy the nature, in that it would not have preserved unaltered the structure by which it is; but if the *mode* [of being] is renewed, while its structure with respect to nature is preserved, it reveals miraculous power, showing its nature as enlivened and enlivening beyond its own normal limits. The *structure* of human nature is the fact that it is soul and body, and that its nature is constituted by soul and body; but its *mode* is the order found in this natural give-and-take of activity, something often varied and altered, yet not altering the nature at all along with itself.[81]

Maximus then gives examples from the Old Testament of people enabled by God to do and experience wonderful things—to act and be acted upon in a divine way—without undergoing any basic alteration in their humanity. He continues:

> Along with all these events, as well as after them, [God] brought to completion what was truly the newest of all mysteries, through which and because of which all these had occurred: his humanization for our sake; in doing this, he renewed our nature not in its structure, but in its mode, by taking up flesh through the mediation of a rational soul, having been ineffably conceived without seed, and having truly become a perfect human being,

80. *Or.* 40.2.
81. *Amb.* 42 (PG 91, 1341D4–14).

free of all corruption, possessing a rational soul with its body as a result of precisely that indescribable conception.[82]

The distinction between a natural structure and its mode of being is a centrally important one for Maximus, because, in his view, the underlying structure or nature of each identifiable thing has permanent validity before God, is what it is because God has made it such, and cannot become something different in that respect without simply ceasing to be: "Those features which their structures [*logoi*] perfectly possess before God, along with their very existence—of these their own growth and substantial development, according to their own structures—are utterly unable to receive any addition or diminution, beyond being whatever they are."[83]

The mystery of renewal, then—redemption from sin and restoration to the fullness of the image of God, for which humanity was originally created—must be, in Maximus's view, a fundamental transformation of the *way* we exist, which leaves intact the inner character of *what* we have been made to be. For one thing, it consists in the renewal of the particular way humans exercise their habitual freedom of choice—γνώμη—which Maximus defines as "a mode of living according to virtue or vice."[84] And since, as Gregory of Nyssa had suggested two and a half centuries earlier, the fallen condition of human nature is above all reflected in our "animal" mode of sexual conception and birth, through which God providentially surrounds our conflicted natures in a merciful mortality,[85] Maximus sees the renewal of our mode of being through Christ as taking place mainly through a renewal of *birth* as well: first through the new and unprecedented manner of Christ's birth, of his origin as a human hypostasis, of his human *hyparxis* or existence; and then, through the rebirth of baptism, made available to all of us after the example and through the activity of Christ.

82. Ibid. (PG 91, 1344D10–1345A5).

83. Ibid. (PG 91, 1345B12–C2). As Madden remarks ("Composite Hypostasis," 193), "The λόγος φύσεως and the τρόπος ὑπάρξεως require each other as the two necessary dimensions of all existents. It is the existent alone that is in reality and that acts in reality."

84. *Dialogue with Pyrrhus* (PG 91, 308B8–12; see also 308D8–10).

85. *On the Making of the Human Person* 16–17. For a recent discussion of this passage, with a survey of the abundant literature on it, and an attempt to reinterpret it as suggesting the positive potential of even human animality, see J. Behr, "The Rational Animal: A Rereading of Gregory of Nyssa's *De hominis opificio*," *Journal of Early Christian Studies* 7 (1999), 219–47.

Maximus makes this point in several places: one is a little work dating from the late 630s, a treatise on the Mystery of Christ addressed to the *higoumen* George (*Opusculum 4*). The Word of God renewed and saved our nature, Maximus says, by reordering not the functioning of our nature in itself, but the way we use it. This means not only that God empowers our wills to choose his will, free of the passionate inclinations that put us at war with him;[86] it also means that he has begun to reform the very way in which we come to live out our natural identity and potential, a way now rooted in the manner of our conception and birth. To do this, the Word himself became perfectly and completely human, but by a new and divine way of birth, and so—as a result of that birth—he now acts with a divinely oriented human will.[87] Maximus writes:

> Having the Logos himself as its own seed, renewing the manner of begetting that had been introduced [into human nature], [Christ's humanity] received in itself, along with its natural way of being, a divine way of concretely existing, so that it might confirm what is ours and give credibility to what is above us. For it is completely necessary that he [the Son] conserve both the nature of the Word of God, who became flesh and perfectly human for our sakes, and the additional nature he took on, with its natural qualities—without which it is, of course, no nature at all, but merely an empty fantasy—and also that he preserve the union. The first is preserved by natural difference, the second recognized in hypostatic identity. So we shall wisely and piously profess the whole structure of God's saving plan, without confusion and without separation.[88]

It is in the hypostatic union of the divine and the human in Christ that our human way of using our natural faculties, and thus of being ourselves, is made new: first in Christ, born of the Father and of the Virgin, and then through him, by a second birth "not of blood, nor of the will of the flesh nor of human will, but of God" (John 1:13), also in us.[89]

A century after Maximus, this Greek Christian tradition of speculation on the meaning of the "mode of union" of two natures in Christ's single,

86. *Opusc.* 4 (PG 91, 60A9–12).

87. Ibid. (PG 91, 60C5–15).

88. Ibid. (PG 91, 61B10–C11).

89. Maximus discusses the peculiar "mode of union" in Christ in a number of passages in his work: see, e.g., Ep. 12, to John the Chamberlain (written towards the end of 641), esp. PG 91, 477B. For further discussion of the "mode of existence" of the Word in his flesh, see also *Dialogue with Pyrrhus* (PG 91, 177AB).

composite hypostasis reached a further degree of synthetic maturity, as well as considerably greater clarity, in the writings of the great patristic systematician, John of Damascus. John, like Maximus, takes over Leontius of Byzantium's analysis of the meanings of substance-, nature-, and hypostasis-language with reference to the Mystery of Christ—without acknowledgment, but also virtually without alteration—and he uses them often as he expounds the orthodox tradition of the faith against its various alternatives.[90] Arguing against the Apollinarian phrase, "one nature of the Word of God, made flesh," used first by Cyril as a convenient christological formula and then by the opponents of Chalcedon as a kind of dogmatic emblem, John argues that the earlier Fathers were clearly speaking of "nature" here in an inexact way (καταχρηστικῶς); in saying that "the Word was made flesh," after all, the Evangelist was clearly referring to a particular hypostasis within the divine being, and not to the whole divine nature. "For the Logos did not have another nature alongside that of the divinity; the Logos is of the same nature as the Father and the Spirit, and all things are common to Father and Son and Holy Spirit except the manner of existence."[91]

In his treatise usually entitled *On the Two Wills in Christ*—actually a full discussion of the person of Christ, directed against the "monenergist" and "monothelite" brands of opposition to Chalcedonian Christology condemned at the Third Council of Constantinople in 681—John develops this understanding of classical terminology more fully:

> One must realize that every human hypostasis receives from the Creator both its being and the fact that it has proceeded from non-being into being. That is, [it has received] its being a creature, alive and active; its possessing sensation and understanding and reason, and appetite according to sensation and reason—in other words, its having a self-determining will; and its concrete existence consisting of substance and accidents. All these things are essential and natural qualities; but the particular mode of motion, particularly chosen by the individual, is the distinguishing mark of the hypostasis [ὑποστατικὴ διαφορά]. For sharing in the former characteristics establishes the identity of nature; but the manner of existing [ὁ τρόπος τῆς ὑπάρξεως] introduces the difference of hypostases, and the separate existence of each, their internal coherence, their peculiar mode of being and

90. See esp. his *Dialectica* 30, 43–45, 67; *Expositio fidei* 47–55, 57, 91; *Contra Jacobitas* 52; *De duabus in Christo voluntatibus* 7.

91. *C. Jac.* 52.24–27 (ed. Kotter, 4. 126).

> movement, and their different use of natural qualities, all make for separate hypostases and allow us to say there are many human beings.[92]

John immediately goes on to observe that the most fundamental difference between the three divine hypostases and any number of human hypostases is that the Trinity wills and acts as one—only their ὕπαρξις, their way of existing determined by their respective origins, differs in any way, so that we may not speak of "three gods" as we might speak of "three human beings."[93] More pointedly, perhaps, than his patristic predecessors who used these terms, John is aware of the inherent difficulty of using hypostasis-language for the persons in God, given the notions of independent subjectivity and self-conscious personhood forced upon us by our experience as human individuals. Unlike his predecessors, too, John sees the defining characteristics of hypostatic being not only in origin and in relationships with other hypostases of the same nature—not only in one's place in the family, one might say—but also in behavior, which for intelligent beings is inseparably rooted in the *will*. So he adopts the distinction Maximus had elaborated, a century earlier, between the "natural will," the innate dynamism towards self-preservation and self-fulfillment shared by every living being, and the particular, "gnomic will"—the human "mode of using the natural will" determined by the inclinations of the individual—which in the present world, after the fall, tends to be self-centered and determined by passion. He writes:

> Willing [θέλησις] is a natural appetite which is rational and living, suited only to what is natural. Natural acts of the will [φυσικὰ θελήματα] include, first, [to will] to be subject to the law of God—for the human person is naturally a servant of God and subject to Him—and next [to will] the things that hold nature together, such as hunger, thirst, sleep and such things.

92. *De duab. volunt.* 7.1–27 (corrected recension) (ed. Kotter, 4. 183–84).

93. Ibid. In the chapter of his *Dialectica* where he deals more generally with the problem of the hypostatic union in Christ, John also seems to be aware that "hypostasis" must be used of the persons in the Trinity in a more restricted sense than what we understand when speaking of created individuals. Having emphasized that no hypostasis can ever have undergone a new beginning in its own concrete being, since a hypostasis is "coming-into-existence for oneself," he adds: "one must know that in the case of the holy Trinity, hypostasis is the mode of each one's eternal existence, which has no beginning" (*Dial.* 67: ed. Kotter, 1. 34–38). The contextual sense of historical contingency, of source and relationship and circumstance, implied in the word *hypostasis*, must clearly be taken analogously if one is to use the term for the inner life of the eternal God.

> Hypostatic, gnomic willing, on the other hand, is an appetite determined by pleasure and by the private opinion of the hypostasis making use of the will, not by the law of God; it is a mode of using the natural will, according to the individual choice [γνώμη] of the hypostasis using it.[94]

John Damascene's analysis of the person of Christ in terms of nature and hypostasis follows generally the lines of earlier tradition. Christ, as a person, is unique—"one cannot find a common form" of Christ, such as would allow one to speak of him as being a single nature or universal substance![95] There never was and never will be another Christ; his coming, his very being, is not the product of the natural functioning of things either divine or human, but something much more mysterious and unpredictable, "a mode of adaptation planned by God [τρόπος οἰκονομικῆς συγκαταβάσεως]."[96] Thus we must speak, in the language of the Second Council of Constantinople, of a "union of two perfect natures, the divine and the human"—not a union by confusion, as the "Monophysites" imply, nor a union of a merely "external or relational kind," as the Nestorians suggest—but a union "by composition or indeed by hypostasis."[97] Following the earlier tradition, John emphasizes that this notion of a "hypostatic union" allows us "to confess that the two natures are preserved in him after the union, not as if we suppose each of them to be by itself or set apart, but [seeing them as] united with each other in the one compound hypostasis."[98] And we can call the union "essential" (οὐσιώδης), not in the sense that the two united natures form a single essence, but "in the sense that they are truly"—in other words, ontologically—"joined to each other to make the one composite hypostasis of the Son of God," even while their "essential" differences remain intact as well.[99]

In the treatise *Against the Jacobites*, too, John emphasizes that the paradoxical end-product (ἀποτέλεσμα) of the incarnation is not something that developed over time, "for ἕνωσις is not like the nature of things that are coming to be but do not yet exist, such as time or dancing or things like that."[100] "Things that are in relation [τὰ πρός τι—the Aristotelian category]

94. *De duab. volunt.* 25 (ed. Kotter, 4. 207–8). For further discussion of the kinds of will and their relation to nature and hypostasis, see ibid. 28.74–77, 82–84; 35.16–19.

95. *Exp. fid.* 47 (ed. Kotter, 2. 113.50). Cf. Leontius of Byzantium, *CNE* 5 (1292A).

96. *C. Jac.* 52 (ed. Kotter, 4. 127.54–55).

97. *Exp. fid.* 47 (ed. Kotter, 2. 114.60).

98. Ibid. (2. 114.65–66).

99. Ibid. (2. 114.67–115.70).

100. *C. Jac.* 45 (ed. Kotter, 4. 124.7–9).

are simultaneous and always remain simultaneous," he asserts a few chapters later; "but *union* and the things united belong to the class of things that are in relation. Union and the things united, therefore, are simultaneous."[101] As a result, any union of two naturally different entities that we can call hypostatic must be temporally co-extensive with their very existence together as a hypostasis; so even in the case of the ordinary human "hypostatic union" of soul and body to form the distinctive human individual, union is complete from the first moment of soul's and body's existence, and does not even come to an end when death separates body from soul. "For the body and the soul remain, always preserving the single principle of their existence and hypostatic being, even if they should be separated from one another."[102] Unlike natures, hypostases are always unique and unrepeatable, and endure as long as their natural powers allow. Yet they are constituted in their being by the very particular way in which their natural parts are related to each other and to the rest of creation—as individuals they are, in a sense, the product and the sum of their ontological circumstances.

IV. Conclusions on the "Manner" of Christ's Mystery

At the end of this rapid survey of the Greek patristic christological vocabulary—more particularly, of the use of the terms "nature," "hypostasis," and the "mode of union" that can constitute the latter, without essentially changing or annihilating its component natural parts—what conclusions might we draw of a more general, theological kind that might help us reflect for ourselves on the "manner" of the Mystery of Christ? Let me suggest at least a few:

1. When Greek theologians in the early Church speak of the "hypostasis" of Christ, or of the three "hypostases" of the Trinity, it is clear that they are not referring to what we moderns might call a "person": an independent subject, constituted by a unique and unrepeatable focus of self-consciousness, practical autonomy, and some measure of psychological freedom, and so able to enter into relationships with genuine commitment, to "give oneself away"; a repository of indestructible value within a world populated by persons, and thus an object of irreducible moral obligation for others; an individual

101. Ibid. 63 (4. 131.1–3).

102. *Dial.* 67 (ed. Kotter, 4. 139.22–24). Gregory of Nyssa had emphasized just this point about the souls and bodies of the dead in his dialogue *On the Soul and the Resurrection.*

whose existence is constituted by a contingent, limited yet authentic "act of being" in its own right. Even language in these works identifying a hypostasis as possessing τὸ καθ' ἑαυτὸ εἶναι ("being by oneself") should not lead us, as it has led a number of twentieth-century readers, to understand this as equivalent to the *Für-sich-sein* of German idealism—as referring to an ontological core of any particular density. For the authors we have been considering, who developed their notion of hypostasis to meet the needs of clarifying the apostolic faith, with the aid of contemporary philosophy but not necessarily determined by its conclusions, a hypostasis was essentially a particular individual within a universal species, identifiable as such or such a thing by the qualities it (or he or she) shared with similar individuals, yet marked off as unique by a set of characteristics all its own. It was the kind of thing so unique and unrepeatable you could call it by name—not just "horse," but "Silver"; not just "man," but Peter or Paul or John, or even Jesus. Beyond this, however, the Greek Fathers we have been considering rarely attempt to "look inside" the hypostasis of Jesus or of anyone else, and offer us little clue as to the peculiar ontological status or psychological character of any hypostasis within itself, besides insisting—as we have tried to show here—that the principal distinguishing characteristic of any individual is its *origin*: where it (or he or she) comes from, how it is situated genetically within the larger field of similar individuals, what its family relations are. In addition to origin, as John of Damascus observes, *behavior*—the actualization of freedom in "movement"—is also an indispensable determinant of the identity of human hypostases: *who we are* is revealed and actualized not only in *where we come from*, but in *how we act*. But whether it is origin or action that serves as our leading clue, for Greek patristic theology "hypostasis," and even *hyparxis*, "existence," were words that referred to the *manner* of being rather than to its general denomination—every "who" was defined in terms of "how" it was what it was recognized to be, rather than simply in terms of its "what," its definition and its intelligible characteristics.

2. To say that Christ is a single hypostasis who joins together two wholly distinct and unequal natures—the transcendent, infinite, foundational reality of God and the limited reality of a historical human being—in a "mode of union" which constitutes his present personal reality is to say that he is a living paradox. It is also to say that his person, his life, the event of his coming and working in our world, are all contingent things, not derivable from our knowledge of human nature or from our speculations about the divine reality that lies at the heart of things. We cannot guess from what we know about humanity, the world, or even absolute reality itself that God would

speak to us in this way, let alone that God's Word should "become flesh and dwell among us" as a Jew in the time of Caesar Augustus. The features and acts that enable us to recognize Jesus as the eternal Word made flesh are all accidental, contingent, historical things, reported to us by historical witnesses: for the Fathers, first of all the extraordinary manner of his birth, his descendence from God's holy people, the holiness of his mother; then his miracles, the moral purity of his teaching, the extraordinary generosity and fidelity of his passion and death, the glorious transformation of Mount Tabor and Easter morning. All these things, as Maximus the Confessor liked to observe, reveal him as "divine in a human way, and human in a divine way."[103] For the Fathers, Christ the Lord is made a person, a hypostasis, precisely by the way God the Word acts in the world through Jesus, and the way the human Jesus is related to the Father and the Holy Spirit. How he exists, how each "part" of him shapes and expresses the other, makes him who he is.

3. The core of the Mystery of Christ, then, for the authors we have been considering, is a mystery of *relationship*: God's relationship to the created world, and especially to the human community, now renewed and transformed by the unique, utterly particular relationship of God the Word to the humanity of Jesus. This is a relationship like no other we have experienced: totally unequal, expressing the total dependence of the human on the divine for its personal as well as its generic being, yet at the same time (as Maximus and John of Damascus recognized) setting this human freer than any human before him to be what all of us are created to be—sons and daughters of God, created in God's image and likeness. The uniqueness of Jesus's relationship to God is that the creative and redeeming presence of God in him—the mission of the Father, the creative ordering and self-revealing illumination of the Logos, the anointing of the Spirit—brings his very person, his hypostasis into being in human terms, makes him who he is. Yet the Mystery of Christ's unique person is also a Mystery that potentially, at least, includes us: the model and source of our own renovation, as Maximus reminds us, the sign of our vocation as human creatures. Our hypostases need to be perfected in their humanity through our relationship to God in Christ.

4. In Christ, the particular and contingent character of the "mode of union" reveals and embodies ultimate and universal things, the eternal, unknowable substance and nature of God, and also reveals and embodies human reality, human nature in its fullest perfection. This, perhaps, is why

103. See, e.g., *Opusc.* 7, to Marinus (PG 91, 84B11–D3); *Dialogue with Pyrrhus* (297D13–298A4).

Greek christological writers continued to insist that for all its relational and "modal" character, the union of divinity and humanity in Christ is also, paradoxically, a *substantial* one. Despite Nestorius's arguments, it was not to be conceived of as *simply* relational, simply a ἕνωσις σχετική. Neither of the realities involved, the divine or the human, could be conceptually plumbed to their depths or delimited, let alone explained in their new, unique christological structure of coinherence. But the struggle over the reception of Chalcedon made it clearer than ever before that the faith of Christianity is quite simply that it is *God* who encounters us personally in Jesus, that the hypostasis formed by Jesus's origin and his relationships and his actions "has its being in the Logos."[104] In recognizing and imitating the human Jesus's "mode of union" with the transcendent substance of God, we discover nothing less than the presence of God here in the human world, inviting us to accept a new origin, a new set of relationships, a new personal identity and "mode of being" that does not destroy what is proper to ourselves, but unites it to him.

104. Leontius of Byzantium, *Epil.* 1944C2–4.

PART 5

Christ in Philosophical and Apocalyptic Traditions

15 *Logos* as Reason and *Logos* Incarnate

Philosophy, Theology, and the Voices of Tradition

One of Pope Benedict XVI's first serious clashes with the "chattering classes" represented by today's media was his now-famous lecture to academic faculties of the University of Regensburg, in September of 2006. As you doubtless remember, that lecture was widely interpreted as a strong critique of Islam on religious grounds, and it inspired heated reactions—against him and against Christian institutions in general—all over the Muslim world. Actually, though, it was not a lecture on Islam and Christianity at all, but a subtle and carefully constructed discussion of faith and human reason. More explicitly, Benedict was really talking about the role of rational thought—of the faculty for argued, ordered thinking, which the Greeks called *logos*—in our understanding of the God who is, by definition, infinitely beyond reason's ability to conceive in rational terms, or to set within the rational boundaries of moral obligation.

In spite of God's ontological and moral transcendence, Benedict apparently wanted to say, the Christian tradition has always, somewhat paradoxically, taken it for granted that God is most closely approached by creatures through the exercise of their reason, and their love of what reason approves. Being an academic, he chose to begin his lecture with a fascinating, slightly off-beat example of this ancient assumption: a passage in one of the Byzantine emperor Manuel II Palaeologus's learned *Dialogues* on Christianity and Islam; composed in the last decade of the fourteenth century, it compares the presentations of God, humanity, and behavioral ideals in the Scriptures of those two traditions. There, in the seventh of the *Dialogues*, Emperor Manuel comments on the ancient Islamic tradition of holy war—of spreading the faith by force of arms—with what Benedict rightly calls "a brusqueness that *we* find unacceptable," but with perceptive depth nonetheless: "God," the emperor straightforwardly says, "is not pleased by blood—and not acting reasonably (σὺν λόγῳ) is contrary to God's nature."[1] Thus the kind of activities that our moral reasoning would reject as repugnant to human goodness, because they contradict our nature at its best, must also be rejected as contrary to what we can know of how God acts in the world, and so of what God is.

Benedict's point, of course, was not to offer a criticism of the Islamic idea of the sovereignty of the divine will, or to summarize the foundational assumptions of late Byzantine theology, but to underline the role that reasoning and our criteria for reasonable behavior have played in development of the thought and life of the Church. Against the suggestion of Harnack and other liberal Protestants of the late nineteenth century that the "Hellenization of Christianity" has been, from the beginnings of the Church, a kind of corruption of the limpidly simple teachings of the rabbi Jesus about "the fatherhood of God and the brotherhood of man," Benedict asks:

> Is the conviction that acting unreasonably contradicts God's nature merely a Greek idea, or is it always and intrinsically true? I believe that here we can see the profound harmony between what is Greek, in the best sense of the word, and the biblical understanding of faith in God. . . . The Faith of the Church has always insisted that between God and us, between his eternal Creator Spirit and our created reason there exists a real analogy, in which—as the Fourth Lateran Council in 1215 stated—unlikeness remains infinitely greater than likeness, yet not to the point of abolishing analogy and its language. God does not become more divine when we push him away from us in a sheer, impenetrable voluntarism; rather, the truly divine God is the God who has revealed himself as *logos* and, as *logos*, has acted and continues to act lovingly on our behalf.[2]

1. Pope Benedict XVI, "Regensburg Lecture of the Holy Father: Faith, Reason and the University; Memories and Reflections" (University of Regensburg, September 12, 2006), citing Manuel II Palaeologus, *Dialogue VII*, 3b–c, ed. Theodore Khoury, in SC 115 (Paris: Les Éditions du Cerf, 1966), 144.

2. Benedict XVI, "Regensburg Lecture," 2–3. Reasoning on the implications of the gospel, and on the person and origin of Jesus, has been central to Christian discipleship from the beginning, despite the contention of some post-Enlightenment critics that Christian theology is a deformation of Jesus's message. Benedict clearly has in mind such passages as this in Harnack's famous Berlin lectures on the "essence of Christianity": "[Jesus's] message is simpler than the churches would like to think it; simpler, but for that very reason sterner and endowed with a greater claim to universality. A man cannot evade it by the subterfuge of saying that as he can make nothing of this 'Christology' the message is not for him. Jesus

To talk about *logos*, the human faculty and process of rational thought in all its manifold aspects and uses, is of course to talk—in the most general terms, at least—about *philosophy*: that collection of strategies and practices by which human beings since ancient times have tried to help each other become wise. Philosophy, more than any other branch of human thought, is ancient Greece's contribution to human culture: it began with the questions Greek poets and pundits asked of each other, especially of the young, about what is most truly real in our world of experience, what goals are most worth pursuing, what beauty and goodness and the well ordered human society really might be like. Benedict's argument—surely not new to anyone who takes the Catholic tradition seriously—is that philosophy has played a distinctive, at times even normative role in the Church's elaboration of what Scripture and the teaching of the disciples of Jesus have to say about these things: that our Christian theology—our language and thought about God in God's deepest reality—has not and really cannot be elaborated meaningfully without the intentional use of what philosophy, since the pre-Socratics, has clarified for us. Philosophy and theology, surely, have distinctively different sources, methods, and goals. If theology, in the Anselmian truism, is "faith seeking understanding," the faith with which the search begins is something quite different from *logos* as analysis: trust in the words of historical persons within a historical community; committed membership in a community which hears the word of God as something strange and totally reorienting, and keeps it.

Theology, then, when seen in this light, bears in itself a certain degree of tension, even of paradox. One might think of it as philosophical discipleship, a self-questioning and world-questioning participation in the open-hearted faith of a group of friends—a life lived in the space between *logos* and love. What I would like to do here is simply to reflect a bit further on that tension, as it has developed through twenty centuries of Christian thought about the person and meaning of Jesus Christ, by singling out a handful of key figures, especially in the early development of the Church's theology, and to ask how this history of reflection—reflection by *logos* as reason on *Logos* as

directed men's attention to great questions. . . . The individual is called upon to listen to the glad message of mercy and the Fatherhood of God, and to make up his mind whether he will be on God's side and the Eternal's, or on the side of the world and of time. The Gospel, as Jesus proclaimed it, has to do with the Father only, and not with the Son." Adolf von Harnack, *What Is Christianity?*, trans. Thomas Bailey Saunders (Philadelphia: Fortress Press, 1937), 143–44.

Word made flesh, God's own *Logos* in person—has invited us to live faithful Christian lives today.

Figures from History

One of the most influential achievements of Pierre Hadot, the distinguished French historian of later Greek philosophy, in recent years has been to remind us of the essentially practical, "pastoral" character of most of what we would characterize as philosophical activity in the ancient world. Although philosophy in ancient Greece, even in its earliest known stages, certainly focused on asking ultimate questions about the nature of reality and the ultimate values human action and human society strive to realize, Hadot insists that most of its ancient practitioners—from the Sophists and Socrates to the Peripatetics, the Stoics, and the Cynics—saw it above all as a way of raising unsettling questions in the minds of their contemporaries: moving ordinary people, especially young people, to develop a critical understanding of their inherited cultural and religious and ethical assumptions, by suggesting a habit of reflective thought—"spiritual exercises," as Hadot calls them—that led to deeper awareness of the truth and to greater personal freedom. Far from being the highly specialized, esoterically cerebral form of discourse that we identify as philosophy in the post-Enlightenment West, philosophy in late Hellenistic times—claiming in its name to be the "love of wisdom"—used a variety of strategies to help people develop focus and self-mastery in day-to-day life.[3] So it was perfectly understandable that early Christian ascetical practice, at least from the early fourth century, was usually called the *bios philosophikos*, even when those who practiced it had little formal education.[4] If one thoughtfully prayed over a selection of memorized Psalms and Gospel sayings, lived a life as free as possible from sensual distraction,

3. See, for example, Pierre Hadot, *What Is Ancient Philosophy?*, trans. Michael Chase (Cambridge, MA: Harvard University Press, 2002), esp. 2–4. Hadot writes (p. 3): "In the first place, at least since the time of Socrates, the choice of a way of life has not been located at the end of the process of philosophical activity, like a kind of accessory or appendix. On the contrary, it stands at the beginning, in a complex interrelation with critical reaction to other existential attitudes, with global vision of a certain way of living and of seeing the world, and with voluntary decision itself. Thus, to some extent, this option determines the specific doctrine and the way this doctrine is taught. Philosophical discourse, then, originates in a choice of life and an existential option, not vice versa."

4. See ibid., 237–52.

and was under the guidance of an experienced spiritual director, one was—in the ancient sense—living as a philosopher.

Justin, writing in the mid-second century, was the first Christian writer to be generally styled "a philosopher" by profession. Originally from Flavia Neapolis in Samaria (present-day Nablus), Justin spent the last few decades of his life as a teacher of the Christian way of life in Rome, and was put to death for it, with a few of his pupils, around the year 165. The first eight chapters of his *Dialogue with Trypho* give us a glimpse—unusual in ancient documents—of his early intellectual formation, which he describes as a continuing, if somewhat circuitous, search for the unitary vision of truth on which a "happy life" is founded.[5] "Philosophy," he says at the start of his narrative, "is in fact the greatest possession, and most honorable before God, to whom it leads us and who alone commends us; and they are truly holy men who have bestowed attention on philosophy."[6]

Philosophy, as Justin understands it, is in itself a pursuit of holiness, a way to God; what disturbed him in his early years was not its secularity, but the variety of schools and competition of theories by which ancient philosophy was characterized. He tells us that, after brief but unsatisfying stints as a pupil of Stoic, Peripatetic, and Pythagorean teachers, he made greater progress toward what he was seeking when he became a Platonist and discovered that the only worthwhile object of contemplation is immaterial reality.[7] Then, however, he says, while walking by the sea he encountered a "venerable old man" who apparently was himself a Christian teacher. Justin recounts their conversation—stylized, probably, to reflect a living genre of philosophical conversion stories[8]—as itself a kind of Socratic dialogue. The old man leads him to clarify his conception of philosophy, as "the knowledge of that which really exists, and a clear perception of the truth"—knowledge that leads to happiness and is rooted in the conviction of a transcendent God.[9] Further, Justin and his teacher agree that such a God *can* be known by the human mind, which has an affinity with God because it is itself "divine and immortal."[10] They also agree that a just life is the prerequisite for the

5. Justin, *Dialogue with Trypho*, in *Ante-Nicene Fathers*, vol. 1, ed. Archibald Roberts and James Donaldson (repr., Grand Rapids: Eerdmans, 1981), chaps. 2, 8.

6. Ibid., chap. 2.

7. Ibid.

8. See Arthur J. Droge, "Justin Martyr and the Restoration of Philosophy," *Church History* 56 (1987): 304.

9. Justin, *Dialogue*, chap. 3 (*ANF* 196).

10. Ibid., chap. 4.

happy survival of the human soul. Finally, Justin's companion leads him to reject Plato's theory of reincarnation and to affirm that our hope for everlasting life is founded not on some primordial identification of the soul with life (as the *Phaedo* suggests), but on the soul's participation in the life of God.[11] Gradually, through these steps, their conversation leads Justin to ask where one might turn to find a reliable teacher for such a path to life with God, and his partner points to the Christian Bible as the source of a philosophy which "alone is safe and profitable":

> There existed, long ago, certain men more ancient than all those who are thought of as philosophers, blessed and righteous and beloved by God, who spoke by the Divine Spirit and foretold events which would take place, and which are now happening. They are called prophets. . . . They did not use demonstration in their treatises back then, seeing that they were trustworthy witnesses to the truth that is above all demonstration. . . . They both glorified the Creator, the God and Father of all things, and proclaimed his Son, the Christ sent by him.[12]

It is the Hebrew prophets, in their Spirit-led witness to Christ who was to come, who are presented here as the teachers of a philosophy that can be relied on, purveyors of a wisdom that alone brings its practitioners to the happy life.

Behind Justin's identification of the biblical prophets as the most trustworthy teachers of the "truth that makes us free" lies the notion, found in a variety of ancient pagan and Christian sources, that Plato, the most religious of Hellenic teachers, had traveled to Egypt on his own quest for wisdom and had learned there from sources more ancient and more venerable than his own Greek contemporaries.[13] Philo and other Hellenistic Jewish thinkers identified this Egyptian source of classical wisdom with the Hebrew Bible, especially the books of Moses—by their time widely available in Egypt in Greek translation. Early Christian writers readily picked up the story. For Justin, the central point is not simply that Plato borrowed from Moses, but that the fullness of the divine wisdom, guiding the world and offering itself

11. Ibid., chaps. 5–6.

12. Ibid., chap. 7 (*ANF* 198; translation altered).

13. For this idea, suggested by Poseidonius, Numenius, and others, that Plato had made contact with an *Urphilosophie* among the Egyptians, see Droge, "Justin Martyr and Restoration of Philosophy," 311, 317.

to us as a norm for right living, is to be found in the one to whom Moses and the prophets pointed in the Scriptures, Jesus Christ.[14] So a key argument in all of Justin's works is that Old Testament prophecy has been fulfilled in the words and deeds of Jesus;[15] in Jesus, in fact, God's own providential wisdom, previously offered to the human race in a variety of forms, has taken human shape, lived a human life, and died a human death on the cross. Interpreting a long series of passages from the Hebrew Bible as prophecies of Christ, Justin insists that "he was 'before the morning star' (Ps 109:3 LXX [110:3]) and the moon, and, when he was made flesh, submitted to be born of this virgin, of the family of David."[16] Assigning the details of human distress and abandonment mentioned in Psalm 22 to Jesus in his passion, Justin asserts: "I have already proved that this man was the unique offspring of the Father of all things, being begotten from him in a distinctive manner, as Word and Power, and afterwards becoming man through the Virgin."[17] That divine "Word and Power," for Justin, is precisely the rational presence of God in creation.[18]

Justin's boldest, most famous statement of Christ's eternal identity as the eternal reason or *Logos* of God, the guiding force in creation and the object of every human search for wisdom, appears in his *First Apology.* Countering the pagan charge that Jesus cannot be a genuinely divine figure of transcendent import, because he lived only a century or so before Justin's own time, the Christian philosopher affirms:

> We have been taught that Christ is the first-begotten of God, and have previously testified that he is the reason [λόγος] of which every race of humanity partakes. Those who lived in accordance with reason are Christians, even though they were called atheists—such as, among the Greeks, Socrates and Heraclitus and others like them; among the barbarians, Abraham, Ananiah, Azariah and Misael,[19] and Elijah, and many others, whose deeds and names I forbear to list for now, knowing that this would be lengthy. So also those

14. This is especially a Lucan theme; see Luke 24:25–27, 32, 45–48; Acts 10:43.

15. See, for instance, Justin Martyr, *First Apology*, trans. Edward R. Hardy, in *Early Christian Fathers*, Library of Christian Classics, vol. 1 (Philadelphia: Westminster John Knox Press, 1953), 1.47–53 (hereafter *Apology*); *Dialogue*, chaps. 13–14, 28–30, 32–34, 36–38, 43–45, 49, 53, 66, 68, 77–78, 98, 125.

16. Justin, *Dialogue*, chap. 45 (translation altered). See also chaps. 48, 63, 68, 75.

17. Ibid., chap. 105 (*ANF* 251; translation altered).

18. Justin, *Apology*, 1.10.

19. These last three names refer to the "three young men" thrown in the furnace by Nebuchadnezzar, in Dan 1:7 (LXX).

> who lived without reason [λόγος] were ungracious,[20] enemies to Christ, and murderers of those who lived by reason; and those who live by reason [λόγος] now are Christians, fearless and unperturbed.[21]

In a single stroke, Justin here identifies the Jesus of the Gospels both with the object of Old Testament prophecy and the content of Old Testament types, on the one hand, and with the divine reason guiding the cosmos, on the other—a divine mind in whose activities and knowledge the searching human mind, at its best, is able to share. The implications, though hardly worked out here with any sophistication, are staggering: philosophical ethics are essentially the same as biblical teaching, for Justin, and are summed up most perfectly in the moral teachings and parables of Jesus; the divine Wisdom by which God shaped and still guides the world[22] is a universal presence, which has become embodied, personified, in the carpenter of Nazareth. Christ has implicitly become for Justin the norm for an adequate philosophical quest for truth and moral righteousness, the implied content of the philosopher's attempts to lead others to freedom and personal integration. On the other hand, the language and concepts of Platonism and Stoicism, which we would call "philosophical" in the more usual sense, are now available to Justin and his colleagues not as religious alternatives, but as tools for deepening their own grasp on biblical images and narratives, and for making them intelligible as religious teachings of universal significance.

For Harnack and other liberal Protestant scholars, at the end of the nineteenth century, this identification of philosophical laws and cosmic teachings with the historical kerygma of Jesus was the first major step in the alienation of the Christian message from its Jewish beginnings: the distancing of the simple, essentially ethical gospel, free from ontological claims, from the person of the rabbi Jesus, and the beginning of a clerical "intellectualism" that even the Reformation—with its presumed emphasis on *sola Scriptura*—was not completely successful in purging from Christian faith.[23]

20. Greek: ἄχρηστοι. Justin is playing on the title "Christ," which, though unrelated, is similar in sound to the Greek word χρηστός: "good," "honest," "upright." So those who live according to reason, he argues a few lines later, are by the very fact of being *chrēstoi*—"upright people"—also *Christianoi.*

21. Justin, *Apology*, 1.46.272 (translation altered).

22. See, for example, Prov 8:22–36; Ps 104:24.

23. Harnack writes wistfully, in the fourth chapter of Book II of his *History of Dogma*: "In the dogmas of the Apologists . . . we find nothing more than traces of the fusion of the philosophical and historical elements; in the main, both exist separately side by side. It was

For the Orthodox and Catholic traditions, on the other hand, it marked the beginning of theology in the full sense, as the engagement of faith by reason and the transformation of reason by faith. The *logos* of the philosophers had become flesh for the Church, tangible and immediately nourishing, because it was embodied in the Church's Lord.

A second phase to which we might fruitfully point, in this challenging yet fruitful dialogue between philosophy and faith, began to unroll toward the end of the fourth century, as worldly and educated Greek Christians—now free and honored citizens in an at least nominally Christian empire—argued earnestly and sometimes heatedly about the proper way to understand the apostolic confession that Jesus is truly the divine savior of the world. What modern historians of theology usually refer to as the "Arian controversy" began in Alexandria, at the end of the second decade of the fourth century, with the reaction of Alexander, the local archbishop, to the preaching and pamphleteering of Arius, a respected local pastor. Arius's position, as far as we can determine it from this distance, was apparently only a somewhat oversimplified—and so radicalized—form of a way of thinking about Christ, the divine *Logos* made flesh, that had been widely accepted since at least Origen, a century earlier. Jesus, as Christian tradition made clear, was the mediator between an utterly transcendent God, about whom the human mind and human speech must remain silent, and this world of limited, intelligible, vulnerable beings. The world was created by the *Logos*, at the behest of his divine Father, and was brought back into a good relationship with the Father through him, after some intellectual creatures had turned away. This *Logos* or Son, as mediator between God and the world, was unquestionably a *divine* figure, for Arius and his forebears; but he was

not till long after this that intellectualism gained the victory in a Christianity represented by the clergy. What we here chiefly understand by 'intellectualism' is the placing of the scientific conception of the world behind the commandments of Christian morality and behind the hopes and faith of the Christian religion, and the connecting of the two things in such a way that this conception appeared as the foundation of these commandments and hopes. Thus was created the future dogmatic in the form which still prevails in the churches and which presupposes the Platonic and Stoic conception of the world long ago overthrown by science. The attempt made at the beginning of the Reformation to free the Christian faith from this amalgamation remained at first without success" (*History of Dogma* II, trans. Neil Buchanan [London: Constable & Robinson, 1900], 229). For Harnack, it would presumably be only in the less institutional, non-clerical form of liberal Protestantism in the late nineteenth and early twentieth centuries that dogma and Hellenistic "intellectualism" would finally come to an end, being replaced by a Christianity of high-minded, middle-class religious and moral sentiment within a culture of scientific enlightenment.

just as clearly *not* divine in the full, unlimited, primordial sense in which God his Father is. As "begotten," generated by God to be the minister of God's will, Arius argued, the Son belonged fundamentally to the realm of creatures: a pre-cosmic mediator created precisely to bring creation into being and to redeem it, "a creature—yet not like one of the creatures; an offspring, yet not like things begotten."[24]

The response of most bishops and theologians, in the early 320s, was to resist this highly structured way of conceiving the position of Christ, the Son of God and redeemer, within the cosmos, even though acceptable alternatives were not immediately clear. Gathered in council at Nicaea in Asia Minor, in the late summer of 325, they approved as normative for faith a revised version of a traditional baptismal creed, which now affirmed that Christ, the Son of God and our Lord, the one who died and rose for us, was "begotten of the Father uniquely: that is, of the substance [οὐσία] of the Father; God of God, light of light, true God of true God; begotten, not made; of the same substance [ὁμοούσιος] as the Father." Language straight from Aristotle's *Categories* had suddenly been introduced into the Church's liturgical profession of faith; and the main subject of theological debate and Church-political wrangling for the next fifty years was precisely how to interpret and apply these terms to the rest of the Christian understanding of God and human history.

In his treatise *In Defense of the Nicene Definition*, written around 356 and usually referred to simply as *De decretis*, Athanasius—successor to Alexander as bishop of Alexandria and a stalwart, if politically savvy, defender of the Council of Nicaea's doctrinal position on the person of Christ—felt compelled to deal with one of the main criticisms that had been raised against the Nicene formula in the intervening thirty years: that its language, in this crucial point of expressing the original identity of the Son of God, was taken from philosophical discourse rather than from Scripture, and could there-

24. So Arius and his early colleagues, in a common profession of faith sent to Bishop Alexander, sometime around 321, present their position this way: "Before everlasting ages [God] begot his unique Son, through whom he made the ages and all things. He begot him not in appearance, but in truth, constituting him by his own will, unalterable and unchangeable, a perfect creature of God, but not as one of the creatures—an offspring, but not as one of things begotten. . . . But as we said, by the will of God he was created before times and before ages and received life and being and glories from the Father, the Father so constituting him" (Hans-Georg Opitz, *Athanasius Werke* III/1 [Berlin: De Gruyter, 1934], Urkunde 6.3, pp. 12–13; translation from *Christology of the Later Fathers*, trans. Edward R. Hardy [Philadelphia: Westminster Press, 1954], 332–33).

fore not be normative for Christian faith in the same way that Scripture is. Athanasius's response to this challenge is to concede, implicitly, that the first choice of theological terms and concepts should normally make use of words taken from the Bible, yet also to affirm that maintaining the central religious understanding of the Christian community, drawn from Scripture—what he calls "reverence" (εὐσέβεια)—must be the Church's first priority, and that this sometimes requires using non-scriptural terminology to clarify Scripture's traditional meaning: "Reverent speech [τὸ δὲ εὐσεβεῖν] is acknowledged by everyone as a holy thing, even if someone should use terms of foreign origin, as long as the one speaking preserves a reverent intention, and wishes to make a reverent statement by what he has in mind."[25] Athanasius then goes on to describe the intention of the Fathers at Nicaea as precisely this: to make the Church's understanding of the biblical portrait of Christ unmistakably clear, by the use of secular philosophical language.

> The Synod wanted to annihilate the impious interpretations of the Arians and to write in the recognized language of the Scriptures, that the Son does not come from what is not but is from God, and is *Logos* and Wisdom, but not a creature or something made, and that he is from the Father as his proper offspring. But those associated with Eusebius [of Nicomedia—one of Arius's main episcopal backers], drawing from their long-standing bad intentions, wanted to say that being "from God" is common to us and to the Word of God, and that in this respect he does not differ from us—since Scripture says, "There is one God *from whom* are all things" (1 Cor 8:6), and again, "What is old has passed away; behold, all has become new—and all is *from* God!" (2 Cor 5:17–18). But the Fathers, recognizing their trickiness and the evil intent of irreverent thinking [ἀσέβεια], were now forced [!] to say more plainly that he is "from God" and so to write that the Son is "from the essence of the Father," for the reason that being from God is not common and equivalent when understood of the Son and of creatures. . . .
>
> And again, the bishops said that the Word is the true Power and Image of the Father, invariably like the Father in every way, unchanging and always in him without division—for the Word never *was not*, but exists always alongside the Father as a ray of his light. Those associated with Eusebius held back, not daring to contradict this out of sheer shame over what had been charged against them, but they were caught again, whispering to each

25. Athanasius, *De decretis* 18.4 (Opitz II/1 [Berlin: De Gruyter, 1935], 15); my translation.

> other and rolling their eyes, to the effect that being "like" and being "always" and the language of "power" and being "in him" is common, once again, to us and to the Son; "No harm [they said] for us to agree with these things!" ... But since the begetting of the Son from the Father is something different when compared to human nature, and he is not simply like but also inseparable from the substance of the Father, and since "he and the Father are one," as he himself says (John 10:30), and the Word is always in the Father and the Father in the Word, just as the ray is related to the light—for this is what the text indicates—therefore the Synod, with this in mind, made the excellent decision to write "of the same substance" [ὁμοούσιον], in order to defeat the bad intentions of the heretics and to indicate that the Word is different from created things.[26]

In this passage, with deep implications for Christian hermeneutics, Athanasius is clearly suggesting that while biblical terminology ought to remain the primary vehicle for the language in which Christian faith is expressed, there are situations in which non-biblical language—specifically, technical language taken from the realm of philosophy—is necessary simply to make clear how the community of faith has, through its history, come to understand the Bible's real meaning.

This same sense of the possible tension between the language of reverence or faith and the (often) more precise language of philosophical analysis emerged again, in an opposite direction, over the next two decades of continuing controversy on the faith of Nicaea. In the late 350s, a new group of anti-Nicene theologians began to form around Eudoxius, the bishop of Antioch (358–360) and later of Constantinople (360–370), who had been promoted to his offices by the emperor Constantius II because of his steadfast rejection of Nicaea. The intellectual leader of the group around Eudoxius was Aetius, a skilled Antiochene grammarian and dialectician of humble origin. In his brief compendium or *Syntagmation*, Aetius argued on the basis of a developed theory of language, and through a chain of tightly constructed syllogisms, that God, if he is real at all, must also be intelligible to us, in terms of the most precise language used of him. So if it is agreed, by Scripture and by the philosophical tradition, that God is the first of causes, the being who simply *is* and who is the cause of all else, then all beings who are in any way caused by God are, by definition, *not* God but creatures. The consequences for understanding Christ, the Son and Word of God, are

26. Ibid., 19.1–2; 20.1, 5 (Opitz II/1, 15–17); my translation.

obvious: if he is truly the offspring of God, he is *produced* or caused; but if God is the Uncaused One (ὁ ἀγένητος), then the Son cannot be God in any true sense, and should not be called so. And if God's *substance* is defined as his being unbegotten, then the Son also cannot be "of the same substance" as the Father, or even *like* the Father in any significant sense. He is simply the first and noblest of creatures.

Aetius's more celebrated and influential pupil was Eunomius of Cyzicus, a Cappadocian also of humble origins, born around 330; he eventually came to Antioch and became a pupil of Aetius and a follower of Bishop Eudoxius, who eventually ordained him bishop of Cyzicus, across the Sea of Marmara from Constantinople. As an outspoken critic of Nicene theology, Eunomius eventually became involved in heated written controversies with Basil of Caesarea, with Basil's younger brother Gregory of Nyssa, and (in more personal encounters) with their friend and colleague Gregory of Nazianzus (after this Gregory was made bishop of the Nicene party in the imperial capital in 378). One of the handful of works of Eunomius that have survived is his *Liber apologeticus*, probably composed in the winter of 360–361 as part of his defense against charges of heresy that appear to have been brought before a local synod in Constantinople at that time.[27] Here Eunomius presents the central arguments proposed by Aetius in a somewhat less terse form. Arguing from the absolute simplicity and primacy of the divine nature, Eunomius concludes: "If it has now been demonstrated that God neither existed before himself nor did anything else exist before him, but that he *is* before all things, then what follows from this is the title Unbegotten—or rather, he is himself unbegotten substance."[28] Eunomius goes on to draw his principal conclusion: "If God is unbegotten in the sense shown by the foregoing demonstration, he could never undergo a generation which involved the sharing of his own distinctive nature with the offspring of that generation, and could never admit of any comparison or association with the thing begotten."[29] Later on in the treatise, Eunomius declares himself ready to accept the fact that the Son is in a genuine sense divine—genuinely the savior of humanity, genuinely the mirror of God's infinite perfections—provided these are understood as *derived* from the Father as his source, and provided we do *not* assert his unity

27. For the dating of this treatise, see the introduction to the edition and translation by Richard P. Vaggione, *Eunomius: The Extant Works* (Oxford: Oxford University Press, 1987), 5–8.

28. Eunomius, *Liber Apologeticus* 7 (Vaggione, 40–41; translation altered).

29. Ibid., 9 (Vaggione, 42–43).

in actual substance with the Father, or even an ontological likeness and parity of ontological status with him.

> We have not used these expressions in order to take away the godhead of the Only-begotten, or his wisdom, or his immortality, or his goodness, but rather to distinguish them with respect to the pre-eminence of the Father. For we confess that the Lord Jesus is himself "Only-begotten God," immortal and deathless, wise, good; but we say too that the Father is the cause of his actual existence and of all that he is, for the Father, being unbegotten, has no cause of his essence or goodness. . . . Rejecting, therefore, any "similarity of essence" and accepting the similarity of the Son to the Father in accordance with his own words, we must mount up in very truth to the one and only font and source of all things, clearly having subordinated the Son to the Father.[30]

Although all three of the "Cappadocian Fathers" were outspoken critics of Eunomius and his "Neo-Arian" colleagues, it was Gregory of Nazianzus who extended his critique not only to their conclusions about the divine status of Christ, but to the philosophical assumptions and methods in which they steadfastly trusted. A highly educated man of letters himself, Gregory was not only a prolific poet and rhetorician, but considered himself a "philosopher," both in the sense of a single-minded ascetic and in that of a speculative thinker.[31] Yet his main critique of the Neo-Arians, as he had come to know them in Constantinople in the debates of the late 370s, was that they prized cleverness of thought and speech, dialectical adroitness, over faithful adherence to the faith of the gospel: they sought to be intelli-

30. Ibid., 21–22 (Vaggione, 60–63).

31. For a fuller treatment of the ways in which Gregory considered himself a "philosopher," and for further bibliography, see my *Gregory of Nazianzus* (London: Routledge, 2006), 34–41. And see especially Gregory's own descriptions of the "philosophic life," in passages such as Oration (Or.) 26.8–17 or Epistle (Ep.) 178. The portrait which emerges is that of a person who has attained a remarkable degree of freedom from anxiety and unbalanced desire by his practice of the Christian virtues. "Let me put it in a nutshell," he writes: "two things stand beyond our control—God and an angel; and in third place comes the philosopher! He is an immaterial being in matter, uncircumscribed while in a body, a citizen of heaven on earth, impassible in the midst of vulnerability, beaten in all things except his thoughts, a conqueror of those who think they have subdued him—simply by letting himself be conquered" (Or. 26.13; ibid., 113). Gregory (who always saw himself as persecuted by his enemies) does not claim to have reached perfection in this way, but presents himself as a committed seeker of genuine philosophic enlightenment.

gent, in a flashy and polemical way, rather than to be religious. In the first of his celebrated *Five Theological Orations*, a five-part treatise on the Trinity probably composed as an anti-Eunomian manifesto in the summer of 379, Gregory calls his opponents "acrobats of words," and compares them to professional wrestlers (who, even in fourth-century Byzantium, were apparently long on display and short on athletic substance!).[32] He cautions:

> Not to everyone, my friends, does it belong to philosophize about God; not to everyone—the subject is not so cheap and so low-flying! And, I will add, not everywhere, nor before every audience, nor on all subjects; but on certain occasions, and before certain persons, and up to certain limits.[33]

To "philosophize about God," was, of course, to carry on the kind of speculative reflection about God's being that we continue to call "theology,"[34] but like all philosophy in the ancient understanding, this reflection had to be carried on by people whose human passions had at least begun to be tamed and integrated, whose mind was broadly educated, and whose desires had matured; and it had to be done in a setting of serious, reverent dialogue. So he continues:

> I am not saying that one should not remember God at all times—lest these swift and eager people fasten on me again like dogs! For we ought to remember God even more often than we draw our breath; indeed, if I may be allowed to say so, we ought to do nothing else but this. . . . It is not the continual remembrance of God that I would hinder, but only talking about God [θεολογία]; nor would I prevent talk about God, as something irreverent, but only when it is out of place; nor teaching itself, but only a lack of moderation.[35]

Gregory then proceeds, in the rest of these five extraordinary "orations" or essays, to sketch out the possibility of our finding indications of God's reality in the natural world, as well as in the world of Scripture (Or. 28),

32. See Or. 27.1–2.

33. Or. 27.4. See Edward R. Hardy, ed., *Christology of the Later Fathers*, trans. Charles Gordon Browne and James Edward Swallow (Philadelphia: Westminster Press, 1954), 129; translation altered.

34. On the relation of "philosophy" and "theology" in ancient Greek thought and in Gregory's work, see my *Gregory of Nazianzus*, 42–43.

35. Or. 27.4 (Hardy, 130; translation altered).

and then (in Ors. 29 to 31) to consider the uniquely Christian conception of God—based on Scripture, especially on the New Testament, and on the present life of the Church, but surely "messy" philosophically: that God is both radically simple and single, and eternally three in his archetypally personal relationships of giving and receiving—the very conception of radically unified divine plurality that the Neo-Arians were bent on denying. At the start of the third "Theological Oration," he writes:

> The three most ancient opinions concerning God are *anarchia* [there are no ultimate causes], *polyarchia* [there are multiple ultimate causes], and *monarchia* [there can be only one ultimate cause]. The first two are the sport of the children of the Greeks [atheists and polytheists]. . . . But monarchy is what we hold in honor. It is, however, not a monarchy that is limited to one acting person, for it is possible for unity—if in a state of tension with itself—to come to be established as many; but a monarchy that is made of an equal dignity of nature, and a harmony of mind, and an identity of motion, and a convergence of its elements to unity [a thing which is impossible to created nature], so that though [the many are] numerically distinct, there is no separation of substance. Therefore that which is One from the beginning, being set in motion toward a Dyad, has come to its steady state as a Triad. This is what we mean by Father and Son and Holy Spirit![36]

Gregory is here bending the language of substance and individual, of identity and plurality, in a way that moves freely beyond the traditionally understood limits of philosophical analysis of divine simplicity, and even hovers on the edge of self-contradiction. Yet it is rooted, as he will go on to show, both in a long array of biblical texts, as they have come to be understood within the community of Christian faith and worship, and in the continuing experience of the Church, where the living presence of the Holy Spirit as the divine sanctifier is revealed in daily action. He writes in the final oration, on the Holy Spirit:

> To us there is one God, for the Godhead is one, and all that proceeds from God is predicated of one, even if we profess faith in three. For one is not more God, and the other less; nor is one before and another after; nor are

36. Or. 29.2. (Hardy, 161; translation altered). Gregory seems here to be deliberately evoking the classic Middle Platonic and Neo-Pythagorean language of a primordial Monad which, in its activities outside itself, develops into a Dyad and a Triad.

they divided in will or parted in power; nor can you find here any of the qualities that exist in divisible things; but the Godhead is, to speak concisely, undivided in its division; and there is one mingling of lights, as it were of three suns joined to each other.[37]

Philosophical discourse is needed, Gregory seems to assume, to identify the scope and implications of Christian faith, to specify what faith does and does not embrace; but philosophical discourse also meets its limits in the paradoxical affirmations of Christian Scripture. So, after a long and painstaking discussion of the passages in the New Testament that present the main paradoxes implied in Christian faith in Jesus—passages that for fifty-some years had been at the heart of the dispute between Arian and Nicene Christians—Gregory boldly affirms this mutual limitation of the concepts of philosophy and faith:

> This, then, is our reply to those who would throw riddles at us . . . that they may be led to see that they are not wise in every respect, nor invincible in those superfluous arguments which empty out the Gospel. For when we give first place to what is attainable by reason alone, and let go of faith, and destroy by our investigations what the Spirit makes credible, and when then our argument is overwhelmed by the sheer size of the subject (and surely it *must* be overwhelmed, since it starts off from the weak instrument of our own reason), what is the result? The weakness of the argument seems to be a weakness in the Mystery, and so elegance in reasoning "makes void the cross," as Paul also thought (1 Cor 1:17). For faith is that which brings our own human reasoning to its fulfillment.[38]

Philosophical dialectics, in Gregory's view, must find their context in the thought and worship of the community of faith, if they are to complement Christian faith in its articulation and not to become an alternative, ultimately a non-Christian, form of theology in themselves.

A third period to which one might point, as significant for the developing relationship between classical philosophy and Christian theology, is the seventh and eighth centuries: a time, in the Greek-speaking world especially, when the portrait of Christ enunciated at the Council of Chalcedon in 451, and reaffirmed in slightly different terms at the Second Council of

37. Or. 31.14 (Hardy, 202; translation altered).
38. Or. 29.21 (my translation).

Constantinople in 553, continued to be analyzed and discussed in what by then was primarily philosophical language. It seems fair to say, in general terms, that what we think of as "scholastic" theology began in earnest in the Eastern Christian world, in the wake of Chalcedon, and that the bitter debates which followed, about the adequacy of that council's dogmatic definition as an expression of the Church's faith, were carried on almost exclusively in the language of the classroom rather than that of the pulpit: in definitions and syllogisms, well-constructed theses and highly technical sets of questions and answers, rather than in the more homiletic and biblical theological style of the third, fourth, and early fifth centuries.[39] By the late fifth century, too, what we understand as philosophy had become more identifiably academic. In the established schools in Athens and Alexandria, for instance, imperially salaried professors lectured on the classical sources of the Greek philosophical tradition: the major dialogues of Plato, Aristotle's *Ethics*, *Physics*, and *Metaphysics*, as well as the *Organon*, and Porphyry's *Eisagōgē*—his introduction to Aristotelian logic. The texts being commented on were mainly familiar representatives of Hellenistic philosophy, reaching back a millennium; but the perspective in which they were construed was, in general terms, Neoplatonic—that more inward-turned, even mystical style of philosophical thought that drew inspiration from both Aristotle and Plato, as well as from the eclectic traditions of the second century.

One might point to the work of a number of sixth- and seventh-century Christian theologians to show the growing influence of Neoplatonic philosophical commentaries on Aristotle within the language and style of theology: to the work of Leontius of Byzantium and Leontius of Jerusalem, to that of the theologian-emperor Justinian I, and especially to the dense and original essays and letters on the ascetical life and the Mystery of Christ by Maximus the Confessor, in the seventh century. Here, however, it might be more helpful simply to consider the relation of school philosophy and the patristic theological tradition to each other in the work of one of the great synthesizers of antique Christian thought, John of Damascus (c. 680–750).

Like the majority of influential Christian writers since Chalcedon, John was not a bishop, but a monk and priest who devoted most of his energies, it seems, to study and writing. A member of the Palestinian monastic community of Mar Saba for almost fifty years, John was a prolific poet, an

39. See my article "Boethius' Theological Tracts and Early Byzantine Scholasticism," *Mediaeval Studies* 46 (1984): 158–91.

accomplished and profound preacher, and above all a philosophically acute theologian who saw his work as one of retrospective synthesis: "I will say nothing of my own," he insists in the preface of his ambitious compendium of philosophical and theological learning, the *Spring of Knowledge* (Πηγὴ γνώσεως), "but will collect into one place the labors of the most respected of our teachers, . . . and keep my language as brief as possible."[40] Like the Western scholastics of the thirteenth century and later, John saw his work, on the surface at least, as one of systematization and integration.

The Damascene begins this monumental treatise with a section usually called the *Dialectica*: a summary of the key concepts and logical rules of late antique reasoning and analysis, largely drawn from Aristotle's *Categories* and Porphyry's *Eisagōgē*, and presented here conveniently in 68 terse chapters.[41] He then offers us, in Part II, 101 chapters outlining the key "heresies" or sects of the early Christian centuries, each focused on a particular misconstrual of the Church's tradition of understanding biblical faith; significantly, the final, "bonus" chapter of the work is a description of Islam—the dominant religious system in John's native Damascus while he was growing up, which John took to be a Judaeo-Christian heresy. Part III—subtitled "On the Orthodox Faith"—contains a further 100 chapters, outlining in contrast the main recognized teachings of mainstream Christianity; Christian doctrine is expressed here in terms that often draw on Hellenistic philosophy, and that stands in contrast to the beliefs of quasi-Christian sects, but its guiding norm is the Scriptures and their interpretation within the Church.[42]

The guiding theme of the whole *Spring of Knowledge* is the unsurpassable importance of knowledge, our access to the truth; this knowledge is grounded in God's being, and is revealed to us both in the historical events

40. John Damascene, *Spring of Knowledge*, in *Die Schriften des Johannes von Damaskos*, vol. 1, ed. Bonifatius Kotter (Berlin: De Gruyter, 1969), Prooemium, 53.

41. Since the second and third parts of the *Spring of Knowledge* consist each of 100 chapters, it is possible that John planned to offer 100 preparatory philosophical chapters as well. This part of the project may not have been finished—a possibility suggested by the somewhat disorganized and repetitive character of the last three chapters of the longer version of the *Dialectica*—or John may simply have run out of suitable material.

42. This final section of the *Spring of Knowledge* was translated several times into Latin in the early Middle Ages, most famously by Burgundio of Pisa in the second half of the twelfth century, and was known in the West as *De fide orthodoxa*. This translation, in which the numbering of chapters is altered to turn the treatise into four "books," corresponding to the parts of Peter Lombard's *Sentences*, was the vehicle through which St. Thomas Aquinas came to know it and to use it so widely as a guide for his own arguments.

and teachings of Scripture and in the operation of human reason. John begins the first chapter of the *Dialectica*:

> Nothing is more precious than knowledge [γνῶσις]. For if knowledge is the light of the rational soul, ignorance, on the other hand, must be darkness. And as the deprivation of light is darkness, so the deprivation of knowledge is a darkness of our reason. But ignorance is proper to irrational beings, knowledge to rational ones. If someone, then, does not possess knowledge, when he is naturally able to know and to give reasons for things, this person—being rational by nature—is, because of indifference and laziness of soul, worse than irrational beasts![43]

Knowledge is the intellectual creature's contact with reality; but it is always precarious and halting for the human mind, because the mind is "covered, as it were, with the veil of the flesh,"[44] and so can mistakenly embrace ignorance rather than real knowledge. As a result, the mind needs to be purified from passionate attachments, and patient in its search; more important still, John points out, it needs a Teacher. He continues:

> Let us draw near to the Truth, the Teacher who does not deceive. But Christ is Wisdom and Truth personified; in him "all the treasures of knowledge are hidden,"[45] and he is "the Wisdom and Power of God" the Father.[46] Let us listen to his voice speaking through the divine Scriptures, and let us learn the true knowledge of all things that are.[47]

To know Christ, who is divine Wisdom in person, and through contact with him to be able to use human reason as a reliable instrument for discovering truth, John is convinced—as Origen and Augustine had been before him—that we need to undertake the laborious task of "knocking at the door" of Scripture, as it points to Christ in figures and discloses his presence in our midst.

> And as we move forward, let us not be satisfied with simply arriving at the gate, but let us knock vigorously, so that the door to the bridal chamber

43. *Dialectica* 1, ed. Kotter, in *Schriften*, vol. 1, p. 53; translation mine.
44. Ibid.
45. Col 2:3.
46. 1 Cor 1:24.
47. *Dialectica* 1, p. 53; translation mine.

> might be opened to us and we might see the beauties within it. The gate, after all, is the letter; but the bridal chamber within the gate is the beauty of the thoughts which it hides, or the spirit of truth. Let us knock vigorously; let us read the scriptural text once, twice, many times, and so—by opening the treasury of knowledge—we shall find it and feast on its riches.[48]

Knowledge of the truth of things, in other words, engages the human mind in the hard labor of analysis and argument—in what we have come to call philosophy—as well as in the equally hard labor of seeking for the real meaning of scriptural revelation, the story of God's unpredictable actions in human history. In the end, knowledge of the truth is an encounter with Christ, the Wisdom of God and the foundation of the truth of all else that is; it depends both on human shrewdness and effort and on God's gratuitous self-disclosure. "If we love to learn," he writes, "we shall learn much! All things can naturally be grasped by concentration and labor, and before and after all else by the grace of God, who has given them all to us."[49]

With this as his presupposition, John then goes on to sketch an outline of what reason can achieve by engaging the world around us; he gives brief definitions of what the Greek world has come to understand by being, substance and accident, genus and species and differentiating characteristic, of what an individual is and how it is related to universals—essentially the kind of philosophical terminology one would need to know, to understand classic Christian discussions of the Trinity and the person of Christ. Yet the focus, even in this essentially philosophical treatise about terminology, is on what the mind can do with Revelation. So in chapter 3, where he offers several definitions of philosophy itself, John begins with a definition one can find in the Neoplatonic commentators on Aristotle: "Philosophy is knowledge of the things that are, insofar as they are—that is, knowledge of the nature of what is."[50] But he concludes, six definitions later, with a characterization of philosophy that is not found in the commentators but may well have grown from his own experience as scholar and monk: "Philosophy, once again, is love of Wisdom. But true Wisdom is God. Therefore the love of God is true philosophy."[51]

48. Ibid., 54; translation mine.
49. Ibid.; translation mine.
50. Ibid., 3, p. 56; translation mine.
51. Ibid.; translation mine.

Christ as the Reason

One might, of course, offer many other examples to illustrate how deeply intertwined Christian theologians, since the second century at least, have seen reason and Revelation to be in God's long history of engagement with the human race. Although he often acknowledged that faith—trust in the word of another, on the basis of the other's known credibility—is essential for all human knowledge, Augustine, for instance, insisted that faith is only a provisional form of knowledge (*scientia*); knowledge of truth in its fullness is to be looked for in the unitive, participative contemplation of God, and of all things in God, which is reserved for the life to come, beyond time, and which Augustine calls wisdom (*sapientia*).[52] He writes in Book 13 of *De Trinitate*:

> Our *knowledge* therefore is Christ, and our *wisdom* is the same Christ. It is he who plants faith in us about temporal things, he who presents us with the Truth about eternal things. Through him we go straight towards him—through knowledge towards wisdom—without ever turning aside from the same Christ, "in whom are hidden all the treasures of wisdom and knowledge" (Col 2:3).[53]

Augustine was always ready, of course, to make use of the best available strategies for reasoning critically and truthfully about the world; for him, this normally involved making limited use of the philosophical strategies of Latin Neoplatonism. He describes at some length, in Book 7 of his *Confessions*, how his engagement with "books of the Platonists" during his time teaching in Milan solved a number of the intellectual problems with orthodox Christianity that had led him to become a Manichee some thirteen years earlier.[54] Yet it was not until he was able to recognize Christ, as God humbling himself out of love for our sakes[55]—a notion that philosophical speculation would doubtless find bizarre—and to discover for himself the equally non-philosophical humility to accept the grace of Christ, by reading

52. This distinction runs throughout his works. On faith as a form of *scientia* based on trusting the credibility of another, see, for instance, *De vera religione* 25.46–47 (written in 390); *De utilitate credendi* 10.23–16.34 (written in 391–92). For the distinction of *scientia* and *sapientia* in a broader sense, see *De Trinitate* 12.15.22–16.25; 13.1.2 (written in 417–419?).

53. *De Trinitate* 13.19.24 (trans. Edmund Hill, OP [Brooklyn, NY: New City Press, 1990], 363–64).

54. See *Confessions* 7.9.13–17.23.

55. Ibid., 7.20.26.

Paul,[56] that he was able to move beyond his questions and accept baptism. Philosophy could take him only so far toward knowing truth in its fullness.

St. Thomas Aquinas, too, is clearly aware both of the importance of the newly rediscovered, Aristotelian philosophical system for ordering and balancing our theological knowledge and of philosophy's limitations for helping us know God, since philosophy is simply an articulation of human reason. In the classic presentation of article 8 of question 1 of the *Summa theologiae*, for instance, he insists that *sacra doctrina*—our knowledge of God, and all things in their relation to God, arranged as a "science" in terms of ordered explanation from first principles—is certainly a realm of human knowing that is open to argument: a place where people of good will and sound mental powers must labor and can plausibly disagree. But because the first principles of the science of theology are affirmed in the Scriptures, and are thus "articulations of faith" (*articuli fidei*) rather than affirmations to be proved by reasoning, one can argue about theological statements only with a person who is able to concede as true at least something of what the Scriptures present of God. Aquinas writes in his famous response to the second objection of this article:

> Arguing on the basis of authority is especially characteristic of this body of knowledge [*doctrina*], for the reason that the principles of this knowledge are possessed through revelation, and thus it is appropriate that the authority of those people is to be believed to whom revelation was made. . . . Sacred doctrine, however, makes use also of human reason: not to prove the content of faith, since through that the merit of believing would be taken away, but to make clear some of the other points that are communicated in this doctrine. . . . That is why sacred doctrine even makes use of the authority of the philosophers, when, by the use of natural reason, they have succeeded in knowing truth. . . . But sacred doctrine makes use of authorities of this kind as extrinsic evidence, forming part of probable arguments; whereas it uses the authorities of canonical Scripture in the full sense, arguing to necessary conclusions.[57]

Clearly, the understanding of religious knowledge that Aquinas shows here, and that is evident in the patristic examples we discussed earlier, leads in a very different direction from the conception of knowledge, on

56. Ibid., 7.21.27.

57. St. Thomas Aquinas, *ST* I, q. 1, a. 8, ad 2 (translation mine).

the one hand, and of religious faith, on the other, that has characterized the modern West since the seventeenth century. In the wake of the Enlightenment, as has often been observed, religious faith came more and more to be considered as part of the realm of interior assumptions, moral convictions, or personal feelings, in contrast to that of empirical, "scientific" knowledge of the objective world. For Harnack and his colleagues, as we have seen, Christianity itself was not originally a set of doctrines at all; it was essentially a moral stance, a trusting benevolence toward one's fellow human beings, grounded in a sense of being creatures of a benevolent God, that was rooted in the teaching and practice of Jesus, but that nineteen centuries of philosophical speculation had simply alienated from its source.

In response to Enlightenment critique, and to the liberal Protestant rejection of historical dogma, much of the effort of nineteenth- and early twentieth-century Catholic scholasticism was to reaffirm the reasonableness and philosophical coherence of faith as officially formulated, and to present Church doctrine as an abstract, tightly reasoned system of principles and conclusions. As the Belgian Dominican M. M. Tuyaerts argued in his work *L'Évolution du dogme: étude théologique* (1919), "The nature of dogma, and of our mind, make possible only one single process in the evolution of dogma: the dialectical process, which is reasoning."[58] Faced with the range of propositions one can identify in Scripture and in the Church's official teachings through the centuries, the theologian's task was simply to draw out their implications in a logically consistent way.

Much of the energy of Catholic theology since the 1930s has come from a reaction against both of these approaches to conceiving the role of philosophical reason in the articulation of the Church's faith: the anti-dogmatic moralism of liberal Protestant historians, and the stiff and exclusive rationalism of some scholastic handbooks. In the writings that represent what came to be called—first disparagingly, then approvingly—*la nouvelle théologie*, an important group of mid-twentieth-century European theologians, mainly French Dominicans and Jesuits, began to raise serious questions about both of these theological styles and to emphasize once again both the importance of historical and cultural context and the possibility of genuine development of new issues and ideas in the articulation

58. M. M. Tuyaerts, *L'Évolution du dogme: étude théologique* (Louvain: Nova et Vetera, 1919), 236; cited by Henri de Lubac, "Le problème du développement du dogme," *Théologie dans l'histoire*, vol. 2 (Paris: Desclée, 1990), 38–39.

of faith, based on the concrete reality of Jesus, the Word made flesh.[59] In an influential article published in 1935, for instance, the French Dominican scholar of twelfth- and thirteenth-century theology, Marie-Dominique Chenu, insisted that, unlike the philosopher,

> the theologian works with a history. His "data" are not the natures of things, or the timeless forms; they are events, corresponding to an *economy*, whose realization is bound to time, just as extension is bound to the body—beneath the order of essences. The *real* world is this one, not the abstraction of the philosopher. The believer, the believing theologian, enters by his faith into this plan of God; what he seeks to understand, *quaerens intellectum*, is a divine initiative, a series of absolute divine initiatives, whose essential trait is to be without a reason—both the general initiatives of creation, the incarnation, redemption, grace, and the particular initiatives of the gracious predestination of individuals: the sweet and terrible contingency of a love which needs give no account of his benefits or his refusal to benefit. This world is the true world of contemplation, and of theological understanding.[60]

So the work of the theologian, however shaped in its articulated form by philosophical discipline and pastoral urgency, is always inseparable from a contemplation of the presence and the saving acts of God in history, as narrated in the Scriptures and as interpreted in the continuing, time-bound tradition of the community of faith. When theology turns from ideas, it turns from Christ, the Word and Wisdom of God; but when it becomes so preoccupied with building a coherent intellectual system of ideas that it loses conscious contact with either Scripture or tradition, it loses its identifying focus on the work of God. As Chenu writes in the same article:

> The philosopher can ignore the history of philosophy—in theory, at least—without suffering any disadvantage; because it is not the historians [of

59. For a fuller treatment of the importance of this movement for the revival of patristic and liturgical studies in the Catholic Church, see my article "The *Nouvelle Théologie* and the Patristic Revival: Sources, Symbols, and the Science of Theology," *International Journal of Systematic Theology* 7 (2005): 362–82; also "Knowing God in History and in the Church: *Dei Verbum* and 'Nouvelle Théologie,'" in *Ressourcement: A Movement for Renewal in Twentieth-Century Catholic Theology*, ed. Gabriel Flynn and Paul D. Murray (Oxford: Oxford University Press, 2012), 333–51.

60. Marie-Dominique Chenu, "Position de la théologie," *Revue des sciences philosophiques et théologiques* 25 (1935): 247; my translation.

> thought] who give him his material, but things in themselves. The theologian, on the other hand, has no object apart from the *auditus fidei*, of which the historian, working in the light of faith, gives him the content—not simply a catalogue of propositions arranged by some Denzinger or other, but living material, in its full abundance, always active in the treasury of the Church, laden with divine intelligibility.[61]

A product of this same movement, arguably, is the Second Vatican Council's *Dogmatic Constitution on Divine Revelation* (November 18, 1965), which attempted to present the whole vexed question of the sources of faith, the "first principles" of the Church's theology, in the light of the historical reality of God's presence in the history of Israel and the Church. So the constitution declares at the outset its distinctive conception of what Revelation is:

> It has pleased God, in his goodness and wisdom, to reveal himself and to make known the secret purpose of his will (see Eph 1:9). This brings it about that through Christ, God's Word made flesh, and in his Holy Spirit, human beings can draw near to the Father and become sharers in the divine nature (I Pt 2:4). By thus revealing himself, God, who is invisible, in his great love speaks to humankind as friends, and enters into their life, so as to invite and receive them into relationship with himself. The pattern of this revelation unfolds through deeds and words bound together by an inner dynamism, in such a way that God's works, effected during the course of the history of salvation, show forth and confirm the doctrine and the realities signified by the words, while the words in turn proclaim the works and throw light on the meaning hidden in them. By this revelation the truth, both about God and about the salvation of humankind, inwardly dawns on us in Christ, who is in himself both the mediator and the fullness of all revelation.[62]

It is hard here not to be reminded of John of Damascus's insistence that it is Christ, made known to us in the challenging yet rich text of Scripture, who is the heart of the wisdom that reason so eagerly seeks, or of Gregory Nazianzen's astonishing affirmation that "faith"—faith in Jesus, the incarnate Word, expressed in the historical and culturally limited words of human speech—"is what brings our own human reasoning to its fulfillment."

61. Ibid., 245.

62. *Dei Verbum*, §2, in *Decrees of the Ecumenical Councils*, vol. 2, ed. Norman P. Tanner (Washington, DC: Georgetown University Press, 1990), 972.

Christian faith, as Pope Benedict reminded his scientist colleagues at Regensburg, has always cherished the assumption that God acts reasonably and that our created reason is grounded in the very reality of God. Hence Christian faith, since Paul's speech on the Areopagus, has attempted to connect the proclamation of God's work in history, which has reached its peak in the death and resurrection of Jesus, with the best instincts of secular literary and intellectual culture, and to see in Christ the embodiment of divine reason, the *Logos* who has become flesh. Christ is, for Christianity, not simply the one on whose identity revelation casts its light, the one about whom theology reasons in often philosophical terms. He is rather, in his own historical human person, the fullness of Revelation, the source of our ideas and understanding about God, the promise of a full share in eschatological wisdom, which will be no more and no less than a share of Christ in his fullness. If philosophy represents the best and most concentrated efforts of human reason, relying on its own powers, to connect and arrange our understanding of the world, philosophy and theology clearly need each other to reach their goals. But philosophy, as Christian theology uses it, can never be left to function on its own, an analytical or deductive system engaging experience as an independent intellectual discipline; it must be, in some sense, a philosophy aimed at making sense of the mystery of Christ's person and work. Without the Word in his flesh, philosophical reasoning struggles on without a reliable teacher, gropes in the dark of language games and rival schools, lacks substance and hope. As St. Paul wrote to the Colossians, "The Mystery hidden for ages and generations"—the lost key to the world's intelligibility, for which philosophers continue to search—"but [which is] now made manifest to the saints . . . is Christ in you, your hope of glory" (Col 1:26–27). What Christian faith has to offer the world—even the world of philosophy—is the challenge and the promise of sharing in that Mystery.

16 "Faithful and True"

Early Christian Apocalyptic and the Person of Christ

Lo, he comes with clouds descending,
Once for favored sinners slain;
Thousand, thousand saints attending
Swell the triumph of his train;
Hallelujah, hallelujah!
God appears, on earth to reign![1]

Charles Wesley's great hymn, linked in the minds of many Western Christians to the start of the Advent season, is but one of many evocations of what has remained, since the time of the earliest church, the centerpiece of Christian hope: the reappearance of Jesus on earth, still bearing on his body what Wesley calls "his glorious scars," "the dear tokens of his passion," yet resplendent now in divine power, triumphant over the enemies of faith, and surrounded by those who have faithfully endured persecution for his name. The scene, as Wesley paints it, is focused on Jesus: Jesus in glory, Jesus bringing to a conclusion the story that began with the Gospel accounts of his resurrection and ascension, Jesus as Savior yet to come. Yet the colors of the scene are borrowed from that particular Jewish and Christian tradition we identify as apocalyptic: from the book of Revelation, the only full exemplar of the genre in the New Testament canon, and from its canonical and postcanonical Jewish sources and parallels. While this may not seem

1. From the 1870 Methodist *Hymnbook*, no. 66; see Frank Whaling, ed., *John and Charles Wesley: Selected Prayers, Hymns, Journal Notes, Sermons, Letters and Treatises* (New York: Paulist Press, 1981), 276.

surprising at first glance, it suggests some important aspects of both classical Christology and Christian apocalyptic that I will explore further here, if only in summary and in a somewhat hypothetical way.

At the risk of saying the obvious, let me characterize what I understand as the principal features of the apocalyptic literary genre, since its form, significance, and history remain the subject of considerable debate.[2] In their classical guise, apocalyptic works are dramatic religious narratives, usually telling of journeys beyond the world of ordinary experience, in dream or vision, in which the narrator is permitted by the sovereign God to glimpse the underlying secrets of human history, past and future. They are normally pseudepigraphic works: the author conceals his or her identity under the name of some already-familiar personality from the biblical past, a strategy calculated both to give credibility to the work's message and to guarantee its continuity with received religious tradition. The scene of the seer's journey is normally set on a grand scale, offering a glimpse of the mechanics and dimensions of the world well beyond the screen of our daily experience. The characters in the drama are also usually fantastic, larger-than-life figures, embodying the forces of good and evil that struggle to control the world's history. Assuming that our present human situation, with all its dangers and ambiguities, is veiled in mystery, its outcome uncertain, the narrative offers a glimpse—a "revelation" or *apokalypsis*—of otherwise inaccessible meaning; and the message, in its simplest terms, is that God remains in control, that God is faithful to his promises, and that he will save his chosen ones from danger. Usually, this message of reassurance is interwoven with strong criticism of the dominant forces behind the social and political situation of believers, and with an equally strong appeal to believers themselves to

2. See my remarks in "Apocalypticism in Early Christian Theology," in *Encyclopedia of Apocalypticism*, vol. 2, *Apocalypticism in Western History and Culture*, ed. Bernard McGinn (New York: Continuum, 1998), 3–6, as well as the discussions of the genre by other authors in the same work, esp. John J. Collins, "From Prophecy to Apocalypticism: the Expectation of the End," in *Encyclopedia of Apocalypticism*, vol. 1, *The Origins of Apocalypticism in Judaism and Christianity*, ed. John J. Collins (New York: Continuum, 1998), 129–61; Florentino García Martínez, "Apocalypticism in the Dead Sea Scrolls," in Collins, *Encyclopedia of Apocalypticism*, 1:162–92; James C. VanderKam, "Messianism and Apocalypticism," in Collins, *Encyclopedia of Apocalypticism*, 1:193–228; David Frankfurter, "Early Christian Apocalypticism: Literature and Social World," in Collins, *Encyclopedia of Apocalypticism*, 1:415–53. For a useful survey of the genre, see Christopher Rowland, *The Open Heaven: A Study of Apocalyptic in Judaism and Early Christianity* (New York: Crossroad, 1982); John J. Collins, *The Apocalyptic Imagination: An Introduction to the Jewish Matrix of Christianity* (New York: Crossroad, 1984).

remain faithful to God and to the moral and religious obligations he has laid on them. Although we can only guess at the actual social context in which particular works in the genre were written, the intended audience was clearly people who felt themselves to be marginalized, under threat by the world's superpowers, struggling for survival; at the same time, apocalyptic works usually convey a sense of privilege, of election, of strong traditional bonding, in which both the personality of the pseudepigraphic speaker and the prophetic rhetoric of his message can be expected to deliver maximum impact. It is a literature that presumes a strong sense of religious boundaries and that seems calculated to reinforce them.

What I want to argue here is that the apocalyptic genre, in the hands of Christians in the patristic era, underwent a fairly rapid transformation, late in the second century, that robbed it of much of its original mystery, drama, and rhetorical tension, even as it wove apocalyptic imagery into a growing common Christian understanding of the identity and person of Jesus, the reality of the material world and its importance in God's plan of salvation, and the nature of the church as God's elect community.

It seems beyond question that both Jesus and his disciples, and Paul, Jesus' earliest written interpreter, were steeped in the motifs and images of Jewish apocalyptic literature.[3] The apocalyptic discourses of Jesus in the Synoptic Gospels, for instance (Matt. 24–25; Mark 13; Luke 17:20–37; Luke 21), suggest clearly that the earliest oral traditions placed his message of the coming kingdom within the context both of the final struggle of cosmic powers and of the accompanying exhortation to fidelity and trust that is characteristic of this late Jewish genre. Paul's earliest letter, 1 Thessalonians, describes the "coming of the Lord," Jesus who has died and is risen, as something to be expected soon, an event that will mean salvation for the faithful, dead or living, and judgment for all (1 Thess. 4:13–5:11). The book of Revelation or

3. See Dale C. Allison Jr., "The Eschatology of Jesus," in Collins, *Encyclopedia of Apocalypticism*, 1:267–302; Richard A. Horsley, "The Kingdom of God and the Renewal of Israel: Synoptic Gospels, Jesus Movements, and Apocalypticism," in Collins, *Encyclopedia of Apocalypticism*, 1:303–44; M. C. DeBoer, "Paul and Apocalyptic Eschatology," in Collins, *Encyclopedia of Apocalypticism*, 1:345–83. For apocalyptic elements in the Synoptic Gospels, see G. R. Beasley-Murray, *Jesus and the Last Days: The Interpretation of the Olivet Discourse* (Peabody, MA: Hendrickson, 1993). For Paul's use of apocalyptic themes, see J. C. Beker, *Paul the Apostle: The Triumph of God in Life and Thought* (Philadelphia: Fortress, 1980). For a discussion of modern scholarly debate about the apocalyptic dimension of Paul's theology, see R. Barry Matlock, *Unveiling the Apocalyptic Paul: Paul's Interpreters and the Rhetoric of Criticism* (Sheffield: Sheffield Academic Press, 1996).

Apocalypse of John—the New Testament's only full example of the genre, and indeed the paradigm of later Christian apocalyptic thought[4]—brings us fully into the visionary world of enormous beasts and world-changing battles, of moral exhortation and urgent reassurance, characteristic of classical Jewish apocalyptic. It weaves into its narrative a multitude of texts and allusions from those sections of the earlier Jewish canon that paved the way for this form of literature, especially Daniel 7–12; Ezekiel 40–48; and sections of the book of Isaiah and the Psalter. This work is, in a sense, a pastiche of powerful apocalyptic images and warnings from earlier Jewish tradition; but here, as in 1 Thessalonians 4 and even, by implication, in the synoptic apocalyptic passages I have mentioned, the central figure of the vision is precisely the crucified and risen Jesus. It is "Jesus Christ, the faithful witness, the firstborn of the dead, and the ruler of the kings on earth" (Rev. 1:5) who is the source of the moral exhortations that the seer sends to the seven churches of Asia; it is Jesus, who remains near to his disciples, "standing at the door, knocking" (Rev. 3:20), who promises them victory over the enemies that now threaten to distract or destroy them. And it is Jesus, "the Lamb that was slaughtered" (Rev. 5:6, 12; 13:8; cf. 7:14)—now standing in the place of honor before the gloriously enthroned God of Israel's prophetic visions (see, e.g., Exod. 24:9–11; Isa. 6:1–4; Ezek. 1:22–28)—who unseals the secrets of God's purpose in history, and who promises to defeat the forces of oppression. The apocalyptic form has become, overtly in these works and as a subtext in other New Testament passages, a central instrument for confessing Jesus as Messiah, enthroned with God, and as Lord of history.

My purpose here, however, is not to characterize the apocalypticism of the New Testament writings, but to survey the changing character of this powerful style of Jewish and Christian thought, and its use in the wider context of an emerging orthodox consensus on the interpretation of Christ's person and work, during the six or seven centuries that followed their composition. What I want to argue here is that even as the drama of Christian apocalyptic narrative lost much of its urgency, as Christian communities came to be more sure of themselves within the wider matrix of late Roman society, the apocalyptic image of the glorified Jesus—"the Lamb who

4. See Richard Bauckham, *The Theology of the Book of Revelation* (Cambridge: Cambridge University Press, 1994); Adela Yarbro Collins, "The Book of Revelation," in Collins, *Encyclopedia of Apocalypticism*, 1:384–414. The most recent and thorough large-scale commentary on the book of Revelation in English is David E. Aune, *Revelation 1–5*, WBC 52a (Dallas: Word Books, 1997); idem, *Revelation 6–16* and *17–22*, WBC 52b–c (Nashville: Nelson, 1998).

was slain"—as judge to come, victor over the demonic powers of evil, and hidden companion of his church in what was assumed to be the continuing, final age of history, took on a formative, even a determining role for the development of doctrine. Christology, cosmology, ecclesiology—to use the distorting categories of modern academic theology—all became, in the course of the patristic period, East and West, "apocalypticized"; but it was an apocalypticism that had become a vehicle for acknowledging Jesus as Lord of history. Apocalyptic prophecy to communities under threat, beginning from what is found in the texts of the Bible and in early post-70 Jewish and Christian works, was gradually transformed into a set of images for the glorified Christ, and a scenario for the present and future course of the age of the church.[5] In broad strokes, at least, let me try to fill out this very general scheme of theological development with some concrete examples.

Early Christian Apocalyptic

Undoubtedly the clearest example of a noncanonical early Christian document fully embodying the apocalyptic genre is the *Ascension of Isaiah*, a work generally thought to have been written in Syria between 112 and 138.[6] Although the language of its composition was probably Greek, only a few fragments of that original version remain; we do have a later Greek paraphrase, as well as partial translations in Latin, Slavonic, and Coptic, and an apparently complete version in Ethiopic, which serves as the foundation for most modern translations. For a long time the work was curiously neglected by students of earliest Christianity, although a spurt of interest, especially among Italian scholars, resulted in a ground-breaking conference in 1981, numerous articles and monographs since then, and a long-awaited critical edition.[7] Well before this trend began, however, Jean Daniélou identified the

5. For an exploration of the impact of apocalyptic imagery for Christ on the catechesis and church iconography of the fourth and fifth centuries, see Geir Hellemo, *Adventus Domini: Eschatological Thought in Fourth-Century Apses and Catecheses* (Leiden: Brill, 1989).

6. For a full discussion of the probable date and place of this work's origin, see esp. Michael A. Knibb, "The Ascension of Isaiah," in *OTP* 2:143–50; Jonathan Knight, *Disciples of the Beloved One: The Christology, Social Setting, and Theological Context of the Ascension of Isaiah* (Sheffield: Sheffield Academic Press, 1996), 33–39.

7. See esp. Mauro Pesce, ed., *Isaia, il Diletto e la Chiesa: Visione ed esegesi profetica cristianoprimitiva nell'Ascensione di Isaia*, Conference in Rome, 1981 (Brescia: Paideia, 1983), with important articles on the work's text, literary background, and theology; Antonio

Ascension as the clearest literary example of what he called "Jewish Christianity":[8] an unambiguously Christian work that presents the gospel of Christ's coming and victory in the full trappings of Second Temple apocalyptic.

The *Ascension* is framed in a narrative of the persecution and martyrdom of the prophet Isaiah, due to the unrelenting enmity of Beliar or Sammael, the "great prince" (*Ascension* 4.2) and leader of the spirits opposed to God and his faithful people.[9] It offers two separate prophetic narratives embodying the Christian gospel of salvation through Christ, God's "Beloved,"[10] both of them presented as the record of an ecstatic vision granted the prophet Isaiah before he was arrested and sawn in two.[11] The first of these begins with a summary of the story of Jesus, as this work presents it:

> Through [Isaiah] the coming forth of the Beloved from the seventh heaven had been revealed, and his transformation, his descent and the likeness into which he was to be transformed, namely, the likeness of a man, and the persecution which he was to suffer. . . . and that he was to be crucified together with criminals, and that he would be buried in a sepulcher, and that

Acerbi, *Serra Lignea: Studi sulla Fortuna dell' Ascensione di Isaia* (Rome: Editrice AVE, 1984), on the literary and theological influence of the work; idem, *L'Ascensione di Isaia: Cristologia e profetismo in Siria nei primi decenni del II secolo* (Milan: Vita e Pensiero, 1989), offering a close exegesis of the text; Enrico Norelli, *L'Ascensione di Isaia: Studi su un apocrifo al crocevia dei cristianesimi* (Bologna: EDB, 1994), a collection of studies by the editor of the Greek versions of the text; Jonathan Knight, *The Ascension of Isaiah* (Sheffield: Sheffield Academic Press, 1995), a concise introduction to the work and analysis of its content; and idem, *Disciples of the Beloved One*, Knight's fuller discussion of the critical problems of the work as well as its theology. The new critical edition of the work, in its Ethiopic, Greek, Coptic, Latin, and Old Slavic or Paleo-Bulgarian versions, including a valuable synopsis of all the versions, has been produced by the first-rate team of Italian scholars originally gathered by Mauro Pesce, in Corpus Christianorum, Series Apocryphorum 7 (Turnhout: Brepols, 1995). This is now the basis for any serious translation or study of the work. There is now also a concordance of the Ethiopic version, which is the only witness to the complete text: Gianfrancesco Lusini, *Ascensione di Isaia: Concordanza della versione etiopica* (Wiesbaden: Harrasowitz, 2003).

8. Jean Daniélou, *The Theology of Jewish Christianity* (London: Darton, Longman and Todd, 1964), 12–14 and passim.

9. That this narrative seems most likely based on oral rather than written Jewish sources is argued by Mauro Pesce in "Presupposti per l'utilizzazione storica dell'Ascensione di Isaia: Formazione e tradizione del testo; genere letterario; cosmologia angelica," in *Isaia*, 13–76; cf. Knight, *Disciples of the Beloved One*, 13–14, 28–29, and further references there.

10. For the use of this title in the New Testament for Jesus, see Matt. 3:17 par; 12:18 par; Eph. 1:6. In the Old Testament, see Isa. 5:1; cf. Gen. 22:2, 12, 16.

11. For the prophet's death, see Matt. 5:11; this same tradition seems to be alluded to in Heb. 11:37.

> the twelve who were with him would be offended because of him, and the watch of the guards of the grave, and the descent of the angel of the church which is in the heavens, whom he will summon in the last days; and that the angel of the Holy Spirit and Michael, the chief of the holy angels, would open his grave on the third day, and that the Beloved, sitting on their shoulders, will come forth and send out his twelve disciples, and that they will teach to all the nations and every tongue the resurrection of the Beloved, and that those who believe in his cross will be saved.[12]

This first prophetic narrative goes on to speak in vivid terms about the problems that will increasingly infect the community of disciples in the time after this first proclamation of Christ: conflicting expectations about his second coming, ambition, lack of holiness among community "shepherds," greed, "respect for persons," slander and boasting, all leading to the radical decline of the prophetic charism among them (*Ascension* 3.22–28). The document then sketches a picture of the final age soon to follow, in which Beliar will descend from heaven in the form of Nero returned from the grave, performing nature-miracles and daring to "speak in the name of the Beloved" (*Ascension* 4.6)—an Antichrist, in other words, who will seduce the faithful into apostasy. After 1,332 days, "the Lord will come with his angels and with the hosts of the saints from the seventh heaven" (*Ascension* 4.14), and will defeat the forces of Beliar; then, in a version of the "rapture" alluded to by Paul in 1 Thessalonians 4:17, the faithful "who are found in the body" will be caught upwards and clothed in the glorious "garments which are stored on high in the seventh heaven"—bodies of light apparently—while their material bodies remain on earth.[13] After this will come further conflict,

12. *Ascension of Isaiah* 3.13–18 (trans. and ed. R. McLaren Wilson, based on the German translation of C. Detlef and G. Muller, in *New Testament Apocrypha*, ed. Edgar Hennecke and Wilhelm Schneemelcher, 2 vols., rev. ed. [Louisville: Westminster John Knox, 1992], 2:608).

13. *Ascension* 4.17. For a rich discussion of the Jewish and early Christian tradition, particularly in early Syriac literature and the ascetic literature of Egypt in the late fourth century, of God's "body of light" and of its implications for the future form of human disciples, see Alexander Golitzin, "Recovering the 'Glory of Adam': 'Divine Light' Traditions in the Dead Sea Scrolls and the Christian Ascetical Literature of Fourth-Century Syro-Mesopotamia," in *Dead Sea Scrolls as Background to Postbiblical Judaism and Early Christianity* (Leiden: Brill, 2003), 275–308; idem, "The Vision of God and the Form of Glory: More Reflections of the Anthropomorphite Controversy of A. D. 399," in *Abba*, ed. John Behr (Crestwood, NY: St. Vladimir's Seminary Press, 2003), 273–97.

resurrection and judgment, and in the end the "Beloved" will send forth fire to consume his enemies completely (*Ascension* 4.18).

The second part of the work presents the christological part of Isaiah's vision—his prophetic glimpse of Jesus' coming, passion, and resurrection as a narrative of "descent" and "ascent"—in new terms, and in much richer detail than the earlier summary given above. Here we are told of the prophet's ecstasy (*Ascension* 6); of his experience of being guided upwards by an unnamed angel through six heavens, each peopled with spirits formally arranged, each bathed in a greater degree of glory (7–8); of his entry into the seventh or uppermost heaven, where God dwells, by the permission of Christ himself (9.1–6); and of his vision there of the "garments" of glory reserved for the elect (9.7–12; cf. 8.26). There Isaiah is allowed to see "one whose glory surpassed that of all" (9.27), "my Lord Christ who shall be called Jesus" (10.7), and standing alongside him a "second angel, . . . the angel of the Holy Spirit" (9.35–36). The prophet is told to join the whole company of the seventh heaven in worshiping these two glorious figures, and is then invited by them to join with them in worshiping "the most high of the high ones, who dwells in the holy world and rests with the holy ones, who will be called by the Holy Spirit, through the mouth of the righteous, the Father of the Lord" (10.6).

This second part of the *Ascension*, then, presents us with an unmistakably Trinitarian portrait of the divine power ruling the cosmos,[14] as well as with a vision of a highly structured cosmos, peopled with mighty invisible powers, that lies beyond the boundaries of normal human sensation. Within this monumental setting, the final two chapters of the document tell the story of the coming of God's Beloved, as Jesus, into the world: a descent in which the prophet is told that he will "become like you in appearance, and it will be thought that he is flesh and a man" (9.13). Disguise, in fact, is central to the narrative's plot: as the Beloved, sent by the invisible Father, descends through the storied layers of the heavens to earth, his appearance changes to resemble that of each heaven's population; he is accepted by each group of angels as one of them, not singled out for special praise. Eventually he comes to the human world, and is born of the Virgin Mary, in a miraculously speedy and painless way, as a human child (11.2–14). Later on, as an adult, he "performs great signs and wonders in the land of Israel and in Jerusalem" (11.18), is crucified, descends into the underworld, and is raised after three days (11.19–21). And when he ascends then into glory, up through the six lower heavens, all

14. For the Trinitarian scheme assumed by this work, see *Ascension* 7.7–8, 23; 9.27–42; 11.32–33.

the spirits now recognize him in his glorious form for who he is, and worship him in wonder, asking themselves, "How did our Lord remain hidden from us when he descended, and we perceived not?" (11.26). At the end of his ascent, he is enthroned "on the right hand of that great glory, whose glory . . . [the prophet confesses,] I was not able to behold," while "the angel of the Holy Spirit" is enthroned on the left (11.32). It is from there that his final path to judgment and victory presumably will begin.

Even more than the New Testament book of Revelation, this work (of almost equal antiquity) uses all the literary techniques of the apocalyptic imagination to present us with a carefully sketched portrait of Christ: as the Beloved of the mysterious, transcendent God, to whom both he and the Holy Spirit pay homage; as Lord of all angels, who himself is sent on a mission of revelation and of engagement with the forces of evil analogous to theirs, but climactic in its importance; as superior to the angels, just as he is superior to humans, yet as capable of assuming the form of all of them in order to disguise his identity. This emphasis on the Son's disguises, on his "appearing" to be like angels or human beings—what Jonathan Knight has called the work's "naïve docetism"[15]—is not to be taken as a denial of his body or his real human experiences; unlike the heavenly savior of Gnostic narratives, he is genuinely born in the flesh, and genuinely dies. It is, rather, a way to explain his mysterious, changing identity: though a divine being, he becomes like all the species of angels, and eventually like us as well, in order to win the worship and confidence of everyone ready to discover the mystery of his coming. Just as the saints may hope one day to put on the "robes" and "crowns" of glory now stored up for them in the upper heavens, the Beloved has put on a form similar to our own, to reveal and to achieve the saving plans of God.

Curiously, perhaps, this work from the earliest period of what is usually called "Judaeo-Christianity" is also the last work to make full use of this Second-Temple genre for entirely Christian purposes. Other early Christian works only partially qualify, at best. The first two and last two chapters of the Latin Vulgate *4 Ezra* (a version of Hebrew *2 Ezra*), usually called 5 and *6 Ezra* respectively, are clearly Christian additions to a late Jewish apocalypse; similarly, a number of passages in the collection of the *Sibylline Oracles* seem to have a Judaeo-Christian origin, and use images borrowed from the apocalyptic tradition. The Coptic *Apocalypse of Elijah*, an Egyptian work probably put together in the late third century, seems to be a Christian

15. Knight, *Disciples of the Beloved One*, 140.

reworking of older Jewish material about the final crisis of the world, but it lacks most of the classic literary features of apocalyptic literature.[16] The Nag Hammadi collection, too, contains a number of texts labeled "apocalypses" most of uncertain date,[17] but for the most part these revelation-discourses have little literary connection with the traditional apocalyptic form.

In the second half of the fourth century, it is true, and for roughly two centuries thereafter, Christian works were again composed with a number of strong apocalyptic features. Two other Nag Hammadi documents, for instance, which seem both to be late fourth-century products, draw on features of the Jewish and Christian apocalyptic traditions to present a dramatic vision of the coming end of material creation, in violence and conflict: *On the Origin of the World* (Nag Hammadi 2.5 and 13.2) and *The Concept [Ennoia] of Our Great Power* (Nag Hammadi 6.4). The second of these describes an age of oppression led by the "Archon of the Western regions"—a kind of Antichrist figure who comes from the West to invade "that place where the Logos first appeared"[18]—and identifies the consummation of the present world with the return of Christ, who will lead purified souls into "the immeasurable light."[19] Neither of these brief works, however, could be called a fully developed apocalypse. Closer to classical apocalyptic form, but still somewhat underdeveloped, is the *Apocalypse of Thomas*, a fifth-century Latin work that may be based on a fourth-century Greek original, and that transforms a scenario for the end of the world and the resurrection of the saints into a new, angelic form that strongly echoes passages from the book of Revelation. The better-known *Apocalypse of Paul*—a Greek work probably composed in the first two decades of the fifth century—uses the narrative form of a visionary tour, granted to the apostle Paul, of regions beyond the present world, as a way to sketch out a picture of the fate of individuals after death, to reinforce moral and ascetical exhortation. All of these works, along with the later Byzantine "political apocalypses," like the fifth-century *Oracle*

16. The best translation of this work, with an authoritative brief introduction, is that of O. S. Wintermute in *OTP* 1:735–53. For a discussion of the work's background and theology, see David Frankfurter, *Elijah in Upper Egypt: The Apocalypse of Elijah and Early Egyptian Christianity* (Minneapolis: Fortress, 1993).

17. The collection contains an *Apocalypse of Paul* (V, 2), not related to the fifth-century *Visio Pauli* or *Apocalypse of Paul*; two *Apocalypses of James* (V, 3 and V, 4); an *Apocalypse of Adam* (V, 5); and an *Apocalypse of Peter* (VII, 3).

18. *The Concept of Our Great Power* 44.1–2, trans. Frederik Wisse, in *The Nag Hammadi Library*, ed. James M. Robinson, 3rd ed. (San Francisco: Harper, 1990), 315.

19. Ibid. 46.9, p. 316.

of Baalbek, which embody social critique within a vision of the coming end of history, make use of themes and narrative elements from earlier Jewish and Christian apocalyptic in order to underline the fragility of human life and the vulnerability of the material world, but (with the exception, perhaps, of the *Apocalypse of Thomas*) they do not attempt to revive the genre in its full literary form. Fascinating works, but marginal in terms of their lasting influence on Christian theology, they are partial heirs of the apocalyptic tradition, rather than its authentic representatives.[20]

The Transformation of Apocalyptic

The more central and lasting imprint of apocalyptic on Christian theology and worship, I suggest, is to be found in the presence of certain themes and images, taken especially from the book of Revelation, which from the mid-second century on continued to find their way into the efforts of Christian thinkers to express their understanding of the reality and importance of the material cosmos, the person of Christ and his ongoing role in history, and the status and hope of the church. All I can hope to do here is simply to point out a few striking examples of this doctrinal, openly christocentric transformation of apocalyptic themes—or perhaps better, the apocalyptic tinting of a developing Christian orthodoxy—as a kind of hybridization that would remain enormously influential in Christian thought.

Apocalyptic Cosmology

One of the first Christian theologians to rely heavily on the Christian apocalyptic tradition in support of a wider theological argument is Irenaeus of Lyons. Irenaeus's five books, *Against Heresies*, written in Gaul around 185, are above all a tortuous but relentless polemic against the Valentinian cosmogonic myth and its implications for Christian teaching and Christian community life: a plea for the importance of the flesh, the visible world, and our daily lives in the world on the grounds of Christ's involvement in all of them, his "recapitulation" of this visible cosmos and its history in his own per-

20. For further discussion and bibliography concerning these later apocalyptic works, see Daley, "Apocalypticism in Early Christian Theology," 35–39; see also my *The Hope of the Early Church*, 2nd ed. (Peabody, MA: Hendrickson, 2003), 26–27, 120–22, 178–79.

son. The fifth book of *Against Heresies* is really Irenaeus's main engagement with the Christian apocalyptic tradition, the section of this massive work in which—by what may seem at first a curiously reversed argument—he looks ahead toward common Christian eschatological hope, and to the typically apocalyptic themes of resurrection, the coming of the Messiah, judgment and a millennial kingdom for the just, precisely as a way to confirm the urgency of rejecting a Gnostic view of the material world.

Irenaeus begins book 5 by pointing out that our only source of knowledge for "the things of God" is Jesus, the Word who became human; because he spoke audible words and performed visible actions, we have communion with the God who is "beyond creation" (*Against Heresies* 5.1.1). His point here is that if we confess Jesus' death on the cross to be a saving act, and look on the Eucharist as our means to share in that saving act—two points of faith he seems to presume among his readers—then clearly both Jesus' flesh and blood and ours must be centrally involved in this act of salvation: Jesus cannot simply be a phantom savior of the inner person.

> If this [flesh] does not attain salvation, then neither did the Lord redeem us with his blood, nor is the cup of the Eucharist a communion in his blood, nor the bread which we break a communion in his body. For blood can only come from veins and flesh, and whatever else makes up the substance of a human person, such as the Word of God was actually made. . . . When, therefore, the mingled cup and manufactured bread receive the word of God, and the Eucharist becomes the body of Christ, and from them the substance of our flesh is increased and supported, how can they [the Gnostic Christians] affirm that flesh is incapable of receiving the gift of God, which is eternal life?[21]

For Irenaeus, the implication is that our bodies must undergo the same process of decay and revitalization that seems to take place in the grain made into bread:

> Just as a grain of wheat, falling into the earth and becoming decomposed, rises with manifold increase by the Spirit of God, who contains all things, and then, . . . having received the Word of God, becomes the Eucharist, which is the body and blood of Christ; so also our bodies, being nourished

21. *Against Heresies* 5.2.2–3, in *ANF* 1 (repr. Grand Rapids: Eerdmans, 1981), 528 (altered); hereafter *AH*.

> by it, and deposited in the earth, and suffering decomposition there, shall rise at their appointed time, the Word of God granting them resurrection to the glory of God. (*AH* 5.2.3)

As his argument develops, Irenaeus insists that the resurrection of the dead reveals God's transcendent power (*AH* 5.3.2), in a way fully commensurate with his power revealed in creating; just as our flesh was brought to life by his original touch, so flesh will receive life again after decomposition. Irenaeus then connects this hope for fleshly resurrection with the kerygma of Christ's resurrection: neither can be conceived by us simply as a spiritual event (*AH* 5.7.1). Christian faith confesses that "the Word has saved that which really was dead humanity, bringing about by means of himself that communion (*koinonia*) which he needed to have with it, and seeking out its salvation" (*AH* 5.14.2). We must understand, then, that the Lord "had, himself, flesh and blood, recapitulating in Himself not some other, but that original handiwork of the Father, seeking out what had perished" (*AH* 5.14.2).

In the last eleven chapters of the book, Irenaeus turns from bodily resurrection to what were for him the other key aspects of the apocalyptic scenario: the coming of the Antichrist, Jesus' second coming and judgment, and between them the millennial kingdom of earthly blessedness promised to the just. Here he alludes frequently to the book of Revelation. Both the mysterious name of the Antichrist and the millennium are solidly witnessed to, he insists, by oral tradition as well as by apostolic text (*AH* 5.30.1; 5.33.4). In his view, too, the earthly millennium is not only required in justice as a reward for those who have suffered bodily persecution (*AH* 5.32.1), but is also the fulfillment of God's promise to Abraham, which was focused not simply on spiritual gifts but on a land (*AH* 5.32.1–2); it also makes intelligible Jesus' assurance at the Last Supper (Matt. 26:29) that he would share the "fruit of the vine" with his disciples in the kingdom of God. For Irenaeus, the earthly millennium is a transitional stage to a more comprehensive and mysterious salvation, allowing the righteous to "become accustomed to partake in the glory of God the Father" (*AH* 5.35.1). But because the flesh, created by God, is made for life, and because the Word took our flesh on himself to save it, the salvation of the flesh must be taken with utter seriousness, and the vision of the latter chapters of the book of Revelation not diluted by typological interpretation. "Since there are real human beings, so must there be a real establishment [*plantatio*], so that we might not vanish away among nonexistent things, but progress among things that have an actual existence" (*AH* 5.36.1). The events promised in the book of Revelation must be part of the real future, if the mainstream Christian confession of the Word made flesh, and the highly physical, eucharistic practice of Christian worship, are not to be made empty gestures. Living as Christians in the present world requires apocalyptic hope if it is to be coherent at all.

Apocalyptic Christology

For Irenaeus, the key to this integration of apocalyptic themes and images into his antignostic apologetic is his understanding of Jesus, not only as Savior (which he also was, of course, for Valentinian theology) but as the Christ of the Judaeo-Christian apocalyptic tradition, ready to come in triumph to raise the bodies of his faithful ones and inaugurate the final drama of the world's judgment. This christological focus remained central to the Christian theological use of apocalyptic images, even as interest in the details of the final conflict and an emphasis on the millennium began, in many places, to wane, from the early third century on.

An important example is Hippolytus's *Commentary on Daniel* (hereafter *Com. Dan.*), usually assumed to have been written by a Greek-speaking presbyter of that name in Rome, around 204, but possibly the work of a theologian from western Asia Minor contemporary with Irenaeus.[22] This earliest Christian Scripture commentary interprets the book of Daniel in a homiletic, heavily moralizing way, and attempts straightforwardly to connect the narrative and visions of the book with subsequent history. Underlying Hippolytus's interpretive scheme, however, is an Irenaean sense of the shape of God's plan for redemption, in which the Logos, the agent of God's saving works through history, is revealed more and more clearly to humanity in

22. The first modern attempt to divide the works ascribed to Hippolytus between two authors was that of Pierre Nautin, *Hippolyte et Josipe* (Paris: Éditions du Cerf, 1947); see also his *Lettres et écrivains chrétiens des IIe et IIIe siècles* (Paris: Éditions du Cerf, 1961). The question was discussed at length in two symposia sponsored by the Institutum Patristicum Augustinianum in Rome: *Ricerche su Ippolito: Studia Ephemeridis "Augustinianum"* 13 (1977), and *Nuove Ricerche su Ippolito: Studia Ephemeridis "Augustinianum"* 30 (1989). Arguing for the unity of authorship of all the works ascribed to Hippolytus, with the exception of *Contra Noetum*, is Josef Frickel, *Das Dunkel um Hippolyt von Rom* (Graz: Grazer Theologische Studien, 1988); see also C. Scholten, "Hippolyt II von Rom," *RAC* 15:492–551, esp. 503–4. The most recent attempt to argue that the commentaries ascribed to Hippolytus, along with the treatise *On the Antichrist*, are the work of a second- or early-third-century Greek author, probably from western Asia Minor, is J. A. Cerrato, *Hippolytus between East and West: The Commentaries and the Provenance of the Corpus* (Oxford: Oxford University Press, 2002).

understandable, human terms. The angel who comes to encourage the three young Jewish men in the furnace and teach them to join all creation in praising God, in Daniel 3, and whom King Nebuchadnezzar recognizes as "like a son of God" (Dan. 3:25 LXX), is clearly the Logos (*Com. Dan.* 2.33), who also submerged the Egyptians in the Red Sea, who rained fire on Sodom and who appeared to Isaiah and Ezekiel—the "angel of great counsel" (Isa. 9:6), whom the Father has appointed judge of the nations (*Com. Dan.* 2.32). Daniel's vision in chapter 7 of "one like a son of man" is a prophetic glimpse of the Logos's "complete humanization" (τὴν καθ' ὅλου ἐνανθρώπησιν—*Com. Dan.* 4.39) that Hippolytus has previously taken pains to date precisely at the midpoint of the fifth millennium of world history.[23] In interpreting the four beasts that precede this vision in Daniel 7, Hippolytus sees already a dramatic tableau of history's end:

> Then earthly things will cease and heavenly things will begin, so that the indestructible and eternal kingdom of the saints might be revealed, and the King of heaven, in addition, revealed openly to all—no longer seen by means of a vision, as on Mount Sinai, nor revealed in a pillar of cloud on a mountaintop, but with the powers and hosts of angels, God enfleshed and a human being, Son of God and of Man, the judge come from heaven to be present in the world. (*Com. Dan.* 4.10)

The real content of this vision, Hippolytus goes on to explain, is really nothing less than a glimpse of God's own being: in Daniel's "ancient of days" (Dan. 7:9, 13), "the Lord of all things, God and King, who is Father of Christ"; and in the "one like a Son of Man," who is given "dominion and glory and kingly power," the incarnate Word still to come on earth, first as humble Son of Mary and then as victorious judge.

> By subjecting all things to his own Son, the Father . . . has clearly shown that he is the first-born of all things: first-born of God, so that he might be revealed as second after the Father, since he is God's Son; first-born before the angels, so that he might appear as lord of angels; first-born from a virgin,

23. *Com. Dan.* 4.23: "The first coming (*parousia*) of our Lord, the fleshly coming which led him to be born at Bethlehem, took place the eighth day before the calends of January, a Wednesday, in the forty-third year of the reign of Augustus, five thousand five hundred years after Adam." Hippolytus goes on to give the precise date of Jesus' passion as well, and suggests that at the end of the sixth millennium of creation—five hundred years after Christ's birth, the "kingdom of the saints" on earth will begin, with Jesus' second coming.

> so that he might be shown to re-shape in himself Adam, the first of creatures; "first-born from the dead" (Col. 1:18), so that he might himself be the "first-fruits" (1 Cor. 15:23) of our resurrection. (*Com. Dan.* 4.11)

In language echoing Irenaeus, Hippolytus finds in Daniel, especially in the chapters that became the model for later Jewish and Christian apocalyptic writing, a revelation not simply of future events, but of the person of Christ and of his ever more manifest role in history.[24] Put in modern terms, Christ's second coming, for Hippolytus, will really be a statement about Christology.

Hippolytus's Alexandrian contemporary, Origen, shares this tendency to read the Christian biblical apocalyptic tradition as primarily revealing Christ, in himself and in his relationship with the church. Origen refers frequently to the book of Revelation in his works, and assumes—unlike his admiring pupil Dionysius of Alexandria[25]—that it was written by the Beloved Disciple, who was also the author of the Fourth Gospel.[26] For Origen,

24. For very detailed discussion of the Christology of the works ascribed to Hippolytus, see Antonio Zani, *La cristologia di Ippolito* (Brescia: Morcelliana, 1984). A good overview of the literary and theological character of the *Commentary on Daniel* is still Gustave Bardy's introduction to the edition and translation of the work in SC 14 (Paris: Éditions du Cerf, 1947).

25. See Eusebius, *Historia ecclesiastica* (hereafter *HE*) 7.25, where Eusebius quotes Dionysius's arguments for a diversity of authorship at some length. Dionysius here expresses his reverence for the book, as containing "a certain concealed and wonderful meaning in every part," even though he finds that that meaning often escapes him (*HE* 7.25.4–5).

26. See, e.g., *Commentary on John* 1.22, 84; 2.45. For a good survey of Origen's use of the book of Revelation and his attitude toward it, see Clementina Mazzucco, "Apocalisse," in *Origene*, ed. Adele Monaci Castagno (Rome: Città Nuova, 2000), 22–24. Origen says, in the *Commentariorum Series in Matthaeum* 49, probably part of a commentary on Matthew written in the late 240s, that he intends to explain some difficult passages in the book of Revelation *tempore suo*. There is no evidence he ever attempted to write a commentary on the work. The fragments published by Constantine Diobouniotis and Adolf von Harnack in 1911, eagerly identified by Harnack as excerpts from such a commentary, are now recognized to come from a variety of authors and represent what A. de Boysson, in his review of their work, called "un Origène simplifié, assagi, . . . mais affaibli et énervé." See C. Diobouniotis and A. von Harnack, *Das Scholien-Kommentar des Origenes zur Apokalypse Johannis*, TU 38 (Leipzig: Hinrichs, 1911); A. de Boysson, "Avons-nous un commentaire d'Origène sur l'Apocalypse?" *RB* 10 (1913): 555–67. For a thoughtful recent discussion of the value and possible identity of these fragments, see Éric Junod, "À propos des soi-disant Scolies sur l'Apocalypse d'Origène," *Rivista di storia e letteratura religiosa* 20 (1984): 112–21.

however, despite the "deep obscurity" of the book's "unfathomable mysteries" (*On First Principles* 4.2.3), its real message is its vision of Christ; none of the other sacred authors, he remarks near the beginning of his commentary on the Gospel of John, "revealed his divinity so clearly as John," and he quotes both the Gospel and the Apocalypse to illustrate his point (*Commentary on John* 1.22; hereafter *Com. Jn.*). One of Origen's favorite passages, it seems, in this regard is the dramatic portrayal, in Revelation 19, of the risen Christ, seated on a white horse, returning at the head of a victorious heavenly army to judge the world for God. Although Origen alludes to this passage forty-seven times in his known works, his most extended exegesis of it is near the beginning of the second book of his *Commentary on John.* Here—having finally reached the Gospel's second verse—he is explaining in detail who and what the Word is, who "was in the beginning with God" (John 1:2). To underline the fact that he is not only "with" God, but God's own Word—the expressive, dynamic force that finds its "beginning" in the divine Wisdom—Origen suddenly turns from the Johannine Gospel to Revelation 19 (*Com. Jn.* 2.42–63). Origen notes that in this passage, the author tells us that the majestic rider is called not only "Faithful and True" (Rev. 19:11) but "Word of God" (Rev. 19:13) and that he bears on his blood-sprinkled robe a third name, "King of kings and Lord of lords" (Rev. 19:16). As Origen reads the text, the evangelist-prophet is offering us a kind of miniature treatise on the divine Logos. He is God's Word, the only Word in the universe—hence he is named without a definite article, so as not to suggest a multiplicity of intellectual mediators between the spiritual world and the world of creatures (*Com. Jn.* 2.43–44). He appears in an "open heaven" (Rev. 19:11) to suggest his role as the sole revealer of divine reality to those who have preserved in themselves something of the image of God (*Com. Jn.* 2.47). His "white horse" (Rev. 19:11) seems to represent his communication of knowledge to created minds, so that they, as members of his army, will eventually ride white horses of their own (*Com. Jn.* 2.62; see Rev. 19.14); he sits on it "firmly" and "royally," "on words that cannot be turned aside," a vehicle "sharper and more swift than any horse," which leaves all hostile simulations of revelatory language—he seems to be thinking of gnostic documents—behind in the dust (*Com. Jn.* 2.48). He is called "faithful and true," as Moses called Israel's God in Deuteronomy (Deut. 32:4 LXX): faithful "not because he believes but because he is believable—that is, worthy of being believed" (*Com. Jn.* 2.49), and true because he realizes God's justice in himself and embodies it for creatures (2.53). His role in the world, as Word of God, is to "make war" against deceit and lies in the heart of every would-be disciple (2.55–56); his eyes "are like a flame of fire," because they consume all the chaff of "gross material thoughts" in those on whom he gazes (2.57). The "many diadems" of the triumphant warrior signify his many victories over forms of false knowledge;[27] he also has "a name written which no one knows but himself," because there are mysteries now known only to God's Word, which may some day be shared at least partially with those who share in his life (2.60). And John emphasizes, as Origen says, that "the Word of God on his horse is not naked," but that he is "wrapped in a robe sprinkled with blood,"

> because the Word who became flesh, and who died because he had become flesh, so that his blood was spilled on the ground when the soldier pierced his side, is wrapped in the marks of that passion. For perhaps even when we come to be in the highest, ultimate stage of contemplating the Word and the Truth, we will not completely forget that our introduction to them took place through him, in this body of ours. (*Com. Jn.* 2.61)

For Origen, here as elsewhere, the real message of Scripture is not so much a key to future events in history as it is a pointer to that education and transformation that are the only really significant history any of us live through. So this scene from the Johannine apocalypse becomes a revelation not simply of future conflicts and victories for God's people, but of Christ, in and through whom victory is modeled and won. Similarly, in his comments on Jesus' apocalyptic discourse in Matthew 24, Origen suggests that the battles Jesus describes are most "worthily" interpreted as the inner battles of the disciple struggling to live by the Truth (*Comm. Ser. Matt.* 35; 38), and that the one who "sees his glorious coming" is the one who perceives "the coming of Wisdom into his soul" (38). Apocalyptic language, for Origen, is a central part of the Bible's way of revealing Christ to us, in symbols that clearly call forth figural interpretation; but the most important stage on which the drama is played out is the present life of faith, the inner apocalyptic of Christ's coming to conquer the warring spirits within us, and to heal and illumine the battleground of the fallen mind.

27. *Com. Jn.* 2.58. In his comments on Christ's conflict with the Antichrist, as represented in Jesus' apocalyptic discourse in Matthew, Origen also insists that what is referred to is really the continuing conflict between the truth taught by Christ and the specious imitations of it promoted by the evil spirits: *Commentariorum series in Matthaeum* 33, GCS 11 (Leipzig: Hinrichs, 1933), 62–63; hereafter *Comm. Ser. Matt.*

Apocalyptic Ecclesiology

In a way typical of his speculative, endlessly suggestive approach to biblical interpretation, Origen also provides us with a different emphasis in the Christian use of apocalyptic imagery that was to become more and more dominant from the third century on, especially as a strategy for interpreting the New Testament's book of Revelation: seeing the drama as referring principally to the present life of the church as she lives out the conflicts of the end time, awaiting Christ's second coming. In the second book of his *Commentary on the Song of Songs*, composed perhaps ten to fifteen years later than the first books of the *Commentary on John*,[28] Origen returns to the vision of the rider on the white horse of Revelation 19 to shed light on Song 1:9 (LXX): "I have compared you to my mare among the chariots of Pharaoh." Here Origen suggests that one might take the "white horse" in Revelation to stand for the body assumed by the Lord, or for his soul, or perhaps for both together; but one might also take it, he suggests, to refer to the church, "which is also called his body," and which "is 'without stain or wrinkle' because he has himself 'made it holy by the bath of water.'" Origen continues:

> To this white horse, then, on which he rides who is called Word of God, or else to this heavenly army that follows him on horses that are equally white, Christ compares his Church, and makes it similar. (*Commentary on Canticles* 2.6.9)

Later patristic exegetes of the book of Revelation attach themselves in varying degrees to Origen's exegetical strategy, seeing the work less as a revelation of unknown things to come than as an affirmation of the victory of Christ and a representation of the life of the church, his body, in its present time of struggle.[29] Such exegesis begins with Victorinus of Poetovio's Latin commentary, written around 300, and continues through the later Latin tradition in such authors as the African Donatist Tyconius, Victorinus's ed-

28. Luc Brésard and Henri Crouzel, the editors and translators of the *Commentary* in SC, suggest a date of composition around 240: see SC 375.11–12. The *Commentary on John* was begun in Alexandria in the late 220s, and Origen had probably completed the first five books before moving to Caesarea in 231.

29. For brief expositions of the commentaries of these authors, see Daley, *Hope of the Early Church*, 65–66 (Victorinus); 127–31 (Tyconius); 210–11 (Primasius and Apringius); 179–83 (Oecumenius); 198–200 (Andrew). See also Daley, "Apocalypticism in Early Christian Theology," 17–18, 24–26, 40–41.

itor Jerome, the mid-sixth-century commentaries of Caesarius of Arles in Gaul,[30] Primasius of Hadrumetum in Africa,[31] Cassiodorus the Senator in southern Italy,[32] Apringius of Beja in the Iberian peninsula,[33] and the eighth-century compendium of the Spanish monk Beatus of Liébana.[34] The only Greek commentaries we possess from the patristic period—the early sixth-century commentary of Oecumenius[35] and that of Andrew of Caesarea,[36] metropolitan of Cappadocia, from the end of the century—also follow Origen's exegetical strategy.

Jerome characterized Victorinus, for instance, as a follower of Origen in his exegesis, even though he was a millenarian—a position that Origen himself despised.[37] Although Victorinus does try to link individual figures and episodes in the work to historical events, his main interest is in the work's portrait of Christ. Tyconius, the fourth-century Donatist whose "keys" for unlocking the puzzling figures of Scripture Augustine adopts in *De Doctrina Christiana* 3, also left a commentary on the book of Revelation that exists in manuscript fragments, and that can to some extent be recovered from later commentaries that made use of it.[38] Here, as in the

30. Dom Germain Morin, the editor of this *Expositio in Apocalypsin*, which was long attributed to Augustine, has called it an "undigested hash." He believes it was meant to serve as a set of homily notes rather than as a full-scale commentary. See *S. Caesarii Arelatensis Opera*, 3 vols. (Maredsous, Belgium: Abbaye de Maredsous, 1942), 2:210–77, with Dom Morin's brief introduction.

31. PL 68:793–934, with omissions supplied in PLS 4:1207–21.

32. This brief, little-known work of Cassiodorus's old age is an attempt to identify the cohesive thread of meaning in the work. So the author called it *Complexiones in Apocalypsi*. See the new critical edition by Roger Gryson, in *Commentaria Minora in Apocalypsin Johannis*, CCL 107 (Turnhout: Brepols, 2003), 101–29.

33. Apringius's commentary, written as a series of homilies or *tractatus*, has also been critically edited by Gryson, *Commentaria*, 13–97.

34. Critical edition by E. Romero-Pose, *Beati in Apocalypsin libri duodecim* (Rome: Typis Officinae Polygraphicae, 1985).

35. This work has now been published in a new critical edition: *Oecumenii Commentarius in Apocalypsin*, ed. Marc De Groote (Leuven: Peeters, 1999).

36. The authoritative edition and textual study of this work is that of Josef Schmid, *Studien zur Geschichte des Griechischen Apokalypse-Textes. 1. Teil: Der Apokalypse-Kommentar des Andreas von Kaisareia*, text: Münchener theologische Studien, Ergänzungsband 1 (Munich: Zink, 1955); *Einleitung* (Munich: Zink, 1956).

37. For Victorinus's Origenism, see Jerome, *Epistles* 61.2; 84.7; *Apologia adversus libros Rufini* 3.14; *Commentarius in Ecclesiasten* 4.13.

38. For a thorough consideration of the issues involved in recovering Tyconius's commentary, as well as a very useful survey of Latin patristic commentaries on this book, see

dependent works of Caesarius and Primasius, the drama of the Johannine Apocalypse is really being played out now in the life of the church. The Antichrist is already active, but held in check by the faith of Christians;[39] the millennial kingdom is already under way, in the church's present time of "rest," which extends "from the passion of the Lord to his second coming" (Beatus 11.5.9). The "first resurrection" referred to in Revelation 20:5 is accomplished now for the Christian in baptism—a notion that has antecedents in Origen (Beatus 11.5.3).[40]

The first extant Greek commentary on the book of Revelation, composed by a certain Oecumenius, probably in the first decade of the sixth century, also interprets the work mainly as a representation of the present spiritual struggles of the church, and the hope of Christians for a largely spiritual form of blessed union with God. Oecumenius interprets the vision of the mounted warrior, in Revelation 19, as a vision of the glorified Jesus, "making war with and for his holy ones, and commanding the forces against their enemies"[41] in the present age; the "white horse" on which he sits reminds us that "Christ rests on none other but the pure, on those not marked by any stain of sin."[42] The "thousand years" in which Satan is bound in the abyss (Rev. 20:2–3) signify, for Oecumenius, not a thousand-year interval of bliss for holy souls, before their own reincarnation, as Plato imagines, but this present age, in which the faithful live in the "daylight" of the Word made flesh:

> The incarnation of the Lord has become "day" and "morning" for us, since "the sun of justice" (Mal. 4:2) shines on us—for that is what Malachi calls him—providing us with "the light of knowledge" (Hos. 10:12 LXX); Zachary announced the coming of this divine light, when he said, "The dawn from on high has overshadowed us, to shine on those seated in darkness and the shadow of death" (Luke 1:78–79). . . . Since Scripture says that a day is counted "as a thousand years" with God (Ps. 90:4; 2 Pet. 3:8), and, in contrast, the Lord's presence on earth is called "day," the author calls this day "a thousand years," since there is no difference with God between one

---

Kenneth B. Steinhauser, *The Apocalypse Commentary of Tyconius: A History of Its Reception and Influence* (Frankfurt: Peter Lang, 1987).

39. See the probable comment of Tyconius in Beatus of Liébana's commentary, 2.6.82–83 (hereafter Beatus).

40. See Origen, *Com. Jn.* 10.243–45; *Hom. Luc.* Greek frag. 83.

41. *Commentary* 10.13 (De Groote, *Oecumenii Commentarius*, 241.255–57).

42. Ibid. (De Groote, *Oecumenii Commentarius*, 241.260–61).

> day and a thousand years. In this "day," the incarnation of the Lord, the devil has been bound, unable to struggle back against the divine revelation of the Savior.[43]

Although Andrew of Caesarea, writing his own commentary at the end of the same century, seems intent on correcting some of the Origenist tendencies in Oecumenius's work, he also identifies the millennium in Revelation 20 with the present life of the church, and stresses the spiritual character of the rewards of the saints. Details of interpretation vary, of course, for particular passages, but in general these later commentators joined Origen's project of reading the book of Revelation, the only apocalypse in the Christian canon, as revealing principally Christ's present relationship to the believer and the community, rather than the shape of things to come.

Maximus the Confessor, the great—and ever-critical—seventh-century synthesizer of the theological and spiritual tradition that reaches back through the sixth-century christological controversialists to Dionysius, Evagrius, the Cappadocian Fathers, and Origen, offers us no direct commentary in his works on the book of Revelation. Apart from a number of allusions to familiar phrases from the work—calling Jesus "alpha and omega" (Rev. 1:8; 21:6; 22:13) or "the fountain of the water of life" (Rev. 21:6)—he seldom averts to it. Yet Maximus, too, offers us a synthetic vision of the person of the glorified Christ, as the center of the life of the church and the guiding norm for the flow of time, that seems embedded in this same Origenist tradition of translating apocalyptic imagery into the present existence of the Christian believer, as he or she looks to the future. In *Replies to Thalassius*, Question 22, for instance, Maximus—writing in the early 630s—struggles with the relationship of future and present eschatology head on: "If God 'will reveal his riches in the ages to come,'" he asks, quoting Ephesians 2:7, "how has 'the end of the ages come upon us'?" (1 Cor. 10:11). Is the fulfillment of God's plan still ahead of us, or do we already live in its spell? Maximus answers by dividing the whole history of creation, in God's providential plan, into two great periods: the first, in which the Word has steadily involved himself more and more in human life, eventually becoming human himself in the Incarnation; and the second, in which human beings, incorporated into him by faith and the life of grace, are gradually allowed to become divine by participation.

43. Ibid. 10.16 (De Groote, *Oecumenii Commentarius*, 248.438–249.451).

> Let us . . . distinguish the ages in our thought, and allot some of them to the Mystery of God's becoming human (*enanthrōpēsis*), and others to the grace of humanity's becoming divine. We shall find that the first set of these (ages) have reached their proper goal, but that the others have not yet arrived. To put it concisely, some of the ages belong to God's descent towards humanity, the rest are part of humanity's ascent towards God. If we understand this, we will not flounder around in unclarity about the sacred words, thinking that the holy Apostle himself was also in the dark. Rather—since our Lord Jesus Christ is the beginning and middle and end of all ages, of those past and those present and those still to come—then the end of the ages really has come upon us in the power of our faith—that end that will be formally brought to realization, by grace, in the divinization of those who are worthy.[44]

We live already in the age of eschatological fulfillment, of the realization of the apocalyptic vision of Daniel and the book of Revelation: Jesus has come, "the Word became flesh . . . and we have seen his glory" (John 1:14). Yet the apocalyptic promise of salvation from the dangers of mortality still waits to be carried out in us, as individuals and as a church; the Messiah who has already come must come again—not alone and obscure this second time, but with "thousand, thousand saints attending," with humanity itself now looking on and sharing openly in his victory.[45] For Maximus and for most of the patristic tradition before him, the apocalyptic promise was really a promise of revelation and participation: the promise that God's faithful ones would not simply be rescued from oppression, but that they would see and share in God's own transformed humanity.

44. *Replies to Thalassius*, Question 22, CCSG 7 (Turnhout: Brepols, 1980), 139–65.

45. Cyril of Alexandria emphasizes this contrast between the secrecy of Jesus' identity in his first coming, necessary in order that his enemies might "crucify the Lord of glory" (1 Cor. 2:8), and the "illustrious and terrible" openness of his second coming; see *Homilies on Luke* 139, trans. Robert Payne Smith (Boston: Stoudion, 1983), 555.

Acknowledgments

Eerdmans gratefully acknowledges the permissions received by Brian E. Daley to reprint the following essays authored by him. Minor editorial adjustments were made in reproducing the following essays in this volume.

1. "Christ and Christologies," in *Oxford Handbook of Early Christianity*, ed. David G. Hunter and Susan Ashbrook Harvey (New York: Oxford University Press, 2008), 886–905.

2. "Seeing God in Flesh: The Range and Implications of Patristic Christology," *Josephinum Journal of Theology* 14 (2007): 27–44.

3. "'One Thing and Another': The Persons in God and the Person of Christ in Patristic Theology," *Pro Ecclesia* 15 (2006): 17–46.

4. "The Word and His Flesh: Human Weakness and the Identity of Jesus in Patristic Christology," in *Seeking the Identity of Jesus: A Pilgrimage*, ed. Beverly Roberts Gaventa and Richard B. Hays (Grand Rapids: Eerdmans, 2008), 265–83.

5. "Antioch and Alexandria: Christology as Reflection on God's Presence in History," in *The Oxford Handbook of Christology*, ed. Francesca Aran Murphy (New York: Oxford University Press, 2015), 121–38.

6. "Divine Transcendence and Human Transformation: Gregory of Nyssa's Anti-Apollinarian Christology," *Studia Patristica* 32 (Peeters: Leuven, 1997): 87–95. [Reprinted in *Modern Theology* 18 (2002): 497–506; also in Sarah Coakley, ed., *Re-thinking Gregory of Nyssa* (Oxford: Blackwell, 2003), 67–76.]

7. "'Heavenly Man' and 'Eternal Christ': Apollinarius and Gregory of Nyssa on the Personal Identity of the Savior," *Journal of Early Christian Studies* 10 (2002): 469–88.

8. "Word, Soul, and Flesh: Origen and Augustine on the Person of Christ," *Augustinian Studies* 36, no. 2 (2005): 299–326.

9. "The Giant's Twin Substances: Ambrose and the Christology of Augustine's *Contra sermonem Arianorum*," in *Augustine: Presbyter Factus Sum*, ed. Joseph T. Lienhard, SJ, Earl C. Muller, SJ, and Roland J. Teske, SJ. Collectanea Augustiniana (New York: Peter Lang, 1993), 477–95.

10. "A Humble Mediator: The Distinctive Elements in St. Augustine's Christology," *Word and Spirit* 9 (1987): 100–117.

11. "Unpacking the Chalcedonian Formula: From Studied Ambiguity to Saving Mystery," *The Thomist* 80 (2017): 165–89.

12. "Apollo as a Chalcedonian: A New Fragment of a Controversial Work from Early Sixth-Century Constantinople," *Traditio* 50 (1995): 31–54.

13. "Leontius of Byzantium and the Reception of the Chalcedonian Definition," in *Jesus der Christus im Glauben der einen Kirche: Christologie, Kirchen des Ostens,* Ökumenische Dialoge, ed. Theresia Hainthaler, Dirk Ansorge, and Ansgar Wucherpfennig (Freiburg: Herder, 2019), 217–35.

14. "Nature and the 'Mode of Union': Late Patristic Models for the Personal Unity of Christ," in *The Incarnation: An Interdisciplinary Symposium*, ed. Gerald O'Collins, SJ, Stephen Davis, and Daniel Kendall, SJ (New York: Oxford University Press, 2002), 164–96.

15. "*Logos* as Reason and *Logos* Incarnate: Philosophy, Theology, and the Voices of Tradition," in *Theology Needs Philosophy*, ed. Matthew L. Lamb (Washington, DC: Catholic University of America Press, 2016), 91–115.

16. "'Faithful and True': Early Christian Apocalyptic and the Person of Christ," in *Apocalyptic Thought in Early Christianity*, ed. Robert J. Daly, SJ (Grand Rapids: Baker Academic, 2009), 106–26.

Index of Authors

Abramowski, Luise, 63n, 70n, 79n, 116, 241n, 317n
Acerbi, Antonio, 371n
Alberigo, Giuseppe, 40n, 48n, 49n, 53n, 105n, 239n, 240n, 241n, 246n, 322n
Alexander, Paul J., 258n
Allison, Dale C., Jr., 368n
Altaner, Berthold, 175n
Anatolios, Khaled, 9n, 22–23, 32, 99n
Anderson, Justin M., 2n
Arnim, H. von, 309n
Aune, David E., 369n
Ayres, Lewis, 34, 64n, 98n

Bacht, Heinrich, 19, 33, 38–39, 41
Baillie, Donald, 17
Balthasar, Hans Urs von, 32, 39, 167n, 236, 254, 284
Bardy, Gustave, 75n, 381n
Barnes, Michel R., 64n, 74n, 77n
Bartelink, Gerard, 175n
Basevi, C., 216n
Bathrellos, D., 32
Batiffol, Pierre, 258n
Bauckham, Richard, 369n
Beasley-Murray, G. R., 368n
Beck, Hans-Georg, 267n
Bedjan, Paulus, 321n
Behr, John, 9n, 34, 64n, 98n, 164n, 327n
Beker, J. C., 368n
Benedict XVI, 2, 11, 339–41
Bergjan, Silke-Petra, 83–84, 85n, 87n, 115, 321n
Berkhof, Hendrik, 90n
Bertrand, Frédéric, 21, 191n
Bidez, J., 271n
Blowers, Paul M., 33
Boeft, J. den, 175n
Bongiovanni, A., 268n
Bonner, G., 201n
Bouchet, Jean-René, 145n, 146n, 149n, 150n, 151n, 163n, 163n
Bouillard, Henri, 39
Boulnois, Marie-Odile, 34
Bourke, V., 210n
Boysson, A. de, 381n
Braun, René, 69n
Brésard, Luc, 384n

Brooke, A. E., 195n
Brooks, E. W., 276n
Browne, Charles Gordon, 155n, 353n
Bruns, I., 308n
Buchanan, Neil, 347n
Buresch, Karl, 258, 270
Busse, A., 308n, 309n
Butterworth, George, 183n, 193n
Butterworth, Robert, 67n, 68n, 68n, 68n

Cameron, Michael, 197n
Cerrato, J. A., 379n
Chabot, I. B., 276n
Chadwick, Henry, 126, 181, 186n, 192, 193n, 257n
Chenu, Marie-Dominique, 39–41, 363
Chesnut, Roberta C., 34
Clark, Elizabeth A., 177n, 195n
Clayton, Paul B., Jr., 34
Collins, John J., 256n, 367n
Combès, J., 310n
Congar, Yves, 39, 51n
Cranz, F. Edward, 90n
Crouzel, Henri, 176n, 384n

Daley, Brian E., 1–12, 18, 32, 115, 165n, 182n, 207n, 236n, 252n, 291n, 292n, 295n, 296n, 300n, 302n, 315n, 376n, 384n, 389
Dalmais, I.-H., 324n
Daniélou, Jean, 39, 141n, 159n, 370, 371n
DeBoer, M. C., 368n
De Ghellinck, J., 207n
De Groote, Marc, 385n, 386n, 387n
Detlef, C., 372n
Devreese, Robert, 83n, 317n
Dewart, Joanne McWilliam, 83n, 114, 130
Diẹhl, E., 225n
Diekamp, Franz, 272
Diobouniotis, Constantine, 381n
Donaldson, James, 96n, 343n
Dräseke, J., 315n
Driver, S. R., 83n, 122–23, 130, 321n
Drobner, Hubertus, 32, 201n, 219n
Droge, Arthur J., 343n, 344n
Duchesne, L., 276n
Dunkle, Brian, 1–2, 9n
Dupuis, J., 16, 94n, 260n
Durand, G. M. de, 86n

Einarson, B., 316n
Eno, Robert B., 204n
Erbse, Hartmut, 258, 269n, 270n, 271n, 272n, 273n, 278
Ettlinger, G. H., 123–24, 127, 320n
Evans, Ernest, 69n, 70n

Fédou, Michel, 182n, 182n
Feige, Gerhard, 77n
Fiedrowicz, Michael, 197n
Fortin, Ernest, 185n, 223n, 225n, 317n
Frankfurter, David, 367n, 375n
Frend, W. H. C., 34, 52n, 243n, 244n, 247n, 260n, 261n, 263n, 265n, 274n, 285n, 289n
Frickel, Josef, 379n

Gaddis, Michael, 239n, 285n, 286n, 287n, 288n
Gallay, P., 143n, 256n
Galot, Jean, 43n
Galtier, Paul, 43n, 288
García Martínez, Florentino, 367n
Gasparro, Giulia Sfameni, 175n
Gavrilyuk, Paul L., 9n, 32
Gebremedhin, E., 126
Geerlings, W., 32, 201n, 215n

Geffcken, J., 256n
Gianotto, Claudio, 66n
Glorieux, P., 219n, 220n, 222n, 224n
Golitzin, Alexander, 176n, 372n
Gray, Patrick T. R., 34, 260n, 261n, 262n, 290n
Greer, Rowan A., 24, 32, 114, 116, 148–49, 154n, 156, 164
Grillmeier, Aloys, 4n, 18–19, 22–23, 24n, 32–34, 38–45, 47–49, 51n, 55, 60n, 84n, 106n, 138n, 150n, 152n, 154n, 158n, 224n, 235, 238, 241, 242n, 244n, 245n, 250, 261n, 262n, 263n, 264n, 265n, 267n, 268n, 276n, 283, 287n, 289n, 290n, 295n, 301n, 316n, 320n
Grossi, Vittorino, 180
Grumel, V., 301n
Gryson, Roger, 385n
Guillaumont, Antoine, 177n

Hadot, Pierre, 313n, 342
Halleux, André de, 62n, 210n, 287n
Hallman, J. M., 127
Hammond Bammel, Caroline P., 175n
Hansen, Günther C., 78n, 264n, 266n
Hanson, Richard P. C., 22, 205n, 206n
Hanssens, M., 203n
Hardy, Edward R., 33, 155n, 157n, 318n, 345n, 348n, 353n, 354n, 355n
Harl, Marguérite, 182n
Harnack, Adolf von, 39, 42, 66, 297–98, 340, 341n, 346, 347n, 362, 381n
Hayduck, M., 308n
Heidl, György, 175n
Heinzer, F., 308n, 313n, 324n
Hellemo, Geir, 83n, 370n
Helmer, S., 262n, 290n
Herrmann, L., 217n
Hespel, R., 245n, 261n, 268n, 273n
Hill, Edmund, 173n, 184n, 191n, 199n, 360n
Himes, Michael J., 51n
Hodgson, L., 83n, 122–23, 130, 321n
Hofer, Andrew, 8n
Holl, Karl, 149n, 150n
Horsley, Richard A., 368n
Horton, F. W., 65n
Hübner, Reinhard M., 140n, 141n, 146n

Jackson, Blomfield, 124
Jaeger, Werner, 308n
Jones, Gareth, 64n
Junod, Éric, 381n

Kalbfleisch, C., 308n, 308n, 309n
Kato, Takeshi, 175n
Keating, D. A., 32
Keenan, Mary Emily, 163n
Kelly, J. N. D., 18, 34, 138n, 150n, 235n, 283n
Khoury, Theodore, 340n
Kilmartin, Edward J., 51n
Klostermann, E., 78n, 271n, 272n, 278
Knibb, Michael A., 370n
Knight, Jonathan, 370n, 371n, 371n, 374
Koch, G., 82n, 114–15
Kolbet, Paul R., 174n
Kotter, Bonifatius, 151n, 314n, 329n, 330n, 331n, 332n

La Bonnardière, Anne-Marie, 203n, 204n, 205n, 216n
Lamberz, E., 315n
Lampe, G. W. H., 142n
Lang, Uwe Michael, 34
Lange, Christian, 247n
Layton, Bentley, 20

Lebon, Joseph, 32, 290n
Lebourlier, J., 141n
Lennon, Paul, 110n
Levering, Matthew, 2n
Lienhard, Joseph T., 76n, 77n
Lies, Lothar, 186
Lieske, A., 146n
Lietzmann, Hans, 79n, 80n, 141n, 142n, 143n, 151n, 152n, 153n, 156n, 159n, 311n, 312n
Logan, A. H. B., 77n
Lonergan, Bernard J. F., 43n, 63n
Loofs, Friedrich, 295, 297
Louth, Andrew, 1, 9n
Lubac, Henri de, 39–40, 362n
Lusini, Gianfrancesco, 371n
Lyman, Rebecca, 187n

Madden, Nicholas, 324n, 325n, 327n
Mai, Angelo, 271n
Marbach, C., 208n
Markus, Robert, 70n
Martens, Peter W., 1–2
Martindale, J. R., 202n
Mateo-Seco, Lucas F., 140n, 146n
Matlock, R. Barry, 368n
May, G., 141n
Mazzucco, Clementina, 381n
McGuckin, John A., 32–33, 114, 124, 127–28, 153n
McInery, J. L., 128,
McLeod, Frederick G., 34
McNamara, K., 84n
Meredith, Anthony, 147
Meslin, M., 203n, 205n
Millar, James, 66n
Mingana, Alfonse, 115, 117–20, 317n
Mioni, Elpidio, 268n
Moeller, Charles, 262n, 290n
Moingt, Joseph, 69n
Morel, W., 208n
Morin, Germain, 385n
Moutsoulas, Elias, 150n, 163n
Mühlenberg, H., 141n
Muller, G., 372n

Nautin, Pierre, 379n
Neuner, J., 16, 94n, 260n
Newton, J. T., 201n
Norelli, Enrico, 371n
Norris, Richard A., 26–28, 32–33, 115, 118–21, 125, 130

O'Collins, Gerald, 34
O'Connell, Robert J., 177n
O'Daly, Gerard P., 177n
O'Keefe, John J., 32, 81n, 124
Oort, Johannes van, 175n, 290n
Opitz, Hans-Georg, 58n, 348n, 349n, 350n
Orlov, Andrei, 176n
Osborn, Eric, 70n
Outler, Albert C., 190n

Patrick, John, 198n
Pelikan, Jaroslav, 149n
Perrone, Lorenzo, 73n
Pesce, Mauro, 370n, 371n, 371n
Peterson, Erik, 90n, 91n
Petterson, Alvyn, 23, 32, 99n
Pidel, Aaron, 2n
Pitra, J., 272n, 273n
Pohle, Joseph, 43n
Portalie, Eugene, 223n
Pottier, B., 146n
Premerstein, Anton von, 272n
Prestige, G. L., 153n
Preuschen, E., 311n
Preuss, Arthur, 43n

Price, Richard, 239n, 285n, 286n, 287n, 288n
Pusey, Philip E., 84n, 85n, 86n, 87n, 104n, 105n, 127, 130, 318n, 319n, 320n

Rahner, Hugo, 39
Rahner, Karl, 16–17, 39 41, 42n, 43n, 45, 54, 60
Régnon, Théodore de, 64n
Remy, G., 201n
Richard, Marcel, 245n, 261n, 290n, 294n, 301n
Richardson, C. C., 176n
Richardson, Cyril G., 315n
Riedinger, Rudolf, 54n, 240n
Riou, A., 324n
Robertson, Archibald, 96n, 100n, 343n
Roldanus, J., 290n
Romero-Pose, E., 385n
Rowland, Christopher, 367n
Russell, N., 127

Sansterre, Jean-Marie, 90n
Scheel, Otto, 201n, 219n, 223n
Schmid, Josef, 385n
Scholten, C., 379n
Schwartz, Eduard, 65n, 152n, 260n, 264n, 265n, 276n, 318n
Scipioni, L. I., 26, 32, 321n
Seibt, Klaus, 77n, 89–90
Sherwood, P., 324n
Siclari, Alberto, 316n
Simonetti, Manlio, 66n, 67n, 205n, 207n
Smith, J. Warren, 32, 104n, 127
Smith, Robert Payne, 388n
Sotiropoulos, C., 324n
Spoerl, Kelley McCarthy, 79, 148–49, 151n
Staab, K., 91n
Steinhauser, Kenneth B., 386n
Stevenson, J., 285n
Straub, J., 240n
Studer, Basil, 23, 61n, 63n, 177n, 201n, 216n
Sumruld, W. A., 203n
Swallow, James Edward, 155n, 353n

Tanner, Norman, 48n, 49n
Telfer, W., 316n
Ternus, Joseph, 43n, 53n, 105n, 239n, 240n, 241n, 246n, 260n, 322n, 364n
Teske, Roland, 177n, 178n
Theiler, Willy, 175n
Tillard, Jean-Marie, 51n
Tillemont, L. Le Nain de, 315n
Tixeront, J., 137–38, 150n
Tonneau, Raymond, 83n, 317n
Torrance, Iain R., 32, 34
Trigg, Joseph, 174n
Tuyaerts, M. M., 362

Uthemann, K.-H., 290n

Vaggione, Richard P., 351n, 352n
Van Bavel, Tarsicius J., 182n, 194n, 201n, 207n, 210n, 214n, 215n, 219n, 220n, 222n, 227n, 231n
VanderKam, James C., 367n
Viteau, J., 271n

Wallis, R. E., 196n
Walpole, A. S., 207n
Weinandy, T. G., 32
Wessel, Susan, 34, 114, 129
Westerink, L. G., 310n
Whaling, Frank, 366n
Wickham, Lionel R., 28, 102n, 103n, 126–27, 129

Wilken, Robert L., 33, 42n, 44–46
Williams, George Huntston, 90n
Williams, Lionel, 33
Williams, Rowan, 98n
Wintermute, O. S., 375n
Wisse, Frederik, 375n
Woude, A. S. van der, 65n

Yarbro Collins, Adela, 369n
Young, Frances M., 81n, 113

Zanetti, A. M., 268n
Zani, Antonio, 67n, 381n
Zarb, S., 203n
Zizioulas, John, 59

Index of Subjects

Acacius of Melitene, 46, 52, 244, 260, 289

Adam, 24, 110, 164, 312–13, 380n; Jesus Christ and, 24, 110, 121, 148, 156, 381; new or second, 110, 121, 142n, 148, 156; sin and, 24, 69, 99, 128

Aetius, 350–51

Alexander of Alexandria, 21, 58, 347–48

Alexandria, 51, 171, 243, 258, 263, 289, 347, 356, 384; Antioch and, 112–31, 150, 237, 261; school of, 26, 81, 129

Ambrose of Milan, 7, 177, 206–14, 215n, 217n; against Arians, 203, 206, 210, 213–14, 216; on the incarnation, 208–9, 211; relationship with Augustine, 11, 177, 203, 206–7, 209–17

Anastasius I (emperor), 259, 261–62, 266–68, 271, 276

anathema, 52, 82, 94, 126, 244, 260, 263, 264n, 266, 276n, 288–89, 318–19

angels, 165, 178, 213, 352, 372–74, 380

anthropology (theological), 10, 56, 164–65, 184, 214, 297, 299, 303–4, 326

anti-Arianism, 23, 76, 99, 117, 203–4, 206, 212, 214–15, 217

Antichrist, 372, 375, 378, 383n, 386

Antioch, 47, 51, 102–6, 243, 257, 260, 264, 276, 283, 288, 294, 351; Alexandria and, 112–31, 150, 237, 261; school of exegesis of, 43, 53, 112–31, 138, 246, 263, 291; Synod of, 74–75, 79, 154; theologians of, 10, 26, 30, 81–84, 86, 88, 90–91, 247, 253, 317

apocalyptic, 12, 366–70; cosmology, 376–79; early Christian, 370–76; ecclesiology, 384–88. *See also* Christology: apocalyptic

Apollinarianism, 23–25, 82–83, 116–17, 237, 241, 285, 297, 301, 322, 329; anti-, 137–47, 202, 218–19; Gregory of Nazianzus and, 154–67

Apollinarius of Laodicea, 79, 122–24, 129, 291, 292, 311; Christology of, 10, 31, 54, 79–81, 113–14, 137–67, 206–10, 312; critics of, 23–24; Gregory of Nyssa and, 10, 148–67, 313

apologetics, 90, 99, 176, 202, 219, 257–59, 272, 275, 345–46, 379

apostles, 6, 8, 74, 256, 269
Arianism, 24, 85, 129, 139, 216; Christology and, 83, 98–99, 101, 122, 203–6, 211, 213; controversy of, 79, 202–3, 347, 355; neo-, 159, 312, 352. *See also* anti-Arianism; Arius
Aristotelian philosophy, 65, 145, 249, 251, 253, 295, 298, 310, 356, 359; categories of, 307–8, 331, 361; terminology of, 107, 309
Aristotle. *See* Aristotelian philosophy
Arius, 21–23, 58, 74–81, 98, 109, 154, 205, 347–48
Athanasius of Alexandria, 7, 32, 46, 64, 88, 95, 113, 130, 248–49, 261; Arius and, 21–23, 154; Christology of, 26–30, 57–58, 81, 97–102, 107–9, 115, 285, 298; Council of Nicaea and, 74, 77, 151, 348–50
Augustine, 7, 10–11, 21, 31–32, 70, 88, 101, 129, 358, 360, 385; Christ and Scripture in, 181–82; Christ as mediator in, 226–32; Christology of, 11, 201–32; Christ's human soul in, 184–87; Christ's person in, 171–200; faith in, 190–92; incarnation in, 192–200, 205, 208, 222–26; letters of, 203–4, 226. *See also* Ambrose of Milan: relationship with Augustine
authority, 20, 89, 91, 260, 287–88, 318, 361

baptism, 27, 86, 124, 172, 177, 218, 230, 326–27, 361, 386; creeds and, 204, 348; Eucharist and, 20, 164; faith and, 146, 197
Basil of Caesarea, 11, 91, 143, 153, 165, 351
Basil of Seleucia, 50, 241
body, 42, 58, 94–97, 102, 138, 155, 159–62, 263, 265, 352, 363; Christ's divine, 156, 377; Christ's human, 19–20, 110, 124, 179, 184–89, 193–94, 215, 225, 311, 366, 374; the church as, 15, 103, 131, 196–200, 218, 372, 383–84; divinity and, 209–14; flesh and, 20, 86, 102, 142, 156; human, 17, 22, 27, 75, 99, 100–101, 128, 143, 224, 323; immortal, 114, 163, 176; living, 24, 141; soul and, 27, 223–27, 252, 292, 296, 299, 301–35; suffering, 28, 125

canon (law), 84, 93, 98, 107, 137, 153, 249, 370, 387; of Chalcedon, 53, 261; of Constantinople, 51, 54, 243, 246, 290, 293–94, 322; doctrinal, 30, 298, 320; of Nicaea, 172
canon (of Scripture), 15, 16, 56, 181–82, 198, 361, 366, 369
Cappadocian Fathers, 7, 11, 50, 62, 88, 91–92, 295, 304, 352, 387; against Apollinarius, 10, 24–27, 137–67; Christology of, 27, 82–84, 90, 137–67, 228, 250, 307, 320. *See also* Basil of Caesarea; Gregory of Nazianzus; Gregory of Nyssa
Chalcedon, Council of, 32–33, 91, 112, 150, 355–56; formula of, 16, 19, 33, 40–44, 55–56, 225, 260–63, 275, 283–302, 322; reception of, 11, 33, 38–39, 105, 107, 109, 111; rejection of, 32, 88, 106, 329. *See also* canon (law): of Chalcedon; Christological definition: Chalcedonian; paradox: Chalcedonian
Christ. *See* Jesus Christ
Christological definition, 54–55, 146, 167, 317, 320, 322, 333, 359; anti-

Chalcedonian, 258–77, 289, 298; Cappadocian, 164, 167; Chalcedonian, 11, 18, 30, 44–47, 55, 106–7, 235–55, 309, 329, 356; Nicene, 348, 350; reinterpretation of, 291, 322
Christology, 15–37, 40–46, 55–57, 62, 64, 79, 81, 87–88, 90, 92, 252; Alexandrian, 88, 112–31; Antiochene, 32, 86, 112–31, 248, 293, 301, 317, 319, 323; apocalyptic, 379–83; early or classical, 1, 9, 12, 23, 26, 31, 367, 370; models of, 303–35; patristic, 1, 9, 93–111, 149
church, 154, 183–84, 197–202, 219, 239, 245, 266, 287, 354; African, 172–73; Alexandrian, 49, 171, 175, 235, 240, 267, 283, 285, 288; Antiochene, 23, 34, 46–47, 237–38, 285; Constantinopolitan, 238, 261, 264, 267; early, 15–31, 235–36, 284, 332, 357, 366–88; Eastern/Byzantine, 246–47, 259–60, 267, 322; faith of, 178, 242–43, 248, 254, 275, 303, 340, 348, 362–64; imperial, 244, 248, 289, 292, 294; Roman, 39–40; service and, 3–12, 164; Syrian, 24, 153; Western, 177, 246
Cledonius, 9, 24, 62, 157
communicatio idiomatum, 215–16
communion, 29, 59, 89, 153, 244, 308n, 325; ecclesial, 24, 29–30, 247, 263, 267, 289–90; in faith and sacrament, 50, 102, 242, 377; with Christ, 119–20, 186n, 197n, 377–78
Constantinople, 46, 83, 236–37, 248, 259, 256–82, 285, 351–52; creeds/formulas of, 49–50, 219, 239–40, 242–44, 246, 294, 323; First Council of, 24, 29, 47, 52, 82, 105, 218, 238, 293; Second Council of, 30–32, 51–54, 94, 219, 246–47, 260–64, 274, 290–93, 300, 322, 331, 356; Third Council of, 31, 51, 54, 219, 329
consubstantiality. *See* substance: consubstantial
controversy, 2, 16–17, 23, 41, 43; between Antioch and Alexandria, 26–29, 81–87; between Marcellus and Eusebius, 76–81; Chalcedonian, 28–31, 53–54, 137; doctrinal, 48–50, 64n; Monarchian, 65–72, 88–89; Nestorian, 26–29, 46. *See also* anti-Arianism; Apollinarianism; Arianism: controversy of; Paul of Samosata
creation, 95–96, 117–18, 142, 154, 184, 191, 197, 250, 332, 380; ancient understanding of God and, 56, 64, 82, 166, 178, 205; distinction between God and, 10, 77, 83–84, 98, 103, 115, 130, 232, 321; the Logos and, 21–22, 68, 99, 145, 152, 185, 188–89, 192, 221, 227, 345; new, 129, 194; order of, 21–22; redemption of, 138, 348, 363, 375; relationship between God and, 236, 284, 377; story of, 185, 387
Cyril of Alexandria, 7, 46–53, 57, 95, 260–62, 268, 272–76, 323, 329; Antiochene theologians and, 10, 81–84, 105, 112–31, 235–38; background of, 26–32; Christology of, 53, 84–86, 91, 102–9, 124–31, 240–49, 317–22; influence of, 147, 224; letters to John of Antioch from, 29, 286; letters to Nestorius from, 28, 49, 52–53, 83, 102–3, 125–26, 240, 244, 286–89, 318; letters to Succensus from, 126–29, 319

David, 116, 118, 208–9, 345
devil, 66, 121, 180, 229, 232, 386–87
Diodore of Tarsus, 24, 81–82, 103, 112–17, 150, 153n, 264n, 276n, 291
Dioscorus of Alexandria, 46–47, 237–38, 285
diphysite, 294, 296, 317n
disciples, 15, 66, 191, 318; of the church, 9, 200, 235; Jesus and, 60, 68–69, 93, 131, 140, 182, 198–99, 341, 368–69, 372, 378
divinization, 25, 108, 115, 129, 146, 164–65, 388
dogma, 17, 44, 56, 60, 146, 201, 219, 242, 347, 362

ecclesiology, 12, 370, 384–88
energy (divine), 22, 24, 54, 62, 100, 108, 163
Ephesus, council(s) of, 28–29, 47–48, 52, 112, 237–39, 244, 264, 285, 293
Epiphanius, 176, 179–80, 206
eschatology, 10, 90, 93, 165, 197, 257n, 365, 387–88; Christian hope and, 12, 157, 377, 388; salvation and, 82, 103, 108, 114, 117, 130
essence (*ousia*), 215, 291–302, 320, 325, 363; of Christ, 116, 144, 155, 352; of God, 116–17, 251–52, 349; unity of, 314, 331. See also *homoousios/homoiousios/homoean*
Eucharist, 20, 97, 153, 164, 377
Eudoxius, 350–51
Eusebius of Caesarea, 22, 65, 73, 76–81, 90, 154, 257–58, 381
Eusebius of Dorylaeum, 46–47, 237
Eusebius of Nicomedia, 74, 349
Eutyches of Constantinople, 46–49, 237, 241, 254, 262–63, 285–86
excommunication, 29, 47, 98, 218, 238
existence, 88, 126, 130, 162, 225–27, 306, 387; eternal, 24, 107, 115; historical, 252, 304; human, 5–6, 43; hypostatic, 332–33; independent, 28, 76, 126, 251, 253; levels of, 105, 325, 357; modes of, 313–14, 328–30; nature and, 297–99, 317; real, 81, 92, 103, 312, 352, 378; substantial, 73, 79

face (*prōsopon*), 50, 66, 77, 120, 122–24, 130, 137, 149, 241, 250, 320; of Christ, 26–27, 112, 299, 320; definition of, 48, 62, 146, 239, 248, 250, 291, 298, 321. *See also* person: the term *prōsopon* and
faith, 18, 52, 99, 127, 243, 349, 360, 363; of the church, 5, 178, 226, 285–87, 291; confession of, 262, 288; in God, 6, 340, 354; in Jesus Christ, 7, 18–19, 46, 97, 105, 153, 221, 237, 254, 355, 364; orthodox, 32, 51, 154, 239, 242, 253, 261–63, 265–66, 285, 329, 357; rule of, 70, 172–73, 181; statement of, 47, 54, 238, 243, 247, 274–75
Flavian (bishop of Constantinople), 49, 217, 240, 248, 285, 287
Flavian (patriarch of Antioch), 263, 276
flesh, 6, 23, 30, 86, 159–61, 208, 260, 273, 317, 326–28, 345, 358, 373–78; of Christ, 19, 21, 23–24, 28, 61, 79–80, 155, 210–11, 246, 288, 322; God in, 38–58, 118, 156, 158, 166, 319; human, 11, 25, 72, 78, 113, 116, 139–47, 151–52, 205–6, 270, 285, 301; of Mary, 27, 69; soul and, 26, 157, 181–200, 216, 231. *See also* Logos, the: as Word-flesh (*logos-sarx*)

Gnostics, 19–20, 95–97, 108, 131, 172, 195, 285, 374, 377, 382
Gregory of Nazianzus, 9, 11, 24, 62, 141, 154–55, 157, 244, 248, 256–57, 300, 351–53
Gregory of Nyssa, 10–11, 32, 119, 129, 298, 312–15, 332, 351; Apollonarius and, 24–25, 137–67; letters of, 139, 141, 151, 153, 314; Maximus the Confessor and, 320–23, 327

Henōtikon, 52, 244–45, 258, 260–64, 267, 276, 289
heresy, 2, 24, 42, 49, 73, 139, 173, 176, 206, 240, 247, 262, 351, 357
Hiba. *See* Ibas (Hiba)
Hippolytus of Rome, 10, 65–92, 213, 379–81
Holy Spirit, the, 8, 21, 93, 159, 161, 308, 364, 372–74; Father, Son, and, 23, 27, 56, 59–60, 63, 68–70, 74, 77, 80, 84, 91–92, 98, 124, 152, 250, 252, 273, 304, 329, 334; power of, 6, 82, 86, 118, 314; presence or gift of, 129–31, 197, 221, 230, 354
homoousios/homoiousios/homoean, 74, 77, 204–5, 314. *See also* essence (*ousia*)
human intelligence (*nous*), 23, 75, 79, 81, 227
humanity, 20, 76, 149, 181, 302, 333, 339; characteristics of, 7, 22, 25, 251–54, 285, 313, 345; Christ as mediator of, 195–96, 218–32; divinity and, 209, 212, 214, 238, 248, 250, 270, 286, 306; of Jesus Christ, 17, 41–46, 64, 75, 93–131, 187–88, 292, 315, 334; restoration or redemption of, 63, 80–81, 148, 213, 228–29, 237, 351, 378–79; sanctification of, 47, 87, 93; transformation of, 10, 57–62, 137–47, 157–58, 160–63, 166–67, 197, 388; union of God and, 254, 260, 318–28, 335; of the Word, 143, 207, 228, 305
humility, 160, 190n, 226, 232, 360; of Christ, 11, 159–60, 189, 194, 200, 202, 217, 229, 360; divine self-emptying as, 11, 109, 159, 182, 217, 229, 232; as a virtue, 189–90; way of, 194, 202
hypostasis, 48, 50, 83–85, 123, 292–302, 307–9, 316, 319–22, 325; of Christ, 57, 126, 146, 149, 246, 262, 306, 323, 327, 331; as a concrete individual, 103, 105, 228, 239, 241, 248, 251–54, 291, 313, 329; divine, 30, 107; person and, 27, 53, 62, 274, 287, 334; of the Trinity, 124, 264, 325; of the Word, 30, 122, 125, 301, 319. *See also* existence: hypostatic; nature(s): hypostasis and; union: hypostatic

Ibas (Hiba), 246, 293–94
identity, 55, 83, 184, 251, 296, 299, 309, 311, 314, 354, 365, 367, 374; divine, 59, 191, 200, 260–61, 270, 274; human, 215, 221, 333; of Jesus Christ, 25, 31, 41, 57, 93–111, 140, 194, 202, 222, 227, 260–62, 304, 345, 348, 368, 388; natural, 328–29; personal, 10, 18, 21, 63, 148–67, 230, 308, 335
Ignatius of Antioch, 7, 19, 61, 63
Ignatius of Loyola, 2
immortality, 100, 124, 128, 191, 264, 343, 352; incorruptibility and, 58, 114, 119–20; mortality and, 11, 25, 270
impassibility (divine), 104, 123, 156
incarnation, 17, 74, 77–78, 117–30, 140–41, 146, 285, 298, 315–25, 331; doctrine of, 272–74, 303; of God, 61, 80; of Jesus Christ, 213, 386–87; of the Son of God, 60, 154; of the Word,

21–25, 70, 93–111, 114, 139, 148–67, 221, 307, 339–65, 380. *See also* Augustine: incarnation in
incorruptibility, 22, 25, 58, 96, 99, 100–101, 114, 119–20, 123, 153
intellect, 23–25, 43, 75, 79, 81, 108, 174, 179, 196, 227, 347, 358
Israel, 4, 6, 15, 22, 56, 60, 71, 90, 93, 113, 188, 364, 368–69, 373, 382

Jerome, 176–78, 180, 195, 256–57, 385
Jesus Christ, 3, 7–12, 146, 268, 274, 341, 344–50, 352, 355–60, 363–65, 369–88; as crucified, 15, 53, 99, 126, 141, 190, 200, 246, 264, 293, 369; divinity of, 256–57, 291; in the form of a servant, 117, 182, 184, 191, 317, 321; identity of, 93–111, 270; as mediator, 11, 58, 96, 185, 187–91, 195, 202, 205–32, 347–48, 364; mystery of, 250, 285; person of, 5–6, 15, 40–92, 171–200, 235–55, 259, 283–84, 301; portrait of, 112–17, 126, 236–40, 266, 287–94, 297–98; transfiguration of, 191, 193–94; unity of, 118–31, 148–67, 242–44, 249, 261–62, 303–35. *See also* humanity: of Jesus Christ
John (apostle), 193, 252, 318, 333
John Chrysostom, 113, 275
John Malalas, 271, 276, 278
John of Antioch, 29, 46, 49, 237, 240, 286
John of Caesarea (the grammarian), 262, 292, 298
John of Damascus, 7, 151, 250, 255, 301, 304, 309, 322–23, 328–35, 356–59, 364
John of Scythopolis, 291–92
Judaism, 56, 115, 266, 269
judgment, 20, 92, 109, 118, 120, 165, 196, 368, 373–74, 377–79
Julian (emperor), 153, 257
Justinian, 30, 52–54, 244–46, 255, 262, 267, 290–92, 322, 356
Justin Martyr, 66, 343–46

Leo I (pope), 29, 51, 147, 240, 243–44, 260, 262; Chalcedon and, 29, 43–44, 47, 217, 262, 287–89, 294; Cyril of Alexandria and, 7, 47, 238, 245, 285–88, 293–94; letters of, including the *Tome*, 49, 72–75, 217n, 240, 263, 285, 287
Leontius of Byzantium, 1, 55, 116, 147, 246, 306n, 311n, 321–23, 329, 356; on the formula of Chalcedon, 11, 53, 250, 253, 255, 291, 294–302, 305–6; on hypostases, 250–53, 291, 295–302, 306–9, 329; late antique philosophy and, 251n, 251n, 252, 291, 297–98, 307, 316n, 323, 356; on the mystery of Christ, 250, 253–55; *vs.* neo-Chalcedonian thought, 53, 291n, 297; *vs.* Nestorianism, 301–2; on ontology, 250–52, 291, 297–99, 314, 316; on union of the natures, 253–55, 295, 299–300, 305–9, 314, 322–23
liturgy, 102, 130, 208, 264–66
Logos, the, 12, 165, 186, 193–95, 198, 241, 311–12, 328–29, 375, 379–80; Christology, 66, 76; as divine, 31, 81, 88, 112, 121, 152–54, 184–85, 223, 293, 308, 325, 382; eternal, 143, 302; of God, 27–28, 75, 77–78, 118–19, 125–26, 149, 345; hypostasis of, 85, 301, 334–35; incarnate, 158, 160, 188, 195, 221–24, 339–65; Jesus Christ and, 50, 89; as reason, 71, 79, 99, 208, 339–65; as Word-flesh (*logos-sarx*), 22–23, 43, 114–16, 158, 206; as Word–human being (*logos-anthrōpos*), 26, 43, 112,

120, 158. *See also* creation: the Logos and; mind, the: of the Logos; soul: of the Logos; union: of the Logos
Lord's Supper. *See* Eucharist

Macedonius II (patriarch), 259, 262–67, 274n1, 275, 277
Manichaeism, 174, 185, 189, 224, 360
Marcellus of Ancyra, 23, 74, 76–80, 89–91, 148, 151, 154
Marcian, 29, 45–47, 51, 236, 238, 243, 246, 284, 286
Mary, 61, 80, 152, 191; as God-bearer (*Theotokos*), 27, 103, 126, 149, 218; as mother of Jesus Christ, 27, 107, 110, 116, 121, 252–53, 264, 285, 293, 380; as virgin, 69, 373
Maximus the Confessor, 7, 31–32, 54, 57, 61, 88, 95, 101, 105–9, 187, 236, 387–88; Christology of, 147, 166, 301, 322–29, 334–35; letters of, 107, 324, 356; reception of Chalcedon by, 250, 254–55, 284
metaphysics, 41, 55, 84, 220, 226–27, 253, 303, 308, 356; framework of, 175, 217; principals of, 193, 299, 310
miaphysite, 30, 32, 294, 296, 299
mind, the, 10, 21, 25, 146–47, 171–74, 184, 190–91, 293, 354, 382–83; body and, 94, 110; divine, 110, 141, 155–58, 223, 346; human, 96, 100, 102, 110, 113, 124, 142–44, 164, 301, 343, 346–47, 358–59; of the Logos, 57, 75, 80, 154–55, 166; philosophical, 229, 277, 311
modalism, 10, 23–24, 63–67, 70, 76–77, 82, 88, 91, 148, 151
monarchianism, 65–68, 88–89
monasticism, 172, 176, 266, 292, 356
monks, 30–31, 46, 106, 120, 218, 236, 249, 284, 324, 359, 385; Antiochene, 243, 276; Constantinopolitan, 263, 265; Eastern, 29, 52, 243, 248, 260, 289; Egyptian, 288–89, 292; Syrian, 29, 264, 288–89
monophysite, 17, 137, 150
monothelitism, 54, 329
mortality, 58, 93, 99, 101, 121, 140, 164, 191, 254, 327, 388
mystery, 4, 56, 59, 101, 110, 125, 163, 205, 232, 240, 305, 355, 368, 374; in Augustine, 182–84, 223; of Christ, 55, 113, 157, 220, 285, 319, 322–23, 328–35, 356; of Christ's person, 127, 130, 200, 216, 219, 235, 283, 294, 304; divine, 60, 62–64, 68, 70, 77, 82, 86–87, 94, 99, 210, 229; of God, 6, 23, 57, 73, 76, 85, 154, 199, 222, 239, 304; hidden, 365, 367; of the incarnation, 31, 44, 49, 56, 58, 209, 306, 311, 315, 388; of redemption, 61, 321, 327; of salvation, 8, 12, 22, 46, 61, 124, 138, 181, 231, 235–55, 306, 321, 327; of the Trinity, 81, 84, 137; of union, 56, 147, 294, 305, 314

nature(s), 24, 116, 221, 230–31, 239, 244, 292, 295–300, 302, 368; of the body, 97, 191–200; in the Chalcedonian formula, 235–55; divine, 104, 117–20, 123–25, 130, 215, 236, 252, 254, 284; of God, 18–19, 26–27, 74, 86, 127, 197, 205–10, 293, 340, 351; human, 25, 93, 103, 108, 117–21, 128–29, 199, 227, 236, 284, 350; hypostasis and, 48, 85, 137–67, 251, 295, 297, 299, 323; mode of union of, 11, 126, 303–35; oneness of, 10, 63, 82, 314; of reality, 342, 354, 358–59, 362–63; single, 29–30, 105–7, 113–14, 124, 247, 261, 288, 293; of the soul, 184–86, 224; the term *physis*

and, 84, 137–67, 291, 298; two, 16, 29–31, 44–56, 80, 84, 107, 110, 122, 127, 220, 260–74, 285–88, 301; twoness of, 10, 64, 201–17; union of, 28, 61, 299
Nemesius of Emesa, 307, 315–16, 323
neo-Chalcedonians, 53, 246, 262, 270, 273, 290–94, 297, 307
Neoplatonism, 115, 122, 185, 201, 214, 241n, 356, 359; Augustine and, 219n, 223–26, 229, 232, 360; commentaries of, 249, 251, 253n; Leontius and, 297, 307–9; Porphyry of Tyre and, 310, 315, 356
Nestorius of Constantinople, 32, 43, 49–53, 81, 83, 103–4, 218; Christology of, 147, 235–36, 254, 263, 283, 286–87, 318–22, 335; Cyril of Alexandria and, 112–31, 237, 240–45
Nicaea, councils of, 29, 51, 64, 98, 154, 242–44, 263, 293, 304, 348–49; creeds of, 29, 47–52, 55, 105, 125–26, 129, 159, 235, 239, 241, 248, 283, 289; faith of, 207, 238, 264, 286, 290, 350; formulas of, 18, 21–22, 77, 82, 109, 172, 289, 348; opponents of, 100, 350. *See also* Athanasius of Alexandria: Council of Nicaea and

ontology, 60, 183, 249, 309, 333
oracles, 256–58, 271n, 272, 374; of Apollo, 11, 258, 268–69, 278; Christian reappropriation of, 259, 269–78; criticism of, 11, 257–58, 274; Delphic, 256, 259, 268, 271, 275
Origen of Alexandria, 7, 11, 22–24, 26, 112, 120, 147, 154; Augustine and, 181–200; Christology of, 66, 75–81, 88, 176–81, 223, 311, 347, 358; exegesis of, 21, 78, 173, 175, 381–87; letters of, 177–78
Origenism, 75, 292, 387
orthodoxy, 19, 24, 42, 53, 75, 80, 102, 248, 293, 312, 369; biblical, 47, 238; of the Chalcedonian formula, 41, 44, 47–48, 50–53, 239, 242–43, 246–47, 249, 259, 268–69, 275, 286, 291; Christian, 93–95, 347, 360, 376; Christological, 45, 55, 81, 124, 245–46, 272, 274, 287, 294, 300–301, 316; debates over, 52, 55, 103, 121, 199, 262, 276, 285; Nicene, 24, 126; theologians and, 8, 249, 261, 309

paradox, 32, 71, 104, 126–27, 130–31, 220, 232, 333, 341; Chalcedonian, 16, 55, 254, 277, 300; of faith, 18, 94, 293; of the incarnation, 21, 23, 166, 183, 215, 219
Paul (apostle), 119, 200, 265, 333, 355, 361, 365, 368, 372, 375
Paulinus of Antioch, 153
Paul of Samosata, 73–77, 81, 89, 154
Pelagians, 175n, 178, 180, 195, 228, 230–31
persecution, 90, 172, 257n, 352n, 366, 371, 378
person, 118–31, 146–47, 341–42, 354, 358–61; in the Chalcedonian formula, 18, 235–55, 259–66, 274, 283–302; divine, 42, 44, 159–60; the divinity of Christ and, 9–12, 17, 22–29, 44–49, 51, 55–92, 103, 109–10, 114–15, 137–39, 143, 348, 365–88; of God, 59–92; the humanity of Jesus and, 5–6, 15, 19–21, 31–32, 40, 43, 49, 96–97, 105–8, 111, 346; hypostasis and, 53; identity of, 99, 148–67; of the

Savior, 41, 52, 112, 164, 235, 243; the term *prosōpon* and, 80, 83–84, 118, 121, 125, 155, 241, 251, 260. *See also* Augustine: Christ's person in
Peter (apostle), 101, 193, 252, 318, 333
philosophy, 84, 109, 129–30, 145, 171, 184, 236, 251, 255, 257, 284, 291, 295, 333; Christ in, 249, 339–65; discourse of, 43, 50, 56, 66–67, 69, 114–15, 175, 193, 195, 297–98, 348, 355; language of, 41–42, 88, 129, 239, 298, 349–50. *See also* Aristotelian philosophy; Neoplatonism; Platonism; Stoicism
Philoxenus of Mabbug, 30, 263, 291
piety, 18, 21, 173, 222, 248, 260, 288
Plato. *See* Platonism
Platonism, 21, 98, 146, 174–75, 299, 346–47, 354
Plotinus, 174, 223n, 225n, 253n
Porphyry, 252, 257–58, 307, 315, 316n, 356–57
preexistence, 91, 177, 186
presence, 17, 22, 32, 46, 52, 71, 88, 158, 182, 316, 345–46, 386; of Christ, 92, 97, 131, 151, 153, 166, 190, 199, 358; divine, 60, 80, 243; of God, 20, 26, 56, 81, 112–31, 142, 160, 304, 315, 335, 364; of the Holy Spirit, 129, 354; ontological, 236, 284; redeeming, 96, 195, 323, 334, 363; of the Word, 57, 78, 99, 100, 118, 198
Proclus of Constantinople, 46, 50, 237, 241
prophecy, 6, 41, 64, 95, 344, 368, 382; concerning Jesus Christ, 344–46, 371–73, 380; divine inspiration and, 68, 344, 373; of the end time, 258, 370; false or pagan, 154n, 256; in the Old Testament, 50, 181, 209, 241, 344–46, 369
Pulcheria, 46–47, 86, 236, 238, 284, 286

reason, 39, 71, 173, 237; critical, 88–89, 321, 329; divine, 79, 99, 339–65; human, 129, 339–65
redemption, 16, 19–20, 95–97, 131, 146, 157, 180, 185, 363; mystery of, 61, 321, 327; plan of, 61, 129, 326, 379. *See also* creation: redemption of; mystery: of redemption; salvation; soteriology
Reformation, 15, 346–47
ressourcement, 18, 39, 43n
resurrection, 61, 69, 86, 92, 93, 100, 119, 200, 372–73, 377, 381, 386; of Christ, 27, 67, 124, 127, 140, 163, 165, 222; of human beings, 20, 97, 163–64, 176, 326, 375, 378; of Jesus Christ, 15, 28, 82, 123, 161–62, 365–66; mystery of, 160, 163
Reunion, Formula of, 46, 236–37, 240
Rufinus of Aquileia, 175n, 177–78

Sabellius, 64, 74, 91, 266
sacrifice, 86, 102
salvation, 19, 25, 57, 60, 63, 79, 82, 115–17, 142, 163, 211, 222, 232, 323; act of, 158, 377; economy of, 67–69, 77, 87, 92, 120, 124, 151, 378; of God, 20, 97, 161, 368; history of, 24, 28, 51, 96, 113, 131, 146, 200, 229, 243, 364, 371; of humanity, 22, 112, 114, 140, 144, 147, 150, 179–82, 192, 237, 317; message of, 101, 103, 108, 129–30, 198; mystery of, 8, 12, 138, 231; plan of, 15, 161, 368, 388; of the world, 21, 80, 176, 196, 255
Satan. *See* devil
scholastic theology, 17–18, 42, 249, 356

Septuagint, 273n, 274n
Sergius of Constantinople, 30, 106–7
Severus of Antioch, 30, 263, 267, 289, 291, 309
sin, 44, 69, 121, 162–64, 178–80, 185–86, 196–97, 202, 211, 218, 231, 386; death and, 20, 86, 109, 157, 163, 193; freedom from, 157, 162, 230, 327; power of, 61, 99, 103, 114, 193
Smyrna, 20, 66
Socrates (Christian historian), 83, 120
Socrates (Greek philosopher), 342, 345
soteriology, 10, 56–57, 104, 156, 163
soul, 79, 138, 141, 157, 162, 164, 171–200, 209, 252, 257, 383–84; body and, 128, 155, 296, 299, 307–11, 314–16, 319–20, 326, 332; of Christ, 22, 26, 44, 207, 292, 311; human, 20, 128, 157, 206, 210–11, 213–16, 232, 301–2, 323, 344; intellectual, 23–24; interior, 22, 44; irrational, 123, 211; of the Logos, 27, 69, 124–25, 171–200, 223–26, 231; rational, 114, 123–25, 143, 326–27, 358
spirituality, 11, 39–40, 52, 61, 88, 91, 154, 158, 176, 190, 202, 243, 386; enlightenment and, 20, 174, 342–43; gifts and, 140, 378; growth in, 112–13, 139, 172, 188, 191, 194; substance of, 186, 223, 314–15; tradition and, 131, 200, 387; world of, 178, 382
Stoicism, 71, 309, 313, 320–21, 343, 346–47
substance, 68, 77, 82, 101, 107, 122–24, 149, 174, 182, 307, 359; consubstantial, 22–23, 98, 101, 159, 314, 324, 348, 350–54; different, 24, 110, 312–14; divine, 71–72, 76, 78, 83, 85, 112, 115, 158, 174, 224, 312, 325; of God, 146, 166, 222–23, 226, 321, 334–35; human, 62, 225, 377; hypostasis and, 48, 239, 298, 308–11, 323, 329; nature and, 10, 27, 31, 64, 110, 239, 251–52, 285, 302–5, 323, 331; soul-, 185–86; twin-, 201–17, 220, 316
Symphōnia, 268, 272–73, 275–78
Syria, 29–30, 52–53, 55, 73, 243, 246, 264, 276, 288–89, 370; Apollinarianism and, 24, 153; churches of, 24, 261
Syriac, 19, 83n, 176, 264n, 273n, 291, 317n, 372n

temple, 26–27, 75, 112, 116–17, 121, 256, 268, 271, 317, 371, 374
temptation, 17, 198–99
Tertullian of Carthage, 10, 65–72, 89, 213
Theodore of Mopsuestia, 26, 32, 103, 246, 264, 322; Christology of, 81–83, 112–20, 123, 129–30, 260, 301, 317–19; school of Antioch and, 81–83, 290–94
Theodoret of Cyrus/Cyrrhus, 26, 84, 103, 127, 286, 294, 319–22; Antioch and, 46, 49, 53, 112, 237, 240, 245–46; Nestorius and, 123–24, 129, 147; Theodore of Mopsuestia and, 114–15, 260, 264
theology, 99, 112, 123, 129, 154, 157, 167, 202, 219, 376, 379; anti-Arian, 21–24, 204–6; Antiochene, 81–87, 103; of Augustine, 202, 219–22, 232; Catholic, 17–18; Chalcedonian, 245, 267, 275; of Christ's divinity, 163; of Christ's person, 38–58, 171–200, 238; Greek, 304, 323, 333; historical, 2–12, 32, 297; patristic, 59–92, 110, 333; philosophy and, 339–65; scholastic,

18, 42, 248–49, 356, 370; Trinitarian, 56, 64, 68, 83, 87, 151, 258, 323–24
Theophilus of Alexandria, 25, 139, 141, 161, 176
Timothy Ailouros, 30, 32, 261, 289, 291
Timothy of Berytus, 311–12
transcendence, 10, 27, 64, 82–85, 117, 122, 130, 137–47, 174, 307, 339
transformation, 15, 56, 114, 187, 214, 231, 327, 334, 347, 368, 371; of apocalyptic thought, 376–88; Christology of, 158–67; human, 10, 25, 52, 57–58, 137–47, 221, 243
Trinity, the, 15, 27, 59–92, 110, 184, 210, 291, 294, 300, 306–8, 353, 359; Christ and, 9, 262; doctrine of, 139, 176, 211, 216, 272–74, 323; God as, 55, 173, 202, 205, 219, 266, 298; hypostases of, 30, 124, 264, 326, 332; members of, 53, 226, 246; persons of, 76, 106, 146, 157, 182, 304, 311, 313, 320, 330

union, 50, 58, 108, 162, 178, 194, 231, 236, 284, 302, 386; formula of, 47, 51, 238, 240, 243, 260, 289; hypostatic, 28–29, 46–47, 51, 61, 85, 126, 262, 325; of the Logos, 123, 127, 311–12, 158, 195, 198, 214, 221, 232, 293; as mixture, 145–52, 225–26, 260, 300; mode of, 11, 253–54, 303–35; mystery of, 56, 73, 255; in nature, 28–29, 46, 49, 53, 105, 126, 241, 247, 260, 285, 299, 301; perfect, 118–20; of persons, 121, 130, 165–66, 230, 250

Valentinianism, 20, 95, 174, 312, 376, 379

will, 78, 110, 180, 187, 193, 317–18, 330–31, 340, 355; of Christ, 24, 31, 78, 101, 106–9, 125, 143, 161, 187, 213, 270, 308; of God, 21, 26, 43, 93, 96, 196, 213, 348, 364; human, 31, 107–8, 143, 161, 195, 328, 361. *See also* monothelitism
wisdom, 141–42, 160, 188, 191, 194, 236, 284, 352, 360; divine, 21, 75, 225, 227, 382–83; of God, 10, 15, 182–84, 214, 345–46, 358–59, 363–65; philosophical, 342, 344; as the Word, 64, 73, 81, 161–62, 184–86, 190, 349, 363

Zeno, 52, 244–45, 258, 260–61, 289